MEDICAL JURISPRUDENCE

MEDICAL JURISPRUDENCE

Jon R. Waltz, LL.B.
PROFESSOR OF LAW, NORTHWESTERN UNIVERSITY
SCHOOL OF LAW, AND LECTURER IN MEDICAL
JURISPRUDENCE, NORTHWESTERN UNIVERSITY
MEDICAL SCHOOL, CHICAGO

Fred E. Inbau, LL.B., LL.M.
PROFESSOR OF LAW, NORTHWESTERN UNIVERSITY
SCHOOL OF LAW, CHICAGO

THE MACMILLAN COMPANY, NEW YORK
COLLIER-MACMILLAN LIMITED, LONDON

PRINTED IN THE UNITED STATES OF AMERICA

Figures 1, 2, 17, 18, 19, 20, and 21 herein are reproduced courtesy of Office of Chief Medical Examiner, State of Maryland; Figure 3, courtesy of Office of Coroner, Orleans Parish, Louisiana; Figure 4, courtesy of Charles M. Wilson and Fred E. Inbau; Figures 5, 9, 10, 11, 12, 13, 14, 15, and 16, courtesy of Chicago Police Scientific Crime Detection Laboratory; Figures 6, 7, and 8, courtesy of Department of Medicine, Indiana University Medical Center.

THE MACMILLAN COMPANY
866 Third Avenue, New York, New York 10022

COLLIER-MACMILLAN CANADA, LTD., Toronto, Ontario

Library of Congress catalog card number: 77–133563

First Printing, 1971

To N. S.

from J. R. W.

To W. R. I. and L. I. B.

from F. E. I.

PREFACE

Everybody talks about "the law" but few, aside from lawyers, judges, and law professors, have more than the vaguest notion of what constitutes "law." The average layman often has about as much accurate information about "the law" as he has about medicine—or life on Venus. And, unfortunately, two professional groups suffer from more ignorance of law and medicine than is good for them: lawyers, at least those who do not constantly deal with medical issues in their legal practice, know very little about the medical profession and its problems; physicians frequently comprehend too little about the law and how it affects them in the practice of their profession.

This treatise is in a sense one-sided. Although law students and lawyers will undoubtedly find it helpful, this book has been written primarily for the practitioner and the student of medicine, to answer their most significant and basic questions about the law and its workings. It will be used by students as a text in medical-legal courses and by practitioners as a reference work.

"The law," of course, is a lot of things. It is the law that one cannot crash red lights at traffic intersections or commit armed robbery, premeditated homicide, rape, or "the unspeakable crime against nature." It is also the law that one cannot practice medicine without a valid license, perform unnecessary hysterectomies, or prescribe morphine for nervousness. In a general way, "the law" is the body of authoritative rules by which a civilized society regulates, minimally, the conduct of its members. It takes its coloration from the authority that lies behind it and gives it force. "Law" may look for its authoritativeness to a legislative body, to a court with its judge and jury, to an agency or commission. The manner in which judges, lawyers, and juries function in our adversary trial system will be the most frequently recurring topic in this book because it is vital that physicians know why lawyers and judges and jurors behave the way they do.

The physician meets the law at every turn. He confronts it when, as the treating doctor, he is subpoenaed as a witness in a personal injury lawsuit; he meets it when his aid is sought as an expert in connection with a claim that another member of his profession has been negligent and when he is faced in his office or clinic by a narcotics addict, a man with a gunshot wound, or a young couple seeking a blood test. He is face-to-face with the law when he is required to render an aggravating array of governmental reports or to preserve physical evidence for the benefit of a law enforcement agency. The physician, in fact, finds a great deal of the law intensely irritating, often because he is not absolutely clear as to its purpose.

This book will explain the important judicial opinions, statutes, rules, and regulations, and also many of the informal practices of lawyers and judges, that impinge on the professional life of a doctor. An innovative early chapter outlines all phases of the trial process as it functions in the United States. So fundamental a topic as medical malpractice is exhaustively treated, with emphasis on recent doctrinal developments and potential defenses. Related subjects, such as liability for emergency treatment, failure to obtain "informed consent," and abandonment, are also carefully considered. The chapters on damages and malpractice insurance are the most comprehensive to be found in any medical-legal text. A unique section is devoted to the physician's relation to the criminal law, stressing the preservation of essential evidence. Chapters and sections on homotransplantation, the new Uniform Anatomical Gift Act, computerized medical records, and liberalized abortion laws make this book as timely as today and tomorrow.

Although this is a one-sided book in the sense that it is written in the main for medical students and practitioners, the authors are optimistic that it will bring the two crucial professions of medicine and law closer by at least partially closing an information gap that has persisted between them for much too long.

We have had a great deal of valuable help in the preparation of this text. Physicians too numerous to mention granted us interviews, corresponded with us, and read portions of the manuscript. The same can be said of a number of attorneys throughout this country and Canada whose practices regularly involve medical-legal problems. Several medical malpractice insurance companies supplied useful data, as did the staff of the American Medical Association's Legal Department. We single out for specific mention those who have made especially heavy and significant investments of time in this project.

The entire manuscript, with the exception of the three criminal law chapters, was read by Doctor James E. Eckenhoff, former Chairman of the Department of Anesthesia and now Dean of the Northwestern University Medical School, and by Doctor Julius Conn of the Department of Surgery at Northwestern. Although they are in no way responsible for the contents of this book, their comments and suggestions helped to form important parts of it. Thomas W. Scheuneman, a member of the Illinois Bar, made invaluable contributions to the author's thinking, particularly in the areas of informed consent and innovative therapy.

For the chapter on "The Medical Practitioner and Physical Evidence in Criminal Cases" we are deeply indebted to Doctor Charles S. Petty, Chief Medical Examiner of Dallas County, Texas, and Director of the Southwestern Institute of Forensic Sciences at Dallas. He supplied many of the ideas and suggested sources for illustrations contained in that chapter. In connection with this chapter we also wish to express our appreciation for suggestions received from Doctor Milton Halpern, Chief Medical Examiner of the City of New York; Doctor Russell M. Fisher, Chief Medical Examiner of the State of Maryland; Doctor Samuel Gerber, Coroner of Cuyahoga County, Ohio; and from the following members of the staff of the Chicago Police Scientific Crime Detection Laboratory: Director David Purtell; John C. Stauffer, Firearms Identification Technician; and Louis R. Vitullo, Microanalyst. Most of the photographs are from the files of the Office of the Chief Medical Examiner of the State of Maryland, the Chicago Police Scientific Crime Detection Laboratory, the Department of Medicine of Indiana University Medical Center, and the Coroner's Office, Orleans Parish, Louisiana. To none of the foregoing individuals or departments, however, must any responsibility be assessed for any of the chapter's shortcomings; that responsibility rests upon the authors alone.

Research assistance of a high order was supplied by a number of students at the Northwestern University School of Law: Thomas W. Bianchi, Michael Bolger, James R. Bronner, Richard C. Fiddes, Richard A. Schiffer, and Jon E. Steffensen. Mrs. Witold Obuchowicz, the ultimate secretary, typed the manuscript with typical but nonetheless extraordinary competence—and patience.

JON R. WALTZ
FRED E. INBAU

CONTENTS

part one

THE PHYSICIAN AND THE CIVIL LAW

chapter 1

THE MEANING OF LAW AND THE ADVERSARY PROCESS

THE MEANING OF "LAW"

This is a book about the law as it applies to physicians and surgeons. It therefore ought to commence with a clear statement of what the term "the law" means. It won't. The vast monument that is "law," or jurisprudence, can comprehensibly be defined only in an aphorism or a treatise since, as Dr. Johnson put it, "The law is the last result of human wisdom acting upon human experience." (That is an aphorism, and this introductory chapter will not be ballooned into a treatise.) But, despite the fact that legal scholars are notoriously reluctant to embark upon a definitive definition of "law," this brief section will have something to say about what we mean in the balance of this text when he speak of "the law."

Other lawyers will say that our discussion of the nature of the law is incomplete. As we have already promised, it will be. In the first place, this book has a limited purpose and a limited audience; physicians and surgeons do not require a close consideration in these pages of "the law" as it applies to corporate mergers, taxation of the petroleum industry, or the capturing of mud turtles and migratory birds. Furthermore, the late Jerome Frank, a most distinguished federal judge, was right when he remarked that a complete definition of "law" would be impossible and that even a good working definition "would exhaust the patience of the reader." We will try not for an across-the-board working definition but for a reasonable description of what this text is all about.

Even in being descriptive rather than definitional we run the risk of criticism from those members of our discipline who love endlessly to worry the question "What is law?" We cannot hope to win, for there resides a certain truth in Sholom Aleichem's cynical comment that "Lawyers are just like physicians: what one says, the other contradicts." The real difficulty, to borrow from Judge Frank again, is that the term "law" fairly "drips with ambiguity" and has "at least a dozen defensible definitions."

Even so, it is not enough for present purposes simply to say, as one undiplomatic jurist once did, that "The law is what the judges say it is." It would not even be accurate.

The law, as we shall be discussing it in this book, means rules that govern one's conduct as that conduct relates to society in general and to individual members of society. There is, in other words, *public law* and *private law*. Criminal law, prohibiting antisocial conduct ranging from the serious to the trivial—from murder to littering—is an example of so-called public law. It is aimed at protecting society at large from evil deeds by punishing their perpetrators and thereby discouraging others from indulging in similar conduct; it levies fines that go into the general treasury and puts persons in prison or the gas chamber, but so far it does nothing whatever, directly, for the criminal's victims. They, if they hoped to be compensated by the criminal for the injuries done to them, would have to look to private law.

There are numerous private or personal interests that the law seeks to protect from invasion by permitting the injured party to recover compensation—money damages—from the wrongdoer. This is the civil law, as distinguished from criminal law. The law of torts, which permits an injured person to recover damages from the person who intentionally or negligently hurt him, is the example of private law with which we shall be primarily concerned, since medical malpractice is an aspect of tort law.

We need not dwell on the need for rules of the sort that make up what we call "the law." There is a need for rules in boxing matches and football games; otherwise the participants could with impunity knee each other in the groin and engage in other tactics which, however effective, are generally thought to be unsportsmanlike. There is a need for rules to keep the conduct of society at large, and special segments of it, within reasonable behavioral bounds. If such rules did not exist, or were not enforced or implemented, society would fly apart. It requires no deep thought to conclude that the alternative to the rule of law is chaos.

Since humans do so many things, there are lots of laws. Ludwig Boerne, the German author, was obviously sighing when he commented that "If nature had as many laws as the State, God himself could not reign over it." Physicians and surgeons are subject to vast numbers of rules governing their conduct. It is, in a sense, part of the price they pay for being in a profession that daily deals intimately with the lives and well-being of others. It is part of the price they pay for being members of a profession in which society at large has a tremendous stake.

Law in the United States is generated in a variety of ways. It might be simpler if it were handed down periodically by an absolute monarch or a dictator, but a democracy such as ours trades harsh and unpredictable simplicity for broad concepts of fairness. And so law comes not only from elected and appointed judges who are hedged about by long traditions of justice and overseen by reviewing courts who think nothing of reversing incorrect lower court decisions; law comes also from state legislatures and city councils, from Congress and from state and federal agencies and commissions. Legislative bodies enact statutes and ordinances; agencies and commissions, empowered by statute to do so, promulgate regulations. Courts interpret statutes, ordinances, and regulations, if they are ambiguous, and enforce them when they are applicable. But legislative and administrative bodies cannot pass laws and draft regulations to channel every aspect of human behavior. Some governing principles are threshed out in courtrooms during what is known as litigation—the resolving of disputes through the elaborate machinery of the adversary judicial process. These principles, some of them downright ancient, make up the great body of the *common law*—law declared by judges functioning in areas not controlled by statutes, ordinances, and governmental regulations. The law of medical malpractice, for example, is mostly common law—judge-made law.

There is nothing unvaryingly certain and static about the common law. That is the very essence of its genius. It is composed of general principles or doctrines, deliberately kept sufficiently flexible—hopefully—to cope with myriad factual variations on a central theme. It is fluid as well as flexible; it may not only bend but change, to bring itself into conformity with the felt needs, the common sense, of contemporary society. We shall see that the law of medical malpractice has been both flexible and fluid; so have other phases of law applicable to physicians and surgeons.

Thus far we have spoken, in the main, of statutory law and common law, public law and private law. We have referred to the forum—the courtroom, be it trial level or appellate—in which statutes are interpreted and enforced and common law is created, interpreted, and implemented, all by means of the adversary trial and appellate process. We should now mention that all law splits into two large categories, *substantive* and *procedural.* The line of demarcation wavers at times, but it is enough here to say that the rules of substantive law regulate the rights and obligations of persons in their daily relations with each other and with society at large, while procedural law is composed of those more or less mechanical rules that govern the means by which substantive rights and duties are vindicated or enforced. By and large, then, procedural rules implement substantive rules. They are the rules by which litigation is conducted. Trial lawyers—litigators—who are perhaps too flip would say that procedural canons constitute the rules of the game; trial lawyers who are too grim about their calling might refer to them as the rules of warfare, after the fashion of the Geneva Convention. Procedural rules govern such questions as the form that suit papers—the plaintiff's Summons and Complaint or Petition, the defendant's Answer, and sometimes the plaintiff's

Reply—must follow, which party goes first in putting on evidence at trial, who can be subpoenaed to testify as a trial witness, and what the distinctive functions of judge and jury are.

THE LITIGATION PROCESS

The adversary trial system is a thing of wonder. One wonders whether it is properly attuned to its announced goal, the ascertainment of relevant truth. Beyond that, one wonders how it ever works at all. There is nothing very scientific about it. As one highly experienced trial lawyer, who believed in straight talk, once described it, ". . . the way we administer justice is by an adversary proceeding, which is to say, we set the parties fighting." Professor Robert E. Keeton of the Harvard Law School has said it more calmly: "A trial is a competition of inconsistent versions of facts and theories of law." Defying all precepts of scientific fact-finding, the system actually works quite well. Adversariness seems to be the best method yet devised by the mind of man for forcing the truth into the open.

Almost everyone has at least a generalized impression of how litigation operates. It is occasionally a very fuzzy impression, drawn more from Perry Mason than from unembellished fact. The skeleton of a civil lawsuit—much simplified—looks like this:

The Complaint

Litigation is commenced by the filing in court of the plaintiff's written Complaint (in some jurisdictions this first piece of paper is called the Petition or Declaration). The Complaint sets forth the basic elements of the plaintiff's claim against the named defendant and demands judgment for money damages in a specified sum. A summons, together with a copy of the Complaint, will be served on the defendant by some court functionary; he is thereby notified of the beginning of suit and of his duty to defend.

Motions

The defendant, through his legal counsel, may file motions attacking the legal sufficiency of the Complaint. Such motions are filed when the defendant admits, for the sake of argument, all the allegations of the Complaint but contends that they do not add up to a claim that the law recognizes as compensable.

The Answer

If the defendant's motions, if any, are denied, he will next file his written Answer, responding specifically to the allegations of the plaintiff's

Complaint. The Answer may admit some of the plaintiff's allegations while denying others; it may also set up affirmative defenses of the sort discussed in Chapter 9 of this book.

The Reply

In some jurisdictions the plaintiff is permitted to file a Reply, responding to affirmative defenses revealed in the defendant's Answer. In all others the defendant's affirmative defenses are simply taken—assumed—to be denied by the plaintiff.

By means of these three pieces of paper (Complaint, Answer, Reply), called the pleadings, the issues for trial are drawn. Only evidence that is relevant to the issues formed in these pleadings will be permitted at trial unless an amendment to the suit papers has been allowed by the trial court; otherwise trials would be unmanageable, with incessant surprise being their principal ingredient.

Pre-Trial Discovery

Plaintiff's counsel will have been investigating the facts of the case from the moment the plaintiff appeared in his office; defendant's counsel will have been digging into the facts from the moment his client advised him of the possibility of suit. This early investigation is conducted on an informal basis without the backing of any judicial machinery. The term "pre-trial discovery" refers to more formal investigatory methods, authorized by enforceable procedural rules and available to the parties only after suit has been instituted. The following discovery devices are typical:

Written Interrogatories to Parties

A party to a lawsuit can require any adverse party to answer, in writing and under oath, relevant written questions propounded to him. Written interrogatories are usually employed to secure detailed information which the answering party must obtain from records in his possession or control.

Oral Depositions

Parties and nonparty witnesses alike can be required, by means of a subpoena, to come to counsel's office for deposition purposes. Counsel will propound oral questions, much as he would at trial, and the questions and the answers, given under oath, will be taken down and transcribed *verbatim* by a high-speed stenographer, usually called a reporter. By this means counsel obtains desired information from the witness; furthermore, the transcription of the witness's deposition testimony will rise to haunt him at trial if he then seeks to change his story in any significant way.

Motions for the Production of Documents and Things

A party can obtain a court order requiring the opposing party to produce relevant documents and objects for inspection, copying, or photographing at the requesting party's expense.

Physical and Mental Examinations

In any action in which the mental or physical condition of a party is in dispute, as it would be in a personal injury action, the court can order him (or her) to submit to a mental or physical examination by a physician. Such an order can be made only on the motion of the adverse party, supported by a showing of legitimate need for such an examination.

Requests for Admissions of Facts

A party can make a request on his adversary for a formal admission of relevant facts set forth in the request, including the genuineness of documents. If the adverse party refuses the requested admission and the party requesting it thereafter establishes the truth of the disputed matters, the adverse party can be required to defray the cost involved in proving the matters in question.

Pre-Trial Conference

In many progressive jurisdictions the trial court, concerned by the backlog of pending cases, will conduct a pre-trial conference concerning the case. Present at this conference will be a judge, the parties (often, but not always), and their attorneys. Settlement possibilities will be explored; if the case cannot be disposed of by settlement, methods of simplifying the trial to cut time-consumption will be considered.

The Trial

A case that has not been settled will be called for trial. The principal phases of a civil jury trial are as follows:

Selection of the Jury

A necessary first step in a civil jury trial is the selection, by court and counsel, of a panel of jurors to hear the case. An American jury trial is something more than twelve good men and true plucked at random from the surrounding community. It is the product of a sometimes lengthy process of questioning and selection. Lawyers call this process the *voir dire,* Norman French for "to tell the truth." During the *voir dire* the trial judge, through his questioning of prospective jurors, simply seeks persons who are qualified under the laws of the jurisdiction to sit as jurors. The two opposing sides seek something more: the plaintiff and the defendant each attempt to find jurors who can most readily be convinced of the rightness of its position. (For example, a defendant relying on complex medical facts will seek educated, intelligent jurors.) The actual picking of jurors is done by calling prospective panelists, either individually or in groups of up to twelve, and questioning them—first by the judge, then by one side, then by the other.

After the questioning, the juror may be accepted or he may be challenged or, more politely, "excused." Two types of challenges are recognized in American trial courts: the challenge for cause and the peremptory challenge. The former must be based on a specific, recognized ground, whether it be statutory or embedded in the common law, while the latter, as its name "peremptory" implies, may be for good reason, bad reason, or no reason at all, provided only that the limited number of such challenges allotted each counsel has not been exhausted. The grounds for challenging a potential juror peremptorily are manifold and often involve a modicum of untested folklore—"Never accept a man wearing a bow tie"—that lies beyond the scope of this text.

Opening Statements

After the jury has been selected and sworn to "well and truly try this case," the lawyers will present their opening statement to the jury's members. These are not arguments; they are statements of what each side expects its evidence to show. They are, to put it another way, previews of the evidence making up each side's case. Since evidence comes into the courtroom in bits and pieces—testimony of witnesses, introduction of tangible objects and documents such as x-rays, hospital records, and the like—it is thought that the lawyers' opening factual statements will aid the jury in following the mosaic of evidence.

Examination of Witnesses and Introduction of Tangible Evidence by the Plaintiff

Plaintiff, having the burden of proof, goes first in the putting on of evidence. He calls his witnesses and questions them in what is referred to as direct examination; the defendant can then engage in cross-examination, which may be followed by re-direct and re-cross. During this entire process the plaintiff's lawyer, with the aid of the court reporter or clerk, will mark for identification and offer any items of tangible (that is, nontestimonial) evidence that he may have—for example, hospital records or x-ray plates. (The trial judge will rule on objections made by defense counsel to the proferred testimony and other evidence.) This testimony—taken down by the court reporter—and tangible evidence constitute the plaintiff's case in chief; when his counsel has completed it he will announce that "The plaintiff rests," meaning that he has concluded his case and that it is now the defendant's turn to put in his case for nonliability.

Motion for a Directed Verdict at the Close of the Plaintiff's Case

If defendant's attorney believes that the plaintiff has failed to make out a case, he will move for a directed verdict in his client's favor at the close of the plaintiff's evidence. The motion will be granted by the judge only if he believes that there exists no factual dispute as to any material issue for the jury to resolve.

Examination of Witnesses and Introduction of Tangible Evidence by the Defendant

If the defendant's motion for a directed verdict, if any, is denied he will then put in his case for nonliability. He will conduct direct examination of defense witnesses, who then will be subject to cross-examination by plaintiff's counsel, and will offer his tangible evidence. Objections will be ruled upon by the judge. When the defense's case in chief has been presented, counsel "rests."

Rebuttal Evidence for the Plaintiff

After the defendant rests the plaintiff will be permitted to introduce evidence to rebut matters introduced by the defense.

Motion for a Directed Verdict at the Close of All the Evidence

After all of the evidence is in, the defendant can again move for a directed verdict. The trial judge may rule on it immediately or reserve his ruling until a later time, preferring to wait and see what the jury does with the case. If the jury finds for the defendant the motion for a directed verdict becomes moot.

Closing Arguments to the Jury

At the close of all the evidence the parties' counsel are entitled to make arguments to the jury, assuming that no directed verdict has been granted. Plaintiff's counsel goes first, followed by defendant's lawyer; plaintiff's counsel is also permitted to make an additional argument following the defendant's. Plaintiff's counsel generally argues the substantive issues of liability during the "opening close," reserving the more emotion-laden damage arguments for his "closing close" so that their impact will still be strong when the jury retires to deliberate and—who knows?—perhaps because defense counsel will have no opportunity to rebut plaintiff's final argument.

The Judge's Instructions to the Jury on the Law

Following the lawyers' closing arguments the trial judge must instruct the jurors on the law applicable to the case. This is the so-called charge to the jury. The judge will advise the jurors that if they find such-and-such facts to have been established by the evidence, then the law is that they must find for the plaintiff; that if, on the other hand, they conclude that certain essential facts were not established by the plaintiff, or that one or more affirmative defenses were proved by the defendant, then their verdict must be for the defendant. He also explains how, if their verdict is for the plaintiff, they shall go about arriving at appropriate money damages.

Deliberation by the Jury

After the charge the jurors retire to a room set aside for the purpose to deliberate upon their verdict. There they elect a foreman, who presides at their deliberations and delivers the jury's verdict to the judge. In some jurisdictions the verdict must be unanimous; in others a majority vote of the jurors is all that is required. If the necessary number of votes cannot be mustered there results what is termed a "hung jury." When a jury deadlocks, a new trial must ordinarily be ordered by the court.

Post-Trial Motions

After a verdict has been rendered the losing side can present various motions, including a motion for a verdict in its favor notwithstanding the adverse verdict of the jury. Such a motion will be granted only if the trial judge believes that the jury's verdict is legally unjustified. The losing side can also move for a new trial on various grounds, such as that the trial judge made prejudicially erroneous rulings on objections to evidence during the trial. If this motion is overruled by the judge, as for some not altogether unfathomable reason it usually is, the losing side has no further recourse at the trial level. It must determine whether to appeal to a reviewing court, asserting that errors of law occurred at the trial.

Distinctive Characteristics of the Adversary Trial System

Although the foregoing is the barest outline of the litigation process, a few distinctive characteristics of the adversary trial system should stand out. The reader will have observed that in Anglo-American jurisdictions civil cases are prosecuted by private parties through their legal representatives who, guided by a judge, control the flow and content of the evidence. And civil cases are two-sided, not one-sided, in the sense that each party has an equal opportunity to investigate the case and present his side of it at trial through evidence and argument. This means, among other things, that each side has the power to require the attendance of desired witnesses; if they ignore a lawful subpoena they will be brought bodily to court by a marshal or deputy sheriff.

The foregoing outline also reveals that the trial judge in a jury case serves only as a sort of umpire; he applies the rules—the law—to the lawyers (procedural law) and explains it to the jurors (substantive law), but generally the jurors, and they alone, decide what facts have been established by a preponderance of the evidence. Put another way, the judge is the arbiter of the law; the jurors are the arbiters of the facts. And the jurors, in reaching their verdict, apply to the facts, as found by them, the law as it is explained to them in the judge's instructions. (If the parties have waived trial by jury, or if the action is of the sort in which the parties are not legally entitled to trial by jury, the judge will himself find the facts and apply the law to them in what is referred to as a bench trial.)

The statement that litigation is party-prosecuted simply means that noncriminal actions are initiated by a supposedly aggrieved private party, not by a court or any other arm of government. An aggrieved person need not file a lawsuit if for some reason he chooses not to litigate. (He may think as did Learned Hand, one of the most perceptive judges ever produced by this country, who commented after long service on the trial bench, "I must say that as a litigant I should dread a lawsuit beyond almost anything else short of sickness and death.") If an adult elects to file suit, he can settle it with the defendant without the court's permission. (The rule is different in cases involving minors.) If the case goes to trial the parties, represented by their attorneys, produce the evidence that the jury is to consider; the judge ordinarily has no authority to tell the parties what evidence to produce or to produce any himself, and the jurors never have any such power. (Occasionally the court may itself call an impartial expert, or panel of experts, to testify in a complex case, but this in fact is not often done in civil cases.)

Although it may at first blush seem strange that the parties, through their lawyers, can freely decide what evidence the jurors will hear and see, the workings of the adversary system usually assure that what one side leaves out the other will triumphantly produce—with the result that the first side will introduce it initially rather than be charged with suppressing relevant data. This process of smoking out the evidence would prove ineffective if one side were unaware of favorable evidence in the possession of the opposite side. In today's practice this rarely occurs, since each side, as our outline suggests, is entitled to penetrating pre-trial discovery of its opponent's evidence.

The Role of Expertise in Medical Litigation

Physicians sometimes are perturbed that twelve laymen are seemingly called upon to resolve complex medical issues that are undeniably beyond their competence. It would be genuinely bizarre if lay jurors in, for example, a medical malpractice case were called upon to decide, unaided, whether a particular diagnostic method or mode of treatment were proper. But this is not the way the litigation process works. Jurors are not permitted to decide esoteric questions without the aid of expert witnesses. It is for this reason, as we shall later discuss in detail, that the plaintiff in a medical malpractice case cannot ordinarily hope to prevail unless he produces favorable testimony by one or more qualified medical experts. The hard and altogether legitimate question comes when both sides in a complex case produce divergent expert testimony. How, when the "battle of the experts" takes place, can untrained jurors be expected to find for one side or the other intelligently? The truth is that jurors do a surprisingly effective job of separating wheat from chaff, but they do it on bases that will remain largely a mystery to those, including trial lawyers, who must remain outside their deliberation room. They can, of course, compare the tangible qualifications of the contesting experts—training, experience, and the like—but they will also take into account less tangible factors such as the witness's demeanor while answering questions. And it must not be forgotten that trial lawyers who have steeped themselves in medical knowledge will aid the jurors through their cross-examination of sometimes not-so-expert witnesses and through understandable and helpful closing arguments.

PUBLISHED SOURCES OF LAW

The literature of the law is staggeringly large. First there are the true sources of basic "law": the innumerable statutes, ordinances, administrative regulations, and judicial opinions. All federal and state statutes and regulations, all municipal ordinances, and all but the most unimportant judicial opinions are published in full, officially or unofficially, in one place or another and sometimes in several. Lawyers refer to published statutes, ordinances, regulations, and court opinions as "primary authority," since they, and they alone, constitute "law" to which citizens must adhere and which courts must enforce. Then there is a mass of secondary authority that expounds and interprets the primary sources of law: encyclopedias, treatises, dictionaries, law reviews published by the nation's top law schools and other legal periodicals, restatements of the law, and so on—and on. Finally, and necessarily, there are elaborate indices, digests, and citators that aid the lawyer in locating relevant primary and secondary authorities.

These various publications are available, for the most part, only in specialized legal libraries and in the offices of those who deal regularly with the law. Law schools maintain the most extensive law libraries. City, county, and state bar associations, as a service primarily to their members, also maintain libraries of legal publications. Nonlawyers can usually secure permission to make at least limited use of law school and bar association collections. Courthouses contain law libraries but these are for the use of the judges and their clerks and are not ordinarily open to the general public. The same is true of the law libraries maintained by some governmental departments such as the United States Department of Justice and the state attorneys general. Law firms and single practitioners invariably have law libraries of their own, occasionally of a highly specialized sort reflecting the restricted nature of their law practice, but they tend not to encourage browsing by nonlawyers. Public libraries and undergraduate university libraries do not have extensive collections of lawbooks, but some of the larger institutions may have the statutory codes and municipal ordinances of the state in which they are located, as well as some explanatory texts, such as the one you are now reading.

Since this book has been prepared principally for the use of medical students and practitioners, it is not as heavily annotated with citations to published judicial opinions and other esoteric legal source materials as are some treatises for lawyers. For example, we do not always footnote judicial decisions that are merely illustrative of factual situations discussed in the text. On the other hand, judicial opinions and other authorities that are genuinely important for the broad-gauge legal principles they enunciate are cited in the footnotes. A bibliography appears at the end of each chapter.

Judicial opinions are printed in books called "reports" or "reporters." For many years there was no organized system for the publication—reporting—of American court decisions. The job was left to private reporters and publishers; the result was a hodgepodge of separate publications that did not lend itself to efficient legal research. Today the situation is different and much improved. The volumes of the National Reporter System include all of the decisions of the highest state courts. This system also incorporates the decisions of all intermediate appellate courts. And it publishes the decisions of federal courts, including the Supreme Court of the United States.

In this book we shall refer the reader, whenever possible, to the volumes of the largely unofficial but highly accurate National Reporter System. A typical citation to a state court decision will look like this: *Brown* v. *Box,* 230 N.E.2d 204 (S. Ct. Ill. 1967). "Brown" and "Box" are the names of the parties to the reported litigation. The intervening "v." stands for *versus,* "against." The initial number, 230, refers, of course, to the volume in the reporter series. The "N.E." refers to the geographic region covered by the volume; "2d" indicates that this system of regional reports has gone into a second series, the preceding series having been denominated simply "N.E." Other phases of the National Reporter System reprint decisions from the Pacific region (Pac. and P.2d), North Western (N.W. and N.W.2d), South Western (S.W. and S.W.2d), Atlantic (Atl. and A.2d), South Eastern (S.E. and S.E.2d), and Southern (So. and So.2d). Separate series are published for New York and California: the New York Supplement (N.Y.S. and N.Y.S.2d) and the California Reporter (Cal. Rptr.). The number 204 in our citation to the case of *Brown* v. *Box* refers to the page of volume 230 of the N.E.2d series on which the opinion in that case begins. Within the parentheses are the name of the court rendering the decision—here, the Supreme Court of Illinois—and the year in which the decision was handed down, 1967. Citations to federal cases are similar in appearance. *United States* v. *Oregon State Medical Soc.*, 343 U.S. 326 (1951), refers to a decision in volume 343 of the National Reporter System's series that reports decisions of the Supreme Court of the United States. *Essington* v. *Parish*, 164 F.2d 725 (7th Cir. 1947), would take the researcher to a volume in the second Federal series that reports decisions of the United States Courts of Appeal, in this instance the one that sits in the Seventh Circuit, embracing Illinois, Indiana, and Wisconsin. *Zucker* v. *Vogt*, 200 F. Supp. 340 (D. Conn. 1961), identifies an opinion written by a federal trial judge sitting on the United States District Court for Connecticut. Where a case is too ancient to have been included in the National Reporter System, we cite the available series of official or private reporters: *Slater* v. *Baker*, 60 Barb. 488 (S. Ct. N.Y. 1871), for example, is a citation to an opinion by a judge of a New York trial court, handed down prior to commencement of the National Reporter System. For a much more detailed description of legal sources and methods of citation, we refer the reader to an excellent reference work: *How to Find the Law*, edited by law librarian William R. Roalfe and published in 1965 by West Publishing Company. We hasten to add, however, that the analysis of "law" is so complex an undertaking that it should ordinarily be left to lawyers.

We conclude this broad view of law and its sources and of the adversary trial process by commenting that the law and the process by which it is applied to all of us are things of genuine wonder—because they regularly serve everyone with an effectiveness that belies the seeming crudity of our man-made system of adjudication. The balance of this text will demonstrate, at that level of detail which will be most useful to the physician, the workings of our legal system as it applies to him. We begin at the beginning, or at least one beginning, by discussing medical licensure laws.

BIBLIOGRAPHY

An exhaustive bibliography on the subjects of law, lawyers, courts, and trials would be very long. We list below a sampling of worthwhile books and articles that amplify the topics discussed in the foregoing chapter.

BOOKS

Blume, W. W.: AMERICAN CIVIL PROCEDURE. Prentice-Hall, Inc., Englewood Cliffs, N.J., 1955.

Frank, J.: LAW AND THE MODERN MIND. Coward-McCann, Inc., New York, 1930.

James, F.: CIVIL PROCEDURE. Little, Brown and Company, Boston and Toronto, 1965.

Johnstone, Q., and Hopson, D.: LAWYERS AND THEIR WORK. The Bobbs-Merrill Company, Inc., Indianapolis, 1967.

Joiner, C. W.: TRIALS AND APPEALS. Prentice-Hall, Inc., Englewood Cliffs, N.J., 1957.

Kalven, H., and Zeisel H.: THE AMERICAN JURY. Little, Brown and Company, Boston and Toronto, 1966.

Kaplan, J., and Waltz, J. R.: THE TRIAL OF JACK RUBY. The Macmillan Company, New York, 1965.

Keeton, R. E.: TRIAL TACTICS AND METHODS. Little, Brown and Company, Boston and Toronto, 1954.

Mayer, M. P.: THE LAWYERS. Harper & Row, New York, Evanston and London, 1967.

Stryker, L. P.: THE ART OF ADVOCACY. Simon and Schuster, New York, 1954.

ARTICLES

Alexander, R. C.: *Discussing Medical Issues in Opening Statements for the Defense,* 14 DEFENSE LAW JOURNAL 633 (1965).

Cobb, K.: *Investigation,* 46 NEBRASKA LAW REVIEW 446 (1967).

Colson, W. R.: *Final Argument,* 36 MISSISSIPPI LAW JOURNAL 500 (1965).

Epton, H.: *Effective Use of Pre-Trial Discovery,* 19 ARKANSAS LAW REVIEW 9 (1965).

Groce, J. H.: *Jury Argument,* 31 INSURANCE COUNSEL JOURNAL 483 (1964).

Handbook for Effective Pre-Trial Discovery, 37 FEDERAL RULES DECISIONS 255 (1965).

Kennelly, J. J.: *Jury Selection in a Civil Case,* 9 TRIAL LAWYERS GUIDE 15 (1965).

Lane, J. A.: *Using Discovery Effectively,* 46 NEBRASKA LAW REVIEW 449 (1967).

Michael, J., and Adler M. J.: *The Trial of an Issue of Fact,* 34 COLUMBIA LAW REVIEW 1224 (1934).

Powers, G. B.: *The Closing Argument,* 19 ARKANSAS LAW REVIEW 58 (1965).

NOTE

Note, *The Opening Statement,* 4 WILLAMETTE LAW JOURNAL 1 (1966).

chapter 2

LICENSING LAWS

Controls on Health Service Quality

The medical profession and the general public, obviously, have a deep and continuing interest in the quality of medical and related health services. The quality of these vital services is regulated in a wide and sometimes bewildering variety of ways. The law probably impinges on the activities of health personnel and facilities to a degree greater than that experienced by any other profession or occupation in the United States. Some of the most potent controls on health service quality are these: (1) professional canons of ethics; (2) city, county, state, and federal licensing laws; (3) criminal laws prohibiting and punishing unauthorized practice of medicine; (4) regulations set up by professional organizations for the certification of medical and dental specialties, the accreditation of hospitals and like institutions, and the approval of training programs; (5) personnel controls maintained by hospital staff organizations; (6) standards written into state and, especially, federally financed health programs; and (7) the common law standards of professional conduct enforced by courts in medical malpractice and related private legal actions. This book will at least touch on most of these mechanisms of control; heavy emphasis will be placed on the law of medical malpractice. In this chapter we shall describe the nature and purpose of licensure laws.

The Purposes of Licensure Laws

Governmental licensing of health personnel, including medical doctors, was not common prior to the late nineteenth century, and most of the present-day licensure statutes were enacted shortly after the turn of the century. Over the years there has been little change, by legislative amendment, in their wording. The content of these enactments varies somewhat from jurisdiction to jurisdiction, but their source, their nature, and their functions can be broadly sketched. Licensing laws are legitimate exercises of a governmental unit's power to legislate for public health, welfare, and safety—a governmental right that flows from the constitutionally authorized "police power." They are designed to protect the public from incompetent and unethical practitioners by regulating the personnel, facilities, equipment, and medications that can be utilized in what is loosely and irreverently referred to as the health service industry. The licensing of individuals to engage in this field is based on minimum qualifications and standards of conduct for entry into, and retention in, the particular health profession or occupation. City, county, state, and now also federal licensing of hospitals and related facilities is aimed at assuring at least minimum levels of quality in these institutions.

Licensing statutes define the functions that specified occupational groups are permitted to perform; they also set forth character, education, and training requirements. Entry into practice is also controlled by provisions for approval of educational institutions and the examination of licensure applicants. The statutes further provide grounds and procedures for renewal, suspension, revocation, and reinstatement of licenses. Agencies are created to administer the licensing statutes.[1]

The mandatory licensing process governs physicians, dentists and dental hygienists, osteopaths, chiropractors, professional and practical (vocational) nurses, physical therapists, optometrists, and podiatrists in every state in the nation. In some states psychologists, dispensing opticians and x-ray and medical technicians or technologists are also subject to licensure. In no jurisdiction are dental assistants or occupational therapists required to obtain a license. The medical doctor receives an unlimited license. Other health personnel, referred to above, receive licenses that are limited in scope, and health services not expressly included within their ambit can be rendered only by a physician.

Reciprocity Between States

Most states recognize the medical licenses of other states, either through reciprocity with the licensing state or through endorsement of an existing license. The licensing authorities in all but six of the forty-nine states that make some provision for recognizing other states' licenses have discretionary power to endorse—that is, accept—licenses issued by nonreciprocating states. Two states, Iowa and Minnesota, have amended their

[1] More detailed descriptions of the mechanics of licensure can be found in Forgotson, E. H., and Cook, J. L.: *Innovations and Experiments in Uses of Health Manpower —The Effect of Licensure Laws,* 32 LAW & CONTEMPORARY PROBLEMS 731 (1967), and Forgotson, E. H., Roemer, R., and Newman, R. W.: *Licensure of Physicians,* (1967) UNIV. OF WASHINGTON LAW QUARTERLY 248.

licensure statutes to specify that their reciprocity requirements are discretionary, not mandatory.[2]

The Grounds for License Revocation or Suspension

Although they may be commingled and there is some overlapping, three groupings of grounds for license revocation or suspension can be discerned in the licensure law of every state. First come *personal disqualifications,* such as mental or physical illness, alcoholism, narcotics addiction, and gross immorality. Next come *criminal acts:* conviction of a felony or misdemeanor involving moral turpitude, performing an unlawful abortion, aiding or abetting an unlicensed person to practice medicine. Finally, *unprofessional conduct,* a sort of grab bag that includes fee splitting, improper advertising, betrayal of a professional secret, gross malpractice, fraud, and so on. There is not much consistency in the licensing laws of the various states. In 1961 it was reported that among the states there were more than ninety grounds for license revocation or suspension.[3] The same report pointed out that no one ground, stated in the same words, was to be found in all of the medical practice acts. Furthermore, as we shall see, the statutes are riddled with that sort of vague language that is the grist of courts.[4]

The Illinois Medical Practice Act [5] is a typical licensure code. It begins by providing that "No person shall practice medicine, or any of its branches, or midwifery, or any system or method of treating human ailments without the use of drugs or medicines and without operative surgery, without a valid, existing license to do so." The third section of the statute provides that no license shall be issued until the applicant has passed "an examination of his qualifications therefor," administered by the Department of Registration and Education. The next section of the statute sets out numerous conditions that must be met by an applicant for licensure. These include the submission to the Department of evidence under oath that the applicant is at least twenty-one years old and of good moral character, that he has the necessary undergraduate and professional education, and that he is either a citizen of the United States or in the process of becoming one. (If the applicant subsequently fails to perfect

[2] IOWA ANN. CODE, §148.5 (Supp. 1968); MINN. STAT., §147.04 (Supp. 1967).

[3] A.M.A. MEDICAL DISCIPLINARY COMMITTEE, REPORT TO BOARD OF TRUSTEES 41 (1961).

[4] One court has pointed out that the phrase "unprofessional or dishonorable conduct," employed in the District of Columbia's licensure law, ". . . is not defined by the common law, and the words have no common or generally accepted signification." *Czarra* v. *Board of Med. Supervisors,* 25 App. D. C. 443, 453 (D. C. Cir. 1905).

[5] ILL. ANN. STAT., ch. 91 (Supp. 1969).

his citizenship, his license will not be renewed.) The applicant must also designate the name, location, and kind of educational institution of which he is a graduate and describe the system of treatment under which he seeks to practice.

There follow the inevitable provisions for the payment of various fees. Three types of licenses are provided for under the Medical Practice Act: (1) an unlimited license "to practice medicine in all of its branches"; (2) a limited license to treat human ailments without the use of drugs, medicines, or operative surgery; (3) a limited license to practice midwifery. Other Illinois statutes, not included within the Medical Practice Act, provide for the limited licensing of dentists, nurses, and others.

The Illinois Medical Practice Act, like all licensure statutes, sets up numerous grounds for revocation or suspension of a license to practice:

1. Conviction of procuring, or of attempting or aiding to procure, an unlawful abortion;
2. Conviction of any crime that would be a felony under Illinois law (a felony, as distinguished from a misdemeanor, is a serious crime punishable by imprisonment in a penitentiary for more than one year);
3. "Gross" malpractice, resulting in the death or permanent injury of a patient;
4. Engaging in dishonorable, unethical, or unprofessional conduct of a character likely to deceive, defraud, or otherwise harm the public;
5. Obtaining a fee or other valuable consideration in exchange for the fraudulent representation that an incurable disease or injury can be permanently cured;
6. Habitual and incapacitating intemperance in the use of "ardent spirits, narcotics, or stimulants";
7. Holding one's self out to treat human ailments under any name other than one's own, or impersonating another physician;
8. Using fraud, deception, or any unlawful means to obtain a license, including the violation of rules concerning examinations;
9. Making false claims regarding one's skill or the efficacy of one's method of treatment;
10. Professional connection with, or lending one's name to, another person for the illegal practice by that person;
11. Revocation or suspension of one's medical license in another state;
12. Advertising or soliciting "by means of handbills, posters, circulars, stereopticon slides, motion pictures, radio, newspapers, or in any other manner for professional purposes" (happily, there is no reported case of license revocation based on advertising by means of a stereopticon);

13. A judicial decree that a licenseholder is in need of mental treatment operates as a suspension of his license; it will not be restored until it has been formally determined that he has recovered from his mental illness.

The Illinois Medical Practice Act provides that proceedings to suspend or revoke a medical license must be commenced within a limited period of time after the occurrence of any of the acts or events catalogued above; with the exception of items 8 and 13, the period is three years. The statute also provides for fair hearing and review procedures.

In Illinois, which again is typical, a physician's license cannot be revoked or suspended until the following procedures have taken place: (1) the filing with the Department of Registration and Education of a sworn Complaint setting forth the improper acts charged against the named physician; (2) the issuance to the named physician by the Department's Director of a summons, together with a copy of the Complaint, requiring the recipient to appear before the Department's Examining Committee at a specified time and place and to file, within twenty days, his sworn written Answer to the charges (if the physician fails to file an Answer, his license can be revoked or suspended without a hearing if the charges warrant such action); (3) a hearing, to take place not less than thirty days after issuance of the summons.

At the hearing the physician will be given ample opportunity to make his defense, in person or with the aid of legal counsel. He can introduce testimony, tangible evidence, written statements, and an argument can be presented by him or on his behalf. Strict courtroom rules of evidence are not imposed. The Department, at its expense, provides a stenographer to take down and preserve a *verbatim* record of the hearing, a copy of which, vital to the perfecting of an appeal, will be made available to the physician upon payment of a nominal fee. The Department cannot suspend or revoke a license except upon the written report and recommendation of the Examining Committee. The Director of the Department has the power to order a rehearing before the same or other examiners if he is not satisfied that substantial justice was done in the initial hearing. Any final decision by the Director is subject to review, on appeal, in the courts of the state.

Courts do not deal cavalierly with statutes that visit the most serious of consequences upon those accused of their violation. The authority to practice medicine is a property right and the possessor cannot be deprived of it arbitrarily. Statutes providing for the revocation or suspension of professional licenses are penal in nature (quasi-criminal), and consequently their wording is strictly construed in favor of a physician against whom charges have been made; any ambiguity in the language of the statute will be interpreted in his favor. Two reported cases illustrate this judicial approach:

A Connecticut licensure statute provides that "habitual negligence" is a ground for license revocation. This phrase was judicially construed to require *repetitious* negligence and to exclude all other forms of negligence; accordingly, a license revocation for "wanton negligence" was overturned since ineptitude might be "wanton" without being "habitual." [6]

The New York licensure statute, like Illinois', is made applicable to a doctor who has offered, undertaken or agreed to cure or treat disease by a "secret method, procedure, or treatment" which he refuses to divulge. A physician's license was suspended by the New York Board of Regents because he had undertaken, successfully, to treat a cancerous growth with a "secret formula." The patient had undergone orthodox medical and surgical treatment, including radiation, without success; her family had been told that she was beyond hope and had only a few weeks to live. The defendant doctor suggested the application of a salve. He secured the consent of the patient and of her relatives to this course of treatment, but the ingredients of the salve were not disclosed to them. The physician, however, knew the salve's components and had previously tested it, without injurious results, on healthy tissue. At a preliminary hearing the physician revealed his salve's ingredients and outlined his method of treatment. A reviewing court,[7] construing the words "secret method, procedure, or treatment," stated that "the commonly accepted and understood meaning of what is secret is that which is intentionally withheld." The court held that in a penal statute the word "secret" means "studiously concealed." Reversing the Board of Regents' findings, the court declared: "It is not fraud or deceit for one already skilled in the medical art, with the consent of the patient, to attempt new methods when all other known methods of treatment had proved futile and least of all when the patient's very life has been despaired of."

The meaning of many of the statutory grounds for license revocation or suspension, typified by the outlined Illinois provisions, is reasonably self-evident. As the Connecticut and New York cases cited in the last paragraph attest, however, some of the statutory provisions have undergone judicial interpretation; some have also been the subject of statutory elaboration.

[6] *Adam* v. *Medical Examining Board,* 79 A.2d 350 (S. Ct. Err. & App. Conn. 1951).

[7] *Stammer* v. *Board of Regents,* 29 N.Y.S.2d 38, *aff'd,* 39 N.E.2d 913 (Ct. App. N.Y. 1942). For another example of strict construction of a medical practice act, see *Magit* v. *Board of Examiners,* 366 P.2d 816 (S. Ct. Cal. 1961).

Procuring, or Attempting or Aiding to Procure, an Unlawful Abortion

Under the wording of typical licensure statutes it is not a prerequisite to license revocation that the accused physician actually has performed an unlawful abortion; a mere offer to do so may be sufficient. In a New York case [8] antedating that state's adoption of a significantly liberalized abortion statute, a physician was visited by three women who did not announce that they were special investigators for the Department of Education. The physician advised each of them that she was pregnant, and that he was willing to abort her. In each case he made a date for the performance of the abortion. His license was revoked. In another New York case [9] in which the accused physician had not himself performed an abortion but had procured its performance by another, the Board of Regents ordered a two-year license suspension, which subsequently was judicially upheld. Liberalized abortion laws, such as the one enacted in New York in 1970, render these opinions, and the licensure provisions underlying them, obsolete.[9a]

Conviction of Crime

In a case [10] involving two physicians who had been convicted of contempt of Congress, the court held that it was of no moment that their crimes bore no direct relation to the practice of medicine and might not be said to evidence moral turpitude. "The conviction for any crime," said the court, "bears some relation to the practice of any profession." The court declined to usurp the examining board's discretion in determining whether the doctors' conduct warranted license suspension or revocation.

The fact that a physician convicted of a crime has received little or no punishment is not determinative. In a California case,[11] for example, a doctor had been found guilty of unlawfully dispensing a morphine preparation. The trial court placed him on probation and thereafter discharged him from probation. The doctor then sought to have the suspension of his license declared invalid. His effort was rebuffed since the criminal court's mitigating action did not detract from the fact that the doctor had

[8] *Kahn* v. *Board of Regents,* 4 N.Y.S.2d 233, *aff'd,* 23 N.E.2d 16 (Ct. App. N.Y. 1939).

[9] *Newman* v. *Board of Regents,* 61 N.Y.S.2d 841 (App. Div. N.Y. 1961).

[9a] See Chapter 24.

[10] *Miller* v. *Board of Regents,* 111 N.Y.S.2d 393 (App. Div. N.Y. 1952); *Barsky* v. *Board of Regents,* 111 N.E.2d 222 (Ct. App. N.Y. 1953). A strong dissenting opinion was filed by one of the court's most distinguished judges, but the Supreme Court of the United States affirmed, 347 U.S. 442 (1954). See also *Erdman* v. *Board of Regents,* 261 N.Y.S.2d 698 (App. Div. N.Y. 1965).

[11] *Meyer* v. *Board of Examiners,* 206 P.2d 1085 (S. Ct. Cal. 1949).

been convicted of the crime charged. Probation is rather frequently granted in income tax cases, and yet conviction for income tax evasion is probably the most commonly encountered ground, under this heading, for the suspension or revocation of a physician's license to practice.[12] In fact, several courts have held that the granting of a full pardon will not affect the power of a regulatory board to revoke a convicted practitioner's license.[13] Conviction in a state other than the one in which the defendant carries on his medical practice is sufficient to support a license revocation.[14]

Gross Malpractice

Something more than simple negligence is obviously required under statutes that provide for license suspension or revocation for "gross" malpractice or "gross" incompetence. No court has ever done a wholly comprehensible job of defining the term "gross." Judges are inclined to say in effect, as they do when confronted by claims of literary obscenity, that "I cannot define it, but I know it when I see it." This much is clear, however: "gross" malpractice or incompetence connotes very great negligence or the lack of even scant care. It has been characterized as a failure to employ even that care which a careless person would use. It involves an extreme departure from the ordinary standard of care. And in licensure matters the traditional standard of care applied in medical malpractice cases [15] cannot be abandoned in favor of some more rigid test even where the accused has proclaimed himself to be "one of the greatest and most skillful plastic surgeons in the world." [16]

Unprofessional Conduct

The phrase "unprofessional conduct" is a legislative catchall and has resulted, predictably, in endless judicial controversy. California's licensure

[12] *E.g., Application of Palermo,* 221 N.Y.S.2d 91 (App. Div. N.Y. 1961); *In re* Kindschi, 319 P.2d 824 (S. Ct. Wash. 1958); *State* v. *Margoles,* 124 N.W.2d 37 (S. Ct. Wis. 1963); see also Note, *Physicians—Unprofessional Conduct—Wilful Evasion of Federal Taxes as an Offense Allowing Summary Action by Disciplinary Board,* 11 VANDERBILT LAW REVIEW 1456 (1958).

[13] *E.g., Hughes* v. *State Board of Medical Examiners,* 142 S.E. 285 (S. Ct. Ga. 1928); *Hughes* v. *State Board of Health,* 159 S.W.2d 277 (S. Ct. Mo. 1942). See also *Hartman* v. *Board of Chiropractic Examiners,* 66 P.2d 705 (Cal. App. 1937) (sentence for first-degree murder commuted). *Contra: Page* v. *State Board of Medical Examiners,* 193 So. 82 (S. Ct. Fla. 1940) (probation).

[14] *E.g., Bancroft* v. *Board of Governors of Registered Dentists,* 210 P.2d 666 (S. Ct. Okla. 1949); *Francisco* v. *Board of Dental Examiners,* 149 S.W.2d 619 (Tex. Civ. App. 1941). See also *State ex rel. Munch* v. *Davis,* 196 So. 491 (S. Ct. Fla. 1940) (conviction in federal court of federal offense); *Barsky* v. *Board of Regents,* 111 N.E.2d 222 (Ct. App. N.Y. 1953), *aff'd,* 347 U.S. 442 (1954) (same).

[15] See Chapter 4.

[16] *Schireson* v. *Walsh,* 187 N.E. 921 (S. Ct. Ill. 1933).

statute, unlike most, attempts to give some specific content to the phrase.[17] It provides that "unprofessional conduct" includes, but is not limited to, (1) violating or attempting to violate, or assisting in or abetting the violation of, or conspiring to violate, any other provision of its licensure code; (2) gross negligence; (3) gross incompetence; (4) gross immorality; (5) the commission of any act involving moral turpitude, dishonesty, or corruption, whether or not the act relates directly to the practice of the accused's profession; and (6) any conduct that would have warranted denial of a license in the first place.

It comes down to this: a broad spectrum of reprehensible conduct may constitute "unprofessional conduct." Whether or not particular conduct falls within the intendment of the statutory language will depend on the attitude adopted by the court considering the conduct. A review of the many decided cases makes it clear that courts will not support license revocation or suspension under so open-ended a statutory phrase unless the accused's deviations were of a gravely serious brand. Some sense of this conclusion's validity can be drawn from a Nevada judicial opinion [18] in which it was held that a doctor's "harshly critical language . . . directed by him at three other doctors . . . and the entire local medical profession" did not constitute such unprofessional conduct as to justify license revocation. However misguided he may have been, the Nevada doctor had not acted out of evil motives or for the purpose of expanding his own medical practice. To be contrasted with this case is an earlier Colorado [19] case in which a chiropractor, to increase his own business, had printed and distributed false charges that a hospital had caused the death of a patient "by inhuman treatment." The chiropractor's enterprising conduct was considered "unprofessional" and a license revocation was judicially upheld. And for an example of a genuinely clear case the reader can consult the New York decision involving a doctor who engaged in clandestine surgery and surreptitiously dismembered a corpse in an effort to conceal a crime.[20] Or the California case involving the statutory rape by a psychiatrist of a youthful patient whom he was treating for sexual promiscuity.[21]

Representations of a fraudulent nature can result in license revocation or suspension. Wholly typical are cases of physicians who advertise, falsely, that they have perfected "sure cures" for sundry ills of mankind.[22]

A physician or surgeon is required to rely on his own reputation. He

[17] CALIF. BUS. & PROF. CODE, §§2416–17 (Supp. 1967).

[18] *Boswell* v. *Board of Medical Examiners,* 293 P.2d 424 (S. Ct. Nev. 1956).

[19] *State Board of Medical Examiners* v. *Spears,* 247 Pac. 563 (S. Ct. Colo. 1926).

[20] *Gilbert* v. *Cole,* 42 N.Y.S.2d 801 (App. Div. N.Y. 1943).

[21] *Bernstein* v. *Board of Medical Examiners,* 22 Cal. Rptr. 419 (Cal. App. 1962).

[22] *E.g., Randall* v. *Board of Medical Examiners,* 293 P. 790 (S. Ct. Cal. 1930).

cannot use a name other than his own; the licensure laws prohibit him from engaging in what lawyers call "palming off." The doctor named Smith or Jones, not yet widely acclaimed, cannot borrow the name of a more renowned practitioner—a Mayo or a Menninger—no matter how much he admires the ring of it. It is equally improper to lend one's name to an unlicensed person.

Understandably, a fraudulently obtained license will be revoked. The use in licensure statutes of such terms as "fraud," "deception," and "unlawful means" has necessitated judicial interpretation. In an influential Illinois opinion [23] the state supreme court held that the fact that a physician was not "a man of good moral character" at the time of his application for a license did not warrant revocation. The court said:

> It is apparent that the legislative intent . . . contemplated that some positive, willful, or intentional act be committed on the part of the registrant which actively induced the issuance of his license. It must have been some overt act in the way of making false answers to material questions affecting his qualifications for the practice of his profession, or of unlawfully concealing from the department the fact, if it was a fact, that he had theretofore been guilty of a violation of some of the causes laid down in the statute for the revocation or suspension of the license of a physician, or some willful misconduct on his part in the taking of an examination, such as having some one else write his examination for him, or willfully cheating in the examination. . . .

The medical profession itself, akin with the legal profession, is opposed to self-advertising to the general public. This ethical determination is reflected in licensure statutes. However, such statutes are not taken to prohibit the listing in a telephone directory of a physician's name, title, office hours, address, telephone number, and professional specialty. Nor do the statutes preclude the use of professional cards or appointment cards. Illinois, by express statutory language, also permits a physician to "list his name, title, address and telephone number and any specialty in public print limited to the number of lines necessary to state that information"; in like manner he may announce a change of office address or his absence from or return to his office. It is prudent to add that a physician taking unduly active advantage of this sort of statutory provision will encounter disapprobation on the part of his professional colleagues.

License Reinstatement

One seeking the restoration of a revoked license to practice medicine has no greater rights than a person seeking a license in the first instance. Although a board of medical examiners usually has broad discretionary

[23] *Schireson* v. *Walsh,* 187 N.E.2d 921 (S. Ct. Ill. 1933).

power to reinstate revoked licenses, the burden is on the petitioner to demonstrate that he has rehabilitated himself. It has been said that only "clear and convincing proof of reform" will discharge this burden.[24] By way of example, it is not enough for one who has been convicted of a felony to show that he has received a full pardon.[25]

Criminal Penalties for Failure to Comply with Licensure Requirements

There is more than one bite in state medical practice acts. Violation of their licensure provisions can result not only in license revocation or suspension but also in a criminal prosecution and penalty. Violation of licensing statutes is generally made a misdemeanor, punishable by fine, imprisonment, or both. The Illinois statute, for example, provides for a fine of not less than $200 nor more than $1,000 and for confinement in a county jail for not more than one year. Practicing without a valid license or exceeding the scope of a limited license is punishable in like manner. Furthermore, unauthorized practice is subject to injunctive proceedings in the courts, whereby a person can be barred, at the behest of a private citizen or a public official such as the state attorney general or a county prosecutor, from continuing his unlicensed activities.

The Effect of Licensure Laws on Health Manpower

Licensure laws pose a problem peculiar to a period of shortages in skilled health personnel. It has been forcefully argued that present legal regulation of health manpower is restricting, unduly, the allocation of vital tasks among auxiliary members of the medical community.[26] Furthermore, it has been suggested that the present regulatory scheme impedes experimentation aimed at utilizing entirely new categories of health professionals.[27] Pressures built up by new health programs will inevitably force state legislatures to redesign their medical practice statutes.

BIBLIOGRAPHY

BOOK

Richardson, J. R.: DOCTORS, LAWYERS AND THE COURTS 1–52. The W. H. Anderson Company, Cincinnati, 1965.

[24] *Housman* v. *Board of Medical Examiners,* 190 P.2d 653 (Cal. App. 1948).

[25] *E.g., People* v. *Rongetti,* 70 N.E.2d 568 (S. Ct. Ill. 1947); *State* v. *Hazzard,* 247 P. 957 (S. Ct. Wash. 1926).

[26] Forgotson, E. H., and Cook, J. L.: *Innovations and Experiments in Uses of Health Manpower—The Effect of Licensure Laws,* 32 LAW & CONTEMPORARY PROBLEMS 731 (1967).

[27] *Ibid.*

ARTICLES

Epstein, D. G.: *Limitations on the Scope of Practice of Osteopathic Physicians,* 32 MISSOURI LAW REVIEW 354 (1967).

Forgotson, E. H., Roemer, R., and Newman, R. W.: *Licensure of Physicians,* [1967] WASHINGTON UNIV. LAW QUARTERLY 249.

Graves, W. B.: *Professional anl Occupational Restrictions,* 13 TEMPLE LAW QUARTERLY 334 (1939).

Grills, N. G.: *Regulation of the Practice of Medicine in the State of Michigan,* 15 UNIV. OF DETROIT LAW JOURNAL 42 (1952).

Monaghan, H. P.: *The Constitution and Occupational Licensing in Massachusetts,* 41 BOSTON UNIV. LAW REVIEW 157 (1961).

NOTES AND COMMENTS

Comment, *Criminal and Tort Liability of Unlicensed Healers,* 41 VIRGINIA LAW REVIEW 961 (1955).

Note, *Entrance and Disciplinary Requirements for Occupational Licenses in California,* 14 STANFORD LAW REVIEW 533 (1962).

chapter 3

PRIVATE CANONS OF PROFESSIONAL AND INTERPROFESSIONAL CONDUCT

The American Medical Association Principles of Medical Ethics

Although the books are brimming with legislative enactments and administrative regulations governing the conduct of medical men, the medical profession itself sets standards of proficiency and propriety that are at least as demanding as those laid down in formal laws such as the licensure statutes considered in the last chapter. Of primary significance are the *Principles of Medical Ethics* of the American Medical Association.[1] This catalog of ethical standards, while not itself a set of formal laws, may be consulted by courts in their efforts to flesh out the common law's standards of professional competence—and these common law standards, as we shall see, are central to that most astringent of professional regulators, the law of medical malpractice.[2] For this reason we include here, *verbatim*, the ethical standards promulgated by the American Medical Association: [2a]

PRINCIPLES OF MEDICAL ETHICS OF THE AMERICAN MEDICAL ASSOCIATION

Preamble. These principles are intended to aid physicians individually and collectively in maintaining a high level of ethical conduct. They are not laws but standards by which a physician may determine the propriety of his conduct in his relationship with patients, with colleagues, with members of allied professions, and with the public.

Section 1. The principal objective of the medical profession is to render service to humanity with full respect for the dignity of man. Physicians should merit the confidence of patients entrusted to their care, rendering to each a full measure of service and devotion.

[1] A.M.A., PRINCIPLES OF MEDICAL ETHICS (1957) (pamphlet).

[2] See Chapter 4.

[2a] Reprinted with permission.

Section 2. Physicians should strive continually to improve medical knowledge and skill, and should make available to their patients and colleagues the benefits of their professional attainments.

Section 3. A physician should practice a method of healing founded on a scientific basis; and he should not voluntarily associate professionally with anyone who violates this principle.

Section 4. The medical profession should safeguard the public and itself against physicians deficient in moral character or professional competence. Physicians should observe all laws, uphold the dignity and honor of the profession and accept its self-imposed disciplines. They should expose, without hesitation, illegal or unethical conduct of fellow members of the profession.

Section 5. A physician may choose whom he will serve. In an emergency, however, he should render service to the best of his ability. Having undertaken the care of a patient, he may not neglect him; and unless he has been discharged he may discontinue his services only after giving adequate notice. He should not solicit patients.

Section 6. A physician should not dispose of his services under terms or conditions which tend to interfere with or impair the free and complete exercise of his medical judgment and skill or tend to cause a deterioration of the quality of medical care.

Section 7. In the practice of medicine a physician should limit the source of his professional income to medical services actually rendered by him, or under his supervision, to his patients. His fee should be commensurate with the services rendered and the patient's ability to pay. He should neither pay nor receive a commission for referral of patients. Drugs, remedies or appliances may be dispensed or supplied by the physician provided it is in the best interests of the patient.

Section 8. A physician should seek consultation upon request; in doubtful or difficult cases; or whenever it appears that the quality of medical service may be enhanced thereby.

Section 9. A physician may not reveal the confidences entrusted to him in the course of medical attendance, or the deficiencies he may observe in the character of patients, unless he is required to do so by law or unless it becomes necessary in order to protect the welfare of the individual or of the community.

Section 10. The honored ideals of the medical profession imply that the responsibilities of the physician extend not only to the individual, but also to society where these responsibilities deserve his interest and participation in activities which have the purpose of improving both the health and the well-being of the individual and the community.

These ten basic ethical principles are not the only professional canons that exist in the medical world. Specialty groups such as the American College of Surgeons, founded in 1913 to advance the welfare of patients, have also drawn up special standards of conduct. But the quoted A.M.A. standards have been the most broadly influential.

The *Principles of Medical Ethics* comport generally with the law. For example, the law supports Section 5 of the *Principles*, having to do with a physician's free choice of patients. Like lawyers and members of other professions, physicians have a powerful moral obligation to serve the public. But doctors are not public servants, obligated to serve any member of the public who seeks him out.[3] The reason underlying this legal conclusion is that a doctor, like most other persons, must be accorded reasonable freedom of contract. The concept of contract is a voluntary sort of thing; one cannot be coerced into entering a contractual relationship. And the doctor-patient relationship is fundamentally contractual in nature. The principle that a physician is free to choose his patients, moreover, has real practical values. It furthers the notion of a personal and confidential relationship between physician and patient. It also furthers concentration on specialized fields of medical science; no physician, in other words, can be forced to hold himself out as a general practitioner if he does not wish to do so. And it permits a physician to restrict his activities to a reasonable number of patients, to the end that they will receive adequate care and attention.[4]

One lower state court has held that a doctor's office is not a place of "public accommodation" in the language of a civil rights statute and that, consequently, a physician or surgeon is not legally obligated—at least in the absence of an explicit statute—to render professional services to everyone who seeks them.[5] It would be unwise in the mid-twentieth century, however, to treat this decision as authorizing conscious racial discrimination by a doctor. It simply means that a physician can limit his practice in a sensible fashion.

Section 5 of the quoted *Principles* adjures private physicians to render emergency service to the best of their ability. Here the *Principles* command more than the law does; no private citizen is obligated under the law to come to the rescue of another, since this involves a moral decision which the law leaves to the conscience of the individual. We shall discuss later in this book the legal liability of the doctor who experiences a bad result while tendering emergency treatment.[6]

Section 9 of the A.M.A. *Principles* also finds a counterpart in the law of some states. That section seeks to prohibit voluntary disclosure by the physician of confidential communications made to him as an outgrowth of the doctor-patient relationship. We shall devote a full chapter to the state physician-patient privilege statutes that enforce a similar rule.[7]

[3] See, *e.g.*, *Agnew* v. *Parks*, 343. P.2d 118 (Cal. App. 1959); *Buttersworth* v. *Swint*, 186 S.E. 770 (Ga. App. 1936); *Childers* v. *Frye*, 158 S.E. 744 (S. Ct. N.C. 1931).

[4] See Louisell, D. W., and Williams, H.: MEDICAL MALPRACTICE, par. 8.02. Matthew Bender, New York, 1969.

[5] *Rice* v. *Rinaldo*, 119 N.E.2d 657 (Ohio C.P. 1951).

[6] See Chapter 8.

[7] Chapter 15.

The Regulatory Role of Medical Organizations

Medical societies, from the American Medical Association to the smallest county organization, serve significant public purposes, including the improvement of standards in the practicing profession, medical schools, and hospitals and the protection of the public from quacks. The American Medical Association, as we have seen, promulgates a code of ethics; through its Joint Commission on Accreditation of Hospitals it also approves and accredits hospitals and medical schools.[8] County medical societies, which are components of the A.M.A., generally have the power to exclude or expel from membership those who fail to conform to the *Principles of Medical Ethics.* Most hospitals will exclude a practitioner who has been excluded or expelled by a county medical society.[9] Any other course might result in loss of accreditation, and an unaccredited hospital cannot effectively conduct internship and nursing programs. Furthermore, loss of accreditation will result in losses within the medical staff.

County Medical Societies

Exclusion, suspension, or expulsion from a county medical society can have serious consequences for a physician.[10] Medical societies are private voluntary associations, and courts are usually reluctant to inject themselves into the internal affairs of such organizations. Nonetheless, a suspended or expelled physician has a limited recourse to the courts. There is

[8] The Commission is made up of representatives of four bodies: the A.M.A., the American Hospital Association, the American College of Physicians, and the American College of Surgeons.

[9] In considering the power of *hospitals* to exclude doctors from the use of their facilities, courts have usually distinguished between public—*i.e.,* governmentally managed and controlled—and private hospitals. Regularly licensed physicians and surgeons are generally considered to be entitled to practice in public hospitals providing only that they comply with all reasonable rules and regulations. See, *e.g., Hayman* v. *Galveston,* 273 U.S. 414 (1927); *Henderson* v. *Knoxville,* 9 S.W.2d 697 (S. Ct. Tenn. 1928). On the other hand, in times past it has been held that private hospitals have the right to exclude licensed physicians and surgeons and that such exclusion rests in the sound discretion of the hospital's managing authorities. See, *e.g., West Coast Hospital Ass'n* v. *Hoare,* 64 So.2d 293 (S. Ct. Fla. 1953); *Natale* v. *Sisters of Mercy of Council Bluffs,* 52 N.W.2d 701 (S. Ct. Iowa 1952); *Van Campeu* v. *Olean General Hospital,* 147 N.E. 219 (App. Div. N.Y. 1925). However, the trend is toward equating public and private institutions. See, *e.g., Griesman* v. *Newcomb Hospital,* 192 A.2d 817 (S. Ct. N.J. 1963). See also Southwick, A. F.: *Hospital Medical Staff Privileges,* 18 DE PAUL LAW REVIEW 655 (1969).

[10] In addition to those previously mentioned, the denial of patient referrals and consultations and difficulty in securing malpractice insurance can be mentioned. See Note, *The American Medical Association,* 63 YALE LAW JOURNAL 938, 949 (1954).

one preliminary requrement: all internal administrative remedies must have been exhausted before a court will take jurisdiction of the physician's complaint.[11] This ordinarily involves an appeal to a state medical society.

Once expulsion is complete and all internal remedies have been exhausted, courts can grant relief on any of three theories. One group of cases requires the plaintiff to demonstrate that he has been deprived of a property right; [12] in the absence of any such right, the courts will decline to act. If, however, a property right can be shown, the courts will then inquire whether the society's expulsion procedures complied with notions of legal "due process"—that is, fairness—and will also determine if the ground of expulsion violated some public policy.

A typical "due process" case is *Reid* v. *Medical Society*.[13] In this early New York case the court, in granting the plaintiff doctor a restoration to membership in a medical association, found that no evidence of guilt had been produced, that the plaintiff had been precluded from presenting his proof, and that prejudicial comments had been made during his hearing. Another case, *Bernstein* v. *Alameda-Contra Costa Medical Ass'n*,[14] supplies an example of a ground for expulsion that was considered violative of public policy. The plaintiff had been expelled from his county medical society for violation of the ethic forbidding a physician to disparage the work of another physician. The disparagement was contained in an affidavit filed in a Workmen's Compensation proceeding. The court held that the plaintiff's affidavit was privileged—in effect, that it constituted legally *required* disparagement—and added that the medical society could not expel a member for performing a public duty or for exercising a citizen's right.

A second legal theory supporting relief in expulsion cases is based on contract notions. The theory is that the medical society's constitution and bylaws form a contract between the society and its members, with the result that expulsion proceedings must comply with the procedural requirements set out in the agreement. In other words, application of this theory requires a determination "whether [the medical society] acted within its powers in good faith, in accord with its laws." [15] If it did, there has been no breach of contract and the expelled doctor is entitled to no

[11] *E.g., Weyrens* v. *Scott Bluff County Medical Soc.*, 277 N.W. 378 (S. Ct. Neb. 1938).

[12] This requirement is undoubtedly a holdover from early cases in which the association actually held property in which the members had an interest. *E.g., Smith* v. *Hollis*, 33 WEEKLY NOTES OF CASES 485 (Pa. C. D. 1893).

[13] 156 N.Y.S. 1129 (App. Div. N.Y. 1917); see also the *dictum* in *People* v. *Medical Society of the County of Erie*, 24 Barb. 577 (S. Ct. N.Y. 1857).

[14] 293 P.2d 862 (Cal. App. 1956).

[15] *Smith* v. *Kern County Medical Association*, 120 P.2d 874, 875 (S. Ct. Cal. 1942); see also *Robinson* v. *Lull*, 145 F.Supp. 134 (N.D. Ill. 1956).

judicial relief. This contractual theory has largely supplanted the "property right" theory.

A third group of cases disregards the fictional conceptions of property and contract altogether. These cases, few in number, go to the heart of the matter and simply inquire into the procedural and substantive validity of the plaintiff's expulsion.[16]

Thus far we have restricted our consideration to suspensions and expulsions from medical organizations. A problem is also posed by *exclusions* from such associations. The bases for relief from suspension and expulsion are narrow; the grounds for relief from exclusion have generally been even more restricted. On the surface, at least, this has resulted from the entanglement of courts and lawyers in their own sometimes sterile concepts. Jurisdictions requiring a showing of "property" cannot find such an interest in one who has never been a member of the society; jurisdictions looking for a "contract" cannot find one between a medical society and a mere applicant for membership. The New Jersey case of *Falcone* v. *Middlesex Co. Medical Soc.*[17] heralds a different approach to exclusion cases. The plaintiff in that case was a Doctor of Osteopathy and had been licensed to practice medicine and surgery. When the Middlesex County Medical Society discovered that plaintiff had not studied for four years in an A.M.A.-approved medical school it refused to admit him to active membership. Membership in the Society was prerequisite to the use of two local hospitals. Plaintiff, after having exhausted nonjudicial remedies, brought a lawsuit to force admission into the Society. He prevailed at the trial court level. The court reasoned that the bylaw excluding plaintiff was against public policy, since the New Jersey examiners had already approved plaintiff's medical education and licensed him to practice in the state.

In the mid-twentieth century it seems appropriate to suggest that medical associations will encounter no interference from courts so long as they function within their proper sphere, advancing medical science and promoting elevated professional standards, but that they will be restrained from acts of discrimination that run counter to public policy.[18]

The Interprofessional Code for Physicians and Attorneys

The professions of medicine and law are frequently thrown together in close relationship. The very existence of this book attests that fact. At

[16] See, *e.g.*, one of the earliest of them, *State* v. *Georgia Medical Society*, 95 Am. Dec. 408 (S. Ct. Ga. 1869); see also *Group Health Cooperative* v. *King County Medical Society*, 237 P.2d 737 (S. Ct. Wash. 1951).

[17] 162 A.2d 324 (N.J. Super. 1960).

[18] See Note, *Legal Limitations on Right of Unincorporated Medical Associations to Expel Members*, 41 MINNESOTA LAW REVIEW 212 (1957).

times, unfortunately, the two professions generate friction—even sparks. The American Medical Association and the lawyers' national professional organization, the American Bar Association, have worked together to dispel the misunderstandings that occasionally contribute to this friction. Out of this cooperative effort, in 1958, came the National Interprofessional Code for Physicians and Attorneys. This code, which follows, was developed by the A.M.A.-A.B.A. Liaison Committee and has been adopted by both Associations.[19]

Preamble

The provisions of this Code are intended as guides for physicians and attorneys in their interrelated practice in the areas covered by its provisions. They are not laws, but suggested rules of conduct for members of the two professions, subject to the principles of medical and legal ethics and the rules of law prescribed for their individual conduct.

This Code constitutes the recognition that, with the growing interrelationship of medicine and law, it is inevitable that physicians and attorneys will be drawn into steadily increasing association. It will serve its purpose if it promotes the public welfare, improves the practical working relationships of the two professions, and facilitates the administration of justice.

Medical Reports

The physicians upon proper authorization should promptly furnish the attorney with a complete medical report and should realize that delays in providing medical information may prejudice the opportunity of the patient either to settle his claim or suit, delay the trial of a case, or cause additional expense or the loss of important testimony.

The attorney should give the physician reasonable notice of the need for a report and clearly specify the medical information which he seeks.

It is improper for the attorney to abuse a medical witness or to seek to influence his medical opinion. Established rules of evidence afford ample opportunity to test the qualifications, competence and credibility of a medical witness; and it is always improper and unnecessary for the attorney to embarrass or harass the physician.

Fees for Services of Physician Relative to Litigation

The physician is entitled to reasonable compensation for time spent in conferences, preparation of medical reports and for court or other appearances. These are proper and necessary items of expense in litigation involving medical questions. The amount of the physician's fee should never be contingent upon the outcome of the case or the amount of damages awarded.

Payment of Medical Fees

The attorney should do everything possible to assure payment for services rendered by the physician for himself or his client. When the physician has

[19] Reprinted with permission.

not been fully paid the attorney should request permission of the patient to pay the physician from any recovery which the attorney may receive in behalf of the patient.

Implementation of this Code at State and Local Levels

In the event similar action has not already been taken this Code should, in the public interest, be appropriately implemented at state and local levels for the purpose of improving the interprofessional relationship between the legal and medical professions.

Consideration and Disposition of Complaints

The public airing of any complaint or criticism by a member of one profession against the other profession or any of its members is to be deplored. Such complaints or criticism, including complaints of the violation of the principles of this Code, should be referred by the complaining doctor or lawyer through his own association to the appropriate association of the other profession; and all such complaints or criticism should be promptly and adequately processed by the association receiving them.

Conferences

It is the duty of each profession to present fairly and adequately the medical information involved in the legal controversies. To that end the practice of discussion in advance of the trial between the physician and the attorney is encouraged and recommended. Such discussion should be had in all instances unless it is mutually agreed that it is unnecessary.

Conferences should be held at a time and place mutually convenient to the parties. The attorney and the physician should fully disclose and discuss the medical information involved in the controversy.

Subpoena for Medical Witness

Because of conditions in a particular case or jurisdiction or because of the necessity for protecting himself or his client, the attorney is sometimes required to subpoena the physician as a witness. Although the physician should not take offense at being subpoenaed, the attorney should not cause the subpoena to be issued without prior notification to the physician. The duty of the physician is the same as that of any other person to respond to judicial process.

Arrangement for Court Appearances

While it is recognized that the conduct of the business of the courts cannot depend upon the convenience of litigants, lawyers or witnesses, arrangements can and should be made for the attendance of the physician as a witness which take into consideration the professional demands upon his time. Such arrangements contemplate reasonable notice to the physician of the intention to call him as a witness and to advise him by telephone, after the trial has commenced, of the approximate time of his required attendance. The attorney should make every effort to conserve the time of the physician.

Physician Called as a Witness

The attorney and the physician should treat one another with dignity and respect in the courtroom. The physician should testify solely as to the medical facts in the case and should frankly state his medical opinion. He should never be an advocate and should realize that his testimony is intended to enlighten rather than to impress or prejudice the court or the jury.

BIBLIOGRAPHY

ARTICLES

Helwig, G.: *Interprofessional Code for Physicians and Surgeons,* 40 PENNSYLVANIA BAR ASSOC. QUARTERLY 84 (1968).

Mack, J. H.: *Physician's Use of Hospital Facilities: Right or Privilege?* 8 CLEVELAND-MARSHALL LAW REVIEW 437 (1959).

Southwick, A. F.: *Hospital Medical Staff Privileges,* 18 DE PAUL LAW REVIEW 655 (1969).

NOTES

Note, *Expulsion and Exclusion from Hospital Practice and Organized Medical Societies,* 15 RUTGERS LAW REVIEW 327 (1961).

Note, *Legal Limitations on Right of Unincorporated Medical Associations to Expel Members,* 41 MINNESOTA LAW REVIEW 212 (1957).

chapter 4

LIABILITY FOR PROFESSIONAL NEGLIGENCE: MEDICAL MALPRACTICE

In England not so long ago a surgeon amputated his patient's left leg. The operation was a complete surgical success. Still, the surgeon was unhappy; shortly after the operation he discovered that he had amputated the wrong limb. With equal proficiency he then removed his patient's other leg. Upon learning of this contretemps, the patient was resentful. A lawsuit of spectacular proportions against the surgeon is in the offing.

A Massachusetts physician injected erythromycin into the low center of his patient's left buttock. Damage to the sciatic nerve resulted, leaving the patient with marked functional deficits in the left leg. He sued his doctor and recovered substantial money damages, testimony having been received during the trial that it was common local practice to make such injections in the upper, outer quadrant of the buttock in order to avoid injury to the sciatic nerve.

In Florida two physicians performed a hemorroidectomy and a spot ligation of varicose veins. The patient went into coma two days after these operations: he had contracted encephalitis and he is now paralyzed from the neck down. For turning him into a "living vegetable," the two physicians and the hospital were ordered by a jury to pay the patient $1,500,000.

In Illinois a jury, after a costly trial, held that an attending physician should not be held responsible for his patient's suicide. The patient, intermittently irrational as the result of medication and toxemia, had barricaded his hospital door with his bed, ripped the galvanized iron screen from his room's solitary window, and leaped to the ground several stories below.

In New Mexico in 1968 a young boy suffered a massive overdose of radiation when a technician failed to place an aluminum filter in an x-ray machine. He lost his hair, and his scalp became ulcerated and then failed to heal because of insufficient blood supply. Expert testimony in his malpractice action was to the effect that the radiation burns would probably result in cancer in the affected area. A jury awarded the boy $950,000 and his father $300,000, for a total of $1,250,000.

In New York, x-ray therapy was negligently administered to a patient, resulting in chronic radiodermatitis. Later, and before her burns were fully healed, the plaintiff was told by a dermatologist that she should have the inflamed area checked periodically, since it might undergo malignant degeneration. The patient developed cancerophobia, the severe apprehension that cancer might in fact develop in the injured area. She recovered damages from her original doctors in the sum of $15,000 for her mental anguish.

GENERAL RULES OF LIABILITY

We are talking about the physician's liability in money damages for negligence or other improper conduct toward his patient. As is true with anyone else, a physician may incur liability for any activity, nonmedical as well as medical, that violates a duty owed to others. It may be an activity closely related to the practice of his profession, or it may be activity of the sort that most adults carry on, be they movie stars, taxi drivers, or septic tank cleaners.

All people who drive automobiles are expected to do so in a reasonably careful fashion so as to avoid cutting down pedestrians in crosswalks and persons sitting on their front porch. Bottlers of soft drinks are subject to successful lawsuits if they include mice, bolts, ground glass, or copper bristles in their refreshments. Lawyers are in trouble if they negligently mislay the funds in trusts and estates that they administer. A doctor, like anyone else, is liable for the consequences of his negligent operation of a motor vehicle. If, on the side, he is bottling and distributing a soft drink of his invention, he had better make certain that it contains no foreign objects. And, like lawyers and other professionals, the physician is liable for negligent or unauthorized actions done within the ambit of his regular professional functions. He is, in short, liable for what is broadly termed *malpractice.*

It is not within the purview of this chapter to instruct physicians and surgeons on automobile negligence law; neither is it our purpose to advise medical men on their obligations as landlords, or as the parents of obstreperous children who smash other people's windows. We shall restrict ourselves to a discussion of the law of medical malpractice. It is a topic of the highest consequence to the medical man.

Although the first reported American malpractice action [1] bears the date 1794, it inspired no rash of similar claims. For a long, long time suits by a patient against his doctor for malpractice were almost unheard of, and substantial damage recoveries, in the few cases filed, were infrequent.

[1] *Cross* v. *Guthery,* 2 Root 90 (S. Ct. Err. & App. Conn. 1794). The first reported English medical malpractice case took place in 1374. See the case of one J. Mort, recorded in Y. B. Hill. 48 Edw III, f. 6, pl. 11 (1374).

But the situation has changed dramatically in the past thirty years or so. Actions for medical malpractice are now common; thousands are filed annually and many of them have resulted in the award of substantial damages. Verdicts in six figures are not rarities; the seven-figure verdict is undoubtedly just around the corner. Have doctors lost their beneficent—and insulating—image? Are plaintiffs' attorneys bolder? Are fraudulent lawsuits being brought in increased numbers? Are physicians more frequently negligent today? Are they more willing than ever before to testify against each other? No one really knows why medical malpractice suits are so markedly on the rise. The realities of the situation are plain enough, however. Ten years ago 18,500 living American physicians, or approximately one in seven, had been the subject of a malpractice claim at some time in their professional careers.[2] Now the upward curve of these claims [3] is such that it would be statistically surprising if almost every current medical school graduate were not eventually charged with or actually sued for professional malpractice at least once during his active professional lifetime. It is for this reason that the writing of medical malpractice liability insurance, which we shall discuss,[4] is now a substantial business in the United States.

Malpractice: Tort or Breach of Contract?

Lawyers categorize the claims of patients against a physician as being either for breach of contract or for the commission of a "tort." The physician-patient relationship is ordinarily considered to be based on contract, express or implied. In other words, the physician promises to perform professional services in exchange for the patient's promise to pay a reasonable fee for them. There may even occasionally be a formal, written con-

[2] See Sandor: *The History of Professional Liability Suits in the United States,* 163 J.A.M.A. 459 (1957). Medical malpractice litigation is also on the rise in Great Britain. See Nathan, H. L. N.: MEDICAL NEGLIGENCE vi. Butterworth, London, 1957.

[3] Statistics are hard to come by; a few can be found in Staff of the Subcommittee on Executive Reorganization, 91st Cong., 1st Sess., REPORT ON MEDICAL MALPRACTICE: THE PATIENT VERSUS THE PHYSICIAN 1009–1060 (Comm. Print. 1969). The authors have been advised by one medical malpractice insurer that malpractice claims increased by 43 percent during the period 1964–1969, and the average cost per claim is reported to have risen 200 percent. It is the conclusion of the Senate Subcommittee on Executive Reorganization, headed by Senator Abraham Ribicoff of Connecticut, that the increasing number of malpractice lawsuits, and the increasing size of judgments, threaten to become a national crisis, perverting "the traditional physician-patient relationship into outright courtroom battle" and forcing the patient to pay more for medical services as doctors pass on the cost of high malpractice insurance premiums. *Id.* at 1–13. And see *Agnew* v. *Parks,* 343 P.2d 118 (Cal. App. 1959) ("We are acutely aware of the problems arising out of the steadily increasing volume of negligence actions plaguing doctors. . . .").

[4] See Chapter 19.

tract between the doctor and the patient; more likely, the agreement simply arises by implication from the behavior of the parties—a person who places himself in the hands of a private physician for treatment implies a willingness to pay for the services he receives, and the physician, of course, impliedly undertakes to perform competently the services required by any patient whom he accepts.[5] Theoretically, many malpractice claims could be cast in terms of a breach by the physician of the physician-patient contract. For a bewildering variety of technical reasons with which, for the most part, we need not burden the readers of this book, claims against physicians are usually expressed in terms of negligent conduct rather than breach of contract. To be somewhat more legally precise, the plaintiff claims not that the defendant physician violated their contract but that he committed a "tort."

The Meaning of "Tort"

The lawyers' term "tort" has an evil connotation, coming as it does from the Latin word *tortus,* meaning twisted or crooked. Lawyers employ the word tort as a label to identify any wrongful act, other than a breach of contract, for which a civil action—as distinguished from a criminal charge—can be maintained.

The Elements of a Tort Claim

A valid tort claim against a physician has three elements. The first element is the *duty* toward the patient which the law imposes on the physician. "Duty" can be translated as "standard of care." Second is the specific *conduct* on the physician's part which, in the law's view, violated his duty to the patient. The physician's actions will be measured against the standard of care applicable to him. Third is the *causal connection* between the physician's conduct and the damages alleged by the patient. To put it absurdly, the law inquires whether the defendant doctor's allegedly improper use of an ice-cold stethoscope was the probable cause of the plaintiff patient's recurrent backache. A litigant cannot recover damages for arguably improper conduct that produced no injury whatever, except perhaps where the conduct can be shown to have been willful and motivated by an evil purpose. Damages for simple negligence, as we shall see, are ordinarily intended to be compensatory, not punitive.

To run the sequence of tort elements backward: (1) *damage* to the patient, *caused by* (2) *conduct* of the physician that fell below (3) the *standard of care* governing the physician.

[5] See, *e.g.*, *Cartwright* v. *Bartholomew,* 64 S.E.2d 323 (Ga. App. 1951); *Klein* v. *Williams,* 12 So.2d 421 (S. Ct. Miss. 1943). See also Comment, *The Implied Contract Theory of Malpractice Recovery,* 6 WILLAMETTE LAW JOURNAL 275 (1970).

The Physician's Legal Duty

It is easy, in a generalized way, to state the physician's legal duty to his patients. The broad and flexible common law rule laid down by the courts is this: a physician has the obligation to his patient to possess and employ such reasonable skill and care as are commonly had and exercised by reputable, average physicians in the same general system or school of practice in the same or similar localities.[6] The courts often add the statement, perhaps superfluous, that a physician is duty-bound "to use his best judgment at all times."[7] These generalizations are applied, with occasional variations, by courts in all jurisdictions in the United States.

Reverting to the general rule mentioned above, it will be observed that doctors pretty much set their own standard of performance. That is, a doctor is expected to do what reputable practitioners of his school of medicine in his sort of locality would do in a particular type of case. He is not expected to be the best-trained, most highly skilled physician in his locale; otherwise all other physicians would have to be considered substandard.[8] But he must possess skill and judgment conforming to the average. And the level of his skill and judgment is not evaluated in terms of the fee he receives; except in certain emergency situations,[9] it is wholly irrelevant to a malpractice action whether the defendant doctor was or was not being compensated for the professional services about which complaint is made.[10]

As Justice Oliver Wendell Holmes once suggested, generalizations do not decide concrete cases. Although Holmes's remark was itself a generalization, it has obvious merit. The standard of care applicable to physicians is, as a generalization, understandable enough; but standing alone, it will not assist lay jurors in deciding most malpractice cases because they cannot figure out, intelligently, whether the defendant's conduct fell below the standard. The quality of the defendant physician's conduct, gauged by the generalized standard, is the crux of a malpractice case. Except in a few self-evident situations, lay jurors are unequipped to determine whether a physician's professional actions violated the generalized standard. The layman cannot be expected to know whether x-rays will reveal the presence of gas gangrene bacillus, and he will not be permitted to specu-

[6] See, *e.g.*, *Loudon* v. *Scott*, 194 Pac. 488 (S. Ct. Mont. 1920); *Pike* v. *Honsinger*, 49 N.E. 760 (Ct. App. N.Y. 1898).

[7] *E.g.*, Regan, L. J.: DOCTOR AND PATIENT AND THE LAW 17, 3d ed. The C. V. Mosby Company, St. Louis, 1956.

[8] *E.g.*, *Davis* v. *Potter*, 2 P.2d 318 (S. Ct. Idaho 1931); *Vaughan* v. *Memorial Hospital*, 130 S.E. 481 (S. Ct. W. Va. 1925).

[9] See Chapter 7.

[10] *E.g.*, *Fortner* v. *Koch*, 261 N.W. 762 (S. Ct. Mich. 1935); *Ritchey* v. *West*, 23 Ill. 385 (S. Ct. Ill. 1860).

late; he does not know whether loss of hearing and compression fractures following electroshock therapy are a sure sign of negligent administration, and he will not be allowed to guess. Such matters are beyond his competence; he would be helpless to make any use of the law's generalized standard of care unless competent guidance were offered him. Thus it is that, in all but self-evident cases, the plaintiff patient must give meaning to the standard of care by presenting expert medical witnesses who are competent to characterize the defendant physician's conduct.[11] This means, among other things, that the test of professional competence has a subjective element.[12]

The Impact of Computerization

The electronic computer may soon have a measure of impact on the medical malpractice field. Although at the present time there is no fully operational system adapted to the purpose, in the near future the computer may be able to assist in determinations as to whether there has been compliance with current medical standards in a given case. Specifically, computerization may permit a physician or, for that matter, a lawyer to review in sequence all of the data relevant to a patient's problem and thereby knowledgeably assess, to a specified degree of probability, whether there was adherence to current medical standards in the patient's case.

However, both the medical and the legal professions will exercise great caution in their use of computerized systems of information retrieval. As one legal observer has warned, "The computer can be no better than the information contained in it, nor any better than its programming." [13] Where, for example, a computer is used to search the medical literature, it may turn up too much or too little. It may, because of programming difficulties, produce much that is irrelevant, or on the other hand, if it is too restrictively programmed it may bypass much information that would be altogether pertinent to the case under assessment. Furthermore, there is always the risk of mechanical failure and operator error, including even the risk of inadvertent erasure of electronically stored data.

With these preliminary remarks the groundwork has been laid for a detailed analysis of the individual elements of a malpractice claim.

[11] See, *e.g.*, *Phillips* v. *Stillwell*, 99 P.2d 104 (S. Ct. Ariz. 1940); *Chubb* v. *Holmes*, 150 Atl. 516 (S. Ct. Err. & App. Conn. 1930). See generally, Morris, C.: *The Role of Expert Testimony in the Trial of Negligence Issues*, 26 TEXAS LAW REVIEW 1 (1947).

[12] The test or standard cannot be considered wholly objective, since it involves the opinion of medical experts regarding "the degree of prudence, caution, or common sense . . . practitioners use in applying their skills." 1 Louisell, D. W., and Williams, H.: *Medical Malpractice* 203. Matthew Bender, New York, 1969.

[13] Hermann, P. J.: *Will Computers Increase Medical Malpractice Claims?* 5(6) TRIAL 50 (1969).

THE DUTY OF POSSESSING NECESSARY TRAINING AND KNOWLEDGE

As an abstract proposition it is true that a doctor is required to have the training and knowledge essential to adequate performance of the professional services required by his patient. If he lacks these things he should make full disclosure of the fact to the prospective patient. The patient is then in a position, supposedly, to decide intelligently whether to accept the present physician's efforts or go to someone possessing the requisite attributes—for example, to a specialist. But even when the patient still desires to be treated by the inadequately prepared physician, there probably is an obligation to refuse to treat him: the risk of liability persists because of the patient's patent inability to determine the best course of action to follow. The risk probably remains even in cases where the physician offers to, and does, secure a consultation with someone fully qualified in the relevant field.

The real point is whether the services performed in a given case by the practitioner were in fact incompetent and resulted in provable damage to the patient. If, by a stroke of luck or because he has been guided by a proficient consultant, the ill-prepared practitioner performs passably and causes no injury, there will be no lawsuit because, as we have said, improper conduct without resultant damage—negligence in the air, so to speak—is not ordinarily actionable. If, on the other hand, the inadequately prepared practitioner forges ahead blindly and does cause injury, the ensuing litigation will focus on his substandard treatment, not on the inadequate level of his training and knowledge—psychologically potent as this underlying factor may be with the jurors.

Court cases purporting to involve the training and knowledge aspect of the practitioner's duty to his patients usually involve persons having restricted licenses to practice—naturopaths, drugless healers, chiropractors, and the like—who have ventured, unsuccessfully, outside their professional bailiwick. The practitioner who permits gangrene to set in because he believes that all wounds can be healed through the application of wet grape leaves is going to be held liable to his victim. In practicality, however, he will be held liable because his mode of treatment was demonstrably improper, not because his education lacked a certain something.[14]

A question, as we have suggested, sometimes arises regarding the obligation of a general practitioner to refer a patient to a specialist. Clearly, the general practitioner today cannot keep up with all the latest developments in every phase of medicine and surgery. In some specialized situa-

[14] See Stryker, L. P.: COURTS AND DOCTORS 52. The Macmillan Company, New York, 1932.

tions, despite the broad wording of his license and his good intentions, he may be unable to render adequate professional services. In such a situation the general practitioner is obligated to refer his patient to a specialist or at least obtain a consultation; otherwise, he proceeds at his peril and will be liable to a damaged patient if his treatment fails to conform to accepted standards in the specialized field.[15] Much will depend on the nature of the particular case. The only appropriate generalization concerning the general practitioner is that he should refer his patient to a specialist whenever it appears to him that this is the course of action that probably would be adopted under like circumstances by reasonably prudent general practitioners. The testimony of qualified medical men as to customary procedure would be essential to support any claim that a general practitioner had improperly retained a patient.[16]

THE DUTY TO EXERCISE REASONABLE SKILL AND CARE

The core of the physician's obligation under the law of medical malpractice lies in the statement that he must employ such reasonable skill and care as are commonly exercised by average reputable physicians in the same general line or school of practice in the same locality or in localities substantially similar to it. The statement is easy to make and endlessly confounding to implement in the context of our adversary trial system.

Before courts and juries can make fair and effective use of this generalized standard, myriad basic questions have had to be worked out in the law—and many of the answers are still evolving, sometimes in a manner sorely vexing to the medical profession. For instance, who shall be permitted to expound for a jury's guidance on the propriety of the defendant doctor's treatment? Can an osteopath testify against a medical doctor in a malpractice case? Can a medical doctor testify against an osteopath? Can a chiropractor testify against an orthopedic surgeon who holds the degree of medical doctor, and *vice versa?* Can a specialist testify against a general practitioner, and *vice versa?* Is a Chinese herb doctor entitled to be judged by the standards of his "school" of treatment?

Who is a "reputable" physician? When are localities sufficiently similar to the one where the defendant practices to provide a source of expert

[15] *E.g., Seneris* v. *Haas,* 291 P.2d 915 (S. Ct. Cal. 1955); *Tvedt* v. *Haugen,* 294 N.W. 183 (S. Ct. N.D. 1940); *Derr* v. *Bonney,* 231 P.2d 637 (S. Ct. Wash. 1951). See also Anno., *Duty to Send Patient to Specialist,* 132 A.L.R. 392. The American Medical Association's *Principles of Medical Ethics,* §8, states: "A physician should seek consultation upon request, in doubtful or difficult cases, or whenever it appears that the quality of medical service may be enhanced thereby."

[16] See McCoid, A. H.: *The Care Required of Medical Practitioners,* 12 VANDERBILT LAW REVIEW 549, 597–98 (1959).

testimony in a malpractice action against him? Is it fair, for instance, for a New York City general practitioner to testify against a general practitioner practicing in Dry Gulch, New Mexico, population 600?

Is it invariably necessary for the plaintiff in a medical malpractice case to support his claim with expert testimony, or does some conduct, by its very nature, eloquently bespeak negligence even to a lay juror? How many medical experts must a plantiff produce to demonstrate that leaving a sponge in his wound is reprehensible?

These and many other questions must be asked and answered in medical malpractice cases. But first we can clarify partially by unequivocally stating some of the things that physicians are *not* obliged to deliver.

In the first place, it can be flatly stated that the law imposes no absolute duty on any physician to treat an injured or sick person. Treatment can be refused and the practitioner's failure to act will not give rise to legal liability.[17] A refusal, of course, can result in very damaging publicity, as recently developed when a doctor in a Southern state declined, for no good reason, to treat a black victim of a particularly cruel rape.

As our statement of the physician's standard of care indicates, unvarying perfection and the working of miracles are no more expected of the medical profession than of any other calling. It has been facetiously remarked that when a doctor says he is "practicing," he really means it. Although such a statement is as unfair as most sarcastic witticisms are, it does reflect a realization that man's knowledge in the field of medicine does not yet permit flat guarantees of total success whenever treatment is undertaken. When a qualified practitioner competently performs the work for which he has been trained, the result may be good or bad; the fact that it sometimes is bad in no way evidences tort or contract liability. For that matter, the complexities of the human machine are such that even an erroneous diagnosis is not always indicative, in the law's eyes, of a lack of proper skill.

In the absence of an express contractual promise, the physician is not considered a guarantor of good results.[18] By embarking upon treatment, however, he has implied something important; in other words, by accepting a patient, he impliedly represents that he has the necessary training, knowledge, and skill and that he will employ these assets in the way any reputable physician ordinarily would.[19] He also impliedly promises that

[17] The leading case is *Hurley* v. *Eddingfield*, 59 N.E. 1058 (S. Ct. Ind. 1901); see also *Findlay* v. *Board of Supervisors*, 230 P.2d 526 (S. Ct. Ariz. 1951); *Childers* v. *Frye*, 158 S.E. 744 (S. Ct. N.C. 1931).

[18] *E.g.*, *Ramberg* v. *Morgan*, 218 N.W. 492 (S. Ct. Iowa 1928); *Williamson* v. *Andrews*, 270 N.W. 6 (S. Ct. Minn. 1936); *McBride* v. *Roy*, 58 P.2d 886 (S. Ct. Okla. 1936).

[19] *E.g.*, *Leighton* v. *Sargent*, 27 N.H. 460 (S. Ct. N.H. 1853); *McCandless* v. *McWha*, 22 Pa. (10 Harris) 261 (S. Ct. Pa. 1853).

he will exercise his best judgment in a good faith effort to produce a satisfactory result.

A physician is not considered by the law to be holding himself out as the most highly qualified of physicians. In accepting a patient the physician tacitly declares not necessarily that he has the highest level of skill or even a high level, if so fuzzy a distinction can be drawn. By accepting the patient he tacitly says to him, "I shall employ at least the level of skill and care ordinarily exercised by the average reputable physician under the same or similar circumstances." It follows that whatever may be the patient's natural hopes, the physician is not an insurer of their fruition—for he is not a magician and never said he was. Only the overreaching quack enters into express agreements to effect a cure. He then becomes legally liable, of course, for the breach of his strange and special covenant.[20] The reputable physician, on the other hand, finds it both wise and possible to reassure an apprehensive patient honestly and without guaranteeing a complete cure in the face of unknown variables.

It is worth pausing briefly here to mention that the law's conception of an enforceable contract is a sometimes subtle thing. It is perhaps easier to stumble into a binding contractual agreement than many doctors realize. All that is required is offer, acceptance, and consideration: the practitioner says, "I offer to accomplish such-and-so"; the patient responds, "Go ahead and do it"; a fee (consideration) for the professional services is promised or paid. Failure to deliver the "such-and-so"—the promised result—gives rise to legal liability. The process can best be demonstrated by reference to an actual lawsuit.

The case of *Noel* v. *Proud*[21] was decided in Kansas in 1961. Defendant physician Proud undertook the treatment of plaintiff Noel for ear trouble, advising him that he should undergo stapes mobilization operations. But Doctor Proud, for some reason, went further. He allegedly told his patient that "while the operations might not have any beneficial effect on . . . [his] hearing, his hearing would not be worsened as a result." Three operations were performed. Not only did Noel's hearing fail to improve, it got much worse. He sued his doctor, alleging the breach of an express contractual warranty that his hearing would not worsen as a consequence of the operations. The Supreme Court of Kansas upheld the trial judge's refusal to dismiss Noel's lawsuit, holding that the facts alleged in his complaint added up to an enforceable contract.

The practitioner who issues specific guarantees may find himself well out toward the end of a legalistic limb. On the other hand, if he foregoes the issuance of promises he will be judged, as he should be, exclusively

[20] *E.g., Robins* v. *Finestone,* 127 N.E.2d 330 (Ct. App. N.Y. 1955); *McAlpin* v. *Browne,* 181 N.Y.S.2d 525 (S. Ct. N.Y. 1958).

[21] 367 P.2d 61 (S. Ct. Kans. 1961).

on the basis of standard professional competence. Basically, the physician violates the standard of care applicable to him in two situations: (1) when he improperly—*i.e.*, unjustifiably—departs from accepted practices, the term "practices" being employed in the triple sense of methods, procedures, and treatments, and (2) when he employs accepted practices but does so ineptly. A special problem, closely related to the field of professional negligence but nonetheless different, is encountered when a practitioner, most commonly a surgeon, employs unimpeachable practices but does so without the informed consent of the patient or someone authorized to speak for him. In this situation the patient may be in a position to recover damages for a bad result even though that result was not caused by any negligence. This problem, involving the scope of a physician's duty to inform the patient regarding the possible consequences of a proposed course of treatment, will be considered in a later chapter.[22]

THE "SCHOOL RULE" AND THE STANDARD OF CARE

The so-called school rule is a qualification said to attach to the general obligation of the practitioner to adhere to acceptable levels of training, knowledge, and skill. Its continuing vitality, at least as it was originally formulated, is now open to some doubt. The rule, first discernible in nineteenth-century judicial pronouncements, was based on the assumption that different schools or systems of medicine had significantly different precepts and methods.[23] So long as the various schools of treatment were respectable, the law was not about to pick and choose among them, opting for one of them as being the best and judging all practitioners, whatever their school, by its standards. The school rule, born of a sense of fairness, declared that a malpractice defendant was entitled to be judged by the standards of his own school, no matter what good things might be said of other schools, so long as his was a recognized one. In times past, the schools of treatment most frequently identified in judicial opinions were the following:

Allopathic: a system that combats disease through the use of remedies producing effects different from those generated by the disease itself

Homeopathic: a system holding, in sharp contrast to the allopathic school, that disease can be cured by remedies that produce on a healthy person effects similar to the symptoms of the particular disease

[22] See Chapter 11.

[23] *E.g., Force* v. *Gregory,* 27 Atl. 1116 (S. Ct. Err. & App. Conn. 1893); *Bowman* v. *Woods,* 1 Greene 441 (S. Ct. Iowa 1848); *Patten* v. *Wiggen,* 51 Me. 594 (S. Ct. Me. 1862).

Eclectic: a system in which the physician selects from the various schools that method of treatment thought to be the best in a given case; particular emphasis is placed on the development of indigenous plant remedies

Osteopathy: a system of therapeutics grounded on the theory that diseases stem chiefly from bone displacements, with consequent pressure on blood vessels and nerves, and can be remedied by manipulation of the skeletal structure and, sometimes, surgery

Chiropractic: a system that operates on the theory that disease is caused by abnormal functioning of the nervous system and combats it by digital manipulation of the joints, especially of the spine

Drugless healing: a system of treatment that employs neither drugs nor penetration of body tissues except for cutting of the umbilical cord at birth

Christian Science: a system of healing by means of prayer and the triumph of mind over matter

In adopting the school rule, the courts did not suggest that every known form of treatment, differing from generally recognized modes, was to be dignified as a "school." It was about as simple to define a "school" of treatment as it is to define the term "religion." Still, the task was an essential one. Were there no reasonably workable definition of "school" of treatment, all manner of potentially harmful quacks would clamor to be judged only against their own curious standards. In an action against a spiritualist, the defendant could successfully assert that he adhered to the customary practices of all clairvoyants; the same defensive stance could be taken by Chinese herb doctors, magnetic healers, and the like. To avoid such grotesque results, the courts placed emphasis on the concept of a governing "system" of treatment.

In one leading decision the court sought to fence out clairvoyants. In a Wisconsin case [24] decided in the latter part of the nineteenth century, the parent of his "patient" sued a spiritualist. The defendant was not allowed to defend on the ground that his mode of treatment was consistent with the usual practices of spiritualists. The Supreme Court of Wisconsin found that the "clairvoyand school" had but one basic tenet, that disease could be detected and treated by means of the trance. The court said:

> To constitute a school of medicine under this rule, it must have rules and principles of practice for the guidance of all its members, as respects principles, diagnosis, and remedies, which each member is supposed to observe in any given case. Thus, any competent practitioner of any given school would treat a

[24] *Nelson* v. *Harrington*, 40 N.W. 288 (S. Ct. Wis. 1888).

given case substantially the same as any other competent practitioner of the same school would treat it.

The court added that the practitioners of a school of treatment, if it is to be recognized as such by the law, must gain professional knowledge through the study of general scientific principles. Plainly enough, under this conception the clairvoyant, the magnetic healer, and the herb doctor fail to make the grade.[25] They are not judged in negligence actions by their own dubious standards; and as we shall see, they are not qualified to condemn, as experts, the conduct of members of recognized schools of treatment (or put it this way: there is no recorded case of a Chinese herb doctor having been permitted to testify in a malpractice action against a medical doctor).

As medical science has deepened and broadened, the notion of separate and distinct schools has been eroded. In its original formulation, the school rule simply gave recognition to divisions of medical dogma. Today, reputable practitioners owe allegiance to fixed rules of practice, to widely accepted precepts, more than to nicely calculated school boundaries. In the twentieth century the regular physician, treating all aspects of disease, summons to his aid a wide variety of procedures and methods, some of which might once have been considered the property of another "school." It therefore often borders on the meaningless to attach to him a specific school label. Rather, we simply say that today's physician is engaged in the regular practice of medicine. And in malpractice cases, we try to determine whether he has unjustifiably departed from regular or fixed rules of practice, whatever their sources, or has followed them incompetently.

Recognition of the notion that there are relatively fixed rules of practice does not mean that a physician who employs procedures developed by himself or adhered to by a minority of practitioners is to be automatically branded guilty of malpractice. The law, whenever the facts dictate, realizes full well that doctors can still differ legitimately as to proper methods of treatment. The medical innovator and the follower of the minority approach will, however, find it crucial in a malpractice action to produce expert opinion other than their own in justification of their mode of treatment. This point is illustrated by a Missouri case.[26] The defendant, at the pertinent time, was the only practitioner in St. Louis who employed a particular treatment. He successfully defended against a claim of malpractice by pointing to approved use of the same procedure in such places as Chicago, Cincinnati, and Vienna, Austria. His was a minority approach,

[25] See McCoid, A. H.: *The Care Required of Medical Practitioners,* 12 VANDERBILT LAW REVIEW 549, 561 (1959).

[26] *McClarin* v. *Grenzfelder,* 126 S.W. 817 (Mo. App. 1910).

but it was shown to be a scientifically supportable one. We shall later have more to say about so-called experimental or innovative medicine.[27]

The school rule has meaning in a few remaining areas, for the practice of medicine still has some relatively tight compartments. They are obvious ones: psychiatry, dentistry, anesthesiology, nursing, veterinary medicine, to name a few. Practitioners in such special fields are entitled, in accordance with the original school rule, to be judged in malpractice cases by the practices and precepts of their particular medical field.

In a sense, the school rule also has modern meaning in connection with the numerous specialties that have developed in medical practice. Today, at least in the larger cities, all sorts of specialty practices exist, from ophthalmology to proctology.[28] The specialty may be limited by the portion of the body or by the ailment or special mode of treatment with which it is concerned. Certifying boards, acting on the basis of an applicant's training and test results, give recognition to proficiency in the various specialties, and many hospitals now require board certification before permitting a doctor to make use of their facilities for specialized purposes. The specialty phenomenon poses for the law the question of whether a new sort of "school" concept should be enforced. The law's answer to this question has been an equivocal "Yes."

A physician's adoption of a specialty does not ease the standard of care governing his professional conduct; quite the contrary. If a practitioner holds himself out as a specialist, he will undoubtedly be held to a higher degree of skill and knowledge than a general practitioner.[29]

So far, at least, the practitioner who disclaims any narrow specialty is not likely to be held to a specialist's standards.[30] It is in this area, however, that the law has commenced a process of equivocation. It is still probably fair to say that the nonspecialist is entitled to be judged in a malpractice case by the standards of his own "school," the school of general practice. For example, a California trial court verdict was reversed by the state's highest appellate court because the judge had instructed the jury that if a doctor undertook to provide professional services in a specialized phase of medicine at a time when other practitioners in his locality had restricted their practice to that specialty, then the doctor must meet the standards of the specialists.[31] The California Supreme Court stated that

[27] See Chapter 12.

[28] The nonsurgical and surgical specialties are cataloged and described in Louisell, D. W., and Williams, H.: *Medical Malpractice,* ch. III. Matthew Bender, New York, 1969.

[29] *E.g., Ayers* v. *Parry,* 192 F.2d 181 (3d Cir. 1951); *Scarano* v. *Schnoor,* 323 P.2d 178 (Cal. App. 1958); *Rule* v. *Cheeseman,* 317 P.2d 472 (S. Ct. Kan. 1957).

[30] *E.g., Sinz* v. *Owens,* 205 P.2d 3 (S. Ct. Cal. 1949); *Marchlewski* v. *Vasella,* 106 A.2d 466 (S. Ct. Err. & App. Conn. 1954).

[31] *Simone* v. *Sabo,* 231 P.2d 19 (S. Ct. Cal. 1951).

this higher duty would apply to the defendant doctor only if he knew or should have known that a general practitioner's knowledge and skill were inadequate to the task at hand. This decision, along with others, contains a veiled warning, however. As the medical schools and certifying boards produce more and more specialists who practice in more and more areas of the country, the courts will hold with increasing frequency that a general practitioner must either possess the knowledge and skill of the specialist or else refer his patient to one. To put it another way, in some instances acceptable procedure in the "school" of general practice will dictate reference to a specialist. If and when the law adopts this view unequivocally, it will have done almost precisely what the hospitals themselves accomplish when they restrict the use of certain of their facilities to accredited specialists such as surgeons, anesthesiologists, and radiologists. The prudent general practitioner, mindful of a shift in the law of medical malpractice, will increasingly limit himself to home and office treatment, referring more complex cases to the specialist.

The school rule, redefined broadly as "the regular practice of medicine," also continues to serve as a device for regulating fringe disciplines such as chiropractic, drugless healing, and others that rely for healing and therapy principally on natural elements such as heat, manipulation, and health foods. Many of these disciplines qualify, to a greater or lesser degree, as "schools" of treatment as the law has defined that term. Each has at least some pervasive rules and principles of practice guiding its adherents, with the result that often any practitioner of one of these disciplines would treat a given condition in much the same manner as would any other member of the same discipline. Each of these schools, in other words, is to some degree systematized, and their members are therefore not ordinarily to be lumped together with the motley array of independent and self-guided entrepreneurs known variously as faith healers, clairvoyants, root-and-berry doctors, and the like. Furthermore, all or most of the aforementioned disciplines have achieved some measure of legislative recognition in the form of licensing laws,[32] with the result that courts are more or less bound to accept them as discrete systems entitled to independent assessment.[33]

Happily, the licensing statutes usually define with reasonable exactitude the ambit of the sundry nonmedical disciplines. They ordinarily do so in terms of the types of disorders treatable and the methods employable by

[32] See Forgotson, E. H., Roemer, R., and Newman, R. W.: *Licensure of Physicians,* (1967) UNIV. OF WASHINGTON LAW QUARTERLY 249, 308–331, for lists of licensing statutes.

[33] *E.g., Bryant* v. *Biggs,* 49 N.W.2d 63 (S. Ct. Mich. 1951) (osteopath); *Hardy* v. *Dahl,* 187 S.E. 788 (S. Ct. N.C. 1936) (naturopath); *Sheppard* v. *Firth,* 334 P.2d 190 (S. Ct. Ore. 1959) (chiropractor).

the specified disciplines. The follower of those disciplines exceeds their defined scope at his peril. Thus a chiropractor who decided to engage in neurosurgery would be held to the skill of a neurosurgeon if he held himself out, expressly or impliedly, as being capable of performing such surgery. He could not expect to be judged by the standards of his own school since chiropractic, by definition and by law, eschews the performance of true surgical procedures and therefore provides no relevant standards. The approach of courts confronted with the limited practitioner who has overstepped the bounds of his discipline has been stated succinctly enough: "[He] must be held to the same standards of skill and care as prevail amongst those who are licensed [to practice medicine]." [34]

Many courts look no farther than the applicable state licensing statute. Thus a Massachusetts court [35] has said, "The [licensing] statute . . . must be construed as intended to afford relief by way of damages to all persons suffering harm where the violation of the statute is the proximate cause of their injuries." It is also worth mentioning here that almost all state licensing statutes regulating the healing professions are criminal in nature and include penalties ranging from license revocation to fines and imprisonment.

Even the practitioner of certain identifiable limited schools who adheres to their fixed precepts may nevertheless be held to the standards of the regular practice of medicine. Dramatic evidence of this fact is provided by two decisions, many years apart, involving the same drugless healer. In the Washington case of *Wilcox* v. *Carroll* [36] the court upheld a damage judgment in favor of the mother of a child who succumbed to peritonitis after a drugless healer had diagnosed the child's condition as an "inflammation of the spine and congestion of the bowels" and treated it accordingly. The court held that fixed precepts governed diagnosis of appendicitis and approved the receipt of testimony by medical doctors against the defendant. Twenty-seven years later the same drugless healer, obviously a slow learner, again failed to diagnose appendicitis.[37] He deterred the patient's wife from bringing in a medical doctor and prescribed "sine wave" treatments and a laxative. Medical doctors testified on behalf of the plaintiff in his lawsuit against the healer. The trial judge refused to instruct the jury that the defendant was entitled to be judged by the standards of drugless healers. A higher court affirmed a judgment in favor of the plaintiff. It bluntly declared that a drugless healer is not a "doctor"

[34] *Monahan* v. *Devinny*, 229 N.Y.S. 60 (App. Div. N.Y. 1928). See also *Bacon* v. *Walsh*, 184 Ill. App. 377 (1913); *Epstein* v. *Hirschon*, 33 N.Y.S. 2d 83 (S. Ct. N.Y. 1942); *Walkenhorst* v. *Kesler*, 67 P.2d 654 (S. Ct. Utah 1937).

[35] *Whipple* v. *Grandchamp*, 158 N.E. 270 (Sup. Jud. Ct. Mass. 1927).

[36] 219 Pac. 34 (S. Ct. Wash. 1923).

[37] *Kelly* v. *Carroll*, 219 P.2d 79 (S. Ct. Wash. 1950).

in the medical sense, does not belong to any school of medicine, and cannot insist upon being judged by any standards other than those generally applicable to the medical profession.

In many states osteopathy, in marked contrast to naturopathy, chiropractic, and other clearly limited disciplines, is considered virtually coexistent with the practice of medicine.[38] Statutory definitions of osteopathic practice are often quite broad, not to say ambiguous. Some of them prohibit osteopaths from administering drugs and some foreclose them from engaging in "operative surgery." On the other hand, a number of licensing statutes permit osteopaths to practice as surgeons. In recent years osteopathy has demonstrated a positive desire to broaden its discipline and to keep abreast of the entire spectrum of innovations in medical science. Osteopaths adhere to a code of ethics similar to that of the American Medical Association, and sanctions against unethical osteopaths are enforced. There are five approved colleges of osteopathy in the United States; they conduct a four-year course of instruction on top of at least three years of preparatory work in an accredited college or university and maintain clinics that permit students to get clinical experience before graduation. Osteopathic hospitals have been established. They provide for internships and residencies for postgraduates. Eleven osteopathic specialties are recognized, including surgery, internal medicine, neurology and psychiatry, obstetrics and gynecology, and radiology. In short, medicine and osteopathy are drawing ever closer.[39] It is not altogether surprising, therefore, that the courts, at least in jurisdictions in which osteopaths are broadly licensed, are today requiring that osteopaths measure up to fixed standards of practice.[40] Moreover, as we shall see in a subsequent section, with increasing frequency osteopaths are being held qualified to testify adversely to medical doctors in malpractice actions, and *vice versa.*

THE REQUIREMENT OF EXPERT TESTIMONY

The plaintiff in a medical malpractice action is ordinarily required to produce, in support of his claim, the testimony of qualified medical

[38] Detailed discussion and comparison of the training of medical doctors and osteopaths can be found in Comment, *Expert Testimony in Medical Malpractice Cases,* 17 UNIV. OF MIAMI LAW REVIEW 182, 185–88 (1962).

[39] Witness, for example, the merger of the California Osteopathic Society and the California Medical Association, with accompanying elimination of all distinctions between the schools of osteopathy and medicine. See Comment, *Expert Testimony in Medical Malpractice Cases,* 17 UNIV. OF MIAMI LAW REVIEW 182, 187 (1962).

[40] See, *e.g.,* the leading case of *Grainger* v. *Still,* 85 S.W. 1114 (S. Ct. Mo. 1905); see also *Josselyn* v. *Dearborn,* 62 A.2d 174 (S. Ct. Me. 1948); Comment, *Medical Malpractice—Expert Testimony,* 60 NORTHWESTERN UNIV. LAW REVIEW 834, 840 (1966).

experts.[41] This is true, as we have earlier said, because the technical aspects of his claim will ordinarily be far beyond the competence of the lay jurors whose duty it is to assess the defendant doctor's conduct. The plaintiff, himself a layman in most instances, is not free simply to enter the courtroom, announce under oath that the defendant surgeon amputated his leg instead of saving it, and then request the jury to find the surgeon negligent.

The jurors, possessing no special expertise in the relevant field, are incapable of judging whether the facts described by the plaintiff, even assuming an accurate narration by him, add up to negligent conduct. And the plaintiff himself is incompetent to supply guidance; he, too, lacks the training and experience that would qualify him to characterize the defendant's conduct. Unless the facts in our hypothetical amputation case spoke for themselves and unmistakably pointed to malpractice (the defendant, although operating in a fully equipped hospital, unaccountably removed plaintiff's leg with a dull ax), the judge would direct a verdict in defendant's favor immediately after the plaintiff's presentation of evidence. The judge would say that there had been a failure of proof on the issue of negligence, as to which the plaintiff had the burden of proof. Since the mere filing of a lawsuit, unsupported at trial by any probative evidence, does not entitle one to the payment of damages, the plaintiff here must lose. The plaintiff could hope to prevail only if he came to court backed by one or more qualified expert witnesses.

There is nothing unique about the requirement of expert testimony in medical malpractice cases.[42] All sorts of lawsuits involve technical issues that exceed the competence of lay witnesses and lay jurors.[43] A successful criminal prosecution may depend on the testimony of a firearms identification expert, a fingerprint expert, a handwriting expert, a pathologist, and a couple of psychiatrists.[44] Many types of civil suits other than malpractice cases may call forth an array of essential experts: mechanical or aeronautical engineers and metallurgists in a case involving an airplane that allegedly crashed as a consequence of metal fatigue in the wing structure; pathologists in a product liability case against a food processor

[41] The following are only a few of the myriad cases on this point: *Phillips* v. *Stillwell,* 99 P.2d 104 (S. Ct. Ariz. 1940); *Sinz* v. *Owens,* 205 P.2d 3 (S. Ct. Cal. 1949); *Hogmire* v. *Voita,* 49 N.E.2d 811 (Ill. App. 1943); *Treptau* v. *Behrens Spa, Inc.,* 20 N.W.2d 108 (S. Ct. Wis. 1945).

[42] See generally, Morris, C.: *The Role of Expert Testimony in the Trial of Negligence Issues,* 26 TEXAS LAW REVIEW 1 (1947).

[43] See Waltz, J. R.: *The Uses of Non-Medical Expert Information in Civil Litigation,* CHICAGO BAR RECORD, Vol. XLVIII, No. 2, p. 15 (1966).

[44] See Waltz, J. R.: *Inadequacy of Trial Defense Representation as a Ground for Post-Conviction Relief in Criminal Cases,* 59 NORTHWESTERN UNIV. LAW REVIEW 289, 335–36 (1964).

(was the corn borer that slipped into defendant's canned corn truly toxic?); handwriting experts in a will contest; accountants, entomologists, civil engineers—the catalog of potentially vital expert witnesses in civil cases goes on and on. It is so lengthy a list because lawsuits so often involve esoteric issues which a jury, unaided, could not possibly resolve on any basis other than guesswork. To the extent that it can, the Anglo-American system of justice prohibits verdicts having baseless speculation as their only support. The requirement of expert testimony on technical issues is one designed to avoid guesswork verdicts.

In short, lay jurors have a reasonable basis in their own life experience for deciding that it is negligent—that it poses an unreasonable risk of harm to others—to drive an automobile down the wrong side of the highway at ninety miles an hour; on the other hand, their life experience gives them no basis for assessing, for example, a delicate and difficult surgical procedure.

In our hypothetical malpractice case involving the defendant's amputation of plaintiff's leg, then, the plaintiff would be required to produce qualified medical experts who were prepared (1) to explain the accepted medical procedures and considerations applicable to plaintiff's condition and (2) to express an opinion, based on the proved facts, that the defendant surgeon had unjustifiably failed to follow those procedures or had followed them incompetently. In a less obvious case the plaintiff's experts would have to provide an answer to a third question—that is, whether the defendant's improper conduct probably was the cause of the plaintiff's injury. Indeed, in a less clear case than one involving an amputation it might even be essential that medical experts establish that the plaintiff had in fact suffered injury.

To recapitulate in sequence, in a typical medical malpractice lawsuit the plaintiff must put qualified medical experts on the witness stand to testify (1) that plaintiff suffered an injury that produced the disability and other ill effects claimed by him; (2) that the cause of this injury, or at least a significant contributing cause of it, was the professional services rendered by the defendant doctor; (3) that the standard methods, procedures, and treatments in cases such as plaintiff's were such-and-so; and (4) that defendant's professional conduct toward plaintiff fell below or otherwise unjustifiably departed from the described standard. In steps 1 and 2 the plaintiff's experts are used to establish damage and the causal connection with that damage of defendant's conduct. These two steps are common to every type of personal injury action, whether it be an automobile collision case or a medical malpractice case. Steps 3 and 4 are peculiar to professional negligence cases for they impart content and meaning to the generalized standard of care uniquely applicable to such cases.

BIBLIOGRAPHY

BOOKS

Long, R. H.: THE PHYSICIAN AND THE LAW, chap. 2, 3d ed. Appleton-Century-Crofts, New York, 1968.

Moritz, A. R., and Stetler, C. J.: HANDBOOK OF LEGAL MEDICINE, 2d ed. The C. V. Mosby Company, St. Louis, 1964.

Prosser, W. L.: TORTS 164–68, 3d ed. West Publishing Company, St. Paul, 1964.

Regan, L. J.: DOCTOR AND PATIENT AND THE LAW, 3d ed. The C. V. Mosby Company, St. Louis, 1956.

Regan, L. J., and Moritz, A. R.: HANDBOOK OF LEGAL MEDICINE, chap. 29, 2d ed. The C. V. Mosby Company, St. Louis, 1964.

Roady, T. G. (ed.): PROFESSIONAL NEGLIGENCE. Vanderbilt Univ. Press, Nashville, 1960.

Staff of Senate Subcommittee on Executive Reorganization, 91st Cong., 1st Sess., REPORT ON MEDICAL MALPRACTICE: THE PATIENT VERSUS THE PHYSICIAN (Comm. Print 1969).

ARTICLES

Ames, F. G.: *Modern Techniques in the Preparation and Trial of a Medical Malpractice Suit,* 12 VANDERBILT LAW REVIEW 649 (1959).

Cline, E.: *Professional Liability,* 35 NEBRASKA LAW REVIEW 547 (1956).

Goldman, M. H.: *Proof and Procedures in Malpractice Cases,* 40 MASSACHUSETTS LAW QUARTERLY 18 (1955).

McCoid, A. H.: *The Care Required of Medical Practitioners,* 12 VANDERBILT LAW REVIEW 549 (1959).

Miller, A. J.: *Contractual Liability of Physicians and Surgeons,* [1953] WASHINGTON UNIV. LAW QUARTERLY 413.

Oppenheim, M.: *Standard of Care of Medical General Practitioners,* 9 CLEVELAND-MARSHALL LAW REVIEW 227 (1960).

Sadusk, J. F.: *Professional Liability Problems of the Medical General Practitioner,* [1958] INSURANCE LAW JOURNAL 335.

Smith, D. S.: *Battery in Medical Torts,* 16 CLEVELAND-MARSHALL LAW REVIEW 22 (1967).

Swan, J. H.: *The California Law of Malpractice of Physicians, Surgeons, and Dentists,* 33 CALIFORNIA LAW REVIEW 248 (1945).

Symposium, *Medical Malpractice,* 25 OHIO STATE LAW JOURNAL 323 *et seq.* (1964).

Wildman, M.: *Trends in Medical Liability Suits,* 15 MEDICAL TRIAL TECHNIQUE QUARTERLY 1 (1969).

NOTES AND COMMENTS

Comment, *An Evaluation of Changes in the Medical Standard of Care,* 23 VANDERBILT LAW REVIEW 729 (1970).

Comment, *Civil Liability of Physicians and Surgeons for Malpractice*, 35 MINNESOTA LAW REVIEW 186 (1951).

Comment, *The Locality Rule in Medical Malpractice Suits*, 5 CALIFORNIA WESTERN LAW REVIEW 124 (1968).

Comment, *Malpractice and the Healing Arts—Naturopathy, Osteopathy, Chiropractic*, 9 UTAH LAW REVIEW 705 (1965).

Note, *Contracts—Physicians and Surgeons—Complaint Alleging Breach of Contract to Cure Held Sufficient*, 31 ST. JOHN'S LAW REVIEW 123 (1956).

Note, *Medical Specialties and the Locality Rule*, 14 STANFORD LAW REVIEW 884 (1962).

chapter 5

THE ELEMENTS OF QUALIFICATION TO TESTIFY AS A MEDICAL MALPRACTICE CLAIMANT'S EXPERT WITNESS

Quite clearly, the efficacy of the standard of care which the law applies to physicians and surgeons depends on the type of expert testimony allowed in malpractice cases. It is not enough to say merely that a malpractice claimant's case must be buttressed by the testimony of someone who owns a license to practice some sort of healing art somewhere in this or another country. The very statement of the practitioner's standard of care forecloses so loose an approach. That statement calls, basically, for such reasonable skill and care as is had by (1) the average reputable physician (2) in the same school of practice (3) in the same or a similar locality.[1] The requirements respecting expect testimony in medical malpractice cases are rather carefully prescribed. However, as we shall presently see, some of the requirements—particularly the so-called locality rule—are gradually being relaxed or abolished.

"AVERAGE AND REPUTABLE"

Average

The first requirement that we have listed might suggest that a malpractice claimant's expert witnesses must be possessed of no more than "average" knowledge and capability. That is not the case. The expert called by the plaintiff need not himself be "average"—he himself may have a reputation for extraordinarily high skill—but he must be familiar, as presumably he would be, with acceptable practice among less able practitioners possessed of only average skill. And he must restrict himself in his deposition and courtroom testimony to a description of acceptable conduct among practitioners of average skill lest he saddle the defendant practitioner with a higher standard of care than the law demands.[2] To

[1] See *Loudon* v. *Scott,* 194 Pac. 488 (S. Ct. Mont. 1920).

[2] *E.g., Adkins* v. *Ropp,* 14 N.E.2d 727 (Ind. App. 1938); *Nelson* v. *Nicollett Clinic,*

put it graphically, plaintiff's expert will not be heard to say, "I, with my unmatched gifts, wouldn't have done it that way." The law is not concerned by a pomposity that has seemingly reached Gilbert and Sullivan proportions, but it assuredly is concerned by the fact that the quoted testimony would be wholly irrelevant in a malpractice action against a defendant less Godlike than the witness. The court desires to know not whether the witness would have "done it that way" but whether reputable practitioners of average training, knowledge and skill "do it that way."

Reputable

Although plaintiff's expert witness need not be an "average" practitioner, he must be a "reputable" one. The word "reputable" does carry with it something of the connotation of "average"; that is, the defendant is held to the standards of the average practitioner—the "reputable" although not necessarily extraordinary practitioner. But the term "reputable" also means something more. It conditions the sort of person who can properly be offered as an expert witness in a malpractice case. Needless to say, neither the plaintiff nor the defendant is permitted to rely on the testimony of one who has lost his license to practice.[3]

THE "SCHOOL RULE" AND EXPERT TESTIMONY

Identity of Precepts

The so-called school rule, which is the second condition delineating the qualifications of an expert witness in a malpractice case, would seem likely, on its face, to limit sharply the availability of expert witnesses in this class of litigation. However, because of the decline of the principle that a physician's professional conduct is to be judged in strict accordance with the tenets of his particular school of treatment to the exclusion of all others, the school rule is no longer as important a limiting factor as it once was. The fundamental question is whether a fixed rule of diagnosis, treatment, or practice is applicable to the complainant's case.[4] Medical

---

276 N.W. 801 (S. Ct. Minn. 1937); *Loudon* v. *Scott,* 194 Pac. 488 (S. Ct. Mont. 1920).

The term "average" is employed in the sense of "ordinary" learning and skill; a true average would involve an uneasy aggregation of the best and the worst, the experienced and the inexperienced, the quack and the specializing medical doctor. It has never been suggested that the law strikes the average from so diverse a totality. See, *e.g., Sim* v. *Weeks,* 45 P.2d 350 (Cal. App. 1935); *Holtzman* v. *Hoy,* 8 N.E.2d 832 (S. Ct. Ill. 1886); *Whitesell* v. *Hill,* 66 N.W. 894 (S. Ct. Iowa 1896).

[3] See, *e.g., Rankin* v. *Mills,* 278 Pac. 1044 (S. Ct. Cal. 1929); *Moeller* v. *Hauser,* 54 N.W.2d 639 (S. Ct. Minn. 1952). See also 1 Louisell, D. W., and Williams, H.: MEDICAL MALPRACTICE 202. Matthew Bender, New York, 1969.

[4] See, *e.g., Foster* v. *Thornton,* 170 So.2d 459 (S. Ct. Fla. 1936).

doctors and osteopathic physicians, for example, may be in perfect agreement as to acceptable procedure in countless situations. If a fixed rule is recognized by all schools of treatment, a practitioner of any school is qualified to testify as to that fixed precept in a malpractice action against a member of any other school of treatment. In other words, all that matters is that methods of diagnosis and therapy are the same in the witness' school and that of the defendant.

Testimony by Osteopathic and Medical Doctors Against Each Other

This notion that identity of precepts is the key accounts for the growing tendency of courts to permit osteopathic and medical doctors to testify against one another in malpractice cases.[5] Judges will look primarily to similarity of training and state licensing practices in determining whether the school rule should block a witness's testimony. Indicia such as the merger in California of the Medical Association and the Osteopathic Society will also be accorded weight. Of course, the differences between osteopathic and medical practice vary markedly from state to state. Under the statutes of some, such as Maine,[6] the osteopathic physician or surgeon is allowed to use drugs and to engage in obstetrics and surgery. Accordingly, the courts in such states consider the two schools virtually coexistent and freely permit testimony by osteopaths against medical doctors and *vice versa*. In other jurisdictions there still exist sharp differences between the practice of osteopathy and the practice of medicine. In Kansas, for example, an osteopath's license does not permit him to employ drug therapy or surgery by means of surgical instruments as distinguished from digital manipulation of the body.[7] Consequently, one would not anticipate allowance in Kansas courts of testimony by an osteopath against a surgeon. On the whole, however, the trend in this country's courts is toward crossover expert testimony in the fields of medicine and osteopathy, based on the demonstrable sharing of precepts by those two schools of treatment.[8]

Testimony by a Chiropractor Against a Medical or Osteopathic Doctor

In contrast to the situation of the osteopath witness, courts are not likely to look with favor on testimony by chiropractors against either

[5] See, *e.g.*, *Musachia* v. *Terry*, 140 So.2d 605 (Fla. App. 1962); *James* v. *Falk*, 360 P.2d 546 (S. Ct. Ore. 1958).

[6] ME. REV. STAT. ANN., tit. 71, §7 (1965).

[7] KAN STAT. ANN., §§65-1201 to 65-1208 (Supp. 1968), interpreted in *State ex rel. Beck* v. *Gleason*, 79 P.2d 911 (S. Ct. Kan. 1938); see also *Cummins* v. *Donley*, 249 P.2d 695 (S. Ct. Kan. 1952).

[8] See Comment, *Medical Malpractice—Expert Testimony*, 60 NORTHWESTERN UNIV. LAW REVIEW 834, 840 (1966).

medical or osteopathic doctors except in limited, special circumstances. The question is completely foreclosed in states such as New York and Massachusetts where chiropractors are not licensed to treat human ailments.[9]

Occasionally a chiropractor will be permitted to testify in personal injury lawsuits other than those involving claims of medical malpractice; his testimony will be a practical necessity where the plaintiff's only treating "doctor" happened to be a chiropractor. In this circumstance the chiropractor will probably be restricted to opinions regarding the nature and extent of physical injury; it is questionable whether he should be allowed to venture a prognosis. Nothing in these suggestions should be read as implying that a chiropractor, whose training and precepts differ so observably from those of medical doctors and osteopaths, would be considered generally competent to assay an opinion respecting treatment accorded by a member of either of those schools. The decided cases are to the contrary.[10]

There may be some isolated instances in which the approach of the medical doctor or osteopath and the chiropractor concur—or ought to. Just as all schools, no matter what their modes of treatment may be, ordinarily ought to recognize a given disease when it exists, some procedures are not properly susceptible to variation. It was for this reason that in an Oregon case a chiropractor was allowed to testify against a physician on the proper use of a diathermy machine.[11] By way of foundation for his testimony it was developed that the diathermy machine is extensively employed in chiropractic practice and that the witness was fully familiar with the mechanism. By the same token, testimony by a nonchiropractic doctor has been allowed against a chiropractor.[12]

Cultists

It will come as no surprise to learn that the courts have never suggested that cultists of one sort and another can be qualified as expert witnesses in medical malpractice cases. A medical doctor or an osteopathic doctor, both members of recognized schools of treatment sharing numerous fixed precepts, can testify adversely to a cultist but the converse is not and never will be true.[13]

[9] See McCoid, A. H.: *The Care Required of Medical Practitioners,* 12 VANDERBILT LAW REVIEW 549, 564 (1959), and cases therein cited.

[10] *E.g., Ness* v. *Yeomans,* 234 N.W. 75 (S. Ct. N.D. 1931).

[11] *Wemmett* v. *Mount,* 292 Pac. 93 (S. Ct. Ore. 1930); see also *Foster* v. *Thornton,* 170 So. 459 (S. Ct. Fla. 1936); *Shockley* v. *Tucker,* 103 N.W. 360 (S. Ct. Iowa 1905).

[12] *Treptau* v. *Behrens Spa, Inc.,* 20 N.W.2d 108 (S. Ct. Wis. 1945).

[13] *E.g., Longan* v. *Weltmer,* 79 S. W. 655 (S. Ct. Mo. 1904) ("magnetic healer"); *Hansen* v. *Pock,* 187 Pac. 282 (S. Ct. Mont. 1920) (Chinese herb doctor).

Testimony by Nonspecialists Against Specialists

The school rule has continuing vitality in one large area: the various fields of specialty practice. The rule demands particularized expertise on the part of anyone seeking to testify on behalf of a claimant in a malpractice case involving dentistry, anesthesiology, veterinary medicine, nursing, and the work of x-ray technicians, to mention only a few examples.[14] Those engaged in such specialized pursuits are entitled to be criticized only by those having adequate knowledge of the precepts and methods peculiar to their field of practice.

No difficulty presents itself when a certified specialist testifies against a practitioner of the same specialty. But is a general practitioner qualified to testify against a specialist? The specialist is held to a loftier standard of care than is the general practitioner; [15] if the specialist has violated the lower standards applicable to a general practitioner, it presumably follows that he has breached the more demanding standards of his specialty. Since a general practitioner is competent to describe his own supposedly lower standards, his testimony is admissible in any case in which it is charged that the defendant specialist's conduct fell below the level expected of a general practitioner.[16] In permitting general practitioners to supply expert testimony in malpractice actions against specialists, courts may occasionally be reacting to the widespread charge that plaintiffs in such suits experience an unaccountably difficult time securing favorable expert testimony. No such consideration should ever result in permitting a general practitioner to testify to the standard of care pertaining to the trained and certified specialist unless he clearly is competent to do so.

Testimony by a Specialist Against a General Practitioner

Our courts have long permitted specialists to testify in malpractice actions against general practitioners.[17] Theoretically, the specialist must restrict himself to testimony concerning the lower standards applicable to the general practitioner. There is a built-in danger here, however: the conscientious specialist who keeps constantly abreast of the latest advances in his small sphere will not always appreciate that the general practitioner may not be cognizant of discoveries known for some time to

[14] See Comment, *Medical Malpractice—Expert Testimony*, 60 NORTHWESTERN UNIV. LAW REVIEW 834, 841–42 (1966).

[15] *E.g., Ayers* v. *Parry*, 192 F.2d 181 (3d Cir. 1951); *Carbone* v. *Warburton*, 94 A.2d 680 (S. Ct. N.J. 1953); *Huttner* v. *McKay*, 293 P.2d (S. Ct. Wash. 1956).

[16] See *Carbone* v. *Warburton*, 94 A.2d 680, 684 (S. Ct. N.J. 1953). See also Comment, *Medical Malpractice—Expert Testimony*, 60 NORTHWESTERN UNIV. LAW REV. 834, 841–42 (1966).

[17] *E.g., Simone* v. *Sabo*, 231 P.2d 19 (S. Ct. Cal. 1951); *Wilson* v. *Corbin*, 41 N.W.2d 702 (S. Ct. Iowa 1950).

the specialist. Since this lack of awareness does not necessarily spell negligence on the general practitioner's part, courts are usually careful to inquire into a specialist's actual knowledge of standards acceptable in the general practice. If in fact the specialist is ignorant of the norms in general practice, he will not be allowed to testify against a defendant general practitioner. Any other ruling by a court would result in the general practitioner's conduct being measured against the higher standards governing specialists.

THE "LOCALITY RULE" AND EXPERT TESTIMONY

The law's formulation of the generalized standard of care governing the physician and surgeon is full of formulas and phrases which, as Justice Oliver Wendell Holmes once observed in another connection, "by their very felicity delay further analysis." The so-called locality rule, tacked on at the end of the generalized standard, is one of these. We usually say, today, that a medical man has the obligation to his patient to possess and employ such reasonable skill and care as are commonly had and exercised by reputable, average physicians in the same general system or school of practice *in the same or similar locality*.[18] On a practical level, the locality rule has influenced not only the professional standards demanded of medical men but also the availability of witnesses to establish, in malpractice actions, their culpable deviation from those standards.

The locality rule possessed a semblance of certainty for only a short time. It has been put through the mill, so to speak, by lawyers and courts and in the process has been significantly revised and refined. Moreover, it is about to disappear almost completely.

Original Formulation of the Locality Rule

The locality rule was a product of the United States; English courts never developed such a principle.[19] In its original formulation, which took shape in the late nineteenth century, the locality rule literally demanded that a medical expert testifying for the plaintiff in a malpractice action must have practiced in the defendant's community.[20] The rule, in its early form, was demonstrably calculated to protect the rural and small-

[18] *E.g., Adkins* v. *Ropp,* 14 N.E.2d 727 (Ind. App. 1938); *Nelson* v. *Nicollett Clinic,* 276 N.W. 801 (S. Ct. Minn. 1937); *Loudon* v. *Scott,* 194 Pac. 488 (S. Ct. Mont. 1920). See also Waltz, J. R.: *The Rise and Gradual Fall of the Locality Rule in Medical Malpractice Litigation,* 18 DE PAUL LAW REVIEW 408, 409 (1969).

[19] See Nathan, H. L. N.: MEDICAL NEGLIGENCE 21. Butterworth, London, 1957.

[20] For three of the earliest formulations of the rule, see *Smothers* v. *Hanks,* 34 Iowa 286 (1872); *Tefft* v. *Wilcox,* 6 Kan. 46 (1870); *Hathorn* v. *Richmond,* 48 Vt. 557 (1876).

town practitioner, who was presumed to be less adequately informed and equipped than his big-city brother.[21] As was said in *Small* v. *Howard*,[22] a case involving a general practitioner in a village of 2,500, the defendant "was not bound to possess that high degree of art and skill possessed by eminent surgeons practicing in larger cities." [23] The residents of our country towns and frontier outposts would have to be satisfied with second-rate health services. The rule that accomplished this result was a frankly expedient one; although their opinions are short on supporting data, courts one hundred years ago were probably justified in adopting a presumption that the large-city practitioner enjoyed a broader experience than his country cousin, and greater access to the latest medical knowledge and to the most advanced and elaborate facilities and equipment. If plaintiff's expert did not come from the defendant's town, he had no business testifying against him; they functioned in different worlds.

Expansion of the Rule to Include "Similar" Localities

The early and most restrictive form of the locality rule was soon relaxed in many jurisdictions,[24] if only because it posed a predictable problem. It effectively immunized from malpractice liability any doctor who happened to be the sole practitioner in his community. He could be treating bone fractures by the application of wet grape leaves and yet remain beyond the criticism of more enlightened practitioners from other communities. And there have been additional reasons for the gradual amelioration of the strict locality rule.

Instead of a "same locality" rule, today the law usually applies a "same *or similar*" locality rule.[25] Furthermore, the definition of "locality" may

[21] *E.g.*, *Force* v. *Gregory*, 27 Atl. 1116 (S. Ct. Err. & App. Conn. 1893); *Burk* v. *Foster*, 69 S.W. 1096 (Ct. App. Ky. 1902). Surprisingly, a few more recent decisions adhere to this early and most restrictive formulation. See, *e.g.*, *Horton* v. *Vickers*, 111 A.2d 675 (S. Ct. Err. & App. Conn. 1955); *Lockhart* v. *MacLean*, 361 P.2d 670 (S. Ct. Nev. 1961); *Huttner* v. *MacKay*, 293 P.2d 766 (S. Ct. Wash. 1956).

[22] 35 Am. Rep. 363 (S. Jud. Ct. Mass. 1880).

[23] See also *Smothers* v. *Hanks*, 34 Iowa 286 (S. Ct. Iowa 1872); *Tefft* v. *Wilcox*, 6 Kan. 46 (S. Ct. Kan. 1876). Consideration for the "isolated" practitioner has lingering force. See, *e.g.*, *Stallcup* v. *Coscarat*, 282 P.2d 791 (S. Ct. Ariz. 1955) (oral surgeon in Phoenix, Arizona; misguided decision); *Josselyn* v. *Dearborn*, 62 A.2d 174 (S. Ct. Me. 1948) (general practitioner in small Maine town 130 miles from hospital and laboratory facilities; rare disease). *Cf. Moeller* v. *Hauser*, 54 N.W.2d 639 (S. Ct. Minn. 1952) (plaintiff, in action against St. Paul practitioner, relied on experts from Mayo Clinic at Rochester; court warned that their level of skill was not conclusive).

[24] *E.g.*, *Pelky* v. *Palmer*, 67 N.W. 561 (S. Ct. Minn. 1896); *McCracken* v. *Smathers*, 29 S.E. 354 (S. Ct. N.C. 1898); *Bigney* v. *Fisher*, 59 Atl. 72 (S. Ct. R.I. 1904).

[25] *E.g.*, *Weintraub* v. *Rosen*, 93 F.2d 544 (7th Cir. 1937); *Lewis* v. *Johnson*, 86 P.2d 99 (S. Ct. Cal. 1939); *Avey* v. *St. Francis Hospital and School of Nursing, Inc.*, 442 P.2d 1013 (S. Ct. Kan. 1968); *Kirchner* v. *Dorsey*, 284 N.W. 171 (S. Ct. Iowa

be an expansive one. In a 1916 case [26] involving practitioners in the village of Cloquet, Minnesota, that state's supreme court, fifty years ahead of its time, suggested that the relevant locality was the entire state. To this day few courts have expressly gone so far but it is clear that the current stress is on similarity of locality and medical practice rather than on geographical proximity. For example, the Iowa Supreme Court in 1950 allowed testimony by physicians from Evanston, Illinois, against physicians practicing in Davenport, Iowa.[27] Its conclusion was that the practice in and around Chicago was essentially comparable to the practice in Davenport. In a still more recent case a Florida appellate court was adverting to the locality rule, and not to more frivolous matters, when it commented that "Miami is at least a community similar to West Palm Beach." [28] It concluded that plaintiff's witness, "though from Miami, was a competent medical expert on the ordinary care required of a doctor in West Palm Beach." In a Washington case [29] the state's supreme court upheld the receipt in evidence of expert testimony from a Portland, Oregon, doctor in a malpractice action that arose in Longview, Washington, fifty miles away. The two communities were hardly similar. The court perceived, however, that this circumstance, and the geographical facts, were virtually irrelevant since the Portland doctor had testified that he was familiar with the standards of medical practice in Longview.[30]

The Supreme Court of California was forced to take a position when two lower California courts went off in seemingly different directions. In *Warnock* v. *Kraft* [31] the appellate court approved the admission of testimony by Los Angeles doctors in a malpractice suit against a Pasadena surgeon. The decision was less than radical; Los Angeles was a larger city than Pasadena but they were both in the same county and, at the time, shared the same general hospital. Even so, two years after the *Warnock*

1939); *Hodgson* v. *Bigelow*, 7 A.2d 339 (S. Ct. Pa. 1939); *Stafford* v. *Hunter*, 401 P.2d 986 (S. Ct. Wash. 1965). For significant statutory changes in the rule, see GA. CODE §84-924 (1955) as interpreted in, *e.g.*, *Murphy* v. *Little*, 145 S.E.2d 760 (Ga. App. 1965), and WIS. STAT. §147.14(2)(a) (Supp. 1969).

[26] *Viita* v. *Dolan*, 155 N.W. 1077 (S. Ct. Minn. 1916).

[27] *McGulpin* v. *Bessmer*, 43 N.W.2d 121 (S. Ct. Iowa 1950).

[28] *Coolz* v. *Lichtblau*, 144 So.2d 312 (Fla. App. 1962).

[29] *Teig* v. *St. John's Hospital*, 387 P.2d 527 (S. Ct. Wash. 1963).

[30] See also *Riley* v. *Layton*, 329 F.2d 53, 57 (10th Cir. 1964), in which a San Francisco practitioner was permitted to testify against a physician practicing in a small Utah town after having testified that "through his experience, reading, lectures and travels [he] was familiar with the practice in small towns throughout the United States with regard to the treatment of . . . fractures [of the type involved in the case]." Additional cases are cited in Note, *An Evaluation of Changes in the Medical Standard of Care*, 23 VANDERBILT LAW REVIEW 729, 730–41 (1970).

[31] 85 P.2d 505 (Cal. App. 1938).

case another California appellate court, in *McNamara* v. *Emmons*,[32] rejected testimony from San Bernardino doctors in a malpractice action against an Ontario physician (the two communities were in geographic proximity but San Bernardino had a population of 50,000 while Ontario's was 15,000). Nine years after *McNamara* the California Supreme Court, in *Sinz* v. *Owens*,[33] reached a somewhat timid compromise. Plaintiff Sinz had charged the defendant general practitioner with malpractice in his treatment of a double comminuted leg fracture. An expert called by the plaintiff testified that "the standard practice *in California*" was to use skeletal traction in double comminuted fracture cases, a procedure that had been omitted by the defendant physician. A verdict for plaintiff resulted. On appeal the defendant contended that plaintiff's expert had not been properly qualified to testify. The contention pushed the locality rule to something of an extreme, since the community from which plaintiff's expert hailed was *smaller* than the town in which the defendant practiced. The plaintiff's witness practiced in the town of Oakdale, about twenty-seven miles south of Stockton in the San Joaquin Valley; defendant practiced in the town of Lodi, some twelve miles on the other side of Stockton. The California Supreme Court, rejecting defendant's argument, stated: "The essential factor is knowledge of similarity of conditions; geographical proximity is only one factor to be considered." But the court insisted that plaintiff's putting forth of the entire San Joaquin Valley as the relevant geographic area was "beyond permissible bounds." Dissenting, one justice thought it obvious that "the qualifications of a physician and surgeon to practice in California does [*sic*] not depend upon the locality in which he is engaged in practice, but upon the education and training which he has received in institutions in which the method and scope of instruction and the technique in training are substantially uniform." He would have held that a physician licensed to practice medicine in California was qualified to testify as an expert in any part of the state. The level of equipment and facilities available to the defendant in his particular locality would simply be a factor that the jurors could take into account in assessing the propriety of his conduct.

The dissenter in *Sinz* v. *Owens* at least partially comprehended the real reasons for a lessening of the locality rule's rigidity. These reasons are to be found in nationwide advances in medical training and improvement in communications and transportation. Today's doctor begins his practice, wherever it may be, with a stronger base of training than was generally true in the late nineteenth century. The proliferation of medical literature and its reasonably rapid delivery enhance and update the

[32] 97 P.2d 503 (Cal. App. 1940).
[33] 205 P.2d 3 (S. Ct. Cal. 1949).

knowledge of practitioners in small communities as well as large; so does attendance at seminars and conferences. Thus the Supreme Court of Florida has commented, in *dicta,* that "this rule [*i.e.,* the locality rule] was originally formulated when communications were slow or virtually non-existent and . . . it has lost much of its significance today with the increasing number and excellence of medical schools, the free interchange of scientific information, and the consequent tendency to harmonize medical standards throughout the country." [34] That the Florida court's suggestion is realistic is demonstrated by Louisell and Williams's more complete listing of the modern-day doctor's learning aids: "The comprehensive coverage of the *Journal of the American Medical Association,* the availability of numerous other journals, the ubiquitous 'detail men' of the drug companies, closed circuit television presentations of medical subjects, special radio networks for physicians, tape recorded digests of medical literature, and hundreds of widely available postgraduate courses." [35] A decade ago, when they made this list, Louisell and Williams insisted that the medical profession was rapidly establishing nationwide standards of proficiency. "Medicine realizes this," they then said, "so it is inevitable that the law will do likewise."

Furthermore, in an era of fast transportation it may be proper practice in the smallest and most remote community to send a patient with a complex malady to a specialist in a metropolitan area that boasts better medical facilities. In *Tvedt* v. *Haugen* [36] a North Dakota court, refusing to limit the pertinent locality to the town of Larimore, said:

> . . . Today, with rapid methods of transportation and easy means of communication, the horizons have been widened, and the duty of a doctor is not fulfilled merely by utilizing the means at hand in the particular village where he is practicing. So far as medical treatment is concerned, the borders of the locality or community have, in effect, been extended so as to include those centers readily accessible where appropriate treatment may be had which the local physician, because of limited facilities or training, is unable to give.

Of course, the quoted language states a double-barreled proposition: (1) acceptable practice in an ill-equipped community may involve sending the patient to an accessible metropolitan area for treatment, time permitting; and (2) a physician from a metropolitan area might be allowed to testify against a rural practitioner that this was an indicated procedure

[34] *Montgomery* v. *Stary,* 84 So.2d 34 (S. Ct. Fla. 1955).

[35] Louisell, D. W., and Williams, H.: THE PARENCHYMA OF LAW 183. Professional Medical Publications, Rochester, N.Y., 1960. See *Kolesar* v. *United States,* 198 F. Supp. 517 (S.D. Fla. 1961); *Douglas* v. *Bussabarger,* 438 P.2d 829 (S. Ct. Wash. 1968).

[36] 294 N.W. 183 (S. Ct. N.D. 1940).

applicable to him. The first point has to do with the physician's standard of care, while the second has to do with the sort of expert who can testify to it.

For the past few years, then, the view of a majority of courts has been that a medical expert is free to testify in a malpractice case if his community or other communities with which he is familiar bear sufficient similarity to the one in which the defendant practices.[37] And in determining similarity, the courts will now look not to such socioeconomic facts as population, type of economy, and income level, but rather to factors more directly relating to the practice of medicine. In the main, an expert practicing in a locality having medical facilities comparable to those existing in the defendant's community is permitted to testify concerning the standard of care governing the defendant. The number and the quality of hospitals, laboratories, and medical schools are typical considerations. Of course, the nature of the community in which the witness currently practices is irrelevant if he happens also to possess familiarity with standards in the defendant's locale or in areas sufficiently similar to it. The law has focused on the witness's place of practice on the assumption that a medical man will be knowledgeable only about standards in his immediate vicinity, but this assumption is not always valid.

The Impending Disappearance of the Locality Rule

It is a safe prognostication of the law's future direction to say that the locality rule, long in the process of shrinking, will gradually disappear almost completely. In 1964, in the third edition of his work on torts, Dean Prosser discerned a "tendency . . . to abandon any such formula [*i.e.*, the locality rule], and treat the size and character of the community, in instructing the jury, as merely one factor to be taken into account in applying the general professional standard." [38] Prosser's observation is beginning to be borne out by the cases. The highest court of Massachusetts has recently indicated, perhaps somewhat too broadly, that it is abandoning the last vestiges of the rule. And this is more than a straw in the wind since Massachusetts, with its decision in *Small* v. *Howard*,[39] was among the first of the states to adopt a locality concept. Now, in the 1968 case of *Brune* v. *Belinkoff*,[40] the state's Supreme Judicial Court has flatly announced that it is abandoning the locality rule. The sweep of this statement is limited only by the fact that *Brune* involved a medical specialist

[37] See, *e.g.*, *Riley* v. *Layton*, 329 F.2d 53 (10th Cir. 1964); *Teig* v. *St. John's Hospital*, 387 P.2d 527 (S. Ct. Wash. 1963).

[38] Prosser, W. L.: TORTS 166–67, 3d ed. West Publishing Company, St. Paul, 1964.

[39] 35 Am. Rep. 363 (S. Jud. Ct. Mass. 1880).

[40] 235 N.E.2d 793 (S. Jud. Ct. Mass. 1968).

as defendant, and it is arguable that the locality rule has long since lost vitality in specialist cases.[41] But a court, when it speaks more broadly than the facts before it require, is usually delivering a preview of things to come.

The *Brune* case involved an action against an anesthesiologist to recover for injuries caused by his alleged negligence in injecting an overdose of Pontocaine when the plaintiff delivered a baby in a New Bedford, Massachusetts, hospital. The defendant practiced in New Bedford, which is a city of 100,000 population slightly more than fifty miles from Boston. Plaintiff complained of persistent postdelivery numbness and weakness in her left leg. The evidence showed that the anesthetic contained 8 milligrams of Pontocaine in 1 cubic centimeter of 10 percent glucose solution. Plaintiff's evidence also tended to prove that good medical practice called for a dosage of 5 milligrams or less; defendant's evidence, including his own testimony, was that an 8-milligram dosage was customary in New Bedford in vaginal deliveries. The plaintiff objected to the trial judge's giving to the jury the following instruction on the governing law:

> [The defendant] must measure up to the standard of professional care and skill ordinarily possessed by others in his profession in the community, which is New Bedford, and its environs, of course, where he practices, having regard to the current state of advance of the profession. If, in a given case, it were determined by a jury that the ability and skill of the physician in New Bedford were fifty percent inferior to that which existed in Boston, a defendant in New Bedford would be required to measure up to the standard of skill and competence and ability that is ordinarily found by physicians in New Bedford.

This charge to the jury was a more or less typical expression of the locality rule as it pertains to the standard of care.

The jury in *Brune* found for the defendant anesthesiologist, and the plaintiff appealed, winning a reversal and a new trial. The core of the higher court's reasoning is found in the following portions of its opinion:

> We are of the opinion that the "locality" rule . . . , which measures a physician's conduct by the standards of other doctors in similar communities, is unsuited to present day conditions. The time has come when the medical profession should no longer be Balkanized by the application of varying geographic standards in malpractice cases. . . . The present case affords a good illustration of the inappropriateness of the "locality" rule to existing conditions.

[41] *E.g., McGulpin* v. *Bessmer,* 43 N.W.2d 121 (S. Ct. Iowa 1950); *Sampson* v. *Veenboer,* 234 N.W. 170 (S. Ct. Mich. 1931); *Carbone* v. *Warburton,* 94 A.2d 680 (S. Ct. N.J. 1953); *Hundley* v. *Martinez,* 158 S.E.2d 159 (S. Ct. W. Va. 1967).

The court observed that New Bedford was close to Boston, "one of the medical centers of the nation, if not the world." A practitioner in New Bedford was "a far cry from the country doctor." The trial judge, said the court, may well have carried the locality rule to its logical conclusion, "but it is, we submit, a *reductio ad absurdum* of the rule." The court went on to expound what it viewed as the proper approach:

> The proper standard is whether the physician, if a general practitioner, has exercised the degree of care and skill of the average qualified practitioner, taking into account the advances in the profession. In applying this standard it is *permissible* to consider the medical resources available to the physician as *one* circumstance in determining the skill and care required. Under this standard *some allowance* is thus made for the type of community in which the physician carries on his practice. . . .
>
> One holding himself out as a specialist should be held to the standard of skill of the average member of the profession practicing the specialty, taking into account the advances in the profession. And, as in the case of the general practitioner, it is permissible to consider the medical resources available to him.

There were harbingers of *Brune* in a 1967 Washington decision. *Pederson* v. *Dumouchel*[42] involved a malpractice action against an Aberdeen, Washington, medical doctor, dentist, and hospital in which the trial court had charged the jury that the standard of care applicable to the defendants "was set by the learning, skill, care and diligence ordinarily possessed and practiced by others in the same profession in good standing, engaged in like practice, in the same locality or in similar localities." The Supreme Court of Washington rejected the locality rule as a binding principle. It stated that "local practice within geographic proximity is one, but not the only factor to be considered." Pointing to expanded means for the dissemination of medical knowledge, the court declared: "No longer is it proper to limit the definition of the standard of care . . . to the practice or custom of a particular locality, a similar locality, or a geographic area." But the court, seemingly on the verge of adopting a nationwide standard, appeared to backtrack, stating that the standard of care applicable to healers is that level of proficiency "established in an area coextensive with the medical and professional means available in those centers that are readily accessible for appropriate treatment of the patient." It can be demonstrated, however, that the Washington court's apparent hedging reflected a necessary exception to the concept of a national standard of care in medical malpractice cases.

[42] 431 P.2d 973 (S. Ct. Wash. 1967). See also *Douglas* v. *Bussabarger*, 438 P.2d 829 (S. Ct. Wash. 1968); *Versteeg* v. *Mowery*, 435 P.2d 540 (S. Ct. Wash. 1967). In July of 1968 a Kansas court had also begun to back away from the locality rule. See *Avey* v. *St. Francis Hospital and School of Nursing, Inc.*, 442 P.2d 1013 (S. Ct. Kan. 1968).

The Significance of the Brune and Pederson Decisions

The *Brune* and *Pederson* decisions herald an important shift at two levels of the law of medical malpractice. The most fundamental shift is in the relevant standard of care. *Brune* seems to suggest a nationwide standard for both specialists and general practitioners: the general practitioner must adhere to "the degree of care and skill of the average qualified [general] practitioner"; the specialist must adhere "to the standard of skill of the average member of the profession practicing the specialty." *Pederson* is more cautious, and rightly so. By holding the medical man to that degree of care and skill established in areas accessible to him the Washington court took into account the possible unavailability in some cases of special facilities, equipment, or devices. It would not do to suggest that a physician could rationally be found guilty of malpractice for failing to employ, for example, an artificial kidney machine if that equipment were unavailable in his community and not accessible elsewhere in time to save his patient's life.

If *Brune* is read to mean that the absolute unavailability of essential "medical resources" is merely a "permissible" consideration for which a jury could make "some allowance," it goes astray. Such a situation would constitute the basis not for "some allowance" but rather for summary judgment or a directed verdict in favor of the defendant doctor. The law of medical malpractice, akin with diplomacy, is an aspect of the art of the possible. If, on the other hand, *Brune* is read to mean that "some allowance" could properly be made where essential resources were unavailable locally (*e.g.*, in New Bedford) but readily accessible elsewhere (*e.g.*, in Boston, a fast fifty miles away), it does not go far enough. In the latter situation it can justly be said, as a matter of law, that the defendant doctor had a duty to remove his patient to the accessible medical facility where crucial resources and medical specialists were available. That is the inferential teaching of the more carefully worded *Pederson* opinion. It is the express teaching of the forward-looking 1940 opinion in *Tvedt* v. *Haugen*,[43] previously quoted.

Putting aside cases involving crucial medical facilities, equipment, devices, and the like, *Brune* and *Pederson* are consistent. In cases involving general professional skill, uncomplicated by any question of available special resources, they strongly suggest the demise of the locality rule as a binding consideration.

At a second level, the *Brune* and *Pederson* decisions are a mandate to malpractice claimants to seek their medical experts in any geographic area in the United States, or perhaps even beyond, so long as they are

[43] 294 N.W. 183 (S. Ct. N.D. 1940). See also *Flock* v. *J. C. Palumbo Fruit Co.*, 118 P.2d 707 (S. Ct. Idaho 1941); *Hodgson* v. *Bigelow*, 7 A.2d 338 (S. Ct. Pa. 1939).

equipped to describe "the degree of care and skill of the average qualified [general or specializing] practitioner." [44]

The locality rule has exerted two interrelated and unfortunate influences. It has rendered all the more shallow the pool of available expertise in legitimate malpractice litigation. And, at least in times past, it has permitted geographic pockets of inferior health service to flourish unchallenged for no better reason than that one or a few less than minimally proficient practitioners have been allowed, by the law's default, to set the standard of a community. The fall of the locality rule will exert pressure for uniformly adequate health services, a goal as to which law and medicine are united. For some time the medical specialist has neither had nor wanted the rule. Its baleful influence has been upon the general practice of medicine. The general practitioner, whether in large city or small town, must soon confront a nationwide standard of competence. But nothing in what has been said here suggests that the general practitioner must now conform to standards set by medical specialists. The general practitioner must adhere only to those standards of unspecialized practice for which his educational resources have equipped him. It is still good law to say, as did Connecticut's highest court fifteen years ago, that "A country general practitioner should not be expected to use the high degree of skill possessed by eminent surgeons living in large cities. . . ." [45]

BIBLIOGRAPHY

BOOKS

Kramer, C.: MEDICAL MALPRACTICE 43–46. Practising Law Institute, New York, 1962.

[44] *Cf. Meiselman* v. *Crown Heights Hospital, Inc.,* 34 N.E.2d 367 (Ct. App. N.Y. 1941) (German-trained physician who had not been practicing in the United States at or before the time of defendant doctor's challenged conduct); *Ramsland* v. *Shaw,* 166 N.E.2d 894 (S. Jud. Ct. Mass. 1960) (proffer of English anesthesia treatise under Massachusetts statute permitting receipt in evidence of authoritative medical treatises).

[45] *Marchlewski* v. *Casella,* 106 A.2d 466, 468 (S. Ct. Err. & App. Conn. 1954). See also, *e.g., Ayers* v. *Parry,* 192 F.2d 181 (3d Cir. 1951); *Worster* v. *Caylor,* 110 N.E.2d 337 (S. Ct. Ind. 1953); *Rule* v. *Cheeseman,* 317 P.2d 472 (S. Ct. Kan. 1957).

As an offshoot of the locality rule, the question occasionally arises whether members of the staff of a teaching institution should be permitted to testify in a malpractice suit against a private practitioner. Professor Allan H. McCoid of the University of Minnesota Law School, a leading student of the medical-legal field, has intimated that the answer should be "No," since "it is expected that in a teaching institution advances in practice may be attempted more rapidly than in clinics or private practice, that a certain amount of 'experimental' medicine may be undertaken." McCoid, A. H.: *The Care Required of Medical Practitioners,* 12 VANDERBILT LAW REVIEW 549, 573 (1959).

Louisell, D. W., and Williams, H.: MEDICAL MALPRACTICE, chap. VII. Matthew Bender, New York, Supp. 1969.

Prosser, W. L.: TORTS 167, 3d ed. West Publishing Company, St. Paul, 1964.

Richardson, J. R.: DOCTORS, LAWYERS AND THE COURTS, §§1.11, 15.13. The W. H. Anderson Company, Cincinnati, 1965.

Wasmuth, C. E.: LAW AND THE SURGICAL TEAM. Williams & Wilkins, Baltimore, 1969.

ARTICLES

McCoid, A. H.: *The Care Required of Me lical Practitioners,* 12 VANDERBILT LAW REVIEW 549, 614–31 (1959).

Waltz, J. R.: *The Rise and Gradual Fall of the Locality Rule in Medical Malpractice Litigation,* 18 DE PAUL LAW REVIEW 408 (1969).

NOTES AND COMMENTS

Comment, *Expert Testimony in Medical Malpractice Cases,* 17 UNIV. OF MIAMI LAW REVIEW 182 (1962).

Comment, *Medical Malpractice and the Expert Witness in the District of Columbia,* 16 AMERICAN UNIV. LAW REVIEW 278 (1967).

Comment, *Medical Malpractice—Expert Testimony,* 60 NORTHWESTERN UNIV. LAW REVIEW 834 (1966).

Note, *Locality Rule in Medical Malpractice Suits,* 5 CALIFORNIA WESTERN LAW REVIEW 124 (1968).

Note, *Malpractice and Medical Testimony,* 77 HARVARD LAW REVIEW 333 (1963).

Note, *Negligence—Medical Malpractice—The Locality Rule,* 18 DE PAUL LAW REVIEW 328 (1968).

chapter 6

RELAXATION OF THE REQUIREMENT OF EXPERT TESTIMONY IN MEDICAL MALPRACTICE CASES

THE UNDERLYING PROBLEM: UNAVAILABILITY OF PLAINTIFFS' EXPERTS

Silence Among Physicians

The requirement of expert testimony in most medical malpractice cases has been sorely vexing to those lawyers who regularly represent the plaintiff's side in such litigation. It cannot be denied that with some frequency plaintiffs find it difficult or impossible to produce medical experts willing to testify adversely to members of their profession who have been sued for alleged malpractice.[1] This stumbling-block to successful malpractice litigation has caused frustrated claimants' counsel to charge that doctors deliberately refuse to provide needed expertise in meritorious cases.[2] These lawyers suggest that the asserted reluctance of doctors to be witnesses in malpractice cases stems either from a conscious desire to provide unwarranted protection to medical colleagues or from a fear of reprisal by medical societies and malpractice insurers. Seldom have the lawyers realized, or been willing to admit, that their difficulties are traceable to a lack of merit in a given lawsuit.

Whatever may be the validity of the claim that medical experts are unduly tightlipped, its acceptance by some courts has contributed to an occasional relaxation of the general rule that expert testimony is essential to a plaintiff's malpractice action. This acceptance has also contributed to the fabrication of a few moderately successful devices for facilitating plaintiffs' efforts to secure needed expertise. Or, as the editor-in-chief of an occasionally shrill journal for claimants' lawyers, who clearly took his

[1] See Note, *Intimidation of Plaintiff's Witness in a Malpractice Suit by Cancellation of Insurance,* 63 Northwestern Univ. Law Review 873, 876 (1969).

[2] See, *e.g.,* Belli, M. M.: *An Ancient Therapy Still Applied: The Silent Medical Treatment,* 1 Villanova Law Review 250 (1956).

job seriously, once put it, "There are perfectly legitimate ways of surmounting, outflanking, getting around, at least to some extent, the conspiracy of silence." [3]

Before considering these outflanking legal principles, which either dispense with expert testimony in malpractice cases or facilitate its production, we should pause to consider the imputation of obstructionism that has been leveled at the medical profession. It is a serious charge, not lightly to be brushed aside: it implies that individual practitioners are conspirators or cowards, or both, and that medical organizations and malpractice insurers are direct contributors to this reprehensible state of affairs.

Coercion, Conspiracy, and Cowardice?

It is, we believe, true that there has been a widespread unwillingness on the part of doctors to testify for malpractice claimants. However, the reasons often advanced by claimants' counsel for this assertedly conspiratorial silence—fear of expulsion from local medical societies and threatened cancellation of medical malpractice liability insurance policies—call for close scrutiny.

The Claim of Pressure by Medical Societies

One finds few reported judicial decisions involving efforts by a physician to be reinstated by a medical society. Since it is undeniable that a number of doctors—an increasing number—have testified on behalf of plaintiffs in malpractice actions, one might anticipate a fair number of reinstatement actions if threats of expulsion from medical societies are employed with frequency by the profession to coerce silence. Where admission to a hospital staff and other benefits essential to a successful medical practice are contingent, as they often are, on medical society membership, an improperly expelled doctor would surely initiate legal proceedings to regain membership. An example, and a sorry one, is the case of *Bernstein* v. *Alameda Contra Costa Medical Ass'n*,[4] involving a doctor who had been expelled from his local medical association because of a report he had prepared for a claimant before the state industrial accident commission. In his report the doctor had charged that another physician, who had written a pathological report for the claimant, was "inept" and "inexpert." The California appellate court ordered the petitioning doctor reinstated to membership in his medical society, declaring that it would not permit enforcement of a medical association bylaw "which holds over each of the

[3] Lambert, T. F.: *Malpractice Concepts Affecting All Professions,* in Harolds, L. R., and Block, M. (eds.): MEDICAL MALPRACTICE 17. The Lawyers Co-operative Publishing Company, Rochester, N.Y., 1966.

[4] 293 P.2d 862 (Cal. App. 1956).

members the threat of expulsion if in his testimony . . . before a court or other judicial body he 'disparages, by comment or insinuation,' another physician." But the limited number of cases like *Bernstein* offers fairly potent evidence that unjustified threats of expulsion, and actual follow-through, are uncommon.[5]

The Claim of Pressure by Malpractice Insurance Companies

The significance of claimed insurance company pressure is at least questionable, but it, like medical society pressures, cannot be completely discounted. There has been a gradual, observable increase in the number of physicians willing to testify on behalf of malpractice plaintiffs, as is evidenced by the increase in successful medical malpractice actions. With this demonstrable increase recently in the number of malpractice actions against doctors there has been a concomitant increase in the purchase of medical malpractice insurance policies. (A 1959 study estimated that more than 92 percent of American doctors then carried professional liability insurance and the percentage is probably higher today. At the time of this study the number of satisfied malpractice claims had increased 84 percent from 1954, and the number of physicians insured had increased 56 percent during the same period.[6]) The physician's obvious need for insurance coverage, coupled with any coercion toward silence exerted by the insurers, should logically have led to a decrease rather than an increase in the number of doctors willing to testify for malpractice plaintiffs. Since an increase in the number of successful malpractice actions bespeaks an increase in the number of doctors willing to testify, the existence of broad-scale insurance company pressure might appear doubtful.

A recent litigation in Ohio indicates that insurance company pressure is not altogether imaginary, however. The plaintiff in *L'Orange* v. *The Medical Protective Company*[7] was a dentist. Since 1938 he had been insured by the defendant against malpractice claims. In 1965, shortly after he had testified against another dentist in a successful malpractice action, plaintiff's policy was cancelled. The policy contained a standard provision giving the insurer an unconditional right to cancel it upon the giving of appropriate notice and the refunding of any unearned premiums. Nonetheless, plaintiff sued for breach of contract, alleging that the cancellation of his insurance was against public policy, and therefore void, because it was "intended to constitute coercion and intimidation of the plaintiff against future court appearance in [malpractice cases]." Plaintiff alleged

[5] See Comment, *Medical Malpractice—Expert Testimony*, 60 NORTHWESTERN UNIV. LAW REVIEW 834 (1966).

[6] *Malpractice*, NEW MEDICA MATERIA, Jan., 1963, pp. 11, 17, and note 5 at p. 16.

[7] 394 F.2d 57 (6th Cir. 1968), discussed in Note, 63 NORTHWESTERN UNIV. LAW REVIEW 873 (1969).

that the insurer's action "was designed to impede and obstruct justice." A federal trial court dismissed his action on the ground that the defendant's right to cancel plaintiff's policy was absolute, but a United States Court of Appeals reversed the lower court, holding that the attempted cancellation was void, as violative of overriding public policy, if done for the reasons alleged by the plaintiff. The court's reasoning is worth quoting:

> A member of the medical profession could hardly be expected to appear in court and testify for a plaintiff in any litigation if the penalty might be the cancellation of his own malpractice insurance. It manifestly is contrary to public policy to permit an insurance company to use policy cancellation as punishment against a doctor or dentist who appears as a witness to protect the rights of a plaintiff who has been wronged by another member of the profession. If the insurance industry can use the cancellation procedure to keep members of the medical profession from testifying as witnesses, malpractice litigation can be stifled.

The court concluded that the trial court, instead of dismissing plaintiff's lawsuit out of hand, should have permitted him an opportunity at trial to prove his claims regarding the defendant insurer's motivations.[8]

All that can fairly be said is that there are far fewer known examples of coercion in this area than would be anticipated if such practices were widespread. And the few litigated cases demonstrate that the law provides a remedy for any medical man who has been unjustifiably punished for expressing a medical opinion. Even so, members of the medical profession are sometimes overly reluctant to testify for claimants in malpractice cases. It is occasionally suggested that this reluctance stems primarily from what can be characterized as the "There-but-for-the-grace-of-God-go-I syndrome." The resulting reticence, although not conspiratorial in nature, is more than enough to vex claimants' counsel to the point that they, and perhaps also the general public, assign ulterior motives to the medical profession.

The Physician's Duty to Provide Relevant Expertise

Stripped of all propagandistic overtones, the pertinent point seems clear enough. Time permitting, a doctor with relevant expertise should feel no reluctance to testify in a case involving what he firmly believes to

[8] For additional insight into the asserted role of insurance companies in fostering a "conspiracy of silence," see *Hammonds* v. *Aetna Cas. & Sur. Co.*, 237 F. Supp. 96 (N.D. Ohio 1965); *Huffman* v. *Lindquist*, 234 P.2d 34, 36 (S. Ct. Cal. 1961) (dissent); *Julien* v. *Barker*, 272 P.2d 718 (S. Ct. Idaho 1954). *See generally*, Comment, *The California Malpractice Controversy*, 9 STANFORD LAW REVIEW 731 (1957).

have been professional malpractice. By the same token, a physician obviously has a duty to decline to aid a claimant whose lawsuit, in the physician's considered and objective opinion, is unmeritorious. It cannot be overstressed that the medical profession, by coming to the aid of plaintiffs with justifiable claims, will help to forestall adoption of expedient rules that unduly dilute the principle that claims of malpractice must be backed by expert evidence.

We take up now those evolving legal rules that make inroads on the orthodox principle that expert testimony is essential in medical malpractice actions.

ESTABLISHING MALPRACTICE THROUGH THE DEFENDANT'S ADMISSIONS

In a very real sense the doctor-defendant in a malpractice action is sometimes the best and most impressive authority on the quality of his own conduct. He knows what he did, how he did it, why he did it and, hopefully, whether his conduct measured up to acceptable standards. And so it is that the necessary expert testimony in a malpractice case may be provided by the defendant doctor's own admissions. It will come as no surprise that a physician's admissions of negligent conduct are receivable as evidence against him.[9]

Admissions have varying degrees of force. They may be of the sort to which a jury can properly attach full weight, little weight, or none at all. Or they may be conclusive against the defendant, rendering a defense against the plaintiff's claim impossible. If the defendant has made a so-called judicial admission—in a sworn deposition, in the suit papers, or in trial testimony, for example—it may be absolutely conclusive in effect; it cannot be explained or otherwise brushed aside and will, by itself, support a verdict against him.[10] If the defendant has made less formal concessions—in conversations with the patient, for example—they will be receivable at trial simply as items of evidence.[11] The physician will be permitted to explain or modify his seemingly embarrassing comments, and the jury will not be conclusively bound by them. The jurors will be free to accept as the truth either the claimed admissions or the defendant's contradicting testimony.

A good example of an evidentiary admission was involved in a 1961

[9] For general discussions of the law relating to the admissibility of a party-opponent's admissions, see McCormick, C. T.: Evidence, ch. 27. West Publishing Company, St. Paul, 1954; Morgan, E. M.: *Admissions*, 12 Washington Law Review 181 (1937).

[10] *E.g., Polk* v. *Missouri-Kansas-Texas R. Co.*, 111 S.W.2d 138 (S. Ct. Mo. 1937).

[11] *E.g., Cooper* v. *Brown*, 126 F.2d 874 (3d Cir. 1942).

Tennessee case.[12] The defendant doctor had admitted to his patient and her family that, had he conducted a proper postoperative examination, the patient's vagina would not have closed following hysterectomy. This expert evaluation of his own conduct was enough to support a verdict against him.

Statements constituting admissions against interest are usually self-evident. Sometimes, however, they are relatively subtle. In a recent Illinois case [13] it was held that a surgeon's statement to his patient, following a bad result, ". . . that he had an insurance policy of $100,000 for malpractice," could be interpreted by a jury as a concession of negligence. It appears questionable whether the quoted statement, which seems somewhat ambiguous, was in fact intended as a knowing admission of improper conduct. But whether it was or was not constituted a question that the jury would be permitted to resolve. The moral is that doctors should weigh their words carefully; loose remarks intended only to placate an unjustifiably irate patient may later return in the form of evidentiary admissions to plague the speaker.

USE OF THE DEFENDANT AS A WITNESS TO ESTABLISH THE FACTS AND THE STANDARD OF CARE

In light of the foregoing discussion, the question arises whether a malpractice defendant can be called to the witness stand by the plaintiff and there be questioned by counsel in such a way as to extract admissions from him. In other words, can the plaintiff, as a part of his own case for liability, call the defendant as a witness in the hope that he will condemn himself? Since malpractice actions are civil in nature and rarely involve criminal conduct, the defendant cannot invoke any privilege against self-incrimination and on that basis refuse to take the witness stand. And the widespread enactment of what are known as "adverse witness statutes," which expressly permit a litigant to call the adverse party for cross-examination, affords the malpractice plaintiff an opportunity to elicit helpful testimony from the defendant physician.[14] The prevalent but waning view is that the defendant's testimony cannot, however, be utilized to establish the applicable standard of care. In most American jurisdictions the defendant physician can be summoned to testify only to facts within his direct

[12] *Wooten* v. *Curry,* 362 S.W.2d 820 (Tenn. App. 1961). See also *Sheffield* v. *Runner,* 328 P.2d 828 (Cal. App. 1958), citing numerous cases in which malpractice was established by the defendant's admissions.

[13] *Asher* v. *Stromberg,* 223 N.E.2d 300 (Ill. App. 1966).

[14] See, *e.g.*, FED. R. CIV. P. 43(b) (1968); CAL. CODE CIV. PRO., §2055 (Supp. 1967); ILL. REV. STAT., ch. 110, §60 (Supp. 1969); MD. ANN. CODE, art. 35, §9 (Supp. 1967); N.J. STAT. ANN., §2A:81-11 (Supp. 1968).

knowledge—what he actually saw and did—and not as to the accepted standard of care among average members of the medical profession.[15] The announced justification for this rule is that notions of fairness preclude courts from forcing a defendant, even in a noncriminal case, to express opinions that might serve to establish the most crucial phase of the plaintiff's case.

Not all courts have felt themselves bound to this view, however. For more than twenty years the courts of California have compelled defendant doctors to testify to the applicable standard of care, making no distinctions based on conceptions of "fact" as distinguished from "opinion." In *Lawless* v. *Calaway*,[16] where this liberalized rule was enunciated, the California Supreme Court said flatly that "Any relevant matter in issue in a case is within the scope of the examination of witnesses called pursuant to the provisions of such [adverse witness] statutes." And in the 1964 case of *McDermott* v. *Manhattan Eye, Ear & Throat Hospital*[17] the influential New York Court of Appeals, the highest court of the state, adopted the same view.

In the *McDermott* case the plaintiff, upon the advice of the defendant doctors, had submitted to three operations for the correction of a corneal condition. One of the defendants was, beyond question, one of the world's leading ophthalmologists and had written a book on corneal operations. Plaintiff's operations, however, resulted in virtual blindness. She sued her doctors and a hospital for malpractice, arguing that in view of the diagnosed condition of her eye—Fuch's dystrophy of the periphery of the cornea; uncorrected eyesight of less than 20/200—surgery was disapproved by accepted medical practice.

At the trial of the *McDermott* case the plaintiff summoned no medical expert of her own to establish standard practice and the defendants' alleged deviation from it. Instead she called to the stand the defendant ophthalmologist and sought to extract his expert testimony as to accepted medical practice and his admission to having departed from that standard. The trial court, in accordance with the general rule, upheld all objections to these lines of questioning, and for want of expert testimony attesting deviation from accepted practice, the plaintiff's suit was dismissed. An intermediate appellate court agreed that plaintiff's maneuver was improper, but the Court of Appeals reversed the lower courts and ordered a new trial. It held unequivocally that the plaintiff in a malpractice action is entitled to elicit pivotal expert testimony from the defendant. The court put it this way:

[15] See, *e.g.*, *Osborn* v. *Carey*, 132 Pac. 967 (1913); *Hunder* v. *Rindlaub*, 237 N.W. 915 (S. Ct. N.D. 1931); *Forthofer* v. *Arnold*, 21 N.E.2d 869 (Ohio App. 1938).

[16] 147 P.2d 604 (S. Ct. Cal. 1944).

[17] 203 N.E.2d 469 (Ct. App. N.Y. 1964).

> . . . [A] plaintiff in a malpractice action is entitled to call the defendant doctor to the stand and question him *as to his factual knowledge of the case* (that is, as to his examination, diagnosis, treatment and the like) and, if he be so qualified, *as an expert* for the purpose of establishing the generally accepted medical practice in the community.[18]

The New York court stated that "There is nothing unfair about such a practice," pointing out that the defendant in a civil lawsuit ". . . has no inherent right to remain silent or, once on the stand, to answer only those inquiries which will have no adverse effect on his case." The court was at pains to put to rest the notion, reflected in many other decisions, "that it is somehow neither sporting nor consistent with the adversary system to allow a party to prove his case through his opponent's own testimony."

The ability to call the defendant doctor as a witness in plaintiff's own case will not solve all of the difficulties complained of by claimants and their counsel. One commentator allied with that segment of the bar which ordinarily represents claimants has summed up the effect of this rule: "The result of this technique will not be a feast of expert testimony for malpractice victims, but it may avoid starvation."[19] Hyperbole aside, it is plain that frivolous malpractice claims will in no way be advanced by placing the defendant physician on the witness stand; indeed, doing so would probably be an unmitigated disaster for the plaintiff. On the other hand, a realization that the defendant can be subjected to a raking examination by plaintiff's counsel, before and during trial, may from time to time promote the equitable pre-trial settlement of valid claims. The rule announced in California and New York is consistent with liberalized pretrial discovery-of-evidence rules now in force in most jurisdictions,[20] and it is likely to be widely adopted by the courts of other states. For example, only recently another important state supreme court, that of Ohio, approved the reasoning of the *McDermott* case.[21]

Compulsion of a Nonparty to Provide Expertise

The emerging rule outlined in the preceding paragraphs will be restricted to adverse parties to a lawsuit. Although other physicians, not named as defendants, can be called by the plaintiff as witnesses in the

[18] Emphasis supplied.

[19] Lambert, T. F.: *Malpractice Liability Concepts Affecting All Professions,* in Harolds, L. R., and Block, M. (eds.): MEDICAL MALPRACTICE 21. The Lawyers Co-operative Publishing Company, Rochester, N.Y., 1966.

[20] See Chapter 1.

[21] *Oleksiw* v. *Weidener,* 207 N.E.2d 375 (S. Ct. Ohio 1965). See also King, L. P.: *The Adverse Witness Statute and Expert Opinion,* 4 WAYNE LAW REVIEW 228 (1958); Spence, J. B.: *Adverse Witness Rule: A Cure for a Conspiracy,* 23 UNIV. OF MIAMI LAW REVIEW 1 (1968).

usual manner, the special rule discussed above does not mean that the plaintiff in a malpractice action can force a person having no relation to the pending matter to come into court and supply expert testimony. Any other rule would impose an unjust burden, akin to involuntary servitude, on at least some practitioners. By a simple exercise of a court's subpoena power a claimant could avail himself of the services of his community's busiest and most distinguished experts in cases with which they had previously had no direct contact. This potential for abuse has consistently led courts to foreclose compulsory expert testimony except where the expert is the named defendant or at least had some direct and relevant connection with the case at hand.[22]

USE OF IMPARTIAL MEDICAL PANELS

Although there appears to be no satisfactory reason for this, malpractice plaintiffs have not generally been tendered the assistance of the impartial medical panels that have been organized in some jurisdictions to supply needed expertise in ordinary personal injury matters, such as automobile collision cases. In partial compensation for this seeming inconsistency, special plans have been devised in some areas to aid the malpractice plaintiff: [23]

Medical Review Committees

Some state and county medical associations have set up medical committees to review malpractice charges levied against doctors and to recommend to the defendant physician that an equitable settlement be accomplished if evidence of malpractice is found. Claimants' counsel are not much enamored of these plans since the resulting reports are usually made available only to the defendant doctor's lawyer. The claimant's attorney does not receive them and no expert witnesses are furnished to him.

The general disenchantment with the Medical Review Committee plan among plaintiffs' attorneys has led to experimentation with two other procedures.

Joint Attorney-Physician Review Panels

One such innovation is the joint attorney-physician review panel, otherwise known as the Pima County (Arizona) Screening Plan. It provides

[22] See *People ex rel. Kraushaar Bros. & Co.* v. *Thorp,* 72 N.E.2d 165 (Ct. App. N.Y. 1947), and numerous cases cited therein. This is also the long-standing English rule. See *Webb* v. *Page,* [1843] 1 Car. & K. 23.

[23] See Comment, *Medical Malpractice—Expert Testimony,* 60 NORTHWESTERN UNIV. LAW REVIEW 834, 842–44 (1966).

for the following procedures: Upon a plaintiff's attorney's receipt of a medical malpractice claim, he writes a letter to the local bar association's Medicolegal Committee. The letter includes a detailed statement of his client's potential claim and requests a screening of it by a panel which is composed of nine physicians and nine lawyers. The doctor against whom the claim has been made is furnished a copy of the letter and is notified of a hearing date. At this hearing each "side" presents its "case" in an informal manner; that is, technical rules of courtroom evidence are not adhered to strictly. The claimant first presents his case through a narrative statement delivered by his counsel, a written statement, witnesses, or a combination of all three. The claimant is then open to questioning by the attorney for the doctor whom he has charged, after which the doctor presents his case. The panel, in reaching its decision, has access to any pertinent medical records since, for the purposes of the hearing, the claimant is deemed to have waived any evidentiary privilege he might otherwise have possessed with regard to such records.[24] At the close of the hearing the panel determines whether the evidence reveals "substantial evidence of malpractice" and, if it does, whether there is "substantial evidence of substantial injury arising out of this malpractice." If the answer to these questions is in the negative, the claimant's counsel is expected, although not required, to refrain from pressing the claim further. If the inquiries are answered in the affirmative, the local medical association produces competent, impartial medical testimony during any subsequent court proceeding involving the matter. This plan has apparently met with qualified success. For example, of fourteen claims referred to the Pima County, Arizona, screening panel between May 1957 and June 1960, four were withdrawn by claimants' counsel prior to any hearing, their own independent investigation having revealed the claims' lack of merit; four were withdrawn prior to any decision by the panel (three were settled and one was dropped for want of merit); six were decided by the panel (two lawsuits resulted).

"California Plan" Advisory Panels

The so-called California Plan, developed by the medical societies of Los Angeles, San Francisco, and San Diego, also involves the use of an advisory panel. A list of qualified physicians who are willing to serve on such a panel is supplied by the local medical society, upon request, to the malpractice claimant's lawyer. The lawyer selects one doctor, who becomes his medical adviser. This doctor either reviews the relevant records or

[24] See Chapters 15–16.

examines the claimant, or both, and then submits a written report to the claimant's lawyer. If the matter goes to trial, the doctor is obliged to testify should he be called upon to do so by the claimant's counsel. If counsel is dissatisfied with his initial choice of doctors, he can request another, but should he do so, he waives the confidential nature of the original examination of his client and thereby releases the first doctor to testify at the request of the defendant. The advantages of this plan are similar to those of the Pima County Plan. There is evidence that it has resulted in the abandonment of unfounded claims and the settlement of meritorious ones. It has also made physicians less reluctant to testify on behalf of plaintiffs in malpractice actions.

USE OF MEDICAL TREATISES AS EVIDENCE

Theoretically at least, the problem of securing expertise in support of meritorious malpractice cases could be neatly solved if only plaintiffs were free to offer in evidence relevant medical treatises instead of having to obtain live witnesses. Plaintiff's counsel, after introducing evidence of what the defendant doctor did, could simply introduce a treatise or other item of medical literature that purportedly lays out the proper procedures —the standard of care—to be followed by doctors in the type of case in question. The jury, optimistically, could then consider the contents of the treatise just as it would weigh the statements of expert witnesses actually testifying in court. But for reasons which we shall presently discuss, this alternative is currently available in only a few jurisdictions.

A few states, by either statute or judicial decision, have taken what might at first appear to be a substantial step toward alleviating malpractice plaintiffs' difficulties in producing expert testimony. Alabama, North Carolina, Kansas, Massachusetts, Nevada, Rhode Island, and perhaps Connecticut, Maine, and Wisconsin will admit into evidence learned books and articles to be used in establishing the standard of care applicable to the defendant physician.[25] Alabama's rule is judge-made as, apparently,

[25] In most jurisdictions it has been explicitly held that medical books are not admissible as direct evidence. See, *e.g., Rice* v. *Clement,* 184 So.2d 678 (Fla. App. 1966); *Koury* v. *Follo,* 158 S.E.2d 548 (S. Ct. N.C. 1968); *Standard Life Ins. Co.* v. *Strong,* 89 S.W.2d 367 (Tenn. App. 1935). Even the use of medical treatises for cross-examination purposes is often sharply restricted. Some jurisdictions permit a medical treatise to be employed to contradict a medical expert only when he concedes that he relied on the particular work in formulating his direct testimony. See, *e.g., Drucker* v. *Philadelphia Dairy Products Co.,* 166 Atl. 796 (S. Ct. Del. 1933); *Percoco's Case,* 173 N.E. 515 (Sup. Jud. Ct. Mass. 1930); *People* v. *McKernan,* 210 N.W. 219 (S. Ct. Mich. 1926). But see *Darling* v. *Charleston Community Memorial Hospital,* 200 N.E.2d 149 (S. Ct. Ill. 1964) (cross-examiner need only show that treatise is authoritative).

is North Carolina's; [26] Massachusetts, Kansas, Nevada, and Rhode Island, have enacted statutes to accomplish the same result. The Massachusetts statute, which is typical, reads as follows:

> A statement of fact or opinion on a subject of science or art contained in a published treatise, periodical, book or pamphlet shall, in the discretion of the court, and if the court finds that it is relevant and that the writer of such statement is recognized in his profession or calling as an expert on the subject, be admissible in actions of contract or tort for malpractice, error or mistake against physicians, surgeons, dentists, optometrists, hospitals sanitaria, as evidence tending to prove said fact or as opinion evidence; provided, however, that the party intending to offer as evidence any such statement shall, not less than three days before trial of the action, give the adverse party notice of such intention, stating the name of the writer of the statement and the title of the treatise, periodical, book or pamphlet in which it is contained.[27]

Nevada's statute is virtually identical with Massachusetts' except that it is made expressly applicable also to cases involving osteopathic physicians or surgeons, chiropractors, chiropidists and naturopathic physicians.[28]

The primary objection to the treatise approach is that it involves massive doses of hearsay, which is ordinarily an inadmissible brand of evidence in our courts. Hearsay evidence, to put it very simply, is the statement of a witness in court as to what another person has asserted out of court, the out-of-court assertion being offered to establish the truth of its contents. Unless the assertion happens to fall within one of the fairly numerous exceptions to the hearsay rule, it is rejected because of its unreliability. One reason for its rejection is that it was not made under oath. More importantly, it is rejected because secondhand assertions depend for their validity on the perception, training, skill, memory, articulateness, and veracity not of the witness on the stand but of the out-of-court declarant. Since the declarant is not on the witness stand, his possession

[26] See *Stoudenmeier* v. *Williamson*, 29 Ala. 558 (S. Ct. Ala. 1857); *Stone* v. *Proctor*, 131 S.E.2d 297 (S. Ct. N.C. 1963). See also *Kaplan* v. *Mashkin Freight Lines, Inc.*, 150 A.2d 602 (S. Ct. Err. & App. Conn. 1959); *Goldthwaite* v. *Sheraton Restaurant*, 145 A.2d 362 (S. Ct. Me. 1958); *Lewandowski* v. *Preferred Risk Mut. Ins. Co.*, 146 N.W.2d 505 (S. Ct. Wis. 1966).

[27] MASS. LAWS ANN., ch. 233, §79(c) (Supp. 1968).

[28] NEV. REV. STAT., §51.040 (1967). See also KANS. STAT. ANN., §60-460(cc) (1964); RHODE ISLAND SESS. LAWS, H. B. 1833 (1969). The New Jersey Supreme Court recently adopted a code of evidentiary rules. One rule, proposed to the court but not adopted by it, would have permitted the use of medical treatises as substantive evidence under certain circumstances. N.J. S. CT. R. 63(31) (not adopted). Section 1341 of the CALIF. EVID. CODE (Supp. 1967) provides that medical books cannot be employed to establish the nature of an injury or its probable effect. See also §721.

of these truth-guaranteeing attributes cannot be tested by means of cross-examination. Furthermore, every statement in medical literature is more or less a generalization; if the author were available for cross-examination it might develop that the fact situation before the court, although apparently the same as that discussed in the witness's book, was different enough to render the author's statement inapplicable to the immediate case.

There are additional dangers in the use of medical books as evidence. An obvious one is their potential for total confusion when placed in the hands of those who are ill-equipped to comprehend their esoteric language. And there is always the risk that jurors will give greater weight to a dubious treatise or article than to the oral testimony of the defendant's experts merely because the plaintiff's case appears in print between impressive cloth covers.

Only the Massachusetts treatise statute has had comprehensive judicial interpretation but the problems that arise under the Massachusetts law are undoubtedly the same as those encountered in the other states that have a treatise rule. Under the Massachusetts law two preliminary requirements must be met before a treatise or other publication will be admitted in evidence. First, the book, or the designated portion of it, must be relevant to material issues in the litigation. Second, and more significantly, the book must be reliable and authoritative. This second requirement has probably forestalled the publication in Massachusetts and elsewhere of a flood of special-interest medical treatises aimed mainly at the courtroom rather than the operating room.

The most difficult hurdle that plaintiff encounters under a treatise rule is the necessity for qualifying the author as a recognized and reliable authority in his field. In the Massachusetts case of *Reddington* v. *Clayman*,[29] medical books were excluded from evidence by the trial judge because he was not satisfied that their authors were recognized experts. If a medical treatise is in fact authoritative, however, plaintiff's counsel can extract this concession from the defendant doctor in a malpractice case by calling him as a witness in the manner previously described in this chapter.

Not surprisingly, it appears that the courts of Massachusetts have looked with disfavor on that state's treatise statute. Lawyers on both sides of the counsel table have agreed that "unsympathetic exercise of the trial judge's discretion has 'emasculated' the Massachusetts malpractice evidentiary statute." [30]

[29] 134 N.E.2d 920 (S. Jud. Ct. Mass. 1956).

[30] Kehoe, W. F.: *Massachusetts Malpractice Evidentiary Statute—Success or Failure?*, 44 BOSTON UNIV. LAW REVIEW 10, 26 (1964).

THE PRINCIPLE OF RES IPSA LOQUITUR

"The Thing Speaks for Itself"

There is one general legal principle of long standing that circumvents, with increasing frequency, the necessity for expert testimony in medical malpractice cases. This is the principle which lawyers, with their love of Latin phrases, have dubbed *res ipsa loquitur*—literally, "the thing speaks for itself." Its very label gives evidence of the principle's function and content, but like many rules that have been crystallized in a short and catchy phrase, the true purpose of the *res ipsa loquitur* doctrine is sometimes misunderstood. It is an extremely important doctrine. Its impact in the field of medical malpractice has been heavy and—to the possible consternation of the medical profession—it is likely to become still greater.

The Origin of the Principle

Most lawyers have tended, erroneously, to associate the *res ipsa loquitur* notion exclusively with tort law. It was S. Burns Weston, a distinguished and scholarly trial lawyer in the city of Cleveland, Ohio, who first gave broad publicity to the fact that the *res ipsa* principle initially arose, in an almost offhand fashion, in a criminal case. It cropped up in oral argument on behalf of the accused. Defense counsel's contention, according to Mr. Weston, went like this:

> Let us . . . consider which party had the better position for an ambush. . . . On this point, gentlemen, is there still room for doubt or further reflection? . . . Was it not rather that my client's arrival was awaited by one who, just because he relied upon the ground, had planned to make his attack there? Facts, gentlemen, are stubborn things but *they speak for themselves* and in this particular case they are eloquent." [31]

This summation, appropriately enough, was delivered in Latin—by Marcus Tullius Cicero, in his defense of Milo for the murder of Clodius, in the year 52 B.C.

The key phrase—*res ipsa loquitur*—found its way into Anglo-Saxon law in 1863 in the case of *Byrne* v. *Boadle*.[32] Byrne, while walking down an English street, was struck on the head by a barrel of flour that had rolled out of a window of Boadle's warehouse. Byrne resented this and went to court. The Baron Pollock, a noted judge, apparently resented it, too; unable

[31] Quoted in Weston, S. B.: *Products Liability and Res Ipsa Loquitur*, 35 CLEVELAND BAR JOURNAL 81 (1964) (emphasis supplied).
[32] 2 H. & C. 722, 159 Eng. Rep. 299 (1863).

to give up the Latin, Pollock, during argument of the case, said, "There are certain things of which it may be said *res ipsa loquitur* and this seems to be one of them." From that day forward the *res ipsa* principle, which we shall now attempt to explain, became ever more deeply embedded in negligence law.

Broadly speaking, the *res ipsa* doctrine applies to cases in which the simple fact that someone was hurt gives rise to an inference that another person, the defendant, was negligent. When an accident occurs and the injured person seeks to recover damages, in all but a limited number of specialized situations he must prove that the defendant was negligent. The injured person, as the plaintiff, has the burden of introducing evidence from which reasonable men (jurors or a judge) could properly conclude that the injury-producing event was more probably caused by the defendant's negligence than that it was not. This is what is meant by the statement that a plaintiff must establish his claim by a "preponderance" of the evidence. In the typical tort case the plaintiff seeks to prove specific, described acts of negligence to support his claim. He will show, for example, that the defendant motorist failed to pay attention to his driving and crossed over the center line in the highway, striking plaintiff's automobile; that the defendant construction contractor failed to place a barricade around a dangerous excavation; that the defendant landlord failed adequately to inspect and repair the elevator in his apartment building. In *res ipsa loquitur* cases, however, a verdict for the plaintiff is supported by proof only of the fact of injury and a few surrounding circumstances. Thoreau was speaking of this type of case when he said, "There are some cases of circumstantial evidence that are overwhelming, as when one finds a trout in the milk"—or, we might add, a sponge in the wound.

The Elements of the Res Ipsa Loquitur Principle

There are three or, it is sometimes said, four elements of the *res ipsa loquitur* principle. First, the accident must have been of the sort that does not ordinarily occur in the absence of negligence. Second, the injury-producing instrumentality or conduct must have been, at some significant time, within the control of the defendant or defendants charged with negligence. To put this second condition another way, the circumstances of the accident must indicate that the negligent person was the named defendant. Third, the injury must not have resulted from a voluntary assumption by the plaintiff of a known and appreciated risk, or from his own contributory negligence. A fourth condition sometimes mentioned in legal treatises and judicial opinions is that evidence explanatory of the accident must be more accessible to the defendant than to the plaintiff. This fourth consideration, even if not a true condition of the *res ipsa* rule, undeniably inspires application of the doctrine in particular cases and especially in medical malpractice cases of certain types.

The Concept of Common Knowledge

The universally accepted rule is that *res ipsa loquitur* will apply only when a layman could infer as a matter of common knowledge that the particular injury would not have occurred unless the defendant was negligent. This rule has evolved as a logical consequence of the first condition for application of the *res ipsa* principle: the injury must be of a kind which would not ordinarily occur in the absence of negligence. Hence, application of the principle is limited, theoretically, to those cases where a jury does not need the assistance of an expert witness to discern negligence. The lay jurors must, supposedly, be competent to determine on the basis of past experience and common knowledge that such-and-such a thing simply does not usually occur unless someone was negligent. As one federal court put it, in the context of a medical malpractice case,

> . . . The lack of the due care, or lack of diligence on the part of a physician in diagnosis, method and manner of treatment ordinarily must be established by expert testimony. . . . Occasionally expert testimony is not required where an injury . . . is of such a character as to warrant the inference of want of care from the testimony of laymen or in the light of knowledge and experience of the jurors themselves.[33]

Expansion of the Common Knowledge Concept

Recent judicial decisions concerning the common knowledge standard in medical malpractice *res ipsa* cases strongly indicate that the standard is being liberalized and that there has been an increase in the number and kind of malpractice cases to which the *res ipsa* principle will be applied. The reasons for this perceptible expansion of what is to be considered within common knowledge are undoubtedly several—a pivotal one being the reaction by our courts to the proof problems confronting the patient who was unconscious at the time of injury or who encounters a reluctance by doctors to testify against other doctors. A widely quoted California opinion discusses courts' reasons for importing the *res ipsa* principle into the malpractice field:

> The application of the doctrine of res ipsa loquitur in malpractice cases is a development of comparatively recent years. Before that time, the facts that medicine is not an exact science, that the human body is not susceptible of precise understanding, that the care required of a medical man is the degree of learning and skill common in his profession or locality, and that even with

[33] *Ayers* v. *Parry*, 192 F.2d 181, 184 (3d Cir. 1951).

the greatest of care untoward results do occur in surgical and medical procedures, were considered paramount in determining whether the medical man in a given circumstance had been negligent. But gradually the courts awoke to the so-called "conspiracy of silence." No matter how lacking in skill or how negligent the medical man might be, it was almost impossible to get other medical men to testify adversely to him in litigation based on his alleged negligence. Not only would the guilty person thereby escape from civil liability for the wrong he had done, but his professional colleagues would take no steps to insure that the same results would not again occur at his hands. This fact, plus the fact that usually the plaintiff is by reason of anesthesia or lack of medical knowledge in no position to know what occurred that resulted in harm to him, forced the courts to attempt to equalize the situation by in some cases placing the burden on the doctor of explaining what occurred in order to overcome the inference of negligence. One other fact contributed to the application of the doctrine, namely that certain medical and surgical procedures became so common that in many of them the layman knew that if properly conducted untoward results did not occur and in others, medical men (when it was possible to get them to admit it) from their specialized knowledge knew that without negligence the result would have been a good one.[34]

Physicians may not agree with some of the statements made in the quoted opinion, but the hard fact remains that there is widespread judicial acceptance of the beliefs reflected in the California court's *dicta.*

The California court adverted to the common knowledge requirement that is generally thought to be built into the *res ipsa loquitur* doctrine. It implied in its opinion an increased confidence in the extent of lay jurors' common knowledge of medical procedures and the outcomes to be expected. It is sometimes difficult to detect the bases for such judicial optimism regarding the level of jurors' specialized knowledge, and physicians may naturally inquire as to the sources from which laymen have extracted their latter-day knowledge. They will be understandably reluctant to conclude that popular periodicals and television serials have contributed altogether reliable information to the general public.

Despite the quoted California court's somewhat sweeping comments, the truth is that cases involving the common knowledge standard cannot be fitted into any nicely logical and consistent framework. Most courts realize that the standard's application in any given litigation involves close and difficult questions of judgment. As would be anticipated in any body of lawsuits involving medical issues, the facts are frequently so complicated and varied that this legal judgment cannot be made to rest on the broad precedent of earlier decided cases; each new litigation must be resolved on its own peculiar facts. The upshot is that there has arisen

[34] *Salgo* v. *Leland Stanford Jr. University Board of Trustees,* 317 P.2d 170, 175 (1957).

a sometimes confusing and seemingly inconsistent welter of decisions concerning the common knowledge standard. We can begin to bring some order to this collection of cases by first discussing the more orthodox applications of the standard.

Foreign Body Cases

In some types of medical malpractice cases *res ipsa loquitur* has traditionally, almost unquestioningly, been applied. Most appellate courts have held the doctrine applicable to the defendant surgeon who left some foreign object in the body of his patient. Wholly typical are the numerous reported sponge cases. An Indiana judge who may have had a bland sense of humor has said, "A surgeon is charged, as a matter of law, with the duty to remove sponges used in the operation, which sponges will not be of use in the abdomen after the operation." [35] The *res ipsa* doctrine has also functioned where forceps, needles, and sundry other items of hardware and soft goods were left within the area of an operation.[36]

The classic example, without doubt, is the celebrated case of *Jefferson* v. *United States*.[37] The plaintiff, a 45-year-old soldier, had undergone an operation for gallbladder trouble at Fort Belvoir, Virginia, on July 23, 1945. In January, 1946, he was discharged from the Army. On March 8, 1946, he went to Johns Hopkins Hospital in Baltimore, complaining of spells of nausea and vomiting that had begun two weeks earlier and were getting worse. On March 13, 1946, he was operated upon at Johns Hopkins. His surgeon found a well-healed medical scar on the plaintiff's abdomen. When he operated through this scar the surgeon came upon a towel which had eroded into the duodenum. The towel was removed, measured, and photographed. It bore the prominent legend, "Medical Department U.S. Army." It was two and one-half feet long by one and one-half feet wide.

[35] *Funk* v. *Bonham,* 183 N.E. 312 (S. Ct. Ind. 1932). Adoption of a before-and-after sponge count by nurses does not relieve the surgeon or surgeons from liability for failing to remove all sponges after an operation. The task of accounting for the sponges is said to be nondelegable so far as liability is concerned. See, *e.g., Davis* v. *Kerr,* 86 Atl. 1007 (S. Ct. Pa. 1913). And where two physicians assisted in placing gauze sponges in plaintiff's body, both have been held liable, under the *res ipsa loquitur* principle, for failure to remove them. *Mitchell* v. *Saunders,* 13 S.E.2d 242 (S. Ct. N.C. 1941). See also *Martin* v. *Perth Amboy General Hospital,* 250 A.2d 40 (N.J. App. 1969).

[36] *E.g., Tiller* v. *Von Pohle,* 230 P.2d 213 (S. Ct. Ariz. 1951) (cloth sack in abdomen); *Bowers* v. *Olch,* 260 P.2d 997 (Cal. App. 1953) (needle in abdomen); *Johnson* v. *Ely,* 205 S.W.2d 759 (S. Ct. Tenn. 1947) (needle in abdomen); *Gray* v. *Wright,* 96 S.E.2d 671 (S. Ct. W. Va. 1957) (hemostat in abdomen). Many additional examples are set forth in 2 Louisell, D. W., and Williams, H.: MEDICAL MALPRACTICE, Appendix A. Matthew Bender, New York, 1969.

[37] 77 F. Supp. 706 (D. Md. 1948), *aff'd,* 178 F.2d 518 (4th Cir. 1949), *aff'd,* 340 U.S. 135 (1950).

The federal courts concluded that these facts bespoke negligence on the part of "agents or employees of the government."

In none of these cases is the plaintiff required to produce expert testimony assessing the defendant surgeon's professional conduct. Courts believe, on the basis of common experience, that "the thing speaks for itself" and that a jury can properly find that it did on the basis of its members' own collective knowledge. In other words, the jurors, unaided by expert witnesses, are permitted to conclude that "everyone knows" that sponges, needles, and packs are not left inside human bodies unless someone was negligent. The defendant surgeon was in control of the foreign object at the pertinent time, and since he has not offered a satisfactory explanation, he is the obvious culprit.

Not all courts regard even the foreign object cases as ripe for application of the *res ipsa* notion, believing as they do that lay jurors lack adequate comprehension of surgery's complexities. English courts often refuse to apply the doctrine in sponge cases, for example. The following is taken from an English opinion reflecting the reasoning of that country's courts:

> . . . It is difficult to see how the principle of res ipsa loquitur can apply generally to actions for negligence against a surgeon for leaving a swab in a patient, even if in certain circumstances the presumption may arise. . . . The nature even of abdominal operations varies widely, and many considerations enter into it. . . . [These] considerations combine together to present a state of things of which the ordinary experience of mankind knows nothing, and therefore, to make it unsafe to beg the question of proof.[38]

It is fair to say, however, that American courts are not as cautious as the English in their application of the common knowledge standard in foreign object *res ipsa* cases. In the United States, as we have indicated, the doctrine is widely considered applicable in such cases.

It may be possible, nevertheless, for a defendant surgeon to rebut the *res ipsa* inference of negligence in certain types of foreign object cases. The defendant in a New York case [39] had a victory of sorts on this front. He had operated on the plaintiff for peptic ulcers. While he was closing the incision a needle broke and a part of it remained in the wound. The surgeon neglected to inform the plaintiff of this fact. The litigation, then, raised two separate issues. The first issue was whether the breaking of the needle was due to negligence. The trial court permitted application of the *res ipsa loquitur* concept in the plaintiff's case to raise an inference of

[38] *Mahon* v. *Osborne,* [1939] 2 K.B. 14. See also *Miller* v. *Tongen,* 161 N.W.2d 686 (S. Ct. Minn. 1968) (leaving sponge in body not necessarily negligent).

[39] *Benson* v. *Dean,* 133 N.E. 125 (Ct. App. N.Y. 1921). See also *Noonan* v. *Sessloch,* 43 N.E.2d 838 (Ct. App. N.Y. 1942) (similar facts; directed verdict for defendant doctor).

negligent conduct. But when the defendant put in evidence that "surgical needles occasionally break, even when the operator uses the highest degree of care," the court decided that, in the absence of counterevidence by plaintiff, the inference of negligence had been satisfactorily rebutted. For the defendant, however, it was a Pyrrhic victory: he was held liable on the second issue involving his failure to disclose the broken needle incident to his patient.

Remote Injury Cases

American courts have also traditionally been willing to employ the *res ipsa loquitur* principle when a healthy part of the body remote from the field of surgery has been injured. The reasoning of the judicial decisions is that even though surgical techniques are not within the common knowledge of laymen, both judges and jurors know that injuries to remote and healthy portions of the body do not ordinarily result from surgery unless there was negligence. Conversely, and logically, the circumstance that the injury was within the field of surgery has been employed by courts as a reason for refusing to apply the *res ipsa* principle.

A Wisconsin decision [40] demonstrates the workings, and the failures, of the common knowledge standard in remote injury cases. The defendant had operated to remove the plaintiff's prostate gland. During the operation he damaged plaintiff's sphincter, making it impossible for plaintiff to control urination. The Wisconsin court recognized the rule that damage to a remote portion of the body during an operation may give rise to the application of *res ipsa loquitur* but suggested the converse: that the proximity of the damage to the field of operation was a factor in finding that the case before it did not fall within the common knowledge standard:

> . . . Those cases [*i.e.*, certain remote injury cases cited by the court] are readily distinguishable from the instant case where the external sphincter was only about one and a half inches from the prostate gland being operated on. It does not lie within the field of common knowledge of laymen that injury to the sphincter ordinarily does not occur if due care is exercised by the surgeon performing the suprapubic prostatectomy.

It is evident that the remoteness from or proximity of the injury to the field of surgery is not absolutely controlling; it is simply a factor in determining whether the *res ipsa* doctrine should be applied. That this is so is attested by several reported cases in which the *res ipsa* principle was applied although the injury was within the field of operation.[41] It should

[40] *Fehrman* v. *Smirl,* 121 N.W. 2d 255, 267 (S. Ct. Wis. 1963).

[41] See *e.g., Cho* v. *Kempler,* 2 Cal. Rptr. 167 (Cal. App. 1960); *James* v. *Spear,* 338 P.2d 22 (Cal. App. 1959); *Guillen* v. *Martin,* 333 P.2d 266 (Cal. App. 1958).

perhaps be added that all of these latter cases arose in California where the courts have been openhanded in their application of the *res ipsa loquitur* concept.

We now take up some less orthodox applications of the *res ipsa* common knowledge standard.

Anesthesia and Drug Injection Cases

Courts in the past have usually been reluctant to apply the *res ipsa* principle in cases where a patient has been harmed by the administration of an anesthetic or the injection of a drug. For example, in *Ayers* v. *Parry* [42] the injection of a spinal anesthetic caused paralysis of the plaintiff's right leg and atrophy of the left. The California court refused to apply *res ipsa loquitur*, holding that the case was one that could be understood and adequately explained only by experts; that, in other words, lay jurors lacked any pertinent common knowledge. The same view was taken in a case arising in Hawaii in which the patient died as a consequence of the administration of ether during a tonsillectomy.[43] Again, the court found that the circumstances were not within the ambit of laymen's common knowledge; the fatality might have resulted even though reasonable care had been exercised, and so jurors would not be heard to say that "the thing speaks for itself."

The law, as we have said, is flexible and fluid, constantly changing as knowledge advances. There is, accordingly, no hard and fast rule that the *res ipsa* formulation cannot be employed in cases involving the administration of anesthetics or drug injections. On the contrary, a few recent decisions indicate that courts have become less reluctant to employ *res ipsa* in this area of medical activity. The trend, if it is one, was once again commenced in California. In two cases [44] the plaintiff had been injured by the injection of drugs, and in each the court held *res ipsa* applicable on the ground that the jurors, on the basis of common knowledge, could infer negligence. The force of these holdings is somewhat blunted by the fact that in each case there was also expert testimony that the injury would not have happened had the defendant exercised reasonable care.

Recent decisions outside California suggest that there is in fact an emerging trend in the anesthesia-drug area. In *Voss* v. *Bridwell* [45] the Kansas Supreme Court held the *res ipsa* doctrine applicable where a patient had incurred permanent brain damage as a result of the admin-

[42] 192 F.2d 181 (3d Cir. 1951).

[43] *Lyu* v. *Shinn,* 40 Hawaii 198 (S. Ct. Hawaii 1953).

[44] *Wolfsmith* v. *Marsh,* 337 P.2d 70 (S. Ct. Cal. 1959); *Seneris* v. *Haas,* 291 P.2d 915 (S. Ct. Cal. 1955).

[45] 364 P.2d 955 (S. Ct. Kan. 1961).

istration of an anesthetic. In *Walker* v. *Distler*[46] the Idaho Supreme Court indicated that *res ipsa loquitur* could properly be invoked in a case involving injury from the injection of a spinal anesthetic. In the New Jersey case of *Terhune* v. *Margaret Hague Memorial Maternity Hospital*[47] the plaintiff alleged that she had sustained a facial burn as the result of negligent administration of an anesthetic during the delivery of her child. The court stated that "the apparently abnormal effect of the anesthesia on [plaintiff's] face" might support an inference of negligence in the absence of any expert testimony. These cases cannot, on their facts, be distinguished from earlier decisions in which the *res ipsa* doctrine was deemed inapplicable and must therefore be taken to evidence a willingness on the part of at least some courts to expand the common knowledge standard.[48]

Diagnosis and Treatment Cases

In two additional types of cases courts have, until recently, been reluctant to apply the *res ipsa loquitur* principle. They are the cases involving asserted error in diagnosis or in the choice of a method of treatment. The theory underlying these decisions is that diagnosis and method of treatment are usually matters of medical judgment and that a doctor should not be held liable for an honest error in judgment. Because lay jurors are not sufficiently knowledgeable to distinguish between errors in judgment and negligence in these cases, they must—the older cases held—be aided by expert testimony. For many years the leading case on the point was *Langford* v. *Jones*,[49] in which the defendant surgeon had removed a tumor from plaintiff's uterus but had failed to detect that she was pregnant. The Oregon court refused to hold the doctor liable, concluding that he had employed reasonable care and skill and had merely made an honest error in diagnosis.

However, uncritical reliance should not be placed on the oft-repeated but incomplete statement that a physician cannot be held liable for honest errors in judgment. This formulation is imprecise. It is more accurate to say that a doctor cannot be held liable for an exercise of medical judgment if he has utilized proper and adequate diagnostic methods. Simply put, a physician cannot be liable for an exercise of *good* judgment. It is fully as possible in the medical profession as elsewhere to employ good judgment in reaching what ultimately proves to be a wrong answer.

If the use of a certain procedure has become, as a matter of common

[46] 296 P.2d 452 (S. Ct. Idaho 1956).

[47] 164 A.2d 75 (S. Ct. N.J. 1960).

[48] See also *Dohr* v. *Smith*, 104 So.2d 29 (S. Ct. Fla. 1958); *Swartout* v. *Holt*, 272 S.W.2d 756 (Tex. Civ. App. 1954); *Kemalyan* v. *Henderson*, 277 P.2d 372 (S. Ct. Wash. 1954).

[49] 22 Pac. 1064 (S. Ct. Ore. 1890).

knowledge, an essential diagnostic method, the courts will invoke *res ipsa* where that procedure has been ignored. The Kentucky Supreme Court supplies an example of this proposition in *Butts* v. *Watts.*[50] In that case a dentist who had extracted a tooth failed to take an x-ray that would have revealed that part of the tooth had not been removed. The court allowed a jury, unaided by expert testimony, to find the dentist negligent because, it held, the making of an x-ray in such cases was commonly known to constitute proper procedure.

"Calculated Risk" Cases

Limitations on the scope of the common knowledge standard can be stated in terms of the so-called calculated risk doctrine. This doctrine is simply a derivative of the notion that *res ipsa loquitur* will not apply when the injury complained of is of a type that may occur even though reasonable care has been employed. The theory of the calculated risk doctrine is that *res ipsa* should not be applied where an accepted method of medical treatment involves hazards which may produce injurious results regardless of the care exercised by the physician. Many courts decline to invoke *res ipsa loquitur* when the known hazards are "a calculated and even an expected risk of the treatment." [51] The point is that it becomes impossible, once the defendant has established that an accepted method of treatment involves inherent risks to the patient, for the judge or jury to determine without the aid of expert testimony whether the claimed injury was unavoidable or resulted from the defendant's ineptitude. Even the California Supreme Court, which originated the calculated risk doctrine and then wavered away from it,[52] seems currently to adhere to it.[53] The doctrine is an important one to any malpractice defendant who can produce expert testimony or statistics demonstrating that the accepted method of treatment he employed posed unavoidable risks. Of course, as we shall later discuss, the physician undoubtedly has an obligation, both moral and legal, to inform the patient fully of these risks.

"Bad Result" Cases

A great many courts refusing to permit use of the *res ipsa loquitur* concept in a malpractice case invoke the so-called bad result rule. These courts reiterate the generalization that evidence of unsuccessful treatment —a bad result—is not in and of itself sufficient to raise an inference of negligence. The extensive reliance on this proposition simply indicates that

[50] 290 S.W.2d 777 (Ct. App. Ky. 1958).

[51] *Farber* v. *Olkon,* 254 P.2d 520, 525 (S. Ct. Cal. 1953).

[52] Compare *Farber* v. *Olkon,* 254 P.2d 520 (S. Ct. Cal. 1953), with *Wolfson* v. *Marsh,* 337 P.2d 70 (S. Ct. Cal. 1959).

[53] See *Silverson* v. *Weber,* 372 P.2d 97 (S. Ct. Cal. 1962).

there exist a wide variety of situations in which neither judge nor jury can say as a matter of common knowledge that the harm was probably caused by negligence.

The traditional bad result rule—if it can fairly be termed a rule—was implemented in the Tennessee case of *Butler* v. *Molinski*.[54] There the defendant treated plaintiff's severely fractured wrist but was unable to prevent development of a deformity. Plaintiff instituted a malpractice action. He could not prove that the defendant had employed improper methods or that the result was particularly unusual. The court held that the *res ipsa* principle was inapplicable, stating that an inference of negligence could not be grounded on mere proof of a bad result. Other courts, however, have been unwilling to invoke the bad result rule in seemingly similar cases. In *Daiker* v. *Martin*[55] the defendant had set a cast overly tight; impaired circulation and an infection in plaintiff's leg resulted. The leg had to be amputated. The Iowa Supreme Court held that the trial judge had erred in refusing to submit the case to the jury for its consideration since "It is a matter of common knowledge that such things do not ordinarily occur in connection with treatment by physicians using ordinary skill." Even more diametrically opposed to the foregoing case of *Butler* v. *Molinski* is *Olson* v. *Weitz*,[56] a Washington case. The plaintiff in *Olson* had suffered a simple fracture in her forearm and the defendant had placed the arm in a cast. The bones showed marked displacement when the cast was removed. An open reduction was required to correct the condition. There was no specific evidence of negligence by the defendant in his treatment of the arm, but the trial court sent the case to the jury on a *res ipsa loquitur* theory. The Supreme Court of Washington, affirming a plaintiff's verdict, said, ". . . such was not the result to be expected from proper treatment of a simple fracture with no complications."

Res Ipsa Loquitur Coupled with Expert Testimony

We have suggested that the observable trend today is toward extension of the *res ipsa loquitur* principle in the malpractice field. One reason for this phenomenon is the gradual broadening of the common knowledge concept. Another reason for increasing application of the doctrine is the development of an exception to the common knowledge rule. The majority of jurisdictions in the United States still hold that "The [*res ipsa*] doctrine does not apply where common knowledge or experience is not sufficiently extensive to permit it to be said that the plaintiff's condition would not have

[54] 277 S.W.2d 448 (S. Ct. Tenn. 1955).
[55] 91 N.W.2d 747 (S. Ct. Iowa 1958).
[56] 221 P.2d 537 (S. Ct. Wash. 1950).

existed but for the negligence of the doctors."[57] However, some courts have recently held that the *res ipsa* principle may apply even though laymen could not properly base an inference of negligence on their common knowledge and experience. These courts have applied *res ipsa loquitur* where an expert witness has testified, on the basis of his specialized knowledge, that the injury probably would not have occurred had the defendant doctor used ordinary care.[58]

There is nothing radical about this exception to the common knowledge rule. Courts have consistently held in nonmalpractice cases that expert testimony can supply a foundation for the *res ipsa* concept when lay jurors could not determine the negligence issue on the basis of their own general knowledge.[59] If an expert can say that certain events do not ordinarily occur unless caused by negligence, the jury is permitted to infer negligence from the happening of such an event. It remains to be seen whether use of this approach will become common in medical malpractice cases. Plaintiffs still may find it difficult to secure the needed expertise even though it is of a different sort than is required in non-*res ipsa* cases. On the other hand, they may find their task somewhat easier. A medical expert, consulted in a malpractice matter, may be reluctant to specify acts of the defendant constituting negligence; he may be much more willing simply to testify that the injury was of a kind that does not ordinarily occur when due care is being exercised. The obvious implication contained in the latter testimony will not escape the average juror.

Res Ipsa Loquitur and Multiple Defendants

Special problems in the application of *res ipsa loquitur* arise in cases where the plaintiff's injury could have been caused by any one of several persons but the evidence does not clearly indicate which of those persons was responsible. As we have previously indicated, one of the conditions limiting application of the *res ipsa* principle is that the inference of negligence must point to the guilty defendant. When "the thing speaks for itself" it must inferentially identify the culprit, since it hardly avails the plaintiff to establish, by inference, that his injury resulted from negligence of a person or persons unknown.[60] Thus, when a circumstantial inference of negligence points to a whole group of persons, none of whom is legally

[57] *Ayers* v. *Parry*, 192 F.2d 181, 185 (3d Cir. 1951).

[58] *E.g., Wolfsmith* v. *Marsh*, 337 P.2d 70 (S. Ct. Cal. 1959); *Walker* v. *Distler*, 296 P.2d 452 (S. Ct. Idaho 1956); *Fehrman* v. *Smirl*, 121 N.W.2d 255 (S. Ct. Wis. 1963).

[59] See Fricke, G. L.: *The Use of Expert Evidence in Res Ipsa Loquitur Cases*, 5 VILLANOVA LAW REVIEW 59 (1959).

[60] See, *e.g., Actiesselskabet Ingrid* v. *Central R. Co. of New Jersey*, 216 Fed. 72 (2d Cir. 1914); *Maybach* v. *Falstaff Brewing Corp.*, 222 S.W.2d 87 (S. Ct. Mo. 1949); *Huggins* v. *John Morrell & Co.*, 198 N.E.2d 448 (S. Ct. Ohio 1964).

responsible for the acts of the others, the question is raised whether the *res ipsa* principle should be applied and, if so, against whom. The multiple defendant situation poses an obvious dilemma. If the *res ipsa* doctrine is applied to the group as a whole, persons who were not in fact negligent may be held liable to the plaintiff; if the doctrine is not applied at all, an injured person with a meritorious claim may be denied a monetary recovery.

Situations sharply posing this dilemma arise with some frequency in medical malpractice cases, especially in those that involve surgical procedures. Modern surgery, obviously, involves highly specialized participants and a complex organization.[61] The surgeon, by and large, no longer controls the entire care of his patient. The hospital provides a trained staff of nurses, supervised by a head nurse. The anesthesiologist performs his duties largely independently of the surgeon. While going to and from the operating room and during his immediate postoperative period of care the patient is usually in the hands of persons other than the surgeon. The availability of *res ipsa loquitur* in so diffused a situation has been the subject of much debate, and the applicable law is currently in a state of flux.[62] A substantial number of courts have held that except in special situations involving vicarious or joint liability, which we shall subsequently discuss, *res ipsa loquitur* cannot be applied in a lawsuit against several defendants, only one of whom—and he being unidentified—could have caused plaintiff's injury.[63] Although there have been some significant inroads, this rule continues to be widely enforced, for two reasons. In the first place, it is thought that holding an entire group of defendants liable is fundamentally unfair to those individual defendants, buried in the pile, who are free of fault. Second, most courts pay more than lip service to the exclusive control element of the *res ipsa* doctrine—or, perhaps more precisely, the requirement that the circumstances relied upon point to the negligence of an identified defendant.

Some courts, however, have been reluctant to deny a chance for recovery in multiple defendant suits by refusing to apply the *res ipsa* principle. These courts look to a landmark California decision, *Ybarra* v. *Spangard*,[64] for support. In that case the plaintiff had undergone an appendectomy. When he regained consciousness following his operation he felt a sharp pain in his right shoulder. Later, paralysis and atrophy of the

[61] See, *e.g.*, Engel, L.: THE OPERATION, McGraw-Hill, New York, 1958 (detailed account of the complex organization involved in open-heart surgery).

[62] See, *e.g.*, Adamson, O. C.: *Medical Malpractice: Misuse of Res Ipsa Loquitur*, 46 MINNESOTA LAW REVIEW 1043 (1962); Renswick, J. C.: *Res Ipso Loquitur in Hospital and Medical Malpractice Cases*, 9 CLEVELAND-MARSHALL LAW REVIEW 199 (1960).

[63] See *Huggins* v. *John Morrell & Co.*, 198 N.E.2d 448 (S. Ct. Ohio 1964), and cases therein cited.

[64] 154 P.2d 687 (S. Ct. Cal. 1944).

muscles of that shoulder developed. He sued the surgeon, his consulting physician, the anesthesiologist, the owner of the hospital and several hospital employees—all the persons who had control of him at one time or another during the period he was anesthetized—on the theory of *res ipsa loquitur.* The trial court directed a verdict for the defendants and the plaintiff appealed. The Supreme Court of California reversed the lower court, holding that the *res ipsa* principle could be applied to multiple defendants even though some of them clearly must have been innocent. The case was retried and resulted in a verdict against all defendants, at least some of whom could not possibly have been the cause of plaintiff's injuries.

Lower California courts, bound by pronouncements of the state's highest court, adhere to the ruling in *Ybarra* [65] and so do courts in some other states. For example, in the Iowa case of *Frost* v. *Des Moines Still College of Osteopathy and Surgery,*[66] plaintiff sued both a surgeon and a hospital on a *res ipsa* theory to recover for burns she had received while anesthetized. The Iowa Supreme Court, holding that the *res ipsa* concept was applicable against both the surgeon and the hospital, relied heavily on *Ybarra* for the conclusion that the plaintiff was not required to show who had been in control of the injury-producing instrumentality. The court said:

> It was sufficient that the plaintiff disclosed that the injury resulted from an external force applied while she lay unconscious in the hospital, and we conclude that it satisfies the requirement that the plaintiff identify the instrumentality causing her injury. It is as clear an identification as such a plaintiff of her own knowledge may ever be able to make, and under the doctrine of res ipsa loquitur the law should require no more.
>
> It is also manifestly unreasonable to insist that she identify any one of the persons who came in or remained in the operating room after the operation, as the person who did the alleged negligent act.

As one prominent legal commentator has remarked, *Ybarra* and its progeny cannot be qualified as orthodox applications of the *res ipsa loquitur* principle; they involve a "striking departure from the idea of exclusive control." [67] They abrogate the limitation that the inference of negligence must point to a particular defendant or defendants; or, put another way, these cases effectively eliminate the general requirement that any person held liable in a civil case must have contributed to the plaintiff's

[65] *E.g., Oldis* v. *La Societé Francaise de Bienfaisance Mutuelle,* 279 P.2d 184 (Cal. App. 1955); *Bowers* v. *Olch,* 260 P.2d 997 (Cal. App. 1953); *Cavero* v. *Franklin General Benevolent Soc'y,* 223 P.2d 471 (Cal. App. 1950).

[66] 79 N.W.2d 306 (S. Ct. Iowa 1956).

[67] Prosser, W. L.: TORTS 227, 3d ed. West Publishing Company, St. Paul, 1964.

claimed injury. It has been suggested that these decisions erect a new and quite revolutionary test which would permit application of the *res ipsa* doctrine whenever the defendants possessed superior knowledge or superior access to information that would explain the plaintiff's injury.[68]

Although *Ybarra* and decisions following it represent a major departure from long-accepted legal dogma, the courts in question justify their decisions by reference to two important factual considerations: the very special relationship between the defendants and their patients and the unconsciousness of the patients at the time of their injuries' infliction. Both of these underlying considerations were featured prominently in the *Ybarra* decision:

> . . . [I]t is difficult to see how the [res ipsa loquitur] doctrine can, without any justification, be so restricted in its statement as to become inapplicable to a patient who submits himself to the care and custody of doctors and nurses, is rendered unconscious, and receives some injury from instrumentalities used in his treatment. Without the aid of the doctrine a patient who received permanent injuries of a serious character, obviously the results of someone's negligence, would be entirely unable to recover unless the doctors and nurses in attendance voluntarily chose to disclose the identity of the negligent person and the facts establishing liability.

The court went on to suggest that it would be highly unfair for a person to submit himself to the care and custody of doctors and nurses and yet be unable to recover for an injury negligently caused during the course of the relationship. The special duty of the defendants to the patient, the California court felt, justified relaxation of the orthodox exclusive control requirement.

Whether these arguments will persuade additional courts to accept the *Ybarra* doctrine is not yet clear. The reaction of legal scholars to the *Ybarra* approach has been distinctly mixed and some have vigorously criticized it.[69] Nonetheless, in a day when courts in other areas of the law are imposing absolute liability regardless of fault (for example, in connection with defective manufactured products), the possibility of widespread adoption of the *Ybarra* approach is altogether real.[69a]

[68] McCoid, A. H.: *Negligence Actions Against Multiple Defendants,* 7 STANFORD LAW REVIEW 480, 505–6 (1955).

[69] See, *e.g.,* Adamson, O. C.: *Medical Malpractice: Misuse of Res Ipsa Loquitur,* 46 MINNESOTA LAW REVIEW 1043 (1962); Seavey, W. A.: *Res Ipsa Loquitur: Tabula in Naufragio,* 63 HARVARD LAW REVIEW 643 (1950). See also Louisell, D. W., and Williams, H.: *Res Ipsa Loquitur–Its Future in Medical Malpractice Cases,* 48 CALIFORNIA LAW REVIEW 252 (1960), for less critical comments.

[69a] See, *e.g., Oldis* v. *La Societé Francaise de Bienfaisance Mutuelle,* 279 P.2d 184 (Cal. App. 1955); *Nicholson* v. *Sisters of Charity of Providence in Oregon,* 463 P.2d 861 (S. Ct. Ore. 1970).

Malpractice plaintiffs can sometimes surmount the problems posed by a multiple defendant situation even in the absence of an *Ybarra*-like rule. The most obvious way is by doing exactly what the law ordinarily requires: developing enough evidence to establish which of the possible defendants actually caused plaintiff's injuries. Modern pre-trial discovery-of-evidence tools, discussed to some extent in the first chapter of this work, can be effective devices for gathering this sort of evidence. The malpractice plaintiff who lacks detailed information regarding the source of his injuries can draft a broadly worded Complaint, engage in sweeping pre-trial discovery to secure the factual details, and thereafter amend his pleadings if necessary. Not much significant evidence can escape the diligent complainant's counsel who subpoenas all relevant records and takes depositions of all persons who might have knowledge of the facts. There are abundant indications that often the malpractice plaintiff who has failed to recover damages did so because his attorney failed to investigate his case adequately. Of course, utilization of discovery procedures may result in plaintiff's counsel realizing that his client's claim is without merit.

Res Ipsa Loquitur and the Master-Servant Doctrine

In those cases where the claimant is unable to determine which person caused his injuries, he may still be able to employ one of several legal theories which legitimately avoid the multiple defendant problem. There is in the law a concept known archaically as *respondeat superior*—literally, "Let the master respond." [70] Lawyers less drawn to the Latin but still tied to antique language will use the term "master and servant." For more than two hundred and fifty years it has been the rule that a master (employer) is liable for the torts of his servants (employees) performed within the scope of their employment.[71] Members of the legal profession say, perhaps also somewhat quaintly, that the employer is "vicariously" liable for the negligent acts of his employee, so long as the employee, at the pertinent time, was not off on a "frolic and detour" all his own. On the theory of *respondeat superior* a malpractice plaintiff may occasionally be able to recover damages from one member of a group for the negligent acts of other members of the group.[72] When the relationship of employer-

[70] The *respondeat superior* principle will be taken up again, and in greater detail, in the next chapter.

[71] Mechem, F. R.: AGENCY, §349, 4th ed. West Publishing Company, St. Paul, 1952.

[72] See, *e.g.*, *Holland* v. *North Shore Hospital*, 206 N.Y.S.2d 177 (App. Div. N.Y. 1960); *Rockwell* v. *Stone*, 173 A.2d 48 (S. Ct. Pa. 1961); *Yorston* v. *Pennell*, 153 A.2d 255 (S. Ct. Pa. 1959). In surgical cases the courts sometimes refer to a captain-of-the-ship principle. See, *e.g.*, the leading case of *McConnell* v. *Williams*, 65 A.2d 243 (S. Ct. Pa. 1949). And see Chapter 7.

employee exists within the group, the employer is liable in the eyes of the law for the negligence of the employees, and the plaintiff can recover from the employer even though he does not know precisely which employee or employees actually caused his injuries.[73] And the plaintiff can have the benefit of the *res ipsa loquitur* doctrine against the employer when an inference of employee negligence is raised by the very nature of plaintiff's injuries.[74]

The *respondeat superior* approach has only limited applicability in the medical malpractice field, however, since the potential employer-defendant is often in fact *not* the employer of all the persons who could have caused the asserted injuries. For example, even though a hospital may be liable for the torts of its employees, it is not usually liable for the negligence of a surgeon who performs an operation in the hospital; the surgeon is not generally to be considered an employee of the hospital. When the surgeon maintains his own private practice, most courts find him to be an "independent contractor" and not an employee of the hospital whose facilities he uses even though he functions as a member of the hospital's staff.[75] The facts of the particular case determine whether an employer-employee relationship exists. Many judicial decisions have held a hospital liable where the plaintiff demonstrated that the defendant physician, resident, or intern was truly an employee, as when his salary was paid by the hospital and he was expected to devote full-time service to it.[76]

Hospitals are sometimes immunized against liability even for the negligent acts of a true employee where those acts took place while the employee was assisting in an operation subject to the control of an independent physician. For instance, in a Vermont case,[77] during the delivery of plaintiff's baby, a nurse employed by the hospital was requested by the independent physician to apply pressure to the mother's ribs. The overzealous or too-strong nurse fractured one of her ribs. The court refused to find the hospital liable for the nurse's negligence on the ground that while she was aiding the outside physician in the delivery room, subject

[73] See Comment, *The Application of Res Ipsa Loquitur in Medical Malpractice Cases*, 60 NORTHWESTERN LAW REVIEW 852, 867–68 (1966).

[74] *Ibid.*

[75] *E.g., Mayers* v. *Litow,* 316 P.2d 351 (Cal. App. 1957); *Wilson* v. *Martin Memorial Hosp.*, 61 S.E.2d 102 (S. Ct. N.C. 1950); *Smith* v. *Duke University,* 14 S.E.2d 643 (S. Ct. N.C. 1941).

[76] *E.g., Garfiend Memorial Hosp.* v. *Marshall,* 204 F.2d 711 (3d Cir. 1957) (physisian); *Bourgeois* v. *Dade County,* 99 So.2d 575 (S. Ct. Fla. 1957) (intern); *Moeller* v. *Hauser,* 54 N.W.2d 639 (S. Ct. Minn. 1952) (resident).

[77] *Minogue* v. *Rutland Hospital,* 125 A.2d 796 (S. Ct. Vt. 1956). See also *St. Paul-Mercury Indem. Co.* v. *St. Joseph's Hosp.*, 4 N.W.2d 637 (S. Ct. Minn. 1942); *Aderhold* v. *Bishop,* 221 Pac. 752 (S. Ct. Okla. 1923).

exclusively to his direction and control, she was not the "servant" of the hospital.

Hospitals, of course, are not the only possible "master" defendants in malpractice matters. A second possible "master" dependant is the surgeon in charge of the challenged operation. He is generally liable for the negligence of those persons who act subject to his direction and control during the course of the operation, whether or not they are in any technical way his employees in the sense that he is paying their salaries or wages.[78]

There have been many cases imposing liability on a supervising surgeon. But a surgeon is not generally held liable for the negligent acts of the anesthesiologist, since the latter usually acts independently of the surgeon's control.[79] In certain other situations it is the hospital, if anyone, and not the surgeon, that is liable for the acts of hospital employees even though their acts could be said to be connected with the operative procedure. Such situations include the preparation of the patient for the operation, postoperative care not controlled by the surgeon, and activities that are purely administrative in nature and not subject to direct control by the surgeon.[80]

Since we are talking about the multiple defendant problem in the context of *res ipsa loquitur,* we should reiterate here that when either a hospital or a surgeon is sued on a *respondeat superior* theory, the *res ipsa* concept will apply against the "master" only if it, or he, was the master of *all* of those persons who could have caused plaintiff's injuries. A jury cannot properly speculate a defendant into liability where it is just as likely that plaintiff's injuries were visited upon him by nonemployees as that they were caused by those under the defendant's direction and control.

Res Ipsa Loquitur and the Concept of Joint Control

A malpractice plaintiff may also legitimately circumvent the multiple defendant dilemma in a *res ipsa loquitur* setting where the defendants had joint control of the injury-producing instrumentality. The orthodox *res ipsa* principle involves a control concept, but the requisite control, which serves to identify the source of the harm, can clearly have been exercised jointly by several persons. In such a situation the control element of the

[78] *E.g., Johnson* v. *Ely,* 205 S.W.2d 759 (Tenn. App. 1947), and cases cited in preceding footnote.

[79] *E.g., Morey* v. *Thybo,* 199 Fed. 760 (7th Cir. 1912); *Jett* v. *Linville,* 259 S.W. 43 (S. Ct. Ky. 1924); *Wiley* v. *Wharton,* 41 N.E.2d 255 (Ohio App. 1941). This is not to imply that the anesthesiologist is necessarily under the *hospital's* control. He sometimes is, but this is becoming less and less frequently the case.

[80] *E.g., Swigerd* v. *City of Ortonville,* 75 N.W.2d 217 (S. Ct. Minn. 1956) (administrative activities); *Clary* v. *Christiansen,* 83 N.E.2d 644 (Ohio App. 1949) (preparation of patient for operation); *Shull* v. *Schwartz,* 73 A.2d 402 (S. Ct. Pa. 1950) (postoperative care).

res ipsa principle is not avoided but rather is fully satisfied. A Kansas decision [81] exemplifies this proposition. A patient was to undergo an operation for a mastoid infection. The Complaint filed in his subsequent lawsuit alleged that the resident who administered the anesthetic had negligently inserted a tube, which was intended to supply oxygen for the anesthetized patient, into the esophagus rather than the larynx, thereby channeling the oxygen into plaintiff's stomach instead of his lungs. The plaintiff became decerebrate secondary to cerebral hypoxia; he thereafter was totally incompetent, unable to talk, see, or move. Suit was instituted against the operating surgeon, the resident, and the head of the hospital's anesthesiology department who was the resident's superior. One phase of the plaintiff's Complaint was couched in terms of *res ipsa loquitur*. He alleged that the instrumentalities causing his injuries "were under the entire, complete and exclusive supervision and control of all of said defendants." The Kansas court declined the request of the defendants that it dismiss the plaintiff's action. It held, in accord with the great weight of judicial authority, that the *res ipsa loquitur* principle could apply against plural defendants when all were jointly in actual or constructive control of the harm-producing instrumentality.[82]

The joint control theory, like the *respondeat superior* theory, has definite limitations. Whenever the injury could have been caused by a person not a joint actor, or a person not in joint control of the patient, the theory is not applicable. The law means it when it says that verdicts of liability cannot be founded upon speculation or conjecture.

Summarization of the Res Ipsa Loquitur Principle

The role of the *res ipsa loquitur* principle in the medical malpractice field can be recapitulated in this fashion: it is applicable whenever a patient is injured by means that were in the exclusive or joint control of one or more other persons, which means, if utilized with due care, would not, in accordance with common knowledge and observation, result in injury. Until relatively recently this principle was rarely invoked in malpractice cases; today the discernible trend is toward more expansive use of the doctrine. It relieves malpractice plaintiffs of the necessity of calling expert witnesses and places upon the defendant doctor the burden of explaining away the inference of negligence which the doctrine generates. Application of the *res ipsa loquitur* doctrine does not inevitably lead to

[81] *Voss* v. *Bridwell,* 364 P.2d 955 (S. Ct. Kan. 1961).

[82] See also *Rodgers* v. *Canfield,* 262 N.W. 409 (S. Ct. Mich. 1935); *Rhodes* v. *Lamar,* 292 Pac. 335 (S. Ct. Okla. 1930). It has also frequently been held that when two or more physicians are jointly engaged to provide treatment they are jointly responsible for the negligence of any one of them. *E.g., Spears* v. *McKinnon,* 270 S.W. 524 (S. Ct. Ark. 1925); *Morrill* v. *Komasinski,* 41 N.W.2d 620 (S. Ct. Wis. 1950).

liability. It simply shifts to the defendant the task of coming forward with evidence—evidence that the plaintiff's injuries were not in fact caused by the defendant's negligence. Analysis of many reported cases reveals that the doctrine is most commonly invoked in the following types of cases:

1. Foreign bodies left in tissues
2. Burns from equipment (including x-ray and lights), hot compresses, and hot water bottles
3. Infections from unsterilized instruments
4. Misuse or slipping of instruments
5. Injuries outside the intended field of surgery

Physicians and surgeons can lessen the incidence of *res ipsa loquitur's* applicability by employing prudence in the selection and training of employees and by giving scrupulous attention to actual procedures and to record-keeping. The surgeon's best protection resides in the competence and conscientiousness of operating room personnel, and in this respect nursing personnel are especially important. The surgeon should take a personal interest in the selection and training of those persons for whose acts he may be held legally responsible. Working through the surgical department of his hospital, and the hospital's administration, he can insist that satisfactory standards of performance be established and maintained. Furthermore, some procedures pose so high a malpractice hazard that specific precautionary measures are indicated. For instance, the claim that teeth have been damaged by bronchoscope, laryngoscope, anesthetic equipment, or surgical instruments is fairly common following surgery of the mouth, head, or neck. It would therefore be prudent to have preoperatively a careful examination of the patient's teeth and, if indicated, an x-ray of the jaw and teeth. A description of the observed condition of the teeth should be entered in the operative record. In short, competence on the part of all concerned, coupled with the making and preserving of complete records, is the answer to the malpractice problem that the law accepts.

BIBLIOGRAPHY

ARTICLES

Binder, R. F.: *Res Ipsa Loquitur in Medical Malpractice,* 17 CLEVELAND-MARSHALL LAW REVIEW 218 (1968).

Fricke, G. L.: *The Use of Expert Testimony in Res Ipsa Loquitur Cases,* VILLANOVA LAW REVIEW 59 (1959).

Hannah, H. W.: *Is Res Ipsa Loquitur for the Dogs?* 3 VALPARAISO UNIV. LAW REVIEW 183 (1969).

Holz, M. C.: *Learned Treatises as Evidence in Wisconsin,* 51 MARQUETTE LAW REVIEW 271 (1967).

Hutton, G. L.: *Res Ipsa Loquitur and Actionable Radiation Injury,* 25 TENNESSEE LAW REVIEW 327 (1958).

Kehoe, W. F.: *Massachusetts Malpractice Evidentiary Statute—Success or Failure?* 44 BOSTON UNIV. LAW REVIEW 10 (1964).

King, L. P.: *The Adverse Witness Statute and Expert Opinion,* 4 WAYNE LAW REVIEW 228 (1958).

Louisell, D. W., and Williams, H.: *Res Ipsa Loquitur—Its Future in Medical Malpractice Cases,* 48 CALIFORNIA LAW REVIEW 252 (1960).

McCoid, A. H.: *The Care Required of Medical Practitioners,* 12 VANDERBILT LAW REVIEW 549 (1959).

Renswick, J. C.: *Res Ipsa Loquitur in Hospital and Malpractice Cases,* 9 CLEVELAND-MARSHALL LAW REVIEW 199 (1960).

Rubsamen, D. S.: *Res Ipsa Loquitur in California Medical Malpractice Law—Expansion of a Doctrine to the Bursting Point,* 14 STANFORD LAW REVIEW 251 (1962).

Seavey, W. A.: *Res Ipsa Loquitur: Tabula in Naufragio,* 63 HARVARD LAW REVIEW 643 (1950).

Seidelson, D. E.: *Medical Malpractice and the Reluctant Expert,* 16 CATHOLIC UNIV. LAW REVIEW 158 (1966).

Spense, J. B.: *Adverse Witness Rule: A Cure for a Conspiracy,* 23 UNIV. OF MIAMI LAW REVIEW 1 (1968).

Thode, E. W.: *Unconscious Patient: Who Should Bear the Risk of Unexplained Injuries to a Healthy Part of the Body?* [1969] UTAH LAW REVIEW 1.

Waltz, J. R.: *Relevant, Material, Competent Evidence in Lawsuits,* in Schreiber, S.: TRIAL EVIDENCE IN CIVIL CASES 1-A. Practising Law Institute, New York, 1969.

COMMENTS

Comment, *Application of Res Ipsa Loquitur in Medical Malpractice Cases,* 60 NORTHWESTERN UNIV. LAW REVIEW 852 (1966).

Comment, *Doctor in Court: Impartial Medical Testimony,* 40 SOUTHERN CALIFORNIA LAW REVIEW 728 (1967).

Comment, *Expert Testimony in Medical Malpractice Cases,* 17 UNIV. OF MIAMI LAW REVIEW 182 (1962).

Comment, *Medical Malpractice—Expert Testimony,* 60 NORTHWESTERN UNIV. LAW REVIEW 834 (1966).

Comment, *Medical Malpractice and Res Ipsa Loquitur,* 5 SOUTH DAKOTA LAW REVIEW 67 (1960).

Comment, *Medical Malpractice—Res Ipsa Loquitur and Informed Consent in Anesthesia Cases,* 16 DE PAUL LAW REVIEW 432 (1967).

Comment, *Medical Treatises as Evidence—Helpful But Too Strictly Limited,* 29 UNIV. OF CINCINNATI LAW REVIEW 255 (1960).

Comment, *Overcoming the "Conspiracy of Silence": Statutory and Common Law Innovations,* 45 MINNESOTA LAW REVIEW 1019 (1961).

chapter 7

THE LIABILITY OF PHYSICIANS FOR THE ACTS OF OTHERS

The Doctrine of Respondeat Superior

The basic concept underlying the law of personal injuries (torts) is that a person who has injured another, either intentionally or through his negligence, must compensate him for the harm done. A variation, almost an exception, to this principle is the doctrine of *respondeat superior:* literally, "Let the master answer" [1] or, as Dean Prosser has said, "Look to the man higher up." [2] Embedded in Anglo-American law is the idea that when a servant, agent, or employee injures someone while acting within the scope of his employment, the master or employer is "vicariously" liable (responsible) for his acts.

No one should be surprised to learn that if he is run over by a train, he need not rely on the limited personal resources of the negligent engineer to pay his damages; he can sue the railroad company. This is an application of the doctrine of *respondeat superior.* It is a legal principle that frequently comes into play in medical malpractice litigation. Thus when Mrs. Wemmett went to her doctor's office for a diathermy treatment and was burned because Nellie Lynch, an assistant to the doctor, forgot for over thirty minutes that she was undergoing treatment, the indignant lady sued the doctor rather than Nellie.[3]

Traditionally, a host of reasons have been advanced in support of the *respondeat superior* doctrine. The negligent employee probably will not have enough money to satisfy a judgment; the doctrine allows the injured party to reach into the employer's deeper pocket. This makes sense, so the argument goes, because the employer has the power to select his employee

[1] Black, H. C.: BLACK'S LAW DICTIONARY 1475, 4th ed. West Publishing Company, St. Paul, 1951; Prosser, W. L.: TORTS 471, 3d ed. West Publishing Company, St. Paul, 1964.

[2] Prosser, W. L.: TORTS 470–71, 3d ed. West Publishing Company, St. Paul, 1964.

[3] *Wemmett* v. *Mount,* 292 Pac. 93 (S. Ct. Ore. 1930).

and to control his acts; making the employer responsible for his employees' negligence will encourage care in the selection of employees and the supervision of their work. Also, since the employer benefits monetarily from his servants' work, it is more fair for him, rather than the injured party, to bear the risk of loss when neither he nor the victim is at fault. Furthermore, the employer is in a position to approximate future damages and treat them as an operating expense, thereby spreading the risk among all who do business with him.[4]

Malpractice insurance—in theory, at least—implements the entrepreneur theory in the professions. Each patient or client pays a fee that includes a part of the cost of professional malpractice insurance. While some professionals understandably complain about the cost of insurance,[5] it is probably their patients or clients who collectively pay the premium; they are the ones who spread the risk of loss among themselves. By making the employer-professional liable, the *respondeat superior* theory has given rise to insurance risk-spreading. It undoubtedly makes more sense than having each employee insure against his own negligence or hoping that each potential victim has insured himself against possible damage, and it saves the uninsured individual[6] from the potential financial loss or ruin of a medical accident.[7]

General Application of the Respondeat Superior Theory to Physicians

Reported judicial opinions involving application of the *respondeat superior* theory to physicians usually involve a surgeon's activities in the operative situation and his liability for the negligent acts of hospital employees. This is true for three reasons: The potential for danger and injury is greater in the operating room, and especially since they are likely to involve higher money damage claims, surgical and anesthesiological cases are more likely to find their way into the courts. Secondly, application of the *respondeat superior* theory is more complex in the operating room situation than in the office situation. Hence there are more legal issues for the parties to dispute and this makes settlement

[4] These arguments are set out in detail in Mechem, F. R.: AGENCY, §§349 *et seq.*, 4th ed. West Publishing Company, St. Paul, 1952.

[5] In 1969 an Illinois anesthetist interviewed by the authors was paying $765.00 for his $100,000/$300,000 malpractice insurance; his California counterpart was paying $12,000.

[6] In the malpractice context, most clients or patients will be without applicable insurance coverage.

[7] In agreement with this view of the insurance question is Comment, *Liability of Surgeons for the Negligent Acts of Servants,* 64 DICKENSON LAW REVIEW 180, 185 (1960). In disagreement is Comment, *Surgeon's Liability and the Concept of Control,* 9 VILLANOVA LAW REVIEW 636, 645 (1964).

without litigation less likely. Finally, the surgeon tends to have more "servants" than do most other doctors.

A part of the *respondeat superior* theory as applied to the physician in the operative situation is the so-called borrowed servant doctrine. Since the negligent employee is often on the payroll of the hospital in these cases, there arises the question of whether he is also the employee of the doctor for the purposes of applying the *respondeat* theory. The borrowed servant doctrine is the legal device by which the physician is rendered liable for the hospital employee's negligence if he used the employee as his own "servant" and had control or the right of control over him when the negligent act was committed.[8]

Historically, the plaintiff in the case where injury was caused by a hospital employee usually had to sue the doctor in charge of the employee because the hospital was immune from suit. The immunity of the hospital rested upon two grounds: it was either immune under the law as a charitable institution, or else it had the benefit of local governmental immunity if it happened to be a public hospital.[9] The reason behind charitable immunity was that the funds of the institution had been given to it for charitable purposes and could not be diverted to other purposes, such as the payment of tort judgments.[10] Governmental immunity rested on the notion that public funds should not be used to satisfy judgments and that "it is better that an individual should sustain an injury than that the public should suffer inconvenience." [11] Both doctrines of immunity have been denounced by modern legal scholars.[12] While the governmental immunity doctrine still has some force, the charitable immunities doctrine is on its way out in the law of the minority of states that originally adopted it.[13] Even where the hospital employer has no immunity today,

[8] This is a simplification of the doctrine and will be expanded upon later. See, generally, Note, *The Borrowed Servant Doctrine as it Applies to Operating Surgeons,* 19 SOUTHWESTERN LAW JOURNAL 179 (1965).

[9] *McDonald* v. *Massachusetts General Hospital,* 120 Mass. 432 (Sup. Jud. Ct. Mass. 1876), brought the charitable immunity doctrine into American law. Governmental immunity can be traced from *Riddle* v. *Proprietor of the Locks and Canals on Merrimack River,* 7 Mass. 169 (Sup. Jud. Ct. Mass. 1810).

[10] *McDonald* v. *Massachusetts General Hospital,* 120 Mass. 432 (Sup. Jud. Ct. Mass. 1876).

[11] *Russell* v. *Men of Devon,* [1789] 2 E.R. 667 (England).

[12] See, *e.g.,* Borchard, E. M.: *Government Liability in Tort,* 34 YALE LAW JOURNAL 1 (1924); Casner, A. J., and Fuller, E.: *Municipal Tort Liability in Operation,* 54 HARVARD LAW REVIEW 437 (1941). See also *Muskopf* v. *Corning Hospital District,* 359 P.2d 457 (S. Ct. Cal. 1961).

[13] See *e.g., Moore* v. *Moyle,* 92 N.E.2d 81 (S. Ct. Ill. 1950); *Haynes* v. *Presbyterian Hosp. Ass'n,* 45 N.W.2d 151 (S. Ct. Iowa 1950); *Noel* v. *Menninger Foundation,* 267 P.2d 934 (S. Ct. Kan. 1954). See also Comment, *Surgeon's Liability and the Concept of Control,* 9 VILLANOVA LAW REVIEW 636, 643 (1964).

and can be held liable for its employees' negligence, the plaintiff usually sues the physician as well as the hospital, since it is to a claimant's advantage to have as many defendants as possible who can satisfy the hoped-for judgment.[14]

Whether or not the physician can be held liable for the hospital employee's negligence depends, as we stated earlier, upon whether he can be said to have "borrowed" and brought that employee under his control. The answer to the question of whether the doctor is or should be exercising control over the employee depends on the facts of the particular situation at the time the tort was committed. There are, at base, three factual situations in which imposition of liability upon physicians for employees' negligence is sought: the preoperative, operative, and postoperative situations. From the multiplicity of American jurisdictions, with their differing and conflicting decisions, certain general rules applicable to each group of fact situations can be extracted.

The Preoperative Situation

The preoperative cases involve acts in preparation for surgery from the time the patient is admitted to the hospital up to and including the administration of the anesthetic. In the first group of cases under this heading the physician was actually present when the assertedly negligent act occurred. The defendant physician in *Beadles* v. *Metayka*[15] was in the room where the plaintiff was being prepared for an operation. He asked an orderly to get a strap to secure the patient, who had been given a general anesthetic. When the orderly left the patient to get the strap, the patient moved, fell to the floor and was injured. The court found that not only was the doctor in charge of and responsible for the acts of the orderly, but the doctor's order to get the strap was itself negligent.[16] In *Benedict* v. *Bondi*[17] the operating surgeon was also present in the room where the patient, an infant, was being readied for an operation. A student nurse prepared two hot water bottles, and the surgeon then requested a registered nurse to place the bottles on either side of the patient's feet. The temperature in the bottles had not been tested and the patient suffered third-degree burns. Both nurses were found negligent, and their negligence was imputed to the doctor on the basis of the *respondeat superior*

[14] Theoretically, a hospital could probably recover indemnification from a doctor for whose negligence it has been held vicariously liable. *Cf. Standard Brands, Inc.* v. *Bateman,* 184 F.2d 1002 (8th Cir. 1950), *cert. denied,* 340 U.S. 942 (1951). The practice is not a common one, however.

[15] 311 P.2d 711 (S. Ct. Colo. 1957).

[16] For additional discussion of this case see, Barlock, E. S.: *Negligence—Physicians and Surgeons—Surgeon's Liability for Negligence of Hospital Employees,* 34 DICTA 351 (1957).

[17] 122 A.2d 209 (S. Ct. Pa. 1956).

theory. In both of these cases the court found the key element of control over the acts of the negligent party at the time the negligent act occurred.[18] In both cases the defendant physician could have ordered some precaution which would have prevented the injury. Conversely, the doctor in *Blackman* v. *Zeligs* [19] was found not liable where he had not been present when the plaintiff was burned by a benzine application prior to an operation.[20]

The second group of cases in this section represents an extension of the control test. In these more recent cases the courts found liability on the *respondeat superior* and borrowed servant theories despite a lack of hard evidence of actual control over the servant tort-feasor.

In *Rockwell* v. *Stone* and *Rockwell* v. *Kaplan*,[21] two cases arising from the same facts, Doctor Jiminez, a hospital resident acting under the direction of Doctor Stone, chief of anesthesiology, injected thiopental sodium (Pentothal) into Rockwell's left arm in preparation for the surgical removal of a bursa on his right arm. The injection was either intraarterial or else there was an extravasation of the drug. This was evident at the time the drug was administered. Doctors Stone and Jiminez administered the general anesthetic because in their judgment this was the best mode of treatment, and brought the patient into the operating room where Doctor Kaplan, the operating surgeon, was waiting, without telling Kaplan what had taken place. As a result of the negligent injection, Rockwell's left arm had to be amputated. Doctor Stone, having been in charge of Doctor Jiminez, was found liable for his own negligence and that of Doctor Jiminez on the *respondeat superior* theory. The court also found Doctor Kaplan liable on the *respondeat* theory. Although Kaplan had not been present when the negligent act took place, the court held that the anesthesiologists had been acting as Doctor Kaplan's servants when the injection was given.[22]

[18] "The question of liability revolves back to the issues of fact. Was the negligent party within the supervision and control of the defendant when the negligent act occurred?" Foote, R. V.: *Malpractice-Liability of Operating Surgeon's Employer,* 27 JOURNAL OF THE BAR ASSOC. OF KANSAS 234, 235 (1958).

[19] 103 N.E.2d 13 (Ohio App. 1951).

[20] See also *Seneris* v. *Haas,* 291 P.2d 915 (S. Ct. Cal. 1955) (obstetrician not liable for negligence of anesthetist who gave spinal prior to delivery); *Salgo* v. *Leland Stanford Jr. University Board of Trustees,* 317 P.2d 170 (Cal. App. 1957) (doctor not liable for negligent aortogram which he requested but took no part in); *Clary* v. *Christiansen,* 83 N.E.2d 644 (Ohio App. 1948) (doctor not liable for preoperative substitution of Fisher machine for the requested Davis Bovie equipment).

[21] 173 A.2d 48 (S. Ct. Pa. 1961); 173 A.2d 54 (S. Ct. Pa. 1961).

[22] For divergent analyses of this case, see Comment, *Surgeon's Liability and the Concept of Control,* 9 VILLANOVA LAW REVIEW 636 (1964); Note, *Pennsylvania's Captain-of-the-Ship Doctrine: A Mid-Twentieth Century Anachronism,* 71 DICKINSON LAW REVIEW 432 (1967).

The control of the surgeon over the negligent party was also tenuous in *Mazer* v. *Lipschutz.*[23] In this case, Professor Israel Abrams entered the hospital for a routine cholecystectomy and was placed in room 807. Another Israel Abrams was admitted to room 342 in the same hospital. Kohn, in charge of the hospital's blood bank, typed the blood of both Abramses. The blood delivered to the operating room for the professor's operation was marked "342 A Positive." During the operation, the surgeon, Doctor Lipschutz, accidentally severed the professor's cystic artery and a transfusion was needed immediately. Doctor Chodoff, the anesthesiologist responsible for giving the transfusion, noticed that the bottle had the wrong room number and called Kohn, who came to the operating room and said that the number was a clerical error but that the blood type was right. Doctor Chodoff then gave the professor the transfusion. Several days later the professor died as a result of acute renal failure. The court held that Kohn was negligent as the agent of Doctor Chodoff, who in turn was the agent of Doctor Lipschutz. Since Kohn had come down to the operating room, where Doctor Lipschutz was in control, he brought himself within that control, which the court found sufficient to hold Doctor Lipschutz liable on the *respondeat* theory. There was some discussion by the court as to whether Kohn actually entered the operating room or talked through an open doorway, demonstrating how slim was the connecting control thread in this case. The court seemed to feel compelled to speak in the traditional language of control while extending liability well beyond the bounds of traditional theory.

The first group of cases in this section teach that when the doctor is present during preparations for a surgical procedure and has authority to direct the activities of those assisting him, he must employ that authority to assure that the work is done properly. He will be held liable for the injury-producing negligence of any employee within his control. The last two cases discussed in this section reflect an occasional judicial tendency to expand the doctor's liability in the preoperative situation.[24]

The Operative Situation

A surgical operation begins when the incision is made and ends when the wound has been properly closed.[25] The law of *respondeat superior,* or vicarious liability, is most clear during this time period: an overwhelming majority of courts find the doctor liable for the acts of his "servants"

[23] 327 F.2d 43 (3d Cir. 1964).

[24] See, Comment, *Surgeon's Liability and the Concept of Control,* 9 VILLANOVA LAW REVIEW 636, 638 (1964).

[25] *Akridge* v. *Noble,* 41 S.E. 78 (S. Ct. Ga. 1902).

during an operation.[26] The courts tend to assume that in the operating room the master-servant relation exists between the doctor and his assistants.[27] The surgeon's very presence in the room is considered tantamount to an exercise of control over subsidiary hospital personnel such as nurses and aides.[28] An anesthesiologist, of course, is not a "servant" of the surgeon; he is an associated but independent expert.[29]

For a time the surgeon's control over the operating room staff was considered so clear and so strong by the courts that his position was often analogized to that of a ship's captain. The captain-of-the-ship doctrine was enunciated in *McConnell* v. *Williams*,[30] where an intern, aiding the defendant doctor in the delivery of the plaintiff's child, negligently put too much silver nitrate in the infant's eyes and failed to irrigate them properly, leaving the infant partially blind in one eye and totally blind in the other. While the court held that the defendant physician's right of control was a question of fact for the jury to determine, it left no doubt that the doctor's position in the operating room would support a finding that he was liable for the intern's negligence.

The doctor was held responsible for the negligence of a nurse during a delivery when he instructed her to apply pressure to the patient's abdomen, in *Minogue* v. *Rutland Hospital, Inc.*,[31] and the nurse broke one of the patient's ribs. The court said, "Where a servant has two masters, a general one [the hospital] and a special one [the doctor], the latter, if having the power of direction or control, is the one responsible for the servant's negligence." [32]

One defense against the application of the *respondeat* theory is that the negligent party is himself an expert who was not under the control of the defendant surgeon. The case of *Thompson* v. *Lillehei* [33] is an example of the successful use of this defense. In the *Thompson* case Doctor C. W.

[26] See Note, *The Borrowed Servant Doctrine as It Applies to Operating Surgeons,* 19 SOUTHWESTERN LAW JOURNAL 179, 180–81 (1965).

[27] See Bradford, A. L., and Carlson, P. A.: *Captain of the Ship,* 27 INSURANCE COUNSEL JOURNAL 156, 163 (1960).

[28] Note, *The Borrowed Servant Doctrine as It Applies to Operating Surgeons,* 19 SOUTHWESTERN LAW JOURNAL 179, 181 (1965).

[29] *E.g., Dohr* v. *Smith,* 104 So.2d 29 (S. Ct. Fla. 1958); *Huber* v. *Protestant Deaconess Hospital Assn of Evansville,* 133 N.E. 2d 864 (S. Ct. Ind. 1956); *Woodson* v. *Huey,* 261 P.2d 199 (S. Ct. Okla. 1953).

[30] 65 A.2d 243 (S. Ct. Pa. 1949).

[31] 125 A.2d 796 (S. Ct. Vt. 1956).

[32] See also *McKinney* v. *Tromly,* 386 S.W. 564 (Tex. Civ. App. 1964) (nurse-anesthetist used ether in conjunction with an electrical instrument; explosion; doctor liable); *Ales* v. *Ryan,* 64 P.2d 409 (S. Ct. Cal. 1936) (nurse told surgeon sponge count correct; it was not; surgeon liable).

[33] 164 F.Supp. 716 (D. Minn. 1958), *aff'd,* 373 F.2d 376 (8th Cir. 1959).

Lillehei, prior to the advent of a successful heart-lung machine, was performing open-heart surgery on the plaintiff's eight-year-old daughter. The plaintiff, on an adjacent table, by cross-circulation supplied oxygenated blood for her daughter. A doctor who was not named as a defendant in the suit was attending the plaintiff when she suffered an air embolism caused when a bottle of glucose and water became empty. The court held that Lillehei could not be held liable since he had been concerned solely with his own operation and there was no evidence that he had directed or had any authority to direct the doctor attending the plaintiff in the operating room.[34] The defense was successful because there were, in effect, two distinct operations being conducted at the same time.

Some writers have been severely critical of the captain-of-the-ship doctrine on the grounds that the doctor cannot possibly observe all of the activities for which he ultimately could be held liable and that he does not in fact possess the authority over the persons aiding in the operation that the doctrine assumes.[35] The captain-of-the-ship concept has lately been giving way to reality. Courts are coming to realize that in fact the surgeon rarely controls everyone in the operating room.[36] Today the surgeon's legal responsibility is likely to be less comprehensive than the older judicial decisions would indicate. Liability will ordinarily be fixed only upon those actually at fault and those whose control over the tort-feasor is demonstrable.[37]

The Postoperative Situation

While the doctor's responsibility for his patient's welfare continues beyond the operation, courts are cautious about extending liability to doctors for the negligent acts of personnel functioning in the postoperative situation.[38] Before a court will apply the *respondeat superior* doctrine in this context there must be a showing by the plaintiff that the doctor

[34] It also appears that Doctor Lillehei did not engage the other doctor to attend the plaintiff. Had he done so, he could have been held liable on the theory that the negligent doctor was his employee. The employment theory will be discussed more fully later.

[35] See, *e.g.*, Bradford, A. L., and Carlson, P. A.: *Captain of the Ship*, 27 INSURANCE COUNSEL JOURNAL 156 (1960).

[36] See, *e.g.*, *McCowen* v. *Sisters of Precious Blood of Enid*, 253 P.2d 830 (S. Ct. Okla. 1953).

[37] See 1 Louisell, D. W., and Williams, H.: *Medical Malpractice*, ch. XVI. Matthew Bender, New York, 1969.

[38] Comment, *Surgeon's Liability and the Concept of Control*, 9 VILLANOVA LAW REVIEW 636, 640 (1964).

was present when the negligent act occurred or otherwise had an opportunity to control the "servant."[39] In this respect these cases are more akin to the preoperative cases, where the courts seek a factual showing of control, than to the operative cases, where the control element may be largely presumed.

For example, the operating surgeon was held not liable in *Sherman* v. *Hartman*,[40] where the plaintiff was injured as a result of a faulty blood transfusion. The defendant surgeon visited the plaintiff's room shortly after her operation and found her in the care of a nurse who was satisfactorily administering the transfusion. After the doctor departed, the nurse left the patient in the care of an orderly. The needle became dislodged and the subsequent extravasation of blood injured the patient's arm. The court held that the doctor could not be charged with any of the employee's negligence once he had left the patient in the care of a seemingly competent nurse.

In *Hunner* v. *Stevenson*[41] the surgeon placed a "cigarette" drain—a rubber drain with gauze packed in it—in the plaintiff's side following an operation to remove a portion of the kidney. Several weeks after the operation some gauze was left in the plaintiff by another doctor, nurse, or intern while changing the bandages around the drain. The Maryland court held that since the operating surgeon was not privy to the aftercare negligence, he could not be held liable. The court also pointed out that the surgeon was an out-of-town specialist who had returned to his home after the operation, with the consequence that he could not have supervised the aftercare.[42]

A physician can be found negligent—directly, and not on any theory of vicarious liability—if he observes someone else's negligence in the aftercare treatment, or should have observed it, and fails to correct the situation. In *Stokes* v. *Long*,[43] for example, the defendant physician reduced the plaintiff's fracture and another doctor placed the plaintiff's leg in traction in such a way that the bone did not heal properly. The defendant saw the plaintiff in traction at the hospital for four days before he left for Florida for the winter. The court held the defendant liable for all of the

[39] See Note, *The Borrowed Servant Doctrine as It Applies to Operating Surgeons*, 19 SOUTHWESTERN LAW JOURNAL 179, 182 (1965).

[40] 290 P.2d 894 (Cal. App. 1955).

[41] 89 A. 418 (Md. App. 1913).

[42] See also *Harris* v. *Fall*, 177 F. 79 (7th Cir. 1910) (doctor not liable for gauze left in patient during aftercare); *Reynolds* v. *Smith*, 127 N.W. 192 (S. Ct. Iowa 1910) (doctor not liable for dressing of wounds by nurses and interns after operation); *Shull* v. *Schwartz* 73 A.2d 402 (S. Ct. Pa. 1950) (doctor not liable for intern's negligent removal of stitches after operation).

[43] 159 P.28 (S. Ct. Mont. 1916).

damage caused by the faulty traction on the grounds that he should have noticed the other physician's negligence and corrected the situation.[44]

While the courts look for an element of actual control or supervision by the doctor over the negligent servant, there has been something of a trend in the postoperative cases, just as has been seen in the preoperative cases, to base liability on a concept of control more legalistic than factual. The case of *Yorston* v. *Pennell*[45] provides an example. The plaintiff, Yorston, went to a hospital following an accident at work in which his right fibula was fractured by a nail driven into his leg. A fourth-year medical student, Mr. Rex, took Yorston's history but failed to note on it that Yorston was allergic to penicillin after being shown a note from Yorston's family doctor that he was never to receive that drug. Doctor Hatemi, a resident physician acting under Doctor Pennell, a staff surgeon, performed an operation to remove the nail from Yorston's leg. During the operation Rex remembered that he had failed to note the allergy on the patient's history. He went to the operating room where he told a nurse of the error. Doctor Hatemi, who had read the history before operating, had prescribed 600,000 units of procaine penicillin every four hours as part of the aftercare treatment. Yorston complained to the nurse administering the injections that he was allergic to the drug, but she gave him the shots anyway since the allergy had not been noted on the chart at that time. (By the time of trial the allergy had been properly noted on the history, but there was no evidence as to when the entry had been made.) The morning after the operation, Doctor Pennell cancelled the order for penicillin after being told about the allergy. One week later Yorston developed an allergic skin reaction and suffered a cerebrovascular accident with physical and personality changes as a direct result of the allergic reaction. The court found that Doctor Hatemi was the agent of and under the general control of Doctor Pennell. Rex, as a servant "borrowed" from the hospital, was found to be the subagent of Doctor Pennell through Doctor Hatemi. The court said, "Defendant [Doctor Pennell] actually assumed the supervision of the plaintiff's treatment [by cancelling the penicillin] and, as he himself testified, he consulted with Doctor Hatemi not only with respect to the surgical procedure but the pre- and postoperative procedures as well." Based on this relationship, the negligence of Rex and the staff which was attributed to Doctor Hatemi was imputed one more rung up the ladder to Doctor Pennell, and he was found liable.[46]

[44] See also *Hale* v. *Alkins,* 256 S.W. 544 (Mo. App. 1923) (duty to detect postoperative negligence).

[45] 155 A.2d 255 (S. Ct. Pa. 1959).

[46] See also *Messina* v. *Sociètè Francaise de Bienfaissance et D'assistance Mutuelle de la Nouvelle Orleans,* 170 S. 801 (La. App. 1936) (extern administered hypo-

The court modified the traditional rule that the person to be charged with *respondeat superior* liability must be in control of the tort-feasor at the time the negligent act occurs and grounded liability on the general relationship of the parties.[47]

In marked contrast to *Yorston* v. *Pennell,* however, is the language of the United States Court of Appeals for the District of Columbia in the more recent case of *Alden* v. *Providence Hospital:* [48]

> Actually, even though a patient has an attending physician selected by him, when that patient goes to a hospital the service rendered by the hospital ordinarily includes medical care from the doctors and nurses employed by the hospital as well as access to any laboratory facilities maintained by the hospital. While it may be that an attending physician remains in charge of the case, the hospital and its agents remain responsible for those services it performs, or should perform, under the circumstances of the case and according to good medical practice.

The Physician as Employer, Partner, and Joint Venturer

In the cases discussed thus far the liability of the physician has generally been for the acts of "borrowed servants." Doctors are, of course, frequently employers in the direct sense and are therefore liable for the negligence of their own employees. For example, the doctor-employer was held liable when Nellie Lynch allowed Mrs. Wemmett to be burned by the diathermy machine.[49] A doctor who engages the services of another doctor is liable for the injuries caused by the associate if he is truly an employee.[50] If a doctor recommends another physician to his patient and the other doctor is in no sense an employee or partner of the recommending doctor, the *respondeat* theory will not apply.[51] A doctor must, however, exercise care in selecting a substitute doctor if he is to avoid being found

---

dermoclysis to plaintiff after operation; hospital not liable; extern responsible to surgeon ordering postoperative treatment).

[47] One author, commenting on the results in *Mazer* v. *Lipschutz, supra,* and *Yorston* v. *Pennell,* was prompted to write: "From these facts we can conclude that a surgeon cannot reasonably rely on hospital personnel to perform their several functions capably." Comment, *Surgeon's Liability and the Concept of Control,* 9 VILLANOVA LAW REVIEW 636, 639 (1964).

[48] 382 F2d. 163 (D.C. Cir. 1967). See also *Graham* v. *St. Luke's Hospital,* 196 N.E.2d 355 (Ill. App. 1964).

[49] *Wemmett* v. *Mount,* 292 P.93 (S. Ct. Ore. 1930).

[50] *Heimlich* v. *Harvey,* 39 N.W.2d 394 (S. Ct. Wis. 1949) (associate on a salary-plus-commission basis).

[51] See Loyd, R. A.: *Physicians and Surgeons—Concurrent Negligence—Joint Liability,* 27 JOURNAL OF THE BAR ASSOC. OF KANSAS 301 (1959).

negligent himself.[52] Courts, needless to say, will frown upon the physician who has referred his patients to quacks and snake charmers.

A physician can be held liable for the acts of equals as well as of servants and employees. While this is not an application of the doctrine of *respondeat superior,* the result is the same: the doctor is held liable for the acts of others. If a doctor practices in partnership, he will be held liable for the negligence of his partners. An Oregon court has described the relevant rule in these terms:

> According to general rules, partners in the practice of medicine are all liable for an injury to a patient resulting from the lack of skill or the negligence, either in the omission or commission, of any of the partners, within the scope of their partnership business.[53]

An unnerving example of the application of the partnership rule is found in *Haase* v. *Morton.*[54] One of two physicians practicing in partnership was wheeling a patient to his room after an operation. He negligently allowed the stretcher to roll through an open elevator door and down the shaft. The court held that the absent partner was also liable because the negligent doctor's acts fell within the scope of the partnership business.

Another aspect of this form of vicarious liability is seen in *Baird* v. *National Health Foundation.*[55] Plaintiff was a member of the defendant health-care association. After being examined by several foundation doctors over a period of ten days, during which her condition became extremely serious, it was discovered that she was suffering from a hemolytic streptococcus infection. Expert testimony indicated that her condition could have been properly diagnosed at least ten days earlier, saving the plaintiff from both danger and pain. Employing partnership principles, the court found the foundation and each doctor member individually and jointly liable for the plaintiff's injury.[56]

In the situation where two or more doctors who are not partners each contribute to a plaintiff's injury, they can be joined as defendants in a single suit and each will be liable for the entire damage regardless of the

[52] *E.g., Gross* v. *Robinson,* 218 S.W. 924 (Mo. App. 1920); *Moore* v. *Lee,* 211 S.W. 214 (S. Ct. Tex. 1919).

[53] *Wemmett* v. *Mount,* 292 P. 93 (S. Ct. Ore. 1930).

[54] 115 N.W. 921 (S. Ct. Iowa 1908).

[55] 144 S.W.2d 850 (Mo. App. 1940).

[56] For additional partnership cases, see *Telanus* v. *Simpson,* 12 S.W.2d 920 (S. Ct. Mo. 1928); *Simons* v. *Northern P.R. Co.,* 22 P.2d 609 (S. Ct. Mont. 1933); *Moulton* v. *Huckleberry,* 46 P.2d 589 (S. Ct. Ore. 1935). The result is different, of course, where a partner's actions were plainly beyond the scope of the partnership's "business." See, *e.g., Hyrne* v. *Erwin,* 23 S.C. 226 (S. Ct. S.C. 1885).

extent of his own wrong.[57] (The law does not permit a double recovery; the device of joining defendants simply frees the plantiff from apportioning damages between defendants and permits a full recovery where one or more co-defendants lack funds to satisfy a judgment.) The co-defendants are often dubbed "joint venturers." An example of this type of case is *Cassity* v. *Brady*.[58] The plaintiff dislocated his knee and went to Doctor Brady, who took x-rays and sent the plaintiff, with the x-rays, to Doctor Frink. Neither doctor reduced the dislocation. The Kansas court held that the plaintiff's complaint properly joined the two defendants, and should the plaintiff's allegations thereafter be proved at trial, both doctors would be liable for his own and the other's negligence.[59]

The joint venture theory has been invoked in the absence of a showing of personal negligence on the part of one of the joint venturers. In *Porter* v. *Puryear*,[60] Doctor Porter arranged to have one of his patients operated on in a hospital that Doctor Porter himself owned. He selected Doctor Finer to perform the operation. Doctor Baker injured the plaintiff while administering a spinal injection under Doctor Finer's instructions. Although the case might seem also to involve the *respondeat superior* theory, the court held the three doctors liable as joint venturers.[61]

The General Rule of Nonliability for the Acts of a Physician Called in as a Consultant, Specialist, or Substitute

A physician who calls in another for consultation or independent assistance in treating a patient is not liable for the latter's malpractice where there was no negligence in the process of selecting him, no agency relationship between them, and no concert of action.[62] By the same token,

[57] *Valdez* v. *Percy*, 217 P.2d 422 (S. Ct. Cal. 1950); *Cassity* v. *Brady*, 321 P.2d 171 (S. Ct. Kan. 1958); *Gibson* v. *Bodley*, 133 P.2d 112 (S. Ct. Kan. 1943).

[58] 321 P.2d 171 (S. Ct. Kan. 1958).

[59] See also *Valdez* v. *Percy*, 217 P.2d 422 (S. Ct. Cal. 1950) (doctor performing operation under instructions from another held joint venturer where plaintiff's breast erroneously removed due to a mislabeled biopsy). *Contra: Morey* v. *Thybo*, 199 F.760 (7th Cir. 1912) (doctor treated as assistant to other doctor; no liability).

[60] 262 S.W.2d 933 (S. Ct. Tex. 1953).

[61] See also *Rodgers* v. *Canfield*, 262 N.W. 409 (S. Ct. Mich. 1935), *Mitchell* v. *Saunders*, 13 S.E.2d 242 (S. Ct. N.C. 1941), which point up the fact that it is legally unimportant that the negligent acts of one joint venturer were neither observed nor acknowledged by the other or that they had no specific common obligation toward the patient.

[62] *E.g., Dill* v. *Scuka*, 175 F.Supp. 26 (E.D. Pa. 1959) (specialist called in to perform aortogram); *Shannon* v. *Ramsey*, 193 N.E. 235 (S. Jud. Ct. Mass. 1934) (physician in charge called in surgeon to set fractured leg); *Brown* v. *Bennett*, 122 N.W. 305 (S. Ct. Mich. 1909) (general practitioner called in surgeon). *Compare Morrill* v. *Komasinski*, 41 N.W.2d 620 (S. Ct. Wis. 1950) (concert of action between family physician and surgeon).

a doctor who merely recommends another doctor is not liable for the negligence of the recommended physician.[63] And, finally, there is no vicarious liability for the malpractice of a substitute physician, assuming that he was not negligently selected and did not act as the agent of the doctor who designated him as his substitute.[64]

The physician, the surgeon, the resident, the intern, the nurse, and other medical personnel, alike with all of us, are amenable to the law of agency. At a given moment, therefore, a physician or surgeon may, in the eyes of the law, be responsible for the conduct of several agents or "servants." He, along with them, must answer in money damages for the negligent acts of associate and assistant alike. Thus when the doctor diagnoses, treats, and operates on his patient in a hospital, the institution and its agents and employees can sometimes be said to subserve the doctor since he, and not them, may be in control of the situation. It is a refrain running through the entire law of torts that control and legal liability move hand in hand.

BIBLIOGRAPHY

ARTICLES

Barlock, E. S.: *Negligence—Physicians and Surgeons—Surgeon's Liability for Negligence of Hospital Employees,* 34 DICTA 351 (1957).

Bradford, A. L., and Carlson, P. A.: *Captain of the Ship,* 27 INSURANCE COUNSEL JOUR. 156 (1960).

Foote, R. V.: *Malpractice—Liability of Operating Surgeon's Employer,* 27 JOURNAL OF THE BAR ASSOC. OF KANSAS 234 (1958).

Hanson, R. L., and Stromberg, R. E.: *Hospital Liability for Negligence,* 21 HASTINGS LAW JOURNAL 1 (1969).

Loyd, R. A.: *Physicians and Surgeons—Concurrent Negligence—Joint Liability,* 27 JOURNAL OF THE BAR ASSOC. OF KANSAS 301 (1959).

Millner, M. A.: *Vicarious Liability for Medical Negligence,* 5 JOURNAL OF FORENSIC MEDICINE 96 (1958).

NOTES AND COMMENTS

Comment, *Liability of Surgeons for the Negligent Acts of Servants,* 64 DICKINSON LAW REVIEW 180 (1960).

[63] *E.g., Oldis* v. *La Sociètè Francaise de Bienfaisance Mutuelle,* 279 P.2d 184 (Cal. App. 1955); *Floyd* v. *Michie,* 11 S.W.2d 657 (Tex. Civ. App. 1929); *Smith* v. *Beard,* 110 P.2d 260 (S. Ct. Wyo. 1941).

[64] *E.g., Norton* v. *Hefner,* 198 S.W. 97 (S. Ct. Ark. 1917); *Nash* v. *Royster,* 127 S.E. 356 (S. Ct. N.C. 1925); *Moulton* v. *Huckleberry,* 46 P.2d 589 (S. Ct. Ore. 1935). *Compare Wilson* v. *Martin Memorial Hospital,* 61 S.E. 2d 102 (S. Ct. N.C. 1950) (hired substitute constitutes agent).

Comment, *Surgeon's Liability and the Concept of Control*, 9 VILLANOVA LAW REVIEW 636 (1964).

Note, *Agency—Borrowed Servant Doctrine—Surgeon Is Responsible for the Pre-Operative Negligence of Anesthetist*, 7 VILLANOVA LAW REVIEW 283 (1962).

Note, *The Borrowed Servant Doctrine as It Applies to Operating Surgeons*, 19 SOUTHWESTERN LAW JOUR. 179 (1965).

Note, *Pennsylvania's Captain-of-the-Ship Doctrine: A Mid-Twentieth Century Anachronism*, 71 DICKINSON LAW REVIEW 432 (1967).

Note, *Torts—Malpractice—Surgeon's Liability for Servant's Pre-Operative Negligence*, 35 TEMPLE LAW QUARTERLY 359 (1962).

chapter 8

LIABILITY FOR TREATMENT RENDERED IN AN EMERGENCY

Emergency Treatment Outside the Office or Hospital

We have previously pointed out that a physician is not obligated by the law to provide professional services to everyone seeking them.[1] However, the American Medical Association's *Principles of Medical Ethics* state that a doctor should "respond to any request for his assistance in any emergency." [2] The physician, in short, is adjured to be a Good Samaritan. Doctors, however, are generally reluctant to be cast in that role. Fearful of malpractice litigation, they are apprehensive about rendering emergency service under less than ideal conditions. The surgeon, for example, accustomed to the sterility and equipment of the modern operating room, is naturally uneasy about using a rusty fishing knife on a traffic accident victim.

Because the law imposes no duty on anyone to volunteer aid to strangers,[3] a physician is free to be a Levite rather than a Good Samaritan. His justification for passing by the accident victim is that the helpful Samaritan may expose himself, at worst, to liability for medical malpractice or, at least, to an involvement of time, effort, emotional drain, and unwanted publicity. It has been reported that one in three physicians would not stop at the scene of an automobile accident where medical services were obviously needed.[4] The result of physicians' failure to provide emergency care must be increased incidence of death and serious but avoidable complications.

[1] See Chapter 3. On the other hand, even a private hospital, because of its public function, has a duty to render emergency service.

[2] See *Manlove* v. *Wilmington Gen. Hosp.*, 169 A.2d 18 (Super. Ct.), *aff'd on other grounds,* 174 A.2d 135 (S. Ct. Del. 1961).

[3] See, *e.g., Hurley* v. *Eddingfield,* 59 N.E. 1058 (S. Ct. Ind. 1901). See also Prosser, W. L.: TORTS 336, 3d ed. West Publishing Company, St. Paul, 1964.

[4] NEWSWEEK, September 4, 1961, p. 41; see also Note, *Florida's Proposed Good Samaritan Statute—It Does Not Meet the Problem,* 17 UNIV. OF FLORIDA LAW REVIEW 586 (1965).

The Common Law Solution

The medical profession's fear of malpractice liability arising from emergency treatment is largely unwarranted; the common law—judge-made law—makes significant allowances for one acting in an emergency. It has long been "established that a physician and surgeon undertaking the treatment of a patient is not required to exercise the highest degree of skill possible." [5] He is simply "required to exercise the care and judgment of a reasonable man" in employing his skill and knowledge.[6] The general standard of care, as enunciated by the Missouri Supreme Court in *Williams* v. *Chamberlain*,[7] is that "a physician is required to use and exercise that degree of care and skill used and exercised by the ordinarily skillful, careful and prudent physician acting under the same or similar circumstances." The law recognizes that the standard of care varies, in a sense, with the attendant circumstances. When the circumstances amount to an emergency—often demanding hasty action under adverse conditions—the standard is not as rigorous as usual. One would not expect the treatment given a stranger lying on the highway to be as comprehensive as that given to a regular patient lying in a hospital bed. Neither does the law.

Several practical considerations reduce the likelihood of success by claimants in malpractice suits arising from an emergency outside the hospital. As is generally true in negligence cases, the burden of proof is on the claimant. This burden requires the plaintiff to demonstrate that the physician did not exercise reasonable care under the circumstances. And this necessitates establishing what constitutes reasonable conduct. Since reasonable medical conduct is usually within the sole knowledge of physicians and not within the knowledge of laymen, the standard ordinarily must be determined by doctors testifying as expert witnesses.[8] Few physicians are willing to criticize the conduct of colleagues who acted under true emergency conditions.

Although this factor, which claimants' compensation counsel will dub a "conspiracy of silence," has been somewhat tempered by decisions enlarging the sources of expertise available to plaintiffs [9] and by extended application by some courts of the doctrine of *res ipsa loquitur*,[10] it is still safe to say that there is little or no need for medical men to fear unfavor-

[5] *Willis* v. *Western Hosp. Ass'n*, 182 P.2d 950, 957 (S. Ct. Idaho 1947).

[6] *Smith* v. *Yohe*, 194 A.2d 167, 170 (S. Ct. Pa. 1963).

[7] 316 S.W.2d 505, 510 (S. Ct. Mo. 1958).

[8] See Comment, *Good Samaritans and Liability for Medical Malpractice*, 64 COLUMBIA LAW REVIEW 1301, 1303 (1964).

[9] See Comment, *Medical Malpractice—Expert Testimony*, 60 NORTHWESTERN UNIV. LAW REVIEW 834, 842–51 (1966).

[10] See Comment, *The Application of Res Ipsa Loquitur in Medical Malpractice Cases*, 60 NORTHWESTERN UNIV. LAW REVIEW 852, 857–74 (1966).

able judgments in malpractice actions arising out of emergency situations. This conclusion is supported by the absence of reported decisions against Good Samaritan physicians who have stopped to aid the injured.

The Statutory Solution: "Good Samaritan" Laws

The mere filing of a negligence claim is an attack on the physician's professional competence. Such an assault may seriously besmirch the practitioner's reputation, particularly in smaller communities where news travels far and fast, even though the jury ultimately finds that he was in no way negligent. And defending against the claim involves loss of time that could be devoted to the treatment of patients. Consequently, doctors understandably fear the bringing of a lawsuit as much as they do the possibility of an adverse judgment, and for this reason are reluctant to render emergency assistance.

Recognizing the reluctance of physicians to render emergency aid, the legislatures of forty-one states and the District of Columbia have responded with a mixed array of statutes designed to encourage the medical man to provide emergency assistance by specifically immunizing him from malpractice liability.[11] South Carolina's enactment is typical of these so-called Good Samaritan laws. It provides:

> Any person, who in good faith gratuitously renders emergency care at the scene of an accident or emergency to the victims thereof, shall not be liable

[11] CODE OF ALA., tit. 7, §121(1) (Supp. 1968); ALASKA STAT. §08.64.365 (1962); ARIZ. REV. STAT., §32-1471 (Supp. 1968); ARK. STAT. ANN., §72-624 (Supp. 1967); CAL. BUS. & PROF. CODE, §2144 (Supp. 1968); COLO. REV. STAT., §41-2-8 (Supp 1966); CONN. GEN. STAT. REV., §52-557b (Supp. 1969); D.C. CODE, §2-142 (Supp. 1968); DEL. CODE ANN., tit. 24, §1767 (Supp. 1969); FLA. STAT. ANN., §768.13 (Supp. 1969); GA. CODE ANN., §84-930 (Supp. 1968); ILL. REV. STAT., ch. 91, §2a (Supp. 1967); IND. ANN. STAT., §63-1361 (Supp. 1968); KAN. STAT. ANN., §65-2891 (Supp. 1968); LA. STAT. ANN., §37:1731 (1964); ME. REV. STAT. ANN., tit. 32, §3151 (1965); MD. ANN. CODE, art. 43, §149A (Supp. 1968); MASS. ANN. LAWS, ch. 112, §12B (Supp. 1968); MICH. STAT. ANN., §14.563 (Supp. 1969); MISS. CODE ANN., §8893.5 (Supp. 1969); MONT. REV. CODES ANN., §17-410 (Supp. 1965); NEB. REV. STAT., §25-1152 (1964); NEV. REV. STAT., §41.500 (1967); N.H. REV. STAT. ANN., §329.25 (1966); N.J. STAT. ANN., §2A-62A-1 (Supp. 1968); N.M. STAT. ANN., §§12-12-3, 12-12-4 (1968); N.Y. EDUC. LAW, §6513(10 (Supp 1968); N.D. REV. CODE, §§43-17-37, 43-17-38 (Supp. 1967); OHIO REV. CODE ANN., §2305.23 (Baldwin Supp. 1964); OKLA. STAT. ANN., tit. 76, §5 (Supp. 1967); ORE. REV. STAT., §30.800 (1968); PA. STAT. ANN., tit. 12, §1641 (Supp. 1969); R.I. GEN. LAWS ANN., §5-37-14 (Supp. 1969); S.C. CODE ANN., §46-803 (Supp. 1968); S.D. COMP. LAWS, §20-9-3 (1967); TENN. CODE ANN., §63-622 (Supp. 1968); TEX. STAT. ANN., art. 1a (1969); UTAH CODE ANN., §58-12-23 (Supp. 1967); VA. CODE ANN., §54-276.9 (Supp. 1968); W. VA. CODE ANN., §55-7-15 (Supp. 1968); WIS. STAT. ANN. §§147.17(7), 149.06(5) (Supp. 1969); WYO. STAT. ANN., §33-343.1 (Supp. 1967).

for any civil damages for any personal injury as a result of any act or omission by such person in rendering the emergency care or as a result of any act or failure to act to provide or arrange for further medical treatment or care for the injured person, except acts or omissions amounting to gross negligence or wilful or wanton misconduct.[12]

Since the Good Samaritan statutes do not extend protection beyond actions for ordinary negligence, they actually do no more than codify existing common law, granting no more immunity than the physician already enjoyed. The similarity between the statutory and the common law rules is especially evident in the wording of the Florida statute, which requires that the physician act "as an ordinary reasonably prudent man would have acted under the same or similar circumstances." [13] A former governor of Illinois, Otto Kerner, recognized this similarity and vetoed a proposed Good Samaritan bill because the Illinois courts already gave full consideration to surrounding circumstances and would not visit unfair consequences upon a physician who responded to an emergency.[14]

Although Good Samaritan legislation does not extend new protection to the physician, it may nonetheless have value in that its reassuring statements of a generous and flexible standard of care should encourage doctors to stop at accidents and render assistance. Furthermore, the statutes may discourage potential plaintiffs from bringing spurious malpractice actions based on a conscientious physician's emergency measures.

These somewhat speculative merits may be offset at least partially by shortcomings common to many of the Good Samaritan statutes. In the first place, the statutes are inconsistent in classifying the objects of their protection. While many of the statutes extend coverage to "any person," nine states, including California,[15] have laws covering only medical personnel licensed in the state that enacted the statute. This curious discrimination may diminish the effectiveness of the enactments. A California physician, for example, knowing that out-of-state doctors are not granted immunity in his home state, might fail to stop at an accident on a Nevada highway because he assumes that only Nevada physicians are statutorily protected there. This, of course, would defeat the purpose of the Nevada statute, which rightly extends immunity to any person in the state.[16]

Additional problems may arise from the conditions and qualifications that hedge the medical man's statutory immunity for acts in an emergency. Many Good Samaritan statutes require that the physician exercise "due

[12] S.C. CODE ANN., §46-803 (Supp. 1968).

[13] FLA. STAT. ANN., §768.13 (Supp. 1969).

[14] A.M.A. NEWS 12 (Oct. 14, 1963). Subsequently, Illinois adopted a limited Good Samaritan statute. ILL. REV. STAT., ch. 91, §2a (Supp. 1967).

[15] CAL. BUS. & PROF. CODE, §2144 (Supp. 1967).

[16] NEV. REV. STAT., §41.500 (1967).

care" or that his actions be free of "gross negligence" and "willful or wanton conduct."[17] Of those states that have enacted Good Samaritan statutes, all except eight specifically demand that the medical aid have been given in "good faith."[18] All of this verbiage is sufficiently vague to invite litigation and to present a hazy image of liability to judge and jury.

Another flaw in the statutes involves uncertainty as to when and where immunity is granted. The laws generally extend protection only for emergency care rendered at the scene of an "accident" or "emergency."[19] While some statutes provide that, for the statute's purposes, an "emergency" cannot occur inside a hospital or in the ordinary course of the physician's practice, very few of them specifically define "emergency." Of those states that have attempted to explain the term, New Mexico frames its definition in terms of various types of accidents or physical causes of injury,[20] while Alaska and Oregon define "emergency" in terms of the seriousness of the injured person's injuries.[21] The absence of consistent definitions raises genuine questions of statutory coverage.[22] This ambiguity could easily be dispelled by uniform legislation.[23]

Further complications might stem from the requirement that the emergency assistance be rendered without remuneration. In *Voss* v. *Bridwell*[24] the Kansas Supreme Court restated the general rule that "The duty of a physician to his patient is not affected by the fact that the service rendered is gratuitous. . . ." Nevertheless, a majority of the states extend protection from civil liability for malpractice only if the emergency aid in question was provided "gratuitously."

Under the common law, ". . . a physician who undertakes to examine or treat a patient and then abandons him, may be liable for malpractice."[25] This means that once the physician-patient relationship has been established, the Good Samaritan must accompany the seriously injured emergency victim to a hospital and either continue to treat him or secure a replacement.[26] Most Good Samaritan statutes provide immunity from

[17] See Long, R. H.: THE PHYSICIAN AND THE LAW 375, 3d ed. Appleton-Century-Crofts, New York, 1968.

[18] See, *e.g.*, N.Y. EDUC. LAW, §6513(10) (Supp. 1968); OHIO REV. CODE ANN., §2305.23 (Baldwin Supp. 1964).

[19] See, *e.g.*, N.J. STAT. ANN., §2A-62A-1 (Supp. 1968).

[20] N.M. STAT. ANN., §12-12-3 (1968).

[21] ALASKA STAT., §08.64.365 (1962); ORE. REV. STAT., §30.800 (1968).

[22] See Comment, *Good Samaritans and Liability for Medical Malpractice.* 64 COLUMBIA LAW REVIEW 1301, 1309–10 (1964).

[23] For a proposed uniform statute, see Long, R. H.: THE PHYSICIAN AND THE LAW 376, 3d ed. Appleton-Century-Crofts, New York, 1968.

[24] 364 P.2d 955 (S. Ct. Kan. 1961).

[25] See *O'Neill* v. *Montefiore Hosp.*, 202 N.Y.S.2d 436 (App. Div. N.Y. 1960).

[26] See Note, *Florida's Proposed Good Samaritan Statute—It Does Not Meet the Problem,* 17 UNIV. OF FLORIDA LAW REVIEW 586, 587 (1965).

liability for injuries caused while *rendering* emergency care. Since abandonment is the intentional *termination* of care, it arguably does not occur in rendering the help and thus is not covered by most immunity statutes.[27] But the duty not to abandon the emergency victim, while burdensome, is an obligation from which the physician cannot fairly be relieved.[28]

Constitutionality of Good Samaritan Statutes

Good Samaritan legislation is subject to constitutional attack. The assault could be framed in terms of unconstitutional vagueness, but a more serious challenge would be that the acts violate the "right to a remedy" guarantee found in many state constitutions. In dealing with this issue, the courts have distinguished those statutes which completely abrogate common law rights of action from those that merely restrict available remedies.[29] While total abrogation of rights of action is probably unconstitutional,[30] a restriction of remedies can often be upheld as a reasonable exercise of police powers in furtherance of a worthwhile aim. The Good Samaritan statutes have a laudable purpose—to encourage emergency treatment by physicians—and probably are safe from successful constitutional attack. In any event, the medical Good Samaritan's best and broadest protection comes from judge-made common law and not from the ineptly drafted statutes discussed in this chapter.

BIBLIOGRAPHY

BOOKS

Chayett, N. L.: LEGAL IMPLICATIONS OF EMERGENCY CARE. Appleton-Century-Crofts, New York, 1969.

Long, R. H.: THE PHYSICIAN AND THE LAW 373–77, 3d ed. Appleton-Century-Crofts, New York, 1968.

NOTES AND COMMENTS

Comment, *Good Samaritans and Liability for Medical Malpractice*, 64 COLUMBIA LAW REVIEW 1301 (1964).

Note, *Physicians—Civil Liability for Treatment Rendered at the Scene of an Emergency*, (1964) WISCONSIN LAW REVIEW 494.

Note, *Statute Relieving Physicians, Surgeons and Nurses from Civil Liability for Emergency Medical Care*, 41 NEBRASKA LAW REVIEW 609 (1962).

[27] See Note, *Negligence—Medical Malpractice—Criticism of Existing Good-Samaritan Statutes*, 42 OREGON LAW REVIEW 328, 334 (1963).

[28] For a detailed discussion of the abandonment concept, see Chapter 10.

[29] *E.g., Emberson* v. *Buffington,* 306 S.W.2d 326 (S. Ct. Ark. 1957).

[30] *E.g., State* v. *Diehl,* 223 N.W. 852 (S. Ct. Wis. 1929).

chapter 9

DEFENSES TO MEDICAL MALPRACTICE ACTIONS

The mere making of a claim or the filing in court of a lawsuit does not by itself establish liability for damages on the named defendant's part. The plaintiff, at trial, must produce admissible evidence supporting the essential elements of his claim. And the defendant, under our two-sided adversary system of litigation, is entitled to make a defense. These fundamental principles are as true in medical malpractice actions as in any other type of litigation.

The law recognizes a number of defenses to malpractice actions. The first and best defense, quite naturally, is a showing that the plaintiff's claim is both factually and legally baseless. A malpractice action is simply a somewhat special type of negligence action; the absence of negligence is a complete defense to any such lawsuit. The defendant in a malpractice action is entitled, in his formal Answer, to deny in good faith all of the plaintiff's allegations of professional negligence and at trial he is free to produce evidence tending to establish the falsity of the plaintiff's charges. Futhermore, the patient, even where capable of demonstrating conduct falling below the law's standard, must show a causal link between the defendant doctor's allegedly substandard conduct and the injury of which the patient complains.[1]

There are also less sweeping defenses to malpractice actions. The following is a sampling; we do not burden the reader with rarer and even more technical defenses.

CONTRIBUTORY NEGLIGENCE

It is a general principle of tort law that the contributory negligence of a plaintiff bars him completely from any recovery of damages from the defendant even though the defendant was himself guilty of negligence in

[1] *E.g., Hunter* v. *United States,* 236 F.Supp. 411 (M.D. Tenn. 1964); *Steele* v. *Woods,* 327 S.W.2d 187 (S. Ct. Mo. 1959).

some degree.[2] Contributory negligence is said to be conduct on the part of the claimant, contributing to his injury, which falls below the standard to which a reasonably prudent person would conform for his own protection.[3] As with most of the law's general principles, however, this one has its refinements and its outright exceptions. For example, contributory negligence on the plaintiff's part is a defense only in cases involving so-called simple negligence; it is not recognized as a defense where the defendant's conduct was intended to inflict harm or was wanton or reckless.[4] Furthermore, a plaintiff's unreasonable conduct will bar him completely from recovery against a defendant only if it cooperated with the defendant's negligent conduct, contemporaneously, as an original cause of the harm of which the plaintiff complains.[5]

The contributory negligence defense does not often arise in medical malpractice cases, since the plaintiff has usually placed himself entirely in the physician's hands and is, at the time of treatment, in no position to do himself harm. The cases commonly cited as examples of the contributory negligence doctrine [6] usually turn out, upon closer examination, to be cases in which the patient's perverse conduct was the sole cause of his injury—in other words, the defendant doctor was not negligent at all; the patient's negligence was exclusive, not contributory. Occasionally imprudent conduct by the patient following malpractice by his physician will exacerbate the harm done the patient; but this, unlike true contributory negligence, will diminish but not preclude the patient's recovery of money damages. Examples of these two sorts of cases are numerous.

In *Smith* v. *McClung* [7] the defendant dentist's Novocaine needle broke off in his patient's gum. The defendant undertook to remove the broken needle "with all the facilities available to him at the time." He then asked the patient to return to his office on the following day, assuring him that he would then be able to remove the needle painlessly. The patient, however, repeatedly refused to permit the defendant or anyone else to remove the broken needle; instead, he sued for malpractice. His claim was rejected. Needles of the sort involved in this case can break in the absence

[2] Harper, F. V., and James, F.: TORTS 1193. Little, Brown and Company, Boston, 1956, and Supp. 1968.

[3] See *Leadingham* v. *Hillman,* 5 S.W.2d 1044 (Ky. App. 1928), for a statement of this principle in the context of a malpractice action.

[4] See Note, *Common Law Exceptions to the Defense of Contributory Negligence,* 32 COLUMBIA LAW REVIEW 493 (1932).

[5] See Bohlen, F. H.: *Contributory Negligence,* 21 HARVARD LAW REVIEW 233 (1908); Lowndes, C. L. B.: *Contributory Negligence,* 22 GEORGETOWN LAW JOURNAL 674 (1934).

[6] See, *e.g.*, Long, R. H.: THE PHYSICIAN AND THE LAW 163–64, 3d ed. Appleton-Century-Crofts, New York, 1968.

[7] 161 S.E. 91 (S. Ct. N.C. 1931).

of any negligence on the dentist's part, said the court; the only negligence in the case was that of the patient.

In *Carey* v. *Mercer* [8] the defendant doctor had advised his patient that an x-ray was required to determine whether his tibia had been fractured. The patient refused, insisting that an x-ray would be too costly. Thereafter the patient, who in fact did have a bone fracture, sued his physician, alleging that he had been negligent in not securing an x-ray. The highest Massachusetts court held, predictably, that "The patient cannot charge the physician with negligence if the patient himself refuses to carry out the directions [of his physician] . . . he cannot attribute to the physician the damages which resulted from his own failure to have something done, when this was caused by his own conduct." The court added: "If the rule were . . . [otherwise] it would place an unreasonable burden upon the physician, and would require of him a much higher standard of care than the law requires." [9] The patient's refusal to have x-rays taken was not contributory negligence; it was the only negligence in the case.[10]

DuBois v. *Decker* [11] is a relatively early exacerbation case. The defendant physician was charged with having so delayed the amputation of a portion of his patient's leg that gangrene set in, necessitating a second operation. The defendant asserted that the patient had contributed to his own injury by refusing to keep the stump of his leg in the position directed by defendant and eventually by refusing further treatment. The New York Court of Appeals rejected the defendant doctor's argument that a contributory negligence instruction should have been given to the jury by the trial judge. The court detected the moderately subtle causation problem. "This [requested instruction] was too broad," said the court, "if the jury found that the defendant was guilty of malpractice *prior* to the disobedience complained of." [12] It held that "these facts would only tend to mitigate the damages, and would not relieve the defendant from the consequences of previous neglect or unskillful treatment."

Leadingham v. *Hillman* [13] is similar to the previous case. There it was charged that the defendant physician had prematurely removed the splints

[8] 132 N.E. 353 (Sup. Jud. Ct. Mass. 1921).

[9] Today a court could be expected to insist that a physician provide a reasonable explanation as to the necessity of recommended treatment, to the end that the patient can employ informed judgment. If the patient is incompetent or incapable of understanding, the physician should communicate, where possible, with the patient's spouse or other relatives. See *Steele* v. *Woods,* 327 S.W.2d 199 (S. Ct. Mo. 1959).

[10] See also *Gentile v. DeVirgilis,* 138 Atl. 540 (S. Ct. Pa. 1927) (patient failed to return, as requested, for follow-up treatment; a no-negligence case from the standpoint of the defendant).

[11] 29 N.E. 313 (Ct. App. N.Y. 1891).

[12] Emphasis supplied.

[13] 5 S.W.2d 1044 (Ct. App. Ky. 1928).

from plaintiff's broken arm, causing damage. The defendant had admitted his fault and recommended that the patient have his arm rebroken and reset. He refused and sued. The Kentucky court, while agreeing that a patient must "use such care as a man of ordinary prudence would ordinarily use under like circumstances," stated that a patient's want of due care would not bar recovery absolutely unless it was "simultaneous with and co-operating with the fault of the defendant." At most, plaintiff's recalcitrance would reduce his recoverable damages. "His refusal to . . . have the arm rebroken and reset only prevented a recovery to the extent the damages were thereby enhanced or increased, if in the exercise of ordinary care he should have done this." And whether the patient should have abided by the negligent physician's advice was held to be a debatable proposition that only the jury could decide.[14]

STATUTES OF LIMITATION

A malpractice claimant cannot indefinitely delay the filing of his lawsuit. One purpose of our legal system is to provide a forum in which legal controversies can be presented and adjudicated by a judge or jury, and it is said that every litigant is entitled to his day in court, but the law usually insists upon reasonable promptness in the initiating of litigation. Adjudication should take place as soon as possible after the occurrence of the alleged wrong, since with the passage of time the memory of witnesses may fade beyond recall or, more devastating yet, the witnesses themselves may die or leave the court's jurisdiction.

The law is necessarily cynical. It recognizes that a person with a questionable claim might delay presentation of it, thereby preventing the defendant from making an effective investigation and defense because favorable witnesses have died, disappeared, or forgotten the facts. To discourage claimants from purposely withholding the filing of a lawsuit, state legislatures have passed what are known as *statutes of limitation.* These laws set the time within which a person must commence a given sort of legal action.

The majority rule in the United States subjects medical malpractice actions to the statute of limitation specifically related to malpractice if the particular state has enacted so explicit a provision; otherwise, malpractice suits are governed by the statute of limitation applicable to tort actions in general.[15] A state's statute of limitation for contract actions, which usually provides for a much longer time within which to bring an action, will not

[14] See also *Flynn* v. *Stearns,* 145 A.2d 33 (N.J. Super. 1958); *Morse* v. *Rapkin,* 263 N.Y.S.2d 428 (App. Div. N.Y. 1965).

[15] See Note, *Theory of a Medical Malpractice Action—Time Limitations and Damages,* 64 WEST VIRGINIA LAW REVIEW 412 (1962). See also *Trimming* v. *Howard,* 16 P.2d 661 (S. Ct. Idaho 1932) (two-year tort statute of limitation applied where

be applied in a malpractice context in the absence of an express contract to effect a cure.[16]

The provisions of statutes of limitation vary markedly from state to state: they differ regarding the length of time allowed for the commencement of suit, and furthermore they differ as to when this time period begins to run against the prospective plaintiff and as to when the time period is prevented from expiring by some special circumstance. We shall not catalog the various statutes of limitation in every American jurisdiction; counsel representing a party to a malpractice action will know the provisions of the applicable statute. For example purposes, however, we can refer to New York's statute of limitation for a medical malpractice action, which is three years,[17] and it has been held to be available not only to medical doctors but to dentists, x-ray technicians, chiropractors, pharmacists, unlicensed as well as licensed practitioners, and others.[18]

Ordinarily a state's malpractice statute of limitation will not apply to an action against a hospital or a nurse; the general and usually longer tort statute of limitation has been held applicable to them.[19]

In the absence of some extraordinary circumstance that tolls (interrupts) the running of the pertinent statute of limitation, an action not commenced within the prescribed period is absolutely barred and will be dismissed on the defendant's motion.[20]

---

plaintiff's basic allegations related to professional negligence even though breach of an implied contract was also suggested).

[16] See, *e.g.*, *Kozan* v. *Comstock*, 270 F.2d 839 (5th Cir. 1959); *Cherry* v. *Falvey*, 68 S.W.2d 98 (S. Ct. Ark. 1934); *Finch* v. *Bursheim*, 142 N.W. 143 (S. Ct. Minn. 1913); *Robins* v. *Finestone*, 127 N.Y.S.2d 330 (Ct. App. N.Y. 1956). Only rarely has there been applied any type of limitation statute other than those relating to torts or contracts. In *Suskey* v. *Davidoff*, 87 N.W.2d 306 (S. Ct. Wis. 1958), the statute of limitation for assault and battery was applied; *contra: Maercklun* v. *Smith*, 266 P.2d 1095 (S. Ct. Colo. 1954). In *Hachmann* v. *Mayo Clinic*, 150 F.Supp. 468 (D. Minn. 1957), the wrongful death statute of limitation was applied but other courts have ruled *contra; e.g., Link* v. *Sorenson*, 276 F.2d 151 (8th Cir. 1960).

[17] N.Y. C.P.L.R., §214(6) (Supp. 1967). In contrast, New York's contract statute of limitation permits a prospective plaintiff to wait six years before filing suit. N.Y. C.P.L.R., §213(2) (Supp. 1967).

[18] *Hurlburt* v. *Gillett*, 161 N.Y.S. 994 (S. Ct. N.Y.), *aff'd*, 162 N.Y.S. 1124 (App. Div. N.Y. 1916) (dentist); *Leitch* v. *Mulcahy*, 31 N.Y.S.2d 874 (S. Ct. N.Y. 1941) (x-ray technician); *Monahan* v. *Devinny*, 229 N.Y.S. 60 (S. Ct. N.Y. 1928) (chiropractor); *Rudman* v. *Bancheri*, 23 N.Y.S.2d 584 (App. Div. N.Y. 1940). Since a psychiatrist is a medical doctor, the statute clearly applies to him. See *Hammer* v. *Rosen*, 165 N.E.2d 756 (Ct. App. N.Y. 1960), so holding.

[19] *Wolff* v. *Jamaica Hosp.* 205 N.Y.S.2d 152 (App. Div. N.Y. 1960) (hospital); *Isenstein* v. *Malcomson*, 236 N.Y.S. 641 (App. Div. N.Y. 1929) (nurse).

[20] See Clark, C. E.: CODE PLEADING 614–15, 2d ed. West Publishing Company, St. Paul, 1947; Atkinson, T. E.: *Pleading the Statute of Limitations*, 36 YALE LAW JOURNAL 914 (1927), and cases cited.

The time for filing an action begins to run when the elements of the particular sort of action have accrued or ripened. The time when a right to file a malpractice action accrues will vary from state to state, and the time from which the period of limitation will begin to run also varies. The three most common points in time at which a medical malpractice action is said to have accrued are (1) the time when the negligent act was allegedly committed;[21] (2) the time when the resultant injury was discovered or should have been discovered had the patient acted with reasonable alertness;[22] and (3) the time when the doctor-patient relationship or the treatments, if there was a continuous series of them, ended.[23]

The clear trend of the cases is toward adoption of the second point, the so-called discovery rule.[24] The discovery rule is an equitable one from the

[21] *E.g., Gangloff* v. *Apfelbach,* 49 N.E.2d 795 (Ill. App. 1943); *Capucci* v. *Barone,* 165 N.E. 653 (Sup. Jud. Ct. Mass. 1919); *Conklin* v. *Draper,* 173 N.E. 892 (Ct. App. N.Y. 1930).

[22] *E.g., Quinton* v. *United States,* 304 F.2d 234 (5th Cir. 1962); *Hungerford* v. *United States,* 307 F.2d 99 (9th Cir. 1962); *Fernandi* v. *Strully,* 173 A.2d 277 (S. Ct. N.J. 1961); *Ayers* v. *Morgan,* 154 A.2d 788 (S. Ct. Pa. 1959). See Hutcheson, S., and Smedley, D. G.: *The Statute of Limitations in California Medical Malpractice Cases,* 28 INSURANCE COUNSEL JOURNAL 269 (1961), concluding, among other things, that nothing short of actual discovery by the patient of a foreign substance left within his body will start the running of the statute. But *compare Stafford* v. *Shultz,* 27 P.2d 81 (S. Ct. Cal. 1954), holding that plaintiff's complaint must state when and how discovery was made, that plaintiff was not at fault for not making earlier discovery, and that he had no actual or presumptive knowledge of facts sufficient to put him on earlier inquiry.

[23] *E.g., DeHaan* v. *Winter,* 241 N.W. 923 (S. Ct. Mich. 1932); *Golia* v. *Health Insurance Plan,* 165 N.E.2d 578 (Ct. App. N.Y. 1958); *Couillard* v. *Charles T. Miller Hosp., Inc.,* 92 N.W.2d 96 (S. Ct. Minn. 1958); *Samuelson* v. *Freeman,* 454 P.2d 406 (S. Ct. Wash. 1969). To be distinguished is the situation in which injury results from a course of treatment and no particular act of negligence can be isolated. Here the date of the course of treatment's termination is deemed to be the date of the wrongful act. See Louisell, D. W., and Williams, H.: TRIAL OF MEDICAL MALPRACTICE CASES 369–70. Matthew Bender, New York, 1960.

[24] A recent and representative case is *Flanagan* v. *Mount Eden General Hospital,* 248 N.E.2d 871 (Ct. App. N.Y. 1969), in which New York's highest court adopted the "discovery" rule. The court noted that eleven states have adopted the discovery rule "regardless of whether a foreign object is involved"; nine states limit the rule to cases where a foreign object has been negligently left in the patient's body; two states have by statute adopted a discovery rule (Alabama and Connecticut); and twenty-one states have not adopted the discovery rule. See also Note, *Limitations of Actions—Physicians and Surgeons—Malpractice,* 18 WESTERN RESERVE LAW REVIEW 1002 (1967). The preferability of the discovery rule has been vigorously argued in the law reviews. See, *e.g.,* Reich, H.: *The Statute of Limitations Applicable to Malpractice Actions in New York,* 11 NEW YORK UNIV. INTRAMURAL LAW REVIEW 190 (1956); Comment, *The Forgotten Sponge and the Statute of Limitations,* 1 WASHBURN LAW JOURNAL 257 (1961); Comment, *Statute of Limitations in an Action for Malpractice,* 64 DICKINSON LAW REVIEW 173 (1960). Its adoption has also been

patient's standpoint. The law, confronted by two competing and important interests, is forging a principle that holds the patient's desire for his day in court higher than it does the physician's wish to be protected from stale claims.[25] The discovery rule removes the bar of the statute of limitation in cases in which, by way of example, the patient could not possibly have discovered a foreign object—forceps, a drill, sponges—in his body until many years after the occurrence of the medical negligence that resulted in its presence there.[26] These cases pose a question as to how a patient can be expected to commence a lawsuit during a period when he does not know and could not reasonably be expected to know that he has one.[27]

A statute of limitation may be prevented from running—the prescribed time period for commencing an action may be "tolled," as lawyers put it—by the fact of the plaintiff's infancy (this, of course, is a common circumstance, particularly in connection with the practice of pediatrics), his insanity, his membership in the Armed Services of the United States, the defendant's absence from the state, or his fraudulent concealment of a basis for suit, or for any other reason specifically set forth in the pertinent statute.

The ground of fraudulent concealment can arise in so-called foreign-object cases if a surgeon is less than candid with his patient. A foreign object left in the patient after surgery may not cause difficulties until long after the statute of limitation would normally have expired, barring any malpractice action. However, if there is evidence that the surgeon knew of the object's presence but did not inform his patient, some courts find that there has been a fraudulent concealment of the patient's cause of

---

opposed, ineptly. See Martin, W. F.: *Comments on the Problem of Malpractice in New York State,* 22 INSURANCE COUNSEL JOURNAL 460 (1955).

[25] See Note, *Limitations of Actions—In a Malpractice Action the Statute of Limitations Does Not Begin to Run Until the Patient Knows or Has Reason to Know of His Injury,* 15 VANDERBILT LAW REVIEW 657 (1962).

[26] *E.g., Spath* v. *Morrow,* 115 N.W.2d 581 (S. Ct. Neb. 1962) (needle discovered ten years after operation; discovery rule applied); *Budoff* v. *Kessler,* 135 N.Y.S.2d 717 (App. Div. N.Y. 1954) (dentist's drill, imbedded in tooth in 1952, not discovered until 1954; discovery rule not applied); *Conklin* v. *Draper,* 173 N.E. 892 (Ct. App. N.Y. 1930 (arterial forceps left in body on May 27, 1925, discovered July 13, 1927, suit commenced July 5, 1929; dismissed for not having been commenced within two years after the operation); *Rappaport* v. *Douglas,* 72 Dauph. 351 (Com. Pl. Pa. 1964) (surgical needle discovered more than two years after operation; discovery rule not applied). *Cf. Ayers* v. *Morgan,* 154 A.2d 788 (S. Ct. Pa. 1959) (injury held to have been "done" when, nine years after operation, sponge discovered). It has been held that the discovery rule is not limited to foreign body cases. See, *e.g., Frohs* v. *Greene,* 452 P.2d 564 (S. Ct. Ore. 1969).

[27] See *Lindquist* v. *Mullen,* 277 P.2d 724 (S. Ct. Wash. 1954) (dissent in sponge case; discovery rule not applied).

action. Accordingly, it has been held that the statute of limitation does not begin to run until the plaintiff discovered the injury done to him or, in the exercise of reasonable diligence, should have discovered it.[28]

RELEASE AND SATISFACTION

The legal terms "release" and "satisfaction" are not as sensual as they sound. A release is an executed writing given by a claimant to an alleged perpetrator of a tort—a "tort-feasor" in the antique lexicon still employed by some courts—which, in exchange for some valuable consideration (typically, a cash settlement), releases the tort-feasor from any further liability regarding the matter specified in the release.[29] If a malpractice claimant has voluntarily accepted a settlement payment from the defendant doctor or, more likely, from his insurer, the wording of that instrument will bar any subsequent litigation by the claimant based on the same underlying set of facts mentioned in the release. This prohibition of renewed litigation is part of the binding bargain entered into by the parties to the settlement. Very often, of course, the cash settlement or other valuable consideration leading to execution of the release will have "satisfied" —reasonably compensated—the plaintiff's claim, and he could not in a later trial obtain a double recovery. A competent defense lawyer will not enter into a settlement without securing a properly worded release from the claimant.

Occasionally the existence of a valid release is significant in more complex situations. Where a plaintiff was injured by the negligence of a tort-feasor and thereafter receives improper medical treatment from a doctor, the original tort-feasor is generally liable under the law not only for the injuries directly caused by him but also for those resulting from the subsequent malpractice of the doctor.[30] Of course, the plaintiff in such a situation will have a potential lawsuit against the doctor as well as the original

[28] Although a few states require an affirmative act of concealment, such as an artifice calculated to deflect inquiry or to mislead the patient, the prevalent view is that, in consequence of the nature of the physician-patient relationship, mere silence is sufficient to constitute fraudulent concealment of professional negligence of which the defendant physician was aware. The following are representative cases: *Acton* v. *Morrison,* 155 P.2d 782 (S. Ct. Ariz. 1945); *Bowman* v. *McPheeters,* 176 P.2d 745 (Cal. App. 1947); *Buchanan* v. *Kull,* 35 N.W.2d 351 (S. Ct. Mich. 1958); *Nutt* v. *Carson,* 340 P.2d 260 (S. Ct. Okla. 1959).

[29] See *DeNike* v. *Mowery,* 41 P.2d 1010 (S. Ct. Wash. 1966).

[30] *E.g., Muse* v. *DeVito,* 137 N.E. 730 (Sup. Jud. Ct. Mass. 1923); *Staehlin* v. *Hochdoerfer,* 235 S.W. 1060 (S. Ct. Mo. 1921); *Martin* v. *Cunningham,* 161 Pac. 355 (S. Ct. Wash. 1916). Compare *Purchase* v. *Seelye,* 121 N.E. 413 (Sup. Jud. Ct. Mass. 1918) (surgeon mistook one patient for another, operated on wrong side; initial tort-feasor held not liable for independent, intervening conduct of surgeon).

wrongdoer. The doctor will be liable only for the injuries directly caused by his malpractice. The significant point is that a release given by the plaintiff to the original wrongdoer has been held by some courts to bar an action against the doctor unless the wording of the release expressly reserved a right on the plaintiff's part to pursue an action against the doctor.[31] Moreover, the plaintiff's entire claim is satisfied if the underlying settlement with the original wrongdoers included full compensation for the injuries caused by the treating doctor; once again, therefore, the plaintiff would not be permitted to seek a double recovery by pursuing an action against the physician.[32] Diligent defense counsel will ascertain whether the plaintiff in a malpractice action has previously executed a significant release to some third party.

PRIOR RELATED OR IDENTICAL LITIGATION

In the state of New York it was once held, many years ago, that if a physician has sued a patient for the value of his medical services and recovered a judgment, even one by default, it serves as a bar against any subsequent malpractice action for injuries caused by those services.[33] This view is a distinctly antiquated one and is not followed in most states.[34] However, it is true that a final judgment on the merits of a case, granted by a court that had the power (jurisdiction) to decide the case, is conclusive of the rights of the parties for all time unless it is overturned by a higher court.[35] This is the principle of *res judicata*—literally, "things adjudicated." It holds that a plaintiff is entitled to a day in court, but only one. Having lost, he cannot go on refiling and retrying the same lawsuit in the valiant but vexatious hope that somehow, someday he will prevail. There must be an end to litigation.

For the *res judicata* principle to apply (1) the evidence in the two lawsuits must be the same; (2) a single right must allegedly have been violated; (3) there must be a single act involved; and (4) the same findings

[31] *E.g., Milks* v. *McIver,* 190 N.E. 487 (Ct. App. N.Y. 1934); *Hartley* v. *St. Francis Hosp.,* 129 N.W.2d 235 (S. Ct. Wis. 1964); *Travelers Indemnity Co.* v. *Home Mut. Ins. Co.,* 111 N.W.2d 751 (S. Ct. Wis. 1961). See Anno., 40 A.L.R.2d 1075. For a case involving a reservation of right, see *Shaw* v. *Crissey,* 43 N.Y.S.2d 237 (S. Ct. N.Y. 1943).

[32] *E.g., Derby* v. *Prewitt,* 187 N.E.2d 556 (Ct. App. N.Y. 1962); *DeNike* v. *Mowery,* 418 P.2d 1010 (S. Ct. Wash. 1966).

[33] *Blair* v. *Bartlett,* 75 N.Y. 150 (Ct. App. N.Y. 1878).

[34] See Anno., *Judgment in Action for Services of Physician or Surgeon as Bar to Action Against Him for Malpractice,* 49 A.L.R. 551.

[35] See *Cromwell* v. *County of Sac,* 94 U.S. 351 (1876). For a painstaking elucidation of what is one of the law's trickier concepts, see James, F.: CIVIL PROCEDURE 549–75. Little, Brown and Company, Boston, 1965.

and judgment must be involved.[36] A relevant illustration can be drawn from lawbooks. A physician sues a patient for the unpaid value of his professional services. The law does not compel the injection into the physician's lawsuit of any claim of malpractice that the patient may think accompanied the physician's services but it does not prevent it, either. If the defendant patient counterclaims for damages for medical malpractice, or if he merely uses this claim defensively, and the entire case ends in a judgment on the merits for the physician, the patient can never again litigate his malpractice claim.[37] He has had his day in court. The result would be the same, of course, in the simpler case in which the patient sues for malpractice and the physician successfully defends against the claim. The judgment in favor of the defendant doctor extinguishes the plaintiff's malpractice claim for all time.

THE MOST COMMON DEFENSE

The foregoing defenses are manifestly uncommon. The great majority of malpractice actions that end in a verdict in favor of the defendant doctor reach that culmination because the doctor was not guilty of malpractice and can prove it. He can prove it because he has witnesses and records that attest his adherence to acceptable professional standards of performance.

The Importance of Adequate and Accurate Records

The importance to physicians and surgeons of adequate and accurate records can hardly be overemphasized. They will frequently serve to refresh the doctor's recollection of events long past. (In several large cities in the United States it now takes more than five years from the time of filing for a lawsuit to come to trial.) Jurors are likely to be suspicious of any physician who lacks a record of some pivotal fact essential to his defense. Where a lawsuit, as lawsuits often do, becomes a Who-do-you-believe? case—the patient testifying "He didn't" and the doctor testifying "I did"—the availability of contemporaneous records corroborating the doctor's recollection will invariably tip the scale of credibility decisively in his favor.

Fields and Home have recommended six categories of records as a

[36] See Clark, C. E.: CODE PLEADING, ch. 7, 2d ed. West Publishing Company, St. Paul, 1947; 1 Louisell, D. W., and Williams, H.: MEDICAL MALPRACTICE, par. 9.04. Matthew Bender, New York, 1969.

[37] *E.g., Barton* v. *Southwick,* 101 N.E. 928 (S. Ct. Ill. 1913); *Leslie* v. *Mollica,* 211 N.W. 267 (S. Ct. Mich. 1926); *Lawson* v. *Conway,* 16 S.E. 564 (S. Ct. W. Va. 1892).

minimum:[38] (1) an exhaustive history; (2) a description, recorded as nearly as possible in the patient's words, of the present ailment or injury; (3) the report of physical examination, showing objective findings and subjective complaints; (4) diagnostic aids used and any reports received concerning the patient; (5) impression or diagnosis (when a physician is able to form only an impression in the absence of additional diagnostic procedures he should avoid use of the word "diagnosis"); and (6) treatment, including medication prescribed, and procedures recommended or performed. A record of any visits to the patient should be carefully maintained lest it later be suggested that the doctor failed to employ due diligence or even abandoned him.[39]

Obtaining adequate written consent to surgical procedures or any extraordinary mode of therapy can be highly significant.[40] Notations on the medical record should be made whenever a patient refuses a diagnostic aid, such as x-ray photographs, or discontinues treatment, as when he rejects his doctor's advice and leaves the hospital to which he has been confined.

Recordation of incidents of treatment in chronological sequence is essential. Any attempt, for whatever reason, to alter the sequence will give rise to a prejudicial inference in the minds of jurors. In fact, *any* alteration of a medical record, no matter how innocently undertaken, can be turned into something ominous by a deft cross-examiner. A large number of medical malpractice actions culminating in a substantial settlement or verdict in favor of the claimant have involved unacceptable record-keeping.

BIBLIOGRAPHY

BOOK

1 Louisell, D. W., and Williams, H.: MEDICAL MALPRACTICE, ch. IX. Matthew Bender, New York, 1969.

ARTICLES

Dorsey, J. W.: *Release of Tortfeasor as Release of Physician,* 15 NORTH CAROLINA LAW REVIEW 293 (1937).

Gress, R.: *Malpractice and the Statute of Limitations,* 16 ST. JOHN'S LAW REVIEW 101 (1941).

Lillick, R. B.: *Malpractice Statute of Limitations in New York and Other Jurisdictions,* 47 CORNELL LAW QUARTERLY 339 (1962).

[38] Fields, A., and Home, D. F.: *Adequate Office Records in Medicolegal Problems,* 33 POSTGRAD. MED. A-62 (1963).

[39] See Chapter 10.

[40] See Chapter 11.

Strandberg, R. J.: *When Statute of Limitations Begins to Run in Malpractice Actions,* 26 MARQUETTE LAW REVIEW 217 (1942).

NOTES AND COMMENTS

Comment, *Contributory Negligence in Medical Malpractice,* 12 CLEVELAND-MARSHALL LAW REVIEW 455 (1963).

Comment, *Malpractice and the Statute of Limitations,* 32 INDIANA LAW JOURNAL 528 (1957).

Comment, *Medical Malpractice: A Survey of Statutes of Limitations,* 3 SUFFOLK UNIV. LAW REVIEW 597 (1969).

Note, *Limitations of Actions—Physicians and Surgeons—Malpractice,* 18 WESTERN RESERVE LAW REVIEW 1002 (1967).

Note, *Release of One Responsible for Injury as Bar to Action Against Physician for Malpractice,* 30 MICHIGAN LAW REVIEW 1349 (1932).

Note, *Release of Tortfeasor as Bar to Claim Against Attending Physician for Malpractice,* 81 UNIV. OF PENNSYLVANIA LAW REVIEW 485 (1933).

Note, *Subsequent Treatment as Postponing the Accrual of a Cause of Action for Malpractice,* 20 MINNESOTA LAW REVIEW 96 (1935).

chapter 10

LIABILITY FOR LACK OF DUE DILIGENCE AND ABANDONMENT OF THE PATIENT

LACK OF DUE DILIGENCE IN CARING FOR THE PATIENT: A BRAND OF MEDICAL MALPRACTICE

Lack of due diligence on the part of a physician in caring for a patient is simply one fairly obvious type of medical negligence (malpractice). For example, a large body of litigation has involved allegedly delayed or insufficiently frequent treatment of the patient.[1]

A physician must employ reasonable care—that is, good medical judgment—in determining the frequency of his visits from or to a needful patient. How much attention a particular patient should be given will depend on custom and good practice and cannot be expressed as an absolute.[2] A physician is under no obligation to remain perpetually at a patient's bedside; he exposes himself to liability only if, although needed, he departs, fails to come at all, or delays too long in coming.[3]

It is essential, of course, that the plaintiff patient establish that the defendant doctor's asserted lack of due diligence was a proximate cause of the injury for which damages are sought.[4] And, except in self-evident

[1] *E.g., Neudeck* v. *Vestal,* 3 P.2d 595 (Cal. App. 1931); *Church* v. *Adler,* 113 N.E.2d 327 (Ill. App. 1953); *Adams* v. *Henry,* 131 N.W. 62 (S. Ct. Mich. 1911).

[2] *Tomer* v. *Aiken,* 101 N.W. 769 (S. Ct. Iowa 1904), and cases cited in preceding footnote.

[3] *Compare Stacy* v. *Williams,* 69 S.W.2d 697 (S. Ct. Ky. 1934) (common knowledge that after broken leg is set and splinted, continuous presence of physician not required), *with Young* v. *Jordan,* 145 S.E. 41 (S. Ct. W. Va. 1928) (physician accelerated plaintiff's labor, then placed himself beyond reach even by telephone; held, liable). See also, *e.g., Thaggard* v. *Vafes,* 119 So. 647 (S. Ct. Ala. 1928); *Levy* v. *Kirk,* 187 So.2d 401 (S. Ct. Fla. 1966); *Gray* v. *Weinstein,* 42 S.E.2d 616 (S. Ct. N.C. 1947); *Nickley* v. *Eisenberg,* 239 N.W. 426 (S. Ct. Wis. 1931).

[4] *E.g. Williams* v. *Tarter,* 151 S.W.2d 783 (Ct. App. Ky. 1941); *Jackowicz* v. *Knobloch,* 265 N.W. 799 (S. Ct. Mich. 1936); *Hurspool* v. *Ralston,* 290 P.2d 981 (S. Ct. Wash. 1955).

cases, expert medical testimony will be required to demonstrate this causal connection.[5]

A different but closely related phenomenon is the intentional severance, by the physician, of the physician-patient relationship.

ABANDONMENT OF THE PATIENT

During the life of the doctor-patient relationship the physician is ordinarily obligated, in the absence of some countervailing agreement with his patient, to provide continued needed care.[6] One who engages a physician to treat him impliedly engages his attendance throughout the illness or until his professional services have been dispensed with; that is to say, the doctor-patient relationship, once initiated,[7] continues until (1) it is ended by the parties' consent, (2) it is revoked by the patient, (3) the doctor's services are no longer needed, or (4) the physician withdraws from the case after reasonable notice to the patient.[8] It is frequently held to be malpractice for a physician unilaterally to sever the doctor-patient relationship.

It has sometimes been thought that the abandonment of a patient is something markedly different from negligence, the notion being that termination of the doctor-patient relationship, being an intentional act, is the antithesis of negligence.[9] While it is true that withdrawal from a medical case is usually a deliberate rather than a careless act, it is usually motivated by a diagnosis or prognosis that was arguably (1) wrong and (2) arrived at through professional negligence. Thus the concept of abandonment has a large malpractice component.[10]

[5] *E.g., Rising* v. *Veatch,* 3 P.2d 1023 (Cal. App. 1931); *McDermott* v. *St. Mary's Hospital Corp.* 133 A.2d 608 (S. Ct. Err. & App. Conn. 1957); *Huggins* v. *Hicken,* 310 P.2d 523 (S. Ct. Utah 1957).

[6] *E.g., Lewis* v. *Johnson,* 86 P.2d 99 (S. Ct. Cal. 1939); *Hall* v. *Nagel,* 39 N.E.2d 612 (S. Ct. Ohio 1942); *Spendlove* v. *Georges,* 295 P.2d 336 (S. Ct. Utah 1956).

[7] The concept of abandonment is, by definition, in no way related to the physician's permissible refusal to enter into a doctor-patient relationship with a particular person; thus the refusal to respond to a call or render treatment to one not yet accepted as a patient is not within the abandonment concept. See, *e.g., Buttersworth* v. *Swint,* 186 S.E. 770 (Ga. App. 1936); *Childers* v. *Frye,* 158 S.E. 744 (S. Ct. N.C. 1931); *Rice* v. *Rinaldo,* 119 N.E.2d 657 (Ohio App. 1951).

[8] A physician, like a civil lawyer, has a right to withdraw from a case if he does so in the proper manner, which involves the giving of reasonable notice to the patient so that he can obtain other medical attendance. Such a withdrawal is not an "abandonment" in the tort sense. See *Capps* v. *Volk,* 369 P.2d 238 (S. Ct. Kan. 1962); *McManus* v. *Donlin,* 127 N.W.2d 22 (S. Ct. Wis. 1964).

[9] See, *e.g.,* Comment, *The Action of Abandonment in Medical Malpractice Litigation,* 36 TULANE LAW REVIEW 834, 836–37 (1962).

[10] The fusing of the two concepts can readily be discerned in cases such as *Groce* v. *Myers,* 29 S.E.2d 553 (S. Ct. N.C. 1944) (inadequate treatment of broken arm;

It has been said, as though three entirely separate and distinct phenomena were being listed, that liability for patient abandonment is based on one or more of the following allegations: (1) a complete and unreasonable refusal to treat the patient, (2) a withdrawal from the physician-patient relationship at a crucial juncture without the patient's consent and without reasonable notice to him, or (3) a premature discharge of the patient.[11] In effect, however, all three of these allegations charge unjustified withdrawal from a medical case.

Refusal to Treat

A physician who unqualifiedly refuses to continue to treat a patient has effectively withdrawn from the case, and if the refusal to continue treatment is not medically justifiable, he has abandoned the patient. The nature and consequences of this form of abandonment are illustrated by a Virginia case. *Vann* v. *Harden*[12] started off unexceptionally enough; the defendant doctor had properly set and placed a cast on a fracture of the plaintiff's lower leg. However, on two subsequent calls, even though the patient complained of extreme pain, the doctor did nothing. He then left town, despite the fact that his patient's chart showed fluctuating fever and low blood count. When the patient's parents were unable to reach the defendant they called another doctor who bivalved the cast and found evidence of acute infection. When the defendant returned he refused to examine the patient's leg and instead discharged him from the hospital, although his temperature had continued to rise and he was still complaining of excruciating pain. Another physician was called; he removed the plaintiff's cast and observed necrotic spots. Eventually it became necessary to amputate the plaintiff's leg. Upholding a verdict against the defendant, the Supreme Court of Virginia held that the jury could properly have found that his refusal to attend and treat the plaintiff was the cause of the ultimate injury.[13]

It is not a prerequisite to liability for abandonment that the defendant doctor expressly and unequivocally refuse to continue needed treatment.

---

court speaks in terms of both abandonment and negligent treatment). See also *Lee* v. *Dewbre,* 362 S.W.2d 900 (Tex. Civ. App. 1962).

[11] See Anno., *Liability of Physician Who Abandons Case,* 57 A.L.R.2d 432.

[12] 47 S.E.2d 314 (S. Ct. Va. 1948).

[13] See also, *e.g., Fortner* v. *Koch,* 261 N.W. 762 (S. Ct. Mich. 1935); *Cazzell* v. *Schofield,* 8 S.W.2d 580 (S. Ct. Mo. 1928); *Burnett* v. *Layman,* 181 S.W. 157 (S. Ct. Tenn. 1915). A showing of causal connection between the abandonment and the plaintiff's injury must be made. It often may be that the defendant physician's refusal to treat in no way contributed to the plaintiff's injury or death; or to put it the other way around, it may be that no amount of treament could have altered the result. See, *e.g., Urrutia* v. *Patino,* 10 S.W.2d 582 (Tex. Civ. App. 1928).

An unexplained failure to supply treatment may be enough.[14] A physician, in other words, must exercise reasonable care in determining when attendance and treatment can safely be interrupted or permanently discontinued. An extreme illustration is the case of *Johnson* v. *Vaughn.*[15] The patient in this case had been in concededly critical condition when admitted to a hospital emergency room at about 1:00 A.M.; a bullet had penetrated his trachea. The defendant doctor arrived shortly thereafter but minimal assistance was rendered although the patient was breathing with difficulty, vomiting, and in "borderline shock." The doctor had been drinking. He returned to his home at about 3:45 A.M., apparently after having paid only one visit to the patient's ward room. At the time of the doctor's departure the patient was experiencing difficulty in breathing. Despite his repiratory difficulty, no tracheotomy was done, nor had the patient received a blood transfusion. At about 4:00 A.M. another physician instituted resuscitative measures. Only after two telephone calls and a time loss of half an hour or more did the defendant physician release the patient to the other physician. The patient died during an operation that was begun at 5:00 A.M. The cause of death was found to be an air embolism due to the escape of air through the patient's punctured trachea. The Kentucky Supreme Court held that there was sufficient evidence of abandonment to carry the case to a jury and to support a verdict against the defendant doctor.

Express Withdrawal

The clearest sort of abandonment is seen when the physician, without legal justification, expressly announces his withdrawal from a medical case. An extreme but nonetheless serviceable example is *Gillette* v. *Tucker,*[16] an old Ohio case in which the defendant, a surgeon, performed an appendectomy on the plaintiff. Although he continued to treat her for a year, her incision failed to heal. When the patient ventured the observation that something might be wrong, the surgeon became furious and informed his patient that if she felt that way about it she could get out. Before their conversation concluded, the doctor had told his patient in no uncertain terms that he would not provide any further treatment and that a police officer would be summoned to eject her from his office. The plaintiff subsequently underwent another operation, performed by another surgeon, and it was then discovered that the defendant had left a sponge in his patient's body when he closed her incision. The Ohio Supreme

[14] *E.g., McGulpin* v. *Bessmer,* 43 N.W.2d 121 (S. Ct. Iowa 1950); *Baute* v. *Haynes,* 104 S.W. 272 (Ct. App. Ky. 1907); *Baird* v. *National Health Foundation,* 144 S.W.2d 850 (S. Ct. Mo. 1940).

[15] 370 S.W.2d 591 (S. Ct. Ky. 1963).

[16] 65 N.E. 865 (S. Ct. Ohio 1902).

Court experienced no difficulty concluding that the defendant had abandoned his patient when he evicted her from his office.[17]

Premature Discharge of the Patient

It is uniformly held by the courts that the premature discharge of a patient constitutes abandonment. It is perhaps in this area that the abandonment concept most noticeably approaches traditional notions of medical negligence: the patient's discharge from a hospital is, of course, deliberate conduct, but the diagnosis or prognosis leading to this intentional conduct may have been the result of medical negligence. Unfortunately, instances of premature discharge abound in the reported cases, and *Morrell* v. *Lalonde* simply provides an aggravated sample.[18]

In *Morrell,* a Rhode Island case, the defendant doctor had operated on the plaintiff for a strangulated hernia. He made an unskillful abdominal incision, sutured it without attempting to relieve the obstructed bowel, and then informed the patient that she was going to die. As if to underscore this gloomy prognosis, he sent his patient home in an undertaker's automobile. Thereafter the defendant neglected to call on his patient, stating he was too busy at his hospital. The Rhode Island Supreme Court, holding that the evidence in support of a verdict for the patient was ample, pointed out that it was the defendant's duty to require his patient to remain in the hospital in order to avoid the risk to her life incident to a premature discharge.[19]

Failure to Instruct the Patient Adequately

An offshoot of the abandonment principle involves a physician's failure to instruct his patient regarding the necessity of future care. It is malpractice of a passive but nonetheless legally actionable sort for a doctor to omit the giving of advice concerning follow-up observation and treatment when this is vital to effect the best possible recovery.[20] There may be nothing more involved than telling the patient to return for further examination and diagnosis. Or there may be something more that is essential, as in the illustrative case of *Doan* v. *Griffith.*[21] The plaintiff, following an accident, had been admitted to a hospital. He was unconscious and had serious injuries, including multiple fractures of the facial bones. The de-

[17] See also, *e.g., Norton* v. *Hamilton,* 89 S.E.2d 809 (Ga. App. 1955); *Gray* v. *Davidson,* 130 P.2d 341 (S. Ct. Wash. 1942).

[18] 120 Atl. 435 (S. Ct. R.I.), *error dismissed,* 264 U.S. 572 (1923).

[19] See also *Mucci* v. *Houghton,* 57 N.W. 305 (S. Ct. Iowa 1894); *Reed* v. *Laughlin,* 58 S.W.2d 440 (S. Ct. Mo. 1933); *Meiselman* v. *Crown Heights Hospital,* 34 N.E.2d 367 (Ct. App. N.Y. 1941); *Vann* v. *Harden,* 47 S.E.2d 314 (S. Ct. Va. 1948).

[20] *E.g., Barnes* v. *Bovenmyer,* 122 N.W.2d 312 (S. Ct. Iowa 1963).

[21] 402 S.W.2d 855 (S. Ct. Ky. 1966).

fendant physician rendered emergency treatment and then made daily visits to the patient until, seven days after his admission, defendant discharged him from the hospital. At the trial of a malpractice claim, expert medical testimony demonstrated that the customary treatment of plaintiff Doan's injuries would have included surgical realignment of the fractured facial bones as soon as the swelling subsided. This would generally be accomplished within ten days of the fracture-producing accident in order to restore normal vision and to reestablish the face's normal contours. Other testimony established that Doan's face was still seriously swollen at the time of his discharge from the hospital; realignment of the facial bones was thus not feasible at or before that time. Doan himself took the stand and swore that the defendant doctor had not informed him of the need to have his facial bones set by a specialist. There was a consequent delay; the bones fused. Doan suffered impairment of his vision and his face was disfigured. The Kentucky Supreme Court held that a jury could properly find that the defendant's failure to give Doan timely advice was the cause of his unfortunate condition. This case supports the proposition that a physician's obligation to his patient does not necessarily terminate when the patient departs the physician's office or a hospital.[22]

DEFENSES TO CLAIMS OF LACK OF DUE DILIGENCE AND ABANDONMENT

Lack of Due Diligence: One Perfect Defense

The best defense to a claim of lack of due diligence, somewhat analogous to the defense of truth in a libel action, is proof of due diligence. It is not only the best defense, it is the only defense—assuming, that is, the unavailability of such technical defenses as the statute of limitations.[23]

Abandonment: The Defense of Proper Withdrawal

There are numerous potential defenses to a claim that a physician abandoned his patient when he was in need of treatment. The most potent of these is proof that the defendant doctor properly withdrew from the patient's case. An effective withdrawal, relieving the physician from civil liability for abandonment, cannot be accomplished by the simple expedient of failing to attend and treat the patient without notification of an intent to leave the case.[24] The patient must be given notice of the physi-

[22] See also *Beck* v. *German Klinik,* 43 N.W. 617 (S. Ct. Iowa 1889); *Orendino* v. *Clarke,* 402 P.2d 527 (S. Ct. Ore. 1965); *Vann* v. *Harden,* 47 S.E.2d 314 (S. Ct. Va. 1948).

[23] See Chapter 9.

[24] *E.g., Bolles* v. *Kinton,* 263 Pac. 26 (S. Ct. Colo. 1928); *Carroll* v. *Griffin,* 101 S.E.2d 764 (Ga. App. 1958).

cian's planned withdrawal in sufficient time to permit the securing of other medical attention.[25] The time period involved in the concept of reasonable notice will vary, depending on the circumstances peculiar to the particular case,[26] but the condition of the patient and the availability of other physicians are the two most clearly material considerations.[27]

A physician, constantly mindful of the possible future need for tangible evidence in the form of records, should communicate his intent to withdraw in an unambiguous writing, preferably a certified letter, and retain a copy in his files.[28]

Designation of a Qualified Substitute Physician

The physician occasionally finds it necessary or desirable to absent himself from his office for a period of time. He may be advancing his knowledge of current developments in his field of medicine by attending professional meetings or he may be taking a sorely needed vacation with his family. On these occasions it is entirely proper for the departing physician to arrange for a substitute doctor to render medical services to his patients.[29] By doing this the departing doctor avoids any possible claim of patient abandonment. However, he runs the risk of liability if he fails to make a reasonable effort to ensure that the substitute is qualified and competent.[30]

Ordinarily the physician should advise his patients of the impending substitution, thereby according them an opportunity to engage the services of other physicians if that is their desire. The physician must be especially sensitive to the wishes of obstetrical patients. A few court cases have held that a physician can properly dispatch a substitute in an obstetrical case without the consent of the patient,[31] but this is not a unanimous view. The court in a Maine case [32] suggested, but did not directly hold, that an obstetrical patient could recover money damages for mental

[25] *E.g., Sibert* v. *Boger,* 260 S.W.2d 569 (S. Ct. Mo. 1953); *Gray* v. *Davidson,* 130 P.2d 341 (S. Ct. Wash. 1942).

[26] *Burnett* v. *Layman,* 181 S.W. 157 (S. Ct. Tenn. 1915).

[27] *E.g., Sibert* v. *Boger,* 260 S.W.2d 569 (S. Ct. Mo. 1953); *Urrutia* v. *Patino,* 297 S.W. 512 (S. Ct. Tex. 1927).

[28] See, *e.g.,* A.M.A., MEDICOLEGAL FORMS WITH LEGAL ANALYSIS 5 (1961).

[29] *E.g., Jackowicz* v. *Knobloch,* 265 N.W. 799 (S. Ct. Mich. 1936); *Stohlman* v. *Davis,* 220 N.W. 247 (S. Ct. Neb. 1928); *Young* v. *Jordan,* 145 S.E. 41 (S. Ct. W. Va. 1928).

[30] *E.g., Stohlman* v. *Davis,* 220 N.W. 247 (S. Ct. Neb. 1928); *Moore* v. *Lee,* 211 S.W. 214 (S. Ct. Tex. 1919).

[31] *E.g., Jackowicz* v. *Knobloch,* 265 N.W. 799 (S. Ct. Mich. 1936); *Young* v. *Jordan,* 154 S.E. 41 (S. Ct. W. Va. 1928).

[32] *Miller* v. *Dore,* 148 A.2d 692 (S. Ct. Me. 1959); see also *Hood* v. *Moffett,* 69 So. 664 (S. Ct. Miss. 1915).

anguish on an abandonment theory where a substitute physician performs the delivery and the patient was not informed in advance of the substitution. The doctor-patient relationship in obstetrical cases is so personal that the patient's written consent to a substitution should be secured whenever possible. Such a consent can properly be obtained at the outset of the doctor-patient relationship.

Consent to Referral to Another Physician

Closely related to the procedure for temporary substitution of a physician is the process of referring a patient to another doctor. Frequently a physician (often a general practitioner) will consider it prudent to refer a patient to a specialist. The patient's consent to the referral should be obtained. The referring doctor is relieved of any ongoing duty to the patient if it is agreed that the specialist is to take over the case completely.[33]

Limited and Special Practice

Because the relationship of doctor and patient is a consensual one, a physician is free to limit the scope of the relationship into which he is willing to enter.[34] He can restrict his practice to his office, and his refusal to make a house call will not constitute abandonment of the patient.[35] The same principle applies to the physician who is brought into a case for consultation only or to conduct a specified series of tests: the doctor-patient relationship terminates with the consultation or testing, and a refusal to provide additional professional services to the patient cannot be characterized as an abandonment of him.[36] By the same token, physicians —whether specialists or general practitioners—can limit their practice to certain ailments or injuries.[37]

Unreasonable Demands by the Patient

It is a valid generalization that a medical man need not respond to the unreasonable demands of a patient. Attempting to determine in advance

[33] *E.g., McLendon* v. *Daniel,* 141 S.E. 77 (Ga. App. 1927); *Engle* v. *Clarke,* 346 S.W.2d 13 (Ky. App. 1961). *But see Welch* v. *Frisbie Mem. Hosp.,* 9 A.2d 761 (S. Ct. N.H. 1939).

[34] *E.g., McNamara* v. *Emmons,* 97 P.2d 503 (Cal. App. 1939); *Young* v. *Crescente,* 39 A.2d 449 (S. Ct. N.J. 1944) See also McCoid, A. H.: *The Care Required of Medical Practitioners,* 12 VANDERBILT LAW REVIEW 549, 550–57 (1959).

[35] *E.g., Nash* v. *Meyer,* 31 P.2d 273 (S. Ct. Idaho 1934); *Urrutia* v. *Patino,* 297 S.W. 512 (Tex. Civ. App. 1927).

[36] *E.g., Tomer* v. *Aiken,* 101 N.W. 769 (S. Ct. Iowa 1919); *Nelson* v. *Farrish,* 173 N.W. 715 (S. Ct. Minn. 1919).

[37] *E.g., McNamara* v. *Emmons,* 97 P.2d 503 (Cal. App. 1933); *Nash* v. *Meyer,* 31 P.2d 273 (S. Ct. Idaho 1934); *Urrutia* v. *Patino,* 297 S.W. 512 (Tex. Civ. App. 1928).

what some court will later agree was an unreasonable demand may seem a dangerous exercise. However, the law's "reasonable man" test is workable here. If the physician behaved as a reasonable physician would under the same or similar circumstances, no jury will be permitted to substitute its hindsight for his judgment. A few examples may give the reader confidence in this assurance.

Rodgers v. *Lawson* is typical.[38] In that case the defendant doctor, who had been treating a postpartum breast infection, was asked to make a house call. He informed the patient that he could not do so during his office hours. The patient, recovering her mobility, then proceeded to the office of another physician for treatment. A federal court, holding that there had been no abandonment of the patient by the defendant, commented pointedly on the fact that the plaintiff's ability to go to another doctor's office branded as unreasonable her insistence that the defendant come to her. Other reported judicial opinions support this decision.[39] There are also opinions standing for the proposition that a patient cannot demand that a physician ignore his other patients[40] and that a patient cannot insist that his doctor attend or treat him at any specified time[41] or at some location far removed from the physician's usual place of practice.[42] Of course, physicians are themselves required to be not merely reasonable but also humanitarian. Thus it has been held that nonpayment of medical fees will not justify the cessation of treatment at a crucial juncture.[43] In truth, this is no more than a reiteration of the medical profession's own canon that the poor as well as the rich are entitled to proper medical treatment.

Lack of Cooperation by the Patient

It is surely self-evident that a patient cannot successfully charge his physician with abandonment when the patient's problems arise from his own failure or refusal to follow a comprehensibly prescribed course of treatment.[44] A patient's outright refusal to cooperate in a course of treat-

[38] 170 F.2d 157 (D.C. Cir. 1948).

[39] *E.g.*, *Nash* v. *Meyer*, 31 P.2d 273 (S. Ct. Idaho 1943); *Urrutia* v. *Patino*, 297 S.W. 512 (Tex. Civ. App. 1927).

[40] *Rodgers* v. *Lawson*, 170 F.2d 157 (D.C. Cir. 1948), discussed above, is such a case but it must not be taken as support for a doctor's accepting more patients than he can effectively attend. See, on this point, *Sinclair* v. *Brunson*, 180 N.W. 358 (S. Ct. Mich. 1920).

[41] *Dabney* v. *Briggs*, 121 So. 394 (S. Ct. Ala. 1929).

[42] *McNamara* v. *Emmons*, 97 P.2d 503 (Cal. App. 1939).

[43] *E.g.*, *Becker* v. *Janinski*, 15 N.Y.S. 675 (App. Div. N.Y. 1891); *Ricks* v. *Budge*, 64 P.2d 208 (S. Ct. Utah 1937).

[44] *Roberts* v. *Wood*, 206 F.Supp. 579 (S.D. Ala. 1962).

ment justifies a breaking off of the doctor-patient relationship;[45] in a clear case it might be considered the equivalent of a discharge of the physician by the patient.[46]

BIBLIOGRAPHY

BOOKS

Chayet, N. L.: LEGAL IMPLICATIONS OF EMERGENCY CARE 177–95. Appleton-Century-Crofts, New York, 1969.

1 Louisell, D. W., and Williams, H.: MEDICAL MALPRACTICE, par. 8.08. Matthew Bender, New York, 1969.

ARTICLE

Levin, M.: *Abandoned Patient,* [1965] INSURANCE LAW QUARTERLY 275.

NOTES

Note, *Abandonment of Patient at Critical Stage Without Reasonable Notice,* 7 NEBRASKA LAW BULLETIN 287 (1929).

Note, *Malpractice—Post-Operative Abandonment of Patient,* 15 ALBANY LAW REVIEW 246 (1951).

[45] *E.g., Dashiell* v. *Griffith,* 35 Atl. 1094 (S. Ct. Md. 1896); *Steele* v. *Woods,* 327 S.W.2d 187 (S. Ct. Mo. 1959); *Urrutia* v. *Patino,* 297 S.W. 512 (Tex. Civ. App. 1927).

[46] *Tomer* v. *Aiken,* 101 N.W. 769 (S. Ct. Iowa 1904).

chapter 11

LIABILITY FOR FAILURE TO OBTAIN "INFORMED CONSENT" TO CUSTOMARY THERAPY

THE CONCEPT OF "INFORMED CONSENT"

Medical Negligence or Assault and Battery?

A doctor, under normal circumstances,[1] cannot properly undertake surgery or critical procedures without the consent of his patient. A general or "blanket" consent, moreover, may have no legal force if the patient was not accorded an opportunity to compare the risks of undergoing treatment with the dangers of foregoing it.[2] The typical patient, largely ignorant of medical science, will be unaware of collateral risks in a proposed therapy unless he is advised of them by his physician. Subsequent to such advice the patient's decision to go ahead with treatment, despite the risks disclosed to him, is said to be the product of his "informed consent." Thus the concept of informed consent has to do with the extent to which a physician must advise his patients of collateral risks attached to a proposed course of treatment.

"Informed consent," seemingly summing up a simple proposition, is another of those expressions, current in the medical-legal lexicon, that may possess more felicity than content.[3] Certainly the so-called informed-

[1] "Normal circumstances," as used here, assumes an adult, mentally competent patient in a nonemergency situation. Consent problems posed by minors and the mentally incompetent are discussed in the next section of this chapter, as are problems of consent arising in an emergency context.

[2] *E.g., Rogers* v. *Lumbermen's Mut. Cas. Co.,* 119 So.2d 649 (S. Ct. La. 1960), in which the court stated that a "blanket" consent form was "almost completely worthless" and could "have no possible weight."

[3] See, generally, Plante, M. L.: *An Analysis of "Informed Consent,"* 36 FORDHAM LAW REVIEW 639 (1968). To be compared with this article is McCoid, A. H.: *A Reappraisal of Liability for Unauthorized Medical Treatment,* 41 MINNESOTA LAW REVIEW 381 (1957).

consent notion has bred both confusion and confusion's outlet, litigation. The confusion stems from courts' unwitting commingling of negligence and battery concepts. To comprehend the confusion it is first necessary to understand the question: Is a physician who implements a therapy without having secured the effective consent of his patient liable for money damages to him on the basis of malpractice (medical negligence), on the one hand, or battery, on the other? To comprehend the question, it is essential to consider the contrasting meaning of the terms *negligence* and *battery*.

Negligence, broadly, consists in a failure to conduct one's self as would a reasonably prudent person in the same or similar circumstances. Battery or, as it is sometimes put, "assault and battery," connotes an unauthorized touching of another person's body. A kiss in the dark, uninvited, can be a battery; so can a punch in the mouth. If a man—be he a doctor or a candlestick maker—deliberately punches another man in the face, he is guilty of an intentional act labeled by the law a battery. This is quite different, obviously, from negligence (carelessness); furthermore, the assaulter's profession or occupation is neither here nor there. It should also be underscored that, by definition, the touching of another person is not wrongful —that is, is not to be characterized a battery—if the touching was with that person's eyes-open consent. Not *all* kisses in the dark are batteries.

Whether a physician's conduct constitutes medical negligence (malpractice) or a battery is not exclusively an exercise in semantics. The selection of a label has significant legal consequences. For example, it is generally thought that expert testimony is essential to a malpractice action but irrelevant to a claim of battery.[4] The selection of a label may also govern the period within which suit must be commenced (the period of the applicable statute of limitations),[5] the nature and measure of recoverable

[4] In an informed consent case based on a *medical negligence* theory the plaintiff will allege that the defendant doctor's insufficient disclosures amounted to a breach of the professional duty to employ reasonable care. The existence and contours of a doctor's duty can usually be established only by expert testimony. The complaint in a *battery* case will allege that the physician's failure to disclose rendered invalid any generalized consent obtained from the patient and terminated the physician's privilege to touch his patient's body. Expertise becomes irrelevant, since the professional standard of care itself becomes irrelevant with the termination of the aforementioned privilege. See, *e.g., Woods* v. *Brumlop,* 277 P.2d 520 (S. Ct. N.M. 1962); *Scott* v. *Wilson,* 396 S.W.2d 532 (Tex. Civ. App. 1965).

[5] In some jurisdictions the period within which actions for malpractice and battery must be brought will differ. The malpractice period is likely to be longer. See *Maercklein* v. *Smith,* 266 P.2d 1095 (S. Ct. Colo. 1954); *Hershey* v. *Peake,* 233 Pac. 1113 (S. Ct. Kan. 1924). The statute of limitations defense is discussed in some detail in Chapter 9.

damages,[6] and the coverage of the defendant doctor's liability insurance policy.[7]

The negligence-battery confusion is not of long standing. The seeds of it are vaguely discernible in a 1957 California case, *Salgo* v. *Leland Stanford Jr. University Board of Trustees.*[8] Plaintiff Salgo suffered paralysis following aortography performed at Stanford University Hospital. One issue on appeal in Salgo's lawsuit was the proper content of a jury instruction on the defendant doctor's duty to disclose to his patient the risks of aortography. The appellate court, no doubt in an effort to be helpful, had this to say:

> A physician violates his duty to his patient and subjects himself to liability if he withholds any facts which are necessary to form the basis of an intelligent consent by the patient to the proposed treatment. Likewise the physician may not minimize the known dangers of a procedure or operation in order to induce his patient's consent. At the same time, the physician must place the welfare of his patient above all else and this very fact places him in a position in which he sometimes must choose between two alternative courses of action. One is to explain to the patient every risk attendant upon any surgical procedure or operation, no matter how remote; this may well result in alarming a patient who is already unduly apprehensive and who may as a result refuse to undertake surgery in which there is in fact minimal risk; it may also result in actually increasing the risks by reason of the physiological results of the apprehension itself. The other is to recognize that each patient presents a separate problem, that the patient's mental and emotional condition is important and in certain cases may be crucial, and that in discussing the element of risk a certain amount of discretion must be employed consistent with the full disclosure of facts necessary to an informed consent.

If the quoted commentary seems at best equivocal, it proved a model of explication when compared with two Kansas opinions handed down

[6] Under a battery theory the defendant doctor would not only be required to compensate the plaintiff for all injury resulting from the operation in question; he might also he held liable for so-called punitive or exemplary damages, which operate as a sort of fine or penalty. See Oppenheim, M.: *Informed Consent to Medical Treatment,* 11 CLEVELAND-MARSHALL LAW REVIEW 249 (1962). He might even be held liable for nominal damages, despite the plaintiff's inability to prove actual injury. The subject of damages is considered in Chapter 19.

[7] Theoretically, at least, battery could be viewed as a criminal act. Many malpractice liability insurance policies specifically disclaim coverage for criminal acts. See Schroeder, O. C.: *Insurance Protection and Damage Awards in Medical Malpractice,* 25 OHIO STATE LAW JOURNAL 323, 330 (1965). Courts are not inclined to construe insurance policies so restrictively, however. See, *e.g., Shehee* v. *Aetna Cas. & Sur. Co.,* 122 F.Supp. 1, 4 (W.D. La. 1954).

[8] 317 P.2d 170 (Cal. App. 1957).

three years later. Both opinions were rendered in phases of the same case. In *Natanson* v. *Kline* [9] the plaintiff had undergone a radical mastectomy. At her surgeon's suggestion, plaintiff had engaged a Doctor Kline to perform radiation therapy at the mastectomy's site. By the time the therapy was concluded, plaintiff had suffered injury to the skin, bone, and cartilage of her chest. She charged Doctor Kline with negligence in two respects: in the administration of the therapy and in failing to warn her of the collateral risks. A jury exonerated the doctor and Mrs. Natanson appealed.

The trial judge had rejected plaintiff's request that the jury be instructed that Doctor Kline was guilty of negligence if it determined that he knew his treatment involved collateral dangers but did not inform plaintiff of them. The Supreme Court of Kansas stated that the requested charge was too broad but that the lower court should have given some form of instruction along the requested lines. The Kansas court then launched into its reasoning. In the process it used negligence and battery terminology interchangeably and so confused the litigants that a rehearing was requested. In a second opinion, denying this request, the court made it reasonably clear that it viewed plaintiff's lawsuit as one for negligence, not for battery or some hybrid.[10]

One commentator, surveying both common sense and the cases, has concluded that the basis of liability in the consent-to-treatment area is always malpractice; the battery theory, in his view, should be confined to those rare punch-in-the-nose cases in which a doctor has engaged in intentional conduct in no way related to therapeutics.[11] A somewhat different analysis has been suggested by another writer, Professor Marcus L. Plante of the University of Michigan Law School.[12] He characterizes as battery cases those in which the patient thought he was going to be touched in a certain way but in actuality was subjected to touching of a substantially different character. *Bang* v. *Charles T. Miller Hospital* [13] provides an illustration. Plaintiff in that case thought he was going to be touched in a certain way: that there would be an operation on his prostate gland and possible bladder surgery. Instead, his vasa deferentia were severed. This, in Professor Plante's view, could properly be characterized a battery. In his view, malpractice principles apply when the patient has been touched in exactly the way that was represented but suffered in-

[9] 350 P.2d 1093, *rehearing denied,* 354 P.2d 670 (S. Ct. Kan. 1960).

[10] *Natanson* v. *Kline,* 354 P.2d 670 (S. Ct. Kan. 1960).

[11] McCoid, A. H.: *A Reappraisal of Liability for Unauthorized Medical Treatment,* 41 MINNESOTA LAW REVIEW 381 (1957).

[12] Plante, M. L.: *An Analysis of "Informed Consent,"* 36 FORDHAM LAW REVIEW 639, 650 (1968).

[13] 88 N.W.2d 186 (S. Ct. Minn. 1958).

jurious results arising from some collateral risk about which he was not warned.[14]

The reported decisions bear out the proposition that the "informed-consent" case involves a negligence issue; [15] theories of assault and battery are to be employed only where the defendant doctor has operated on a part of the body as to which no consent was obtained [16] or where the doctor has simply acted viciously and committed a true battery.[17]

The hard questions do not involve the sort of conceptual confusion or legalistic gamesmanship that we have just described. They involve the nature of the duty imposed upon physicians and surgeons by the informed-consent principle and the means open to claimants seeking to establish a breach of that duty. The answers to these questions have special importance in the field of experimental or innovative therapy and will be considered separately.[18] We deal in this section with somewhat less sophisticated and complex factual contexts.

The Elements of the Informed-Consent Concept

It is clear enough that the informed-consent concept separates into two elements: *information* and *consent*. A twofold duty is imposed: (1) the physician must disclose certain information about risks collateral to proposed therapy, and (2) he must not proceed without consent to the risks that have been, or should have been, disclosed. The judicial opinions have been concerned primarily with the duty of information disclosure, but the scope and content of both duties must be considered, since each poses separate and sometimes difficult legal puzzles.

Information Disclosure

The "information" element of informed consent concerns the scope of the physician's duty to disclose risks collateral to a contemplated therapy. This duty becomes relevant when the patient neither knows nor could be expected to know of particular collateral risks. There is no duty to disclose collateral risks that ought to be known by everyone [19] or that are in fact

[14] *E.g., Mitchell* v. *Robinson,* 334 S.W.2d 11 (Mo. App. 1960), *aff'd,* 360 S.W.2d 673 (S. Ct. Mo. 1962) (insulin shock treatment; fractured vertebrae).

[15] See, *e.g., Bowers* v. *Talmage,* 159 So.2d 888 (S. Ct. Fla. 1963); *DiRosse* v. *Wein,* 261 N.Y.S.2d 623 (App. Div. N.Y. 1965); Note, 75 HARVARD LAW REVIEW 1445, 1446 (1962).

[16] *E.g., Mohr* v. *Williams,* 104 N.W. 12 (S. Ct. Minn. 1905); *Darrah* v. *Kite,* 301 N.Y.S.2d 286 (App. Div. N.Y. 1969).

[17] *E.g., Keen* v. *Coleman,* 20 S.E.2d 175 (Ga. App. 1942).

[18] See Chapter 12.

[19] *E.g., Roberts* v. *Young,* 119 N.W.2d 627 (S. Ct. Mich. 1963); *Starnes* v. *Taylor,* 158 S.E.2d 339 (S. Ct. N.S. 1968).

known to the patient because of his prior experience with the therapy.[20]

With respect to risks unknown to the patient, a distinction must be drawn between risks that a physician *could* disclose and risks that he *should* disclose. The cases and commentators have focused on the second facet [21] without emphasizing that the class of risks that *should* be disclosed is limited to those that *could* be disclosed. Again, blurred analysis of the informed-consent concept has sometimes resulted.

Risks That Could Be Disclosed

A consensus could be obtained on the proposition that it is impossible to disclose something of which one is unaware. Literally, the physician's duty to disclose can encompass only those risks known to him at the time he administers a therapy. This point is not made in reported cases because most informed-consent cases have involved collateral risks attaching to widely used therapies; the courts thus were probably correct in assuming that the physician-defendant actually knew of the risks posed.[22] If a risk is not actually known to the physician, however, it is inappropriate to speak solely of a duty to disclose. Instead, the issue is the physician's duty to have known of the risk so that he could have disclosed it. This adds a second dimension to the class of risks that a physician could disclose.

The duty to know of a risk has two branches: the duty to learn of risks known to others in the profession, and the duty to investigate to discover whether there are risks unknown to others in the profession. When a risk is known to some part of the profession but not to the treating physician, the question is whether he should have possessed equal knowledge. Here, familiar notions of a physician's duty provide a relatively easy solution. A physician is duty-bound to have the knowledge of a reasonably well-trained and knowledgeable physician practicing under like circumstances.[23] If the defendant doctor's knowledge of collateral risks did not meet this standard, liability will be based on that shortcoming, not on failure to disclose.

[20] *E.g., Roberts* v. *Wood,* 206 F.Supp. 579 (S.D. Ala. 1962); *Yeates* v. *Harms,* 393 P.2d 982 (S. Ct. Kan. 1964).

[21] See, *e.g.,* Kelly, E. J.: *The Physician, the Patient and the Consent,* 8 KANSAS LAW REVIEW 405 (1960); Powell, R. E.: *Consent to Operative Procedures,* 21 MARYLAND LAW REVIEW 189 (1961); Note, 18 WESTERN RESERVE LAW REVIEW 1089 (1967).

[22] *E.g., DiFilippo* v. *Preston,* 173 A.2d 333 (S. Ct. Del. 1961) (vocal cord paralysis resulting from thyroidectomy); *Bowers* v. *Talmage,* 159 So.2d 888 (Fla. App. 1963) (injury to function of arm due to arteriogram); *Gray* v. *Grunnagle,* 223 A.2d 663 (S. Ct. Pa. 1966) (paralysis of leg resulting from exploratory laminectomy); *Scott* v. *Wilson,* 396 S.W.2d 532 (Tex. Civ. App. 1965), *aff'd,* 412 S.W.2d 299 (S. Ct. Tex. 1967) (loss of hearing resulting from stapedectomy).

[23] See 2 Harper, F. V., and James, F.: THE LAW OF TORTS §§17.1-.2. Little, Brown and Company, Boston, 1956, and Supp. 1968.

The logical first step to liability for failure to disclose a collateral risk is the demonstration that the defendant doctor either knew or, because of the state of knowledge in the profession, should have known of the particular risk. It is fair to impute this breadth of knowledge to the modern-day physician, because medical knowledge is highly accessible, and it is therefore reasonable to say that the class of collateral risks that *could* be disclosed should extend this far. Risks that are unknown to the medical profession pose a different problem that will arise most frequently in cases of innovative or experimental therapy, a subject that we take up in a separate chapter.[24]

Risks That Should Be Disclosed

We have attempted to define those collateral risks of therapy that *could* be disclosed by a medical man. This leaves the crucial additional question, what risks *should* be disclosed to the patient? It is a question difficult to answer and about which there has been much controversy.

A physician probably need not disclose every risk that *could* be disclosed, if only because of the time that would be consumed in describing every remote risk.[25] Less than "total" disclosure will satisfy the law's demands, but how much less? The opinions addressing this issue have been legion, if not always uniform.[26] Some courts require "full" disclosure, which apparently is something vaguely less than "total" disclosure.[27] The great majority of courts follow some professional standard, variously worded.[28] The largest group within this majority would measure the duty

[24] See Chapter 12.

[25] One commentator has convinced himself that the principle of informed consent should be given very narrow application so that a physician could spend less time informing patients of risks and more time treating patients. Karchmer, W. H.: *Informed Consent: A Plaintiff's Medical Malpractice "Wonder Drug,"* 13 MISSOURI LAW REVIEW 29, 41 (1966). The point would seem to be that disclosure of all risks would be prohibitive but that disclosure which will enable the patient to make an intelligent decision is part of the physician's duty.

[26] The following is a sampling of the most recent decisions: *Patrick* v. *Sedwick,* 391 P.2d 453 (S. Ct. Alaska 1964); *Pedesky* v. *Bleiberg,* 59 Cal. Rptr. 294 (Cal. App. 1967); *Ditlow* v. *Kaplan,* 181 So.2d 226 (Fla. App. 1965); *Grosjean* v. *Spencer,* 140 N.W.2d 139 (S. Ct. Iowa 1966); *Aiken* v. *Clary,* 396 S.W.2d 668 (S. Ct. Mo. 1965); *Kaplan* v. *Haines,* 232 A.2d 840 (N.J. Super. 1967); *Mayor* v. *Dowsett,* 400 P.2d 234 (S. Ct. Ore. 1964).

[27] *E.g., Salgo* v. *Leland Stanford Jr. University Board of Trustees,* 317 P.2d 170 (Cal. App. 1957); *Woods* v. *Brumlop,* 377 P.2d 520 (S. Ct. N.M. 1962).

[28] Professor Plante believes that this approach, which requires the production by the plaintiff of expert testimony, now has almost unanimous support in the courts. Plante, M. L.: *An Analysis of "Informed Consent,"* 36 FORDHAM LAW REVIEW 639, 666 (1968). This possibility has been lamented elsewhere. See Comment, *Informed Consent in Medical Malpractice,* 55 CALIFORNIA LAW REVIEW 1396 (1967).

according to the custom and practice of physicians within the "community." [29] Some courts within the majority group state that they would require the disclosure that a reasonable practitioner would make under the circumstances; [30] others require disclosure consistent with "good medical practice." [31] Whatever the verbal formula, these courts regularly require expert testimony to prove a duty of disclosure.[32]

The Professional Standard

The empirical validity and fairness of using a professional standard have been challenged [33]—and defended.[34] It has been questioned, first, whether there in fact exists any discernible professional standard or procedure concerning risk disclosure.[35] Second, use of a professional standard is viewed by some as imposing an unfair burden on claimants to extract expert testimony from some member of the medical profession's asserted "conspiracy of silence." [36] But the principal weakness of the professional standard may be that it confuses two issues in one concept.

The question of what collateral risks of therapy should be disclosed to the patient involves two interests. The first interest is the patient's desire and right, at least under other than life-preserving conditions, to make his own decision whether to undergo a particular therapy.[37] The law, to serve

[29] *E.g., DiFilippo* v. *Preston,* 173 A.2d 333 (S. Ct. Del. 1961); *Roberts* v. *Young* 119 N.W.2d 627 (S. Ct. Mich. 1963); *Kaplan* v. *Haines,* 232 A.2d 840 (N.J. Super. 1967); *Govin* v. *Hunter,* 374 P.2d 421 (S. Ct. Wyo. 1962).

[30] *Ditlow* v. *Kaplan,* 181 So.2d 226 (Fla. App. 1965).

[31] *Shetter* v. *Rochelle,* 409 P.2d 74 (Ariz. App. 1965), *modified,* 411 P.2d 45 (S. Ct. Ariz. 1966).

[32] *E.g., Grosjean* v. *Spencer,* 140 N.W.2d 139 (S. Ct. Iowa 1966); *Haggerty* v. *McCarthy,* 181 N.E.2d 562 (S. Jud. Ct. Mass. 1962); *Roberts* v. *Young,* 119 N.W.2d 627 (S. Ct. Mich. 1963); *Aiken* v. *Clary,* 396 S.W.2d 668 (S. Ct. Mo. 1965).

[33] *E.g.,* Comment, *Informed Consent in Medical Malpractice,* 55 CALIFORNIA LAW REVIEW 1396 (1967).

[34] *E.g.,* Plante, M. L.: *An Analysis of "Informed Consent,"* 36 FORDHAM LAW REVIEW 639 (1968).

[35] *E.g.,* Comment, *Informed Consent in Medical Malpractice,* 55 CALIFORNIA LAW REVIEW 1396 (1967); Comment, *Valid Consent to Medical Treatment: Need the Patient Know?,* 4 DUQUESNE LAW REVIEW 450 (1966); Note, 75 HARVARD LAW REVIEW 1445 (1962).

[36] The term refers to the asserted phenomenon that physicians will avoid testifying against each other in malpractice litigation. See *Huffman* v. *Lindquist,* 234 P.2d 34, 46 (S. Ct. Cal. 1951) (dissent). *Compare* Comment, *Medical Malpractice—Expert Testimony,* 60 NORTHWESTERN UNIV. LAW REVIEW 834, 835–37 (1966).

[37] The most frequently cited statement of this principle is Cardozo's in *Schloendorff* v. *Society of N.Y. Hosp.,* 105 N.E. 92, 93 (Ct. App. N.Y. 1914): "Every human being of adult years and sound mind has a right to determine what shall be done with his own body." See also 2 Harper, F. V., and James, F.: THE LAW OF TORTS §17.1, n. 15, Little, Brown and Company, Boston, 1956, and Supp. 1968.

this interest, must assess the significance of a risk in terms of its potential effect on the patient's decision. The law must, as a matter of policy, set the level of effect which will be deemed legally significant. The traditional legal litmus for measuring the significance of information in decision-making is "materiality." Since the patient's interest in making an informed decision is paramount, the first principle is that all material risks must be disclosed to him. The meaning of materiality will therefore determine the scope of the disclosure duty. Materiality of risk is thus the first issue in the duty to disclose.

The second interest, sometimes at odds with the first,[38] is the physician's desire to withhold information about risks whose disclosure may have a harmful effect on the patient's well-being.[39] The law, to serve this interest, must set boundaries to the exercise of professional judgment in withholding risk information.[40] The exercise of this professional judgment will function as an exception to the basic principle of disclosure of all material risks. The existence of a privilege to withhold disclosure is the second, subordinate issue bound up in the duty to disclose.

Materiality of Risks

The first task, then, is to determine what risks are material and therefore to be disclosed to the patient in the absence of any privilege to withhold. While judicial opinions have not clearly articulated standards of

[38] In 2 Harper, F. V., and James, F.: THE LAW OF TORTS §17.1, n. 15, Little, Brown and Company, Boston, 1956, and Supp. 1968, the authors point out that in the administration of therapy the interests of the physician and the patient coincide in effecting a cure, whereas in the disclosure of risks the physician may be interested in concealing facts that would induce the patient to forego a therapy that the physician desires to administer.

[39] It is accepted in the medical profession that disclosure of risks may harm some patients psychologically or result in an irrational decision to reject therapy because of the anxiety that accompanies treatment. See, *e.g.*, Laufman, H.: *Surgical Judgment,* in CHRISTOPHER'S TEXTBOOK OF SURGERY 1459, 9th ed., Davis, L. E., ed., W. B. Saunders Company, Philadelphia, 1968.; Nemiah, J. C.: *Psychological Aspects of Surgical Practice,* in SURGERY: A CONCISE GUIDE TO CLINICAL PRACTICE 9, 2d ed., Nardi, G. L., and Zuidema, G. D., Little, Brown and Company, Boston, 1965.

[40] Dr. Harold Williams, co-author of Louisell, D. W., and Williams, H.: MEDICAL MALPRACTICE, Matthew Bender, New York, 1969, reportedly would use this interest as a basis for placing the physician in the role of question-answerer, rather than requiring him to initiate disclosure of risks. Williams' principal justifications for this tack are (1) the fact that the patient asks questions indicates that had he been told of the risks he would not have consented, and (2) it shields patients from being told things that they do not want to know. Comment, *Informed Consent in Medical Malpractice,* 55 CALIFORNIA LAW REVIEW 1396, 1407, n. 70 (1967). The first justification seems to ignore the point that the patient must be given the opportunity to decide on the basis of information that usually is *not* within his knowledge. The second justification ignores the awkward circumstance that the patient cannot ordinarily decide whether he *wants* to know something before he knows it.

materiality,[41] two such standards have been advanced by commentators. It has been suggested, at one extreme, that any risk that might have any influence, however slight, on the patient's decision to accept a therapy should be disclosed.[42] At the other extreme, it has been argued that only risks which would cause the patient to forego the therapy need be divulged.[43]

The latter standard is myopic. It does not take into account the fact that although a single risk of a given magnitude may not cause a patient to forego a therapy, two or more such risks in combination might have that result.[44] A standard of materiality limited to risks that, in isolation, would cause a patient to refuse a therapy deprives the patient of the opportunity to contemplate possible combinations of risks. On the other hand, a rule inflexibly dictating disclosure of all risks, however unlikely they are to affect a patient's judgment, is unrealistic. Fortunately, a middle ground is available.

Since the materiality of a risk must be determined in the first instance by the physician, the issue should be approached from his point of view.[45] He must first know how much impact a risk must have on the patient's judgment before its disclosure is dictated. The ideal rule would require

[41] In some of the very few cases in which the defendant physician prevailed, it is difficult to determine whether the court is deciding on the basis (1) that the physician need not have known of it or (2) that even if risk had been disclosed, the patient would have consented to the procedure. See, *e.g.*, *Stottlemire* v. *Cawood*, 213 F. Supp. 897 (D.D.C. 1963) (no liability for failure to disclose 1:800,000 chance of aplastic anemia resulting from injection of chloromycetin for minor ear infection); *Yeates* v. *Harms*, 393 P.2d 982 (S. Ct. Kan. 1964) (no liability for failure to disclose 1.5 percent chance of loss of eye due to infection following cataract surgery); *Starnes* v. *Taylor*, 158 S.E.2d 339 (S. Ct. N.C. 1968) (no liability for failure to disclose 1:250–500 chance of perforation of esophagus during esophagoscopy, the court using language—in one sentence —of due care, and lack of requisite causation).

[42] Oppenheim, M.: *Informed Consent to Medical Treatment*, 11 CLEVELAND-MARSHALL LAW REVIEW 249 (1962); Comment, *Valid Consent to Medical Treatment: Need the Patient Know?*, 4 DUQUESNE LAW REVIEW 450 (1966).

[43] Johnson, R. F.: *Medical Malpractice—Doctrines of Res Ipsa Loquitur and Informed Consent*, 37 UNIV. OF COLORADO LAW REVIEW 169 (1965); Comment, *Informed Consent in Medical Malpractice*, 55 CALIFORNIA LAW REVIEW 1396, 1407, n. 68 (1967); Note, *Physician's Duty to Warn of Possible Adverse Results of Proposed Treatment Depends Upon General Practice Followed by the Medical Profession in the Community*, 75 HARVARD LAW REVIEW 1445 (1962).

[44] Furthermore, this standard of materiality confuses that issue with the issue of causation, *i.e.*, the question whether there existed some causal connection between the failure to disclose and the injury resulting from the occurrence of an undisclosed risk.

[45] This is not to suggest that the standard is subjective to the physician, although some cases decided under the majority disclosure standard might seem to indicate precisely that. The point, rather, is that the standard of materiality cannot be set with the benefit of hindsight. It must consider that the physician must be the first decision-maker and that the correctness of his decision must be assessed on the basis of the data then available to him.

that a risk be disclosed when the patient would attach importance to it, alone or in combination with others, in making his decision whether or not to consent to the treatment in question.[46] But a physician obviously cannot be required to know the inner workings of his patient's mind. He can, however, employ his general experience with people; he can be required to exercise a sense of how the average, reasonable man would probably react. Additionally, he will know, or can reasonably be required to know, his patient's background, present circumstances, and prognosis. In resolving the materiality issue the physician—and the courts—can apply the standard of the reasonable man who finds himself in the position of the patient.

A risk is thus material when a reasonable person, in what the physician knows or should know to be the patient's position, would likely attach significance to the risk or cluster of risks in deciding whether or not to undergo the proposed therapy. And we think that a basic consideration underlying the materiality of all collateral risks of any therapy is the extent of the particular therapy's prior use. As we shall later reiterate, it is reasonable to require that more be disclosed about an innovative therapy than a customary one, since a patient will probably want to consider acceptance of an innovative therapy more thoroughly.[47] In other words, the fact that a therapy is experimental has the effect of increasing the number of potentially material risks; it does not, however, alter the standard of materiality. Beyond this, the basic factors to be considered are the nature of the overall risk, its severity, and the likelihood of occurrence. Each factor must be weighed in combination with the others to determine whether a particular risk is material and therefore subject to disclosure in the absence of a supportable claim of privilege.

Privilege to Withhold Collateral Risk Data

We next consider the extent to which medical judgment can be exercised to withhold material risks from a patient. The cases have frequently stated that a physician is privileged to withhold information on specific risks when disclosure would be detrimental to his patient's well-being.[48]

[46] See Prosser, W. L.: TORTS 554–55, 3d ed. West Publishing Company, St. Paul, 1964.

[47] See Ritts, R. E.: *A Physician's View of Informed Consent in Human Experimentation,* 36 FORDHAM LAW REVIEW 631, 635 (1968); Note, *Experimentation on Human Beings,* 20 STANFORD LAW REVIEW 99, 102–11 (1967).

[48] While the principle is recognized, judicial formulations of it vary. For example, *Lester* v. *Aetna Cas. & Sur. Co.,* 240 F.2d 676, 679 (5th Cir. 1957), holds that there is a limited privilege to withhold disclosure to "avoid frightening" the patient. In *Roberts* v. *Wood,* 206 F. Supp. 579, 583 (S.D. Ala. 1962), the court stated that "the anxiety, apprehension, and fear generated by a full disclosure may have a very detrimental effect on some patients." The most equivocal statement is by the court in *Salgo v. Leland Stanford Jr. University Board of Trustees,* 317 P.2d 170, 181 (Cal.

Although to some it may seem questionable whether disclosure of risk information would result in psychological damage [49] or permanent rejection [50] of a needed therapy with significant frequency, these possibilities comprise recognized assumptions in medical practice [51] and must be accorded consideration in any formulation of disclosure principles.[52]

No resulting exception can be permitted to swallow the rule requiring disclosure of material risks. A physician is not privileged to withhold disclosure whenever the existence of a risk might cause a patient to refuse a therapy which, in the physician's view, would be "good for him." [53] So paternalistic an attitude is unjustifiable; a medical patient is a free agent, entitled—usually—to make even a wrong decision.[54]

It must, however, be conceded that there may be cases in which a patient is irrationally apprehensive or where disclosure of a risk might be psychologically detrimental.[55] In such a case the physician's training and

---

App. 1957): ". . . while the patient's mental and emotional condition is important and in certain cases may be crucial [the privilege to withhold data must be] consistent with the full disclosure of facts necessary to an informed consent." The most unequivocal *dictum* supporting a privilege to withhold is in *Watson* v. *Clutts,* 136 S.E.2d 617, 621 (S. Ct. N.C. 1964), where the court declares that the doctor's primary duty is to do what is best for the patient, even if that means not disclosing a collateral risk of therapy.

[49] It has been suggested that if emotional harm resulted, the disclosing doctor would be liable for resulting damages. Smith, H. W.: *Therapeutic Privilege to Withhold Diagnosis from Patient Sick with Serious or Fatal Illness,* 19 TENNESSEE LAW REVIEW 349, 354 (1946). However, this proposition is currently untenable in most jurisdictions in the United States, where recovery for emotional harm in the absence of some physical impact has been allowed only where a malicious intent or moral outrage was present. See Prosser, W. L.: TORTS §55, 3d ed. West Publishing Company, St. Paul, 1964. But see *Furniss* v. *Fitchett,* [1958] N.Z.L.R. 398 (New Zealand) (plaintiff was a mental patient to whose husband the defendant physician disclosed the painful facts of her condition; plaintiff later learned of the facts disclosed, reacted adversely, and was allowed to recover for emotional injury).

[50] Probably what is directly at stake here is the possibility that the patient will so delay consent that the proposed therapy will become useless.

[51] See, *e.g.,* Laufman, H.: *Surgical Judgment,* in CHRISTOPHER'S TEXTBOOK OF SURGERY 1459, 1461, 9th ed., Davis, L. E., ed. W. B. Saunders Company, Philadelphia, 1968.

[52] Courts appear to accept the proposition without proof, *i.e.,* they take "judicial notice" of it. See, *e.g., Lester* v. *Aetna Cas. & Sur. Co.,* 240 F.2d 676 (5th Cir. 1957); *Salgo* v. *Leland Stanford Jr. University Board of Trustees,* 317 P.2d 170 (Cal. App. 1957); *Watson* v. *Clutts,* 136 S.E.2d 617 (S. Ct. N.C. 1964).

[53] See, *e.g., Yeates* v. *Harms,* 393 P.2d 982 (S. Ct. Kan. 1964).

[54] A possible exception involves life-preserving therapy that is substantially certain of success. See, generally, Comment, *Unauthorized Rendition of Lifesaving Medical Treatment,* 53 CALIFORNIA LAW REVIEW 860 (1965).

[55] See Nemiah, J. C.: *Psychological Aspects of Surgical Practice,* in SURGERY: A CONCISE GUIDE TO CLINICAL PRACTICE 9, 2d ed., Nardi, G. L., and Zuidema, G. D., Little, Brown and Company, Boston, 1965.

responsibilities may well warrant acting on the basis of his judgment and not the patient's. The doctor will be permitted to establish the medical propriety of his decision not to disclose the collateral risk. He must do so in terms of the patient in question. The relevant question is whether the physician acted in accordance with sound medical judgment when confronted by risk data that he could reasonably conclude would pose a substantial threat to the patient's well-being if disclosure were made.

Consent

The decided cases have paid scant attention to the consent element of the informed-consent concept. This element has seldom been reached because most of the reported litigations have involved only the disclosure issue.[56] Some discussion is essential here, however, since the physician can ordinarily proceed with therapy only after the patient's consent to confront each material risk disclosed.

Consent connotes the dual ingredients of *awareness* and *assent*. To establish consent to a risk it must be shown that the patient was aware of the risk and assented to the encountering of it. The more difficult question involves the kind of evidence that will be admitted at trial to establish these two elements.

It is obvious that a risk must be understandably communicated before the element of awareness can be demonstrated.[57] Communication involves the manner in which the physician must disclose risks—the vocabulary that he must adopt and the degree of elaboration in which he must engage. While the cases rightly indicate that technical language will not ordinarily suffice to disclose a risk to an untutored layman,[58] they are unclear as to what more is required. The physician could be required, absolutely, to use language that his patient will in fact understand. Such a requirement, again, would demand clairvoyance on the part of doctors. Furthermore, any such requirement would be semantically impossible. One

[56] The disclosure cases, of course, are numerous. The following is a representative sample: *Hall* v. *United States,* 136 F. Supp. 187 (W. D. La. 1955), *aff'd,* 234 F.2d 811 (5th Cir. 1956); *Dunlap* v. *Marine,* 51 Cal. Rptr. 158 (Cal. App. 1966); *Block* v. *McVay,* 126 N.W.2d 808 (S. Ct. S.D. 1964); *Scott* v. *Wilson,* 396 S.W.2d 532 (Tex. Civ. App. 1965), *aff'd,* 412 S.W.2d 299 (S. Ct. Tex. 1967).

[57] It is for this reason that statements in standardized consent forms that the patient has been informed of "all" risks are unavailing. Awareness requires that specific risks have been communicated in fact. See, *e.g., Rogers* v. *Lumbermen's Mut. Cas. Co.,* 118 So.2d 649 (S. Ct. La. 1960); *Bowers* v. *Talmage,* 159 So.2d 888 (Fla. App. 1963); *Corn* v. *French,* 289 P.2d 173 (S. Ct. Nev. 1955). Examples of suitably flexible consent forms are set forth in Long, R. H.: THE PHYSICIAN AND THE LAW 50–54, 3d ed. Appleton-Century-Crofts, New York, 1968. See also A.M.A. MEDICO-LEGAL FORMS WITH LEGAL ANALYSIS 30–43 (1961).

[58] See, *e.g., Corn* v. *French,* 289 P.2d 173 (S. Ct. Nev. 1955).

can only communicate in terms one believes the listener will comprehend, based on one's perception of the listener's capacity. This means that the doctor should be required to disclose collateral risks in terms that a reasonable man would believe the particular patient would understand. The disclosure should elaborate, in the same sort of terms, the nature and severity of the risk and the likelihood of its occurrence.[59] In short, the physician, employing language within the grasp of the patient, should paint a complete picture of the situation facing the patient.[60]

Unfortunately, a few courts apparently adopt the position that only the patient's subjective state of mind should be considered in establishing the elements of awareness and assent.[61] Under this approach, the physician could proceed with treatment only where the patient subjectively understood a given risk and intended to manifest his assent to encountering it. One difficulty with this view is that the patient's testimony, undeniably admissible in evidence at trial, would in fact control the issue of consent. And the trial lawyer's healthy cynicism tells him that claimant's testimony is sometimes susceptible to modification based upon hindsight. Another difficulty with this approach is that it leaves no room for reasonable mistakes by the physician; he assumes the risk of incorrectly concluding that the patient understood and assented to the risks communicated. As the whole history of contract law attests, legal relationships based upon communication ought not to depend on the vagaries of the parties' subjective understanding and intent.[62]

The basic question in establishing consent is whether the physician was reasonable in proceeding after a risk was disclosed to the patient in a generally understandable manner. An objective test is therefore appropriate. The proper question is whether a reasonable man would conclude from the patient's behavior that he was aware of the particular risk and manifested a willingness to encounter it. The patient's testimony would be

[59] See Davis, A. G.: *Duty of Doctor to Inform Patient of Risks of Treatment,* 34 SOUTHERN CALIFORNIA LAW REVIEW 217 (1961); see also *Kenny* v. *Lockwood,* [1932] 1 D.L.R. 507 (Canada).

[60] The medical profession has seemed entirely willing to accept this requirement. See, *e.g.*, Laufman, H.: *Surgical Judgment,* in CHRISTOPHER'S TEXTBOOK OF SURGERY 1459, 1461, 9th ed., Davis, L. E., ed., W. B. Saunders Company, Philadelphia, 1968: "A patient is entitled to know everything pertinent both to his condition and to the course of probable treatment. . . . Professional jargon has no place in talking with a patient; it is designed to impress rather than to inform. Oversimplification is equally out of taste; it is a condescension the patient is quick to sense and which he may justifiably resent."

[61] See, *e.g.*, *DiFilippo* v. *Preston,* 173 A.2d 333 (S. Ct. Del. 1961); *Gray* v. *Gunnagle,* 223 A.2d 663 (S. Ct. Pa. 1966).

[62] See generally, 1 Corbin, A. L.: CONTRACTS §107, West Publishing Company, St. Paul, 1963; 1 Williston, S.: CONTRACTS §21, 3d ed., Jaeger, W. H. E., ed., Baker, Voorhis & Co., Inc., Mount Kisco, N.Y., 1957.

relevant but not conclusive. All of the circumstances of the communication and the patient's reaction should be considered by the fact-finder in arriving at a judgment as to whether a reasonable man would conclude that the elements of awareness and assent were present.[63]

So far our discussion of consent has assumed that the physician will disclose material risks and then wait more or less passively until the patient has manifested his understanding of and assent to the proposed therapy. In fact, this may not often be the physician's way. He will probably engage in a measure of salesmanship to persuade his patient to consent, particularly when time is short and treatment must be commenced quickly. The permissible limits of this sort of persuasion are difficult to define short of the point where it might legitimately be said that the patient's consent was actively induced by the physician when, because of the risks involved, he would not otherwise have consented. Such coercion will always be difficult to prove. This much can be said, however: the physician, who may be permitted a privilege to withhold risk-disclosures because of his patient's fears, should be slow to use those same fears to induce consent to treatment.[64]

Causation

Where the physician has breached his duty to disclose, later development of a material risk is insufficient, in and of itself, to fix liability for damages. There must have been some causal connection between the failure to disclose and the alleged injury resulting from the occurrence of the undisclosed risk.[65]

Most commentators assume that this casuation issue can be resolved only by testing the credibility of plaintiff's testimony to the effect that he

[63] Here again the keeping by the physician of adequate and accurate records may prove crucial. See A.M.A., REPORT OF THE COMMITTEE ON MEDICOLEGAL PROBLEMS, PROFESSIONAL LIABILITY AND THE PHYSICIAN 11, 25 (1963).

[64] But the unusual case of *Kraus* v. *Spielberg*, 236 N.Y.S.2d 143 (S. Ct. N.Y. 1962), should be considered. Plaintiff in that case had a tuberculosis phobia as well as acute stomach pains from some undisclosed source. Defendant doctor, to induce plaintiff's consent to chemotherapy for her stomach condition, told her that she had "tuberculosis germs" in her stomach. Although there were apparently unpleasant side effects, the trial court directed a verdict for the defendant physician on the ground that his statement was necessary to induce plaintiff to undergo treatment.

[65] This fundamental principle of tort law has been alluded to more frequently by commentators than courts in the medical malpractice area. See, *e.g.*, Johnson, R. F.: *Medical Malpractice—Doctrines of Res Ipsa Loquitur and Informed Consent,* 37 UNIV. OF COLORADO LAW REVIEW 182 (1965); Comment, *Informed Consent in Medical Malpractice,* 55 CALIFORNIA LAW REVIEW 1396 (1967). The only reported medical cases to state the causation principle clearly are *Shetter* v. *Rochelle,* 409 P.2d 74, *modified,* 411 P.2d 45 (S. Ct. Ariz. 1965), and *Aiken* v. *Clary,* 396 S.W.2d 668 (S. Ct. Mo. 1965).

would not have consented to the therapy at all had the risk that materialized been disclosed.[66] This assumption seems unsound for two reasons. First, it again puts the physician at the mercy of his patient's hindsight. Quite plainly, the patient's trial testimony will tend to take into account the occurrence of the risk, whereas the point in time relevant to the question of causation is the juncture at which his consent was given. Second, this solution does not consider the issue of materiality as we have previously defined it.

While it is true that the duty of risk-disclosure principally serves the patient's interest in deciding whether to undergo a therapy, it must be realized that whether he would have refused the therapy in the face of known collateral risks poses an altogether hypothetical question.[67] It goes like this: "Viewed from the point in time at which he had to decide, would the patient have decided differently had he known something that he did not know?" The answer to this hypothetical question, in the context of courtroom litigation, must be determined by the fact-finder (usually a jury), whether or not the plaintiff's own testimony is accorded any weight. Because any answer to the hypothetical question—"What would the patient in fact have done?"—can only be a guess, posing the causation issue in that form does not promote rational decision-making. Additionally, plaintiff's testimony on the issue will be assessed primarily on the basis of its reasonableness in the fact-finder's view. Accordingly, to provide a realistic framework for rational decision, it would seem that the causation issue should be posed to the jurors in terms of the effect of disclosure or nondisclosure of all material risks on a reasonable person in the plaintiff's position.[68]

[66] See, *e.g.*, Plante, M. L.: *An Analysis of "Informed Consent,"* 36 FORDHAM LAW REVIEW 639 (1968); Comment, *Informed Consent in Medical Malpractice,* 55 CALIFORNIA LAW REVIEW 1396 (1967). The assumption was undoubtedly inspired by such cases as *DiFilippo* v. *Preston,* 173 A.2d 333 (S. Ct. Del. 1961), and *Natanson* v. *Kline,* 350 P.2d 670 (S. Ct. Kan. 1960).

[67] The point is most clearly made in *Aiken* v. *Clary,* 396 S.W.2d 668, 676 (S. Ct. Mo. 1965), the only reported informed consent case in which the patient, having died before trial, did not testify in his own behalf. The court rejected an argument by the defendant physician that the jury could not resolve the causation issue in the absence of the patient's testimony. The court said: "The matter of causation still must be submitted to the jury. Obviously, if the jury was convinced from all the evidence that a more complete disclosure would have made no difference to the plaintiff and that he still would have consented to the therapy or procedure, then plaintiff has not established a right to recovery. . . . On the other hand, a jury could find from all the facts and circumstances in a particular case that had plaintiff been properly informed he would not have consented to the treatment, and this is so even though plaintiff did not so testify."

[68] The court in *Aiken* v. *Clary,* 396 S.W.2d at 676, seems to have adopted this approach.

The causation issue, then, is resolved on the basis of all material risks disclosed or undisclosed. If disclosure of all material risks would have made no difference in the decision of a reasonable person in the position of the particular plaintiff, there is no causal connection between nondisclosure and the plaintiff's injury.[69] Probably the only situation in which the element of causation would become irrelevant would be where death was substantially certain and the proposed therapy had an extremely high probability of success. There is authority that the physician can proceed with treatment in such a situation even in the face of the patient's adamant refusal of consent.[70]

Damages

Only one appellate court has considered the measure of damages for failure to obtain informed consent. In *Natanson* v. *Kline*[71] the court, in the sort of judicial aside that lawyers refer to as *dicta,* stated that the appropriate measure is the loss resulting from the risk that materialized, whether or not the therapy was performed carefully.

This measure of damages would be correct if there were malpractice in the performance of the therapy as well as the absence of informed consent. It seems an unduly harsh measure, however, where the physician's only shortcoming was failure to obtain informed consent. The basis of liability in such a case is that a reasonable person in the patient's position would not have undergone the procedure had he been informed of a material risk which in fact occurred. That being the basis of liability, it would appear that plaintiff's recovery should be the monetary measure of the difference between his condition with no treatment and his condition after the undisclosed risk materialized.

[69] It will be perceived that the causation issue is not identical with the problem of materiality. The materiality of risks must be determined separately and individually, while the issue of causation encompasses *all* risks held to be material. The fact that one undisclosed risk is material does not necessarily force the conclusion that its disclosure would cause refusal of the proposed therapy.

[70] See, *e.g., Application of President of Georgetown College, Inc.*, 331 F.2d 1000 (D.C. Cir.), *cert. denied,* 377 U.S. 987 (1964) (blood transfusions authorized over protests of Jehovah's Witness, mother of 7-month-old child); *Raleigh Fitkin-Paul Morgan Memorial Hosp.* v. *Anderson,* 201 A.2d 537 (S. Ct. N.J.), *cert. denied,* 377 U.S. 985 (1964) (blood transfusion authorized during delivery for a pregnant Jehovah's Witness); *Leigh* v. *Gladstone,* [1909] 26 T.L.R. 139 (fasting suffragette prisoner forcibly fed by prison officials to preserve life). *Contra: In re* Estate of Brooks, 205 N.E.2d 435 (S. Ct. Ill. 1965) (sustaining first amendment right of Jehovah's Witness to refuse treatment); *Erickson* v. *Dilgard,* 252 N.Y.S.2d 705 (S. Ct. N.Y. 1962) (refusal of treatment held a medical decision that court cannot reverse). See, generally, Comment, *Unauthorized Rendition of Lifesaving Medical Treatment,* 53 CALIFORNIA LAW REVIEW 860 (1965).

[71] 350 P.2d 670 (S. Ct. Kan. 1960).

CONSENT IN EMERGENCY SITUATIONS

The informed-consent problem has been thought to be at its most complicated in emergency care situations, when the physician may be confronted by conscious, unconscious, or semiconscious adults and minors and persons who are mentally incompetent.[72] And it is true that every admittance to an emergency ward poses potentially unique consent problems. The applicable law, however, is quite simple and workable.

Conscious, Mentally Competent Adults

When a conscious, competent adult patient enters the hospital emergency room, the medical personnel in charge should, if possible, obtain a written [73] consent to emergency care. A person who is twenty-one years old and of sound mind is presumptively qualified to give or withhold consent.[74] This presumption is rebuttable; it falls away in the face of evidence that the person was delirious or comatose,[75] intoxicated,[76] under the influence of drugs,[77] or otherwise incapable of exercising rational judgment. Under these exceptional circumstances the law will infer consent if the patient's life was at stake and it was not practicable to obtain consent from some authorized person other than the patient. The fact that a patient is being cared for gratuitously, or at the expense of some other person, does not obviate the necessity for securing his consent to treatment.[78] The consent of a husband to an operation on his wife is not essential; the wife's consent is sufficient.[79] Nonetheless, it is the better part of wisdom to have the spouse join in the consent, especially if the contemplated operation involves danger to life, may limit or destroy sexual functions,[80] or may result in the death of an unborn infant.

[72] See, *e.g.*, Chayet, N. L.: LEGAL IMPLICATIONS OF EMERGENCY CARE 96. Appleton-Century-Crofts, New York, 1969.

[73] Theoretically, oral consent would be sufficient. See, *e.g.*, *Maercklein* v. *Smith*, 266 P.2d 1095 (S. Ct. Colo. 1954). But, because of the practical difficulty of making effective proof at trial that oral consent was given, physicians are well advised to obtain written witnessed consents.

[74] See, *e.g.*, *Knowles* v. *Blue*, 95 So. 481 (S. Ct. Ala. 1923); *Meek* v. *City of Loveland*, 276 Pac. 30 (S. Ct. Colo. 1929); *Pratt* v. *Davis*, 79 N.E. 562 (S. Ct. Ill. 1906).

[75] *Arballo* v. *Nielson*, 166 P.2d 621 (Cal. App. 1946).

[76] *Barker* v. *Heaney*, 82 S.W.2d 417 (Tex. Civ. App. 1935).

[77] *Wheeler* v. *Barker*, 208 P.2d 68 (Cal. App. 1949); *Moore* v. *Webb*, 345 S.W.2d 239 (S. Ct. Mo. 1961).

[78] *Bonner* v. *Moran*, 126 F.2d 121 (D.C. Cir. 1941).

[79] *Kritzer* v. *Citron*, 224 P.2d 808 (Cal. App. 1950).

[80] As a legal proposition, however, the spouse's consent is not essential even in the case of a sterilization operation. See, *e.g.*, *Burroughs* v. *Crichton*, 48 App. D.C. 596 (1919); *State* v. *Housekeeper*, 16 Atl. 382 (S. Ct. Md. 1889); *Rytkonen* v. *Lojacono*, 257 N.W. 703 (S. Ct. Mich. 1934).

If it is not feasible to secure written consent to emergency care, the patient should be requested to execute an emergency care acknowledgment and referral notice after treatment but before being discharged. The patient acknowledges receipt of specified emergency care, including the taking of any x-rays, and the fact that described findings were made. He affirms also his understanding that this emergency care was not intended to constitute a definitive diagnosis or complete treatment. Finally, he acknowledges that he has been instructed to obtain continued and adequate diagnosis and care from a physician of his choice.

Unconscious Adults

The emergency ward physician is often confronted by the semicomatose or unconscious adult. It is settled that in this situation the doctor is legally entitled—even obligated—to provide all life-supportive efforts that appear reasonably necessary.[81] The law simply infers consent to such emergency procedures. (There is probably also an implied obligation on the patient's part to pay for the emergency services rendered.[82])

Conscious Minors

As a general rule, minors—usually those under the age of twenty-one—are not empowered to give or withhold consent to therapy. It is usually necessary to secure consent to treatment from the infant's next of kin or guardian. However, it is clear in the United States that necessary emergency care can be given to a minor even though not specifically authorized by a parent or guardian. For example, in a Louisiana case [83] a seven-year-old child died while anesthetized for treatment of a broken arm. An unsuccessful effort had been made to reach the child's mother at her place of employment. In subsequent litigation, based on the notion that an unauthorized procedure had been performed, the court held for the defendant doctor on the ground that an emergency existed. A liberal view of what constitutes an emergency may have been involved in a New York case [84] in which a young man over twenty years of age had broken his ankle during a baseball game. The defendant surgeon had advised him that it would be necessary to anesthetize him before the ankle could be treated. The youth responded, "Well, if you think best, go ahead"—and the surgeon did. The young man's father later brought suit on a battery theory, although the surgeon had caused no physical injury to the patient, alleging that the anesthetic had been administered without his consent.

[81] See Regan, L. J.: DOCTOR AND PATIENT AND THE LAW 64, 2d ed. The C. V. Mosby Company, St. Louis, 1949.

[82] See *In re* Crisans' Estate, 107 N.W.2d 907 (S. Ct. Mich. 1961).

[83] *Wells* v. *McGehee*, 39 So.2d 196 (S. Ct. La. 1949).

[84] *Sullivan* v. *Montgomery*, 279 N.Y.S. 575 (S. Ct. N.Y. 1935).

The court, however, concluded that the operation had been necessary to halt needless pain and held in favor of the surgeon. It is fairly clear that no true emergency existed. The court was undoubtedly impressed by the fact that this "infant" was only eight months shy of being twenty-one.

A few courts have decided that a consent given by one technically a minor is nonetheless effective if he was sufficiently mature to comprehend the full significance of the proposed therapy, especially if the contemplated procedure is a simple one. In one Mississippi case,[85] for example, a seventeen-year-old boy was held to have the capacity to consent to a smallpox vaccination, which the court described as "usually a very simple operation" and one that the boy had sufficient intelligence to understand. Similarly, in an Ohio case [86] it was decided that an eighteen-year-old could effectively consent to simple plastic surgery to her nose. In a Michigan case [87] it was concluded that a nineteen-year-old boy had the legal capacity to consent to a local anesthetic in preference to the general anesthetic that had been specified by his mother. The case of *Bonner* v. *Moran* [88] provides a contrast. There a fifteen-year-old boy served, voluntarily, as a skin and blood donor in a plastic surgery procedure. The consent of his parents had not been obtained. The trial judge concluded that a boy of fifteen could consent on his own behalf; on appeal, a federal court held that the parents' consent should have been secured. The appellate court indicated that only a mature person could fully comprehend the character and consequences of the procedure in question. There is language in the court's opinion that indicates that there might have been a different result had the boy been closer to majority or, for that matter, had the procedure been for his benefit rather than another's.[89]

Some judicial decisions, and much common sense, strongly suggest that, when possible, some effort should be made to reach a minor's parents or guardian prior to the performance of a serious emergency operation.[90] This effort, which could lead to authorized consent for the operation after an explanation of its character and likely consequences, need not be extensive. A telephone call to an apparently correct number would suffice; if there were no answer or the physician or hospital were otherwise

[85] *Gulf & Ship Island R.R.* v. *Sullivan,* 119 So. 501 (S. Ct. Miss. 1928).

[86] *Lacey* v. *Laird,* 139 N.E.2d 25 (S. Ct. Ohio 1956).

[87] *Bishop* v. *Shurly,* 211 N.W. 75 (S. Ct. Mich. 1926).

[88] 126 F.2d 121 (D.C. Cir. 1941).

[89] There may also be instances in which a minor cannot effectively *withhold* consent to treatment. See, *e.g., Ollet* v. *Pittsburgh, C.C. & St. L. Ry.,* 50 Atl. 1010 (S. Ct. Pa. 1902), in which a seventeen-year-old boy's foot had been crushed. The defendant doctor was held justified in amputating the foot over the boy's protestations that he wished to be treated by his own physician.

[90] See, *e.g., Jackovach* v. *Yocom,* 237 N.W. 444 (S. Ct. Iowa 1931); *Luka* v. *Lowrie,* 136 N.W. 1106 (S. Ct. Mich. 1912).

unable to locate the parents or guardian, it would be lawful to proceed with the operation.[91] It might in fact be a ground for malpractice liability that a hospital or individual physician delayed emergency treatment unduly while seeking authorized consent to it.[92]

Unconscious Minors

Almost everything said in the preceding paragraphs is equally applicable to cases involving unconscious and semiconscious minors. There is, in law, no difference between a conscious and an unconscious minor. An effort should be made to contact the parents or guardian but under no circumstances should life-supportive measures be delayed.

Mentally Incompetent Adults

It has been said, correctly, that "The consent of a person *non compos mentis* is no consent at law." [93] The consent of one who stands in the position of guardian is required for an operation on a mentally incompetent person.[94] Again, the solitary exception is the emergency situation.[95] When medical personnel have reason to believe that their emergency patient is mentally incompetent, he should be treated much as a child would be.[96] While a prolonged search for the guardian or next of kin is to be avoided, some effort to secure authorized consent to treatment should be undertaken.

Refusal of Consent to Emergency Treatment

We have previously mentioned the existence of legal authority for the performance of lifesaving treatment even in the face of adamant refusal by the patient or someone acting on his behalf.[97] The situation is rare; it arises most frequently in connection with members of the Jehovah's Witness religious sect who refuse authorization for blood transfusions on the basis of a literal reading of the Bible's prohibition against blood-drinking.

Courts, often aided by legislative enactments, are not usually reluctant to order transfusions and other life-preserving procedures when an infant,

[91] *Ibid.*

[92] See Chayet, N. L.: LEGAL IMPLICATIONS OF EMERGENCY CARE 102. Appleton-Century-Crofts, New York, 1969.

[93] Regan, L. J.: DOCTOR AND PATIENT AND THE LAW 61, 2d ed. The C. V. Mosby Company, St. Louis, 1949.

[94] This may be a spouse or some other person who has been appointed legal guardian. See, *e.g., Farber* v. *Olkon,* 254 P.2d 520 (S. Ct. Cal. 1953); *Rothe* v. *Hull,* 180 S.W.2d 7 (S. Ct. Mo. 1944).

[95] *Pratt* v. *Davis,* 79 N.E. 562 (Ill. App. 1906).

[96] *Rogers* v. *Sells,* 61 P.2d 1018 (S. Ct. Okla. 1936).

[97] See footnote 70, this chapter.

born or unborn, is involved and a parent or guardian has withheld consent. Statutes in some states empower the juvenile court to order necessary medical and surgical care for a minor despite the lack of consent of the child's parents or guardian.[98] In other jurisdictions, courts have relied on general statutes dealing with neglected and dependent children in depriving parents of custody and appointing guardians who are authorized to supply necessary medical attention.[99]

Courts do not lightly breach the parents' right to the custody of their children, of course. They will weigh the risks posed by the proposed therapy against the dangerousness of the infant's condition. Thus blood transfusions have been judicially ordered, over parents' objections, for children afflicted with an Rh complication.[100] Courts realize that such a transfusion poses only minimal risks while, without it, the child will almost certainly die or suffer from impaired mentality.[101]

A more complex situation is posed by the adult, not pregnant, who refuses lifesaving procedures. It has generally been thought that a patient has a right to refuse consent to lifesaving treatment.[102] In a few quite recent cases, however, a court has ordered life-preserving treatment for a nonconsenting adult.[103]

Hospital administrators should ascertain the location of the local judge with jurisdiction to issue orders of the sort discussed in this section.[104] A judge having jurisdiction—that is, power—to issue such orders can do so at any time of the day or night, without regard to whether he is in his courtroom at the time.

[98] See, *e.g.* *In re* Vasko, 263 N.Y.S. 552 (App. Div. N.Y. 1933), upholding the validity of New York's statute. See also MICH. STAT. ANN. §§27.3178 (598.2(b)(1), 27.3178 (598.18)(h) (Supp. 1968).

[99] *E.g., People ex rel. Wallace* v. *Labrenz,* 104 N.E.2d 769 (S. Ct. Ill. 1952); *Morrison* v. *State,* 252 S.W.2d 97 (S. Ct. Mo. 1952); *Mitchell* v. *Davis,* 205 S.W.2d 812 (Tex. Civ. App. 1947).

[100] *E.g., People ex rel. Wallace* v. *Labrenz,* 104 N.E.2d 769 (S. Ct. Ill. 1952); *Morrison* v. *State,* 252 S.W.2d 97 (S. Ct. Mo. 1952). See also *In re* Seiferth, 127 N.Y.S.2d 63 (S. Ct. N.Y. 1954), in which a parent had refused permission for corrective operations for a twelve-year-old boy with a congenital harelip and cleft palate. The court held that the boy should be permitted, without parental interference, to determine his own fate. The court added that for a younger child it would itself have ordered the operations.

[101] But see *In re* Hudson, 126 P.2d 765 (S. Ct. Wash. 1942) (court refused order for amputation of minor's enlarged arm; operation too grave a threat to life).

[102] See, *e.g., Schloendorff* v. *Society of N.Y. Hospital,* 105 N.E. 92 (Ct. App. N.Y. (1914).

[103] *E.g., Application of President of Georgetown College, Inc.,* 331 F.2d 1000 (D.C. Cir.), *cert. denied,* 377 U.S. 978 (1964); *United States* v. *George,* 239 F. Supp. 752 (D. Conn. 1965).

[104] It will usually, but not always, be the judge(s) of the probate court.

EXTENSION OF THE FIELD OF OPERATION

Somewhat analogous to the law of the emergency ward, outlined in the preceding section, is the body of law governing extension of the field of operation in the course of surgery. In discussing the role of assault and battery theory in the medical-legal field, we previously mentioned one writer's view that its application should be restricted to those situations in which the defendant surgeon operated on a part of the body as to which no consent had been obtained.[105] His analysis was founded upon the common law rule that the right of a physician to extend an operation beyond that which has been authorized is limited to emergency situations demanding immediate action.[106] In other words, the only circumstance in which a surgeon can go beyond the agreed field of surgery is where he comes upon a condition posing a threat to the patient's life.[107] This restrictive rule was formulated prior to the discovery of anesthesia, when the patient frequently remained conscious throughout the surgical ordeal and could be called upon to assent to expansions of the operative field.[108] Furthermore, even if he lapsed into unconsciousness, the surgical patient in earlier times was often surrounded by family and friends who could speak for him. Today the common law rule seems too rigid; it is not surprising that inroads upon it are being made.

In the first place, courts can probably be counted upon to accord a liberal interpretation to the concept of emergency.[109] This is entirely justifiable where a surgeon has conformed to accepted medical practice in extending the operation, even where the additional procedure could not properly be termed life-preserving.

Two cases will serve as contrasting examples. As a result of an injury, the patient in *Franklin* v. *Peabody*[110] had a stiff finger. He was anes-

[105] See Plante, M. L.: *An Analysis of "Informed Consent,"* 36 FORDHAM LAW REVIEW 639, 650 (1968).

[106] *E.g. Rogers* v. *Lumbermen's Mut. Cas. Co.*, 119 So.2d 649 (S. Ct. Ga. 1960); *Wells* v. *Van Nort*, 125 N.E. 910 (S. Ct. Ohio 1919).

[107] See, *e.g.*, *Emery* v. *Fisher*, 148 Atl. 677 (S. Ct. Me. 1930); *Robinson* v. *Wirts*, 127 A.2d 706 (S. Ct. Pa. 1956).

[108] See *McGuire* v. *Rix*, 225 N.W. 120 (S. Ct. Neb. 1929).

[109] See, *e.g.*, *Bennan* v. *Parsonnet*, 83 Atl. 948 (N.J. App. 1912); *King* v. *Carney*, 204 Pac. 270 (S. Ct. Okla. 1922). The very treatment consented to may generate an emergency. For example, in *Delahunt* v. *Finton*, 221 N.W. 168 (S. Ct. Mich. 1928), a bougie that had been passed through plaintiff's urethral canal during a diagnostic examination, performed under anesthesia, looped so that it could not be withdrawn. It was held that the surgeon conducting the examination could operate to remove the bougie without waiting for the patient's consent. See also, *e.g.*, *Higley* v. *Jeffrey*, 8 P.2d 96 (S. Ct. Wyo. 1932) (incision reopened to recover needle; held incidental to and part of authorized operation).

[110] 228 N.W. 681 (S. Ct. Mich. 1930).

thetized and an operation to correct the condition was undertaken. During the operation it was discovered that additional fascia lata was needed to separate the superficial and deep tendons. The operating surgeon removed some from the plaintiff's thigh. Claiming that this caused a muscle hernia, plaintiff brought an assault and battery action against him. He contended, uncontrovertibly, that the cutting in his thigh was without his consent. The trial court entered judgment for the defendant surgeon, but on appeal the plaintiff obtained a reversal of this decision. The Supreme Court of Michigan stated the rule in such cases:

> . . . if in the course of an operation to which the patient has consented a physician discovers conditions not anticipated, before it was commenced, and which if not removed, will endanger the life of the patient, he will, although no express consent be obtained or given, be justified in extending the operation to remove and overcome them. . . .

The court held, however, that since, in the case before it, the operation being performed on the plaintiff had been of a minor character and no genuine emergency had developed, the taking of tissue from the thigh was unauthorized and thus actionable. The court held this despite its realization that it had been "good surgery" for the defendant surgeon to proceed in the manner described.

The case of *Barnett* v. *Bachrach,*[111] although involving a curious twist, is more typical. In this case the plaintiff complained of pains in the lower abdominal area and the defendant surgeon diagnosed a tubular pregnancy. He operated but when he opened the patient's abdomen he discovered instead that she had a normal pregnancy but also an acute appendicitis. He concluded, of course, that the appendicitis was the cause of the patient's pain and immediately removed her appendix. She experienced an uneventful recovery and later delivered a normal baby. The plaintiff's husband, apparently seeking to achieve new heights of penuriousness, refused to pay the surgeon's fee, asserting that the appendectomy had been unauthorized. A judgment in favor of the surgeon was affirmed on the ground that the surgeon was faced with an emergency situation giving rise to implied consent.[112]

A second and more commendably candid judicial approach to this problem flatly rejects the old common law rule. A few courts have held that the situations in which a surgeon can properly extend an operation without explicit consent are not restricted to emergencies. Under this more enlightened view a surgeon is empowered by law to extend the

[111] 34 A.2d 626 (Mun. Ct. App. D.C. 1943).

[112] See also *Jackovach* v. *Yocom,* 237 N.W. 444 (S. Ct. Iowa 1931); *Stone* v. *Goodman,* 271 N.Y.S. 500 (App. Div. N.Y. 1934).

operation to any abnormal condition discovered during the operation if doing so is advisable for the patient's welfare and comports with the accepted practice of surgeons generally.[113] For example, the court in *Barnett* v. *Bachrach* [114] asked the following rhetorical questions: "What was the surgeon to do? Should he have left her on the operating table, her abdomen exposed, and gone in search of her husband to obtain express authority to remove the appendix? Should he have closed the incision on the inflamed appendix and subjected the patient, pregnant as she was, to a general spread of the poison in her system, or to the alternative danger and shock of a second independent operation to remove the appendix? Or should he have done what his professional judgment dictated . . . ?"

It is unarguable that the court in *Barnett* v. *Bachrach* would have found itself in agreement with later decisions such as that reached in the case of *Kennedy* v. *Parrott* [115] in 1956. There the defendant surgeon, while performing an authorized appendectomy, found enlarged follicle cysts on the patient's ovaries and punctured them. The patient thereafter developed phlebitis and brought a malpractice action on the theory that her infection stemmed from the puncturing of the cysts. The trial court dismissed the case and the North Carolina Supreme Court affirmed, holding that a surgeon is authorized to extend the operation to any abnormal condition in the vicinity of the original incision, when, in his informed judgment, it is essential to the patient's welfare and constitutes generally approved surgical practice. This decision reflected the court's realization that where an internal operation is required, both doctor and patient comprehend that no definite diagnosis is possible until the incision has been made. Since the patient is under a general anesthetic and unable to engage in conversation, and there is ordinarily no one present to consent on his behalf, he inferentially consents to necessary extensions of the field of surgery.

Occasionally, of course, actual consent to a diagnostic operation—the so-called exploratory operation—can be found in the patient's language even though it was less than precise or explicit. The key case is *King* v. *Carney*.[116] The plaintiff had been advised by her family doctor that a lacerated uterus was causing her frequent miscarriages. Later she told the defendant surgeon that she desired, as she put it, to be "fixed up" so that she could have children. When he operated the surgeon discovered that the patient's ovaries were infected and that her fallopian tubes were sealed, with the consequence that she could never hope to bear children.

[113] *E.g.*, *Bennan* v. *Parsonnet*, 83 Atl. 948 (S. Ct. N.J. 1912); *Kennedy* v. *Parrott*, 90 S.E.2d 754 (S. Ct. N.C. 1956).
[114] 34 A.2d 626, 629 (D.D.C. 1943).
[115] 90 S.E.2d 754 (S. Ct. N.C. 1956).
[116] 204 Pac. 270 (S. Ct. Okla. 1922).

He then removed the diseased organs, although this was not necessary for the protection of the patient's life or general health. The Supreme Court of Oklahoma interpreted the plaintiff's request to be "fixed up" as authority for a diagnostic operation and such additional surgery as might be necessary to rectify her condition. Since her condition before the removal of the diseased organs already made it impossible for her to bear children, and this condition could not be reversed, the surgeon was free to act as he did.

There is much to be said for a rule permitting a surgeon to utilize his training, experience, and judgment in extending an operation when the advisability of additional surgery, under accepted practice, becomes apparent during the operation. Any other course is likely to subject the patient to a second operation, with its costs and collateral risks.[117] In practicality, any different rule frustrates sound medical practice for the sake of securing a formalistic consent which the patient undoubtedly would have given in any event. Of course, it cannot be overly stressed that this seemingly senseless result could be avoided if all surgeons would obtain presurgical consent of sufficient breadth to cover necessary extensions of the contemplated operation.[118]

BIBLIOGRAPHY

BOOKS

Chayet, N. L.: LEGAL IMPLICATIONS OF EMERGENCY CARE 93–113. Appleton-Century-Crofts, New York, 1969.

2 Harper, F. V., and James, F.: THE LAW OF TORTS §17.1, n. 15. Little, Brown and Company, Boston, 1956, and Supp. 1968.

Stetler, C. J., and Moritz, A. R.: DOCTOR AND PATIENT AND THE LAW 135–38. The C. V. Mosby Company, St. Louis, 1962.

ARTICLES

Davis, A. G.: *Duty of Doctor to Inform Patient of Risks of Treatment: Battery or Negligence?* 34 SOUTHERN CALIFORNIA LAW REVIEW 217 (1961).

Jacobson, H. L.: *Informed Consent in Illinois?* 18 DE PAUL LAW REVIEW 458 (1969).

[117] No authority need be cited for the proposition that surgery is costly in both time and money. Furthermore, the risk of anesthesia deaths, paralysis, embolization, and infection, while remote, is always present.

[118] The following language is standard: "I consent to the performance of operations and procedures in addition to or different from those now contemplated, whether or not arising from presently unforeseen conditions, which the above-named doctor or his associates or assistants may consider necessary or advisable in the course of the operation." A.M.A. MEDICOLEGAL FORMS WITH LEGAL ANALYSIS 33 (1961).

Johnson, R. F.: *Medical Malpractice—Doctrines of Res Ipsa Loquitur and Informed Consent,* 37 UNIV. OF COLORADO LAW REVIEW 169 (1955).

Karchmer, W. H.: *Informed Consent: A Plaintiff's Medical Malpractice "Wonder Drug,"* 31 MISSOURI LAW REVIEW 29 (1966).

Kelly, E. J.: *The Physician, the Patient and the Consent,* 8 KANSAS LAW REVIEW 405 (1960).

Levin, M.: *Consent to Medical Procedures,* 1963 INSURANCE LAW JOURNAL 711 (1963).

McCoid, A. H.: *Reappraisal of Liability for Unauthorized Medical Treatment,* 41 MINNESOTA LAW REVIEW 381 (1957).

Oppenheim, M.: *Informed Consent to Medical Treatment,* 11 CLEVELAND-MARSHAL LAW REVIEW 249 (1962).

Plante, M. L.: *An Analysis of "Informed Consent,"* 36 FORDHAM LAW REVIEW 639 (1968).

Powell, R. E.: *Consent to Operative Procedures,* 21 MARYLAND LAW REVIEW 189 (1961).

Proctor, K. C.: *Consent to Operative Procedures,* 22 MARYLAND LAW REVIEW 190 (1962).

Waltz, J. R., and Scheuneman, T. W.: *Informed Consent to Therapy,* 64 NORTHWESTERN UNIV. LAW REVIEW 629 (1970).

Wasmuth, C. E.: *Consent to Surgical Procedures,* 6 CLEVELAND-MARSHALL LAW REVIEW 235 (1957).

NOTES AND COMMENTS

Comment, *Consent to Medical and Surgical Treatment,* 14 DRAKE LAW REVIEW 101 (1966).

Comment, *Informed Consent: Malpractice,* 18 BAYLOR LAW REVIEW 137 (1966).

Comment, *Informed Consent in Medical Malpractice,* 55 CALIFORNIA LAW REVIEW 1396 (1967).

Comment, *Physician and Patient: Some Problems of Consent,* 2 WASHBURN LAW JOURNAL 158 (1962).

Comment, *Physicians and Surgeons: Informed Consent,* 20 OKLAHOMA LAW REVIEW 214 (1967).

Comment, *Valid Consent to Medical Treatment: Need the Patient Know?,* 4 DUQUESNE LAW REVIEW 450 (1966).

Note, *Malpractice—Duty of Doctor to Disclose Risk Involved in Operation,* 40 MINNESOTA LAW REVIEW 876 (1956).

Note, *Malpractice—Physician Has a Duty to Inform Patient of Risk Inherent in Proposed Treatment,* 109 UNIV. OF PENNSYLVANIA LAW REVIEW 768 (1961).

chapter 12

PROBLEMS OF EXPERIMENTAL AND INNOVATIVE THERAPY

THE JUSTIFIABILITY OF INNOVATIVE THERAPY

Recent medical advances—particularly those involving new drugs and organ transplantation—have aroused fresh interest in the legal aspects of so-called experimental medicine. Commentators have written from both legal and medical viewpoints, but their contributions have tended to be cursory.[1] A dearth of reported judicial opinions dealing directly with medical "experimentation" of at least arguable legitimacy has contributed to the inadequacy of the literature. The few decisions producing current legal doctrine have dealt mainly with instances of quackery[2] or demonstrably inappropriate treatment.[3] A second factor is the assumption, frequently made but seldom articulated, that since "experimentation" is a unique problem for medical jurisprudence, existing legal structures and concepts are inadequate to the solution of issues associated with it. As a consequence of this assumption, much of what has been written has been devoted to suggesting entirely new legal doctrines, forums, and procedures to deal with medical experimentation.[4] The result has sometimes been luxurious oversimplification.[5]

[1] The bibliography at the end of this chapter collects the more valuable contributions.

[2] *E.g., Brinkley* v. *Hassig,* 83 F.2d 351 (10th Cir. 1936) (goat gland transplant to cure impotency, high blood pressure, epilepsy, *dementia praecox* and kidney disease); *Graham* v. *Dr. Pratt Inst.,* 163 Ill. App. 91 (1911) (use of undiluted carbolic acid to remove facial smallpox scars); *Board of Medical Regis.* v. *Kaadt,* 76 N.E.2d 669 (S. Ct. Ind. 1948) (use of high-sugar diet in treatment of diabetes).

[3] *E.g., Langford* v. *Kosterlitz,* 290 Pac. 80 (Cal. App. 1930) (improper use of Novocaine in treatment of asthma); *Fortner* v. *Koch,* 261 N.W. 762 (S. Ct. Mich. 1935) (improper treatment of tertiary syphilis gumma); *Owens* v. *McCleary* 281 S.W. 682 (S. Ct. Mo. 1926) (caustic chemotherapy of hemorrhoids).

[4] See, *e.g.,* Burger, W. E.: *Reflections on Law and Experimental Medicine,* 15 UNIV. OF CALIFORNIA LAW REVIEW 436 (1968); Kaplan, L. V.: *Experimentation—An Articulation of a New Myth,* 46 NEBRASKA LAW REVIEW 87 (1967); Morse, H. N.:

It might be appropriate to devise new doctrines applicable to therapeutic medical experimentation and to remove the resolution of medical experimentation problems from the arena of common law trial. One solution would be to create a governmental agency at the federal level to deal with the subject, since the history of federal agencies reflects a measure of success in coping with uncharted problems.[6] This has been the approach of the federal Food and Drug Act which, in its creation of an agency to regulate the development, clearance, and marketing of new drugs, already governs much of what is commonly understood to be medical experimentation.[7] Panels of experts might also be organized, for similar purposes, at local levels.[8] But there are obvious differences between testing a new drug of identifiable composition, on the one hand, and, on the other, assessing a technique to be used by and applied to human beings under widely variant circumstances.[9] Any such steps, imposing additional

---

Legal Implications of Clinical Investigation, 8 WILLIAM & MARY LAW REVIEW 359 (1967); Ritts, R. E.: *A Physician's View of Informed Consent in Human Experimentation,* 36 FORDHAM LAW REVIEW 631 (1968).

[5] Part of the difficulty, which we shall amplify later, may also stem from the common failure to distinguish between experimentation employed as a method of treatment and experimentation aimed exclusively or primarily at the accumulation of scientific knowledge. Regulation of clinical investigation of the second sort is not hard to justify. There is time for extended appraisal of its potential value and costs and, as was evidenced by *Hyman* v. *Jewish Chronic Disease Hospital,* 248 N.Y.S.2d 245 (S. Ct.), *rev'd,* 251 N.Y.S.2d 818 (App. Div. 1964), *rev'd,* 206 N.E.2d 338 (Ct. App. N.Y. 1965) (experimental injection of live cancer cells into patients to determine existence of inherent immunity), an apparent need for it.

[6] See generally, Davis, K. C.: ADMINISTRATIVE LAW, ch. 1. West Publishing Company, St. Paul, 1959.

[7] 21 U.S.C. §§301 *et seq.* (1964). The statute has been expanded significantly in connection with the experimental use of new drugs. The expansion has been accomplished by means of regulations promulgated by the Food and Drug Administration, 21 C.F.R. §§130.1 *et seq.* (1968). See Boyer, F.: *Medical Liability in Drug Trials,* 270 NEW ENGLAND JOURNAL OF MEDICINE 777 (1964); Schreiner, G. E.: *Limb to Limbo—The Moral and Legal Entanglement of the Clinical Investigator,* 11 CLINICAL RESEARCH 127 (1965); Note, *Drug Liability,* 16 WESTERN RESERVE LAW REVIEW 392 (1965).

[8] *Cf.* the 1949 directive of New York City's Department of Hospitals prohibiting nontherapeutic clinical and laboratory research involving patients and requiring that any "proposed clinical or laboratory investigations in any hospital or institution . . . be submitted for review and approval by the Executive Committee of the Medical Board of the hospital concerned." N.Y.C. DEPT. OF HOSPITALS, GEN. ORDER 462, CONCERNING RESEARCH PROPOSALS (Oct. 27, 1949), quoted in Beecher, H. K.: *Experimentation on Man,* 169 J.A.M.A. 461, 478 n. 23 (1959).

[9] One such circumstance will often be the need, in connection with therapeutic experimentation, for a speedy decision. Agencies, panels, committees, and the like are not usually conducive to rapid decision-making, especially when they are far removed from the site at which the decision is needed.

layers of bureaucracy upon the nation's most regulated profession, will be taken only if it can fairly be concluded that existing tools are inadequate. We suggest that existing legal doctrines, with some needed refinements, provide an adequate framework within which problems of medical experimentation in a doctor-patient therapeutic setting can be effectively and appropriately resolved. We devote two brief sections to the necessary clarification of terms; we then describe and analyze the law's approach to innovative medicine.

Therapeutics and Research

The problems of medical "experimentation" in a pure research situation are different from those arising in a therapeutic context and thus require separate consideration. One of the analytic shortcomings of existing legal commentary is its failure consistently to distinguish these disparate situations.[10] In a therapeutic situation the problem involves resolution of issues of liability for a bad result, framed in a professional malpractice setting. In a research situation the problems involve regulation of the use of human subjects for scientific research and pose moral and political questions about the nature and degree of prior control over the investigator and his techniques. The principal distinguishing factor is the experimenter's motivation. In one instance he is concerned primarily with improving the condition of a particular patient under treatment; in the other he is concerned primarily, if not always exclusively, with using a human subject as a means of expanding scientific knowledge for the benefit of all living persons.

The therapy-research distinction, although occasionally slippery, will be maintained here. We consider in detail here only therapeutic "experimentation."[11] To the extent that the propriety of an "experiment" or the liability of the experimenter hinges on the distinction, any close choice between "research" and "therapy" will be resolved in favor of the former

[10] See, *e.g.*, Morse, H. N.: *Legal Implications of Clinical Investigation,* 8 WILLIAM & MARY LAW REVIEW 359 (1967); Note, *Experimentation on Human Beings,* 20 STANFORD LAW REVIEW 99 (1967). The distinction is carefully made in the A.M.A.'s *Ethical Guidelines for Clinical Investigation,* Appendix III.

[11] There is a worthwhile discussion of the ethical aspects of research, usually physiological or pharmacological, on human volunteers in Ratnoff, M. F., and Smith, J. C.: *Human Laboratory Animals: Martyrs for Medicine,* 36 FORDHAM LAW REVIEW 673 (1968). This article is more objective than its title might suggest. See also the bibliography in Note, *Medical Experiment Insurance,* 70 COLUMBIA LAW REVIEW 965, n. 1 (1970). For the only reported instance of damages awarded a volunteer for injury resulting from tests conducted solely for purposes of medical research, see *Halushka* v. *University of Saskatchewan,* [1966] 53 D.L.R.2d 436 (1965) (Canada) (ineffective consent to anesthetic tests; injuries included "diminution of mental ability"; verdict for $22,500).

in order to sharpen the illustration, since the presence of some interest other than the welfare of the subject always tends to render the physician's actions more difficult to justify legally.

"Experimentation" and "Innovation"

Thus far we have employed the terms "experiment" and "experimentation" in a loose and undefined fashion. We shall become more precise. Rather than referring in the abstract to some sort of new or unusual procedure, "experiment" will be taken here to refer to the nature of every therapeutic situation that a physician or surgeon faces.

An "experiment" is usually defined as an act or operation, carried out under conditions determined by the experimenter, to test, establish, or illustrate some suggested or known "truth." Every instance of medical treatment, in this broad sense, is an "experiment." On the basis of data produced by an investigative examination the physician arrives at a hypothesis of his patient's status: a diagnosis.[12] He then makes a prediction that certain specified changes in the patient's environment, physical structure, or functions will tend to produce a favorable change in the patient's status. If and when favorable change occurs, the experimental hypothesis and prediction are affirmed and the known probability of success of the experimental procedure is increased. In this way some therapeutic "experiments," as defined here, become customary. Strangely as it may strike the ear of the layman, physicians are recurringly called upon to undertake *customary experiments*. Those therapeutic procedures that have not yet earned a place in medical custom can be termed *innovative experiments*. Henceforth we shall speak of *customary therapy* and *innovative therapy*. It is innovative therapy that foments controversy and, occasionally, litigation.

Origins of the Legal Standards Governing Innovative Therapy: An English Case and an American Case

The only English case and the first American case on the subject reflect different approaches to the problem of therapeutic innovation and serve to sketch the broad outlines of the legal issues. We take up first the English case, *Slater* v. *Baker*.[13]

In 1767 an English physician named Baker, assisted by an apothecary, undertook to treat the improperly healed leg fracture of one Slater by a method of traction apparently unorthodox for that time or any time since.

[12] Diagnosis itself may involve innovative methods. See, *e.g.*, *Ball* v. *Mallinckrodt Chem. Works*, 387 S.W. 563 (S. Ct. Tenn. 1964) (contrast medium of relatively high toxicity used in performance of aortogram; although risk of injury high, use sustained on testimony that it gave a superior diagnostic x-ray).

[13] 95 Eng. Rep. 860 (K. B. 1767).

Doctor Baker refractured the leg and then applied "an heavy steel thing that had teeth, and would stretch or straighten the leg." When the leg again did not heal properly the patient sued both men. In *Slater* v. *Baker* the Court of King's Bench affirmed a jury verdict for plaintiff Slater on two grounds.

The court first held that the treatment constituted an unwarranted "experiment," saying:

> . . . For anything that appears to the Court, *this was the first experiment made with this new instrument; and if it was, it was a rash action,* and he who acts rashly acts ignorantly; and although the defendants in general may be as skillful in their respective professions as any two gentlemen in England, yet the Court cannot help saying, that in this particular case they have acted ignorantly and unskillfully, contrary to the known rule and usage of surgeons.[14]

The court also held that the surgeon had not procured an effective consent to the treatment he employed. Although Slater had apparently consented generally to undergo treatment, Doctor Baker had not informed him of the details of the procedure or of the fact that it was innovative.

Slater v. *Baker* defined what to this day remain the boundaries of the law of innovative medicine. The English court articulated a rather crude basis of liability for the unsuccessful use of an innovative therapeutic procedure and broached the issue of the scope of consent required from a patient before an innovative procedure can properly be utilized. These two issues coexist in most medical innovation cases and courts are still struggling with them.

In the United States the two issues have emerged in separate bodies of case law, one dealing with "experimentation," the other dealing with "informed consent." We focus now on the problem of medical innovation.[15] The first reported American case was *Carpenter* v. *Blake,*[16] arising in New York in 1871. The opinion's treatment of the facts is scanty; the case apparently involved a leg fracture and an unusual therapeutic device similar to the one involved in the *Slater* case. The trial court set out what has become the most frequently adopted approach to medical innovation in the United States:

> . . . Some standard by which to determine the propriety of treatment must be adopted; otherwise experiments will take the place of skill and the reckless experimentalists the place of the educated, experienced practitioner. . . .

[14] Emphasis supplied.

[15] The general topic of informed consent was considered in Chapter 11. The narrower subject of consent to innovative therapy will be discussed later.

[16] 60 Barb. 488 (S. Ct. N.Y. 1871). A hint of things to come was contained in *Landon* v. *Humphrey,* 9 Conn. 209 (S. Ct. Err. & App. Conn. 1832).

[W]hen the case is one as to which a system of treatment has been followed for a long time, there should be no departure from it, unless the surgeon who does it is prepared to take the risk of establishing by his success the propriety and safety of his experiment.

A close comparison of the *Slater* and *Carpenter* cases reveals similarities and differences. Perhaps the most striking distinction lies in the reaction of the two courts to the possibility, voiced explicitly in *Carpenter,* of reckless experimentation and quackery replacing sound medical practice. Because of this concern the American court in *Carpenter* seemed willing to lump together legitimate experimentation and abject quackery, imposing strict liability for a bad result in either case. The *Slater* court was less panicky; it appeared less willing to equate justifiable innovation and undeniable quackery for purposes of legal liability.

Neither the English nor the American judicial opinion defined "experiment." *Slater,* the English opinion, evidently viewed experimentation as anything that diverged from existing medical practice. *Carpenter* seems to have assumed that experimentation is an *a priori* identifiable phenomenon with unique characteristics including, but not limited to, departure from medical custom.

The courts also differed in their bases for imposing liability for a bad result in a case involving "experimentation," however that term might be defined. The English court focused on the proposition that the experiment in *Slater* involved the first use of the apparatus in question and was therefore "rash." It was this rashness in implementing an untried innovative technique, rather than the fact of its uniqueness, that resulted in the defendant's liability. *Slater,* in other words, did not decree the imposition of absolute liability for a bad result in any case of medical innovation. The English court seemed prepared to recognize justifications for innovation that would free the physician from civil liability no matter what the result of his innovation may have been. The American court in *Carpenter,* on the other hand, sought a simple rule of general and inflexible application, imposing strict liability for any deviation from customary procedures.

The Arguments for and Against Strict Liability

Carpenter's strict liability for use of any medical procedure other than one customarily employed by the profession is a defensible way to resolve the problems posed by medical innovation. It can be justified as an avoidance of overwhelming complexity: judges and lay juries are arguably inadequate to the task of settling issues that pass beyond reasonably clear-cut questions of customary medical practice.[17] Some would also say that

[17] *Cf.* James, F.: *Particularizing Standards of Conduct in Negligence Trials,* 5 VANDERBILT LAW REVIEW 697, 709–12 (1952).

the imposition of strict liability can be related to the potential dangers inherent in abandoning a patient to the mercy of the medical profession's notions as to when innovative techniques should be invoked. It has been suggested by the man who is now Chief Justice of the United States that liability for experimentation is a reasonable *quid pro quo* for the right to engage in experimental methods.[18] And, on the basis of risk-allocation theories, it could be argued that the medical profession is better able, through the mechanism of liability insurance, to bear the loss stemming from a bad result than is the patient.[19]

Counterarguments abound. The contention that the medical profession is too quick to innovate runs counter to conservative professional codes that limit the circumstances in which innovation will be considered appropriate. The Hippocratic Oath, father of them all, puts in the mouths of young doctors the promise that "I will follow that method of treatment which according to my ability and judgment I consider for the benefit of my patients and will abstain from whatever is deleterious and mischievous." The American Medical Association's Law Department has stated that experimental procedures must not vary too radically from accepted methods and that customary methods must first have been tried without success.[20] The Declaration of Helsinki, a prestigious international code, is somewhat more liberal: ". . . In the treatment of the sick person the doctor must be free to use a new therapeutic measure if *in his judgment* it offers hope of saving life, re-establishing health, or alleviating suffering." [21] While risk-allocation analysis has the appearance of simplicity and justice, it is probably appropriate only to large-scale enterprises having statistically predictable loss levels.[22] This hardly describes the medical

[18] Burger, W. E.: *Reflections on Law and Experimental Medicine,* 15 UNIV. OF CALIFORNIA LAW REVIEW 436 (1968). Chief Justice Burger is apparently struck by the seeming nonchalance inherent in statements that "the inevitable cost [of new medical procedures] is the inescapable risk to those on whom the innovations were first tried." Ratnoff, M. F., and Smith, J. C.: *Human Laboratory Animals: Martyrs for Medicine,* 36 FORDHAM LAW REVIEW 673, 676 (1968).

[19] A claim for damages resulting from medical innovation appears to be covered by existing malpractice liability insurance policies examined by the authors. The typical policy covers "any claims for damages . . . based on professional services rendered or which should have been rendered . . . in the practice of the insured's profession. . . ." The subject of medical malpractice insurance is taken up in detail in Chapter 20.

[20] A.M.A., PRINCIPLES OF MEDICAL ETHICS (1957) (pamphlet), quoted in Appendix III.

[21] 67 ANNALS OF INTERNAL MEDICINE, Supp. 774–75 (1967) (emphasis supplied), quoted in Appendix II. See also THE NUREMBERG CODE, 2 TRIALS OF WAR CRIMINALS BEFORE THE NUREMBERG MILITARY TRIBUNALS UNDER CONTROL COUNCIL LAW No. 10. 181–82 (1949), quoted in Appendix I.

[22] See, *e.g.*, Ehrenzweig, A. A.: *Negligence Without Fault,* 54 CALIFORNIA LAW

profession. Moreover, all justifications for strict liability in this context center on the proposition that the problems of medical innovation are inordinately complex.

Many contested matters that are put into courts for decision are complicated, but the litigation process continues to function, once it reaches the trial stage, with an efficiency and perceptivity that surprise everyone except judges, trial lawyers, and other close observers of the system. Perhaps it is enough to say that complexity is no justification for abandoning reasoned analysis and established procedures. Furthermore, the imposition of strict liability for medical innovation is arguably unacceptable as a matter of overriding policy since it would probably be antithetical to medical progress. Everything any physician or surgeon does today as a matter of course—and sound medical practice—was once done for the first time. There must be (so the argument runs) a place in the law for medical progress unhampered by a liability that has no reasoned basis.

A Flexible Approach

Perhaps in realization and acceptance of this need, some American courts have adopted more flexible positions on experimentation than the one outlined in *Carpenter* v. *Blake*. For example, the Colorado court in *Brown* v. *Hughes*,[23] although obscure, seems less rigid. It announced that a physician "must first have left and entirely abandoned all knowledge acquired in the fields of exploration and adopted some rash or experimental methods before [he will] approach the danger zone of liability." And the Michigan court in *Fortner* v. *Koch* [24] went a bit farther, however timidly, in allowing for therapeutic innovation. "We recognize the fact," the court said, "that, if the general practice of medicine and surgery is to progress, there must be a certain amount of experimentation carried on; but such experimentation must . . . not vary too much from the accepted mode of procedure."

A Dilemma: The Duty to Keep Abreast of New Developments

The more liberal courts, to sum up, take the position that a physician must not be too radically experimental, a position to which organized medicine has apparently specifically subscribed.[25] With this recent, flex-

REVIEW 1422 (1966); Note, *Experimentation on Human Beings*, 20 STANFORD LAW REVIEW 99, 115 (1967). Additionally, it may seem repugnant to place the practice of medicine on the same plane as the manufacture of widgets or the bottling of soft drinks. Decent policy may dictate retention of the principle that the stigma of liability should not attach to the practice of medicine in the absence of fault.

[23] 30 P.2d 259 (S. Ct. Colo. 1934).

[24] 261 N.W. 762 (S. Ct. Mich. 1935).

[25] See A.M.A., PRINCIPLES OF MEDICAL ETHICS (1957) (pamphlet), quoted in Ap-

ible approach apparently available, it may be that the needs of medical progress can be satisfied. About all that remains to be done is to impart practical significance to the legal standard.

There is one other difficulty, too, since the practicing physician has a duty to keep abreast of and apply new developments in his profession.[26] This obligation poses a seemingly dangerous dilemma for the medical man. He now must determine when a particular procedure ceases being an innovation, for the use of which he may expose himself to strict liability, and becomes instead a new development which he will be required to use if he is to meet his duty of keeping abreast of his profession's advances.[27] The dilemma will be obviated, however, by further analysis of the nature of medical experimentation and the legal standard applicable to it.[28]

The Definitional Approach to Medical Experimentation

The traditional approach to medical experimentation has been to distinguish permissible from impermissible innovations by means of definition.[29] This approach has serious defects. Semantically, "innovation" or "experimentation" has numerous connotations. Either term may refer to nothing more than thoughtless tinkering. Farther along the line of negative implication, the terms may mean the use of procedures unfounded on any scientifically "valid" theory. The court in the previously discussed case of *Carpenter* v. *Blake* seems to have had at least these two connotations in mind when it employed the term "experiment," and this may account for its unbending legal standard. In an even more extreme sense, the terms

---

pendix III. But note that this admonition was not carried over explicitly to the A.M.A.'s *Ethical Guidelines for Investigation,* Appendix III.

[26] See, McCoid, A. H.: *The Care Required of Medical Practitioners,* 12 VANDERBILT LAW REVIEW 549, 575–81 (1959). *Compare* Evans, F. J.: *New Drugs in Medical Practice: Onus of "Experimentation" as a Medicolegal Hazard,* 6 JOURNAL OF FORENSIC SCIENCE 10 (1961) (taking the position that a physician should never deviate from customary therapy).

[27] We are not the first to be reminded of Alexander Pope's difficult admonition: "Be not the first by whom the new are tried/Nor yet the last to cast the old aside." See Ratnoff, M. F., and Smith, J. C.: *Human Laboratory Animals: Martyrs for Medicine,* 36 FORDHAM LAW REVIEW 673, 676 (1968).

[28] The dilemma is probably obviated by administrative fiat in the case of new drugs. A new drug continues to be an "investigational" drug until it receives Federal Drug Administration approval, and a physician must obtain his patient's express permission for its use. Use of a drug following FDA approval probably cannot properly be deemed innovative in the sense in which we are employing that term. See, *e.g.,* Schreiner, G. E.: *Liability: Use of Investigational Drugs,* 18 FOOD, DRUG & COSMETIC LAW JOURNAL 403 (1963).

[29] See, *e.g.,* Morse, H. N.: *Legal Implications of Clinical Investigation,* 8 WILLIAM & MARY LAW REVIEW 359 (1967); Smith, H. W.: *Antecedent Ground of Liability in the Practice of Surgery,* 14 ROCKY MOUNTAIN LAW REVIEW 233 (1942).

evoke the image of the mad scientist engaged in fantastic manipulations aimed at some absurd, impossible, or depraved result. In a more neutral or even approving sense, the two terms can refer to any attempt to advance scientific knowledge. Similarly, they may indicate the use of advanced but not yet widely employed procedures to improve the condition of a patient under treatment.

Undoubtedly a broad but clearly articulated definition of legitimate medical innovation could be devised. Rules of liability could then be structured to govern the defined class of cases. With that thought in mind, it has been suggested:

> The term "experimentation" . . . [indicates] an application of a new, insufficiently proved drug, instrument or method of treatment, the validity of which has neither been accepted nor rejected by the medical profession and the purpose of which is to help the patient and to advance medical science.[30]

The major difficulty is that this definition, as well as any other that could be constructed, necessitates the drawing of a distinction between permissible and impermissible experimentation on the basis of some meaningful conception of scientific "validity."

Although it might seem easy to distinguish scientifically valid innovation from scientifically invalid quackery, one case alone will illustrate the difficulty of applying any definition that assumes that "validity" is a simple thing to discern in a given case. In the California case of *Kershaw* v. *Tilbury*[31] an osteopathic physician was sued for malpractice in treating a child with osteomyelitis. The method of treatment was "radio therapy," a procedure involving a black box with assorted dials and electrodes, run on standard electric power. Connecting one electrode to an assistant and another to various parts of the patient's body, the physician made a diagnosis of meningitis based on his assistant's reactions. In some undescribed way, involving the use of "radio waves," the physician then purported to use his black box to cure the diagnosed malady. When the procedure, claimed to have been successful previously, failed in the case at hand and the child's condition deteriorated as a consequence of the delay in treating her true illness, the patient's parents sued the physician for money damages. Harking back to the definition previously quoted, the black box might have been considered to be a device "the purpose of which is to help the patient and to advance medical science." But what of its "validity"? Was this a device "the validity of which has been neither

[30] Note, *Liability for Medical Experimentation,* 40 CALIFORNIA LAW REVIEW 159, 162 (1952).
[31] 8 P.2d 109 (S. Ct. Cal. 1932).

accepted nor rejected by the medical profession"? The trial testimony was inconclusive. Plaintiff's expert witness could say only that he had never heard of the technique and personally doubted whether it was scientifically sound; he could not make a categorical judgment. Nevertheless, equivocal as the record was, the California Supreme Court affirmed a verdict for the plaintiff. In doing so it found it necessary to revert to the strict liability approach of *Carpenter* v. *Blake:*

> This court passes no judgment on the theory of . . . [defendant's] profession, the source from whence it came, nor the appliances with which he works. With these we have no concern, but rather look to the results. The law holds him responsible if he does his work unskillfully, although he does the best he can. He assumes the risk of the quality and accuracy of his genius or inventions. On the same principle one who holds himself out as a medical expert and accepts employment as a healer of diseases, but who relies for diagnosis and remedies on some mechanical invention of his own, which invention is unknown to all schools of medical science, in like manner takes the risk of the quality and accuracy of such mechanical invention. If these move so imperfectly or inaccurately that he fails to treat the patients with reasonable skill, he is liable for the consequences.

If orthodoxy is the test, the result in *Kershaw* was unquestionably correct. But the *Kershaw* case was resolved not upon any successful definition of scientific validity but upon a rough nineteenth-century notion that all healers—the reputable along with the disreputable—must innovate at their peril.

Efforts to resolve medical innovation cases by reference to a conception of scientific validity will always fail. Any effort to determine "validity" is limited by the assumptions, knowledge, and techniques of empirical science. A physician, as a man of science, can say what physicians do when confronted with a particular type of case, but he cannot state whether what they do is "valid" in a philosophical sense. He can speak about whether what physicians do tends to improve the condition of the patient, but even here he can talk only in terms of the known probabilities. Given sufficient data, the physician can say this about procedures that are familiar or unfamiliar to him. And, on the same basis, he can talk about collateral risks of various procedures, their nature, likelihood, and severity. In short, the only correct answer to the question of whether a given procedure is scientifically valid is "Maybe." That is all that plaintiff's expert said in *Kershaw* v. *Tilbury,* and that is all that any man of science could say while testifying in a litigated matter. The definitional approach to the problem of medical innovation fails because lawsuits cannot be decided on the basis of a "Maybe."

The Reasonability of Therapeutic Innovation

The legal problems associated with innovative therapy will be solved not by recourse to semantics or rigid formulas but by analysis of its reasonability.

It does not follow from the fact that a method of treatment is innovative that it is not reasonable medical practice to use it. Expert testimony on this issue can evaluate the defendant physician's innovative therapy on the basis of the condition of the patient, the probability of success of the therapy, and the nature, severity, and probability of collateral risks. Such expert testimony would be responsive to the fundamental and long-familiar inquiry: Did the defendant doctor conform to the standard of care of a reasonable practitioner under the circumstances confronting him? It seems, after all, that conventional legal principles—the flexible principles of reasonability—may function to advantage in the field of innovative therapy.

The Relation of Innovative Therapy to Customary Practice

A prime policy reason for permitting therapeutic innovation is that the law must be sensitive to the need for medical progress. Consistency with this policy requires that an innovative therapy represent, in some significant respect, an improvement on existing, available procedures.[32] Where some customary therapy exists, there exists also a body of prior professional judgment concerning its propriety and efficacy. The physician who says that a particular therapy is customary (or "accepted") in the profession for the treatment of a given condition is making a shorthand statement. He is saying that, in the judgment of at least part of the medical profession,[33] it is consistent with reasonable medical practice to use that therapy for that condition. However, in the experimental situation typical of all therapy, three principal factors will determine whether a particular

[32] Putting the question in terms of an *improvement* eliminates those instances in which an innovative procedure has been specifically *disapproved* by the medical profession for reasons relating to probability of success or to the incidence of collateral risks. An example is *Reed* v. *Church,* 8 S.E.2d 285 (S. Ct. Va. 1940), in which a physician attempted to justify use of tryparsamide for treatment of cerebrospinal syphilis. The drug was then in a developmental stage but available data disclosed a significant risk of ocular disturbance, and the drug had been disapproved for use by the medical profession. The defendant's arguments of justifiable innovation and conformity to a recognized minority procedure did not prevail. See also, *e.g., Owens* v. *McCleary,* 281 S.W. 682 (S. Ct. Mo. 1926) (disapproved method of treating hemorrhoids); *Sawdey* v. *Spokane Falls & N. Ry.,* 70 Pac. 972 (S. Ct. Wash. 1902) (disapproved failure to use extension or counterextension in setting of fractured leg).

[33] This parenthetical qualification is to indicate that a therapy's customary status is largely a matter of counting noses and that more than one method of treatment can be customary at the same time.

course of treatment will be used: (1) the present and predicted condition of the patient; (2) the probability of success of a given therapy; and (3) the probability, type, and severity of risks collateral to the therapy.

The customary status of a therapy reflects the judgment of medical practitioners that the patient's condition and the probability of the therapy's success outweigh the nature, probability, and severity of collateral risks.[34] This collective judgment can only be an imperfect generalization, but it commands respect. The potential innovator must justify his actions against this background of professional judgment concerning an already tried and accepted therapy.

A Preliminary Question: What Does the Physician Know About the Innovation?

There is a complex threshold problem in the justification of any therapeutic innovation. Before any other question becomes relevant the innovator must show that he possessed sufficient prior knowledge of the probability of success of the medical technique and of its collateral risks.[35] This showing involves, basically, the physician's level of preparation for use of the innovative technique, including his knowledge of the technique itself and his planning for its implementation. The innovator, in order to decide whether the proposed technique will create an unreasonable risk of harm to his patient, must know whether the probable success of the technique outweighs its collateral risks. He must take the steps that a reasonable practitioner would consider necessary to acquire this information so that the balance can be struck between success and risk. The problem, then, is the proper standard regarding the amount and type of investigation that should be undertaken prior to therapeutic use of an innovative technique.

As to both the amount and type of prior investigation, the standard is again one of reasonable medical practice, as to which any experienced medical witness can testify. What sort of prior investigation, and how much of it, would the reasonable medical practitioner conduct before adopting the particular innovative technique in a therapeutic situation? Did *this* practitioner's prior investigation conform to that standard? Did he make a reasonable assessment of the propriety of using the technique

[34] See DeBakey, M. E.: *Medical Research and the Golden Rule,* 203(8) J.A.M.A. 574 (1968).

[35] See *Board of Medical Regis.* v. *Kaadt,* 76 N.E.2d 689 (S. Ct. Ind. 1948). "A physician is not limited to the most generally used of several approved modes of treatment and the use of another mode known and approved by the profession is proper, but every new method of treatment should pass through an experimental stage in its development and a physician is not authorized in trying untested experiments on patients."

in question? These inquiries must be posed from the viewpoint of the reasonable medical practitioner confronted with circumstances similar to those facing the innovator.

Since the standard governing the type and amount of prior investigation should be a flexible one, drawing upon reasonable medical practice for its content, it is neither wise nor easy to formulate more particularized legal rules. However, certain recurring considerations can be catalogued. One such consideration is whether, and the extent to which, animal research should precede the use of an innovative technique on humans.

Animal Research

Most commentators consider extensive animal research an absolute prerequisite to the use of an innovative technique in the treatment of humans, thus elevating it to a place in the overall legal standard.[36] The American Medical Association, in connection with its *Principles of Medical Ethics,* decreed that "Medical ethics prohibit human experimentation except . . . after the danger of the experiment has been investigated previously by animal experimentation." [37] And the Nuremberg Code provides that "[an] experiment should be so designed and based on the results of animal experimentation and a knowledge of the natural history of the disease . . . that the anticipated results will justify the performance of the experiment." [38]

Perhaps so flat a requirement of antecedent animal research is unwarranted. The need for animal research can be assessed only on the basis of medical knowledge and judgment. The very nature of the innovative technique involved may determine whether animal research will be possible and informative of the technique's effect on human subjects.[39] It would be absurd to insulate a physician from liability simply because he performed extensive but uninformative animal research before embarking upon an innovative technique; it would be equally absurd to fix liability upon a physician for the sole reason that he had foregone useless research.

The most difficult innovation cases will be those in which prior animal

[36] See, *e.g.,* Markel, M. F.: *Legal Considerations in Experimental Design in Testing New Drugs on Humans,* 18 FOOD, DRUG & COSMETICS LAW JOURNAL 219, 223 (1963); Ratnoff, M. F., and Smith, J. C.: *Human Laboratory Animals: Martyrs for Medicine,* 36 FORDHAM LAW REVIEW 673, 681 (1968). For a discussion of the problems surrounding animal experimentation, see Sembower, J. F.: *Animal Experimentation,* in REPORT, NATIONAL CONFERENCE ON THE LEGAL ENVIRONMENT OF MEDICAL SCIENCE 40–49. National Society for Medical Research and the University of Chicago, Chicago, 1959.

[37] Appendix III.

[38] Appendix I.

[39] *Cf.* Ritts, R. E.: *A Physician's View of Informed Consent in Human Experimentation,* 36 FORDHAM LAW REVIEW 631, 632 (1968).

research is impossible or would be uninformative. In such a case the legal question will be the reasonableness of the innovating physician's reliance on scientific principles or upon data gleaned from collateral research.[40] These sources might be informative of an innovative technique's probability of success. But since such data are derived from indirect sources and not from the innovative procedure in question, they will probably not be informative of the nature, likelihood, and seriousness of collateral risks. This sort of case will involve a complicated medical judgment based on the reasonableness of the innovator's actions in light of what he in fact knew about the technique. The fact that the first therapeutic use on a human being is also the first use of the technique on animal life will place the level of the innovator's knowledge much more clearly at the investigative stage than would otherwise be the case; indeed, in this sort of case therapeutic innovation closely approximates experimental research.

Reasoned professional judgment—which is what the law demands—will require soundness of technique in scientific principle and a high level of collateral research.

Consideration of the Patient's Present and Predicted Condition

Any appraisal of an innovative technique's propriety on the basis of what a reasonable practitioner would conclude from the available data must be made in light of the patient's interests, having in mind particularly his present and predictable condition. An actual case may help to illustrate the point.

Baldor v. *Rogers*,[41] a 1955 Florida case, involved unsuccessful chemotherapy of cancer with glyoxylide. The patient contended in a malpractice action that the only proper treatment was with x-rays, radium, or surgery. The Florida Supreme Court emphasized the nature of plaintiff's disease and his discouraging condition in sustaining the propriety of the defendant doctor's method of therapy even though it was innovative.[42]

The world's first heart transplantation operation provides another possible example.[43] It was performed against a background of extensive animal research. However, a complication developed that had been unforeseen, due in large part to the fact that the technique had never before been used on a human: the patient died of pneumonia contracted as a

[40] We are assuming, obviously, that antecedent clinical or laboratory investigation involving human subjects, including the particular patient, is not possible or proper.

[41] 81 So.2d 658 (S. Ct. Fla. 1955).

[42] It should be noted that courts have generally been protective of physicians in cases involving innovative treatment of cancer. Some of the cases are collected in Anno., 55 A.L.R.2d 461.

[43] See *An Unexpected Difficulty, Details of Heart Transplant Reported,* 202(12) J.A.M.A. 23 (1967).

result of lowered resistance caused by the administration of drugs designed to combat the rejection phenomenon. The condition of the patient's original heart was such that his life was unbearable and his condition terminal. The reasonableness of the surgeon's proceeding on the basis of existing but incomplete knowledge becomes legally defensible when the patient's condition is considered.

This proposition has its limits, however. It is doubtful whether a patient's condition would ever be wretched enough to justify a physician's use of an innovative technique about which he knew nothing whatever, but this suggestion may arise as much from feelings of morality as from law or medical judgment. There is probably some point at which it is rightly felt that the dying should be left to die and that doctors should not be allowed to innovate with insufficient prior knowledge on the blind chance that a patient's fatal syndrome might be reversed.

A Return to the Relation of Innovative Therapy to Customary Practice

Once the preliminary issue of the physician's level of knowledge concerning an innovative therapy has been resolved, the next question is the pivotal one of whether the innovative technique can be justified as a medical advance in light of available customary methods.[44] Again the question is one to be posed from the standpoint of the reasonable medical practitioner; the question is whether a reasonable medical practitioner would consider innovation justified in the face of customary alternatives. And again the question must be resolved against the background of the patient's present and predicted condition.

As every trial lawyer and judge know, a technique of long standing for proving both conformity to and departure from the law's standard of care —the "reasonable man" standard—is to show what the relevant group, be it of physicians or construction contractors, customarily does under like circumstances.[45] The existence of this evidential approach poses a potential for confusion in the area of innovative medicine: it might be thought that an innovative therapy could always be attacked successfully by a malpractice claimant's attorney since it could always be proved by means of knowledgeable witnesses that the defendant physician had diverged

[44] In cases where there is *no* customary therapy, courts have indicated that a physician will not be found negligent if he uses a method of treatment that is consistent with reasonable medical practice. See, *e.g., Baldor* v. *Rogers,* 81 So.2d 658 (S. Ct. Fla. 1955); *Smith* v. *Beard,* 110 P.2d 267 (S. Ct. Wyo. 1941); see also Stetler, C. J., and Moritz, A. R.: DOCTOR AND PATIENT AND THE LAW 309, 4th ed. The C. V. Mosby Company, St. Louis, 1962.

[45] *Texas & Pac. R.R.* v. *Behmeyer,* 189 U.S. 468 (1903). See also James, F.: *Particularizing Standards of Conduct in Negligence Trials,* 5 VANDERBILT LAW REVIEW 697, 709–12 (1952); Morris, C.: *Custom and Negligence,* 42 COLUMBIA LAW REVIEW 1147 (1942).

from customary practice. Any such thinking erroneously commingles an evidentiary process and the applicable legal standard.

Despite the tendency of some opinions to elevate custom to the level of legal standard,[46] the fact is that customary behavior and the judgment it implies are only *evidence* of the standard of care in certain types of cases, rather than the standard itself. Dean John H. Wigmore, the master of the law of evidence, saw this. "The proper method," he said, "is to receive [evidence of custom], with an express caution that it is merely evidential and is not to serve as a legal standard." [47] The legal yardstick remains that of reasonable prudence under like circumstances. This has not always been discerned by courts dealing with medical malpractice cases. Some of them have continued to treat customary practice as though it constituted an inflexible legal standard. Thus, if a physician demonstrates adherence to some customary method of treatment, no other evidence can establish lack of due care.[48] This is not disturbing if a national standard, rather than a depressed local one, is being applied. Conversely, however, departure from customary methods of treatment has been held conclusively to establish violation of the legal standard applicable to physicians.[49] Courts announcing this conclusion are in danger of overlooking an important distinction.

Accurate analysis of custom's role in malpractice litigation requires a clear distinction between the use of *adherence* to custom to demonstrate due care and the use of *deviation* from custom to demonstrate negligence. When adherence to custom is held to demonstrate due care in a malpractice context, the policy being served is the protection of the practitioner from having to conform to any higher standard. It is generally agreed that it would be unfair to require the medical practitioner to exceed the dictates of custom. This commendable policy ceases to be relevant, however, when a practitioner voluntarily goes beyond customary practice

[46] *E.g.*, *Ellis* v. *Louisville & N. Ry.*, 251 S.W.2d 577 (S. Ct. Ky. 1952); *Wommack* v. *Orr*, 176 S.W.2d 477 (S. Ct. Mo. 1943); *Shadford* v. *Ann Arbor St. R.R.*, 69 N.W. 661 (S. Ct. Mich. 1897).

[47] 2 Wigmore, J. H.: EVIDENCE 489, 3d ed. Little, Brown and Company, Boston, 1940. See also *Troune* v. *Chicago D. & G. Bay Trans. Co.*, 234 F.2d 253 (2d Cir. 1956); *Uline Ice Co.* v. *Sullivan*, 187 F.2d 82 (D. C. Cir. 1950); *Ramsey* v. *Mellon Nat'l Bank*, 251 F.Supp. 646 (W. D. Pa. 1966); *Donnelly* v. *Fred Whittaker Co.*, 72 A.2d 61 (S. Ct. Pa. 1950).

[48] *E.g.*, *Ales* v. *Ryan*, 64 P.2d 409 (S. Ct. Cal. 1936); *Halliman* v. *Prindle*, 62 P.2d 1075 (S. Ct. Cal. 1936). Cases recognizing that a customary medical practice may nonetheless be a negligent one are *Lundahl* v. *Rockford Memorial Hospital Ass'n*, 235 N.E.2d 671 (Ill. App. 1968); *Favorola* v. *Aetna Casualty & Surety Co.*, 144 So.2d 544 (La. App. 1962); *Toth* v. *Community Hospital*, 239 N.E.2d 368 (Ct. App. N.Y. 1968); *Morgan* v. *Sheppard*, 188 N.E.2d 808 (Ohio App. 1963).

[49] *E.g.*, *Jackson* v. *Burnham*, 39 Pac. 577 (S. Ct. Colo. 1895); *Hodgson* v. *Bigelow*, 7 A.2d 338 (S. Ct. Pa. 1939); *Smith* v. *Beard*, 110 P.2d 267 (S. Ct. Wyo. 1941).

and seeks to justify an innovative technique as constituting an exercise of good medical judgment under the circumstances. In such a case the indiscriminate invocation of custom may turn a rule devised for the practitioner's protection into a rule that punishes him blindly for innovative advances. Custom has its evidentiary function in cases involving medical innovation, as we shall several times suggest, but its purpose will never be more than to supply the background of available alternatives against which a physician's innovative technique must be assessed.

The problem of justification for innovative conduct increases in difficulty when the physician has declined to use one or more customary methods of therapy. It might well be concluded in such a case that innovation was not legally justified. The American Medical Association's Law Department has taken the position that "In order to avoid legal liability for use of experimental procedures in treatment of a patient, . . . usual and accepted procedures must have been tried previously without success." [50] The Declaration of Helsinki, as was previously pointed out, adopts a stance that is only slightly more flexible.[51] If a condition is common, and an available therapy will with high probability produce a satisfactory result,[52] there is little reason for the practitioner to innovate. Justification for innovation may be impossible. The only tenable justification might arise from a delicate time element generated by the patient's condition. If his condition is deteriorating rapidly and there is arguably sufficient time only for innovative conduct, no court is likely to condemn the physician to legal liability even if bases for suggesting causation and damage could be worked out by the claimant.

If the practitioner has in fact exhausted all known and available methods of therapy, it can be argued that he is fully justified in turning to an innovative technique.[53] In a somewhat sophisticated sense the unsuccessful use of every customary technique could be said to establish, in a negative way, that an innovative procedure held out some promise of being an improvement. However, as we have previously indicated, this will not be

[50] A.M.A., PRINCIPLES OF MEDICAL ETHICS (1957) (pamphlet), quoted in Appendix III. It is worth noting again that the A.M.A.'s House of Delegates made no reference to this requirement in its 1966 *Ethical Guidelines for Clinical Investigation*, Appendix III.

[51] Appendix II.

[52] Probability of "satisfactory result," as that phrase is employed here, implies a low probability of the materialization of collateral risks.

[53] It has been asserted that doctors, even in such a case, are reluctant to attempt an innovative procedure for fear of a malpractice action. See Stetler, C. J., and Moritz, A. R.: DOCTOR AND PATIENT AND THE LAW 309–10, 4th ed. The C. V. Mosby Company, St. Louis, 1962. One overwrought commentator has gone so far as to suggest that "in the final analysis, the physician should apply the maxim: run no risks, better let the patient die from disease than from attempted uncertain experiments with the surgeon's knife or by use of dangerous drugs." Evans, F. J.: *New Drugs in Medical Practice: Onus of Experimentation as a Medicolegal Hazard!*, 6 JOURNAL OF FORENSIC SCIENCE 10, 16 (1961). Responsible medical men will discount statements of this sort.

true in all cases because the balance of probability of success and of collateral risks must still be made in the light of the patient's present and predicted condition. It is altogether conceivable that an innovative method might increase the probability of success only slightly while at the same time increasing the probability of significant collateral risks to an unreasonable degree. The hard question here is determining when the collateral risk factor is increased to the point that it poses an unreasonable threat to the patient's life or welfare. To posit an admittedly extreme example, the law of homicide might be at least theoretically relevant in a situation where, even though the patient was dying, there was invoked an innovative technique involving a minimal chance of success and a very high probability of accelerated death.[54]

As was intimated earlier, the converse of the problem of exhaustion of customary procedures is presented when the use of all such procedures to no avail would constitute no treatment at all, leading to deterioration of the patient's condition. Perhaps exhaustion of known procedures should not be required to the point that the patient's condition becomes irreversible. Precisely when this point will be reached is, of course, a question of medical judgment, as is the propriety or duty of innovation at that juncture. We shall shortly revert to the subject of a possible legal *obligation* to engage in medical innovation.

Additional Factors Justifying Innovative Therapy

Various other factors might contribute to the justification of an innovative medical technique, but their weight is likely to be slight. Mere comfort on the part of the patient will not justify innovative measures unless his condition and the level of his suffering are such that his comfort assumes independent significance.[55] Convenience to the physician merits virtually no consideration.

A Legal Duty to Innovate?

A proposition that so far has not been directly considered by the courts is whether a physician might in some circumstances have an affirmative obligation to use an innovative treatment in the course of a patient's care.

[54] In theory, the killing of a dying man by means of an act whereby death is rendered a substantial certainty constitutes unlawful homicide no matter what the motivation, just as the intentional killing of a dying person is homicide. See Chapter 24; see also Williams, G. L.: THE SANCTITY OF LIFE AND THE CRIMINAL LAW 318–26. Knopf, New York, 1957. The question of damages in the event of civil liability would be vexing; it is difficult to ascertain the loss resulting from early termination of a dying man's life. See 2 Harper, F. V., and James, F.: THE LAW OF TORTS, §§25.13–16. Little, Brown and Company, Boston, 1956, and Supp. 1968; McCormick, C. T.: DAMAGES, §§93–98. West Publishing Company, St. Paul, 1935.

[55] The Declaration of Helsinki lists "alleviating of suffering" as a consideration in the use of innovative procedures. See Appendix II.

The proposition is a natural outgrowth of the preceding discussion; it would crop up in cases in which the physician had employed all applicable customary therapies without success or had halted their use because they gave no promise of success and the patient's condition was deteriorating rapidly. It might be contended in such cases that failure to use an innovative technique constituted a technical abandonment of the patient.[56] While most abandonment cases have involved premature and unwarranted severing of the doctor-patient relationship,[57] there are some judicial decisions that tend to support the idea that failure to use an available method of treatment while the relationship continued would constitute abandonment.[58]

The suggested argument could not be made with any hope of success unless at least three key facts were established: first, that the physician knew of a relevant innovative technique; second, that the physician was sufficiently familiar with the technique to be able to implement it skillfully; and, third, that essential facilities and equipment were available. Once more, the overriding consideration will be whether use of the innovative therapy would have constituted due care under the particular circumstances.

While in general the notion of a duty to innovate will undoubtedly be rejected by courts as being both radical and unworkable, it could become more palatable if the attending physician were himself the originator of the innovative technique in question. Even this possibility seems excessively remote, however.

INFORMED CONSENT TO INNOVATIVE THERAPY

Known Collateral Risks

In Chapter 11 we discussed in detail the concept of informed consent to customary therapy. Everything said there about accepted modes of therapy and their collateral risks applies with equal if not greater force to innovative therapy.

Innovative treatments may pose known risks; they may also, by their very novelty, pose the possibility that risks unknown in advance will materialize. If a physician fails to disclose to his patient a known material risk of proposed innovative therapy, liability for the risk's ultimate

[56] The subject of abandonment is treated in detail in Chapter 10.

[57] *E.g., McNamara* v. *Emmons,* 97 P.2d 503 (Cal. App. 1939); *Meiselman* v. *Crown Heights Hospital,* 34 N.E.2d 367 (N.Y. App. 1941); *Gray* v. *Davidson,* 130 P.2d 341 (S. Ct. Wash. 1942).

[58] *E.g., Dale* v. *Donaldson Lumber Co.* 2 S.W. 703 (S. Ct. Ark. 1886); *Norton* v. *Hamilton,* 89 S.E.2d 809 (Ga. App. 1955); *Vann* v. *Harden,* 47 S.E.2d 314 (S. Ct. Va. 1948).

materialization is likely to follow under the legal principles previously enunciated in Chapter 11.

If, on the other hand, a known collateral risk of an innovative therapy is fully disclosed and subsequently materializes, the effect of the patient's consent will probably depend on the propriety of using the therapeutic procedure in the first place. Principles discussed in the initial section of the present chapter come into play. If use of the innovative therapy constituted reasonable medical practice, as that standard has been explained, consent by the patient to a disclosed collateral risk should relieve the physician of legal liability. The result should be different, however, if use of the therapy was itself unreasonable. The principle that a patient's consent to a therapy and its risks will not relieve the physician of liability for negligence in utilizing a therapy should also apply in a case where use of an innovative procedure is negligent in light of its known and significant collateral risks. In both instances the physician has breached his duty of care to the patient in the manner of treatment, and the patient's consent to disclosed risks becomes irrelevant.[59]

At this juncture the reader will sense the authors' fear that the American Medical Association's *Ethical Guidelines for Clinical Investigation* [60] make too casual an assumption that a patient's consent is an almost complete answer to every potential problem posed by innovative therapeutics.[61] The Association's third and lengthiest guideline is devoted to the securing of reasonably informed and voluntary consent to clinical investigation. It provides for disclosure to the patient that the physician intends to use an investigational drug or innovative technique and calls for an explanation of the procedure's character, including its risks and potential benefits; it requires the physician to offer to answer the patient's questions concerning the drug or technique and, finally, requires disclosure of available therapeutic alternatives. Arguably, the *Ethical Guidelines* do not delineate with sufficient sharpness the vital threshold question—whether the use of an innovative technique under the circumstances of a given case constitutes good medical practice. The point is there, however. For example, the *Ethical Guidelines* insist that the innovator or researcher "should demonstrate the same concern for the welfare, safety and comfort of the person involved as is required of a physician who is furnishing medical

[59] See, *e.g.*, *Roberts* v. *Wood*, 206 F.Supp. 579 (S. D. Ala. 1962); *Valdez* v. *Percy*, 217 P.2d 422 (S. Ct. Cal. 1950); *Natanson* v. *Kline*, 350 P.2d 1093 (S. Ct. Kan. 1960). *Cf. Spead* v. *Tomlinson*, 59 Atl. 376 (S. Ct. N.H. 1904).

[60] Appendix III.

[61] *Cf.* Beecher, H. K.: *Consent in Clinical Experimentation: Myth and Reality*, 195 J.A.M.A. 34 (1966), in which the author suggests that the defect in all the codes of medical ethics is a bland assumption that a patient's consent can invariably be obtained merely for the asking.

care to a patient independent of any clinical investigation." Moreover, and most importantly, the *Guidelines* adjure the innovator to "recognize that the physician-patient relationship exists and that he is expected to exercise his professional judgment and skill in the best interest of the patient."

Unknown Collateral Risks

Inevitably, innovative therapy raises the problem of consent to unknown risks. Two principal questions are posed: Should there be disclosure to the patient of the possibility of unknown risks? What should be the legal effect of a patient's unrestricted consent to the possibility of unknown risks if one or more eventually materialize?

As to the first inquiry, it seems axiomatic that in all cases of optional innovative therapy the possibility of unknown risks should be disclosed, since it may bear heavily on the patient's decision whether to consent to use of the therapy.[62] However, the effect of a patient's consent in the face of possible unknown risks when one later materializes is somewhat more troublesome. It could be maintained that a blanket agreement to confront the possibility of unknown risks will constitute consent to any unknown danger that may subsequently materialize. A supposed difficulty with this proposition is that it does not accord precisely with orthodox legal concepts of consent, which have traditionally involved two elements: awareness and assent. Just as one cannot disclose something he does not know, so one cannot assent to something of which he is unaware. It may therefore seem both anomalous and unfair to suggest that agreement to accept the unknown constitutes knowing, binding consent.[63]

In fact, however, thinking in terms of consent to unknown risks raises a phantom issue. The threshold question must again be whether the decision to employ an innovative therapy was reasonable in light of the physician's level of knowledge concerning it. Where use of an innovative technique is unreasonable because it prompts too many unanswered questions, introduction of a concept of consent to unknown risks assumes that advance consent relieves an innovator of liability for negligence in going forward with a therapy. No such concept obtains in cases of customary therapy, and none should apply in cases of innovative treatment. Consent is simply irrelevant. If a physician acted improperly by going ahead with an innovative technique as to which there were too many

[62] See Hershey, N.: *Problems of Consent in Clinical Investigation,* in REPORT, NATIONAL CONFERENCE ON THE LEGAL ENVIRONMENT OF MEDICAL SCIENCE 67. National Society for Medical Research and the University of Chicago, Chicago, 1959.

[63] Notions of contributory negligence and assumption of risk (see Chapter 9) are likewise inapplicable, since these defenses also involve the elements of awareness of a particular risk and assent to the taking of it. See Symposium, *Medical Malpractice in Illinois,* 44 CHICAGO-KENT LAW REVIEW 106, 154 (1967).

unplumbed questions involving its potential risks, liability will flow from the physician's unreasonable conduct. If, on the other hand, he acted reasonably in going forward on the basis of existing knowledge, the patient's consent even to the possibility of unanticipated risks is again irrelevant, since the physician had no legal duty to disclose risks about which he neither knew nor should have known, and for that reason alone is immune from liability.

BIBLIOGRAPHY

BOOKS

Beecher, H. K.: EXPERIMENTATION IN MAN. Charles C Thomas, Springfield, Ill., 1959.

Bernard, C.: AN INTRODUCTION TO THE STUDY OF EXPERIMENTAL MEDICINE. Dover Publications, New York, 1967.

Markowitz, J.: EXPERIMENTAL SURGERY. Williams and Wilkins Co., Baltimore, 1949.

Pappworth, M. H.: *Human Guinea Pigs.* Routledge & Kegan Paul, Ltd., London, 1967.

Smith, A. E., and Herrick, A. D.: DRUG RESEARCH AND DEVELOPMENT. Revere Publishing Company, New York, 1948.

ARTICLES

Archambault, G. F.: *Investigational Drugs and the Law,* 16 CLEVELAND-MARSHALL LAW REVIEW 487 (1967).

Beecher, H. K.: *Consent in Clinical Experimentation: Myth and Reality,* 195 J.A.M.A. 34 (1966).

Beecher, H. K.: *Some Fallacies and Errors in the Application of the Principle of Consent in Human Experimentation,* 3 CLINICAL PHARMACOLOGY & THERAPEUTICS 141 (1962).

Curran, W. J.: *A Problem of Consent: Kidney Transplantation in Minors,* 34 NEW YORK UNIV. LAW REVIEW 891 (1959).

Curran, W. J., and Beecher, H. K.: *Experimentation in Children,* 10 J.A.M.A. 77 (1969).

Freund, P. A.: *Ethical Problems in Human Experimentation,* 273 NEW ENGLAND JOURNAL OF MEDICINE 687 (1965).

Kaplan, L. V.: *Experimentation—An Articulation of a New Myth,* 46 NEBRASKA LAW REVIEW 87 (1967).

Kidd, A. M.: *The Problem of Experimentation on Human Beings: Limits of the Right of a Person to Consent to Experimentation on Himself,* 117 SCIENCE 211 (1953).

Ladimer, I.: *Ethical and Legal Aspects of Medical Research on Human Beings,* 3 JOURNAL OF PUBLIC LAW 467 (1954).

Ladimer, I.: *Human Experimentation: Medicolegal Aspects,* 257 NEW ENGLAND JOURNAL OF MEDICINE 18 (1959).

Ladimer, I.: *Medical Experimentation: Legal Considerations,* 1 CLINICAL PHARMACOLOGY & THERAPEUTICS 674 (1960).
Markel, M. F.: *Legal Considerations in Experimental Design in Testing New Drugs on Humans,* 18 FOOD, DRUG & COSMETICS LAW JOURNAL 219 (1963).
Morse, H. N.: *Legal Implications of Clinical Investigation,* 8 WILLIAM & MARY LAW JOURNAL 359 (1967).
Ritts, R. E.: *A Physician's View of Informed Consent in Human Experimentation,* 36 FORDHAM LAW REVIEW 631 (1968).
Schreiner, G. E.: *Liability: Use of Investigation Drugs,* 18 FOOD, DRUG & COSMETICS LAW JOURNAL 403 (1963).
Smith, H. W.: *Antecedent Grounds of Liability in the Practice of Surgery,* 14 ROCKY MOUNTAIN LAW REVIEW 233 (1942).
Swetlow, G. I.: *What the Law Says About Experimental Therapy,* 32 MEDICAL ECONOMICS 181 (1954).
Symposium, *Human Experimentation—A World Problem From the Standpoint of Spiritual Leaders,* 7 WORLD MEDICAL JOURNAL 80 (1960).
Waltz, J. R., and Scheuneman, T. W.: *Informed Consent to Therapy,* 64 NORTHWESTERN UNIV. LAW REVIEW 629 (1970).

NOTES AND COMMENTS

Comment, *Patient Selection for Artificial and Transplanted Organs,* 82 HARVARD LAW REVIEW 1322 (1969).
Note, *Experimentation on Human Beings,* 20 STANFORD LAW REVIEW 99 (1967).
Note, *Liability for Medical Experimentation,* 40 CALIFORNIA LAW REVIEW 159 (1952).
Note, *Medical Experiment Insurance,* 70 COLUMBIA LAW REVIEW 865 (1970).

chapter 13

LIABILITY FOR UNAUTHORIZED AUTOPSIES AND RELATED PROCEDURES

THE PURPOSE OF AUTOPSY PROCEDURES

An autopsy is a comprehensive study of a dead body, performed by a trained physician employing recognized dissection procedures and techniques.[1] It may be official or nonofficial in nature. Nonofficial autopsies are those that are not required by law to be conducted by a coroner or medical examiner.

Autopsy and related procedures have a variety of purposes. Their most common function is to determine the cause or causes of death.[2] Such a determination serves various informational needs. In cases of death by violence or poisoning it may be crucial to the question of possible criminal conduct. In cases of death by noncriminal casualty it may illuminate the issue of medical causation that lies at the heart of many civil tort actions. In other cases autopsy serves valuable medical education functions, leading to improved health services. The regular performance of autopsies may serve as an aid in measuring the quality of hospital services. And autopsy techniques are employed for teaching purposes in medical schools.

Procedures related to the autopsy process are used for homotransplantation, the removal from a dead body of organs for the rehabilitation of a living person.[3] In short, autopsy and related procedures can be vital to the understanding and control of disease and traumatic injuries and to the education of physicians and other medical personnel. But cadavers are

[1] See Woodburne, R. T.: *Use of Cadavers, Organ Transplants, and Autopsy Procedures,* in REPORT ON THE NATIONAL CONFERENCE ON THE LEGAL ENVIRONMENT OF MEDICAL SCIENCE 11. National Society for Medical Research and the University of Chicago, Chicago, 1959.

[2] See Monger, R. H.: *Functions and Limitations of an Autopsy,* 24 TENNESSEE LAW REVIEW 159 (1956).

[3] The legal issues related to homotransplantation, which are of substantially more far-reaching significance than those considered in this chapter, are taken up in Chapter 14.

not automatically the property of physicians and surgeons, to be dismantled at will. The performance of postmortem examinations and connected procedures is closely regulated by state law. The key question is whether the personnel involved possess the requisite authority to undertake procedures that will result in the mutilation of a dead body.

Although our primary focus will be on the principles regulating nonofficial autopsies and related procedures, some reference to the role of official examinations should be made.

OFFICIAL AUTOPSIES BY A CORONER OR MEDICAL EXAMINER

The Limited Role of Surviving Spouse or Kin

It is a general but not unvarying rule, to be discussed subsequently in greater detail, that a surviving spouse or the next of kin has the legal power to grant or deny authority for an autopsy. Like all general precepts, however, this one has its exceptions. As one court has remarked, "The right to have a dead body remain unmolested is not an absolute one; it must yield where it conflicts with the public good or where the demands of justice require such subordination." [4] The demands of justice—that there be as few "perfect" (that is, undetected) criminal homicides as possible—have inspired the enactment in every state of statutes permitting a coroner or medical examiner to perform an autopsy when death was caused by casualty or violence or when there exist reasonable grounds for concluding that one of these contributive factors was present. Autopsy is also statutorily sanctioned in some jurisdictions when death occurred under merely suspicious circumstances, as where the deceased had been in apparent good health or where no physician had been in attendance prior to death. In New York, for example, a medical examiner's statutory authority has been broadly interpreted to permit autopsy upon the body of a person who expired under any "unusual" circumstances. The issue arose in the 1966 case of *Cremonese* v. *City of New York*.[5] Physicians had been unable, despite extensive testing, to determine the cause of a patient's death. Her husband refused permission for an autopsy and the cause of death was reported as "peritonitis due to perforation of viscus." The Board of Health declined to accept this vague diagnosis and a medical examiner thereafter conducted an autopsy. The surviving spouse's damage action, claiming an unauthorized autopsy, was dismissed with a holding that the examination had been within the medical examiner's statutory power. The New York court held that "the inability of the physicians to diagnose the

[4] *Stastny* v. *Tachovsky*, 132 N.W.2d 317 (S. Ct. Nebr. 1964).

[5] 267 N.Y.S.2d 897 (Ct. App. N.Y. 1966).

nature of . . . [the deceased's] illness or to determine the cause of her death after following procedures customary in a modern hospital was an 'unusual' termination of life." The mystery could not be permitted to go unresolved, the husband's sensitivities to the contrary notwithstanding. The court said, "If a hospital leaves uncertain or indifferently explained how a patient entrusted to its care dies, it is manifestly the duty of the medical examiner in the public interest to find out if he can."

The Legal Definition of "Autopsy"

The term "autopsy" has been defined expansively. For example, the taking of a blood sample from a dead body probably constitutes a partial autopsy.[6]

Statutory authorization to conduct an autopsy carries with it an implied power to remove from the cadaver anything that is essential for purposes of examination, and this has been held to include blood samples.[7]

Autopsy Subsequent to Interment

An official autopsy may be authorized by statute or court order even after interment. For example, in *Donaldson* v. *Holcomb* [8] the deceased had apparently been in good health shortly before her demise; she had not been attended by a physician during her final illness, whatever that illness was; she had been talking about securing a divorce and had expressed a fear of being done in; and to climax it all, after her death her husband vociferously opposed exhumation of her body. An Arkansas court granted a petition for exhumation and autopsy under a statute that provided for such action in any case of "sudden, violent, or suspicious death."

In *Stastny* v. *Tachovsky* [9] the so-called simultaneous-death conundrum was posed. Often it is essential for purposes of estate distribution to determine which spouse died first. For example, did the husband, involved with his wife in a fatal automobile accident, die before his wife, with the result that his estate passed to her for a few seconds and thence to *her* heirs, or was it the other way around? In the *Stastny* case a court directed exhumation and autopsies to resolve this sort of riddle.

The Right of a Coroner or Medical Examiner to Act in the Absence of an Inquest

In some states the coroner or medical examiner is required to convene an inquest before autopsy will be proper; in others he is free to act on his own initiative. His role in criminal matters can be of the weightiest im-

[6] See, *e.g.*, OPINIONS, MISSOURI ATTORNEY GENERAL, Nos. 327, 487 (1964); Nos. 28, 110 (1966).

[7] *Rose Trucking Company* v. *Bell*, 426, P.2d 709 (S. Ct. Okla. 1967).

[8] 396 S.W.2d 281 (S. Ct. Ark. 1965).

[9] 132 U.W.2d 317 (S. Ct. Neb. 1964).

portance. A dispiriting case in point occurred following the assassination of President John F. Kennedy. It is possible that some of the more phantasmagorical theories surrounding that event would have been obviated had a prompt and competent autopsy been performed by the staff of the local Dallas, Texas, medical examiner prior to the return of the deceased President's body to Washington.[10]

Exceeding the Scope of Statutory Authority; the Defense of Good Faith

From the foregoing discussion it can be discerned that the root of an official medical examiner's authority to conduct autopsies lies in pertinent statutes.

Official autopsies are performed for limited purposes—in the main, detection of crime—and conduct that exceeds statutory bounds can supply a basis for civil litigation against a medical examiner. It has been held, for example, that a coroner lacked authority to conduct an autopsy on the body of a city employee for the private benefit of the municipality's Workmen's Compensation insurer.[11] On the other hand, a medical examiner will be insulated from civil liability if the order for an autopsy is based on a reasonable belief that a statutory ground for postmortem examination exists. In a Massachusetts case,[12] by way of example, an autopsy was held proper where there were indications of death by poisoning even though the autopsy turned up no evidence of foul play. Preliminary hospital diagnoses had differed, and the county medical examiner was found to have acted in good faith.

Duty to Surrender the Body and Parts Thereof

Statutory authority for an official autopsy does not carry with it a right to retain the body of the deceased for an unreasonable period of time. It is the duty of a coroner or a medical examiner, after completion of an autopsy, to surrender the body promptly to a person authorized to receive it, such as an undertaker selected by the surviving spouse or other relative or the executor of the deceased's estate. Refusal to do so for an unconscionable period of time gives rise to liability for money damages.[13] The survivor's right to possession of the body for burial also dictates that

[10] For a legally confused but perhaps factually accurate account of the Dallas County Medical Examiner's frustrated efforts, see Manchester, W.: THE DEATH OF A PRESIDENT, ch. 5. Harper & Row, New York, Evanston, and London, 1967.

[11] *Patrick* v. *Employers Mutual Liability Ins. Co.*, 118 S.W.2d 116 (Mo. App. 1938).

[12] *Gahn* v. *Leary*, 61 N.E.2d 844 (Sup. Jud. Ct. Mass. 1945). Compare *Jackson* v. *Rupp*, 228 So.2d 916 (Fla. App. 1969).

[13] *Hirko* v. *Reese*, 40 A.2d 408 (S. Ct. Pa. 1945).

a medical examiner not retain parts of the cadaver unnecessarily.[14] In the absence of valid consent or overriding need, they must be returned to the body cavity prior to interment.

NONOFFICIAL AUTOPSIES

The Necessity and Sources of Authorization for Nonofficial Autopsies

The state, by legislative enactments, grants authority for official autopsies. It is empowered to do so, even though relatives of the deceased may oppose any mutilation of his body, because the state has a paramount interest in, among other things, the detection of unlawful homicide. Except in one pathetic situation, involving unclaimed bodies, the state plays no part in nonofficial autopsies and related procedures such as the securing of organs for homotransplantations. The fact that the state is not a source of permission for unofficial autopsies does not mean, however, that no authority for them is necessary. Authority for nonofficial procedures must be secured if civil as well as possible criminal liability is to be avoided by the physician. Consent to nonofficial autopsies and connected procedures must come, ordinarily, from the deceased during his lifetime or, failing that, from a surviving spouse or next of kin. The reasons for this lie deep in some colorful Anglo-American history.

The History, Function, and Effect of "Anatomy" Laws

It was indicated in the preceding section that, as a general proposition, the common law recognizes a right in the surviving spouse or next of kin to give or withhold authority for an autopsy. This rule—it can, with a double propriety, be referred to as a "body" of law—has had a long history.

In England, long ago, it was the ecclesiastical courts that wrestled with such problems as which survivor had the right to authorize the place and method of interment and possible exhumation and reinterment of a dead body. There were no ecclesiastical courts in the American colonies,

[14] *E.g., Gray* v. *Southern Pac. Co.*, 68 P.2d 1011 (Cal. App. 1937); *Patrick* v. *Employers Mut. Liab. Ins. Co.*, 118 S.W.2d 116 (Mo. App. 1938); *Phillips* v. *Newport*, 187 S.W.2d 965 (Tenn. App. 1945). But see CALIF. HEALTH & SAFETY CODE ANN., §7115 (1955), giving coroners "or any other duly authorized public officer" the right to authorize the removal, during an official autopsy, of tissue for therapeutic or scientific use. To the same effect is a recent amendment to Hawaii's medical examiner law: "The coroner's physician or medical examiner . . . shall have the right to retain tissues, including fetal material, of the body removed at the time of autopsy to be used for necessary or advisable scientific investigation, including research, teaching and therapeutic purposes." No. 188, §2, [1967] HAWAII SESS. LAWS 183, *amending* HAWAII REV. LAWS, §260-14 (1955). See also VA. CODE ANN., §19.1–46.1 (Add. Supp. 1968), giving Chief Medical Officer the power, under stated circumstances, to provide organs for homotransplantation.

however, so the civil courts were occasionally confronted by litigation involving corpses. Some, but by no means all, of these courts gradually circumvented the English common law *dictum* that there could be no property interest in a corpse.[15] But it was the legislatures that first took a consistent position respecting dead bodies. They had to: America in the late eighteenth century saw the emergence of a singularly ghoulish calling that had earlier become a public scandal in Europe. The advance of medical science had by then made it essential that medical students and practitioners obtain cadavers for dissection and study, but no regularized source of supply existed and so the concept of free enterprise gave rise to the grave robber or, more elegantly, the resurrectionist.[16] The medical profession, in the name of science, purchased cadavers from anyone offering them. Cemeteries were defiled by the resurrectionists, and on occasion there was strong reason to believe that the law of supply and demand had compelled an entrepreneur to resort to murder in order to augment his stock. The public, however, was disapproving and in the first third of the nineteenth century a number of states enacted statutes making a crime of grave robbing and other molestations of the dead. At about the same time "unclaimed body" or "anatomy" laws were passed. (The first of these was drawn up in Massachusetts in 1831.) These enactments, which are still on the books, provided that deceased and unclaimed indigents, who ordinarily would be buried at public expense in some "Potter's Field," could be turned over to a state anatomical board, to medical schools, or even to private physicians for distribution and study.[17] This is the solitary situation in which the state is the source of authority for nonofficial autopsy and dissection procedures.

Section 4211 of the New York Public Health Law [18] is a relatively typical "anatomy" law. It defines unclaimed cadavers as those not claimed by relatives or, curiously enough, in certain specified counties by friends,

[15] Typical of the English precedents are *Williams* v. *Wiliams,* 20 Ch. Div. 659 (1882) (body not property, cannot be part of decedent's estate and, therefore, person cannot dictate the manner of his burial); *Regina* v. *Sharpe,* 169 Eng. Rep. 959 (Ct. Crim. App. 1857) (no property right in body of deceased person). American cases avoiding the English precedents are, *e.g., Fidelity Union Trust Co.* v. *Heller,* 84 A.2d 485 (N.J. Super. 1951); *Wilson* v. *Reed,* 68 Atl. 37 (S. Ct. N.H. 1907); *In re* Johnson's Estate, 7 N.Y.S.2d 81 (N.Y. Surr. 1938) (involving a body bequeathed for medical research). See Note, *The Law of Testamentary Disposition—A Legal Barrier to Medical Advance!,* 30 TEMPLE LAW QUARTERLY 40 (1956).

[16] Perhaps the most famous resurrectionist was a fictional one: Jerry Cruncher of Charles Dickens' *A Tale of Two Cities.*

[17] The "unclaimed body" or "anatomy" laws—44 of them—are cited and discussed in Comment, *The Law of Dead Bodies: Impeding Medical Progress,* 19 OHIO STATE LAW JOURNAL 455 (1958).

[18] N.Y. PUB. HEALTH LAW, §4211 (Supp. 1969).

within forty-eight hours after death. Under detailed provisions set out in the statute, an unclaimed cadaver can be delivered to medical schools within the state for study. Similarly, a hospital cannot authorize an autopsy on a dead body without the written consent of those authorized by law to give it unless the body has been unclaimed for forty-eight hours, and notice is required to be given to those entitled to object.

The anatomy statutes drove the resurrectionists out of business and, for a time, resulted in an adequate supply of dead bodies for legitimate study. Grave robbing is still a profitless undertaking but no longer does medical science achieve an adequate supply of cadavers through the operation of the anatomy statutes.[19] Among the factors restricting the number of dead indigents available for dissection are the onset of a generally affluent society, the rise of fraternal orders and welfare agencies offering burial benefits, and the burial benefits accorded to veterans and persons covered by the Social Security Act. It has also been reported that in some prisons the convicts have instituted their own burial societies to ensure that no member's body goes unclaimed.[20]

At a 1959 national conference on medical-legal problems it was announced that "There are areas in the United States and Canada in which the only hope for improving the supply of cadavers for teaching and research appears to be a properly organized system of bequests."[21]

Civil Liability for Unauthorized Nonofficial Autopsy Procedures

Physicians do not always insist on having and keeping the entire cadaver. Often they simply wish to conduct an autopsy for scientific or therapeutic purposes, after which all or most of the deceased's body will be available for interment even though it has been at least partially disassembled. Nevertheless, there still remain impediments, criminal as well as civil, to any such procedure if it has not been properly authorized.

In New York, for example, section 2214 of the Penal Law provides that "Any person who makes, or causes or procures to be made, any dissection

[19] See, *e.g.*, Couch, N. P.: *Supply and Demand in Kidney and Liver Transplantation: A Statistical Survey*, 4 TRANSPLANTATION 572 (1966); Jones, O. P.: *Cadavers, Autopsy and Transplantation*, in REPORT ON THE NATIONAL CONFERENCE ON THE LEGAL ENVIRONMENT OF MEDICAL SCIENCE 14, National Society for Medical Research and the University of Chicago, Chicago, 1959; *The Supply of Cadavers*, 10 BULL. FOR MEDICAL RESEARCH 11 (1955).

[20] Comment, *The Law of Dead Bodies: Impeding Medical Progress*, 19 OHIO STATE LAW JOURNAL 455, 463 (1958).

[21] Woodburne, R. T.: *Use of Cadavers, Organ Transplants, and Autopsy Procedures*, in REPORT ON THE NATIONAL CONFERENCE ON THE LEGAL ENVIRONMENT OF MEDICAL SCIENCE 10. National Society for Medical Research and the University of Chicago, Chicago, 1959.

of the body of a human being, except by authority of law, or in pursuance of a permission given by the deceased, is guilty of a misdemeanor." And section 4201(1) of New York's Public Health Law warns that "A person has the right to direct the manner in which his body shall be disposed of after death."

The courts of New York have held that the deceased during his lifetime, or his surviving spouse or next of kin, has a right to dictate the disposition of the dead body and that survivors are entitled to recover damages for unauthorized interference with this right. A husband, a wife, children, the mother of an infant, the mother of an adult bachelor, and a sister have been held entitled to damages for the unauthorized dissection or disposition of the body of a deceased.[22]

The liability of a hospital for unauthorized dissection has also been considered by the New York courts. In *Darcy* v. *Presbyterian Hospital*[23] it was held that a lawsuit could be maintained against a hospital that refused to deliver the body of a deceased infant to its mother and instead induced a coroner to have an autopsy performed. Unauthorized dissection by hospital staff members has been held, *a fortiori*, to impose liability upon the hospital.[24] However, no liability was found in one New York case in which the plaintiff failed to establish that the defendant hospital in which the deceased reposed had knowingly permitted a dissection by independent agents.[25] On the other hand, failure by a hospital to take reasonable precautions against unauthorized dissection by nonemployees would probably be considered actionable.[26]

Similar results have been achieved in states without statutes comparable to New York's. A leading decision, frequently relied upon by other courts, is that in *Larson* v. *Chase*.[27] An unhappy widow sought damages from the doctor who had dissected the body of her deceased husband without her consent. The Minnesota Supreme Court concluded that it was immaterial whether the widow had a property interest, in a com-

[22] *Jackson* v. *Savage*, 96 N.Y.S. 366 (N.Y. App. 1905) (husband); *Foley* v. *Phelps*, 37 N.Y.S. 471 (N.Y. App. 1896) (wife); *Brown* v. *Broome County*, 207 N.Y.S.2d 657 (Ct. App. N.Y. 1960) (children); *Darcy* v. *Presbyterian Hospital*, 95 N.E. 695 (Ct. App. N.Y. 1911) (mother of infant); *Hassard* v. *Lehane*, 128 N.Y.S. 161 (N.Y. App. 1911) (mother of adult bachelor); *Trammell* v. *City of New York*, 82 N.Y.S.2d 762 (S. Ct. N.Y. 1948) (sister).

[23] 95 N.E. 695 (Ct. App. N.Y. 1911).

[24] *Torres* v. *State*, 228 N.Y.S.2d 1005 (Ct. Claims N.Y. 1962); *Gould* v. *State*, 43 N.Y.S.2d 313 (Ct. Claims N.Y. 1944).

[25] *Hasselbach* v. *Mt. Sinai Hospital*, 159 N.Y.S. 376 (App. Div. N.Y. 1916).

[26] See *Grawunder* v. *Beth Israel Hospital*, 272 N.Y.S. 171 (App. Div. N.Y. 1934), *affirmed without opinion*, 195 N.E. 221 (Ct. App. N.Y. 1935).

[27] 50 N.W. 238 (S. Ct. Minn. 1891).

mercial sense, in the body of her spouse. "The important fact," said the court, "is that the custodian of it has a legal right to its possession for the purpose of preservation and burial, and that any interference with that right by mutilating or otherwise disturbing the body is an actionable wrong." Money damages for the widow were affirmed.

Other states have followed a similar route. Basing their decisions on common law concepts of required permission or upon an express permission statute akin to New York's, they have inquired whether the requisite authority for autopsy was present; if it was not, the only remaining question has been that of damages.[28] Some of the older cases have held that there can be no recovery of money damages for "mental anguish" alone, but this rule is rapidly crumbling.[29] In the 1967 case of *French* v. *Ochsner Clinic and Ochsner Foundation Hosp.*[30] a Louisiana court said, "We . . . find the general rule . . . is that an unauthorized autopsy is a tort giving rise to a cause of action for damages; and . . . the courts are not primarily concerned with the extent of the physical mishandling, injury or mutilation to the body *per se,* but rather with the effect of the same on the feelings and emotions of the surviving relatives who have the duty of burial." However, juries in jurisdictions that permit damage recoveries for mental anguish have been reluctant to return large verdicts. A 1964 survey turned up one award of $5,000; the highest verdict on record in New York was for $3,500. Most were for smaller sums.[31]

A California court has held that the unauthorized retention of body parts will justify only nominal damages, traditionally the munificent sum of six cents.[32] And the highest court of Massachusetts has said that the mere photographing of a corpse is not actionable by the survivors because it in no way interferes with their right to possession of the cadaver.[33]

[28] For representative cases, see *Painter* v. *United States Fidelity and Guaranty Co.,* 91 Atl. 158 (S. Ct. Md. 1914); *Burney* v. *Children's Hospital,* 47 N.E. 401 (Sup. Jud. Ct. Mass. 1897); *Deeg* v. *City of Detroit,* 76 N.W.2d 16 (S. Ct. Mich. 1956).

[29] See, *e.g., Hendriksen* v. *Roosevelt Hospital,* 297 F. Supp. 1142 (S.D.N.Y. 1969); *Jackson* v. *Rupp,* 228 So.2d 916 (Fla. App. 1969); *Chapman* v. *Commonwealth,* 267 S.W. 181 (S. Ct. Ky. 1924); Prosser, W. L.: TORTS 41–54, 348–49, 3d ed. West Publishing Company, St. Paul, 1964.

[30] 200 So.2d 371 (La. App. 1967).

[31] N.Y. LAW REVISION COMMISSION, ACTS, RECOMMENDATION AND STUDY RELATING TO LAWS GOVERNING AUTOPSIES AND DONATIONS OF BODIES OR PARTS OF BODIES 19, 24 (1964).

[32] *Gray* v. *Southern Pac. Co.,* 68 P.2d (Cal. App. 1937).

[33] *Kelley* v. *Post Publishing Co.,* 98 N.E.2d 286 (Sup. Jud. Ct. Mass. 1951), discussed in Note, 4 BAYLOR LAW REVIEW 553 (1952). But see *Bazemore* v. *Savannah Hosp.,* 155 S.E. 194 (S. Ct. Ga. 1930) (hospital permitted newsman to photograph deceased child; cause of action for violation of parents' right of privacy sustained), discussed in Chapter 18.

Summarization of Rules Affecting Autopsy in the Absence of Valid Consent

The currently operative rules to be extracted from the decided cases and the statutes can be summed up.

Although it is undoubtedly still true in the United States that a cadaver is not "property" in the ordinary commercial sense,[34] rights in a dead body do exist for the purpose of decent and proper disposal.[35] It can properly be put this way: a living person has a right, to be accorded to him after death, to have his body disposed of decently. A "decent" disposal, today, means burial or cremation of the intact body as soon as possible after death. In the case of burial, the right connotes permanent burial; the deceased, decently buried, cannot be exhumed at will for belated non-official autopsy purposes. A correlative duty and right devolve upon those whom the deceased has left behind.

The person having the right or duty of disposal is entitled to possession of the body for that purpose; furthermore, that person is entitled to receive the body as soon as possible, and in the same condition it was in at the time of death. The duty of according to the deceased a decent disposition of his remains falls upon the surviving spouse, first; if there is no spouse, the duty falls upon the next of kin. If there is neither spouse nor kin, the obligation may fall upon the person, agency, or institution under whose roof the death occurred. In practicality, if there is neither spouse nor kin the duty of disposal is the public's.

Effective Authorization for Nonofficial Autopsy

The only factor having any impact on the foregoing principles is the existence of effective authorization for nonofficial autopsy. In one sad and rare instance the authorization may be statutory. As we have stated, if there is no one to claim the deceased's body and the duty of disposal has devolved upon the state, it may be empowered by statute to permit medical students to dissect the cadaver. But there are other possibilities that are less coldly automatic.

Our discussion of general legal principles will have made it obvious

[34] It seems thoroughly doubtful, for example, that an English or American court would permit a cadaver to be seized and sold to pay the deceased's debts. See *Long* v. *Chicago, R.I. & P.R. Co.* 86 Pac. 289 (S. Ct. Okla. 1905), where the court indicated as much.

[35] A true lawyer will call this a "qualified property interest in trust for burial." See Kuzenski, W. F.: *Property in Dead Bodies,* 9 MARQUETTE LAW REVIEW 17, 19 (1924). For a comprehensible, common-sense description of the nature of these rights, see *Pierce* v. *Swan Point Cemetery,* 10 R.I. 227 (S. Ct. R. I. 1872).

that the deceased, while still living, is a potential source of permission to dissect his body after death. Some states have enacted statutes specifically authorizing persons to direct the manner of disposition of their remains, whether by interment, cremation, or dissection.[36] Ever since 1881, for example, New York has had a statute providing that "A person has the right to direct the manner in which his body shall be disposed of after death."[37] In the absence of such a statute, however, a person's efforts to authorize his own autopsy may prove unavailing. It might be thought that he could simply bequeath his remains to medical science by means of a provision in his will. He could, but there are practical as well as legalistic problems that may frustrate the intention expressed in his will. There are only two reported cases and they are singularly unhelpful.

In *Holland* v. *Metalious*[38] the author of the best-selling novel *Peyton Place,* perhaps seeking to atone for her prose style, had willed her body to either of two medical schools "for purposes of experimentation in the interest of medical science." Nothing much came of her effort, however; both schools declined to accept the body. In *In re* Johnson's Estate[39] the New York County Surrogate Court considered a codicil (that is, a supplement) to a will in which the testator bequeathed her body for medical research. The court upheld the codicil, but this was to be anticipated in view of New York's statute and the fact that no next of kin had contested the donation.

On a purely practical level the difficulties attending testamentary authorization for autopsy procedures are considerable. For example, the testator's body will ordinarily have been buried or otherwise disposed of long before his will has been read or admitted to probate. Additionally, on a legalistic level there are potential difficulties in those jurisdictions that do not view one's body as a form of property that can be made the subject of testamentary disposition. There is, for example, a line of cases to the effect that a testamentary disposition of a decedent's body is not binding on his spouse or next of kin.[40] In short, the law is sufficiently confused that in the absence of explicit legislative authority a person has only a minimal assurance that the testamentary disposition he makes of his own mortal remains will ever be honored. Surviving relatives can block a testator's attempted authorization for autopsy and tissue removal.

[36] See Sadler, A. M., and Sadler, B. L.: *Transplantation and the Law: The Need for Organized Sensitivity,* 57 GEORGETOWN LAW JOURNAL 5, 37–54 (1968).

[37] N.Y. PUB. HEALTH LAW, §4201 (Supp. 1969).

[38] 198 A.2d 654 (S. Ct. N.H. 1964).

[39] 7 N.Y.S.2d 81 (N.Y. Surr. 1938).

[40] *E.g., Enos* v. *Snyder,* 63 Pac. 170 (S. Ct. Cal. 1900); *Guerin* v. *Cassidy,* 119 A.2d 780 (N.J. Super. Ct. Ch. 1955).

Informal consents, accomplished by means of a simple form that has no statutory or judicial *imprimatur,* are used with some frequency but, here again, their effectiveness depends upon the cooperation of the deceased donor's survivors at a juncture when time is often of the essence—unless, of course, advance consent has also been obtained from them. A variation, and probably an effective one, involves the consent of a living person, such as an executor, whom the deceased during his lifetime designated to take charge of his body after death.

By statute in many states and custom in all others, a deceased person's surviving spouse or next of kin can effectively consent to an autopsy or postmortem examination. In fact, a few states have enacted nonofficial autopsy statutes that lodge the right to disposition of the deceased's body with certain survivors, usually the spouse or designated next of kin, without making any reference to the desires of the deceased.[41] It is questionable, however, whether these statutes accomplish anything not already secured by custom and common sense. If a deceased person's survivors consent to an autopsy, with or without statutory authority, any arguable violation of the deceased's right to a decent and proper burial becomes academic since, having no living champion, it is, practically speaking, unenforceable.[42]

The Need for Uniform Legislation

As the preceding discussion should amply demonstrate, the current state of the law regarding dead human bodies is unsatisfactory. The existing patchwork of judicial decisions and statutes does not make clear the rights of those concerned with orthodox official and unofficial autopsies and postmortem examinations. Far less does it sensibly and sensitively resolve the rights and duties of those interested in the increasingly important subject of homotransplantation and such directly related matters as the legitimate stocking of blood and tissue banks. There is, manifestly, a need for uniform and comprehensive legislation. In the next chapter we discuss a long and commendable step that is responsive to this need.

[41] ALA. CODE, tit. 14, §109 (Supp. 1967); CONN. GEN STAT., §19-143 (Supp. 1969); HAWAII REV. LAWS, §64-14 (Supp. 1961); IND. STAT. ANN., §35-4404 (Supp. 1969); MICH. STAT. ANN., §14-524 (Supp. 1969); NEV. REV. STAT., §451.010 (1967); TENN. CODE ANN., §39-2105 (Supp. 1968).

[42] See Sadler, A. M., and Sadler, B. L.: *Transplantation and the Law: The Need for Organized Sensitivity,* 57 GEORGETOWN LAW JOURNAL 5, 12 (1968). Perhaps the statutes possess some value to the surgeon in that they provide an indication of which survivors are authorized to give binding consent to autopsy in the particular jurisdiction. However, some of them are vague even in this respect.

BIBLIOGRAPHY

BOOK

Polson, C. J.: THE DISPOSAL OF THE DEAD. J. B. Lippincott Company, Philadelphia, 1953.

ARTICLES

Gerber, S. R.: *Postmortem Examinations,* 6 CLEVELAND-MARSHALL LAW REVIEW 194 (1957).

Jones, O. P.: *Cadavers, Autopsy and Transplantation,* in REPORT ON THE NATIONAL CONFERENCE ON THE LEGAL ENVIRONMENT OF MEDICAL SCIENCE 13. National Society for Medical Research and the University of Chicago, Chicago, 1959.

Kuzenski, W. F.: *Property in Dead Bodies,* 9 MARQUETTE LAW REVIEW 17 (1924).

McCormack, L. J.: *The Pathologist and the Autopsy,* 6 CLEVELAND-MARSHALL LAW REVIEW 205 (1957).

Monger, R. H.: *Functions and Limitations of an Autopsy,* 24 TENNESSEE LAW REVIEW 159 (1956).

Sadler, A. M., and Sadler, B. L.: *Transplantation and the Law: The Need for Organized Sensitivity,* 57 GEORGETOWN LAW JOURNAL 5 (1968).

Vestal, A. D., Taber, R. E., and Shoemaker, W. J.: *Medico-Legal Aspects of Tissue Homotransplantation,* 18 UNIV. OF DETROIT LAW JOURNAL 171 (1955).

NOTES AND COMMENTS

Comment, *The Cadaver Business,* 159 J.A.M.A. 21 (1955).

Comment, *California's Response to the Problems of Procuring Human Remains for Transplantation,* 57 CALIFORNIA LAW REVIEW 671 (1969).

Comment, *The Law of Dead Bodies: Impeding Medical Progress,* 19 OHIO STATE LAW JOURNAL 455 (1958).

Comment, *The Legal Problems in Donations of Tissue to Medical Science,* 21 VANDERBILT LAW REVIEW 352 (1968).

Comment, *Mutilation of Dead Body,* 27 CALIFORNIA LAW REVIEW 217 (1939).

Comment, *Property Interest in a Dead Body,* 2 ARKANSAS LAW REVIEW 124 (1947).

Comment, *Property Rights in Dead Bodies,* 71 WEST VIRGINIA LAW REVIEW 377 (1969).

Note, *Donation of Dead Bodies and Parts Thereof for Medical Use,* 21 UNIV. OF PITTSBURGH LAW REVIEW 523 (1960).

Note, *Indecent Treatment of Corpse as Common Law Crime,* 4 ARKANSAS LAW REVIEW 480 (1950).

Note, *The Law of Testamentary Disposition—A Legal Barrier to Medical Advance!* 30 TEMPLE LAW QUARTERLY 40 (1956).

Note, *Relational Concept in Dead Body Cases,* 42 ILLINOIS LAW REVIEW 393 (1947).

chapter 14

HOMOTRANSPLANTATION OF TISSUE AND ORGANS: THE PARTS PROBLEM

THE UNIFORM ANATOMICAL GIFT ACT

The History of Homotransplantation

The impressive chronicle of medical science's advances in the field of transplantation has been set out in both the medical and the legal literature, some of the best of which is cited in this chapter's footnotes. There is provided here, as background for a discussion of the Uniform Anatomical Gift Act, only the briefest of reminders.

Although the first transplantation, on December 3, 1967, of a human heart understandably attracted unprecedented attention,[1] human tissue transplants were not themselves without precedent. The first skin autograft was reported in the year 1804.[2] During the nineteenth century, efforts had also been made to transplant teeth, bone, cornea, and other human structures.[3] Except as to corneal transplantations, where the rejection reaction is insignificant, these efforts slackened temporarily during the same century because of inability to solve the rejection problem.[4]

Experimental work involving organ transplantation was carried on by Carrel at the beginning of the twentieth century.[5] The transfusing of human blood began shortly before World War I.[6] Initially hazardous, transfusion is now a commonplace procedure in hospitals large and small.[7]

[1] See, *e.g.*, N.Y. Times, Dec. 4, 1967, §A, p. 1.

[2] Baronio, Degli Innesti Animali (1804).

[3] See Wasmuth, C. E., and Stewart, B. H.: *Medical and Legal Aspects of Human Organ Transplantation,* 14 Cleveland-Marshall Law Review 442 (1965).

[4] *Id.* at 443.

[5] Carrel, A.: *Results in the Transplantation of Blood Vessels, Organs and Limbs,* 51 J.A.M.A. 1662 (1908).

[6] See Vestal, A. D., Taber, R. E., and Shoemaker, W. J.: *Medico-Legal Aspects of Tissue Homotransplantation,* 18 Univ. of Detroit Law Journal 171 (1955).

[7] Vestal, A. D., Taber, R.E., and Shoemaker, W. J.: *Medico-Legal Aspects of Tissue Homotransplantation,* 18 Univ. of Detroit Law Journal 171 (1955).

After World War II, Carrel's experiments in organ transplantation, which had never been given human application because of inadequate supportive facilities, were revived,[8] and in 1948 the first series of successful human arterial transplantations was accomplished.[9] By 1954 it was possible, by building upon some of Carrel's early work and by taking advantage of the development by Kolff and others of an artificial kidney, to transplant a healthy kidney from one twin to another who was dying of kidney failure.[10] By January 1, 1969, well over two thousand kidney transplantations had been performed throughout the world.[11] Bone and skin homotransplantations now constitute practical surgical procedures.[12] Liver and lung transplant procedures, along with human heart transplantation, are now in advanced developmental stages as medical science solves the rejection reaction puzzle.[13] In fact, in animals and in humans there has emerged a long and encouraging catalog of tissue and organ transplantations, including most vital organs and all culminating in what has been described as "a good functional result": [14] arteries, blood, bone, bone marrow, cartilage, cornea, endocrine glands, heart, intestine, kidney, liver, lung, lymph nodes, ovaries, pancreas, skin, spleen, and veins.[15] Multiorgan transplants are also in the offing.[16] And continued progress in developing techniques of tissue storage is further enhancing the prospects for widespread applications of the new knowledge concerning autografts, homografts, and homotransplantations.[17]

[8] See Hufnagle, C. A.: *Preserved Homologous Arterial Transplants,* 32 BULL. AM. COLL. SURG. 231 (1947).

[9] See Gross, R. E., Bill, A. H., and Pierce, E. C.: *Methods for Preservation and Transplantation of Arterial Grafts,* in *Report of Transplantation of Preserved Arterial Grafts in Nine Human Cases,* 88 SURG., GYNEC., AND OBSTET. 689 (1949).

[10] Merrill, J. P., *et al.: Successful Homotransplantation of the Human Kidney in Identical Twins,* 160 J.A.M.A. 277 (1956).

[11] *Seventh Report of the Human Kidney Transplant Registry,* Advisory Committee, 1969 (mimeograph).

[12] See, *e.g.,* Brown, J. B., *et al.: Postmortem Homografts as "Biological Dressings" for Extensive Burns and Denuded Areas,* 138(4) ANNALS OF SURGERY 618 (1953).

[13] See Starzyl, T. E., *et al.: Immunosuppression After Experimental and Clinical Homotransplantation of the Liver,* 160 ANNALS OF SURGERY 411 (1964); Titus, J. L., *et al.: Transplantation of the Lung,* 48 MED. CLIN. N. AM. 1089 (1964).

[14] Stickel, D. L.: *Organ Transplantation in Medical and Legal Perspectives,* 32 LAW & CONTEMPORARY PROBLEMS 597, 597–98 (1967).

[15] See Woodruff, M. F.: THE TRANSPLANTATION OF TISSUES AND ORGANS, 291–615 (1960); Billingham, R. E.: *Tissue Transplantation; Scope and Prospect,* 153 SCIENCE 266, 267 (1966).

[16] See, *e.g.,* Kelly, W. D., *et al.: Allotransplantation of the Pancreas and Duodenum Along With the Kidney in Diabetic Nephropathy,* 61 SURGERY 827 (1967).

[17] See, *e.g.,* Brown, J. B., *et al.: Establishing a Skin Bank,* 16 PLASTIC & RECONSTRUCTIVE SURG. 337 (1955); Cullipher, E. W.: *The Organization and Operation of a Bone Bank,* 20 AM. JOUR. MED. TECHNOLOGY 354 (1954); Shafter, D. M.: *The Role*

The optimism of medical science in the area of homotransplantation is perhaps best evidenced by the grudging quality of Doctor Delford L. Stickel's concession that "The brain and spinal cord may for all practical functional purposes be regarded as not transplantable in the foreseeable future." [18] But, the same authority has understated, "It would appear that there will be further advances. . . ." [19]

The Inadequate Supply of Materials for Homotransplantation

It is obvious, in view of medical science's headlong progress, that mankind will encounter an ever increasing need for human tissue and organs for grafting and transplantation purposes. In 1958 it was being reported that demand was running well ahead of supply at tissue and organ banks.[20] One year later a distinguished medical commentator said, "Quite naturally, after these [various] techniques [of transplantation] have been developed, there will be an even greater demand for human material than exists today." [21] By early 1964 it had become apparent "that there were many more patients dying of kidney failure than there were available living human donors." [22] In 1969 the President of the American Society of Anesthesiologists was to say, "With the present rate of scientific progress, the medical profession and the public can no longer afford the static luxury of outmoded customs and the traditions of committing to the ground by burial bodies whose organs could have been recovered while viable and used to offer continued life to other persons." [23]

The Present Inadequacy of the Law Respecting Tissue and Organ Donations

The law as it presently exists does not provide an efficient mechanism for the donation of cadaver material usable for grafting and homotrans-

and Function of the National Eye Bank, 56(2) JOUR. KENTUCKY STATE MED. ASSOC. 141 (1958); Williams, D. N., and Hyatt, G. W.: *The Tissue Bank of the Naval Medical School and You,* 126(6) MILITARY MEDICINE 407 (1961).

[18] Stickel, D. L.: *Organ Transplantation in Medical and Legal Perspectives,* 32 LAW & CONTEMPORARY PROBLEMS 597, 598 (1967).

[19] *Ibid.*

[20] Comment, *The Law of Dead Bodies: Impeding Medical Progress,* 19 OHIO STATE LAW JOURNAL 455, 461 (1958).

[21] Jones, O. P.: *Cadavers, Autopsy and Transplantation,* in REPORT ON THE NATIONAL CONFERENCE ON THE LEGAL ENVIRONMENT OF MEDICAL SCIENCE 16. National Society for Medical Research and the University of Chicago, Chicago, 1959.

[22] Wasmuth, C. E., and Stewart, B. H.: *Medical and Legal Aspects of Human Organ Transplantation,* 14 CLEVELAND-MARSHALL LAW REVIEW 442, 444 (1965).

[23] Wasmuth, C. E.: *The Physician's Role in Organ Transplantation,* 37(13) MODERN MEDICINE 70 (1969). See also Dukeminier, J.: *Supplying Organs for Transplantation,* 68 MICHIGAN LAW REVIEW 811 (1970).

plantation.[24] The common law, as we indicated in the preceding chapter, is vague and unreliable in this area. Autopsy statutes and custom, empowering survivors to authorize the conventional autopsy or postmortem examination, do not encompass the permanent removal of tissue and organs for grafting or homotransplantation. The so-called anatomy or unclaimed body statutes do not channel a sufficient amount of cadaver material to medical science even for educational purposes in the schools. Furthermore, those statutes usually call for waiting periods of twenty-four hours or more before a cadaver can properly be considered "unclaimed." Such provisions serve society's need for some assurance that the deceased was in fact alone in the world when he died, but at the same time they preclude utilization of most cadaver parts for therapeutic transplantation.[25]

The usual coroner and medical examiner statutes, with but two recent exceptions,[26] extend to public medical personnel no authority beyond that of conducting orthodox official autopsies. The true donation statutes enacted in one form or another in forty-one jurisdictions, while representing a genuine improvement over the preexisting judicial and legislative picture, are an imperfect means for bringing together medical science, on the one hand, and, on the other, those who wish to donate their remains for

[24] Removal of tissue from competent, adult *living* persons for purposes of homotransplantation ordinarily poses no large legal problems, since effective authorization (consent) can be secured from the donor himself. See Sadler, A. M., and Sadler, B. L.: *Transplantation and the Law: The Need for Organized Sensitivity,* 57 GEORGETOWN LAW JOURNAL 5, 8 (1968). There may be legal hurdles, not insurmountable, if the prospective donor, although living, is himself incompetent to consent to surgical removal of tissue. See Curran, W. J.: *A Problem of Consent: Kidney Transplantation in Minors,* 34 NEW YORK UNIV. LAW REVIEW 891 (1959). Of course, living donors are not a prime source of organs for transplantation since the removal of most such organs would kill the donor. This is called murder. See Vestal, A. D., Tabor, R. E., and Shoemaker, W. J.: *Medico-Legal Aspects of Tissue Homotransportation,* 18 UNIV. OF DETROIT LAW JOURNAL 171, 183 (1955).

[25] "For a few minutes after death cellular metabolism continues throughout the majority of the body cell mass. Certain tissues are suitable for removal only during this brief interval, although improvements in storage and preservation may permit a short delay in actual implantation in the recipient . . . there are 'critical' tissues, such as the kidney and liver, which must be removed from the deceased within a matter of thirty to forty-five minutes." Stason, E. B.: *The Role of Law in Medical Progress,* 32 LAW & CONTEMPORARY PROBLEMS 563, 568 (1967).

[26] See No. 188, §2, [1967] HAWAII SESS. LAWS 183, amending HAWAII REV. LAWS, §260-14 (1955) (medical examiner authorized to retain tissue, removed during autopsy, "for necessary or advisable scientific investigation, including research, teaching and therapeutic purposes"); VA. CODE ANN., §19.1-46.1 (Add. Supp. 1968) (medical examiner authorized, under some circumstances, to provide organs for homotransplantation). See section on official autopsies in Chapter 13.

mankind's good.[27] The present donation statutes, in the main drafted in another era so far as the state of the medical art is concerned, suffer from some of the same inadequacies as does the common law of testamentary disposition, discussed in the preceding chapter. The result is that they frequently fail to make usable material available for grafting or transplanting.

The Uniform Anatomical Gift Act: Origin and Text

It was in an effort to sweep away the previously analyzed ineffectual hodgepodge of law that in 1965 the Commissioners on Uniform State Laws set up a special committee to draft a model uniform donation statute for possible adoption by the several states. On July 30, 1968, the Commissioners approved their committee's product, the Uniform Anatomical Gift Act; the American Bar Association later added its endorsement.[28]

The Uniform Anatomical Gift Act, where adopted, creates a more favorable legal environment for tissue and organ donation than formerly existed anywhere in the United States. By mid-1970 the Act, with occasional modifications, had been adopted by forty-one state legislatures [29]

[27] These statutes have been cited and analyzed in Appendix C, Sadler, A. M., and Sadler, B. L.: *Transplantation and the Law: The Need for Organized Sensitivity,* 57 GEORGETOWN LAW JOURNAL 5, 37–54 (1968). Most of them will be rendered obsolete by state adoption of the Uniform Anatomical Gift Act, to be discussed in this chapter.

[28] The Uniform Anatomical Gift Act has not been without its critics, however. See, *e.g.,* Dukeminier, J., *Supplying Organs for Transplantation,* 68 MICHIGAN LAW REVIEW 811 (1970).

[29] ALA. CODE tit. 22, §§184(4)–(11) (Supp. 1969); No. 4, 2 (1969) ARK. ACTS 1; CAL. HEALTH & SAFETY CODE §§7150–58 (West Supp. 1969); ch. 239 (1969) COLO. ACTS; No. 425 (1969) CONN. ACTS 458; DEL. CODE ch. 24, §§1780–88 (Supp. 1969); ch. 69–88 (1969) FLA. ACTS; GA. CODE ANN. §§48-401 to -409 (Supp. 1969); IDAHO CODE ANN. §§39-3401 to -3411 (Supp. 1969); ILL. ANN. STAT. ch. 3, §§551–61 (Smith-Hurd Supp. 1970); ch. 166 (1969) IND. ACTS 343; ch. 137 (1969) IOWA ACTS 171; ch. 301 (1969) KAN. ACTS 832; LA. REV. STAT. §§17:2351–59 (Supp. 1969); ME. REV. STAT. ANN. tit. 22, §§2201–9 (Supp. 1970); ch. 490, 2 (1969) MD. ACTS 1192; No. 189 (1969) MICH. ACTS 347–51; ch. 79 (1969) MINN. ACTS 132; MO. ANN. STAT. §§194.210–.290 (Supp. 1969); MONT REV. CODE §§69-2315 to -2323 (Supp. 1969); ch. 119, 1 (1969) NEV. ACTS 158; N.H. REV. STAT. ANN. ch. 291-A (Supp. 1969); ch. 161, (1969) N.J. ACTS; N.M. STAT. §§12-11-6 to -14 (Supp. 1969); N.C. GEN. STAT. §§90-220.1 to -220.9 (Supp. 1969); N.D. CENT. CODE §§23.06.1-01 to -09 (1969); OHIO REV. CODE ch. 2108 (Supp. 1969); OKLA. STAT. ch. 63, §§2201-09 (Supp. 1969); ch. 175 (1969) ORE. ACTS 295, ch. 161 (1969) PA. ACTS; R. I. GEN. LAWS §§23-47-1 to -7 (Supp. 1969); S.C. CODE §§32-711 to -720 (Supp. 1969); S.D. COMP. LAWS §§34-26-20 to -41 (Supp. 1969); TENN. CODE ANN. §§53-4201 to -4209 (Supp. 1969); ch. 375, 1 (1969) TEX. ACTS 1176; UTAH CODE ANN. §§26-26-1 to -8 (Supp. 1969); VT. STAT. ANN. tit. 18,§§5231–37 (Supp. 1969); WASH. REV. CODE §§68.08.500-.610 (1969); H.B. 537 (1970) W. VA. ACTS; ch. 90 (1969) WIS. ACTS 266; WYO. STAT. ANN. §§35-221.1 to -221.9 (Supp. 1969).

Nine states and the District of Columbia have organ donation laws that were enacted and was pending, with early enactment predicted, in several others.[30]

There follows the full text of the Act:

AN ACT AUTHORIZING THE GIFT OF ALL OR PART OF A HUMAN BODY AFTER DEATH FOR SPECIFIED PURPOSES

SECTION 1. **[Definitions.]**

(a) "Bank or storage facility" means a facility licensed, accredited or approved under the laws of any state for storage of human bodies or parts thereof.

(b) "Decedent" means a deceased individual and includes a stillborn infant or fetus.

(c) "Donor" means an individual who makes a gift of all or part of his body.

(d) "Hospital" means a hospital licensed, accredited or approved under the laws of any state and includes a hospital operated by the United States government, a state, or a subdivision thereof, although not required to be licensed under state laws.

(e) "Part" includes organs, tissues, eyes, bones, arteries, blood, other fluids and other portions of a human body, and "part" includes "parts".

(f) "Person" means an individual, corporation, government or governmental subdivision or agency, business trust, estate, trust, partnership or association or any other legal entity.

(g) "Physician" or "surgeon" means a physician or surgeon licensed or authorized to practice under the laws of any state.

(h) "State" includes any state, district, commonwealth, territory, insular possession, and any other area subject to the legislative authority of the United States of America.

SECTION 2. **[Persons Who May Execute an Anatomical Gift.]**

(a) Any individual of sound mind and 18 years of age or more may give all or any part of his body for any purposes specified in Section 3, the gift to take effect upon death.

(b) Any of the following persons, in order of priority stated, when persons in prior classes are not available at the time of death, and in the absence of actual notice of contrary indications by the decedent, or actual notice of opposition by a member of the same or a prior class, may give all or any part of the decedent's body for any purposes specified in Section 3:

(1) the spouse,

(2) an adult son or daughter,

---

prior to 1968. ALAS. STAT. §13.035 (Supp. 1969) (applies only to eyes); ARIZ. REV. STAT. §§36-841 to -845 (1967); D.C. CODE §§2-251 to -260 (1967); HAWAII REV. LAWS §§327-1 to -24 (1968); KY. REV. STAT. §§311.352–.356 (1962); MASS. GEN LAWS ANN. ch. 113, §§7–10 (Supp. 1969); MISS. CODE §278.5 (Supp. 1966); NEB. REV. STAT. §§71-1339 to -1341 (1966); N.Y. PUB. HEALTH LAW §§4201 (1)–(4) (Supp. 1969); VA. CODE ANN. §32-364.1 (1969).

[30] See *Anatomic Gift Act Widely Supported,* 5(4) TRIAL 63 (1969).

(3) either parent,
(4) an adult brother or sister,
(5) a guardian of the person of the decedent at the time of his death,
(6) any other person authorized or under obligation to dispose of the body.

(c) If the donee has actual notice of contrary indications by the decedent, or that a gift by a member of a class is opposed by a member of the same or a prior class, the donee shall not accept the gift. The persons authorized by this subsection (b) may make the gift after death or immediately before death.

(d) A gift of all or part of a body authorizes any examination necessary to assure medical acceptability of the gift for the purposes intended.

(e) The rights of the donee created by the gift are paramount to the rights of others except as provided by Section 7 (d).

SECTION 3. [Persons Who May Become Donees, and Purposes for Which Anatomical Gifts May Be Made.]

The following persons may become donees of gifts of bodies or parts thereof for the purposes stated:

(1) any hospital, surgeon, or physician, for medical or dental education, research, advancement of medical or dental science, therapy or transplantation; or

(2) any accredited medical or dental school, college or university for education, research, advancement of medical or dental science or therapy; or

(3) any bank or storage facility, for medical or dental education, research, advancement of medical or dental science, therapy or transplantation; or

(4) any specified individual for therapy or transplantation needed by him.

SECTION 4. [Manner of Executing Anatomical Gifts.]

(a) A gift of all or part of the body under Section 2 (a) may be made by will. The gift becomes effective upon the death of the testator without waiting for probate. If the will is not probated, or if it is declared invalid for testamentary purposes, the gift, to the extent that it has been acted upon in good faith, is nevertheless valid and effective.

(b) A gift of all or part of the body under Section 2 (a) may also be made by document other than a will. The gift becomes effective upon the death of the donor. The document, which may be a card designed to be carried on the person, must be signed by the donor, in the presence of 2 witnesses who must sign the document in his presence. If the donor cannot sign, the document may be signed for him at his direction and in his presence, and in the presence of 2 witnesses who must sign the document in his presence. Delivery of the document of gift during the donor's lifetime is not necessary to make the gift valid.

(c) The gift may be made to a specified donee or without specifying a donee. If the latter, the gift may be accepted by the attending physician as donee upon or following death. If the gift is made to a specified donee who is not available at the time and place of death, the attending physician upon or following death, in the absence of any expressed indication that the donor desired otherwise, may accept the gift as donee. The physician who becomes a donee under this subsection shall not participate in the procedures for removing or transplanting a part.

(d) Notwithstanding Section 7 (b), the donor may designate in his will, card or other document of gift the surgeon or physician to carry out the appropriate procedures. In the absence of a designation, or if the designee is not available, the donee or other person authorized to accept the gift may employ or authorize any surgeon or physician for the purpose.

(e) Any gift by a person designated in Section 2 (b) shall be made by a document signed by him or made by his telegraphic, recorded telephonic or other recorded message.

SECTION 5. [Delivery of Document of Gift.]

If the gift is made by the donor to a specified donee, the will, card or other document, or an executed copy thereof, may be delivered to the donee to expedite the appropriate procedures immediately after death, but delivery is not necessary to the validity of the gift. The will, card or other document, or an executed copy thereof, may be deposited in any hospital, bank or storage facility or registry office that accepts them for safekeeping or for facilitation of procedures after death. On request of any interested party upon or after the donor's death, the person in possession shall produce the document for examination.

SECTION 6. [Amendment or Revocation of the Gift.]

(a) If the will, card or other document or executed copy thereof, has been delivered to a specified donee, the donor may amend or revoke the gift by:

(1) the execution and delivery to the donee of a signed statement, or

(2) an oral statement made in the presence of 2 persons and communicated to the donee, or

(3) a statement during a terminal illness or injury addressed to an attending physician and communicated to the donee, or

(4) a signed card or document found on his person or in his effects.

(b) Any document of gift which has not been delivered to the donee may be revoked by the donor in the manner set out in subsection (a) or by destruction, cancellation, or mutilation of the document and all executed copies thereof.

(c) Any gift made by a will may also be amended or revoked in the manner provided for amendment or revocation of wills, or as provided in subsection (a).

SECTION 7. [Rights and Duties at Death.]

(a) The donee may accept or reject the gift. If the donee accepts a gift of the entire body, he may, subject to the terms of the gift, authorize embalming and the use of the body in funeral services. If the gift is of a part of the body, the donee, upon the death of the donor and prior to embalming, shall cause the part to be removed without unnecessary mutilation. After removal of the part, custody of the remainder of the body vests in the surviving spouse, next of kin or other persons under obligation to dispose of the body.

(b) The time of death shall be determined by a physician who attends the donor at his death, or, if none, the physician who certifies the death. This physician shall not participate in the procedures for removing or transplanting a part.

(c) A person who acts in good faith in accord with the terms of this Act, or under the anatomical gift laws of another state [or a foreign country] is not liable for damages in any civil action or subject to prosecution in any criminal proceeding for his act.

(d) The provisions of this Act are subject to the laws of this state prescribing powers and duties with respect to autopsies.

SECTION 8. [Uniformity of Interpretation.]

This Act shall be so construed as to effectuate its general purpose to make uniform the law of those states which enact it.

SECTION 9. [Short Title.]

This Act may be cited as the Uniform Anatomical Gift Act.

Key Provisions of the Uniform Anatomical Gift Act

The recommended statute, although not a long one, is quite comprehensive. In its second section (§2(a)), one sentence in length, it accomplishes what the common law never managed to do: it unequivocally lodges with anyone eighteen years of age or older the power to make an antemortem gift of his remains. The age of eighteen was apparently considered by the Commissioners to herald the onset of mature judgment.

Section 2(b) of the Act gives next of kin the power to donate all or a part of a deceased's body, thereby doing away with an ambiguity that previously existed in a large number of jurisdictions. By virtue of section 2(c), the next of kin can make such a gift either after or immediately before death. A scale of priority, commencing with the surviving spouse, is set up.

In sections 2(b) and (c) the Act attempts to avoid the confusion that would confront donees (recipients) of cadaver material whenever disagreement existed between the deceased and his next of kin or between the next of kin themselves. The deceased's wishes, of course, are always paramount: his next of kin cannot override his stated desire not to have his body donated; neither can the next of kin override a donation made by the deceased. If a donee has actual notice that a donation by a member of one class of kin (for example, an adult brother) is opposed by a member of the same class (for example, an adult sister) or of a class that is assigned a higher priority (for example, a surviving spouse, an adult son or daughter, or either surviving parent), he (or it, if an institution) must forego the donation.

Nothing in the Act would prohibit a survivor from donating all or part of the body of a deceased who was less than eighteen years of age at the time of his death.

Section 3 of the Act restricts donees, with one obvious exception, to those persons and institutions that are authorized to practice medicine or dentistry, to engage in medical or dental research and education, or to act as tissue banks. The solitary exception is a predictable one: the Act allows direct donation to a specified person "for therapy or transplantation needed by him."

If experience with "professional" blood donors teaches anything it is that tissue will occasionally be donated at a price, especially if commercial tissue banks become a reality—as they almost inevitably will. The Uniform Act does not make any provision for compensation for tissue donations and does not itself provide for the licensing and regulation of tissue banks. (Of course, the Act speaks in terms of a "gift," and the gift concept is at least impliedly inconsistent with a sale.) The Commissioners felt that these subjects were not appropriate for uniform legislation; they did not, however, express any notion that they could not become fit subjects of future state legislation.[31]

Sections 2(a) and 4(a) of the Act eliminate the problems flowing from earlier common law and statutory reliance on the law of wills. Under the Act a donation constitutes not a testamentary bequest but a "gift" and takes effect immediately upon the giver's death, not after admission of his will, if any, to probate. No longer will the time lag between death and the admission of the decedent's will to probate frustrate intended donations of usable cadaver material. This is not to say that a tissue donation cannot be accomplished by last will and testament. The Act provides several methods for executing anatomical gifts, including the use of will provisions. However, the will is merely a sort of documentary vehicle for conveying the gift; the donation is good to the extent that it has been acted upon, even though the will is never probated at all or is declared invalid as a will.

Section 4 of the Act provides that an anatomical donation can be made in four different ways: (1) by will; (2) by means of a card or (3) other "document"—presumably a letter or the like—or (4) by means of telegraphic or recorded telephonic consent of next of kin authorized under section 2(b) to make an effective donation. The card or other document

[31] Sec. 1(a) of the Uniform Act assumes the existence of at least some form of state approval of tissue banks. It defines "bank or storage facility," as those terms are employed in the text of the Act, as "a facility licensed, accredited or approved under the laws of any state for storage of human bodies or parts thereof."

The legal ramifications of the sale and purchase of human organs are considered in detail in Dukeminier, J., *Supplying Organs for Transplantation,* 68 MICHIGAN LAW REVIEW 811 (1970).

must be signed by the donor or, with his authorization, on his behalf in the presence of two witnessing signatories. Formal delivery of the card or other writing to the donee or anyone else during the donor's lifetime, while undoubtedly both helpful and prudent,[32] is not essential to an anatomical gift's validity; the card or other paper simply serves as tangible evidence of the donor's intent. As a practical matter the use of small cards of uniform format will be encouraged, since such a card can conveniently be carried on the donor's person, to be located quickly and easily in cases of sudden or accidental death. It is not enough that the donor's will, card, or other gift-writing, or an executed copy thereof, has been delivered to his specified donee during the donor's lifetime, since he may expire at a place far from his donee's location. In this eventuality a local attending physician, finding the deceased's card on his person, can act as a donee under section 4(c) of the Act.

There is no witness requirement in connection with donations made by survivors under the authority of section 2(b), and they can implement their intent by means of a signed letter or, since time may be of the essence in connection with a contemplated transplantation procedure, and survivors may be at a distance, by telegram or recorded telephone message.

An anatomical gift can be made with or without the naming of a specific donee. A person is free to name his own physician as donee. And section 4(c) of the Act provides that the deceased's attending physician can accept the donated body if there is no named donee or, unless the donor has stipulated otherwise, if the named donee is for some reason unavailable at the time and place of death. The Act does not provide for the situation in which, in addition to the absence of any named donee, there is no attending physician at or about the time of the donor's death.

Some members of the lay public—and perhaps also of the medical profession—have a tendency to believe that a physician who anticipates taking part in a contemplated transplantation operation may be tempted to employ overreaching techniques to persuade a patient to name him as the donee of his body or some needed part of it. (The same suspicion may arise whenever a lawyer turns up as the principal beneficiary under a will that he prepared for an elderly, suggestible client.)

To avoid the appearance of impropriety, section 4 provides that a physician who becomes a donee under section 4(c) shall not take part in removing or transplanting a part of the donee's body. He can make a further gift of the body to another person for any authorized purpose. It is unclear, however, whether section 4(d) would permit a donor, despite 4(c), to name one and the same person both as donee and as the surgeon to carry out the appropriate procedures.

[32] Sec. 5 of the Act suggests that the card, etc., "may be delivered to the donee to expedite the appropriate procedures immediately after death."

Since underlying the Uniform Anatomical Gift Act is a desire to effectuate the final wishes of a donor, section 6 of the Act provides six methods for modifying or revoking a donation.[33] If the card, letter, or will has been given to the named donee, modification or revocation can be accomplished in four different ways: (1) delivery to the donee of an appropriate signed statement; (2) an oral statement made in the presence of two witnesses and conveyed to the donee; (3) a statement made by the donor to an attending physician during the donor's terminal illness or injury and thereafter conveyed to the donee; or (4) a signed writing ("card or document") found among the donor's effects. Of course, if the instrument of gift has not been delivered to the donee, the donor, pursuant to section 6(b), can simply destroy it or in some other unmistakable fashion cancel it and all executed copies, or he can take his pick of the methods listed in section 6(a). If the donation was incorporated in a will, it can be modified or revoked, under 6(c), in the manner prescribed by the particular jurisdiction's laws regarding the modification and revocation of testamentary bequests or in any of the four ways listed in section 6(a).

The donee is free, under section 7 of the Act, to reject an anatomical gift and is empowered by section 2(d) to conduct any examination necessary to determine a donation's medical acceptability. Section 7 also serves to insulate from either civil or criminal liability all persons—donee, survivors, attending physicians, medical examiners, funeral directors—who have acted in good faith pursuant to the terms of the Act.

The donee of an anatomical gift can remove the donated part or parts immediately after death. Unnecessary mutilation should be avoided since any undonated portion of the body should be surrendered to surviving relatives for final disposition.[34] The donee can authorize embalming or cremation and funeral services where the gift was of the entire body.[35] A physician should secure a clearance from the local coroner's or medical examiner's office before removing cadaver material where such an office has potential jurisdiction.[36]

[33] Sec. 6 of the Act is by its terms applicable only to a "donor" and sec. 1(c) defines "donor" as "an individual who makes a gift of all or part of *his* body" (emphasis supplied). Thus the Act makes no provision for revocation of a gift made by a survivor of the deceased. The reason for this omission is not entirely clear. Presumably the Commissioners thought that surgical removal and use of tissue and organs would ordinarily occur so soon after a survivor's gift—which can be made only after or immediately before death—to make revocation a realistic possibility. Perhaps, too, the drafters felt that only the owner of a body should have the privilege of vacillation.

[34] See, *e.g.*, N.J. REV. STAT., §26:6-55 (Supp. 1968); OHIO REV. CODE ANN., §2108.01 (1968).

[35] See CALIF. HEALTH & SAFETY CODE, §7156(a) (Supp. 1968).

[36] The subject of official autopsies is considered in Chapter 13. See also Comment, *California's Response to the Problems of Procuring Human Remains for Transplantation*, 57 CALIFORNIA LAW REVIEW 671, 680–81 (1969).

THE CONCEPT OF DEATH

Time of Death

We have been talking, in the main, about the use of dead bodies for purposes of homotransplantation. Tissue for transplantation must be removed after the donor's death but before the death of the tissue itself. It has been stressed repeatedly that the time lapse between donor death and tissue use is of critical importance. Kidneys to be transplanted should be removed within thirty minutes of the donor's death, lest postmortem deterioration preclude their use. The liver, lungs, and heart also must be removed soon after the donor's death.[37] Thus the pinpointing of the time of death is of great importance in the field of homotransplantation of cadaveric material. The medical profession realizes that "It . . . would be medically, legally, and ethically wrong to do anything at the expense of the life or the comfort of the dying patient who is a prospective donor, just to secure a healthy transplant."[38] But the medical profession also comprehends that a medical man ought not be required to delay the pronouncement of death for insubstantial reasons where such a delay may jeopardize treatment of a transplant recipient.[39]

Clinical Death and the Need for Redefinition

Traditionally, death has been said to have taken place, both medically and legally, whenever it could be declared that both the heart and lungs had irrevocably ceased to function.[40] This phenomenon is generally referred to as "clinical death." Today, primarily because of advances in transplantation and in the use of resuscitative devices, it is with mounting insistence being suggested that the concept of death be redefined[41] and that the new definition be imbedded in statutory law for the guidance of all who must make death and time-of-death determinations.[42] The first

[37] See Wasmuth, C. E., Jr.: *The Concept of Death,* 30 OHIO STATE LAW JOURNAL 32, 34–39 (1969).

[38] Stickel, D. L.: *Organ Transplantation in Medical and Legal Perspectives,* 32 LAW & CONTEMPORARY PROBLEMS 597, 607 (1967).

[39] *Ibid.*

[40] Sadler, A. M., and Sadler, B. L.: *Transplantation and the Law: The Need for Organized Sensitivity,* 57 GEORGETOWN LAW JOURNAL 5, 27 (1968).

[41] *E.g.* Wasmuth, C. E.: *The Physician's Role in Organ Transplantation,* 37(13) MODERN MEDICINE 70 (1969); Williamson, W. P.: *Life or Death, Whose Decision?* 197 J.A.M.A. 793 (1966).

[42] Editorial, WASHINGTON POST, §A, p. 14, col. 4 (May 18, 1968): "Sooner or later the courts will have to face up to a corollary which can be referred to as the right to die. It involves persistent attempts to cause survival in a patient who has a terminal disease. Such patients are frequently subjected to extreme measures, only to succumb

proposition is defensible on scientific, legal, and moral grounds; the second proposition has nothing to recommend it.

The Sources of Redefinition

A preliminary question, which is neither as complex nor as controversial as some have feared, concerns the appropriate source or sources of a redefinition of death. Lawyers and theologians have flocked to the podium, along with doctors, to have their say. All three groups are certain that they have something to contribute to any description of the phenomenon of death. In truth, the determination of an overall concept of death remains as peculiarly medical a judgment as does the actual diagnosis of death under whatever the prevailing concept of death may be. Criteria for determining death will change in the future, just as they currently are changing, but they will change in consequence of advances in medical knowledge and not because courts and lawyers have become expert in things medical.

The concept of death and the question of precise time of death have never been particularly vexing to the law. Although the *fact* of death is obviously of recurring significance in our legal system (which makes premeditated homicide a crime and lets living persons inherit property from dead ones), the law has rarely in the past been faced with a need to fix the precise *time* of death. Any concept of death, so long as it possessed certainty, was satisfactory to the law. And the precise time of death became legally significant, by and large, only in extraordinary cases involving rights of inheritance where there arose a question as to which of two persons had died first. Here the law's only real concern has been, not with the concept of death that medical men might decree, but with the fact that no medical man was present at the crucial juncture to determine the precise time, or at least sequence, of death. And so the law, forced to accept nonexpert testimony as to the facts, has necessarily employed a concept of clinical death: laymen can take a pulse and detect breathing but they do not often have an electroencephalograph handy at the vital moment. A Pennsylvania case is illustrative.

In re Saligman's Estate [43] involved the classic who-went-first problem. An eyewitness, a layman, had observed a husband and wife shortly after they had been trapped in a fire. The husband was not breathing and his body was cold to the touch; in contrast, the wife's body was warm and she was breathing. No physician had arrived on the scene for almost half

---

after incurring large hospital bills. A physician must do everything in his power to prolong life. But is he obligated to prolong death?" *Cf.* Fletcher, G. P.: *Prolonging Life*, 42 WASHINGTON LAW REVIEW 999 (1967).

[43] 130 D. & C. 432 (Pa. Orphan's Ct. 1957).

an hour so there was no direct medical evidence as to who had died first. On the basis of the layman's testimony it was held that the wife had survived her husband; she thus had briefly become the sole owner of property jointly held with her husband, and her heirs, not his, inherited.[44]

The advent of homotransplantation as a medical reality adds a new reason for the law to concern itself with the concept of death in general, and the time of death in particular. Courts might be content to continue their reliance on clinical death as the controlling concept. They cannot jettison the clinical concept in those cases in which lay testimony alone is available—the layman eyewitness, for example, in a who-died-first situation. He can still testify only that "His heart wasn't beating and he wasn't breathing but she had a pulse and I could see she was breathing." However, there are complicating factors where a medical patient, prognosis terminal, is involved. In the first place, a delay in the pronouncement of death may no longer be an inconsequential matter: the urgent needs of a tissue recipient may be at stake. Here recourse to the concept of clinical death may, for no medically or legally justifiable reason, unduly delay the pronouncement of death. This possibility is especially real if the donor has been resuscitated and is being kept "alive" by artificial means.

Proposed Redefinitions of the Concept of Death

One medical authority has advocated that death be pronounced as soon as *one* irreplaceable vital organ has ceased irrevocably to function.[45] Efforts within the medical profession now seem to be aimed principally at achieving a consensus in favor of a definition based on neurological criteria.

Rosoff and Schwab, in a 1967 paper presented before the American Electroencephalographic Society, suggested a three-phase test: (1) no reflexes, spontaneous breathing, or muscle activity; (2) no clinical or electroencephalographic response to noise or pinching; and (3) a repetition of tests 1 and 2 after twenty-four or forty-eight hours.[46]

A faculty committee of the Harvard Medical School has defined irreversible coma as a new criterion of death. The committee sets out four

[44] See also *Smith* v. *Smith*, 317 S.W.2d 275 (S. Ct. Ark. 1958).

[45] Couch, J. R.: *The Legal Aspects of Human Organ Transplantation*, in PROCEEDINGS OF FIRST INTERNATIONAL CONGRESS OF THE TRANSPLANTATION SOCIETY (1967). See Stickel, D. L.: *Organ Transplantation in Medical and Legal Perspectives*, 32 LAW & CONTEMPORARY PROBLEMS 597, 607–608 (1967), citing Couch.

[46] Rosoff, S. E., and Schwab, R. S.: *EEG in Establishing Brain Death: 10-year Report, with Criteria and Legal Safeguards in 50 States*, at American Electroencephalographic Society meeting (June 8, 1967). Additionally, it would have to be demonstrated that the patient was not under the influence of hypothermia or anesthetic drugs that could depress the central nervous system.

indicia of a permanently nonfunctioning brain: (1) unreceptivity and unresponsiveness to inner need and external stimuli; (2) no breathing or movement; (3) no reflexes; and (4) a flat isoelectric electroencephalogram, all four tests to be run again with no change after at least twenty-four hours.[47]

The similarity of these and other [48] efforts to promulgate neurological criteria—a concept of "brain death"—strongly suggests that medical science is moving toward a workable consensus.[49]

The Uniform Anatomical Gift Act Provision: A Medical Prerogative

The medical profession, which for many years has had the prerogative of pronouncing the body's death, should be free, for medical purposes, to shift to a concept of brain death. It will do so only after a consensus has been established within the profession. The law, however, need not settle upon a single concept of death; on the contrary, there is no reason that the law, to meet varying adjudicative situations, should not be at liberty to employ multiple concepts of death. It should be free to rely on a concept of clinical death in cases where there is available only the testimony of laymen as to the observable facts. When the law is not forced by circumstances to be content with such crude estimations it should avail itself of the latest criteria as to which medical science substantially concurs. It can do so in the transplantation field since a physician will usually be present during a tissue donor's final moments.

The Uniform Anatomical Gift Act eschews any attempt at a statutory definition of death. Section 7(b) of the Act states that "The time of death shall be determined by a physician who attends the donor at his death, or, if none, the physician who certifies his death." In case anyone might be prepared to harbor the notion that a physician would accelerate the pronouncement of one patient's death in order to enhance the prognosis of another, section 7(b) also provides that neither an attending nor a certifying physician will be permitted to participate in the procedures for removing or transplanting a donated part. Nothing in the statute prevents the attending physician, however, from communicating with the transplant team. As the drafters of the Act have pointed out, "This communication is essential to permit the transfer of important knowledge concerning the donor, for example, the nature of the disease processes affecting

[47] Ad Hoc Committee of the Harvard Medical School to Examine the Definition of Brain Death, *A Definition of Irreversible Coma,* 205 J.A.M.A. 337 (1968).

[48] See the report of Pittsburgh's Ad Hoc Committee on Human Tissue Transplantation, reproduced in Wecht, C. H., and Aranson, M. J.: *Medical-Legal Ramifications of Human Tissue Transplantation,* 18 DE PAUL LAW REVIEW 488, 493–95 (1969).

[49] See Sadler, A. M., and Sadler, B. L.: *Transplantation and the Law: The Need for Organized Sensitivity,* 57 GEORGETOWN LAW JOURNAL 5, 28 (1968).

the donor or the results of studies carried out for tissue matching and other immunological data."[50]

The drafters of the Uniform Act were satisfied that "No reasonable statutory definition [of death] is possible."[51] They observed that medical authorities are presently working toward a consensus and added that "The real question is when have irreversible changes taken place that preclude return to normal brain activity and self-sustaining bodily functions." The drafters of the Act realized that reliance must be placed upon the medical profession and, in particular, upon the attending physician. The refusal of the Act's drafters to assay an arbitrary definition of death is practical evidence of the wisdom of Doctor Carl E. Wasmuth's comment: "While criteria for . . . [death] determinations have changed in the passage of time and with advances in medical knowledge and instrumentation, the determination of death remains a medical judgment and of necessity must remain a service of the medical profession."[52]

BIBLIOGRAPHY

In addition to the sources cited in the Bibliography appended to Chapter 13, the following articles are valuable:

Baker, J. C.: *Liability and the Heart Transplant,* 6 HOUSTON LAW REVIEW 85 (1968).

Brickman, M. J.: *Medical-Legal Problems with the Question of Death,* 5 CALIFORNIA WESTERN LAW REVIEW 110 (1968).

Dukeminier, J.: *Supplying Organs for Transplantation,* 68 MICHIGAN LAW REVIEW 811 (1970).

Dunphy, J. E.: *The Story of Organ Transplantation,* 21 HASTINGS LAW JOURNAL 67 (1969).

Louisell, D. W.: *The Procurement of Organs for Transplantation,* 64 NORTHWESTERN UNIV. LAW REVIEW 607 (1969).

Richards, V. R.: *Medical-Legal Problems of Organ Transplantation,* 21 HASTINGS LAW JOURNAL 77 (1969).

Savage, J. C.: *Organ Transplantation with an Incompetent Donor,* 58 KENTUCKY LAW JOURNAL 129 (1969–70).

Stickel, D. L.: *Organ Transplantation in Medical and Legal Perspectives,* 32 LAW & CONTEMPORARY PROBLEMS 597 (1967).

[50] NAT'L CONF. OF COMM'RS ON UNIFORM STATE LAWS, UNIFORM ANATOMICAL GIFT ACT WITH PREFATORY NOTE AND COMMENTS 20 (1968).

[51] NAT'L CONF. OF COMM'RS ON UNIFORM STATE LAWS, UNIFORM ANATOMICAL GIFT ACT WITH PREFATORY NOTE AND COMMENTS 19 (1968).

[52] Wasmuth, C. E.: *The Physician's Role in Organ Transplantation,* 37(13) MODERN MEDICINE 70, 71 (1969).

Wasmuth, C. E., Jr.: *The Concept of Death,* 30 OHIO STATE LAW JOURNAL 32 (1969).

Wasmuth, C. E., and Stewart, B. H.: *Medical and Legal Aspects of Human Organ Transplantation,* 14 CLEVELAND-MARSHALL LAW REVIEW 442 (1965).

Wecht, C. H., and Aranson, M. J.: *Medical-Legal Ramifications of Human Tissue Transplantation,* 18 DEPAUL LAW REVIEW 488 (1969).

Wheeler, D. E.: *Anatomical Gifts in Illinois,* 18 DEPAUL LAW REVIEW 471 (1969).

chapter 15

THE PHYSICIAN-PATIENT TESTIMONIAL PRIVILEGE

> Whatsoever things I see or hear concerning the life of men, in my attendance on the sick or even apart therefrom which ought not to be noised abroad, I will keep silence thereon, counting such things to be as sacred secrets.
>
> —HIPPOCRATES, on the physician's buttoned lip.

A Testimonial Privilege, Not an Ethical Canon

Every medical student knows what Hippocrates said about the doctor's duty of confidentiality. He was speaking of an ethical norm. In this chapter, however, we are not primarily concerned with professional etiquette or even with medical ethics as they apply to conduct outside the courtroom. We deal here with a testimonial privilege, or ban, that prohibits the physician-witness, called to testify in a legal proceeding,[1] from divulging information obtained by him during his professional attendance upon a patient.

The Origins and Bases of a Questionable Privilege

If ethical considerations are put to one side, the physician-patient privilege becomes a somewhat surprising one in the context of judicial proceedings. On debatable policy grounds it serves, with some frequency, to frustrate the discovery of truth in our courts. Our judicial system is interested in accurate fact-finding; the purpose of a trial is the ascertainment of truth. And yet the law declares that certain information, which might very well shed significant light, is privileged from disclosure because given and received in confidence. This stems from the notion, strongly

[1] The phase "legal proceeding" may embrace legislative proceedings as well as judicial (courtroom) proceedings. See, *e.g., New York City Council* v. *Goldwater,* 31 N.E.2d 31 (Ct. App. N.Y. 1940), holding that the privilege was applicable to a legislative investigation.

imbedded in Anglo-American law, that some values are more important than accurate adjudication. As one legal authority has put it, "One of them is the right to be left by the state unmolested in certain human relations. . . . It is the historic judgment of the common law . . . that whatever handicapping of the adjudicatory process is caused by recognition of the [evidential] privileges, it is not too great a price to pay for secrecy in certain communicative relations. . . ." [2]

One of the communicative relations that the law protects is the physician-patient relationship. No matter how relevant to a lawsuit they may be, communications made in confidence between patient and doctor can be suppressed from disclosure by the patient. The underlying principle—a debatable one—is that the crafting of such a rule of evidence will encourage the full and frank disclosures so essential to the diagnostician.[3]

The law did not always recognize a physician-patient privilege.[4] The common law recognized only one professional relationship to which there was attached a privilege against divulgence of confidential communications. It is the attorney-client privilege, which has been around since the latter part of the sixteenth century.[5] Two hundred years later the courts that had established the attorney-client privilege gave short shrift to the suggestion of a comparable physician-patient rule. When, in the eighteenth century, a doctor posed to the English jurist Lord Mansfield the question of whether he was bound to disclose a confidence received during the doctor-patient relationship, the Chief Justice replied: "If a surgeon was voluntarily to reveal these secrets, to be sure, he would be guilty of a breach of honor and of great indiscretion; but to give that information in a court of justice, which by the law of the land he is bound to do, will never be imputed to him as any indiscretion whatever." [6] Lord Mansfield put accurate adjudication first.

[2] Louisell, D. W.: *Confidentiality, Conformity and Confusion: Privileges in Federal Court Today,* 31 TULANE LAW REVIEW 101, 109 (1956).

[3] See *Edington* v. *Mutual Life Ins. Co.,* 67 N.Y. 185, 194 (Ct. App. N.Y. 1876), for the most frequently quoted judicial articulation of this policy. See also *Stiles* v. *Clifton Springs Sanitarium Co.,* 74 F.Supp. 907 (W.D.N.Y. 1947); *Ascherman* v. *Superior Court in and for County of San Francisco,* 62 Cal. Rptr. 547 (Cal. App. 1967); *Howard* v. *Porter,* 35 N.W.2d 837 (S. Ct. Iowa 1949); *Metropolitan Life Ins. Co.* v. *Ryan,* 172 S.W.2d 269 (Mo. App. 1943).

[4] See, *e.g., Rhodes* v. *Metropolitan Life Ins. Co.,* 172 F.2d 183 (5th Cir.), *cert. denied,* 337 U.S. 930 (1949); *Edington* v. *Aetna Life Ins. Co.,* 77 N.Y. 564 (Ct. App. N.Y. 1879).

[5] See Comment, *The Lawyer-Client Privilege: Its Application to Corporations, the Role of Ethics, and Its Possible Curtailment,* 56 NORTHWESTERN UNIV. LAW REVIEW 235 (1961).

[6] *The Duchess of Kingston's Trial,* 20 HOW. STATE TRIALS 355, 573 (1776).

The Rule Today

In many American jurisdictions—about two thirds of them so far [7]—the common law's omission of any doctor-patient privilege has been remedied by the legislature by the enactment of statutes creating a physician-patient privilege. The first of these statutes was enacted in New York in 1828.[8] It was uncomplicated in form:

> No person authorized to practice physic or surgery shall be allowed to disclose any information which he may have acquired in attending any patient, in a professional character, and which information was necessary to enable him to prescribe for such patient as a physician, or to do any act for him as a surgeon.

The most recently enacted physician-patient privilege statute forms a part of the California Evidence Code,[9] effective in 1967. It is a far more elaborate and sophisticated enactment than its New York forerunner.

ARTICLE 6. PHYSICIAN-PATIENT PRIVILEGE

SECTION 990. "Physician"

990. As used in this article, "physician" means a person authorized, or reasonably believed by the patient to be authorized, to practice medicine in any state or nation.

[7] Specifically, 32 states and several territories. *States:* ALAS. R. CIV. PROC. R., §43(h)(4) (Supp. 1964); ARIZ. STAT. ANN., §12-2235 (Supp. 1967); ARK. STAT. ANN., §28-607 (Supp. 1967); CALIF. EVID. CODE, §§990-1007 (Supp. 1967); COLO. REV. STAT., §153-1-7(4) (Supp. 1961); HAWAII REV. LAWS §222–20 (1955); IDAHO CODE, §9-203(4) (Supp. 1967); ILL. STAT. ANN., ch. 51, §5.1 (Supp. 1967); IND. STAT. ANN., §2-1714(550) (1968); IOWA CODE ANN., §622.10 (Supp. 1968); KAN. STAT. ANN., §60–427 (Supp. 1967); MICH. STAT. ANN., §274.2157 (Supp. 1968); MINN. STAT. ANN., §595.02 (Supp. 1967); MISS. CODE ANN., §1967 (Supp. 1966); MO. ANN. STAT., §491.060 (Supp. 1967); MONT. REV. CODE ANN., §93-701-4(4) (Supp. 1967); NEB. REV. STAT., §25-1206 (1964); NEV. REV. STAT., §48.080 (1967); N.Y. C.P.L.R., §4504 (Supp. 1967); N.D. REV. CODE, §31-01-06(3) (Supp. 1967); OHIO REV. CODE, §2317.02 (Supp. 1966); OKLA. STAT. ANN., tit. 12, §385 (Supp. 1967); ORE. REV. STAT., §44.040(1)(d) (Supp. 1967); PA. STAT. ANN., tit. 28, §328 (Supp. 1967); S.D. CODE, §36.0101(3) (Supp. 1960); UTAH CODE ANN., §78-24-8 (Supp. 1967); VA. CODE, §8.289.1 (Supp. 1966); W. VA. CODE ANN., §50-6-10(e) (Supp. 1967); WASH. REV. CODE, §5.60.060 (Supp. 1967); WIS. STAT., §885.21 (1965); WYO. STAT., §1-139 (Supp. 1967). *Other:* D.C. CODE ANN., §14-307 (Supp. 1965); P.R. LAWS ANN., tit. 32, §1734(4) (Supp. 1968); CANAL ZONE CODE, tit. 5, §2855 (Supp. 1968); V.I. CODE ANN., tit. 5, §855 (Supp. 1966).

[8] N.Y. REV. STAT., Part III, ch. 7, art. 8, §73 (1829).

[9] CALIF. EVID. CODE, §§990–1007 (Supp. 1967).

SECTION 991. "Patient"

991. As used in this article, "patient" means a person who consults a physician or submits to an examination by a physician for the purpose of securing a diagnosis or preventive, palliative, or curative treatment of his physical or mental or emotional condition.

SECTION 992. "Confidential Communication Between Patient and Physician"

992. As used in this article, "confidential communication between patient and physician" means information, including information obtained by an examination of the patient, transmitted between a patient and his physician in the course of that relationship and in confidence by a means which, so far as the patient is aware, discloses the information to no third persons other than those who are present to further the interest of the patient in the consultation or those to whom disclosure is reasonably necessary for the transmission of the information or the accomplishment of the purpose for which the physician is consulted, and includes [a diagnosis made and the] [10] advice given by the physician in the course of that relationship.

SECTION 993. "Holder of the Privilege"

993. As used in this article, "holder of the privilege" means:

(a) The patient when he has no guardian or conservator.

(b) A guardian or conservator of the patient when the patient has a guardian or conservator.

(c) The personal representative of the patient if the patient is dead.

SECTION 994. Physician-Patient Privilege

994. Subject to Section 912 and except as otherwise provided in this article, the patient, whether or not a party, has a privilege to refuse to disclose, and to prevent another from disclosing, a confidential communication between patient and physician if the privilege is claimed by:

(a) The holder of the privilege;

(b) A person who is authorized to claim the privilege by the holder of the privilege; or

(c) The person who was the physician at the time of the confidential communication, but such person may not claim the privilege if there is no holder of the privilege in existence or if he is otherwise instructed by a person authorized to permit disclosure.[11]

SECTION 995. When Physician Required to Claim Privilege

995. The physician who received or made a communication subject to the privilege under this article shall claim the privilege whenever he is present

[10] As amended CALIF. STAT. 1967, ch. 650, p. 2006, §4.

[11] Amended in 1968 to include medical corporations and physicians and surgeons employed by them.

when the communication is sought to be disclosed and is authorized to claim the privilege under subdivision (c) of Section 994.

SECTION 996. Exception: Patient-Litigant Exception

996. There is no privilege under this article as to a communication relevant to an issue concerning the condition of the patient if such issue has been tendered by:

(a) The patient;

(b) Any party claiming through or under the patient;

(c) Any party claiming as a beneficiary of the patient through a contract to which the patient is or was a party; or

(d) The plaintiff in an action brought under Section 376 or 377 of the Code of Civil Procedure for damages for the injury or death of the patient.

SECTION 997. Exception: Crime or Tort

997. There is no privilege under this article if the services of the physician were sought or obtained to enable or aid anyone to commit or plan to commit a crime or a tort or to escape detection or apprehension after the commission of a crime or a tort.

SECTION 998. Exception: Criminal Proceeding

998. There is no privilege under this article in a criminal proceeding.

SECTION 999. Exception: Proceeding to Recover Damages for Criminal Conduct

999. There is no privilege under this article in a proceeding to recover damages on account of conduct of the patient which constitutes a crime.

SECTION 1000. Exception: Parties Claiming Through Deceased Patient

1000. There is no privilege under this article as to a communication relevant to an issue between parties all of whom claim through a deceased patient, regardless of whether the claims are by testate or intestate succession or by inter vivos transaction.

SECTION 1001. Exception: Breach of Duty Arising Out of Physician-Patient Relationship

1001. There is no privilege under this article as to a communication relevant to an issue of breach, by the physician or by the patient, of a duty arising out of the physician-patient relationship.

SECTION 1002. Exception: Intention of Deceased Patient Concerning Writing Affecting Property Interest

1002. There is no privilege under this article as to a communication relevant to an issue concerning the intention of a patient, now deceased, with respect to a deed of conveyance, will, or other writing, executed by the patient, purporting to affect an interest in property.

SECTION 1003. Exception: Validity of Writing Affecting Property Interest

1003. There is no privilege under this article as to a communication relevant to an issue concerning the validity of a deed of conveyance, will, or other writing, executed by a patient, now deceased, purporting to affect an interest in property.

SECTION 1004. Exception: Commitment or Similar Proceeding

1004. There is no privilege under this article in a proceeding to commit the patient or otherwise place him or his property, or both, under the control of another because of his alleged mental or physical condition.

SECTION 1005. Exception: Proceeding to Establish Competence

1005. There is no privilege under this article in a proceeding brought by or on behalf of the patient to establish his competence.

SECTION 1006. Exception: Required Report

1006. There is no privilege under this article as to information that the physician or the patient is required to report to a public employee, or as to information required to be recorded in a public office, if such report or record is open to public inspection.

SECTION 1007. Exception: Proceeding to Terminate Right, License, or Privilege

1007. There is no privilege under this article in a proceeding brought by a public entity to determine whether a right, authority, license, or privilege (including the right or privilege to be employed by the public entity or to hold a public office) should be revoked, suspended, terminated, limited, or conditioned.

This comprehensive formulation of the physician-patient privilege, to which additional references will be made later on, will probably be a model not only for most future statutory provisions but also for courts that must decide privilege questions in the absence of so detailed a statute. (The proposed *Rules of Evidence for the United States District Courts and Magistrates,* if adopted, may also be influential. The preliminary draft of these rules, deliberately, contains no provision whatever for a general physician-patient privilege.)[12]

The Essential Element of Consultation for Diagnosis or Treatment; the Legal Meaning of the Terms "Patient" and "Physician"

The principal prerequisite of the statutory physician-patient privilege is that the patient must have consulted the doctor for treatment or for

[12] Adv. Comm. note to Rule 5-04 COMM. ON RULES OF PRAC. & PROC. OF THE JUD. CONF. OF THE U.S., PRELIMINARY DRAFT OF PROPOSED RULES OF EVIDENCE FOR THE UNITED STATES DISTRICT COURTS AND MAGISTRATES, 46 F.R.D. 161, 259–60 (1969). See the concluding section of this chapter, on the future of the physician-patient privilege.

diagnosis preparatory to treatment.[13] Theoretically, it is immaterial whether the doctor was employed by the patient or by someone else.[14] As a practical matter, however, treatment will not ordinarily have been the motivation behind a visit to a physician engaged by someone other than the patient. And the privilege will not shield communications between the patient and the doctor if treatment was not the ultimate goal. Thus it is firmly settled that the physician-patient privilege is inoperative where examination of a prospective employee was conducted by a company doctor solely to determine his fitness for hiring; [15] where the physician was designated by a life insurance company to examine an applicant for a policy; [16] or where the examining physician has been either court-appointed or employed by the opposing side in litigation, as when the defense secures an order for a physicial examination of the plaintiff in personal injury litigation.[17]

A doctor can be required to relate what he has learned from purely social contacts with his patient. For example, he can be directed to testify to having heard the patient threaten his wife, since the patient's abuse of his spouse was in no way an aspect of his professional relationship with his physician.[18] This is not to say, however, that the existence of a true doctor-patient relationship is invariably essential. For example, a sick or injured person may be examined by a physician selected by someone else or in the interest of someone other than the patient; in such a situation, if the doctor acts in a fashion calculated to inspire belief that his examination is for the patient's benefit, the physician-patient privilege will apply to information garnered during the examination. An example, drawn from an actual case,[19] will illustrate the point. The plaintiff, having sustained an

[13] *E.g. Taylor* v. *United States,* 222 F.2d 398 (D.C. Cir. 1955); *Hierl* v. *McClure,* 56 N.W.2d 721 (S. Ct. Minn. 1953); *Schwartz* v. *Schneuriger,* 69 N.W.2d 756 (S. Ct. Wis. 1955); *State* v. *Riggle,* 298 P.2d 349 (S. Ct. Wyo. 1956), *cert. denied,* 352 U.S. 981 (1957). The controlling factor is the reasonable belief of the "patient" as to whether treatment was contemplated. *E.g., Brown* v. *Brook,* 236 F.2d 686 (D.C. Cir. 1956); *People* v. *Decina,* 138 N.E.2d 799 (Ct. App. N.Y. 1956).

[14] *E.g., Malone* v. *Industrial Comm.,* 43 N.E.2d 266 (S. Ct. Ohio 1942) (company doctor); *Russell* v. *Penn Mutual Life Ins. Co.,* 41 N.E.2d 251 (Ohio App. 1941) (physician employed by insurance company).

[15] *Montzoukos* v. *Mutual Ben. Health & Accident Ins. Co.,* 254 Pac. 1005 (S. Ct. Utah 1927).

[16] *McGinty* v. *Brotherhood of Railway Trainmen,* 164 N.W. 249 (S. Ct. Wis. 1917).

[17] *E.g., People* v. *Austin,* 92 N.E. 57 (Ct. App. N.Y. 1910) (appointed by public prosecutor to determine sanity); *Heath* v. *Broadway S.A. Ry. Co.,* 8 N.Y.S. 863 (Super. Ct. N.Y. 1890) (employed by opposing party); *Smiecek* v. *State,* 10 N.W.2d 161 (S. Ct. Wis. 1943) (court-appointed to assess sanity).

[18] *Myers* v. *State,* 137 N.E. 547 (S. Ct. Ind. 1922). See also *Watkins* v. *Watkins,* 106 So. 753 (S. Ct. Miss. 1926).

[19] *Arizona & N.M. Ry.* v. *Clark,* 207 F.2d 817 (9th Cir. 1913), *aff'd,* 235 U.S. 669 (1915). See also *Ballard* v. *Yellow Cab Co.,* 145 P.2d 1019 (S. Ct. Wash. 1944).

eye injury, was taken to a hospital where Doctor A, the physician in attendance, advised him that the hospital had no eye specialist and urged that one be procured to examine his eye. Plaintiff then permitted Doctor B, a specialist secured by Doctor A, to examine him, supposing all the while that Doctor B was acting with Doctor A. What plaintiff did not know was that Doctor B was making his examination on behalf of the railroad company that had injured the plaintiff. At the trial of the plaintiff's personal injury action the defendant railroad called Doctor B as one of its witnesses; but upon objection by plaintiff's lawyer, the trial judge foreclosed Doctor B from testifying, citing the physician-patient privilege.

The courts make no differentiation between voluntary and involuntary initiation of the doctor-patient relationship. In a case amply attesting the truth-frustrating potential of the physician-patient privilege it was held to be applicable even where the patient had protested against being given any treatment at all. In *Meyer* v. *Supreme Lodge Knights of Pythias,*[20] hotel employees had called a physician to attend a guest who had taken poison. The guest objected strenuously to being treated although the doctor did succeed in administering a hypodermic. In a suit on the patient's life insurance policy, which contained a clause excluding recovery in suicide cases, the doctor was barred from testifying about the poison.

The fact that a patient is not always the direct employer of the doctor who ministers to him usually has no bearing on the doctor-patient privilege. For example, staff physicians in the employ of a hospital are subject to the privilege, since a true doctor-patient relationship exists between them and persons admitted to the hospital.[21] By the same token, an assisting or consulting physician is bound by the privilege.[22] And the majority of jurisdictions hold that the fact that the afflicted person is a patient in a public institution, such as a hosptial for the insane or mentally ill, does not strip him of the physician-patient privilege.[23]

The term "patient" in the privilege statutes has not been particularly bothersome. However, since a deceased person offers poor prospects for recovery, it has been held that a cadaver is not a "patient" and that evi-

[20] 70 N.E. 111 (Ct. App. N.Y. 1904), *aff'd,* 198 U.S. 508 (1905). See also *Union Pac. R. Co.* v. *Thomas,* 152 Fed. 365 (8th Cir. 1907).

[21] *E.g. Carlton* v. *Superior Court for Los Angeles County,* 67 Cal. Rptr. 568 (Cal. App. 1968); *Smart* v. *Kansas City,* 105 S.W. 709 (S. Ct. Mo. 1907); *People* v. *Decina,* 138 N.E.2d 799 (Ct. App. N.Y. 1956).

[22] *E.g., Manufacturer's Life Ins. Co.* v. *Brennan,* 270 Fed. 173 (1st Cir. 1921); *Lamarand* v. *National Life & Acc. Ins. Co.,* 16 N.E.2d 701 (Ohio App. 1937). In *Franklin Life Ins. Co.* v. *William J. Champion & Co.* 353 F2d 919 (6th Cir. 1965), the privilege was held to apply to an intern who was on medical service at a hospital and whose functions included the taking of histories.

[23] *E.g., Taylor* v. *United States,* 222 F.2d 398 (D.C. Cir. 1955); *Linscott* v. *Hughbanks,* 37 P.2d 26 (S. Ct. Kan. 1934); *McGrath v. State,* 104 N.Y.S.2d 882 (Ct. Cl. N.Y. 1950).

dence obtained from a postmortem examination is therefore not privileged.[24]

The term "physician" has been read to include interns [25] but not practitioners with limited licenses, such as dentists.[26] (New York's statute, however, is made expressly applicable to dentists.[27])

Unlawful Medical Procedures

The term "treatment" does not include unlawful procedures or those calculated to facilitate criminal conduct. One who has sought an illegal abortion cannot claim the doctor-patient privilege; [28] neither can it be invoked by one who has attempted to secure narcotics unlawfully.[29] The privilege would undoubtedly be held inapplicable to a fugitive who sought to have a police-inflicted gunshot wound treated or to have his appearance altered through plastic surgery.[30]

The Legal Meaning of the Term "Communications"

The term "communications" employed in many physician-patient privilege statutes is not so restrictive as it might seem. Courts generally interpret the statutes to cover all information obtained by the physician, even though it may have been secured through observation or examination rather than by oral or written "communication." [31] But the statutes are restricted to *information* imparted by the patient; they do not shield from disclosure the bare facts of consultation and treatment, the dates thereof, or the names and addresses of the doctors involved.[32] For example, defense

[24] *E.g., Harrison* v. *Sutter Street Ry.,* 47 Pac. 1019 (S. Ct. Cal. 1897); *Chadwick* v. *Beneficial Life Ins. Co.,* 181 Pac. 448 (S. Ct. Utah 1919).

[25] *E.g., Eureka-Maryland Assur. Co.* v. *Gray,* 121 F.2d 104 (D.C. Cir), *cert. denied,* 314 U.S. 613 (1941); *Greenbaum* v. *Columbian National Life Ins. Co.,* 62 F. 2d 56 (2d Cir. 1932), *cert. denied,* 293 U.S. 616 (1934).

[26] *E.g., People* v. *DeFrance,* 62 N.W. 709 (S. Ct. Mich. 1895); *Gulf, M. & N.R.R.* v. *Willis,* 57 So. 899 (S. Ct. Miss. 1934).

[27] N.Y. C.P.L.R., §4504 (Supp. 1967).

[28] See *State* v. *Karcher,* 98 N.E.2d 308 (S. Ct. Ohio 1951). However, a communication about a *past* crime or tort might be privileged. *Ibid.*

[29] See DeWitt, C.: PRIVILEGED COMMUNICATIONS BETWEEN PHYSICIAN AND PATIENT 187–88. Charles C Thomas, Springfield, Ill., 1958; Comment, *Physician-Patient Privilege as Affected by Mode of Gaining Information,* 1 WESTERN RESERVE LAW REVIEW 142 (1949).

[30] See §997, CALIF. EVID. CODE, quoted *supra.*

[31] *E.g., Sher* v. *ReHaven,* 199 F2d 777 (D.C. Cir. 1952), *cert. denied,* 345 U.S. 936 (1953); *Howard* v. *Porter,* 35 N.W.2d 837 (S. Ct. Iowa 1949); *Westphal* v. *State,* 79 N.Y.S.2d 634 (Ct. Cl. N.Y. 1948).

[32] *E.g., In re* Albert Lindley Lee Memorial Hosp., 209 F.2d 122 (2d Cir. 1953), *cert. denied sub nom. Cincotta* v. *United States,* 347 U.S. 960 (1954); *Wolf* v. *People,* 187 P.2d 926 (S. Ct. Colo. 1947), *aff'd sub nom. Wolf* v. *Colorado,* 338 U.S. 25 (1949).

counsel in personal injury actions, seeking to determine whether the plaintiff required medical attention, will often rightfully seek at an early stage of the litigation to obtain this sort of data by means of interrogatories or depositions. Furthermore, the privilege has been held not to reach communications having no immediate relevance to diagnosis or treatment; thus, most courts agree that descriptions of how an accident took place are unprivileged.[33] Oddly enough, however, a number of maverick judicial opinions hold that a physician called to treat a person involved in an automobile accident cannot testify to having smelled alcohol on the driver-patient's breath.[34]

Hospital Records

To the extent that hospital records include confidential information supplied by a patient to his physician and the physician's diagnostic findings, they too are privileged.[35] Some courts, believing that privilege statutes should be narrowly construed because of their truth-frustrating attributes, do not extend the privilege to information obtained and recorded by someone other than a physician. These courts exclude, for example, histories taken and charts and progress notes maintained by a nurse.[36] This restrictive rule is by no means universal, however. In the first place, nurses are expressly included in a few physician-patient privilege statutes, notably New York's.[37] And in some other states the courts have held that nurses are, by implication, within the privilege statute if, at the pertinent time, they were acting under a doctor's supervision in his treatment of a patient.[38]

[33] *E.g., Van Wie* v. *United States,* 77 F.Supp. 22 (N.D. Iowa 1948); *Cooper* v. *State,* 223 S.W.2d 507 (S. Ct. Ark. 1949); *Garrett* v. *Butte,* 221 Pac. 537 (S. Ct. Mont. 1923). See also *Edwards* v. *State,* 429 S.W.2d 92 (S. Ct. Ark. 1968).

[34] *E.g., Freeberg* v. *State,* 138 N.W. 143 (S. Ct. Neb. 1912); *Clapp* v. *State,* 124 P.2d 267 (Okla. Crim. App. 1942). There are a few cases to the contrary. *E.g., State* v. *Aguirre,* 206 F.2d 118 (S. Ct. Kan. 1949); *Perry* v. *Hannagan,* 241 N.W. 232 (S. Ct. Mich. 1932).

[35] *E.g., In re* Coddington's Will, 120 N.E.2d 777 (Ct. App. N.Y. 1959) (hospital records); *Hurd* v. *Republic Steel Corp.,* 87 N.Y.S.2d 64 (App. Div. N.Y. 1949) (x-ray and physician's and nurse's reports); *Kinbacher* v. *Schneider,* 89 N.Y.S.2d 350 Super. Ct. N.Y. 1949) (hospital records); *Weis* v. *Weis,* 72 N.E.2d 245 (S. Ct. Ohio 1947) (hospital records).

[36] See *Leusink* v. *O'Donnell,* 39 N.W.2d 675 (S. Ct. Wis. 1949).

[37] N.Y. C.P.L.R., §4504 (Supp. 1967). See also Cady, E. J.: *Law and Contemporary Nursing* 86–87. Littlefield, Adams & Co., Paterson, N.J., 1961; Crawfix, E. H.: *The Physician and the Privileged Communications as They Relate to Mental States,* 46 OHIO MED. JOUR. 1082 (1950).

[38] *E.g., State* v. *Anderson,* 78 N.W.2d 320 (S. Ct. Minn. 1956); *Mississippi Power & L. Co.* v. *Jordan,* 143 So. 483 (S. Ct. Miss. 1932); *Gilham* v. *Gilham,* 110 A.2d 915 (Pa. Super. 1955). However, this is probably not yet the majority rule. For rep-

Disclosures Made in the Presence of Third Persons

Because a patient's possible fear of widespread disclosure of confidences is thought to underlie the doctor-patient privilege, courts refuse to enforce the privilege where the patient apparently had no wish for secrecy. Consequently, no privilege will attach where a stranger was present at a consultation with the acquiescence, express or tacit, of the patient.[39] In that type of situation the doctor, often, and the stranger and the patient always, can be judicially required to divulge disclosures made by the patient.[40] The rule is usually different, of course, where the third person is no stranger but rather a customary participant in confidential medical consultations, such as a nurse or technician who aids the doctor, or a close relative or friend who has accompanied the patient to provide moral support.[41]

Required Public Reports

There is one counterpolicy that generally overrides the policies favoring a cloak of secrecy around the physician-patient relationship. That is the policy requiring full disclosure in required public reports.[42] Consequently, the privilege is usually deemed inapplicable to the contents of a death certificate, including the physician's opinion as to cause of death, despite the fact that this opinion may have been based in part on information secured from the decedent while he was a patient.[43] (Some public

---

resentative cases *contra,* see *First Trust Co.* v. *Kansas City Life Ins. Co.* 79 F.2d 48 (8th Cir. 1935); *General Acc., Fire & Life Assur. Co.* v. *Tibbs,* 2 N.E.2d 229 (Ind. App. 1936); *State* v. *Bounds,* 258 P.2d 751 (S. Ct. Idaho 1953). These cases, which fail to focus on the purpose of the physician-patient statutes, are criticized in McCormick, C. T.: EVIDENCE 214–15. West Publishing Company, St. Paul, 1954. The privilege plainly does not apply where the nurse has acted independently of any physician. *E.g., Culver* v. *Union Pac. R.R.,* 199 N.W. 794 (S. Ct. Neb. 1924); *Wills, Adm'r* v. *National Life & Acc. Ins. Co.,* 162 N.E. 882 (Ohio App. 1928).

[39] *E.g., State* v. *Thomas,* 275 P.2d 408 (S. Ct. Ariz. 1954), *aff'd sub nom. Thomas* v. *Arizona,* 356 U.S. 390 (1958) (deputy sheriffs); *People* v. *Dutton,* 145 676 (Cal. App. 1944) (policemen).

[40] A substantial number of courts have held that the doctor's lips are sealed even where a third person was casually present. *E.g., Gilham* v. *Gilham,* 110 A.2d 915 (Pa. Super. 1955). See Comment, *The Physician-Patient Privilege,* 56 NORTHWESTERN UNIV. LAW REVIEW 263, 272 (1961).

[41] See, *e.g., Ostrowski* v. *Mockridge,* 65 N.W.2d 185 (S. Ct. Minn. 1954); and see §992, CALIF. EVID. CODE, quoted *supra.*

[42] *E.g., People* v. *Nisonoff,* 59 N.E.2d 420 (Ct. App. N.Y. 1944), *cert. denied,* 326 U.S. 745 (1945) (autopsy findings); *Thomas* v. *Morris,* 36 N.E.2d 141 (Ct. App. N.Y. 1941) (reports required under Public Health law). See §1006, CALIF. EVID. CODE, *supra.*

[43] *E.g., Polish Roman Catholic Union* v. *Palen,* 5 N.W.2d 463 (S. Ct. Mich. 1942); *Prudential Ins. Co.* v. *Vozzella,* 274 N.Y.S. 774 (App. Div. N.Y. 1934). There are a

health statutes and municipal ordinances requiring reports by physicians, such as those calling for the reporting of cases of venereal disease, specifically render the report itself confidential, which may provide some solace to the patient who apprehends that no privilege can preclude the filing of the report.)

The Privilege Is the Patient's, Not the Physician's

Occasionally one encounters the doctor or hospital administrator who is firmly of the notion that the physician-patient privilege statutes were promulgated for his benefit. They were not. The privilege is personal to the patient; it belongs to him, not to his physician.[44] For the most part, it can be invoked only by the patient himself or by those acting on his behalf. As Professor McCormick, one of the great legal scholars in the field of evidence, has said, "It is a rule of privilege protecting the extrinsic interest of the patient and designed to promote health and truth. It encourages free disclosure in the sick-room by preventing such disclosure in the courtroom. The patient is the person to be encouraged and he is the holder of the privilege."[45] Section 994 of the new California Evidence Code, previously quoted, is typical in its cataloging of those who, on behalf of the patient, can summon up the privilege.

Waiver of the Privilege

During the lifetime of the patient he alone, or his agent, has the power to invoke the physician-patient privilege. By the same token, he can dispense with its enforcement, since it belongs to him. Such a waiver of the privilege can be either express or by implication.[46]

Except in a minority of states, Michigan being the most important,[47] the courts give effect to an express waiver of the doctor-patient privilege contained in applications for health or life insurance or in the policy it-

---

few reported cases *contra*. *E.g.*, *National Benevolent Society* v. *Russell*, 48 P.2d 1047 (S. Ct. Okla. 1935).

[44] *E.g.*, *Tweith* v. *Duluth, M. & I.R. Co.*, 66 F.Supp. 427 (D. Minn. 1946); *Snyker* v. *Snyker*, 72 N.W.2d 357 (S. Ct. Minn. 1955); *State* v. *Fackrell*, 271 P.2d 679 (S. Ct. Wash. 1954). A doctor who persists in refusing to testify even though the patient has waived the privilege can find himself the recipient of a costly contempt of court citation. See *Markham* v. *Hipke*, 171 N.W. 300 (S. Ct. Wis. 1919).

[45] McCormick, C. T.: EVIDENCE 216. West Publishing Company, St. Paul, 1954.

[46] *E.g.*, *Ranger, Inc.* v. *Equitable Life Assur. Soc'y of United States*, 196 F.2d 968 (6th Cir. 1952); *Wimberley* v. *State*, 228 S.W.2d 991 (S. Ct. Ark. 1950); *Jasper* v. *State*, 269 P.2d 375 (Okla. Crim. App. 1954). It is important to note that 21 of the 32 state privilege statutes contain specific waiver provisions.

[47] See *Gilchrist* v. *Mystic Workers of the World*, 163 N.W. 10 (S. Ct. Mich. 1917), holding that such a stipulation is "against public policy."

self.[48] Moreover, the possibilities for waiver by implication are manifold. The clearest of all occurs when the patient is in a position to assert the privilege and fails or declines to do so.[49] Of course, there is a general waiver when the patient himself calls his physician as a witness at trial and extracts testimony from him as to matters ordinarily privileged; the opposing side can then question the physician as to other matters disclosed to him.[50] And the principle goes farther. If a number of physicians took part jointly in a consultation, the calling of one by the patient to reveal part of the shared information opens the others to wide-ranging questioning by the other side.[51] Furthermore, some courts declare that the patient's summoning of one physician to testify to privileged information authorizes the opposite side to call other doctors consulted by the patient at other times.[52] These additional doctors can then be asked about any facts pertinent to the issues raised by the testimony of the physician called by the patient. Although this approach is rejected by a significant number of courts,[53] it seems a fair one, for it prevents a litigant from limiting the roster of witnesses at trial to those consultants who happen to be favorable to his claims.[54]

A highly important question is whether a plaintiff waives the doctor-patient privilege by the very act of suing for personal injuries. Can the plaintiff bring a lawsuit based on an alleged condition as to which he

[48] *E.g., Murphy* v. *Mut. Life Ins. Co.,* 112 P.2d 993 (S. Ct. Idaho 1941); *Templeton* v. *Mut. Life Ins. Co.,* 57 P.2d 841 (S. Ct. Okla. 1936). See Note, *Waiver Clauses in Insurance Applications,* 16 NORTH CAROLINA LAW REVIEW 53 (1938), and additional cases cited therein.

[49] See *People* v. *Bloom,* 85 N.E. 824 (Ct. App. N.Y. 1908); *State* v. *Koenig,* 36 N.Y.2d 765 (S. Ct. Iowa 1949); *Armstrong* v. *Topeka Ry.,* 144 Pac. 847 (S. Ct. Kan. 1914).

[50] *E.g., Patrick* v. *Smith Baking Co.,* 129 P.2d 651 (S. Ct. Idaho 1942); *Maas* v. *Laursen,* 18 N.W.2d 233 (S. Ct. Minn. 1945); *Williams* v. *State,* 226 P.2d 989 (Okla. Crim. App. 1951).

[51] *E.g., Doll* v. *Scandrett,* 276 N.W. 281 (S. Ct. Minn. 1937); *Morris* v. *New York, O. & W.R. Co.,* 42 N.E. 410 (Ct. App. N.Y. 1895). The *Doll* case is discussed in Note, 22 MINNESOTA LAW REVIEW 580 (1937).

[52] In *Weissman* v. *Wells,* 267 S.W. 400 (S. Ct. Mo. 1924), for example, plaintiff called a doctor to testify to her condition following an alleged injury; in so doing she waived any objection to defendant's calling another of her doctors to testify that she had had the same condition prior to the claimed injury. *Steinberg* v. *New York Life Ins. Co.,* 188 N.E. 152 (Ct. App. N.Y. 1933), is a similar case. See also *McUne* v. *Fuqua,* 253 P.2d 632 (S. Ct. Wash. 1953).

[53] *E.g., Acme-Evans Co.* v. *Schnepf,* 14 N.E.2d 561 (S. Ct. Ind. 1938); *Johnson* v. *Kinney,* 7 N.W.2d 188 (S. Ct. Iowa 1942); *United States Nat. Life & Cas. Co.* v. *Heard,* 298 Pac. 619 (S. Ct. Okla. 1931).

[54] See *Smart* v. *Kansas City,* 105 S.W. 709 (S. Ct. Mo. 1907) ("A litigant should not be allowed to pick and choose. . . . He may choose a serviceable and mellow one out of a number of physicians to fasten liability upon the defendant, and then, presto! change! exclude the testimony of those not so mellow and serviceable. . . .").

sought medical advice and treatment and yet foreclose the defendant from obtaining relevant information from the doctors who examined the plaintiff? This issue has inspired legal commentators, bent on turning a phrase, to inquire whether the privilege can be both shield and sword.

Section 996 of the quoted California Evidence Code, which we have suggested is certain to be influential in other jurisdictions, provides that no physician-patient privilege exists "as to a communication relevant to an issue concerning the condition of the patient if such issue has been tendered [*i.e.*, raised] by . . . the patient." [55] Few courts, unaided by so specific a statute, have reached the same result. New York is the most important state to conclude, by way of judicial decision alone, that the bringing of a personal injury action itself waives the privilege.[56] The trend of decisions is likely to be in this direction.[57] As Wigmore pointed out long ago, "The whole reason for the privilege is the patient's supposed unwillingness that [his] ailment should be disclosed to the world at large; hence the bringing of a suit in which the very declaration, and much more the proof, discloses the ailment to the world at large, is of itself an indication that the supposed repugnancy to disclosure does not exist." [58]

The Physician-Patient Privilege in Medical Malpractice Actions and Other Categories of Litigation

All of the preceding discussion leads to a question of immediate and obvious significance to the physician: Can the plaintiff in a medical malpractice action assert the physician-patient privilege with respect to relevant data imparted during the course of consultation with the defendant, thereby barring the defendant physician from making a defense? If such were the rule, many a physician would echo Dickens' character by suggesting "then the law's an arse!" Statutes obviating so grotesque a result

[55] The privilege statutes of Hawaii, Nebraska, Nevada, and Pennsylvania provide for a waiver when the patient sues for personal injuries. HAWAII REV. LAWS, §222-20 (1955); NEB. REV. STAT., §25-1207 (1964); NEV. REV. STAT., §48.080 (1967); PA. STAT. ANN., tit. 28, §328 (Supp. 1967). The statutes of Illinois and Virginia work a waiver whenever the physical or mental condition of a patient is an issue in a lawsuit. ILL. STAT. ANN., ch. 51, §5.1 (Supp. 1967); VA. CODE ANN., §8-289.1 (Supp. 1966). The Illinois statute is considered in *Webb* v. *Quincy City Lines, Inc.*, 219 N.E.2d 165 (Ill. App. 1966). See also KAN. STAT. ANN., §60-421 (Supp. 1967), containing a waiver provision so broad as to be susceptible to the interpretation that the physician-patient privilege has been wholly abrogated in that state.

[56] See *Van Heuverzwyn* v. *State*, 134 N.Y.S.2d 922 (Ct. Cl. N.Y. 1954); *Elder* v. *Cashin*, 120 N.Y.S.2d 165 (App. Div. N.Y. 1953); *Scolavino* v. *State*, 62 N.Y.S.2d 17 (Ct. Cl. N.Y. 1946). See also *Koump* v. *Smith*, 250 N.E.2d 857 (Ct. App. N.Y. 1969).

[57] See *Mathis* v. *Hildebrand*, 416 P. 2d 8 (S. Ct. Alas. 1966); *Collins* v. *Blair*, 252 N.E.2d 448 (Ind. App. 1969); *Randa* v. *Bear*, 312 P.2d 640 (S. Ct. Wash. 1957).

[58] 8 Wigmore, J. H.: EVIDENCE 832, 3d ed. Little, Brown and Company, Boston, 1940.

have existed for some time in several states;[59] section 1001 of the new California Evidence Code, previously quoted, is the most recent enactment to provide that no physician-patient privilege operates in any lawsuit alleging a breach of duty stemming from the physician-patient relationship. Furthermore, even in the absence of express statutes our courts have held that a defendant—the privilege to the contrary notwithstanding—must be allowed to bring out facts essential to his defense.[60] In this respect at least, the law has not been "an arse."

By statute, the physician-patient privilege has been withdrawn from certain other categories of litigation: will contests, lunacy proceedings, murder prosecutions. Sections 998–1004 of the California Evidence Code are typical in this respect.

The Physician's Duty to Invoke the Privilege on Behalf of His Patient

Although the privilege is that of the patient, not his doctor, there are times when it is incumbent upon the doctor himself to invoke it. This is as much a matter of medical ethics as it is of law—but the law is usually clear on the point.[61]

If apparently privileged matter is inquired into when the patient is not present, in person or through counsel, the doctor should suggest the applicability of the privilege and refuse disclosure unless and until instructed to the contrary by a judge. As a matter of fact, a judge, in the absence of a waiver by the patient, is free on his own motion to enforce the physician-patient privilege in a lawsuit not directly involving the patient.[62] The party seeking the privileged information lacks standing to complain of this discretionary action on the court's part, since the privilege is not his to claim.[63]

The Impact on the Physician-Patient Privilege of Pre-Trial Discovery Rules

There are a number of judicial opinions that attempt to define the impact of pre-trial discovery rules[64] on the physician-patient privilege. The

[59] DeWitt, C.: PRIVILEGED COMMUNICATIONS BETWEEN PHYSICIAN AND PATIENT 248. Charles C Thomas, Springfield, Ill., 1958.

[60] *E.g. Cramer* v. *Hurt,* 55 S.W. 258 (S. Ct. Mo. 1900); *May* v. *Northern Pac. Ry.,* 81 Pac. 328 (S. Ct. Mont. 1905). Furthermore, the principle of waiver will come into play in virtually any malpractice action.

[61] See, *e.g.,* CALIF. EVID. CODE, §§994-5, quoted *supra.*

[62] See McCormick, C. T.: EVIDENCE 216. West Publishing Company, St. Paul, 1954.

[63] *E.g., Olson* v. *Court of Honor,* 110 N.W. 374 (S. Ct. Minn. 1907); *Hier* v. *Farmers Mut. Fire Ins. Co.,* 67 P.2d 831 (S. Ct. Mont. 1937).

[64] For a discussion of pre-trial discovery by means of interrogatories, depositions, motions for production of records, physical and mental examinations, and requests for admissions, see Chapter 1.

problem is that the defense in a personal injury case may wish to take a deposition of the plaintiff's treating doctor, subpoena hospital and other medical records, or engage in other methods of discovering medical information at a time well in advance of trial when it is not yet known definitely whether the plaintiff will have to waive his physician-patient privilege. If plaintiff can successfully employ the privilege to frustrate pre-trial discovery efforts, he can cripple his adversary's efforts to prepare an effective defense. An enforced waiver of the privilege at the time of trial may come too late to do defendant's counsel much good, since few lawyers can investigate a case and try it at the same time. As it happens, courts seem to realize this.[65]

Although Federal Rule of Civil Procedure 26(b), for example, limits pre-trial discovery to "any matter, *not privileged*," [66] the federal courts have tended to permit discovery of medical information whenever it appears that the plaintiff could not hope to persist in claiming the physician-patient privilege at the trial stage due to principles of waiver previously discussed in this chapter. For example, in *Mariner* v. *Great Lakes Dredge & Dock Co.*[67] the trial court required the pre-trial production of medical information which the plaintiff could not hope to suppress at the trial stage by recourse to the physician-patient privilege. As the trial judge somewhat awkwardly put it, "I feel it appropriate that production be made at this time of that matter as to which it is contemplated any privilege will be waived at the time of trial." [68] In *Burlage* v. *Haudenshield* [69] the court put it succinctly: "Discovery of privileged matter should be allowed when waiver of the privilege at trial seems reasonably probable."

A blunter approach is taken by some courts. A few have held that a plaintiff who invokes the physician-patient privilege at the pre-trial discovery stage cannot go forward with his lawsuit. He can insist on his right to the privilege but, where the protected information is essential to his adversary's defense, only at the cost of a dismissal of his action. The leading case is *Kriger* v. *Holland Furnace Co.*,[70] decided in 1960. There the court said, ". . . the [privilege] statutes [although applicable], do not give her [*i.e.*, the plaintiff] the right to force the defendants to trial or to require the court to proceed with trial of her action so long as she is un-

[65] They recognize, for example, that if a plaintiff avoids pre-trial discovery of medical information by asserting the privilege and then engages in a surprise waiver of the privilege at trial, the defendant will be given either a stay of proceedings or an outright mistrial. See, *e.g.*, *Kriger v. Holland Furnace Co.*, 208 N.Y.S.2d 285 (App. Div. N.Y. 1960).

[66] Emphasis supplied.

[67] 202 F. Supp. 430 (N.D. Ohio 1962).

[68] See also *Greene* v. *Sears, Roebuck & Co.*, 40 F.R.D. 14 (N.D. Ohio 1966).

[69] 42 F.R.D. 397 (N.D. Iowa 1967).

[70] 208 N.Y.S.2d 285 (App. Div. N.Y. 1960).

willing to permit pretrial inquiry with respect to the injuries for which she seeks to recover damages."

The *Kriger* approach was followed by a federal court in *Awtry* v. *United States,*[71] an action for malpractice which was said to have taken place in a government hospital. The government, as defendant, demanded in advance of trial that the plaintiff produce the names and addresses of anyone who had provided prior medical or psychiatric services to him and a description of symptoms, diagnoses, and treatment. The court found it unnecessary to decide whether the physician-patient privilege was available to the plaintiff. It held that even if the privilege were applicable and had not been waived by the very bringing of plaintiff's action, "plaintiff may not continue his action and at the same time deny to defendant the right to avail itself of the pre-trial procedures necessary to prepare its defense." The court decreed that plaintiff's action would be dismissed if he did not comply with defendant's requests for pre-trial discovery.

Decisions such as *Kriger* and *Awtry* simply accelerate to the pre-trial stage the time at which a plaintiff must decide whether he is going to forego reliance on the physician-patient privilege.

The Right to a Mental or Physical Examination of a Claimant

As an important aspect of pre-trial discovery, a substantial number of jurisdictions, including the federal, have rules providing for a court-ordered examination of a party to litigation when his physical or mental condition is in issue.[72] In *Simon* v. *Castille* [73] the court held that it was impermissible for an examined party to decline to answer questions propounded by an examining physician and to tender instead a written "medical history" that had been prepared by counsel. The court stated that the examining doctor had "the right to elicit the medical history which he reasonably deems relevant and necessary." [74] Moreover, Federal Rule of

[71] 27 F.R.D. 399 (S.D.N.Y. 1961).

[72] Urbom W. K.: *Medical Discovery in the Fifty States Plus Two,* 33 INSURANCE COUNSEL JOURNAL 376 (1966), lists 34 state statutes or rules. In addition, see ALAS. R. CIV. PRO., R. 35 (1966); ARK. STAT. ANN., §28-357 (Supp. 1967); CALIF. CODE CIV. PROC., §§1871, 2032 (Supp. 1967); MD. R. PRO., R.420 (Supp. 1967); VA. S. CT. OF APP. R. 3.23(d); WYO. R. CIV. PRO., R. 35 (Supp. 1967).

[73] 174 So.2d 660 (La. App. 1965).

[74] Courts are split on the right of a party to have his own lawyer present during an examination conducted at the request of the opposing party in litigation. See, *e.g.*, *Durst* v. *Superior Court for the County of Los Angeles,* 35 Cal. Rptr. 143 (Cal. App. 1963) (not allowed where examining physician was independently selected by the court); *Pemberton* v. *Bennett,* 381 P.2d 705 (S. Ct. Ore. 1963) ("The medical examination is not an occasion when assistance of counsel is normally necessary. . . . The presence of an attorney . . . would probably tend to prolong the examination and could create an atmosphere in which it would be difficult to determine the examinee's true reactions. . . .").

Civil Procedure 35(b) not only provides for an exchange of medical reports by the parties to a lawsuit but provides under certain circumstances for a broad-scale waiver of the physician-patient privilege. Under 35(b)(1) the party examined by his opponent's medical expert is entitled, upon request, to a written report of the examination.[75] Under 35(b)(2), if the examined party requests and obtains such a report, or takes the deposition of the examining expert, he is deemed to have waived the physician-patient privilege with respect to the physical or mental condition in controversy.

Continuance of the Privilege After the Patient's Death

Mention has been made of the policy underpinnings of the privilege: that the law should take cognizance of a person's legitimate fear that the confidences of the consulting room will be broadcast elsewhere. The idea that this fear may discourage frank disclosures to a treating doctor seems markedly speculative except in cases involving mental illness and, perhaps, venereal disease. There seems even less reason to conclude that anyone other than a celebrity would be influenced by fears that disclosure of medical information might occur after his death. Accordingly, it might be anticipated that the doctor-patient privilege terminates with the patient's death. For the most part, it does not; a number of courts have held that the physician-patient privilege continues after the patient's death.[76] The law does not say *de mortuis nil nisi bonum;* it says *de mortuis nil.* It is in part because of this legal background, but primarily in consequence of the ethical considerations surrounding gratuitous revelations of medical information, that Lord Moran was so soundly criticized for having revealed medical secrets about his distinguished patient in *Winston Churchill: The Struggle for Survival,* an intimate biography published in 1966. *The Lancet* stated:

> The public's trust in the medical profession derives largely from its conviction that what transpires between patient and doctor will not be bandied about. If this confidentiality is owed to the living, it is doubly owed to the dead. . . . The point is that Lord Moran, by writing publicly about the medical condition

[75] Proposed amendments to the Federal Rules of Civil Procedure would require that this report include the results of any tests made and the diagnosis or other conclusions of the examining expert. See COMM. ON PROPOSED AMENDMENTS TO RULES OF CIVIL PROCEDURE FOR THE UNITED STATES DISTRICT COURTS RELATING TO DEPOSITION AND DISCOVERY, 43 F.R.D. 257–58 (1967).

[76] *E.g., Bassil* v. *Ford Motor Co.,* 270 N.W. 258 (S. Ct. Mich. 1936); *State* v. *Karcher,* 98 N.E.2d 308 (S. Ct. Ohio 1951); *In re* Will of Hunt, 100 N.W. 874 (S. Ct. Wis. 1904). Some statutes empower specified survivors of the deceased patient, such as an executor, to waive the privilege. See, *e.g., In re* Cashman's Will, 289 N.Y.S. 328 (Surr. N.Y. 1936), *aff'd,* 21 N.E.2d 193 (Ct. App. N.Y. 1939).

of his identified patient, is creating a modern precedent. It is a bad precedent which none should follow.[77]

M. A. Shapiro, writing in the *Journal of Forensic Medicine*,[78] has rightly added that "prospective moranographers" should hold in mind not only the ethics and the laws of confidentiality but also the law of libel (discussed elsewhere in this text [79]). While it is generally true, legalistically speaking, that the dead cannot be defamed, the secrets of the dead sometimes cast reflections on the living. If these reflections bring a survivor into disrepute, the death of the patient will be no bar to the survivor's libel action against the deceased's literary doctor.

The Future of the Physician-Patient Privilege

For a number of years almost no one has had anything good to say about the physician-patient privilege. Dean John Henry Wigmore, the preeminent authority of the law of evidence, thought the privilege a worthless encrustation.[80] "It is certain," he insisted, "that the practical employment of the privilege has come to mean little but suppression of useful truth—truth which ought to be disclosed and would never be suppressed for the sake of any inherent repugnancy in the medical facts involved." Professor Charles T. McCormick, an evidence scholar second only to Wigmore, has lamented "the suppression of what is ordinarily the best source of proof, namely, the physician who examined and treated the patient, upon what is usually a crucial issue, namely, the physical or mental condition of the patient." [81] In his view, the physician-patient privilege "runs against the grain of justice, truth and fair dealing."

While it is an exaggeration to say that its exceptions leave "virtually nothing covered by the privilege," [82] it is evident that the privilege is rapidly being consumed by its exceptions. The Advisory Committee on Rules of Evidence appointed by the Chief Justice of the United States has compiled a list of nine exceptions, the more important of which have been described in this chapter: communications not made for the purposes of diagnosis and treatment; commitment proceedings; issues as to wills;

[77] LANCET, Oct. 16, 1965, pp. 785–86.

[78] Shapiro, M. A.: *Moranography, Or What the Doctor Must Not Tell,* 13 JOURNAL OF FORENSIC MEDICINE 41–43 (1966).

[79] See Chapter 17.

[80] 8 Wigmore, J. H.: EVIDENCE 828–32, McNaughton rev. Little, Brown and Company, Boston, 1961.

[81] McCormick, C. T.: EVIDENCE 223. West Publishing Company, St. Paul, 1954. See also commentaries cited *id.* at 221, n. 1.

[82] Adv. Comm. note to Rule 5-04, COMM ON RULES OF PRAC. & PROC. OF THE JUD. CONF. OF THE U.S., PRELIMINARY DRAFT OF PROPOSED RULES OF EVIDENCE FOR THE UNITED STATES DISTRICT COURTS AND MAGISTRATES, 46 F.R.D. 161, 260 (1969).

actions on insurance policies; required reports (venereal disease, gunshot wounds, child abuse); communications in furtherance of crime or fraud; mental or physical condition put in issue by the patient (personal injury actions); malpractice actions; and some or all criminal prosecutions.[83] This proliferation of judicial and statutory exceptions evidences a growing dissatisfaction with the workings of the general physician-patient privilege. It is not surprising, therefore, that serious efforts to eliminate the privilege are now under way.

On January 30, 1969, the Chief Justice's Advisory Committee transmitted to the appropriate committee of the Judicial Conference of the United states a preliminary draft of an evidence code for federal trial judges and magistrates.[84] As we have previously indicated, this proposed code contains a conspicuous omission: there is no provision for a general physician-patient privilege.[85] The Advisory Committee took this action not only because "the exceptions which have been found necessary in order to obtain information required by the public interest or to avoid fraud are so numerous as to leave little or no basis for the privilege" but also because of "doubts attendant upon the general physician-patient privilege."

A death knell for the general physician-patient privilege has been sounded. The law is on the verge of letting medical truth—and all of it—be known in the courtroom while relegating idle and improper gossip to the sphere of medical ethics, where it has always belonged.

BIBLIOGRAPHY

BOOKS

Chayet, N. L.: LEGAL IMPLICATIONS OF EMERGENCY CARE 212–19. Appleton-Century-Crofts, New York, 1969.

DeWitt, C.: PRIVILEGED COMMUNICATIONS BETWEEN PHYSICIAN AND PATIENT. Charles C Thomas, Springfield, Ill., 1958.

McCormick, C. T.: EVIDENCE, ch. 11. West Publishing Company, St. Paul, 1954.

8 Wigmore, J. H.: EVIDENCE, §§101–8, McNaughten rev. Little, Brown and Company, Boston, 1961.

ARTICLES

Baldwin, R. W.: *Confidentiality between Physician and Patient,* 22 MARYLAND LAW REVIEW 181 (1962).

[83] *Id.* at 259–60.

[84] Adv. Comm. note to Rule 5-04, COMM. ON RULES OF PRAC. & PROC. OF THE CONF. OF THE U.S., PRELIMINARY DRAFT OF PROPOSED RULES OF EVIDENCE FOR THE UNITED STATES DISTRICT COURTS AND MAGISTRATES, 46 F.R.D. 161, 161–485. (1969).

[85] The proposed rules do, however, provide for a comprehensive psychotherapist-patient privilege. See Chapter 16.

Chafee, Z., Jr.: *Privileged Communications: Is Justice Served or Obstructed by Closing the Doctor's Mouth on the Witness Stand?* 52 YALE LAW JOURNAL 607 (1943).

Curd, T. H. S.: *Privileged Communications Between Doctor and Patient—An Anomaly,* 44 WEST VIRGINIA LAW QUARTERLY 165 (1938).

Lipscomb, H. S.: *Privileged Communications Statute—Sword and Shield,* 16 MISSISSIPPI LAW JOURNAL 181 (1944).

Long, R. H.: *The Physician-Patient Privilege Statutes Obstruct Justice,* 25 INSURANCE COUNSEL JOURNAL 224 (1958).

Morgan, E. M.: *Suggested Remedy for Obstruction to Expert Testimony by Rules of Evidence,* 10 UNIV. OF CHICAGO LAW REVIEW 285 (1944).

Purrington, W. A.: *An Abused Privilege,* 6 COLUMBIA LAW REVIEW 388 (1906).

Robitscher, J. B.: *The Doctor's Privileged Communications, Public Life, and History's Rights,* 17 CLEVELAND-MARSHALL LAW REVIEW 199 (1968).

Sawyer, C. T.: *The Physician-Patient Privilege: Some Reflections,* 14 DRAKE LAW REVIEW 83 (1965).

Welch, D. C.: *Another Anomaly—The Patient's Privilege,* 13 MISSISSIPPI LAW JOURNAL 137 (1941).

NOTES AND COMMENTS

Comment, *Legal Protection of the Confidential Nature of the Physician-Patient Relationship,* 52 COLUMBIA LAW REVIEW 383 (1952).

Comment, *Waiver of the Physician-Patient Privilege,* 51 MINNESOTA LAW REVIEW 575 (1967).

Note, *Evidence—Physician-Patient Privilege—Compelling Disclosure of Privileged Information—Discretion of Trial Judge,* 41 NORTH CAROLINA LAW REVIEW 627 (1963).

chapter 16

THE PSYCHOTHERAPIST-PATIENT TESTIMONIAL PRIVILEGE

Applicability of the Physician-Patient Privilege to Psychiatrists and Psychologists

In the preceding chapter we discussed in detail the statutory privilege that is wrapped about information imparted during the relationship between physician and patient. When used in a legislative enactment the word "physician" is what lawyers call a "term of art"—a term, that is, that has a special, restricted meaning to which courts must strictly adhere. A "physician," in statutory parlance, is a licensed or "authorized" medical doctor.[1] A psychiatrist will inevitably be a medical doctor, and so communications between a patient and his psychiatrist are protected by the general physician-patient privilege if the particular state has enacted one but has linked it with no independent privilege applicable specifically to psychiatric consultations.[2] But a consultation with a psychologist will not be covered by the general privilege, since he is not a "physician" within the intendment of the statute.[3]

The typical general physician-patient privilege statute, riddled with exceptions, is not well suited to the psychiatrist-patient situation, and the problems posed by the absence of any protection whatever for the psychologist-patient relationship are obvious. It has long been thought, therefore, that there should be a special evidentiary privilege pertaining specifically to the psychotherapist, be he a psychiatrist or a clinical psychologist.[4]

[1] See, *e.g.*, CALIF. EVID. CODE, §990, quoted in the preceding chapter.

[2] See Guttmacher, M. S., and Weihofen, H.: *Privileged Communications Between Psychiatrist and Patient,* 28 INDIANA LAW JOURNAL 32, 37 (1952).

[3] *Ibid.*

[4] See Chadbourne, J. H.: *A Privilege Not Covered by the Uniform Rules—Psychotherapist-Patient Privilege,* in CALIF. LAW REV. COMM., REPORTS, RECOMMENDATIONS AND STUDIES 417 *et seq.* (1964), reprinted in LOUISELL, D. W., KAPLAN, J., AND WALTZ, J. R.: CASES AND MATERIALS ON EVIDENCE 752–63 (1968); Slovenko, R.:

Emergence of a Psychotherapist-Patient Privilege

Just as the common law never developed a physician-patient privilege, so it has never created a privilege that would apply to consultations with a clinical psychologist.[5] However, as these lines are written, nineteen states have provided explicit statutory protection to the psychologist-client relationship.[6] Oddly enough, a number of these jurisdictions lump psychologists under the orthodox attorney-client privilege, which is a very broad one.[7] The new California Evidence Code [8] is more sophisticated. It sets up an independent psychotherapist-patient privilege, applicable to psychiatrists and psychologists alike.[9] For the first time psychologists are not thrown in with the lawyers and psychiatrists are not made to function under a statute designed for physicians. The psychotherapist in California now has a privilege statute specifically drawn to conform to his special situation. Because, once again, the California statute

Psychiatry and a Second Look at the Medical Privilege, 6 WAYNE LAW REVIEW 175 (1960).

[5] See Note, *Confidential Communications to a Psychotherapist: A New Testimonial Privilege,* 47 NORTHWESTERN UNIV. LAW REVIEW 384 (1952), describing an Illinois trial court's tortured efforts to provide protection in the absence of an applicable statute.

[6] ALA. CODE, tit. 46, §297(36) (Supp. 1967); ARK. STAT. ANN., §72-1516 (Supp. 1967); CALIF. EVID. CODE, §§1010–1026 (Supp. 1967); COLO. REV. STAT., 154-1-7(8) (1963); CONN. GEN. STAT., §52-146a (Supp. 1966); DELA. CODE ANN., §3534 (Supp. 1968); GA. CODE ANN., §38-418 (Supp. 1961); IDAHO CODE, §54-2314 (Supp. 1967); ILL. ANN. STAT., ch. 51 §5.2 (Supp. 1967); KY. REV. STAT., §319.110 (1962); MASS. SESS. LAWS, chap. 418 (June 18, 1968); MONT. REV. CODE ANN., §93-701-4(6) (Supp. 1967); NEV. REV. STAT., §48.085 (1967); N. H. REV. STAT. ANN., §330-A:19 (Supp. 1967); N.Y. C.P.L.R., §4507 (Supp, 1968); ORE. REV. STAT., §44.040 (Supp. 1967); TENN. CODE ANN. §63-117 (1955); UTAH CODE ANN., §58-25-9 (Supp. 1967); WASH. REV. CODE, §18.83.110 (Supp. 1967).

[7] *E.g.,* ALA. CODE, tit. 46, §297(36) (Supp. 1967); DELA. CODE ANN., §3534 (Supp. 1968); IDAHO CODE, §54-2314 (Supp. 1967); N.Y. C.P.L.R. §4507 (Supp. 1968). It has been recognized that fundamental differences between the attorney-client and psychotherapist-patient relationships render application of the attorney-client privilege to the latter relationship altogether inappropriate. See Goldstein, J., and Katz, J.: *Psychiatrist-Patient Privilege: The GAP Proposal and the Connecticut Statute,* 36 CONNECTICUT BAR JOURNAL 175, 182 (1962).

[8] CALIF. EVID. CODE, §§1010–26 (Supp. 1967).

[9] The proposed code of evidence for the federal judicial system also contains a psychotherapist-patient privilege. In its preliminary form it is more streamlined than California's. It provides for only three exceptions to the rule of privilege: (1) in proceedings for hospitalization; (2) where the examination is by order of a judge; and (3) where the patient's mental condition is an element of a legal claim or defense. COMM. ON RULES OF PRAC. & PROC. OF THE JUD. CONF. OF THE U.S., PRELIMINARY DRAFT OF PROPOSED RULES OF EVIDENCE FOR THE UNITED STATES DISTRICT COURTS AND MAGISTRATES, 46 F.R.D. 257–59 (1969).

—enacted only after careful consideration by a knowledgeable Law Revision Commission—is certain to influence other jurisdictions, we set it forth verbatim:

ARTICLE 7. PSYCHOTHERAPIST-PATIENT PRIVILEGE

SECTION 1010. "Psychotherapist."

As used in this article, "psychotherapist" means:

(a) A person authorized, or reasonably believed by the patient to be authorized, to practice medicine in any state or nation who devotes, or is reasonably believed by the patient to devote, a substantial portion of his time to the practice of psychiatry; or

(b) A person licensed as a psychologist under Chapter 6.6 (commencing with Section 2900) of Division 2 of the Business and Professions Code.

SECTION 1011. "Patient."

As used in this article, "patient" means a person who consults a psychotherapist or submits to an examination by a psychotherapist for the purpose of securing a diagnosis or preventive, palliative, or curative treatment of his mental or emotional condition or who submits to an examination of his mental or emotional condition for the purpose of scientific research on mental or emotional problems.

SECTION 1012. "Confidential Communication Between Patient and Psychotherapist."

As used in this article, "confidential communication between patient and psychotherapist" means information, including information obtained by an examination of the patient, transmitted between a patient and his psychotherapist in the course of that relationship and in confidence by a means which, so far as the patient is aware, discloses the information to no third persons other than those who are present to further the interest of the patient in the consultation or examination or those to whom disclosure is reasonably necessary for the transmission of the information or the accomplishment of the purpose of the consultation or examination, and includes [a diagnosis made and the [10]] advice given by the psychotherapist in the course of that relationship.

SECTION 1013. "Holder of the Privilege."

As used in this article, "holder of the privilege" means:

(a) The patient when he has no guardian or conservator.

(b) A guardian or conservator of the patient when the patient has a guardian or conservator.

(c) The personal representative of the patient if the patient is dead.

[10] As amended CALIF. STATS. 1967, ch. 650, p. 2006, §5.

SECTION 1014. Psychotherapist-Patient Privilege.

Subject to Section 912 and except as otherwise provided in this article, the patient, whether or not a party, has a privilege to refuse to disclose, and to prevent another from disclosing, a confidential communication between patient and psychotherapist if the privilege is claimed by:

(a) The holder of the privilege;

(b) A person who is authorized to claim the privilege by the holder of the privilege; or

(c) The person who was the psychotherapist at the time of the confidential communication, but such person may not claim the privilege if there is no holder of the privilege in existence or if he is otherwise instructed by a person authorized to permit disclosure.

SECTION 1015. When Psychotherapist Required to Claim Privilege.

The psychotherapist who received or made a communication subject to the privilege under this article shall claim the privilege whenever he is present when the communication is sought to be disclosed and is authorized to claim the privilege under subdivision (c) of Section 1014.

SECTION 1016. Exception: Patient-Litigant Exception.

There is no privilege under this article as to a communication relevant to an issue concerning the mental or emotional condition of the patient if such issue has been tendered by:

(a) The patient;

(b) Any party claiming through or under the patient;

(c) Any party claiming as a beneficiary of the patient through a contract to which the patient is or was a party; or

(d) The plaintiff in an action brought under Section 376 or 377 of the Code of Civil Procedure for damages for the injury or death of the patient.

SECTION 1017. Exception: Court-Appointed Psychotherapist.

There is no privilege under this article if the psychotherapist is appointed by order of a court to examine the patient, but this exception does not apply where the psychotherapist is appointed by order of the court upon the request of the lawyer for the defendant in a criminal proceeding in order to provide the lawyer with information needed so that he may advise the defendant whether to enter [or withdraw [11]] a plea based on insanity or to present a defense based on his mental or emotional condition.

SECTION 1018. Exception: Crime or Tort.

There is no privilege under this article if the services of the psychotherapist were sought or obtained to enable or aid anyone to commit or plan to commit a crime or a tort or to escape detection or apprehension after the commission of a crime or a tort.

[11] As amended CALIF. STATS. 1967, ch. 650, p. 2007, §6.

SECTION 1019. Exception: Parties Claiming Through Deceased Patient.

There is no privilege under this article as to a communication relevant to an issue between parties all of whom claim through a deceased patient, regardless of whether the claims are by testate or intestate succession or by inter vivos transaction.

SECTION 1020. Exception: Breach of Duty Arising Out of Psychotherapist-Patient Relationship.

There is no privilege under this article as to a communication relevant to an issue of breach, by the psychotherapist or by the patient, of a duty arising out of the psychotherapist-patient relationship.

SECTION 1021. Exception: Intention of Deceased Patient Concerning Writing Affecting Property Interest.

There is no privilege under this article as to a communication relevant to an issue concerning the intention of a patient, now deceased, with respect to a deed of conveyance, will, or other writing, executed by the patient, purporting to affect an interest in property.

SECTION 1022. Exception: Validity of Writing Affecting Property Interest.

There is no privilege under this article as to a communication relevant to an issue concerning the validity of a deed of conveyance, will, or other writing, executed by a patient, now deceased, purporting to affect an interest in property.

SECTION 1023. Exception: Proceeding to Determine Sanity of Criminal Defendant.

There is no privilege under this article in a proceeding under Chapter 6 (commencing with Section 1367) of Title 10 of Part 2 of the Penal Code initiated at the request of the defendant in a criminal action to determine his sanity.

SECTION 1024. Exception: Patient Dangerous to Himself or Others.

There is no privilege under this article if the psychotherapist has reasonable cause to believe that the patient is in such mental or emotional condition as to be dangerous to himself or to the person or property of another and that disclosure of the communication is necessary to prevent the threatened danger.

SECTION 1025. Exception: Proceeding to Establish Competence.

There is no privilege under this article in a proceeding brought by or on behalf of the patient to establish his competence.

SECTION 1026. Exception: Required Report.

There is no privilege under this article as to information that the psychotherapist or the patient is required to report to a public employee or as to information required to be recorded in a public office, if such report or record is open to public inspection.

With certain exceptions set forth in section 1016 *et seq.*, the California psychotherapist-patient privilege provides absolute protection against legally coerced divulgence of communications made during the course of the psychotherapist-patient relationship in all circumstances except that of voluntary, knowing waiver by its holder, the patient. The California privilege, perhaps because of sticky definitional problems, is not specifically limited to communications between a patient and his psychiatrist or psychologist for the purpose of psychodiagnosis or psychotherapy. It is, however, plainly aimed at psychiatrists and psychologists alone in the field of psychotherapy. The definitional section of the statute, section 1010, forecloses assertion of the new privilege by those who have consulted social workers, marriage counselors, and others who, although neither a psychiatrist nor a certified psychologist, employ psychotherapeutic techniques as an aspect of their professional activities.

The Distinctive Nature of the Psychotherapist-Patient Privilege

To some persons it may seem odd that a psychotherapist-patient privilege has been developed at the very time when the physician-patient privilege is under heavy fire. Many students of the law of evidence do contend, of course, that the physician-patient privilege should be abolished on the ground that it frustrates the discovery of truth and in fact serves no useful legal purpose. (They deprecate the notion that anyone in his right mind would fail to disclose essential information to a treating doctor out of fear that it might later be revealed in court.) But the same criticisms cannot rightfully be leveled at the psychotherapist-patient privilege.[12] There exists a peculiarly close and essential relationship of confidence and trust between the patient and his psychotherapist. It is probably fair to say that the psychotherapist-patient relationship is unique in this respect. Ferenczi, one of the founders of modern psychotherapy, said that "The fundamental rule of analysis, on which the whole of our technique is built up, calls for the true and complete communication by the patient of all his ideas and associations." [13] Little wonder then that a perceptive federal judge has written that "Many physical ailments might be treated with some degree of effectiveness by a doctor whom the patient did not trust, but a psychiatrist must have the patient's confidence or he cannot help him." [14]

The physician-patient privilege may not always be with us, but the

[12] See generally, Slovenko, R.: *Psychiatry and a Second Look at the Medical Privilege,* 6 WAYNE LAW REVIEW 175 (1960).

[13] Ferenczi, S.: FINAL CONTRIBUTIONS TO THE PROBLEMS AND METHODS OF PSYCHOANALYSIS 77, Balint, M., ed. Hogarth, London, 1955.

[14] *Taylor* v. *United States,* 222 F.2d 398 (D.C. Cir. 1955), opinion of Judge Edgerton.

psychotherapist-patient privilege, because of the special nature of the relationship involved, is here to stay.

BIBLIOGRAPHY

BOOKS

Chayet, N. L.: LEGAL IMPLICATIONS OF EMERGENCY CARE 212–28. Appleton-Century-Crofts, New York, 1969.

DeWitt, C.: PRIVILEGED COMMUNICATIONS BETWEEN PHYSICIAN AND PATIENT 87–90. Charles C Thomas, Springfield, Ill., 1958.

Slovenko, R.: PSYCHOTHERAPY, CONFIDENTIALITY AND PRIVILEGED COMMUNICATION. Charles C Thomas, Springfield, Ill., 1966.

ARTICLES

Crawfis, E. H.: *The Physician and Privileged Communications as They Relate to Mental State,* 46 OHIO STATE MEDICAL JOURNAL 1082 (1950).

Diamond, B. L., and Weihofen, H.: *Privileged Communications and the Clinical Psychologist,* 9 JOURNAL OF CLINICAL PSYCHOLOGY 388 (1953).

Goldstein, J., and Katz, J.: *Psychiatrist-Patient Privilege: The GAP Proposal and the Connecticut Statute,* 36 CONNECTICUT BAR JOURNAL 175 (1962).

Guttmacher, M. S., and Weihofen, H.: *Privileged Communications Between Psychiatrist and Patient,* 28 INDIANA LAW JOURNAL 32 (1952).

Hollender, M. H.: *The Psychiatrist and the Release of Patient Information,* 116 AMERICAN JOURNAL OF PSYCHIATRY 828 (1960).

Sidel, V. W.: *Confidential Information and the Physician,* 264 NEW ENGLAND JOURNAL OF MEDICINE 1133 (1961).

Slovenko, R.: *Psychiatry and a Second Look at the Medical Privilege,* 6 WAYNE LAW REVIEW 175 (1960).

NOTES AND COMMENTS

Comment, *Legal Protection of the Confidential Nature of the Physician-Patient Relationship,* 52 COLUMBIA LAW REVIEW 383 (1952).

Note, *Confidential Communications to a Psychotherapist: A New Testimonial Privilege,* 47 NORTHWESTERN UNIV. LAW REVIEW 384 (1952).

Note, *Group Therapy and Privileged Communications,* 43 INDIANA LAW JOURNAL 93 (1967).

Note, *Psychiatrist-Patient Relationship—A Need for Retention of the Future Crime Exception,* 52 IOWA LAW REVIEW 1170 (1967).

chapter 17

THE PHYSICIAN'S LIABILITY FOR DEFAMATION

The Meaning of "Defamation"

The tort known as "defamation" denotes an invasion of a person's interest in good name and reputation by means of a false communication that tends to lower the esteem in which the subject of the communication is held.[1] "Defamation" is a general term which, in law, breaks down into the twin torts known as libel and slander.[2] By and large, libel means written defamation, or an electronically transmitted one, such as one made on nationwide television, that is likely to have a heavy, and therefore permanent, impact upon those hearing it. Slander means oral defamation.

The law of defamation, which is both complex and specialized, need not be spelled out in full detail since medical men do not frequently run afoul of it. However, passing reference to this esoteric body of law should

[1] See 1 Harper, F. V., and James, F.: TORTS 349–62, Little, Brown and Company, Boston, 1956, and Supp. 1968; Prosser, W. L.: TORTS 756–61, 3d ed. West Publishing Company, St. Paul, 1964. The shotgun definition of defamation undertaken in *Kimmerle* v. *New York Evening Journal,* 186 N.E. 217 (Ct. App. N.Y. 1933), is one of the most frequently quoted: "Words which tend to expose one to public hatred, shame, obloquy, contumely, odium, contempt, ridicule, aversion, ostracism, degradation or disgrace, or to induce an evil opinion of one in the minds of right-thinking persons, and to deprive one of their confidence and friendly intercourse in society." Thus defamation has nothing to do with one's *feelings;* it has to do with one's *reputation.* However, courts and commentators have disagreed with the notion that one can be defamed only in the eyes of "right-thinking persons." Judge Learned Hand once said, "A man may value his reputation even among those who do not embrace the prevailing moral standards." *Grant* v. *Readers Digest,* 151 F.2d 733 (2d Cir. 1945). Justice Oliver Wendell Holmes stated the governing principle: "No conduct is hated by all. That it will be known by a large number and will lead an appreciable fraction of that number to regard the plaintiff with contempt is enough to do her practical harm." *Peck* v. *Chicago Tribune,* 214 U.S. 185 (1909).

[2] See 1 Harper, F. V., and James, F.: TORTS, §5.9, Little, Brown and Company, Boston, 1956, and Supp. 1968; Prosser W. L.: TORTS 769–85, 3d ed. West Publishing Company, St. Paul, 1964.

be made, for some diagnostic statements could be considered defamatory if they are incorrect and unprotected by any legal privilege. Quite aside from considerations of unprofessional conduct and of the physician-patient privilege's applicability, a patient might legitimately resent a doctor's false and public imputations of, for example, insanity or, in the law's quaint phrase, "loathesome disease," because of their potentially adverse impact on the patient's reputation.

The Essential Element of "Publication"

A defamatory statement is not actionable unless it has been "published." [3] It must have been communicated to persons other than the one defamed; otherwise it would lack any tendency to diminish the subject's reputation in the community. In this sense the law favors defaming a man to his face rather than behind his back. It has been held, however, that defamation, though unintended by the defendant and occurring through no fault of his own, will support a lawsuit if the defendant himself was responsible for the release of the offending communication to third persons.[4]

It is a fair generalization that liability for defamation is strict—absolute—once the fact of publication, not consented to by the subject, is established, unless the defamatory matter is immunized from legal action for special policy reasons recognized by the law.

The Defense of "Privilege"

May a statement made by a physician as an aspect of his professional opinion form the basis for a defamation action? In other words, are a physician's words "privileged" by reason of his professional status? Most of the decided cases—and there have not been many—attest that the physician's status does not, in and of itself, resolve the privilege issue. The law treats a medical man no differently than any other person when it comes to liability for defamation. Whether a doctor's comments are privileged has been determined by our courts under the same orthodox rules applicable in all defamation cases.

[3] *E.g., Tocker* v. *Great* A. & *P. Tea Co.*, 190 F.2d 822 (D.C. Cir. 1963); *Insurance Resarch Service* v. *Associates Finance Corp.*, 134 F. Supp. 54 (M.D. Tenn. 1955); *Yousling* v. *Dare*, 98 N.W. 371 (S. Ct. Iowa 1904). And see 1 Harper, F. V., and James, F.: TORTS, §5.15, Little, Brown and Company, Boston, 1956, and Supp. 1968; Prosser, W. L.: TORTS, 785–91, 3d ed. West Publishing Company, St. Paul, 1964.

[4] The leading case, upon which all others build, is the English *Hulton & Co.* v. *Jones*, [1909] 2 K.B. 44, *aff'd*, [1910] A. C. 20 (fictitious newspaper account linking "Artemus Jones" with a woman not his wife; successful suit by a lawyer whose real name was Artemus Jones). See also *Laudati* v. *Stea*, 117 Atl. 422 (S. Ct. R.I. 1922) ("The question is not who was aimed at, but who was hit").

Qualified or Conditional Privilege

It is a general rule that defamatory publications made in good faith to protect or advance a legitimate and significant interest of the speaker or writer, or to discharge a legitimate duty with which he is charged, are not actionable if made to one having a corresponding interest or responsibility.[5] The interest or duty need not necessarily be a purely legal one; it may be moral or social. However, the privilege attaching to such statements is said to be qualified or conditional, not absolute or automatic, since a prerequisite is the absence of malice in the making of the challenged statement. Two judicial decisions involving physicians serve to exemplify the "publisher-recipient interest" privilege.

In a California case [6] the defendant physician had made an allegedly false and therefore slanderous statement to the plaintiff patient that she had gonorrhea. This statement, which was based on information furnished the doctor by a reputable laboratory to which he had sent test specimens, was made in the presence not only of the patient but also her mother and her landlady. The California court held that the statement had been made by one (the doctor) who was obviously legitimately interested in its subject matter to one (the patient) who possessed an obvious corresponding interest. A special statute, reflective of the general state of the law, also excused the defendant doctor's communication to third parties under these circumstances.[7]

The existence of malice as a motivation for defamatory comment changes the legal picture drastically. In an Ohio libel case [8] the defendant physician, whom plaintiff had apparently consulted as a private patient, filed a written report with the patient's employer during Workmen's Compensation claim negotiations. The report stated that the patient had a venereal disease; it had been filed without the patient's knowledge or consent. A jury's finding that the defendant doctor had not only breached professional ethics but had been actuated by malice was upheld on appeal, with the consequence that the physician was shorn of any protective privilege and could be held liable to the patient for damages.

A Utah decision [9] sets forth helpful guidelines for the physician. The

[5] See 1 Harper, F. V., and James F.: TORTS, §5.26, Little, Brown and Company, Boston, 1956, and Supp. 1968; Prosser, W. L.: TORTS 805–12 3d ed. West Publishing Company, St. Paul, 1964.

[6] *Shoemaker* v. *Friedberg*, 183 P.2d 318 (Cal. App. 1947).

[7] See also *Campbell* v. *Jewish Committee for Personal Service*, 271 P.2d 185 (Cal. App. 1954) (adverse report to a charitable corporation dedicated to assisting state hospital patients).

[8] *Beatty* v. *Baston*, 13 Ohio L. Abs. 481 (Ohio App. 1932).

[9] *Berry* v. *Moench*, 331 P.2d 814 (S. Ct. Utah 1958).

case involved a doctor who, at the request of another physician, provided information about the plaintiff's mental condition. This information was passed on to the parents of a girl who had been keeping company with the plaintiff; eventually it reached the girl herself, dampening her ardor. The Utah Supreme Court declared that a physician's responsibility to keep a confidence stemming from the professional relationship might be outweighed by some higher duty to supply even defamatory information if there existed a sufficiently important interest deserving of protection. However, the conditional privilege attaching to such communications was to be exercised in accordance with the following guidelines: (1) it must be exercised by the medical man in good faith and with due regard for truth; (2) the information must be reported fairly; (3) only that information should be supplied as is essential for the legitimate purposes for which the qualified privilege exists; and (4) dissemination of the information must be exclusively to those persons having a valid interest in it. The Utah court concluded that reasonable minds could differ as to the defendant doctor's adherence to the foregoing cautions. It appeared that he was uncertain regarding the sources of some of his information; that he based his opinion concerning the young man's present condition on treatment rendered some seven years previously; that in certain specific instances the physician had made no reasonable effort to secure accurate information; that neither the young man nor his girl friend or her parents were patients of the defendant at the time of his comments, and the girl's parents were not then the patients of the doctor who had requested the anti-romantic information.

The privilege we have been discussing has often been applied to reporting physicians employed by hospitals and similar institutions to whom persons go voluntarily for examination. In an Alabama case [10] a letter concerning a student, transmitted to the dean of her school by an examining physician on the school's staff, was held privileged. A suit involving a report that a student was "a high-grade moron" reached an identical result.[11] And in several instances where physicians were engaged to examine and report on the fitness of prospective employees it has been held that assertedly defamatory statements based on such examinations were qualifiedly privileged.[12]

[10] *Kenney* v. *Gurley,* 95 So. 34 (S. Ct. Ala. 1923).

[11] *Iverson* v. *Frandsen,* 237 F.2d 898 (10th Cir. 1956). See also *Previn* v. *Tenacre, Inc.,* 70 F.2d 389 (3d Cir.), *cert. denied,* 291 U.S. 677 (1933); *Collins* v. *Oklahoma State Hospital,* 184 Pac. 946 (S. Ct. Okla. 1916).

[12] *E.g., New York & P.R.S.S. Co.* v. *Garcia,* 16 F.2d 734 (1st Cir. 1926); *Leonard* v. *Wilson,* 8 So.2d 12 (S. Ct. Fla. 1942).

Absolute Privilege

Some communications are *absolutely* privileged. Of first importance to the physician is the circumstance that relevant statements made during the course of judicial and quasi-judicial proceedings, such as trials and administrative hearings, are absolutely immune from legal challenge. This rule has been applied in a number of cases involving certificates, affidavits, and testimony by doctors functioning in lunacy proceedings,[13] Workmen's Compensation claim hearings,[14] will probate proceedings,[15] and other sorts of litigation.[16] The rule of absolute privilege would also apply to any doctor testifying on behalf of the plaintiff in a medical malpractice action.

Statements made to the disciplinary arm of a medical association are qualifiedly privileged; they are immune from legal action if made without malice to advance the common interest of the medical profession in the competency and honesty of its members.[17] And the general rule of absolute privilege attending the report of a public officer to his superior, made in the course of his duties, has been applied to a psychiatrist attached to the Medical Center for Federal Prisoners.[18]

In the limited number of cases in which the question has been discussed, there has been recognized an absolute privilege surrounding communications from one physician to another regarding a patient.[19] Implicit in this rule is the condition that the communication shall have been necessary and relevant to the patient's treatment.[20]

[13] *E.g., Mezullo* v. *Maletz,* 118 N.E.2d 356 (Sup. Jud. Ct. Mass. 1954); *Dunbar* v. *Greenlaw,* 128 A.2d 218 (S. Ct. Me. 1956); *Bailey* v. *McGill,* 100 S.E.2d 860 (S. Ct. N.C. 1957). On the related question of suits for malicious prosecution or false imprisonment predicated on lunacy proceedings, see cases cited in Anno., 145 A.L.R. 711, 733–35.

[14] See *Mickens* v. *Davis,* 294 Pac. 896 (S. Ct. Kan. 1931). The result may be different when the information is disclosed without authority to a patient's employer outside the formal framework of a Workmen's Compensation Commission's procedures. See *Beatty* v. *Baston,* 13 Ohio L. Abs. 481 (Ohio App. 1932).

[15] See *Noll* v. *Kerby,* 15 N.Y.S.2d 665 (App. Div. N.Y. 1939).

[16] *E.g., Boyd* v. *Wynn,* 150 S.W.2d 648 (S. Ct. Ky. 1941) (suit on policy of accident insurance); *Hager* v. *Major,* 186 S.W.2d 564 (S. Ct. Mo. 1945) (action by insurers for declaratory judgment that they were not liable to plaintiffs under fire insurance policies; neuropsychiatrist testified that a defense witness was given to exaggerated and false statements).

[17] See *Judge* v. *Rockford Memorial Hospital,* 150 N.E.2d 202 (Ill. App. 1958).

[18] *Taylor* v. *Glotfelty,* 201 F.2d 51 (6th Cir. 1952).

[19] See, *e.g., Thornburg* v. *Long,* 101 S.E. 99 (S. Ct. N.C. 1919); *Berry* v. *Moench,* 331 P.2d 814 (S. Ct. Utah 1958).

[20] See *Parsons* v. *Henry,* 164 S.W. 241 (Mo. App. 1914) (communication not essential to therapy).

Mistake: No Defense

The physician is not immunized from liability for defamation merely because he genuinely, though mistakenly, believes his comments to be true. Courts have expressly suggested that the very fact of being a physician should constitute a ground for caution, rather than license, in expressing opinions.[21] If a physician's information is derived from hearsay or is otherwise open to suspicion, he should at the very least report these circumstances along with the information. A physician's statements, if not hedged, are generally endowed with more than ordinary credibility—a fact that may cut both ways in defamation actions. Comments touching adversely upon the competence of another medical practitioner are subject to the law of defamation and should be scrupulously avoided unless based upon a sure knowledge of all the relevant facts.

The Defense of Truth

It may properly be reiterated that there is one absolute and glorious defense to a charge of defamation: truth.[22] The law of libel and slander applies only to statements that, through design, negligence, or mistake, are false. But the medical man should hold in mind the legal dictum that in defamation actions the burden of proving truth rests upon the defendant.[23]

Defamation of a Physician

For the sake of symmetry, it should be added that physicians are themselves subject to being libeled or slandered and, akin with any other person, are free to sue their defamers.

The 1963 California case of *Hanley* v. *Lund* [24] possesses a certain appropriateness as an example, for it involved a successful slander action by a physician against an overzealous attorney. The defendant lawyer had

[21] See, *e.g., Alpin* v. *Morton,* 21 Ohio St. 536 (S. Ct. Ohio 1871).

[22] See 1 Harper, F. V., and James, F.: TORTS, §5.20 Little, Brown and Company, Boston, 1956, and Supp. 1968; Prosser, W. L.: TORTS 823–26, 3d ed. West Publishing Company, St. Paul, 1964.

[23] See *Bingham* v. *Gaynor,* 96 N.E. 84 (Ct. App. N.Y. 1911). And see Prosser, W.: TORTS 825–26, 3d ed. West Publishing Company, St. Paul, 1964. And there is a danger: in many states an unsuccessful plea of truth, constituting a reiterated defamation, can be considered by the jury in aggravation of damages. *E.g., McMullen* v. *Corkum,* 54 A.2d 753 (S. Ct. Me. 1947); *O'Malley* v. *Illinois Publ. Co.,* 194 Ill. App. 544 (1915).

[24] 32 Cal. Rptr. 733 (Cal. App. 1963).

represented the plaintiffs in a malpractice action against the doctor, a pediatrician. The lawyer had conveyed false accusations about the pediatrician to a newspaper reporter, resulting in a damaging article that charged the doctor with a faulty diagnosis leading to an infant's death. The doctor won the malpractice action and then filed a defamation action against both the plaintiffs' lawyer and the newspaper that had published his false account. The newspaper, apparently sensing the merit of the doctor's claim, settled with him in advance of trial for $1,500. The doctor's action against the lawyer went to trial. It was held that the defendant attorney's comments had not been privileged under the rule, previously discussed, pertaining to statements made during judicial proceedings, since his inaccurate remarks to the newspaperman went far beyond anything contained in the formal malpractice complaint filed in court. A jury awarded the pediatrician $13,500 in compensatory damages and, to teach the lawyer a needed lesson, added another $5,000 in punitive damages. (In many types of tort actions involving intentional and malicious conduct, the jury can compensate the plaintiff for out-of-pocket monetary losses and also assess a fine—punitive damages—against the defendant, the amount of the fine going to the plaintiff personally as an aspect of the total award.)

The principle that accusations of the charging of excessive fees are actionable as libel or slander has also been recognized in a number of cases involving medical men.[25]

BIBLIOGRAPHY

BOOKS

1 Harper, F. V., and James, F.: TORTS, ch. V. Little, Brown and Company, Boston, 1956, and Supp. 1968.

Phelps, R. H., and Hamilton, E. D.: LIBEL. The Macmillan Company, New York, 1966.

Prosser, W. L.: TORTS, ch. 21, 3d ed. West Publishing Company, St. Paul, 1964.

ARTICLES

Donnelly, R. C.: *The History of Defamation,* [1949] WISCONSIN LAW REVIEW 99.

Leflar, R. A.: *Defamation,* 66 LAW QUARTERLY REVIEW 348 (1950).

Veeder, V. V.: *History and Theory of the Law of Defamation,* 3 COLUMBIA LAW REVIEW 546 (1904).

[25] *E.g., Loewinthan* v. *Beth David Hospital,* 9 N.Y.S.2d 397 (S. Ct. N.Y. 1938); *Clemmons* v. *Danforth,* 32 Atl. 626 (S. Ct. Vt. 1895). *Compare DePasquale* v. *Westchester Newspapers, Inc.,* 8 N.Y.S.2d 829 (App. Div. N.Y. 1938).

NOTES AND COMMENTS

Comment, *Developments in the Law—Defamation,* 69 HARVARD LAW REVIEW 875 (1956).

Note, *Liability of Physician for Publication of Fact of Patient's Venereal Disease,* 23 NOTRE DAME LAWYER 377 (1948).

chapter 18

LIABILITY FOR INVASION OF THE PATIENT'S RIGHT OF PRIVACY

The Origin and Development of the General Right of Privacy

Loosely related to the law of defamation, which we discussed in Chapter 17, and somewhat more closely tied to legal and ethical requirements of confidentiality in the doctor-patient relationship discussed in Chapter 15, is the so-called right of privacy. Sometimes referred to as "the right to be let alone," it often connotes something slightly different: a right to be free from unwanted publicity.

A large number of courts and a few statutes now protect private citizens against serious or outrageous interferences with their interest in reasonable privacy. The privacy principle shields against publicity given to the plaintiff's name, likeness, and private data about him, among other things. It is a principle of relatively recent origin, having been unheard of prior to 1890. In that year there appeared in the *Harvard Law Review* an influential article by Samuel D. Warren and Louis D. Brandeis (who later became a distinguished Supreme Court Justice) entitled "The Right of Privacy." [1] The authors surveyed those cases in which damages had been awarded for defamation, breach of confidence or of some implied contract, or invasion of a property right. They decided that many of these cases were in fact grounded upon a separate and broader principle of privacy that deserved to be specifically recognized for what it was. Twelve years passed before a court was confronted by the Warren-Brandeis theory and then it fared poorly. In 1902, in *Roberson* v. *Rochester Folding Box Company*,[2] the defendant had used the picture of an attractive girl, without her permission, to advertise its flour. The New York Court Appeals shied away from any theory that there existed a legally enforceable right of privacy. It pointed to the lack of precedent (aside from the Warren-Brandeis article); to the purely subjective nature of the claimed injury which

[1] 4 HARVARD LAW REVIEW 193 (1890).

[2] 64 N.E. 442 (Ct. App. N.Y. 1902).

made it difficult of reliable proof; to the vast amount of litigation that any such principle would probably inspire (the "floodgates" or "Pandora's Box" argument of which many lawyers and some courts are enamored); to the difficulty involved in drawing a necessary line between "public" and "private" persons (surely a celebrity, especially a self-perpetuated one, could not complain of publicity); and to its fear that such a legal principle would unduly restrict the constitutionally protected freedoms of speech and publication.

The *Roberson* decision was considered unnecessarily timid and evoked a flurry of criticism in the law journals.[3] Two years later the Supreme Court of Georgia, viewing an essentially similar fact situation, declined to follow *Roberson.*[4] It adopted the Warren-Brandeis thesis and held that invasion of privacy was a separate compensable tort. Today some form of privacy right is recognized by statute in four states (New York, Oklahoma, Utah, and Virginia) and by judicial decision—common law—in thirty other states (Alabama, Alaska, Arizona, Arkansas, California, Connecticut, Delaware, Florida, Georgia, Illinois, Indiana, Iowa, Kansas, Kentucky, Louisiana, Maryland, Michigan, Mississippi, Missouri, Montana, Nevada, New Jersey, North Carolina, Ohio, Oregon, Pennsylvania, South Carolina, South Dakota, Tennessee, and West Virginia).[5]

The Four Branches of the Right of Privacy

Use of Plaintiff's Personality for Commercial Purposes

The right of privacy is a fuzzy one, unsusceptible of sharp delineation. It is defined narrowly in some states, such as New York, and broadly in some others. An analysis of cases across the country reveals that the right of privacy actually has four different branches. The first of these, and the one most consistently recognized, consists of the unauthorized appropriation of elements of the plaintiff's personality for commercial purposes. As in *Roberson* and in the cited Georgia lawsuit, the typical case under this branch involves the use of someone's picture or name in advertising, creating the impression that the person endorses the defendant's product or service.[6] Cases of this sort, in effect, recognize an exclusive property right in

[3] This inspired one of the concurring judges in *Roberson* to adopt the unprecedented tactic of writing a law review article defending the court's decision. O'Brien, D.: *The Right of Privacy,* 2 COLUMBIA LAW REVIEW 437 (1902). The result of all the furor was the enactment of a privacy statute. N.Y. CIV. RIGHTS LAW, §50-51 (Supp. 1967).

[4] *Pasevich* v. *New England Life Ins. Co.,* 50 S.E. 68 (S. Ct. Ga. 1904).

[5] For a collection of the cases and statutes, see Prosser, W. L.: TORTS 831–32, 3d ed. West Publishing Company, St. Paul, 1964.

[6] *E.g., Kerby* v. *Hal Roach Studios,* 127 P.2d 577 (Cal. App. 1942) (name); *Brociner* v. *Radio Wire Television,* 183 N.Y.S.2d 743 (App. Div. N.Y. 1959) (name); *Olan Mills, Inc. of Texas* v. *Dodd,* 353 S.W.2d 22 (S. Ct. Ark. 1962) (face); *Eick* v.

one's name and face. Movie stars and baseball players do not praise vodka and toothpaste for nothing.

Intrusion into Plaintiff's Seclusion

A second privacy tort involves gross intrusions into a person's seclusion, such as tapping his telephone,[7] peering through his (or her) windows,[8] or bursting unannounced into his home.[9] A Michigan physician committed a breach of this branch of the privacy tort when he brought an unmarried layman friend with him to observe the delivery of plaintiff's baby.[10]

Placing the Plaintiff in a False and Embarrassing Position

A third branch of the privacy tort consists of placing the plaintiff in a position that is false and embarrassing, although not necessarily defamatory. Examples include signing another's name to a published message such as a letter, telegram, or petition that misrepresents his actual views on some controversial subject,[11] and employing a person's photograph to illustrate an embarrassing article about a news event with which he had no connection.[12]

Revealing Confidential Information About the Plaintiff

In the final cluster of cases, which is of particular significance to the medical profession, courts have upheld a legal action where the defendant abridged the ordinary decencies surrounding information that was private

---

Perk Dog Food Co., 106 N.E.2d 742 (Ill. App. 1952) (face). A large number of cases of this sort are cited and described in *Ettore* v. *Philco Television Broadcasting Corp.*, 229 F.2d 481 (3d Cir. 1956).

[7] *La Crone* v. *Ohio Bell Tel. Co.* 182 N.E.2d 15 (Ohio App. 1961).

[8] *Sounder* v. *Pendleton Detectives, Inc.*, 88 So.2d 716 (La. App. 1956). Cases of this ilk permitted one law student to demonstrate that the titles of law review pieces need not always be dull. See Note, *Crimination of Peeping Toms and Other Men of Vision*, 5 ARKANSAS LAW REVIEW 388 (1951).

[9] *Welsh* v. *Pritchard*, 241 P.2d 816 (S. Ct. Mont. 1952) (landlord moved in on tenant).

[10] *DeMay* v. *Roberts*, 9 N.W. 146 (S. Ct. Mich. 1881). See also *Carr* v. *Shifflette*, 82 F.2d 874 (D.C. Cir. 1936) (medical treatment of woman, requiring exposure of body to layman); *Inderbitzen* v. *Lane Hospital*, 12 P.2d 744 (Cal. App. 1942) (subjection of pregnant woman to numerous vaginal and rectal examinations by young male medical students who had not first sterilized their hands; plaintiff poked and prodded and uterus torn; screams induced only laughter). See also *Savage* v. *Boies*, 272 P.2d 349 (S. Ct. Ariz. 1954); *cf. Stone* v. *Eisen*, 114 N.E. 44 (Ct. App. N.Y. 1916) (attempted rape).

[11] *Hinish* v. *Meier & Frank Co.*, 113 P.2d 438 (S. Ct. Ore. 1941). See Wigmore, J. H.: *The Right Against False Attribution of Belief or Utterance*, 4 KENTUCKY LAW REVIEW, No. 8, p. 3 (1916).

[12] *Semler* v. *Ultem Publications*, 9 N.Y.S.2d 319 (City Ct. N.Y. 1938) (picture in sex magazine).

even though, once again, not necessarily defamatory. A case involving a medical subject provides a useful initial example of this phase of the right of privacy.[13] In 1939 the news magazine *Time* published in its "Medicine" section an account of the physical ailment for which a young and attractive woman was receiving hospital treatment. The article, naming the woman and illustrated with a photograph of her clad in a hospital gown, detailed her symptoms: uncontrollable gluttony apparently induced by a condition of the pancreas. The patient sued the magazine on a right-of-privacy theory, pointing out that far from consenting to such publicity, she had vigorously protested against it to agents of the defendant. The Missouri Supreme Court, upholding a $1,500 verdict (but striking down an additional $1,500 in punitive damages because the magazine had not been motivated by malice), commented that the nature of plaintiff's malady could have been conveyed to the defendant's readers without revelation of her name and likeness. The court added that it made not the slightest legal difference, aside from a possible impact on the level of recoverable damages, the *Time*'s account had been scrupulously accurate; the magazine was charged not with defamation but with an unauthorized invasion of the plaintiff's right to a decent degree of privacy.

There have been successful right-of-privacy actions against physicians and hospitals that adopted a too-casual view of their relationship with patients. In a 1930 Georgia case [14] the parents of a deceased child sued a hospital, among others, for an injunction and damages in connection with an unauthorized newspaper publication of a picture of their child, which had been born with its heart on the outside of its body. The hospital had permitted a news photographer to take the offending picture. The Georgia Supreme Court held that the parents' Complaint, alleging mental anguish generated by the hospital's unauthorized conduct, stated a good cause of action.[15] A New York case [16] is out of the same mold. A federal judge excoriated two osteopathic surgeons for their conduct in turning over to a newspaper reporter x-rays disclosing a six-inch hemostat that had been lodged in the plaintiff's abdomen for some four years. The x-ray pictures made a good feature story—and a good lawsuit for violation of the plaintiff's right of privacy.

The case of *Griffin* v. *Medical Society of State of New York* [17] demon-

[13] *Barber* v. *Time, Inc.*, 159 S.W.2d 291 (S. Ct. Mo. 1942).

[14] *Bazemore* v. *Savannah Hosp.*, 155 S.E. 194 (S. Ct. Ga. 1930).

[15] See also *Douglas* v. *Stokes*, 149 S.W. 849 (S. Ct. Ky. 1912) (photographs of deceased infant's deformities). *Compare Waters* v. *Fleetwood*, 91 S.E.2d 344 (S. Ct. Ga. 1956), which questions the holding in the *Bazemore* case.

[16] *Banks* v. *King Features Syndicate, Inc.*, 30 F.Supp. 352 (S.D.N.Y. 1939). See also *Feeney* v. *Young*, 181 N.Y.S. 481 (App. Div. N.Y. 1920) (motion pictures of plaintiff's cesarean section).

[17] 11 N.Y.S.2d 109 (S. Ct. N.Y. 1939).

strates that wanton irresponsibility does not always lie at the root of privacy actions. In that lawsuit the plaintiff alleged that plastic surgeons had taken photographs at the commencement of treatment and after its conclusion and that a total of four of these before-and-after pictures were published without her authority in the co-defendant society's journal in an article unflatteringly entitled "The Saddle Nose." The defendant doctors argued, under New York's restrictively worded privacy statute, that their article had not been published "for advertising purposes." A New York judge, refusing to dismiss the plaintiff's action before she had had her day in court, stated that "An article, even in a scientific publication, may be nothing more than someone's advertisement in disguise." The judge, who was either cynical or perceptive, harbored the notion that the two plastic surgeons might have had less than altruistic reasons for displaying their prowess to other members of the medical profession. (This judge may also have lost sight of the necessity for publishing medical data for the benefit of other practitioners, who might be labeled medical gamblers if they could not point to published research and experience underlying their seemingly unorthodox procedures.) During the plaintiff's day in court in the foregoing case—that is, at the trial—the defendant doctors would be free to prove, if they could, that the photographs "were used solely for illustrative or scientific purposes."

Not all courts take so restrictive a view of publications in scientific journals. Speaking of a statute similar to New York's in that it prohibited "the appropriation of the name, picture, or personality of an individual for advertising purposes, or for purposes of trade," a United States Court of Appeals has insisted that "It does not undertake to forbid publication . . . of matters essentially educational or informative, even though the name or picture of an individual is used incidentally in connection therewith." [18]

The Special Bases of the Right of Privacy in Medical Cases

In cases involving the release of damaging medical information the courts have especially solid foundations upon which to erect an actionable right of privacy. They need not rely exclusively on the Warren-Brandeis theory; they could, if they chose, announce that the Warren-Brandeis conception of the right of privacy is irrelevant to cases involving medical information. The courts in such cases, unlike most other privacy cases, can cite express legislative enactments requiring physicians to preserve the confidentiality of medical data. We refer, of course, to licensure statutes and to the statutory physician-patient privilege.[19]

[18] *Donahue* v. *Warner Brothers Pictures, Inc.*, 194 F.2d 6 (10th Cir. 1952).

[19] See Chapters 2 and 15.

In *Simonsen* v. *Swenson*,[20] a landmark case in which the defendant physician informed plaintiff's landlady that her tenant had a loathsome disease, the Nebraska Supreme Court sustained a cause of action by pointing to the state's licensing law, which provided that a physician's license could be revoked for any unauthorized or unprivileged betrayal of a patient's communications. The court concluded that this portion of the licensure statute was a sufficient expression of public policy upon which to build a right of redress against a voluble physician unless his breach of confidentiality could somehow be justified.

Other courts have adopted the *Simonsen* approach. In *Berry* v. *Moench*[21] the Utah Supreme Court recognized the availability of a cause of action for wrongful disclosure of medical information, basing its decision on a public policy of nondisclosure as evidenced by the state's physician-patient privilege statute. And in *Hammonds* v. *Aetna Casualty & Surety Co.*[22] a federal court looked to both the licensure and the privilege statutes of Ohio in holding that the leakage of confidential medical information constitutes an actionable wrong.[23]

Defenses to Right-of-Privacy Actions

The defenses to a patient's right-of-privacy action are few. The truth of the medical data disclosed is no defense whatever; simple privacy, not defamation, is at stake.[24] The fact that the patient is not a "private" person but rather a celebrity who customarily feeds on publicity, usually thought to be a defense in cases involving relatively innocuous information, will probably be considered of no consequence where intimate medical data, covered by explicit legal and ethical requirements of confidentiality, are

[20] 177 S.W. 831 (S. Ct. Neb. 1920).

[21] 331 P.2d 814 (S. Ct. Utah 1958).

[22] 237 F.Supp. 96 (N.D. Ohio 1965).

[23] Plaintiff Hammonds had sued a hospital for damages resulting from the collapse of a hospital bed. In preparation for defense of that suit the hospital's attorney allegedly requested the Cleveland, Ohio, office of Aetna Casualty & Surety Co. to obtain all medical information about plaintiff from his treating doctor on the pretext that Aetna, the doctor's malpractice insurer, was investigating a claim by plaintiff against the doctor. The doctor complied with Aetna's request for information, thereby assertedly prejudicing plaintiff's negligence action against the hospital, and he also allegedly discontinued treatment of the plaintiff. The court held that the doctor's breach of confidence was actionable and that the insurance company's conduct in inducing the doctor to behave improperly was also actionable. See also *Alexander* v. *Knight*, 177 A. 2d 142 (Pa. Super, 1962). *Compare Quarles* v. *Sutherland*, 389 S.W. 2d 249 (S. Ct. Tenn. 1965), refusing to hold that a licensure statute gives rise to an action for unauthorized disclosure of confidential medical information.

[24] See *Afro-American Publishing Co.* v. *Jaffe*, 366 F.2d 649 (D.C. Cir. 1966); *Barber* v. *Time, Inc.*, 159 S.W.2d 291 (S. Ct. Mo. 1942); *Smith* v. *Driscoll*, 162 Pac. 572 (S. Ct. Wash. 1917).

involved. The fact that medical data are newsworthy or will advance science is likewise not controlling.[25]

A reporting duty imposed by law will immunize a physician from liability. In almost every jurisdiction, for example, there exist statutes and ordinances requiring doctors to report cases of venereal and other contagious diseases to specified public health authorities. Other laws require the reporting of criminal abortions, narcotics addiction, and gunshot wounds. Since it would be more than faintly incongruous to hold a doctor liable in damages for doing what the law required him to do,[26] it is safe to predict that a physician complying with reporting statutes will not be answerable in damages to his patient for a breach of confidentiality.[27] Similarly, required testimony given in the course of a judicial proceeding is absolutely privileged.[28]

The circumstance that a disclosure was made in good faith to protect third persons from a serious risk of harm will also insulate a physician from liability for the unauthorized disclosure of medical information, just as it will in a libel or slander suit. The leading case leaves one with vague sensations of sympathy for the unsuccessful plaintiff. The physician-defendant in *Simonsen* v. *Swenson* [29] thought that he was advancing laudable ends when he took it upon himself to advise his patient's landlady that he

[25] See, *e.g.*, *Bazemore* v. *Savannah Hospital*, 155 S.E. 194 (S. Ct. Ga. 1930); *Barber* v. *Time, Inc.*, 159 S.W.2d 291 (S. Ct. Mo. 1942); *Clayman* v. *Bernstein*, 38 Pa. D. & C. 543 (Phila. County Ct. Pa. 1940). On the other hand, courts would probably find a way to immunize from challenge the issuance of medical bulletins regarding the condition of a national leader even though they were not specifically authorized. An incumbent President's privacy, no matter how much he might long to preserve it, probably must bow to the public's right to obtain important information. Perhaps the same thing can be said about announcements of the progress of those who have undergone significant new surgical procedures. Thus in the late 1960's the public press reported almost daily on the condition of various recipients of heart transplants.

[26] See *Boyd* v. *Wynn*, 150 S.W.2d 648 (S. Ct. Ky. 1941); *McGuire* v. *Amyx*, 297 S. W. 968 (S. Ct. Mo. 1927).

[27] *Cf. Clark* v. *Geraci*, 208 N.Y.S.2d 564 (S. Ct. N.Y. 1960). The patient, a civilian employee of the Air Force, had asked his doctor to make an incomplete disclosure to Air Force authorities as to the nature of his illness. The court held that the patient was "estopped" from complaining that the physician, in order to correct the impression created by the patient, had informed the authorities that his absences from work were due to alcoholism. The court conceded that disclosures of medical information could be actionable but stated that the physician's duty to his government overrode his duty to his patient.

[28] See *Smith* v. *Driscoll*, 162 Pac. 572 (S. Ct. Wash. 1917). This is only equitable since a physician called as a witness in a lawsuit can be required, on pain of a contempt-of-court citation, to divulge medical information unless his patient has effectively asserted the doctor-patient privilege. See Chapter 15 and Note, *Legal Protection of the Confidential Nature of the Physician-Patient Relationship*, 52 COLUMBIA LAW REVIEW 384 (1952).

[29] 177 S.W.831 (S. Ct. Neb. 1920).

(the patient) was afflicted with a "contagious disease"—h
did not have syphilis—and that she should "be careful to
[plaintiff's] bedclothing, and to wash her hands in alcoh
Acting upon this dire warning, the landlady removed a
belongings to a hallway and fumigated his room. The Neb
Court held that the physician's conduct was a justifiable e
others.[30]

Although the Nebraska court in the foregoing case may have given the defendant doctor more credit for humanitarianism than he deserved, it is obvious that the law cannot reasonably require a physician to keep silent while one of his patients irresponsibly exposes others to a risk of serious infection.

The New Jersey case of *Hague* v. *Williams*[31] arose out of a claim under a policy insuring the life of an eight-month-old child. The infant, during the first four months of its life, had been examined by a pediatrician on numerous occasions. According to the child's parents, the doctor had reported no abnormality of any kind. One night, however, the little girl became ill and was taken to a hospital, where she died the same day. An autopsy revealed a congenital heart defect. When purchasing a $1,500 insurance policy on her life, the child's father had represented that his daughter was, to the best of his knowledge, in good health. During its investigation of the father's claim the insurance company requested medical data from the pediatrician and was informed by him that the child had had heart trouble from birth. The insurer thereupon denied the father's claim, apparently intimating that he had attempted to defraud the company. The father sued the pediatrician, alleging not only that the doctor's disclosures had frustrated his insurance claim but that they had caused him humiliation. The New Jersey Supreme Court rebuffed the plaintiff's action. Observing that it could point to no state statutory physician-patient privilege as a crystallization of public policy favoring nondisclosure of medical information, the court held that divulgence without consent was proper "where the public interest or the private interest of the patient so demands." The court concluded that the public interest in fair and honest resolution of legal claims justified disclosure of a patient's physical condition when that condition was relevant to the claim.

Occasionally a physician must make disclosures of medical information

[30] *Cf.* also *Berry* v. *Moench,* 331 P.2d 814 (S. Ct. Utah 1958) (libel action; defendant doctor sent unauthorized letter, containing embarrassing data, to former patient's prospective inlaws; held: "[The girl's] concern for her well-being and happiness was a sufficient interest to protect, and . . . it was within the generally accepted standards of decent conduct for the doctor to reveal the information which might have an important bearing thereon"). This case is discussed in Chapter 18.

[31] 181 A.2d 345 (S. Ct. N.J. 1962).

for the good of his patient, and the law will protect the physician in this circumstance. *Iverson* v. *Frandsen,*[32] although involving a claim of libel, is the most significant case in support of this prediction. A child's parents had taken her to a mental institution to secure help in overcoming her claustrophobia. The results of tests revealing the patient to be a "feebleminded" high-grade moron were recorded in a standard hospital report along with the prediction that "at the time she is about sixteen, she should have progressed to about the fourth grade level in reading, arithmetic, writing, etc." A copy of the hospital report was transmitted to the guidance director at the girl's school, at his request, and thereafter painful rumors about the child spread throughout the school. *Iverson* contains a strong intimation that a conditional privilege attaches to reports of this sort.[33]

The most potent defense to an action for invasion of a patient's privacy is consent. Informed consent to disclosure of data that would otherwise be confidential, or to other breaches of privacy, is a complete defense to a right-of-privacy action.[34] Accordingly, many of the principles discussed in our chapter on liability for failure to obtain "informed consent" to customary therapy [35] are broadly applicable here.

The law implies consent to those invasions of privacy that any reasonable person would anticipate as being essential for effective diagnosis and treatment.

It is difficult for one to undergo a thorough physical checkup while fully clothed. It is also difficult to diagnose and treat a patient without maintaining detailed records of his case.[36] But submitting to examination and treatment by a physician does not imply consent to the presence of

[32] 237 F.2d 898 (10th Cir. 1956).

[33] A Note, *Medical Practice and the Right to Privacy,* in 43 MINNESOTA LAW REVIEW 943, 960 (1959), persuasively argues that since only the welfare of the patient is concerned in cases such as *Iverson,* either he or those authorized to act on his behalf should control the disclosure of data concerning him.

[34] See Prosser, W. L.: TORTS 850–51, 3d ed. West Publishing Company, St. Paul, 1964. A patient's consent is invalid if it was induced by words or conduct of a deceitful nature. See, *e.g., DeMay* v. *Roberts,* 9 N.W. 146 (S. Ct. Mich. 1881) ("The fact that at the time . . . [plaintiff] consented to the presence of . . . [the defendant doctor's layman friend], supposing him to be a physician, does not preclude her from maintaining an action and recovering substantial damages upon afterwards ascertaining his true character. . . . [Defendant] was guilty of deceit . . ."). Moreover, any conditions or restrictions attached to the patient's consent must be strictly observed. See, *e.g., Feeney* v. *Young,* 181 N.Y.S. 481 (App. Div. N.Y. 1920) (plaintiff consented to taking of motion pictures of her cesarean for scientific purposes only; public showing of the film, as part of motion picture entitled "Birth," was held actionable). See also *Douglas* v. *Stokes,* 149 S.W. 849 (S. Ct. Ky. 1912).

[35] Chapter 11.

[36] *Cf. Iverson* v. *Frandsen,* 237 F.2d 898 (10th Cir. 1956).

nonessential individuals, in person or with the aid of closed-circuit television.[37] Furthermore, courts do not consider submission for diagnosis or treatment as implying any consent to the taking, let alone publishing, of still or motion pictures or videotapes of the patient.[38]

The current state of the law was accurately capsuled in a Pennsylvania case: "While the court appreciates the development of the art of photography generally, and in the medical profession particularly, not only as a means of diagnosis and treatment, but also as a means of instruction, its progress has not yet reached a stage at which physicians have been accorded the right to photograph their patients without their consent." [39] In short, publicity can be given to a patient's condition, nonessential observers can be admitted, and pictures can be taken and published only with the explicit consent of the patient and, for that matter, of any bystanders (such as nurses or other aides) who will show up in the photograph.

If effective medical teaching methods or the expansion of scientific knowledge suggest the filming of surgical procedures, publication of illustrated articles in learned journals (not in titillating best-sellers aimed at a mass audience), and the like, the physician should obtain his patient's written authorization.

Any mention of medical photography raises a question concerning a procedure that is rapidly becoming standard practice in the medical profession. Many medical men, heeding warnings that tangible evidence is often the best evidence with which to combat malpractice claims, have adopted the practice of taking before-and-after photographs of their patients or series of photographs depicting step-by-step improvement in each patient's condition. The taking of such photographs, as a manifestation of the principle that one picture is worth a thousand words in courtrooms as well as newspapers, is now standard practice for many orthopedic surgeons, plastic surgeons, and dermatologists. No reported judicial decision has ruled on the propriety of these procedures. And there probably will be no such decision in the future, for it seems unlikely that the practice of taking progress photographs will inspire a patient to litigate, or a court to rule adversely to the defendant physician, where the physician has been scrupulous in maintaining the photographs as a part of the patient's confidential medical record.

[37] *E.g., Savage* v. *Boies,* 272 P.2d 349 (S. Ct. Ariz. 1954); *DeMay* v. *Roberts,* 9 N.W. 146 (S. Ct. Mich. 1881).

[38] *E.g., Banks* v. *King Features Syndicate,* 30 F.Supp. 352 (S.D.N.Y. 1939); *Bazemore* v. *Savannah Hosp.,* 155 S.E. 194 (S. Ct. Ga. 1930); *Griffin* v. *Medical Society of State of New York,* 11 N.Y.S.2d 109 (S. Ct. N.Y. 1939).

[39] *Clayman* v. *Bernstein,* 38 Pa. D. & C. 543 (Phila. County Ct. Pa. 1940).

Any possible issue regarding the propriety of progress photographs can be obviated, of course, by securing the patient's consent to the taking of them.[40]

The American Medical Association also broadly recommends that prior to the use of motion pictures of surgical procedures the patient be called upon to waive any rights he might otherwise have "to any claims for payment or royalties in connection with any exhibition, televising, or other showing of this [described] motion picture film, regardless of whether such exhibition, televising, or other showing is under philanthropic, commercial, institutional, or private sponsorship, and irrespective of whether a fee of admission or film rental is charged."[41] The patient is asked to grant his consent to the filming of his operation "as a voluntary contribution in the interest of medical education and knowledge" and subject only to the condition that he will not be identified by name in the film. Such authorization clauses are responsive to judicial decisions recognizing an exclusive property interest in one's face.[42]

It is the teaching of the law in this area that without the patient's full knowledge and consent there ought generally to be no broadcasting of a medical case record and no publication of a still photograph or showing of a motion picture film or videotape from which the identity of a patient can be discerned. Man cherishes his privacy, and in many jurisdictions the law offers a means of enforcing it.

BIBLIOGRAPHY *

BOOKS

Prosser, W. L.: TORTS, chap. 22, 3d ed. West Publishing Company, St. Paul, 1964.

Rosenberg, J. M.: THE DEATH OF PRIVACY 47–51. Random House, New York, 1969.

ARTICLES

Brittan, L.: *Right of Privacy in England and the United States,* 37 TULANE LAW REVIEW 235 (1963).

[40] See, *e.g.*, A.M.A., MEDICOLEGAL FORMS WITH LEGAL ANALYSIS 12 (1961), Form 13.

[41] The American Medical Association has published a collection of authorization forms that facilitate proof of consent. The suggested forms cover "Authorization for Disclosure of Information by Patient's Physician," "Authorization for Examination of Physician's Records," "Authority to Admit Visitors," "Consent to Taking and Publication of Photographs," "Consent to Televising Operation," and "Consent to Taking of Motion Pictures of Operation." A.M.A., MEDICOLEGAL FORMS WITH LEGAL ANALYSIS 6–12 (1961).

[42] *Id.* at 12.

* See also the bibliography appended to Chapter 17.

Challener, W. A.: *The Doctor-Patient Privilege and the Right to Privacy,* 11 UNIV. OF PITTSBURGH LAW REVIEW 624 (1950).
Feinberg, W.: *Recent Developments in the Law of Privacy,* 48 COLUMBIA LAW REVIEW 713 (1948).
Nizer, L.: *The Right of Privacy,* 39 MICHIGAN LAW REVIEW 526 (1941).
Prosser, W. L.: *Privacy,* 48 CALIFORNIA LAW REVIEW 383 (1960).
Wade, J. W.: *Defamation and the Right of Privacy,* 15 VANDERBILT LAW REVIEW 1093 (1962).
Warren, C., and Brandeis, L. D.: *The Right of Privacy,* 4 HARVARD LAW REVIEW 193 (1890).
Yankwich, L. R.: *The Right of Privacy,* 27 NOTRE DAME LAWYER 429 (1952).

NOTES AND COMMENTS

Comment, *Physician's Liability for Improper Disclosure,* 198 J.A.M.A. 331 (1966).
Comment, *Right to Privacy: Social Interest and Legal Right,* 51 MINNESOTA LAW REVIEW 531 (1967).
Note, *Medical Practice and the Right of Privacy,* 43 MINNESOTA LAW REVIEW 943 (1959).

chapter 19

THE ASSESSMENT OF MONEY DAMAGES IN A JURY TRIAL

THE GENERAL NATURE OF A DAMAGE VERDICT

At the end of a civil jury trial, after all the evidence is in and the jurors have heard the lawyers' closing arguments and the instructions of the judge, the jury must deliberate secretly and render its verdict. The jurors' deliberations must focus first on the ultimate issue—that of the defendant's liability to the plaintiff. If the jurors find for the defendant on the liability issue they need do nothing more than announce their determination of nonliability in open court. If, on the other hand, they decide that the defendant is liable to the plaintiff, under the facts as found by them and upon the law as it was explained to them by the trial judge, the jurors must proceed to deliberate upon the second crucial issue posed in all tort cases—the issue of monetary damages.

The general legal principles governing the form and content of verdicts in all personal injury actions are applicable to actions for medical malpractice and related torts. It is, for example, a proposition of general application to jury trials that the financial worth of the parties, including the defendant's coverage by liability insurance, is irrelevant to the assessment of damages and cannot, upon pain of a mistrial, be disclosed to the jurors by counsel.[1] It is also held almost universally that the tax-exempt

[1] *E.g., Blankenship* v. *Rowntree,* 219 F.2d 597 (10th Cir. 1955) (wealth); *Lutz Industries* v. *Dixie Home Stores,* 88 S.E.2d 333 (S. Ct. N.C. 1955) (wealth); *Smithers* v. *Henriquez,* 15 N.E.2d 499 (S. Ct. Ill. 1938) (insurance). Louisiana is the only state holding, unaccountably, that "ability to pay" is relevant to the amount of a compensatory damage award. See *Smith* v. *Freeman,* 31 So.2d 524 (La. App. 1947). (It has long been held that the defendant's wealth can properly be divulged to the jury when punitive or exemplary damages, discussed *infra,* are sought. See Morris, C.: *Punitive Damages in Personal Injury Cases,* 21 OHIO STATE LAW JOURNAL 216, 221–22 (1960).) Sly plaintiff's counsel may advert to insurance during the juror-selection process—the *voir dire* (see Chapter 1)—but at best this maneuver probably does nothing more than confirm some jurors in their already firm assumption that nowadays all

status of compensatory damage awards cannot be revealed to the jury.[2]

General and Special Verdicts

Procedural rules in many jurisdictions provide for a special type of verdict in which the jurors spell out their findings in some detail rather than merely stating that they find the defendant liable or not liable.[3] Jurors may be required, for example, to list items of damage separately if the defendant requests this form of verdict prior to commencement of the jury's deliberations. This procedure may help to avoid errors in damage calculations and can be strongly recommended in cases presenting multiple items of major damage.

Despite provision for special verdicts, the typical damage verdict in tort cases, such as malpractice action, is a general one; that is, the jury, having found liability, returns a lump-sum award of damages. The verdict will read something like this: "We, the jury, find for the plaintiff and against the defendant and assess damages in the sum of $15,000." The trial court, in accordance with the request invariably contained in the plaintiff's Complaint, will provide that the verdict include interest and the plaintiff's court costs (not, however, including attorney fees in the usual case).[4]

General and Special Damages

Although damage verdicts are usually general, they in fact encompass various categories of damage which the law recognizes as compensable. Lawyers somewhat loosely refer to *general* and *special damages*.[5] Here they are employing the terms differently than they do when they speak of "general" and "special" verdicts.

General damages are those that are presumed to follow inevitably from the type of injuries alleged; in a personal injury action such as one for malpractice the general damages are ordinarily the more intangible aspects of the plaintiff's claim, such as generalized pain and suffering, which

---

responsible persons carry appropriate forms of insurance. For the courts' attitude toward such efforts to inject insurance into the courtroom, see *Dowd-Feder, Inc.* v. *Truesdell,* 200 N.E. 762 (Ohio App. 1936).

[2] *E.g., Hall* v. *Chicago R. Co.,* 125 N.E.2d 77 (S. Ct. Ill. 1953); *Louisville & N.R. Co.* v. *Mattingly,* 318 S.W.2d 844 (S. Ct. Ky. 1958).

[3] See James, F.: CIVIL PROCEDURE 246, 293–99. Little, Brown and Company, Boston, 1965; Nordbye, G. H.: *Use of Special Verdicts Under Rules of Civil Procedure,* 2 F.R.D. 138 (1943).

[4] See McCormick, C. T.: DAMAGES 255. West Publishing Company, St. Paul, 1935. And see cases therein cited.

[5] *Id.* at 32–39.

are sometimes hard to isolate and define precisely but which necessarily flow from a given sort of injury.[6] Those damages that in the natural and normal course of events can be expected to attend a given type of injury need not be particularized by the plaintiff in his Complaint.[7] Special damages must be set forth with some degree of care, for they are the sorts of damage that are not ordinarily presumed to flow from a particular type of injury and the defendant must be given reasonable notice that plaintiff claims them.[8]

"Special" damages are those that might not ordinarily be anticipated by the defendant in a given sort of case. They are the natural but not the necessary—in the sense of inevitable—consequences of the incident in question.[9] If the defendant negligently causes a compound, comminuted fracture of the plaintiff's leg, he would anticipate that pain would result, since pain necessarily accompanies such a fracture; he would have no particular reason for presuming that the plaintiff would find it necessary to hire a temporary maid. The cost of hiring household help, therefore, is special damage. On the principle of fair pre-trial notice to the defendant, such items of special damage must be spelled out in the plaintiff's Complaint or he may be precluded from proving them at trial.

A "general" verdict may include both "general" and "special" damages, and the latter category may be made up of numerous separate items, all of which the plaintiff is required to plead in his Complaint and establish in the evidence.

Some typical items of special damage that the law regards as compensable are (1) past and future medical, surgical, hospital, and related costs; (2) past and future loss of income (wages, salary, profits); (3) the necessary hiring of a substitute; (4) in a death case, funeral expenses; and (5) unusual physical or mental consequences of the injury alleged, such as aggravation, through malpractice, of a preexisting condition; miscarriage or disturbance of menstruation; and neurosis or psychosis, such as a conversion syndrome.[10] It is generally said that permanence of disability

[6] *E.g.*, *Brockbank* v. *Reorganized Mining Co.*, 237 Pac. 377 (S. Ct. Nev. 1925); *Gumb* v. *Twenty-Third Street Ry. Co.*, 21 N.E. 993 (Ct. App. N.Y. 1889); *Parsons Trading Co.* v. *Dohan*, 167 Atl. 310 (S. Ct. Pa. 1933).

[7] See James, F.: CIVIL PROCEDURE 123–25. Little, Brown and Company, Boston, 1965. And see cases therein cited.

[8] *Ibid.* The main function of the allegations in the papers filed in a lawsuit is the giving of notice of one's factual claims to the other side so that it can admit or deny them and thus delineate the issues to be threshed out at trial.

[9] See, *e.g.*, *Baldwin* v. *Robertson*, 172 Atl. 859 (Ct. Err. & App. Conn. 1934); *Moore* v. *St. Louis Transit Co.*, 126 S.W. 1013 (S. Ct. Mo. 1910).

[10] See James, F.: CIVIL PROCEDURE 124–25. Little, Brown and Company, Boston, 1965.

is an item of special damage that must be both specifically pleaded and proved by the plaintiff.[11]

The law does not recognize claims that cannot be established with reasonable certainty. This is as true with respect to damages as it is with respect to the fundamental liability issue. In an early but still respectable New York case the court said: "The damages must be certain both in their nature and in respect to the cause from which they proceed." [12] The certainty mentioned by the New York court refers to provability. A plaintiff must prove, by a preponderance of the evidence, not only the cause of his asserted damages but also the amount of them. Speculative or conjectural damages are not recoverable.[13] On the other hand, mathematical precision in assessing the amount of damages is not required, and difficulty in calculating damages is not always fatal to the plaintiff's claim, especially if the difficulty stems from the defendant's wrongdoing—as when his conduct aggravated a condition brought on by an earlier injury or disease and an allocation or apportionment of damage is necessary.

GENERAL DAMAGES FOR PHYSICAL PAIN AND MENTAL ANGUISH

A personal injury plaintiff who has established the defendant's legal liability is entitled to recover general damages for provable past and future physical pain and mental anguish attributable to the defendant's negligence.[14] These two closely related classes of damage include fright and shock at the time of the injury (assuming that the plaintiff was capable of experiencing those emotions [15]), apprehension concerning future

[11] *E.g., Fournier* v. *Great Atlantic & Pacific Tea Co.,* 148 Atl. 147 (S. Ct. Me. 1929); *Gurwell* v. *Jefferson City Lines,* 192 S.W.2d 683 (Mo. App. 1946).

[12] *Griffin* v. *Colver,* 16 N.Y. 489 (Ct. App. N.Y. 1858).

[13] At least, not in theory. But it has been pointed out that "the warrant to add [damages for] pain and suffering gives the jury immediate freedom to price the injury subjectively." Kalven, H.: *The Jury, the Law, and the Personal Injury Damage Award,* 19 OHIO STATE LAW JOURNAL 158, 161 (1958). Other ambiguities arise inevitably from the fact that *future* losses and expenditures are compensable.

[14] *E.g., Davis* v. *Green,* 188 F.Supp. 808 (W.D. Ark. 1960); *Hert* v. *City Beverage Co.,* 94 N.W.2d 27 (S. Ct. Neb. 1959); *Heimlick* v. *Harvey,* 39 N.W.2d 394 (S. Ct. Wis. 1949).

[15] Not surprisingly, recovery for pain and suffering is not allowed in cases involving instantaneous death. See *Missouri P.R. Co.* v. *Creekmore,* 102 S.W.2d 553 (S. Ct. Ark. 1937); *Ratushny* v. *Punch,* 138 Atl. 220 (Ct. Err. & App. Conn.) *Chanson* v. *Morgan's L. & T.R. & S.S. Co.,* 136 So. 647 (La. App. 1931). Similarly, there cannot be a recovery for pain and suffering where the injured person was unconscious at the pertinent time. See *Missouri P.R. Co.* v. *Creekmore,* 102 S.W.2d 553 (S. Ct. Ark. 1937).

disability or complications,[16] humiliation produced by disfigurement[17] and "phantom pain" following the amputation of a limb.[18] Pain and, especially, mental distress are subjective, but our legal system does not consider their manifestations too slight or delicate to be weighed in the law's scales. They may be subjective but, legally speaking, they can be proved.[19]

Proof of Physical Pain

Pain, although subjective, is often not at all difficult for plaintiff's counsel to establish by admissible evidence. In all but wrongful death cases the injured party himself can be expected to take the witness stand and testify to his past and present torment.[20] (He is not competent to express an opinion regarding the likelihood of future pain.) Some judges permit in-court demonstrations by the plaintiff, abetted by counsel, that are aimed at evidencing both pain and disability: "Rotate your neck until you experience pain, Mrs. Bushmat." [21] However, such subjective tests, wholly within the control of an interested party, are frequently prohibited on grounds of

[16] *E.g., Gentile* v. *United States,* unreported (E.D.N.Y. 1969); *Ferrara* v. *Galluchio,* 162 N.E.2d 241 (Ct. App. N.Y. 1958). The *Gentile* case, *supra,* involved a $92,500 verdict for an anxiety neurosis generated when doctors at a veterans hospital lost a catheter somewhere in the claimant's bloodstream. *Ferrara* is the famous "cancerphobia" case. See Notes, 25 BROOKLYN LAW REVIEW 264 (1959); 34 NEW YORK UNIVERSITY LAW REVIEW 545 (1959); 10 WESTERN RESERVE LAW REVIEW 322 (1959).

[17] *E.g., Missouri Pac. R. Co.* v. *Riley,* 128 S.W.2d 1005 (S. Ct. Ark. 1939); *Patterson* v. *Blatti,* 157 N.W. 717 (S. Ct. Minn. 1916). A decision to the contrary, but out of the mainstream, is *Colonial Coal Co.* v. *Hobson,* 271 S.W. 680 (S. Ct. Ky. 1925). The cost of plastic surgery is recoverable in disfigurement cases even where damages for embarrassment produced by the disfigurement are not. See, *e.g., Roland* v. *Murray,* 239 S.W.2d 967 (S. Ct. Ky. 1951).

[18] *Hickenbottom* v. *Delaware, L. & W. R. Co.,* 25 N.E. 279 (Ct. App. N.Y. 1890).

[19] A few courts have suggested that mental anguish cannot be considered a separate element of damage since it might overlap physical pain. *E.g., Trotter* v. *United States,* 95 F.Supp. 65 (W.D. La. 1961); *Norton* v. *Hamilton,* 89 S.E.2d 809 (Ga. App. 1955). Trial lawyers themselves tend to lump physical and mental anguish under the heading "pain and suffering" when presenting their cases. Although physical suffering and mental anguish often overlap, some types of mental distress are separate and distinct from physical pain and will support separate allocations of money damages. Embarrassment occasioned by disfigurement is an example; so are the so-called cancerphobia cases.

[20] *E.g., Judd* v. *Rudolph,* 222 N.W. 416 (S. Ct. Iowa 1928); *Jones* v. *Village of Portland,* 50 N.W. 731 (S. Ct. Mich. 1891).

[21] *E.g., Florida Motor Lines* v. *Bradley,* 164 So. 360 (S. Ct. Fla. 1936) (claimant, demonstrating extent to which he could bend leg, cried out in pain); *Happy* v. *Walz,* 244 S.W.2d 380 (Mo. App. 1951) (manipulation of feet and legs by physician; no outcry); *Wilson & Co.,* v. *Campbell,* 157 P.2d 465 (S. Ct. Okla. 1945) (numbness of claimant's leg demonstrated with pin-prick test).

unreliability; claimants, however misguidedly, occasionally fancy themselves adept at feigning impairment and pain.[22]

Other witnesses are permitted to relate apparently spontaneous indications of pain that they have heard or seen.[23] Thus, the claimant's wife will be allowed to testify, "After my husband came home from the hospital he constantly complained about a stabbing pain in his abdomen," or "Every night he would wake up groaning and ask me to massage his aching back." Statements regarding current symptoms, including pain, made in a history taken by or for a treating doctor are admissible at trial.[24] And a medical expert will be permitted to express his opinion that a specified event or condition would be expected to cause moderate, severe, or great pain.[25] Except in self-evident cases, only a medical expert can testify to the probability of future pain and suffering,[26] and jurors cannot properly award damages for future ill effects unless they are reasonably certain to occur.[27] Sometimes certain medical records provide eloquent and reliable indicia of pain. Jurors comprehend the significance of hospital records revealing the repeated administration of narcotics.[28]

[22] *E.g., Meyer* v. *Johnson,* 30 S.W.2d 641 (Mo. App. 1930) (manipulation of spine; outcries); *Lampa* v. *Hakola,* 55 P.2d 13 (S. Ct. Ore. 1936) (back injury demonstrated with bending and cries of pain).

[23] *E.g., Northern Pac. R. Co.* v. *Urlin,* 158 U.S. 271 (1895); *Yellow Cab Co.* v. *Henderson,* 39 A.2d 546 (S. Ct. Md. 1944); *Sherman* v. *Southern Pacific Co.,* 111 Pac. 416 (S. Ct. Nev. 1910).

[24] *E.g., McDuffie* v. *Root.* 1 N.W.2d 544 (S. Ct. Mich. 1942); *Moore* v. *Summers Drug Co.,* 175 S.E. 96 (S. Ct. N.C. 1934). Enlightened courts permit treating doctors to testify to the claimant's statements concerning past as well as present symptoms. See, *e.g.,* the superbly articulated opinion by Judge Learned Hand in *Meaney* v. *United States,* 112 F.2d 538 (2d Cir. 1940); see also *Roosa* v. *Boston Loan Co.,* 132 Mass. 439 (S. Jud. Ct. Mass. 1882); *Missouri, K. & T. R. Co. of Texas* v. *Dalton,* 120 S.W. 240 (Tex. Civ. App. 1909).

[25] See Plante, M. L.: *Damages for Pain and Suffering,* 19 OHIO STATE LAW JOURNAL 200, 203–4 (1958), and cases cited therein. The medical profession has developed more or less scientific methods for measuring the duration and intensity of pain. See, *e.g.,* Beecher, H. K.: *Limiting Factors in Experimental Pain,* 4 JOURNAL OF CHRONIC DISEASES 11 (1956); Beecher, H. K.: *Methods of Quantifying the Intensity of Pain,* 118 SCIENCE 322 (1953); Hardy, *The Nature of Pain,* 4 JOURNAL OF CHRONIC DISEASES 22 (1956); and see also the additional sources listed in Curran, W. J.: LAW AND MEDICINE 524–25. Little, Brown and Company, Boston, 1960.

[26] See *Schackelford* v. *Commercial Motor Freight Co.,* 65 N.E.2d 879 (Ohio App. 1945); *cf. Lowman* v. *Kreeker,* 71 N.W.2d 586 (S. Ct. Iowa 1955) (expert testimony on need for future treatment).

[27] *E.g., Coppinger* v. *Broderick,* 295 Pac. 780 (S. Ct. Ariz. 1931); *Schwarting* v. *Ogram,* 242 N.W. 273 (S. Ct. Neb. 1932).

[28] See, *e.g., Ferne* v. *Chadderton,* 69 A.2d 104 (S. Ct. Pa. 1949) (administration of morphine shots). See also Curran, W. J.: LAW AND MEDICINE 137–38. Little, Brown and Company, Boston, 1960.

Proof of Mental Anguish

Only the plaintiff can provide direct testimonial evidence of mental suffering that has not elevated to the level of an outwardly discernible neurosis or psychosis. However, some types of injuries are their own evidence of probable mental distress. From the very fact of blindness, for example, a jury could properly infer mental suffering.[29] But psychiatric testimony would be essential to any effective claim that the plaintiff was suffering from an injury-produced neurosis or psychosis.[30]

Compensation for Intangible Harms: The Per Diem and "Golden Rule" Arguments

The law's difficult question is not so much how to prove pain and suffering but how sensibly to compensate for physical agony or for other intangible harms such as the humiliation to a woman of a facial scar or to a man of the loss of virility. If the woman cannot be made beautiful again, nor the man potent, the law permits the only compensatory gesture open to it: payment of money damages. But in levying money damages for intangible harms—pain, humiliation, and the like—jurors are on an uncharted sea. As the Illinois Supreme Court has commented, "Pain and suffering . . . has no commercial value to which a jury can refer in determining what monetary allowance should be given to the plaintiff for the pain and suffering he has experienced and is reasonably certain to experience in the future." [31] Pain and suffering have never been appraised in terms of dollars and cents; nothing in the evidence introduced during a personal injury trial will have served to place a value on these conditions of mind and body. And so the courts are sharply split on the question of whether plaintiffs' counsel, in argument to a jury, can even suggest a *per diem* sum for pain and suffering. Lawyers for injured plaintiffs would like to argue to juries that they should compensate the claimant for his continuing torment at the rate of such-and-such a sum per day for the remainder of his anticipated life expectancy. But some courts decline to permit this sort of argument, pointing out that it goes far beyond the evidence of record—and perhaps perceiving that a seemingly modest $5.00 a day for the balance of a young plaintiff's life expectancy may add up to

[29] See Plante, M. L.: *Damages for Pain and Suffering*, 19 OHIO STATE LAW JOURNAL 200, 204 (1958).

[30] The plaintiff, of course, is free to testify in nontechnical language that he suffers from "nervousness," *e.g.*, *Redick* v. *Peterson*, 169 Pac. 804 (S. Ct. Wash. 1918), or a morbid fear of death, *e.g.*, *Elliot* v. *Arrowsmith*, 272 Pac. 32 (S. Ct. Wash. 1928), and the "cancerphobia" cases.

[31] *Caley* v. *Manicke*, 182 N.E.2d 206 (S. Ct. Ill. 1962). See Comment, *Damages—Pain and Suffering—Use of a Mathematical Formula*, 60 MICHIGAN LAW REVIEW 612 (1962).

an unconscionable total, far outdistancing his computable losses. Without explaining precisely how they are to go about it, these courts demand that the assessment of general damages be left entirely to the jurors:

> . . . This determination, like many others that a jury must make, is left to its conscience and judgment. . . . We are of the opinion that an impartial jury which has been properly informed by the evidence and the court's instructions will, by the exercise of its conscience and sound judgment, be better able to determine reasonable compensation than it would if it were subjected to expression of counsels' partisan conscience and judgment on the matter.[32]

Other courts, bewildered as to the stuff upon which the jurors' judgment is supposed to feed, allow the *per diem* argument as constituting the only yardstick by which plaintiffs' counsel can aid the jurymen in measuring pain and suffering. These courts insist that the *per diem* argument be kept within sensible bounds and, as we shall shortly see, reserve the power to reduce damage verdicts that seem to them excessive.[33] By way of example, the Florida Supreme Court approved the *per diem* yardstick for measuring pain and suffering in a case [34] in which the attorney for a nine-year-old amputee employed the following chart before the jury:

Pain and suffering experienced in accident	$ 5,000
Pain and suffering in hospital 12 days	$ 1,200
Pain and suffering first 30 days at home	$ 300
Pain and suffering for 350 days to date of trial	$ 700
Pain and suffering for life expectancy—20,440 days	$20,440

One sort of jury argument is universally condemned. No claimant's counsel will be allowed to inquire of jurors along this line: "How much would I have to pay you to let me come into the jury box and negligently amputate your leg?" This brand of argumentation is deemed irrelevant and inflammatory. A variation, also placed beyond the pale, is the so-called Golden Rule argument or instruction on damages. This argument or charge calls upon each juror to award those damages that he would wish to receive were he the plaintiff in the lawsuit. Again the courts demand that jurors base their verdicts on the evidence of the particular plaintiff's losses and suffering and not on potentially irrelevant notions of what a similar injury would mean to a particular juror.[35]

[32] *Caley* v. *Manicke,* 182 N.E.2d 206 (S. Ct. Ill. 1962). See also *Continental Bus System, Inc.* v. *Toombs,* 325 S.W.2d 153 (Tex. Civ. App. 1959); *Ahlstrom* v. *Minneapolis, St. Paul & S.S.M.R. Co.,* 68 N.W.2d 873 (S. Ct. Minn. 1955).

[33] The leading case supporting the *per diem* gambit is *Botta* v. *Brunner,* 138 A.2d 713 (S. Ct. N.J. 1958); see also *Imperial Oil, Ltd.* v. *Drlik,* 234 F.2d 4 (6th Cir. 1956), *cert. denied,* 352 U.S. 941 (1957).

[34] *Seaboard Airline R. Co.* v. *Braddock,* 96 So.2d 127 (S. Ct. Fla. 1957).

[35] See *Callaghan* v. *A. Lague Exp. Co.,* 298 F.2d 349 (2d Cir. 1962).

Judicial Methods of Adjusting the Size of Jury Verdicts

However much they may trust the good sense of lay jurors in assessing compensation for intangible harms, courts nevertheless retain some devices for remedying the injustices done by occasional runaway juries. One such device is the granting to the defendant of a new trial when the court that tried his case believes the damage verdict to be excessive.[36] But new trials are costly and time-consuming. To avoid this burden courts devised the practice of ordering a new trial conditionally; the new trial will be had only if the plaintiff refuses to consent to the reduction of the damage verdict to a specified amount.[37] The Latin term by which lawyers identify this practice is *remittitur.* The analogous practice of conditioning a new trial on defendant's refusal to consent to an increase in the verdict (*additur*), where plaintiff complains of its inadequacy, has not often been implemented. The Supreme Court of the United States has strongly suggested that the practice is improper.[38] A remitted verdict is within the amount agreed upon by the jury: an *additur,* involving an increase above the limits of the jury's verdict, may do violence to the defendant's constitutional right to trial by jury on all legal issues, which include the issue of damages.

Polling the Jury

Another safety device involves the polling—interrogating—of the jurors to ascertain by what means they arrived at their verdict. A number of jurisdictions allow this procedure in order that the court and the parties can satisfy themselves that the jurors did not employ some interdicted scheme of chance in arriving at their verdict.

Verdicts by lot are prohibited.[39] In casting lots the individual jurors

[36] See, *e.g., Capital Traction Co.* v. *Hof,* 174 U.S. 1 (1899); *Smith* v. *Times Publishing Co.,* 36 Atl. 296 (S. Ct. Pa. 1897). See also Hinton, E. W.: *Power of Federal Appellate Court to Review Ruling on Motion for New Trial,* 1 UNIV. OF CHICAGO LAW REVIEW 111 (1933).

[37] See *Sinz* v. *Owens,* 205 P.2d 3 (S. Ct. Cal. 1949). The procedure of *remittitur* and the related procedure of *additur* are discussed in *Dimick* v. *Schiedt,* 293 U.S. 474 (1935). See generally Carlin, L.: *Remittiturs and Additurs,* 49 WEST VIRGINIA LAW QUARTERLY 1 (1942). It has been held that a reviewing court, believing a damage award to be excessive, can order a new trial on the damage issue. *Larson* v. *Lindahl,* 450 P. 2d 77 (S. Ct. Colo. 1968).

[38] *Dimick* v. *Schiedt,* 293 U.S. 474 (1935). But some state courts have awarded *additurs.* See, *e.g., Bachmann* v. *Passalacqua,* 135 A.2d 18 (N.J. Super. 1957); *Bodon* v. *Suhrmann,* 327 P.2d 826 (S. Ct. Utah 1958). See Note, *Civil Procedure: New Trial: Validity of Order Granting New Trial Unless Defendant Accepts Additur,* 6 UNIV. OF CALIFORNIA LAW REVIEW 441 (1959).

[39] See, generally, Comment, *Impeachment of Jury Verdicts,* 25 UNIV. OF CHICAGO LAW REVIEW 360 (1958).

write a suggested amount on a slip of paper to be drawn blindly from the hat; the amount drawn by chance then becomes the jury's damage verdict.[40] A certain sort of "quotient" verdict is also prohibited.[41] Under this scheme each of the twelve jurors writes on a piece of paper the amount which he believes the plaintiff is entitled to recover. The total of these amounts is divided by twelve, and the figure thus reached may become the final verdict. A verdict reached in this manner is unlawful if the jurors have agreed in advance to be bound by the quotient. (And so lawyers are almost always suspicious of personal injury verdicts in an uneven sum with odd cents.) The system has been permitted, however, where the jurors merely used it to reach a working figure upon which free debate is then focused.[42]

SPECIAL DAMAGES

Recovery of Past Losses

Those damages labeled "special" are susceptible to more or less precise computation by the jury on the basis of the evidence before them. Unless the defendant has stipulated—agreed—to their amount, the plaintiff's out-of-pocket expenditures must be proved by him; he can ordinarily do this easily by introducing his bills and establishing their reasonableness.[43] Another possible out-of-pocket loss (actually, it never got *in* the plaintiff's pocket) is past income lost as a consequence of his disabling injuries.[44] If his injuries kept him from his work he can usually attest whatever

[40] Coin-flipping is also frowned upon. See James, F., CIVIL PROCEDURE 309. Little, Brown and Company, Boston, 1965, and Supp. 1968.

[41] See *United Iron Workers* v. *Wagner*, 167 Pac. 1107 (S. Ct. Wash. 1917); see, generally, Comment, *Impeachment of Jury Verdicts*, 25 UNIV. OF CHICAGO LAW REVIEW 360 (1958).

[42] *Benjamin* v. *Helena Light & R. Co.*, 255 Pac. 20 (S. Ct. Mont. 1927). See McCormick, C. T.: DAMAGES 65. West Publishing Company, St. Paul, 1935.

[43] *E.g.*, *Honaker* v. *Crutchfield*, 57 S.W.2d 502 (S. Ct. Ky. 1933); *Thomas* v. *Lobrano*, 76 So.2d 599 (La. App. 1955); *Torgeson* v. *Hanford*, 139 Pac. 648 (S. Ct. Wash. 1914) (medical expenses). The claimant can also recover for the probable cost of necessary future treatment. See, *e.g.*, *Sotebier* v. *St. Louis Transit Co.*, 102 S.W. 651 (S. Ct. Mo. 1907); *Cornell* v. *Great Northern R. Co.*, 187 Pac. 902 (S. Ct. Mont. 1920).

[44] Courts argue the semantic question of whether recovery is allowed for loss of earnings or for loss of the value of the plaintiff's time. *Compare Reynolds* v. *Clark*, 92 Atl. 873 (S. Ct. Del. 1914) (loss of wages), with *Donoghue* v. *Holyoke St. R. Co.*, 141 N.E. 278 (Supp. Jud. Ct. Mass. 1923) (value of time). The argument becomes important when a claimant seeks to recover for his "lost time" although he was unemployed during the pertinent period. See, *e.g.*, *Cincinnati, N.O. & T.P.R. Co.* v. *Perkins*, 266 S.W. 652 (S. Ct. Ky. 1924) (allowed).

wages or other items of income went by the boards as a result of his period of enforced inactivity.[45]

Damages for Impairment of Future Earning Capacity

A personal injury litigant can recover for impairment of future earning capacity if he can prove temporary or permanent disability, partial or complete.[46] Damages of this sort depend on a number of factors implicit in the last sentence. Damages for loss of earning power depend on the extent and probable duration of disability. It can be temporary and partial, temporary and total, permanent and partial, or permanent and total.[47] If a permanent disability is established to a reasonable degree of medical certainty, plaintiff's life expectancy becomes material. The probable length of the plaintiff's life can be evidenced by expert medical prognosis, taking into account plaintiff's age, health, and occupation, and by actuarial mortality tables which show average life expectancy for persons of a given age.

The "Present Worth" Rule

The plaintiff is not usually permitted to recover the full amount of prospective earnings which will be prevented by his disability. Until quite recently it was universally held that he can recover as special damages only the present worth of the total amount of anticipated lost income.[48] Annuity tables and other aids are employed to calculate the present worth of this total sum.[49] Richardson, in his *Doctors, Lawyers and the Courts,* published in 1965, gives the example of a plaintiff who has sustained a 25 percent permanent, partial disability; who was earning $4,000 per year prior to the disabling event; and who has a life expectancy of 20 years.

[45] The matter may be more complex where the claimant was self-employed. See McCormick, C. T.: DAMAGES 311–14. West Publishing Company, St. Paul, 1935, for a detailed discussion of the potential problems.

[46] *Id.* at 299–309. See also Slagle, L. O.: *The Role of Profits in Personal Injury Actions,* 19 OHIO STATE LAW JOURNAL 179 (1958), and cases therein cited.

[47] See Curran, W. J.: LAW AND MEDICINE 312–17. Little, Brown and Company, Boston, 1960; Richardson, J. R.: DOCTORS, LAWYERS AND THE COURTS 380–85. The W. H. Anderson Company, Cincinnati, 1965, for discussions of disability evaluations.

[48] See, *e.g., Chesapeake & Ohio Ry.* v. *Kelly,* 241 U.S. 485 (1916).

[49] The testimony of expert witnesses may also be allowed on the supportable theory that the wisdom and the method of determining present worth is beyond most lay jurors. Nonetheless, the trial court will go through the motions of advising the jurors that the experts' opinions, the actuarial tables, and average life-expectancy calculations should not be deemed conclusive. See *e.g., Thompson* v. *Camp,* 163 F.2d 396 (6th Cir.), *cert. denied,* 333 U.S. 831 (1947); *Allendorf* v. *Elgin, J. & E. Ry.,* 133 N.E.2d 288 (S. Ct. Ill. 1956).

Barring extraordinary factors, his loss of earning power is therefore at least $1,000 a year; over a 20-year period it would total $20,000.[50] This sum must be reduced to present worth. A 6 percent annuity table reveals that the present worth of a one dollar annuity over a period of 20 years is 11.467. Plaintiff's annual loss ($1,000) will be multiplied by 11.467. The resulting $11,467 is the present worth of annual earnings of $1,000 spread over a period of 20 years. Of course, a jury is not restricted to an inflexible mathematical formula in determining loss of future income.[51] It can take into account the plaintiff's lost prospects of financial advancement, having in mind his apparent capacity and ambition.[52] That is why we suggested, in connection with the foregoing example, that the hypothetical plaintiff's loss of earning power was "at least" $1,000 a year. By the same token, however, a jury can take into account the fact that few men can be expected to work every week until the day of their death.[53]

The "present worth" rule is currently in some jeopardy. The Supreme Court of Alaska, in an unprecedented 1967 opinion,[54] held that jurors need not be instructed to reduce future earnings to present worth, since this process ignores such factors as rising wage levels and inflation. It has been suggested that the computation called for in the Alaska decision is "economically and statistically crude," since it depends on the assumption, demonstrably false, that inflationary earnings increases will offset the future interest on a present sum.[55] The equitable solution probably lies in permitting trained economists to testify to the present value of lost earning power.

A physician called as a witness on the issue of physical disability must be alert to legal nuances. The medical expert can usually determine the degree or percentage of traumatic impairment of a limb or organ with reasonable certitude.[56] But this is a purely medical judgment. The law is interested in the degree to which the physical impairment disables a compensation claimant from performing income-producing work and enjoying life. A high degree of physical impairment may have minimal impact on

[50] Richardson, J. R.: DOCTORS, LAWYERS AND THE COURTS 382. The W. H. Anderson Company, Cincinnati, 1965.

[51] It probably *cannot* be; see, *e.g.*, *Kroger Co.* v. *Rawlings*, 251 F.2d 943 (6th Cir. 1958); *Brooks* v. *United States*, 273 F.Supp. 619 (D.S.C. 1967).

[52] See, *e.g.*, *Loftin* v. *Williams*, 67 So.2d 185 (S. Ct. Fla. 1953).

[53] *E.g.*, *Louisville, N.A. & C.R. Co.* v. *Miller*, 37 N.E. 343 (S. Ct. Ind. 1895).

[54] *Beaulieu* v. *Elliott*, 434 P.2d 665 (S. Ct. Alas. 1967).

[55] Peck, C. J., and Hopkins, W. S.: *Economics and Impaired Earning Capacity in Personal Injury Cases*, 44 WASHINGTON LAW REVIEW 351, 354 (1969). Other courts do not appear to be rushing to apply the Alaskan approach.

[56] See, *e.g.*, Houts, M.: MEDICAL PROOF, §§35.07 *et seq.* Matthew Bender, New York, 1966.

one's ability to carry on an occupation that entails little physical exertion. Conversely, even partial impairment of one finger's function would be significantly disabling to a concert pianist.

The medical witness must separate impairment and disability in his testimony. After describing the degree of impairment the medical expert will be allowed to express his opinion as to the plaintiff's physical capacity to engage in specified types of work or play. The witness may not wish to embark upon such an evaluation, however. A special *ad hoc* Committee of the American Medical Association on Medical Rating of Physical Impairment has categorically stated, "It is not and never can be the duty of physicians to evaluate the social and economic effects of permanent impairment.[57]

Damages for Exacerbation of a Preexisting Condition

In medical malpractice and related cases the courts frequently encounter the claim that the defendant doctor's negligent conduct aggravated or intensified a preexisting condition. Although the rule is often easier to state than to apply, it is generally held, as in logic and justice it ordinarily must be, that the defendant is liable only for the increased pain, disability, and losses occasioned by his conduct.[58]

Plaintiff's Duty to Minimize Damages

One who claims to have been wrongfully injured by another is obligated to use reasonable means to minimize his damages.[59] Putting it another way, he cannot recover for damage that he could readily have avoided without undue risk or expense; a negligently injured person cannot recover for elements of damage caused by his own unreasonable conduct.[60] What is unreasonable depends on surrounding circumstances. A

[57] A.M.A., GUIDE TO EVALUATION OF PERMANENT IMPAIRMENT OF THE EXTREMITIES AND BACK (1958), reprinted in Curran, W. J.: LAW AND MEDICINE 313–17. Little, Brown and Company, Boston, 1960.

[58] See *Guillory* v. *Godfrey*, 286 P.2d 474 (S. Ct. Cal. 1955). *Compare Beauchamp* v. *Davis*, 217 S.W.2d 822 (S. Ct. Ky. 1949) ("But where, as here, the negligence not only caused the plaintiff to incur extraordinary expenses but in addition thereto destroyed the possibility of any benefit whch could have been anticipated under skillful treatment in the first instance, the plaintiff is entitled to recover all expenses incurred by him in the entire course of treatment").

[59] *E.g., Lewis* v. *Pennsylvania R. Co.*, 100 F.Supp. 291 (E.D. Pa. 1951); *Sanders* v. *Beckwith*, 284 P.2d 235 (S. Ct. Ariz. 1955); *Quaranto* v. *Silverman*, 187 N.E.2d 559 (Sup. Jud. Ct. Mass. 1963).

[60] He cannot, for example, refuse to undergo safe and simple measures calculated to correct the condition of which he complains. *E.g., King* v. *St. Louis*, 155 S.W.2d 557 (Mo. App. 1941). This does not mean that he must undergo serious surgery, hazarding his life for the benefit of a wrongdoer. *E.g., Dodds* v. *Stellar*, 175 P.2d 607

person is not required to act if he is understandably ignorant of facts making action necessary. He clearly will be excused for his inaction if the wrongdoer advised him that action was not necessary.

This principle of avoidable consequences has not often come into play in medical malpractice and related cases, but it would be available in any case in which the plaintiff has refused, unreasonably, to undergo corrective procedures following a result claimed to have been caused by malpractice. This does not mean, however, that he must undergo a serious or hazardous operation where the outcome is unpredictable or where it would be reasonable to anticipate a cure without recourse to such an operation.[61]

The Collateral Source Rule

A legal doctrine that may seem to cut across the principle that a litigant must minimize his losses is the collateral source rule. What if the injured plaintiff has received compensation or idemnification, or cost-free services, from a source other than the defendant? A personal injury claimant may have been indemnified by accident and hospitalization insurance; his employer may have continued his salary during a period of recuperation; a close relative may have supplied temporary nursing and household assistance. Are these compensating sums and services, received from a collateral source, to be excluded or deducted from the plaintiff's recovery of damages from the defendant? The law's usual answer is that they are not to be deducted; in this situation the law permits what frequently amounts to a double recovery by the plaintiff.

The collateral source rule is somewhat punitive in nature. The underlying idea is that a tort-feasor—a wrongdoer—should not be allowed to benefit from the plaintiff's prudence in securing insurance or other collateral aid; people, it is said, do not pay insurance premiums for the benefit of the negligent. If this notion seems more emotional than logical, if it seems to violate the law's theory that damages are meant to provide compensation and not a windfall, it nonetheless is widely accepted by courts.[62] It involves a simple, albeit arguable, balancing of equities.

The general rule is that a compensation claimant can recover medical and hospital expenses from a tort-feasor even though the claimant has been idemnified wholly or in part by insurance. Thus, in a leading Kentucky case it was held that the injured plaintiff could recover medical and hospital costs despite the fact that he had been reimbursed for them by a welfare fund to which contributions were made by him or on his behalf.

(Cal. App. 1946); *Sette* v. *Dakis,* 48 A.2d 271 (Ct. Err. & App. Conn. 1946); *Jones* v. *Eppler,* 266 P.2d 451 (S. Ct. Okla. 1953).

[61] See *Dodds* v. *Stellar,* 175 P.2d 607 (Cal. App. 1946).

[62] See McCormick, C. T.: DAMAGES 310. West Publishing Company, St. Paul, 1935, and cases therein cited.

The prevailing rule is the same with respect to income continuation. The fact that the wages or salary of an injured person have been paid by his employer during a period of disability is no ground for mitigation or diminution of damages recoverable from the one who caused the claimant's injuries. The philosophy behind the collateral source rule can be detected in the language of a Wisconsin judicial opinion:

> We see no reason why one whose acts have caused injury to another should reap the entire benefit that comes from the payment of wages made by an employer, either as a gratuity to a faithful employee or because such payments are required by contract. Such payments do not change the nature of the injury which the employee sustains through the wrongful acts of the tortfeasor. If either is to profit by the payments made by the employer, it should be the person who has been injured—not the one whose wrongful acts caused the injury.[63]

Other courts have suggested that an injured plaintiff is entitled to recover even the value of gratuitous services. Thus the highest court of Connecticut has stated: "The majority rule of the cases is that an injured person is entitled to recover as damages for reasonable medical, hospital or nursing services rendered him, whether these are rendered him gratuitously or paid for by his employer." [64]

With the proliferation of social welfare programs, including Medicare, it is possible that courts will commence to erode the collateral source rule. As yet, however, no strong trend in that direction can be discerned.

PUNITIVE OR EXEMPLARY DAMAGES

The Function of Punitive Damages

The usual function of damages in civil cases is compensation to the plaintiff for provable suffering and loss. Theories of deterrence and punishment, concededly central to the criminal law, do not often enter into the civil side of the law. In one area of civil law, however, all but a few courts have allowed juries to award *punitive* or *exemplary* damages on top of compensatory damages. Such damages, sometimes referred to as "smart money" because the defendant will presumably feel the smart of a punitive verdict, are occasionally presented to the victorious tort claimant over and above full compensation for his injuries. They are intended as a sort of fine and serve the same purpose that a criminal fine is supposed to serve: (1) punishment of the defendant; (2) deterrence of the defendant from re-

[63] *Campbell* v. *Sutliff,* 214 N.W. 374 (S. C. Wis. 1927).
[64] *Roth* v. *Chatlos,* 116 Atl. 332 (Ct. Err. & App. Conn. 1922).

peating the same reprehensible conduct; and (3) deterrence of others from following the defendant's poor example.

Factors Supporting the Award of Punitive Damages

Punitive damages are obviously to be awarded only in extreme cases.[65] They are ordinarily permitted only where the defendant's wrongdoing has been deliberate and has displayed overtones of malice, spite, fraudulent or evil motive, or conscious disregard of the interests of others.[66] In other words, the defendant's conduct must possess the outrageous character frequently associated with actual crime; it must be, it is sometimes said, willful or wanton.[67] Typical of the torts for which such damages are occasionally allowed are true, as distinguished from technical, assault and battery; [68] deceit; seduction; trespass; and libel and slander.[69]

The professional conduct of reputable physicians, even when demonstrably negligent,[70] almost never gives rise to punitive damages.[71] It is, however, altogether conceivable that punitive damages would be supported in a medical malpractice case in which the defendant doctor forged perversely ahead with a disastrous procedure despite ample contraindications. Punitive damages might also be assessed where the defendant improperly abandoned his patient.[72] In recent times punitive damages have been increasingly sought, and recovered, in cases involving the manufacture and distribution of dangerously defective consumer

[65] See *Smith* v. *Little, Brown & Co.*, 273 F.Supp. 870 (S.D.N.Y. 1967).

[66] *E.g., Los Alamos Medical Center* v. *Coe,* 275 P.2d 175 (S. Ct. N.M. 1954) (gross negligence amounting to reckless indifference; bad motives or actual intent to injure the patient; utter indifference to the effect of a procedure on the patient); *Noe* v. *Kaiser Foundation Hospitals,* 435 P.2d 306 (S. Ct. Ore. 1967) (particularly aggravated disregard of the professional duty to preserve life and health); *Baxter* v. *Campbell,* 97 N.W. 386 (S. Ct. S.D. 1903) (oppression, fraud or malice, actual or presumed).

[67] See *Roginsky* v. *Richardson-Merrell, Inc.*, 378 F.2d 382 (2d Cir. 1967).

[68] See Chapter 11.

[69] See McCormick, C. T.: DAMAGES 286–91. West Publishing Company, St. Paul, 1935, for discussion and citation to numerous cases. As to the law of libel and slander, see Chapter 17.

[70] Negligence alone, however culpable, is insufficient to support punitive damages. See *Moore* v. *Wilson,* 20 S.W.2d 310 (S. Ct. Ark. 1929).

[71] For a sampling of cases in which plaintiff failed to recover punitive damages from a medical man, see *Kelly* v. *Chillag,* 381 F.2d 344 (4th Cir. 1967); *Cholia* v. *Kelty,* 63 P.2d 895 (S. Ct. Ore. 1937); *Hellend* v. *Bridenstine,* 104 Pac. 626 (S. Ct. Wash. 1909).

[72] *E.g., Rennewanz* v. *Dean,* 229 Pac. 372 (S. Ct. Ore. 1924) (patient suffered rectal hemorrhage; physician did nothing to halt flow of blood, instead compelled patient to lie on couch in adjacent office, leaving patient unattended for 48 hours); *Morrell* v. *Lalonde,* 120 Atl. 435 (S. Ct. R.I. 1923) (patient sent home from hospital in hearse).

products.[73] The same trend in the field of medical malpractice will probably be forestalled only by adherence to acceptable standards of practice.[74]

THE IMPACT ON DAMAGES OF THE CONTINGENT FEE SYSTEM

Although it cannot be documented, it is an inescapable inference that jurors are aware that the loser in an American lawsuit is not ordinarily required to pay the winner's attorney fees. Jurors know, because it is common knowledge, that the fee of a personal injury claimant's trial lawyer will be deducted from any judgment or out-of-court settlement obtained on the claimant's behalf. The trial lawyer will have entered into a so-called contingent fee agreement with his client.

Historically, an attorney who agreed to institute a lawsuit in exchange for a promised share in the recovery found himself liable to conviction for the criminal offense known as champerty.[75] Today, however, what was once called champerty has been dignified and, in most jurisdictions, legalized under the less evil-sounding contingent fee label.[76] That is, an attorney's fee in personal injury matters and in some other types of litigation is made contingent on whether he secures some money for his client. If he obtains a recovery—if he "wins"—he is entitled to a fixed percentage of the recovery; if he "loses"—that is, gains nothing for his client—he takes no fee at all for his unproductive labors.[77] In times past a typical contingent fee schedule has been 25 percent of the amount recovered if no lawsuit is filed (that is, the claim has been settled without litigation having been formally commenced); 33⅓ percent of the recovery if suit is filed (even though it does not go to trial); and 40 percent of the amount eventually recovered where the defendant has perfected an appeal from a verdict and judgment for the claimant but has failed to secure a reversal.[78] In some localities, in some sorts of cases, however, the contingent fee has climbed as high as 50 percent.[79]

[73] See Chapter 9.

[74] This trend was lamented in *Roginsky* v. *Richardson-Merrell, Inc.*, 378 F.2d 832 (2d Cir. 1967). *Compare Noe* v. *Kaiser Foundation Hospitals,* 435 P.2d 306 (S. Ct. Ore. 1967).

[75] See Radin, M.: *Maintenance by Champerty,* 24 CALIFORNIA LAW REVIEW 48 (1935).

[76] The contingent fee is still completely outlawed in England; it is disapproved but allowed in Massachusetts. See MacKinnon, F. B.: CONTINGENT FEES FOR LEGAL SERVICES 37–38. Aldine Publishing Company, Chicago, 1964.

[77] See, generally, *ibid.*

[78] See Combs, W. A.: *The Contingent Fee Contract,* 28 TEXAS BAR JOURNAL 949 (1965).

[79] See, *e.g., Taylor* v. *Bemiss,* 110 U.S. 42 (1883).

What bothers many, including physicians, is the inference that jurors will return hugely inflated money damage verdicts to ensure that the plaintiff has a sizable sum left after his attorney has skimmed off his agreed percentage.[80] That this inference may be valid, at least occasionally, cannot be denied. Furthermore, there is sometimes no rational relation between the fee assessed and the legal services rendered; the lawyer who can settle his client's claim for $600,000 after three hours of negotiation is still entitled, in many states, to a fee of $200,000 under his one-third contingency agreement with the client.[81]

There is one significant justification for the contingent fee system. It permits those who are without substantial resources to obtain the services of a lawyer. This, in turn, occasionally facilitates the vigorous pursuit of legitimate claims that might otherwise be abandoned because of the claimant's poverty. The Supreme Court of the United States has pointed out, in a different context, that there can be no equal justice where the kind of trial a man gets depends on the amount of money he has.[82]

One approach to the problem of exorbitant contingent fees has been absolute prohibition of this method of compensating lawyers. The contingent fee system has been outlawed in criminal matters, divorce proceedings, lobbying activities, and government contract negotiations.[83] Nowhere, however, has it been prohibited in personal injury cases. It has been regulated in some jurisdictions, notably New York. A court can punish attorneys who charge unconscionable fees, and fee schedules can be enforced.[84] Furthermore, emerging forms of group legal service promise to reduce the legal expenses of some classes of clients. The members of some organizations, such as labor unions, are entitled to low-cost legal assistance as one of the benefits of membership.[85] In 1964 the United States Supreme Court struck down efforts by the states to restrict the group legal assistance program of the Brotherhood of Railroad Trainmen,[86] and such programs can now be expected to proliferate.

[80] See Johnstone, Q., and Hopson, D.: LAWYERS AND THEIR WORK 64. Bobbs-Merrill Company, Inc., Indianapolis, 1964.

[81] In New York, however, the courts have implemented a scheduled reduction in contingent fees in inverse proportion to the amount of money recovered. See Johnstone, Q., and Hopson, D., *op. cit. supra,* at 63, n. 127.

[82] *Griffin* v. *Illinois,* 351 U.S. 12 (1956).

[83] See Johnston, Q., and Hopson, D., *op cit. supra,* at 64.

[84] See, *e.g., Gladstone* v. *State Bar,* 6 P.2d 513 (S. Ct. Cal. 1931); *Berkos* v. *Aetna Life Ins. Co.,* 279 Ill. App. 243 (1935).

[85] See Symposium, *The Availability of Counsel and Group Legal Services: A Symposium,* 12 UNIV. OF CALIFORNIA LOS ANGELES LAW REVIEW 279 (1965); Note, *Group Legal Services,* 79 HARVARD LAW REVIEW 416 (1965).

[86] *Brotherhood of Railroad Trainmen* v. *Virginia ex rel.* Virginia State Bar Assoc., 377 U.S. 1 (1964). See also *United Mine Workers of America, Dist. 12* v. *Illinois State Bar Assoc.,* 389 U.S. 217 (1967).

For the foreseeable future, however, the contingent fee, accompanied perhaps by a somewhat increased measure of regulation and supervision, will continue as the most common method for compensating lawyers in personal injury cases, including medical malpractice actions. Continuation of the contingent fee arrangement will permit some claimants to have the "day in court" that they might otherwise be unable to afford. Regrettably, it will also contribute to the problem of vexatious lawsuits and excessive damage awards.

BIBLIOGRAPHY

BOOKS

Dublin, L. I., and Lotka, A. J.: THE MONEY VALUE OF A MAN. The Ronald Press Company, New York, 1930.

MacKinnon, F. B.: CONTINGENT FEES FOR LEGAL SERVICES. Aldine Publishing Company, Chicago, 1964.

McBride, E. D.: DISABILITY EVALUATION, 6th ed. Lippincott, Philadelphia, 1963.

McCormick, C. T.: DAMAGES. West Publishing Company, St. Paul, 1935.

ARTICLES

Bauer, R. S.: *Fundamental Principles of the Law of Damages in Medico-Legal Cases,* 19 TENNESSEE LAW REVIEW 255 (1946).

Cutler, C. R.: *Taxation of the Proceeds of Litigation,* 57 COLUMBIA LAW REVIEW 470 (1957).

Jaffe, L. J.: *Damages for Personal Injuries: The Impact of Insurance,* 18 LAW & CONTEMPORARY PROBLEMS 219 (1953).

James, F.: *Social Insurance and Tort Liability: The Problem of Alternative Remedies,* 27 NEW YORK UNIV. LAW REVIEW 537 (1952).

Maxwell, R. C.: *The Collateral Source Rule in the American Law of Damages,* 46 MINNESOTA LAW REVIEW 669 (1962).

Miller, V. X.: *Assessment of Damages in Personal Injury Actions,* 14 MINNESOTA LAW REVIEW 216 (1930).

Morris, C.: *Punitive Damages in Tort Cases,* 44 HARVARD LAW REVIEW 1173 (1931).

Peck, C. J., and Hopkins, W. S.: *Economics and Impaired Earning Capacity in Personal Injury Cases,* 44 WASHINGTON LAW REVIEW 351 (1969).

Schumacher, B. E.: *Rights of Action Under Death and Survival Statutes,* 23 MICHIGAN LAW REVIEW 114 (1924).

Symposium, *Damages for Personal Injuries,* 19 OHIO STATE LAW JOURNAL 155 *et seq.* (1958).

Welch, E. P.: *Permanent Disability Evaluation,* 82 CAL. MED. 35 (1955).

NOTES AND COMMENTS

Comment, *Damages for Shortened Life,* 10 FORDHAM LAW REVIEW 219 (1941).

Comment, *Exemplary Damages in Medical Malpractice,* 6 WILLAMETTE LAW REVIEW 265 (1970).

Comment, *Life Expectancy and Loss of Earning Capacity,* 19 OHIO STATE LAW JOURNAL 314 (1958).

Comment, *The Measure of Damages for a Shortened Life,* 22 UNIV. OF CHICAGO LAW REVIEW 505 (1955).

Note, *Damages for the Wrongful Death of Children,* 22 UNIV. OF CHICAGO LAW REVIEW 538 (1955).

Note, *Damages—Proving Medical and Hospital Bills Necessary and Reasonable,* 27 UNIV. OF CINCINNATI LAW REVIEW 176 (1958).

chapter 20

MEDICAL MALPRACTICE LIABILITY INSURANCE

Adequate Medical Malpractice Insurance: Necessity and Purpose

In medical malpractice actions, as in all other categories of personal injury litigation, there has been an increasing incidence of what plaintiffs' lawyers call "the adequate verdict" and what the insurance companies call disasters—in other words, staggeringly high verdicts for money damages. In early 1968, for example, a Chicago jury returned a verdict for $900,000 on behalf of a single plaintiff; a woman in her forties, she had been blinded in both eyes. Nor is this the highest personal injury jury verdict on record; there have been recent verdicts substantially in excess of a million dollars. As of 1970 the record medical malpractice verdict was $750,000. Whether or not the upward curve of verdict figures, and the attendant upswing in settlement sums, is simply an aspect of inflation's spiral, the active physician must face the necessity of sufficient malpractice liability insurance. The only other course involves potential financial ruin.

Although physicians' malpractice liability insurance is in some ways a specialized sort of coverage, written for the most part by only half a dozen insurance companies in the United States, it has the same basic function and features with respect to professional liability that public liability and automobile liability insurance have in their spheres. Medical malpractice liability insurance is a contract under which the insurer agrees, in exchange for the payment of premiums, to indemnify the physician named in the insurance policy against loss by reason of liability imposed upon him by law as a consequence of his claimed professional negligence. A significant corollary of this coverage is the insurer's undertaking to defend the insured physician against malpractice claims.

Factors in Selection of a Malpractice Insurer

In selecting a malpractice insurer the physician should inquire into seven key factors: (1) the stability of the insurance carrier, including the level and location (domestic or foreign) of its financial reserves; (2) the attitude and experience of the company in handling claims and defending lawsuits, and the apparent effectiveness of these services; (3) the extent and sufficiency of coverage afforded for the acts of the physician, his partners, if any, and his employees; (4) the availability of supplementary coverage of the physician's exposure as the owner or tenant of the space occupied by his office (this is an important coverage, sometimes overlooked); (5) the size of the premium and the existence of any hidden extra charges; (6) the nature of any exclusion and cancellation clauses and the carrier's policy regarding renewals; [1] and (7) the carrier's willingness to engage in malpractice liability prevention programs.

It is a foolhardy physician who selects an insurance policy on the basis of low premiums alone.[2] Adequacy of coverage and the carrier's reliability are considerations of primary importance. The level of coverage required by a physician will depend somewhat on the state and community in which he practices (California, for example, is a high verdict state), on the nature of his practice (predictably, settlements and judgments are the highest and most frequent in the field of surgery, where the risk of permanent disablement of the patient is greatest), and on the physician's own financial situation.

Amount of Coverage

At one time some insurance companies recommended very low malpractice coverage—$5,000/$10,000—on the theory that claimants' counsel would be discouraged from litigating when apprised of the small amount of insurance available to pay any judgment. These carriers anticipated that settlements could regularly be achieved within this low coverage, no matter how serious the claim. But physicians, some of whom had been held personally liable for the difference between their insurance coverage and the amount of a judgment against them, became disenchanted with the theories underlying low coverage. Today no active practitioner, and particularly no surgeon, should consider carrying malpractice insurance at a protective level lower than that of his automobile liability insurance. It is neither uncommon nor extravagant for practitioners to have $100,000/

[1] See *L'Orange* v. *Medical Protective Co.*, 394 F.2d 57 (6th Cir. 1968) (impropriety of refusal to renew malpractice insurance of dentist who had testified for plaintiff in a malpractice suit). This case is discussed in Chapter 6, and in Note, 63 NORTHWESTERN UNIV. LAW REVIEW 873 (1969).

[2] Of course, it is an unavoidable fact that not all physicians can simply select an insurer. The high-risk physician—the surgeon and the anesthesiologist, for example—must find an insurer that is willing to accept him as a risk. It has been reported to the authors that in 1967 one prominent practitioner, acting as the spokesman for a group of specialists, was rejected by no fewer than 18 insurers although the group had experienced no malpractice problems. Incidents of this sort enhance the likelihood of increased governmental regulation of the insurance industry.

$300,000 or $200,000/$600,000 protection, and some policies in excess of a million dollars in coverage have been written. Current verdict and settlement reports amply justify such protection, and the additional premium cost of coverage in excess of minimum limits, while no longer insignificant, is not prohibitive.

Terms of the Policy

The terms of malpractice liability insurance policies need not be outlined in substantial detail; there are agents who are happy enough to do that and they will usually do it competently.[3] However, some notion of the appropriate content of a medical malpractice liability insurance policy should be imparted.

Some American malpractice insurers employ a form of insurance contract developed by the National Bureau of Casualty Underwriters; others have developed their own contract format. In any event, malpractice insurance policies are fairly uniform in basic content. The typical policy has three parts: (1) the insuring agreement itself; (2) exclusionary clauses; and (3) conditions.

The Insuring Agreement

The insuring agreement simply serves to set out the insurer's promise to pay damages, up to the specified policy limits, arising out of the insured physician's asserted malpractice or that of any persons for whose conduct he is legally responsible (excepting, ordinarily, responsibility that stems solely from the insured's membership in a partnership). It is in this part of the contract that the insurer also agrees to provide legal counsel to defend any lawsuit against the insured. A standard clause of this type provides that the insurer, upon receipt of notice from the insured, will immediately assume the defense of any covered claim and will retain counsel for that purpose. The insurer will continue to defend until final judgment in favor of the insured or until all remedies by appeal or other means have been exhausted, at the insurer's cost and without limit as to the amount expended. The insurer undertakes to furnish a bond in any amount required to appeal a judgment against the insured in the event that the judgment is not in excess of the minimum coverage contracted for; if it

[3] This apparently is not invariably the approach of all insurers and their agents, however. Physicians interviewed by the authors stated that in some instances medical malpractice insurers were reluctant, sometimes to the point of adamant refusal, to discuss the following questions: (1) the identity and qualifications of the insurer's local legal counsel; (2) the scope of policy coverage for the physician's association with others (including supervisory activities), such as physicians in training, medical students, nurses, and technicians; and (3) the scope of coverage for outside professional activities, such as membership on a certifying board, a residency review committee, or the credentials committee of the local medical society.

is in excess of that amount, the insurer will furnish a bond to secure its *pro rata* share of the judgment.

Coverage extends only to professional services rendered during the life of the policy.[4] Protection is not limited to injuries to patients; it covers also the claims of persons other than the patient who, directly or indirectly, have also been damaged by the insured's wrongful conduct. It would, by way of example, extend to a claim by a married person for loss of marital services of a spouse. To pick a more bizarre example, it would probably also extend to bystanders—presumably grouped close to the operating table—who were injured when a surgeon's scalpel slipped. Protection has been extended to cover a claim for injuries inflicted upon a third person by a patient while under the effects of medication administered by or at the direction of the defendant doctor.[5]

Malpractice insurance protection need not be confined to orthodox claims of bodily injury and mental anguish. It may include assault and battery, breach of implied warranty, property damage, false imprisonment, invasion of privacy, and defamation, so long as the events giving rise to such claims were directly related to the insured's practice of his profession.[6]

As we have indicated, the liability of an insurance carrier is expressly limited to the sum set forth in the insuring agreement. In exceptional circumstances, however, insurers have been held liable for sums in excess of the stated coverage. This occurs when a carrier, through negligence, bad faith, or outright fraud, rejects an offer of settlement by the plaintiff that is within the policy limits and thereafter a judgment exceeding those limits is obtained. To date, however, there are no reported cases of this sort involving medical malpractice liability insurers.

We have pointed out that protection against liability created by the conduct of a medical partner is not ordinarily provided in malpractice insuring agreements. Physicians in a partnership practice, akin with other sorts of partners, are legally responsible for each other's conduct; and this liability, unlike that of a corporation stockholder, may be unlimited. Accordingly, if a judgment is rendered against a partner who lacks sufficient

[4] See *Aetna Life Ins. Co.* v. *Maxwell,* 89 F.2d 988 (4th Cir. 1937) (patient treated from March 26 to August 7; malpractice insurance policy issued on July 23; held: insurer liable only for malpractice occurring between July 23 and August 7). See also *Shaw* v. *United States Fid. & Guar. Co.* 101 F.2d 92 (3d Cir. 1938); *Waterman* v. *Fidelity & Cas. Co.,* 209 Ill. App. 284 (1917); *Lehr* v. *Professional Underwriters,* 296 N.W. 843 (S. Ct. Mich. 1941).

[5] See *Bullock* v. *Parchester General Hosp.,* 160 N.Y.S.2d 117 (App. Div. N.Y. 1957).

[6] See, *e.g., Maier* v. *United States Fid. & Guar. Co.,* 298 P.2d 391 (S. Ct. Colo. 1956) (libel); *American Policyholders Ins. Co.* v. *Michota,* 103 N.E.2d 817 (S. Ct. Ohio 1952) (injury due to chiropodist's failure to "lock" hydraulic chair).

insurance coverage and personal assets to satisfy it, the balance can be collected from his partners. A similar situation arises when a claim has been made against a deceased partner whose estate has already been distributed. Insurance protection against partnership liability can be purchased, at additional premium cost, and constitutes a prudent investment on the part of physicians engaged in such a practice.

Exclusionary Clauses

Certain classes of liability are expressly excluded from coverage by malpractice insurance policies. The standard exclusions are three in number: (1) liability for injuries arising out of the performance of a criminal act, such as an unlawful abortion;[7] (2) liability for injuries caused by x-ray apparatus used for therapeutic purposes; and (3) liability of the doctor as the proprietor or executive officer of a hospital or like institution. At one time insurers also excluded liability for injuries caused by a doctor while under the influence of intoxicants or narcotics and liability assumed by the doctor under a contract guaranteeing the result of treatment, but this is no longer the case. In times past some insurers expressly excluded coverage for the following procedures: cosmetic plastic surgery; the fitting of contact lenses; shock therapy; nontherapeutic sterilization; anesthesiology; the use of hand fluoroscopes; the use of nuclear energy; the conduct of employees who are not medical doctors; and the employment of a surgeon without the patient's knowledge or consent. These exclusions have also fallen into general disuse, although the facts that inspired them may now influence insurers to divide physicians into risk groups, with internists at one end of the scale and neurosurgeons, orthopedists, obstetricians, plastic surgeons, and anesthesiologists at the other end.

Conditions

All insurance agreements impose certain conditions upon the insured, and this is true of malpractice liability policies. Failure of the physician-insured to abide by these conditions may result in a loss of coverage. The most important conditions expressed in malpractice policies are those requiring the insured to notify the insurer promptly of any malpractice claim against him and to cooperate with the carrier in its defense on his behalf of any claim or suit.[8]

[7] See, *e.g.*, *Glesby* v. *Hartford Acc. & Indem. Co.*, 44 P.2d 365 (Cal. App. 1935) (patient's injuries attributable to use by insured physician of unlicensed assistant in violation of California law). *Cf. Shehee* v. *Aetna Cas. & Sur. Co.*, 122 F.Supp. 1 (W.D. La. 1954) (failure to obtain patient's consent to operation not "assault and battery" as that term employed in policy's exclusionary clause).

[8] See *Coleman* v. *New Amsterdam Cas. Co.*, 160 N.E. 367 (Ct. App. N.Y. 1928)

No amount of irritation or embarrassment should deter a doctor from supplying immediate notice of any malpractice claim at its earliest stage, since prompt investigation of the claim by the insurer, while the evidence is still available, can be of the greatest benefit to the insured. Annoying as it may sometimes be, as in the case of a patently frivolous or fraudulent lawsuit, the necessity of continuing cooperation with the insurer and its legal counsel is undeniable.

One policy condition redounds to the potential benefit of the insurer as well as the insured. In most malpractice insurance policies the carrier reserves the right, with the written consent of the insured, to compromise —settle—any claim or suit. Older policies put teeth in this reservation: if the physician-insured refused authority for a reasonable and recommended settlement offer, the policy coverage was automatically restricted to the sum of the settlement offer. This type of provision is now obsolete.

The recommendations of malpractice insurers regarding settlement can properly be accorded substantial weight by the practitioner, since they are customarily based on the advice of highly knowledgeable legal counsel. Present-day malpractice insurers generally adhere to that course which best serves the medical profession: determined defense of the unmeritorious claim and just settlement of the comparatively few cases involving physician negligence.

Occasionally vexing questions arise as to whether the physician's malpractice insurance policy provides coverage in the case at hand. For one reason or another, the insurer may believe that it is not obligated under the terms of its policy to defend or indemnify the physician-insured against a claim that has been asserted. The insurer can do one of three things when notified of a claim or suit: (1) it can, of course, simply assume its responsibilities under the insuring agreement and abandon any question of coverage; (2) it can send to the policyholder a notice of disclaimer of liability; or (3) it can send the policyholder a letter reserving its right thereafter to assert its noncoverage contention or, alternatively, it can require the insured to agree, in exchange for a defense, that the insurer has not waived its right to contest coverage.[9] A notice of reservation of rights advises the insured that the carrier will investigate, negotiate, defend, or take any other appropriate action without waiving its right there-

("Cooperation does not mean that the assured is to combine with the insurer to present a sham defense. Cooperation does mean that there shall be a fair and frank disclosure of information reasonably demanded by the insurer to enable it to determine whether there is a genuine defense . . ."). It is an insured's duty to appear at and assist in the conduct of trial. *Medical Protective Co.* v. *Light*, 194 N.E. 446 (Ohio App. 1934).

[9] See, *e.g.*, *Ancateau* v. *Commercial Cas. Ins. Co.*, 48 N.E.2d 440 (Ill. App. 1943); *Hinchcliff* v. *Insurance Co. of North America*, 277 Ill. App. 109 (1934).

after to contest the basic question of coverage. The alternative nonwaiver agreement permits the carrier to handle the claim and defend any lawsuit without thereby impliedly surrendering its right later to disclaim coverage. Sometimes these coverage issues can be threshed out in a so-called declaratory judgment action in advance of trial of the malpractice claim against the physician-insured, with the laudable result that the parties know where they stand before it becomes necessary to cope with the malpractice claim. Fortunately, coverage questions are infrequent in the area of malpractice liability insurance.

BIBLIOGRAPHY

BOOKS

Long, R. H.: THE PHYSICIAN AND THE LAW 360–72, 2d ed. Appleton-Century-Crofts, New York, 1968.

Staff of Senate Subcommittee on Executive Reorganization, 91st Cong., 1st Sess., REPORT ON MEDICAL MALPRACTICE: THE PATIENT VERSUS THE PHYSICIAN 1009–60 (Comm. Print 1969).

ARTICLES

Franklin, S.: *What Should Be in a Malpractice Insurance Policy,* 14 CLEVELAND-MARSHALL LAW REVIEW 478 (1965).

Hirsh, H. W.: *Insuring Against Medical Professional Liability,* 12 VANDERBILT LAW REVIEW 667 (1959).

Uhthoff, D. R.: *Medical Malpractice–The Insurance Scene,* 43 ST. JOHN'S LAW REVIEW 578 (1969).

chapter 21

PUBLIC HEALTH AND CHILD ABUSE REPORTING REQUIREMENTS OF PHYSICIANS

The idyllic purpose of government is to "establish justice, insure the domestic tranquillity, provide for the common defense, and promote the general welfare of its citizens."[1] Maintaining wholesome and sanitary conditions in the community is an obligation of government aimed at promoting general welfare, and the enactment of health measures is designed to satisfy this duty. The power of the state to carry out its functions of general health protection has been called its "police power" and includes the power to make laws as well as to enforce them. The reasons usually assigned for the exercise of this police power—sometimes labeled "environmental law"—are the prevention of air and water pollution; the prevention of epidemic; the abatement of public nuisances; and the registration of vital statistics.[2]

To be effective in these vital areas, the government must be able to enlist the aid of its individual citizens. This chapter is concerned with the aid that is requested of the nation's physicians. When considering the various reporting duties placed upon the physician it is necessary to emphasize their positive significance. Although in a sense they call for the production of "red tape," they are not designed to hinder the physician's practice of medicine but rather to allow him to make an even greater contribution to the general welfare than his limited medical practice would otherwise permit. By reporting the various diseases that he daily treats, the physician is able to contribute to governmental control of crime and epidemic and to progress in the prevention and cure of disease.

The physician is called upon to report a broad range of diseases and conditions. These reporting requirements may be separated into two categories: those that deal with the detection and prevention of disease and

[1] Preamble, United States Constitution.

[2] See Stetler, C. J., and Moritz, A. R.: Doctor and Patient and the Law 83, 4th ed. The C. V. Mosby Company, St. Louis, 1962.

those that deal with the detection and prevention of crime. The physician's role in criminal law enforcement is discussed in later chapters.[3] Before consulting typical public health reporting procedures it is necessary to understand the scope of state public health programs.

STATE PUBLIC HEALTH PROGRAMS

What is to be included in the domain of public health is largely a matter of time and place, but it has a solidly accepted meaning which tends to expand with expanding technology and with the expanding functions of government in the service and protection of its citizens. It is the duty of government to protect its citizens; as the duty expands, so must the measures used to discharge it. Often these measures will conflict in some degree with personal interests of the citizen, but the right to adopt health measures under the police power means that the state can constitutionally enact laws that may interfere with the private property and business interests of the citizens.[4]

State and local health agencies derive their power by delegation from the state legislature. The delegation may be of merely administrative functions, such as the power and duty to enforce the state health codes, or it may be broader and include a delegation of regulatory or rule-making powers. If the legislature delegates only an administrative function, the manner of performing this function may be explicitly detailed or it may be a general delegation under which the agency has broad discretion as to the manner in which it will operate its programs. If the legislature delegates the power to make rules and regulations as well, the power to do so will be specifically limited by the scope of the delegation. Any health regulation enacted by a health agency, if outside its delegated power, would be declared invalid if challenged in court. However, delegations of rule-making power are liberally construed; courts will usually uphold an agency's health regulations. In all such cases the constitutional due process requirement that the legislature, in granting rule-making power, set reasonable guidelines and standards must be observed. But again, this requirement is liberally construed, and a standard such as that an agency's regulations be for "the protection of public health" will generally be judicially acceptable.[5] Standards that carry with them criminal penalties are construed more strictly. Only state legislatures are authorized to define penalties, and these must be definite. What occurs is that the state legisla-

[3] See Chapters 22–24.

[4] See Grad, F. P.: PUBLIC HEALTH LAW MANUAL 5. American Public Health Association, Washington, D.C., 1965.

[5] Grad, F. P.: PUBLIC HEALTH LAW MANUAL 12. American Public Health Association, Washington, D.C., 1965.

ture decides that a violation of a health statute enacted by it will be a misdemeanor (a petty crime) and determines what the penalty for committing the misdemeanor will be; but the local health agency decides, in effect, what constitutes a violation of the statute.[6]

A state's public health system may be organized along two lines. The first involves a highly centralized system in which the state legislature passes a public health law providing for a state board of health. The local subdivisions—counties, cities, towns, and villages—act primarily as health law enforcers and are subject to supervision by the state board of health.[7] The second and contrasting type of system is decentralized, with all detailed implementation left to local officials. Because of the increasing complexity of modern health problems, few local subdivisions are equipped to handle procedural details as well as enforcement. Consequently, the completely decentralized public health system is becoming rare.

"Promoting the general welfare" of its citizens requires that government keep itself abreast of all diseases that could have an adverse effect upon the populace. Acquisition of this information poses two questions: how the government is able to require its reporting, and to whom it is to be reported. Information concerning the existence of these conditions can best be obtained from those who treat them, the members of the medical profession, but they are not the only source.

There are, at base, two methods by which public health departments are able to obtain the information needed to complete their records. The first is through the voluntary submission of information by the general

[6] Under this system, state law reposes discretion in the party who prosecutes for the violation. For example, Art. 23 N.Y. PUB. HEALTH LAW (Supp. 1969), covers control of venereal disease. Sec. 2309 of the article states that any violator of a section of this article shall be guilty of a misdemeanor. Sec. 2300, which is concerned with the required examination for venereal disease, provides that the health officer can order an examination only when he has "reasonable grounds" to believe that a person within his jurisdiction is afflicted. Thus although the state has set a penalty, the health officer has the prosecutorial discretion to decide whether to order the examination. Only upon issuance of that order, and a failure to comply, will there be a statutory violation.

[7] An example of a centralized public health system is New York State's. N.Y. PUB. HEALTH LAW, §201 (Supp. 1969), designates the functions, powers, and duties of the State Department of Health. Its first concern is to "supervise the work and activities of the local boards of health and health officers throughout the state." §201 (1)(a). To facilitate the state board's control, the statute creates a Public Health Council whose primary responsibility is to consider any matter relating to the preservation and improvement of public health, at the request of the state commissioner. The enforcers of the state public health system are the local boards of health and the local health officer, who is the local board's chief executive. §308. Pursuant to §324 of the act, the general duty of the local health officer is to enforce the public health laws and the sanitary code.

public. This creates no legal problems; the only difficulty is communicating with the public. To satisfy this need for communication, the public health services conduct extensive advertising campaigns portraying the duty of the citizen to report cases of communicable disease. The second method is through compulsory disclosure. The state legislature may grant the public health authorities the power to require the filing of reports. This power is exercised to ensure the filing of birth and death certificates. Health authorities may also have the power to order the keeping of certain records, subject, at all times, to inspection.[8] This power is exercised particularly with respect to the keeping of drugs and narcotics by physicians. For example, section 17.2 of the New York Sanitary Code requires doctors to keep records showing shipment, receipt, and delivery of poliomyelitis vaccine. Section 22-19 of the Illinois Uniform Narcotic Drug Act requires the keeping of detailed records showing all narcotic drugs received, administered, and dispensed by a physician.[9] Records and documents required to be kept for purposes of inspection assume the character of quasi-public documents, with the result that there can be no objection to their official inspection.[10]

It would be repetitious to list the state reporting requirements of physicians in all fifty states. Instead this chapter focuses upon requirements in three major states: California, Illinois, and New York. This focus is designed primarily to make the physician broadly aware of his role in the reporting of disease rather than merely to enumerate the mechanical techniques of reporting. The reporting requirements of most states parallel those of our three example states. However, all physicians and surgeons will consult the public health service of their state of practice to secure current and detailed instructions on reporting and records requirements.

REPORTING VITAL STATISTICS

Public health reporting requirements are divided into two categories: "vital statistics" and "contagious, infectious, or communicable diseases." Vital statistics involve the filing of birth, fetal death, and death certificates. Every state requires the filing of birth and death certificates, and the methods of reporting are relatively uniform as a consequence of recommendations made by the National Office of Vital Statistics and the World Health Organization.

[8] Grad, F. P.: PUBLIC HEALTH LAW MANUAL 176. American Public Health Association, Washington, D.C., 1965.

[9] ILL. STAT. ANN., ch. 38, §22-19 (Supp. 1969).

[10] See, *e.g.*, *United States* v. *Pine Valley Poultry Distributing Corp.*, 187 F.Supp. 455 (S.D.N.Y. 1960).

A birth certificate is important to every citizen. It is required upon entering school; in obtaining a driver's or marriage license; in obtaining a passport; for voting rights and for joining the armed forces. Death certificates are often essential to the resolution of probate, pension, and life insurance questions. The recommended birth certificate form requires the child's name, sex, and race; the exact time and place of birth; the names of the father and mother (unless the child was illegitimate, in which case consent to the inclusion of the parents' names must be secured from them); and the names of all previous children by the mother. Some states go farther, requiring information about the mother's pregnancy; blood types; the result of the prenatal venereal disease examination; type of delivery; and any malformations.

The form of the death certificate most often used is that recommended by the National Office of Vital Statistics. It states the name and address of deceased, time and place of death, marital status, occupation, sex, race, name of parents, and cause of death.[11] In stating the cause of death it may be necessary to distinguish between primary and immediate causes, on one hand, and, on the other, contributory causes or complications.[12] The physician who last treated the deceased is responsible for the execution of the death certificate except where the death falls within one of those categories commonly referred to as "coroner's cases." In such cases, the obligation of the physician is only to report the death. "Coroner's cases"—those in which a coroner or medical examiner is required to determine the cause of death and sign the death certificate—generally include cases of violent or suspect death, whether homicidal, suicidal, or accidental; cases in which no doctor is in attendance at the time of death, or in which the attending physician is unable to ascertain the cause of death by the usual clinical means; and cases in which it appears that a criminal act may have been a contributing cause.[13] Circumspection will always be exercised by the physician in signing death certificates; he will not sign the certificate until certain of both death and its cause. In the California case of *Thayer* v. *Board of Osteopathic Examiners*[14] the court affirmed the decree of the Board of Osteopathic Examiners that the defendant doctor's license be revoked for aiding an unlicensed person to practice osteopathy and for signing a death certificate representing that the doctor had attended a decedent whom he had never in fact seen.

In Illinois the filing of birth and death certificates falls under the Illi-

[11] See Stetler, C. J., and Moritz, A. R.: DOCTOR AND PATIENT AND THE LAW 78, 4th ed. The C. V. Mosby Company, St. Louis, 1962.

[12] See Regan L. J., and Moritz, A. R.: HANDBOOK OF LEGAL MEDICINE, 83, 3d ed. The C. V. Mosby Company, St. Louis, 1956.

[13] See Chapter 13.

[14] 320 P.2d 28 (S. Ct. Cal. 1958).

nois Vital Statistics Act.[15] When the birth occurs in a medical institution the doctor in attendance must verify or provide the date of birth and all medical information required by the certificate. When the birth occurs outside an institution the physician in attendance at or immediately after birth shall complete and file the birth certificate. Medical certificates of death must be completed within twenty-four hours after death by the physician in charge of the patient's care for the illness or condition that resulted in the death. Any person who knowingly or willfully makes a false statement on either of these certificates or willfully supplies false information is guilty of a misdemeanor which is punishable by a fine of between $25 and $100 or imprisonment for not more than thirty days, or both.[16]

New York requires that the birth of every child shall be reported within five days after birth, and if a physician is present at birth it is his duty to file the report.[17] The New York certificate of death must be filed within seventy-two hours following the death.[18] These requirements are based on the general right of the Health Commissioner of the State of New York to demand all information concerning births and deaths. The information must be given on forms supplied by his office. At any time after birth, and within one year after death, the Commissioner may demand that such certificate be filed and, upon refusal or neglect to do so, can prosecute the deficient party.[19] The failure to supply the required information or any willful alteration of a birth certificate is a misdemeanor, the penalty for which, on first offense, is a fine of between $5 and $50 and, for repeated offenses, between $10 and $100, with a maximum of thirty days' imprisonment.[20]

California requires that all births and deaths be registered, on prescribed certificate forms, with the State Department of Public Health. In addition, it is the duty of all citizens, including physicians, to supply information they may possess concerning births and deaths.[21] For live births that occur in a hospital, it is the duty of the physician in attendance to register the certificate with the local registrar. For live births that occur outside the hospital, a physician in attendance is responsible for the filing; if there was no attending physician, either of the parents shall be responsible for entering the information on the certificate and filing it with the

[15] ILL. STAT. ANN., ch. 111-1/2, §§73-12, 73-18 (Supp. 1969).
[16] *Ibid.*, §73-27.
[17] N.Y. PUB. HEALTH LAW, §4130 (Supp. 1969).
[18] *Ibid.*, §4140.
[19] N.Y. PUB. HEALTH LAW, §4175 (Supp. 1969).
[20] *Ibid.*, §4102.
[21] CALIF. HEALTH & SAFETY CODE, §§10000, 10005 (Supp. 1970).

Registrar.[22] Death certificates must be registered in the district where the death was officially pronounced, or where the body was found, within five days after death and, most importantly, prior to any disposition of the human remains. It is the responsibility of the physician last in attendance to state on the certificate of death the disease or condition directly leading to the death; any antecedent causes; the last time he examined the patient; the last time he saw the decedent alive; and the hour and day when the death occurred.[23] As in Illinois and New York, the failure to furnish correct information for birth and death certificates is a misdemeanor punishable by a fine of not less than $10 for the first offense and a fine of not less than $50 for each subsequent offense, plus possible imprisonment for up to sixty days.[24]

A third type of certificate filed under the Vital Statistics category is for fetal or stillborn deaths. Usually a special form of certificate is used. The first part of the certificate is virtually the same as a death certificate, while the second part requires information of the sort called for on a birth certificate. When a state does not use this convenient hybrid type of certificate it will often require the filing of both a birth and a death certificate.[25] The California and New York fetal death certificates are divided into two sections, the first containing the items necessary to establish the fact of the fetal death, and the second containing questions relating to medical and health data.[26] All three example states concur in the definition of stillborn death as one that occurs after a gestation period of not less than twenty weeks. In such cases all three states require that the proper certificate be filed with the local registrar of the health district in which the delivery occurred.[27]

Each of the example states requires, in addition, that reports be filed concerning the health of newborn infants. In Illinois it is the duty of any physician or nurse attending a newborn child to report to the local health authority within six hours any diseased condition of the eyes, characterized by redness or swelling (ophthalmia neonatorum), of an infant less than two weeks old.[28] In addition, every newborn child must be subjected to an examination for phenylketonuria, and the results of this test

[22] *Ibid.*, §§10101–10102.

[23] CALIF. HEALTH & SAFETY CODE, §10225 (Supp. 1970).

[24] *Ibid.*, §10679.

[25] See Stetler, C. J., and Moritz, A. R.: DOCTOR AND PATIENT AND THE LAW, 4th ed. The C. V. Mosby Company. St. Louis, 1962.

[26] CALIF. HEALTH & SAFETY CODE, §10190 (Supp. 1970); N.Y. PUB. HEALTH LAW, §4160(2) (Supp. 1969).

[27] CALIF. HEALTH & SAFETY CODE, §10190 (Supp. 1970); ILL. STAT. ANN., ch. 111-1/2, §73-20 (Supp. 1969); N.Y. PUB. HEALTH LAW, §4160(1) (Supp. 1969).

[28] ILL. STAT. ANN., ch. 91, §106.107 (Supp. 1969).

must be passed on to the Illinois Department of Public Health.[29] New York has a similar statute relating to ophthalmia neonatorum,[30] and also requires that all birth defects and birth-allied diseases be reported to the local authorities by the doctor in attendance.[31] In an attempt to prevent inheritable disorders leading to mental retardation or physical defects, the California Department of Health exrcises the power to order medical tests for all newborn children. It becomes the duty of the doctors and hospitals caring for the infants to administer tests as soon as the department informs them that they are required.[32]

REPORTING CONTAGIOUS, INFECTIOUS, OR COMMUNICABLE DISEASES

The second category of the public health reporting requirements—the reporting of contagious, infectious, or communicable diseases—is the basis for attempted governmental control of epidemic disease. These reports are the basis for quarantine regulations, mass inoculations, vaccinations, and compulsory isolation of infected persons. State health authorities are usually authorized by their enabling legislation to specify the diseases to be reported, and because of the vital need for these reports, most states fix heavy penalties for failure to comply. The report supplies the name and address of patient; the disease; the time of onset; and the name of the reporting doctor.[33]

In California it is the duty of all physicians to report to the local public health officials the names and addresses of all persons whom they have treated for an infectious, contagious, or communicable disease. This requirement is contained in the general section of the California Health and Safety Code delegating to the state department of health the power to quarantine areas exposed to disease whenever in its judgment such action is necessary to protect or preserve public health.[34] An indication of those diseases that fall within the broad category of "infectious, contagious, or communicable diseases" is supplied by the California statute, which authorizes local health officials to take whatever action they may deem necessary to stop the spread of "cholera, plague, yellow fever, malaria, leprosy, diphtheria, scarlet fever, smallpox, typhus fever, typhoid fever, paratyphoid fever, anthrax, glanders, epidemic cerebro-spinal meningi-

[29] *Ibid.*, ch. 91, §113(f).

[30] N.Y. PUB. HEALTH LAW, §2502 (Supp. 1969).

[31] *Ibid.*, §2733.

[32] CALIF. HEALTH & SAFETY CODE, §280 (Supp. 1970).

[33] See Stetler, C. J., and Moritz, A. R.: DOCTOR AND PATIENT AND THE LAW 82, 4th ed. The C. V. Mosby Company, St. Louis, 1962.

[34] CALIF. HEALTH & SAFETY CODE, §3051 (Supp. 1970).

tis, tuberculosis, pneumonia, dysentery, erysipelas, hookworm, trachoma, dengue, tetanus, measles, German measles, chickenpox, whooping cough, mumps, pellagra, beriberi, Rocky Mountain spotted (or tick) fever, syphilis, gonococcus, rabies, or poliomyelitis." [35] It is within the power of the state health department, operating through local health officials, to isolate and disinfect the diseased persons; destroy such objects as bedding, carpeting, and household goods which are considered a menace to public health; exclude pupils from school; and, if necessary, take possession of the body of living or deceased persons. Any person who fails to perform his duty to report diseases or refuses to comply with the isolation order will be guilty of a misdemeanor, punishable by a fine of not less than $25 nor more than $500 or by imprisonment for a term of up to ninety days, or both. A violator can be prosecuted for a separate offense for each day that the violation continues.[36]

New York operates under the same kind of statutory scheme for the reporting of communicable diseases. The New York State Sanitary Code states that it is the duty of every physician to report to the local health officer the name, age, and address of every person afflicted with a communicable disease within twenty-four hours after the disease is first diagnosed by him.[37] Such reports may be made by telephone or telegraph, but they must be finalized in writing. In cases where the diagnosis of a communicable disease is not made until after death, the same reporting requirements must be followed. Whenever it appears to the local health officer that an unusual number of cases of a particular communicable disease are being reported, it becomes his duty to report this fact to the state health authorities. The state department of health may then request that physicians who attended the diseased persons submit such specimens and laboratory tests as the department feels it may need. Pending official action by the state health officials, it is the duty of the attending physician to keep the patient isolated and to make other members of the family aware of necessary precautions. Any violation of these requirements is a misdemeanor and is punishable by a fine of not more than $50 or by imprisonment for not more than six months, or both. (New York used to have a statute that required that a physician give immediate notice of every case of communicable disease to the local health officer. For each case he reported the physician was entitled to a twenty-five-cent fee. This statute was repealed in April of 1966 and the present Sanitary Code provision replaced it. We regret to report that the new provision does not include a reward.)

Illinois operates under a slightly different statutory scheme. The state

[35] CALIF. HEALTH & SAFETY CODE, §2554 (Supp. 1970).
[36] *Ibid.*, §§3350 *et seq.*
[37] N.Y. SANITARY CODE, ch. 2, reg. 9 (Supp. 1969).

legislature has not passed specific requirements that the physician must report instances of communicable disease. The state department of public health has the power to make such rules and regulations and investigations as it may deem necessary for the public health.[38] Periodically the department publishes a pamphlet enumerating the rules and regulations currently in force. The most recent edition was published on June 1, 1965, and is still applicable. Cities and townships may adopt ordinances and additional regulations which are supplementary to, or which amplify, those of the state. The only requirement is that they must be reasonable.[39] The pamphlet enumerates the reportable diseases, reporting requirements, general and detailed procedures for the control of communicable diseases, rules and regulations applying specifically to venereal disease, and regulations relating to the conduct of funerals when the death occurs from a communicable disease. The scope of these requirements is coextensive with those that have been described for New York and California. Any violation of Illinois' regulations is considered a misdemeanor, and any violator is liable to a fine not to exceed $200 or imprisonment not to exceed six months, or both.[40]

Venereal disease is considered an extremely critical problem by state health officials. Once such a disease has been diagnosed, it falls within the general category of communicable diseases and is reported in the usual way. A great deal of effort is aimed at disease prevention. As a means both to detect the disease and to prevent any further communication of it, all three of our example states require both premarital and prenatal venereal disease examinations. In reporting every birth and stillbirth the Illinois physician must state on the certificate whether a syphilis test was taken, the date of the test, and the laboratory that received the specimen.[41] In addition, all persons making application to marry within Illinois must have a blood test within fifteen days prior to the application, and an examining physician must certify that the person tested is free from venereal disease.[42] A false statement in either of these certificates will expose the physician to liability for a fine of $100 to $500 for each offense.

In New York a health officer who has reasonable grounds to believe that a person is infected with a venereal disease can order him to have an examination. The physician who performs the examination must report the result to the health officer who demanded it. A licensed physician is

[38] ILL. STAT. ANN., ch. 111-1/2, §22 (Supp. 1969).

[39] ILL. DEPT. OF PUB. HEALTH, RULES AND REGULATIONS FOR THE CONTROL OF COMMUNICABLE DISEASE 4 (June 1, 1965 ed.).

[40] ILL. STAT. ANN., ch. 111-1/2, §24 (Supp. 1969).

[41] *Ibid.*, ch. 89, §113(b).

[42] ILL. STAT. ANN., ch. 89 §6(a) (Supp. 1969).

the only person who can treat or prescribe a treatment for venereal diseases.[43] New York's prenatal examination requirement provides that every physician attending a pregnant woman shall cause a blood sample to be taken and that he shall submit the sample to an approved laboratory. Failure to satisfy these requirements is a misdemeanor.[44] No application for a marriage license will be accepted unless it is accompanied by a certificate signed by a licensed physician stating that both parties have been given the standard serological examination within thirty days prior to the making of the license application and that neither is inflicted with syphilis in the communicable stage.[45]

California requires that a physician attending a person whom he suspects of being infected with a venereal disease must submit a blood specimen for examination; not to do so is a misdemeanor.[46] Every physician engaged in prenatal care of a pregnant woman or attending such a woman at the time of delivery must obtain a blood specimen at the time of his first professional visit or within ten days thereafter. The specimen must be designated as one obtained either during a prenatal examination or following delivery. A violation of any of these requirements is a misdemeanor. However, if the request for a blood specimen is refused by the woman, the physician cannot be prosecuted for failure to obtain it.[47] California's marital examination requirements are identical with those described for New York State.[48]

The physician in these three example states is also called upon to report diseases and conditions that are not considered communicable. The state's interest in such afflictions as blindness and deafness is not one of protecting the public from an outbreak of disease; its interest is in maintaining the general welfare of all its citizens. If reported cases of blindness or deafness increase, presumably the state will consider the establishment of added facilities for education and maintenance. In New York it is the physician's duty to report, in writing, the name, age, and address of all blind persons [49] and of every child under six years of age who is either totally deaf or has impaired hearing.[50] California requires that every doctor who examines anyone under twenty years of age and finds either impaired hearing or total deafness shall report to the Department of Education the name, age, and address of the minor.[51] In addition, all

[43] N.Y. PUB. HEALTH LAW, §§2300 *et seq.* (Supp. 1969).
[44] *Ibid.*, §2308.
[45] N.Y. DOMESTIC RELATIONS LAW, §13(a) (Supp. 1969).
[46] CALIF. HEALTH & SAFETY CODE, §3198 (Supp. 1970).
[47] *Ibid.*, §§3222 *et seq.*
[48] CALIF. CIVIL CODE, §79.01 (Supp. 1970).
[49] N.Y. UNCONSOLIDATED LAWS, tit. 24, §8704 (Supp. 1969).
[50] N.Y. PUB. HEALTH LAW, §2584 (Supp. 1969).
[51] CALIF. EDUCATION CODE, §12802 (1969).

doctors must report to the local health officer, in writing, the name, age, and address of every person diagnosed as an epileptic or victim of any similar disorder characterized by lapses of consciousness.[52]

REPORTING CASES OF CHILD ABUSE: THE "BATTERED BABY" SYNDROME

The problem of child abuse in this country achieved notoriety with the advent of the 1960's. Typical of the publicity that engendered alarm over the battered child phenomenon were two major studies released in 1962 and 1963.

One, published by the American Medical Association, involved inquiries of 70 hospitals and 77 district attorneys as to incidents of abused children over a one-year period. The hospitals reported over 300 known cases of battery, with 33 deaths; district attorneys responded with evidence of 447 victims, including 45 deaths.[53] The second survey, undertaken by the Children's Division of the American Humane Association, documented 662 instances of child battery that left 178 children dead in 1962 alone.[54]

Legislatures reacted speedily to this unsettling publicity. From 1962 through 1967 each of the fifty states established statutory machinery to deal with child abuse.[55] At the heart of each legislative initiative were measures designed to facilitate the discovery of battered children.

This discovery function has been allocated to the medical profession. Every state now permits, and most compel, physicians to bring to the attention of appropriate authorities any suspected case of child battery. The legislatures, in effect, have codified the public's trust in physicians' ability to recognize in children injuries that evidence human abuse. Child battery most often occurs in the privacy of the home, and a doctor is frequently the only outsider contacted. Physicians can recognize trauma or neglect consistent with possible abuse, such as "fractures of any bone, subdural hematoma, multiple soft tissue injuries, poor skin hygiene, or malnutrition." [56] While barbarous parents may attempt to cover up battery with accounts of everyday child mishaps, the physician can detect discrepancies between clinical findings and the parents' story of how the

[52] CALIF. HEALTH & SAEFTY CODE, §211(a) (Supp. 1970).

[53] Kempe, C. H., *et al.*: *The Battered Child Syndrome,* 181 J.A.M.A. 17 (1962).

[54] Quoted in McCoid, A. H.: *The Battered Child and Other Assaults upon the Family,* 50 MINNESOTA LAW REVIEW, 1, 15 (1965).

[55] For the citations of all but the Hawaii statute, HAWAII STAT., ch. 350, 350-1, to -5 (Supp. 1969), see Paulsen, M. G.: *Child Abuse Reporting Laws: The Shape of the Legislation,* 67 COLUMBIA LAW REVIEW 1, 1-2 (1967).

[56] Kempe, C. H., *et al.*: *The Battered Child Syndrome,* 181 J.A.M.A. 17 (1962).

injuries occurred. He remains the ready source of information on suspected victims.

A model reporting statute proposed by the Children's Bureau of the United States Department of Health, Education, and Welfare in 1963 read in part as follows:

Any physician, including any licensed osteopathic physician, intern and resident having reasonable cause to suspect that a child under the age of [the maximum age amenable to juvenile court proceedings] brought to him or coming before him for examination, care, or treatment has had serious physical injury or injuries inflicted upon him other than by accidental means by a parent or other person responsible for his care, shall report or cause reports to be made in accordance with the provisions of this act: provided that when the attendance of a physician with respect to a child is pursuant to performance of services as a member of the staff of a hospital or similar institution, he shall notify the person in charge of the institution, or his designated delegate who shall report or cause reports to be made in accordance with the provisions of this Act.

An oral report shall be made immediately by telephone or otherwise and followed as soon thereafter as possible by a report in writing, to an appropriate police authority. Such reports shall contain the names and addresses of the child and his parents or other persons responsible for his care, if known, the child's age, the nature and extent of the child's injuries (including any evidence of previous injuries), and any other information that the physician believes might be helpful in establishing the cause of the injuries and the identity of the perpetrator.[57]

The fifty states vary in the degree to which the quoted language has been followed. The nature of the duty to report differs with respect to (1) whether reports are mandatory or voluntary; (2) if mandatory, the sanctions for failure to report; (3) what injuries are to be reported; (4) to whom the report must go; and (5) the precise content of the report.

All but six of the fifty states (the six are Alaska, Missouri, New Mexico, North Carolina, Texas, and Washington) make reporting a mandatory function of the examining physician. In the wake of this legislation the American Medical Association objected to the designation of doctors as the key reporting agents.[58] It was feared that if physicians alone were required to report cases of suspected child abuse, guilty parents would fail to bring their battered children for medical treatment.

The case of *People* v. *Forbs*[59] in the California Supreme Court con-

[57] Children's Bureau, U.S. Dept. of Health, Education, and Welfare, *The Abused Child—Principles and Suggested Language for Legislation and Reporting of the Physically Abused Child* 11–13. U.S. Govt. Ptg. Off., Washington, D.C., 1963.

[58] See, *e.g., Battered Child Legislation,* 188 J.A.M.A. 386 (1964).

[59] 402 P.2d 825 (1965).

tributed some weight to the Association's theory. There a mother struck her son in anger at his conduct. The child fell to the floor unconscious. The parent telephoned a relative and told her that her son was hurt but that she "had not called a doctor because she feared that he might report her." The boy died without attention.

Yet the number of parents who would abuse their children and leave them unattended is probably small. Furthermore, the medical profession's required cooperation has proven invaluable in obtaining aid for victims of child battery. The mandatory reporting statute in Illinois alone led to information and preventive action on behalf of 363 children in the first nine months after its inception.[60]

Though most of the states require reporting of suspected cases of child abuse, only twenty-seven impose specific penal sanctions for failure to report (Arizona, Arkansas, California, Delaware, Florida, Georgia, Kansas, Kentucky, Louisiana, Maine, Michigan, Minnesota, Nebraska, Nevada, New Jersey, Ohio, Oklahoma, Oregon, Pennsylvania, South Carolina, South Dakota, Tennessee, Utah, Vermont, Virginia, West Virginia, Wyoming).

Those not imposing specific penalties include Alaska, Missouri, New Mexico, North Carolina, Texas, and Washington, where the reporting function is not mandatory. Statutes in Alabama, Colorado, Connecticut, Hawaii, Idaho, Illinois, Indiana, Iowa, Maryland, Massachusetts, Montana, Mississippi, New Hampshire, New York, North Dakota, Rhode Island, Wisconsin speak in mandatory terms but carry no penalty provisions.

Where provided, specific penalties will be imposed only in instances of "knowing or willful" violation of the reporting requirement. Pennsylvania's sanctions are representative: a fine of $300 or ninety days imprisonment in case of conviction for violation of the statute.[61] Convictions are rare, however, because of the difficulty of proving that a physician "willfully" avoided his duty to act.

The degree of injury requiring a doctor's report is described in various ways. New York calls for reports of "serious injuries"[62] and is joined by Kansas, Kentucky, Louisiana, Massachusetts, New Jersey, North Dakota, Oklahoma, and South Dakota. Pennsylvania cites the need for information in the event of "gross physical neglect or injury."[63] California and Illinois specify no standard of seriousness and refer to any "physical

[60] Paulsen, M. G.: *Child Abuse Reporting Laws: The Shape of the Legislation,* 67 COLUMBIA LAW REVIEW 1, 38 (1967).

[61] PA. STAT. ANN., tit. 18, §2109 (Supp. 1969).

[62] N.Y. PENAL LAW, §483-d (Supp. 1969).

[63] PA. STAT. ANN., tit. 18, §4103 (Supp. 1969.

injury" or "evidence of injury" as grounds for a doctor's cooperation.[64] Statements on the degree of harm necessitating reports are lacking as well in the Arizona, Florida, Hawaii, Idaho, Indiana, Iowa, Maine, Michigan, Minnesota, North Carolina, Ohio, Oregon, Rhode Island, Tennessee, Texas, Utah, and Wyoming statutes.

Designation of reportable injuries often goes beyond a measure of seriousness, however, and requires of the physician the making of significant substantive judgments. Thirteen states demand reporting of injuries inflicted by "other than accidental means" (California, Florida, Illinois, Indiana, Kentucky, Louisiana, Maine, New Jersey, North Dakota, Rhode Island, South Dakota, Washington, Wyoming). Michigan, Nebraska, Oregon, and Wisconsin look for reports when the injuries discovered were, in the view of the physician, "intentionally or wantonly inflicted." Others require information only when injuries are "the result of abuse" (Hawaii, Kansas, Massachusetts, New York, North Carolina, Oklahoma, Texas, Utah).

Legal writers have questioned the propriety of demands upon a doctor for substantive determinations as to whether injuries are "wanton," "intentional," "accidental," or the result of "abuse."[65] They suggest that a physician should not be asked to resolve such mixed issues of law and fact. Investigatory agencies and the courts are perhaps better equipped to deal with such questions. The doctor, it is thought, should only be asked to raise suspicions of simple battery, when they are warranted, since his skills serve him best in an assessment of the physical manifestations of injury. The doctor, as we have said before, can also decide whether the harm done coincides with any account of the injuries given by the parents or others.

The question may arise as to how positive the doctor must be before he is required or permitted to report. The statutes speak of this problem. Information is generally required or encouraged only if there are "reasonable grounds" or "reasonable cause" to "believe" or "suspect" that a reportable injury has occurred. For instance, Illinois refers to the requisite degree of certainty in terms of "having a reasonable cause to believe." [66] California demands cooperation when there is an "appearance of child abuse." [67] New York looks for reports from physicians "having reason to believe" that the defined types of injuries have occurred.[68] Unique among

[64] CAL. PENAL CODE, §11161.5 (Supp. 1968); ILL. ANN. STAT., ch. 23 §2042 (Supp. 1968.)

[65] See McCoid, A. H.: *The Battered Child and Other Assaults Upon the Family*, 50 MINNESOTA LAW REVIEW 1, 45 (1965).

[66] ILL. ANN. STAT., ch. 23, §2042 (Supp. 1969).

[67] CAL. PENAL CODE, §11161.5 (Supp. 1968).

[68] N.Y. PENAL LAW, §483-4 (Supp. 1969).

the reporting laws remains Pennsylvania's, requiring information on injuries without regard to cause to believe, reasonable cause to suspect, or appearance of child abuse.[69]

Once a physician determines that a report must or ought to be made, state laws differ as to the identity of its recipient. Distinctions among the statutes can be drawn along three lines.

Illinois and New York are representative of those states that designate public or private welfare agencies as the principal recipients of the medical profession's reports. Illinois physicians must inform the State Department of Children and Family Services. New York reports are to be received by any "society for the prevention of cruelty to children or other duly authorized child protective agency"; [70] the same approach is taken in Hawaii, Idaho, Iowa, Massachusetts, North Carolina, Rhode Island, and Wyoming.

A number of statutes provide for initial reports to police or similar law enforcement authorities. California, for example, dictates that information on victims of child abuse be sent "to the local police authority having jurisdiction and to the juvenile probation department." [71] California is joined in this respect by Arizona, Louisiana, Maryland, Missouri, Montana, Nebraska, New Jersey, Ohio, Tennessee, Virginia, Washington, West Virginia, and Wisconsin. Juvenile courts are the primary receiving agents in Florida, Kansas, Mississippi, and South Dakota.

A third group of statutes—those in Alabama, Connecticut, Maine, Oklahoma, Pennsylvania, South Carolina, Texas, and Utah—permit a choice between two or more agencies to which the report must go. Michigan, meanwhile, denies any discretion and dictates that reports be drawn in triplicate with provision of copies to "the local prosecuting attorney, the probate court and the Department of Social Welfare." [72]

The lawmakers in many instances have specified the content of the physician's report. Among others, California insists on the "name of the minor, his whereabouts, and the character and extent of the injuries." [73] Reports in Illinois must contain the "names and addresses of the child and his parents or other persons having his custody; the child's age; the nature of the child's condition including any evidence of previous injuries or disabilities; and any other information that the reporter be-

[69] The statute reads, "Any physician whose examination of a child less than eighteen years of age discloses evidence of gross physical neglect or injury not explained by the available medical history . . . shall immediately report. . . ." PA. STAT. ANN., tit. 18, §2103 (Supp. 1969).

[70] N.Y. PENAL LAW, §483-d (Supp. 1969).

[71] CAL. PENAL CODE, §11161.5 (Supp. 1968).

[72] MICH. STAT. ANN., §14.564(2) (1969).

[73] CAL. PENAL CODE, §11161.5 (Supp. 1968).

lieves might be helpful in establishing the cause of such physical abuse, neglect, or injury, and the identity of the perpetrator."[74] Such are the standard specifications among those states defining the content of a report. Michigan and Texas fail to specify the need to relate evidence of either prior injury or the identity of the perpetrator. The Pennsylvania and Tennessee statutes require the name of the victim and the character and extent of the injuries but remain silent as to the need for any information on the possible cause of injury. As a rule of thumb, physicians in those states without content specification should at least set out their medical findings, noting any inconsistencies between the injuries as diagnosed and the purported medical history.

One additional type of rule concerning the reporting mechanism is frequently laid down. Illinois and California are typical of the many states that order an immediate oral report to the appropriate authorities, followed by a more comprehensive written record. Only Idaho, Maryland, Massachusetts, New York, North Carolina, Oregon, Tennessee, and Wisconsin fail to specify whether a report should be oral or written. Florida, Louisiana, Maine, and Michigan designate written reports alone.

Initial proposals for the child abuse statutes in 1962 and 1963 raised fears among spokesmen for the medical profession that mandatory reporting might pose a threat to doctor-patient confidentiality. Alarms were also sounded regarding the possibility of suits against reporting physicians for libel, slander, or invasion of privacy. The champions of battered child legislation assuaged these fears with their insistence upon the inclusion of immunity clauses in every reporting statute. The fifty states unanimously promulgated immunity provisions that typically read:

> Any person or institution participating in good faith in the making of a report . . . shall have immunity from any liability, civil or criminal, that might otherwise be incurred or imposed because of the making of such a report.[75]

Furthermore, any fears that reports of instances of child abuse overstep the bounds of confidentiality and trust between doctor and patient appear to be unfounded. Section Nine of the American Medical Association's *Principles of Medical Ethics* asserts:

> A physician may not reveal the confidences entrusted to him in the course of medical attendance or the deficiencies he may observe in the character of patients, unless he is required to do so by law or unless it becomes necessary in order to protect the welfare of the individual or of the community.[76]

[74] ILL. ANN. STAT., ch. 23, §2044 (Supp. 1969).

[75] N.Y. PENAL LAW, §483-4 (Supp. 1969).

[76] This rule was promulgated in 1957, years before the enactment of child-abuse reporting legislation.

A doctor must remember that his patient, in the circumstances under discussion, is the child and not the apparently abusive parents whom he might be tempted to insulate from prosecution for assault and battery or, worse, attempted homicide. Required reports benefit the battered infant patient, to whom attending physicians owe a moral and, now, a statutory duty of protection. The duty is not onerous. The thorough physician gathers and maintains detailed histories on each patient examined. In the case of a child whose history appears suspicious, the reporting statutes demand nothing more than a good-faith sharing with appropriate police and welfare authorities of the information gathered.

BIBLIOGRAPHY

BOOKS

Richardson, J. R.: DOCTORS, LAWYERS, AND THE COURTS, ch. 6. The W. H. Anderson Company, Cincinnati, 1965.

ARTICLES

Garve, K., and Wilhelm, L. F. X.: *Medical and Legal Aspects of Damage Suits Due to Erroneous Reporting and Quarantining of Communicable Diseases,* 49 MEDICAL LEGAL JOURNAL 69 (1932).

McCoid, A. H.: *The Battered Child and Other Assaults upon the Family,* 50 MINNESOTA LAW REVIEW 1 (1965).

Paulsen, M. G.: *Child Abuse Reporting Laws: The Shape of the Legislation,* 67 COLUMBIA LAW REVIEW 1 (1967).

part two

THE PHYSICIAN AND THE CRIMINAL LAW

chapter 22

THE MEDICAL PRACTITIONER AND PHYSICAL EVIDENCE IN CRIMINAL CASES

The usual role of a physician is in diagnosis and treatment. Whether he is a specialist or not, he is comfortable in that role. He tends to view any unrelated responsibility as an unwarranted encroachment upon his time and energy. Nevertheless, he will sometimes find himself in a professional situation where he must become interested in matters other than those of a strictly medical nature. This will occur whenever he is the attending physician to a victim of a criminal offense or of an accident with possible criminal implications.

There are times when a physician will be the only one who can adequately observe the fresh and unaltered wounds caused by firearms, knives, or other objects. It is upon him that police investigators will have to rely for an accurate observation and documentation of the nature and characteristics of such wounds and the proper collection and preservation of criminal evidence.

A proper examination and documentation of a wound may reveal the nature of the wounding object, the direction of force, the approximate time between the infliction of the wound and the physician's observations, and other factors of importance to police investigators. The proper collection and preservation of whatever physical evidence he can obtain may be essential in a subsequent prosecution of the person responsible for the injury. In all of this the physician's cooperation is indispensable.

The medical practitioner very frequently fails to record what he sees at the time of an examination of a patient. He is preoccupied with diagnosis and therapy and feels that written or other documentation is of secondary importance. In this he is quite correct; documentation must take a secondary role to the saving of the patient's life and to prompt and efficient treatment of his traumatic problems. But many times, after the completion of the therapeutic efforts, a physician will either deliberately or inadvertently neglect to document what he has seen. He may harbor a concern about "getting involved" in a police matter—especially one that may culminate in a court trial, either criminal or civil. As a consequence he may deliberately avoid recording observations of vital significance to the police investigators and to the courts. At other times the physician may simply neglect even to consider the importance of documentation, and either omit it altogether or else perform it inadequately.

In cases involving patients who have been wounded by someone else, it is not only the physician's moral and social obligation but also at times a legal obligation to document the nature and extent of the wound to the best of his ability. He should note, sketch, diagram, or perhaps even have a photograph made of the wound, subject to the reservation, of course, that such efforts will not adversely affect the diagnosis, treatment, or the outcome of the patient's traumatic disability. Most certainly, however, whenever the welfare of the patient is no longer a pressing matter, there is no justification for omitting proper documentation. A failure to do so constitutes a breach of the physician's obligation to both the patient and the public.

Although documentation is imperative, a risk is incurred whenever the practitioner goes beyond that responsibility and ventures into the area of interpretation of his recorded observations. Lacking the benefit of special training in such matters, or the opportunity for a visual internal examination of the wounded patient, he may well come up with an erroneous conclusion. His job, therefore, is documentation, not interpretation. The latter must be left to the expert in injuries due to trauma.

Nothing is more disconcerting to law enforcement officers, and on occasion to the courts, than to have to contend with an inadequate or improper interpretation by a physician who was not adequately qualified for the task. The risk of an unqualified interpretation is well illustrated in Figures 1 and 2. These two figures demonstrate the difficulty of distinguishing between an entrance and an exit bullet wound. Figures 1*A* and 1*B* are remarkably similar, as are 2*A* and 2*B*. Accurately distinguishing between the two is a hazardous task for the unqualified observer.

The need for documentation of external wounds prior to any alteration by therapeutic endeavors arose in the case of the assassination of President John F. Kennedy. If proper notation had been made of the exit bullet wound in the front of the President's neck prior to the tracheostomy incision, much subsequent confusion would have been avoided regarding the course of the bullet.

The necessity for documentation of wounds as the physician sees them initially is demonstrated by Figure 3. It shows how an alteration of evidence by scrubbing the skin surface around a bullet wound can destroy the only means of subsequently establishing facts such as the approximate distance from which a bullet wound was inflicted. A reliable con-

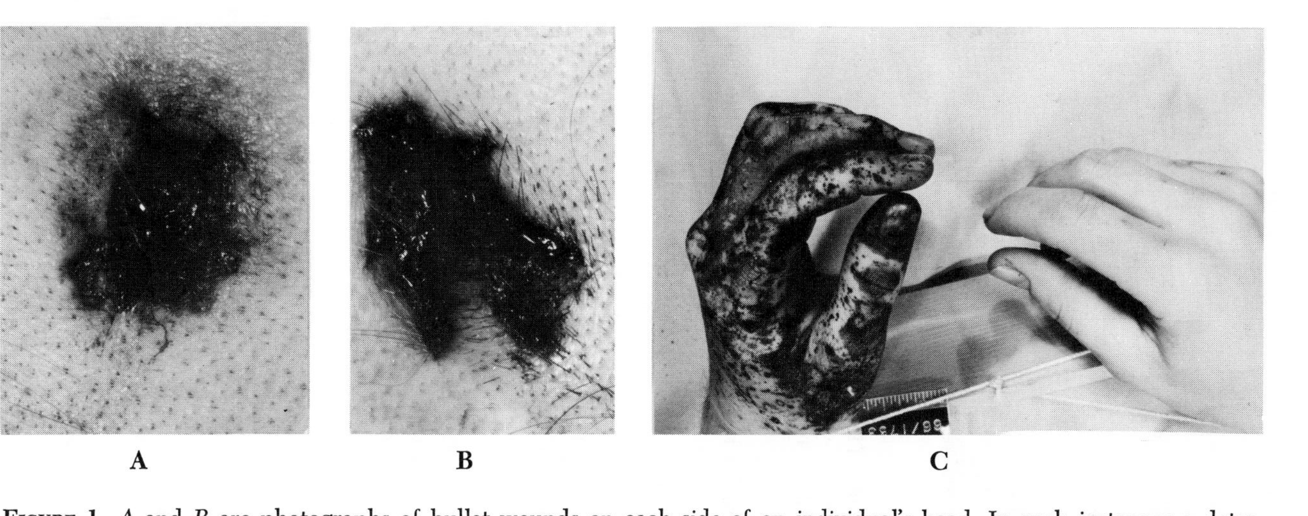

A B C

Figure 1. *A* and *B* are photographs of bullet wounds on each side of an individual's head. In such instances a determination of which is the entrance wound and which is the exit is often a crucial issue for the police and the courts. It is a determination that must be made by someone specially trained and experienced in such matters.

A is the entrance (inshoot) wound in the right temple; *B* is the exit (outshoot) wound.

In *C* observe the blood on the victim's left hand. He had committed suicide by holding a pistol against his right temple with his left hand and pulling the trigger with a finger of his right hand.

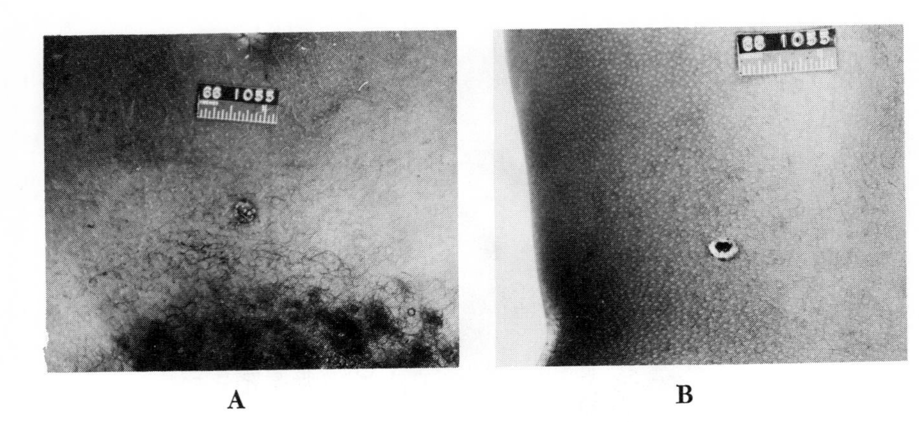

FIGURE 2. *A* is an entrance (inshoot) bullet wound in the lower abdominal wall. *B* is the exit (outshoot) wound in the left back. To the inexpert eyes the opposite conclusion might be reached.

clusion of suicide or murder may depend upon a proper documentation of physical evidence of this type.

It is not enough for the examining and treating physician merely to make note of, or otherwise document, the nature and area of the wound itself. Other parts of the body should also be scrutinized and appropriate documentation made of anything out of the ordinary. Figure 1*C* is a good illustration of the point. The documentation of the blood on the victim's left hand was extremely important in establishing the fact of suicide.

Whenever it becomes necessary for a physician to remove a bullet from the body of a patient the physician should exercise whatever reasonable caution he can to avoid a mutilation of the bullet, or even the bullet fragments. The gun barrel impressions on a bullet, or on a portion of a bullet, can serve to identify the weapon from which it was fired. (See Figure 4.)

A surgeon uses instruments as extensions of his fingers, and the majority of surgical procedures are performed without the fingers ever touching the body tissues to any significant degree. It is a natural act for the surgeon, therefore, to remove bullets with forceps and surgical clamps. But unjacketed bullets fired from rifled arms (pistols and rifles) are composed of a soft lead alloy, and surgical forceps or clamps may damage the bullet to such an extent as to destroy its value as a possible means for identifying the weapon from which it was fired. Such bullet mutilation may deprive the police and prosecution of an indispensable piece of evidence for the establishment of the guilt of the assailant or killer.

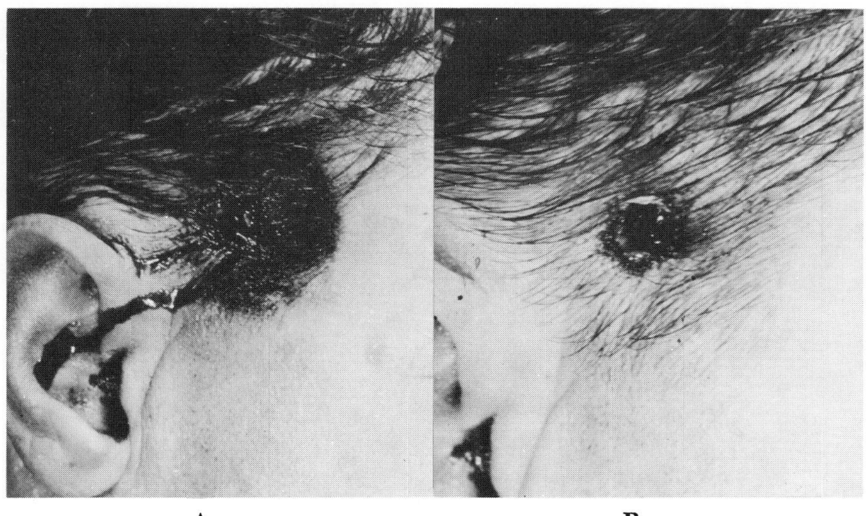

FIGURE 3. *A* is a photograph of an unaltered bullet wound in an individual's right temple. Observe that the point of entry, the inshoot wound, is surrounded by a nearly symmetrically placed zone of fouling caused by powder gas from the barrel of the weapon.

B is the same wound after the powder residues had been completely removed with a damp sponge. The small, grayish-black ring on the periphery of the entrance area was caused by the "wiping" effect of the bullet as it entered the stretched skin.

A is a typical example of a wound caused by a bullet fired at very close range, whereas *B* typifies a long-range wound, falsely created in this instance by the sponge scrubbing.

Where alteration of evidence is necessary for diagnosis or treatment purposes, there should be documentation by one means or another so as to avoid the possibility of a subsequent erroneous interpretation of what remains. In cases where the victim is already dead there should be no tampering whatsoever with the wound area; the evidence should be left untouched for expert examination.

Whenever possible, under conditions that will not impair the welfare of the patient, a bullet should be removed with the fingers or by the use of a clamp with the jaws covered with rubber tubing.

For an illustration of the damage that a surgical removal process can cause to the surface of a bullet, see Figure 5.

After the proper removal of a bullet from a gunshot victim, it should be placed on a piece of gauze and left within sight of the surgeon or other assistant or staff member who may later arrange for its preservation as evidence. Then, when time and circumstances permit, the bullet should be labeled and stored in a secure place.

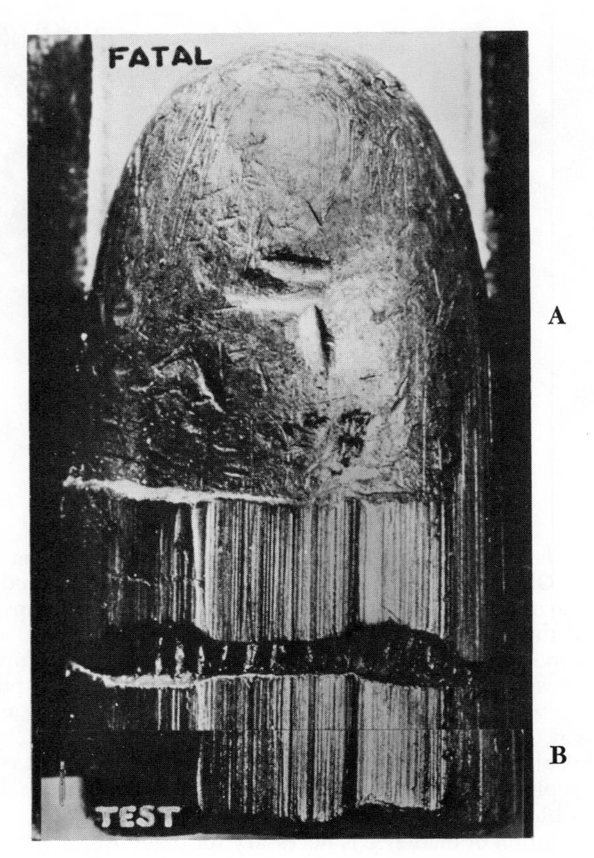

FIGURE 4. *A* represents a section of an enlarged photograph of a bullet removed from the body of a shooting victim; *B* is a section of a photograph of a similar area of a bullet fired from a suspected weapon. Observe the matching of the two sets of impressions which had been left on the lead alloy bullets as they traveled through the gun barrel.

The markings that are thus transmitted from the interior of the barrel to the bullets are the result of the gun barrel manufacturing process. They are caused primarily by the scraping effect of the rifling cutter used to create the slightly twisting lands and grooves (usually five or six in number) that give gyroscopic effect to the bullet as it emerges from the gun.

It is mathematically improbable that any two rifle barrels will possess the same set of markings; in fact, even within the same barrel, no two grooves and no two lands will bear the same markings. Upon this principle, an expert comparison of two bullets under a comparison microscope will reveal whether or not they were fired from the same weapon. It is essential, therefore, that there be no avoidable mutilation of these telltale impressions on a bullet in the process of its removal from the body of a shooting victim.

FIGURE 5. Photograph of a portion of a bullet showing the damage that can be caused by surgical instruments used in its removal from a body. Damage of this nature may render it impossible to determine whether or not the bullet was fired from a suspected weapon.

A removed bullet should be marked with an identifying set of letters (and in some instances with numbers as well). Preferably, the surgeon himself should do this. However, any assistant or staff member who witnessed its removal would be a satisfactory substitute. The important thing is that the markings be placed upon it by someone who can later tell the police, and perhaps a judge or jury, that upon the basis of his identifying markings the bullet is the one he saw removed from the victim's body. In some instances it may be of importance to further state from which portion of the body, or from which internal organ, it was removed. This is one reason the surgeon or an assisting physician is the preferred person for identification purposes whenever there is any indication that such details may be of some future value. Ordinarily, however, where the precise cause of death is not an issue, and the only fact that need be established is that "this is the bullet that was removed from the body," any witness to the removal would suffice. Perhaps the most cautious procedure to follow is to have the surgeon place the markings on the bullet while one or two other persons witness the markings *and* make their own records of what the markings were, the date and place of removal, the name of the victim, and the like. In this way a prosecuting attorney would not have to rely upon one person alone as an identifying witness; he could use the one upon whom the courtroom appearance would impose the least inconvenience.

A removed bullet should be marked with an identifying set of letters or numbers at the *base* of the bullet, or perhaps on the nose, but never on the circular surface containing the gun barrel impressions. Then the bullet should be placed in a suitable envelope, and sealed, by that individual or some other witness to the removal and marking. Across the sealed flap the sealer should write his name or initials.

Where more than one bullet or other foreign object has been removed from the body of a victim, or found in or about his clothing, each one should be labeled and placed in separate envelopes, on which should be noted the location where it was found, either inside or outside the body. The location could be indicated by a number on the base or nose of the bullet, and this location identifying number could be noted in a record book kept by the surgeon or some other witness to its removal. At a later date this detail of location might become a crucial issue, especially in situations where it may be necessary to decide which particular bullet was the actual cause of death.

Bullets preserved as suggested above should be put into a locked container by the same person who handled the evidence from the outset. By confining the various procedures to one person, the need for the court appearance of other tracing-the-evidence or chain-of-custody witnesses will be obviated.

In addition to bullets, other foreign objects removed from a patient can be of great importance in the investigation of criminal cases. An illustration of this is Figure 6, a photograph of three shotgun wads, several pellets, and the inner lining of a shotgun shell. These objects were recovered from a debridement of the shoulder of the victim of a shotgun blast. From the wads the gauge of the shotgun was determined; from the inner lining of the shotgun shell blown into the shoulder muscles the police were able to ascertain the specific kind of ammunition. This information enabled the investigating officers to determine which of two potential assailants, each armed with a shotgun, actually fired the shot.

Figure 7 shows shotgun wads, pellets, and the polyethylene liner of a relatively new type of shotgun shell. All of these objects were removed from the body of a shotgun victim. The exact ammunition used was determined by an examination of these foreign bodies.

Figure 8 shows a piece of plastic table cloth removed from the depths of an abdominal wound. From this evidence the investigators were able to establish that the victim had fallen across a glass-topped table, breaking it and injuring himself.

Objects such as the above-described ones (Figures 6, 7, and 8) are not susceptible to marking, so they need only be placed in suitable envelopes, labeled, and stored in the manner previously suggested for bullets.

FIGURE 6. Three shotgun shell wads, several pellets, and the inner lining of the shell removed from the body of a victim. This evidence served to identify the gauge of the shotgun and the manufacturer of the ammunition. This, in turn, distinguished which of two potential assailants actually fired the shot.

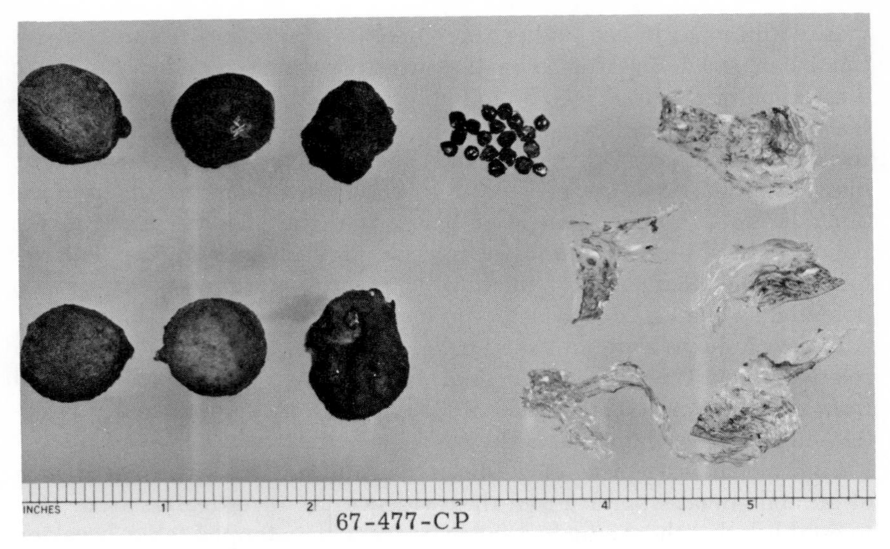

FIGURE 7. Shotgun shell wads, pellets, and the polyethylene liner of a shell which were removed from a body. They permitted a determination of the ammunition used.

When the time comes for turning over bullets or other small foreign objects to the police, another and larger envelope should be used as the container for all of the small ones. This, too, should be sealed, with the sealer's name or initials placed across the sealed flap. Again we urge that whenever possible only one person should be involved in the process of handling the evidence from the time of its recovery until delivery to the police. (For an illustration of a suitable envelope and the labels it should bear, see Figure 9.) Before relinquishing any evidence to the police, a receipt should be obtained and kept in the files along with all other records in the case.

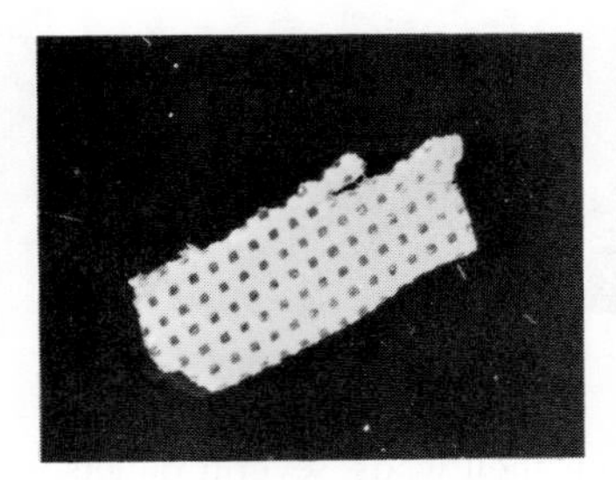

FIGURE 8. A piece of plastic tablecloth removed from the depths of an abdominal wound, which established the fact that the source of injury was a broken glass-topped table.

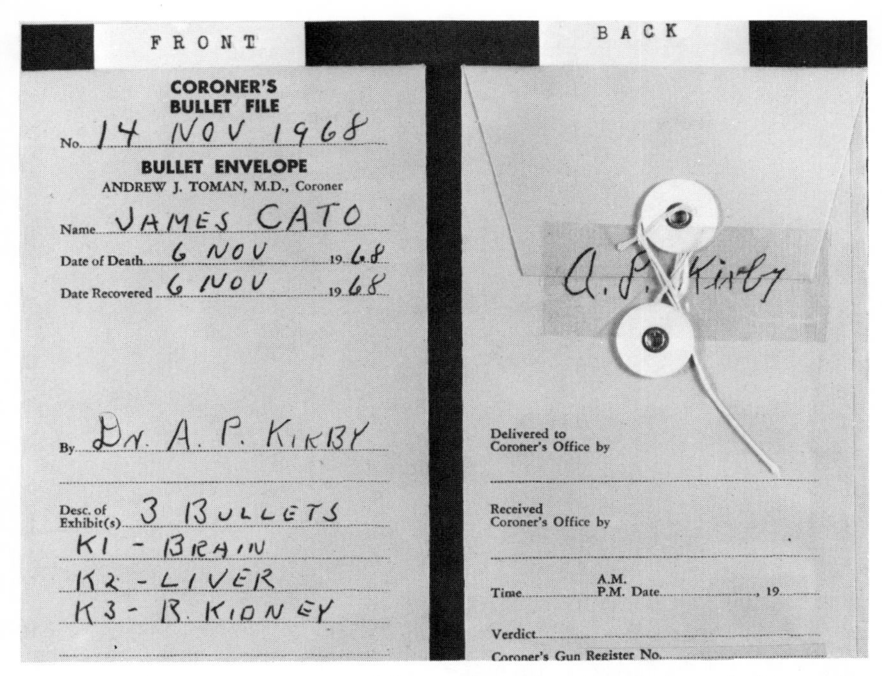

FRONT

CORONER'S
BULLET FILE

No. 14 NOV 1968

BULLET ENVELOPE
ANDREW J. TOMAN, M.D., Coroner

Name JAMES CATO

Date of Death 6 NOV 19 68

Date Recovered 6 NOV 19 68

By Dr. A. P. KIRBY

Desc. of Exhibit(s) 3 BULLETS
K1 - BRAIN
K2 - LIVER
K3 - R. KIDNEY

BACK

A. P. Kirby

Delivered to
Coroner's Office by

Received
Coroner's Office by

Time A.M. P.M. Date , 19

Verdict

Coroner's Gun Register No.

FIGURE 9. Illustration of a suitable envelope for the placing of the smaller envelopes or boxes used by the surgeon or assistant for the preservation of individual bullets removed from the body of a shooting victim. The placing of the name over the flaps of the envelope will simplify the chain-of-evidence problem at the time of a court trial.

The clothing worn by victims of accidents, criminal homicides, and suicides may be of utmost importance in criminal case investigations and court trials. It would be ideal, of course, if clothes worn by accident and crime victims could be gently removed without cutting or tearing. It is recognized, however, that in many instances quick removal is required so as to expose the areas of the body involved by trauma. Consequently, cutting or tearing away of the clothing is an acceptable practice insofar as diagnosis and therapy are concerned. Nevertheless, whenever it is possible to do so without impinging upon the physician's primary responsibility to the patient, the clothing should be cut or torn in an area away from any bullet hole or any wound caused by knives or other instrumentalities or objects. A preferred area is along a seam in the garment, as illustrated in Figure 10.

Clothing removed from the victim of an accident or possible crime should not be thrown on the ground or floor or otherwise discarded or destroyed. A simple example of the inadvisability of this is the victim of a

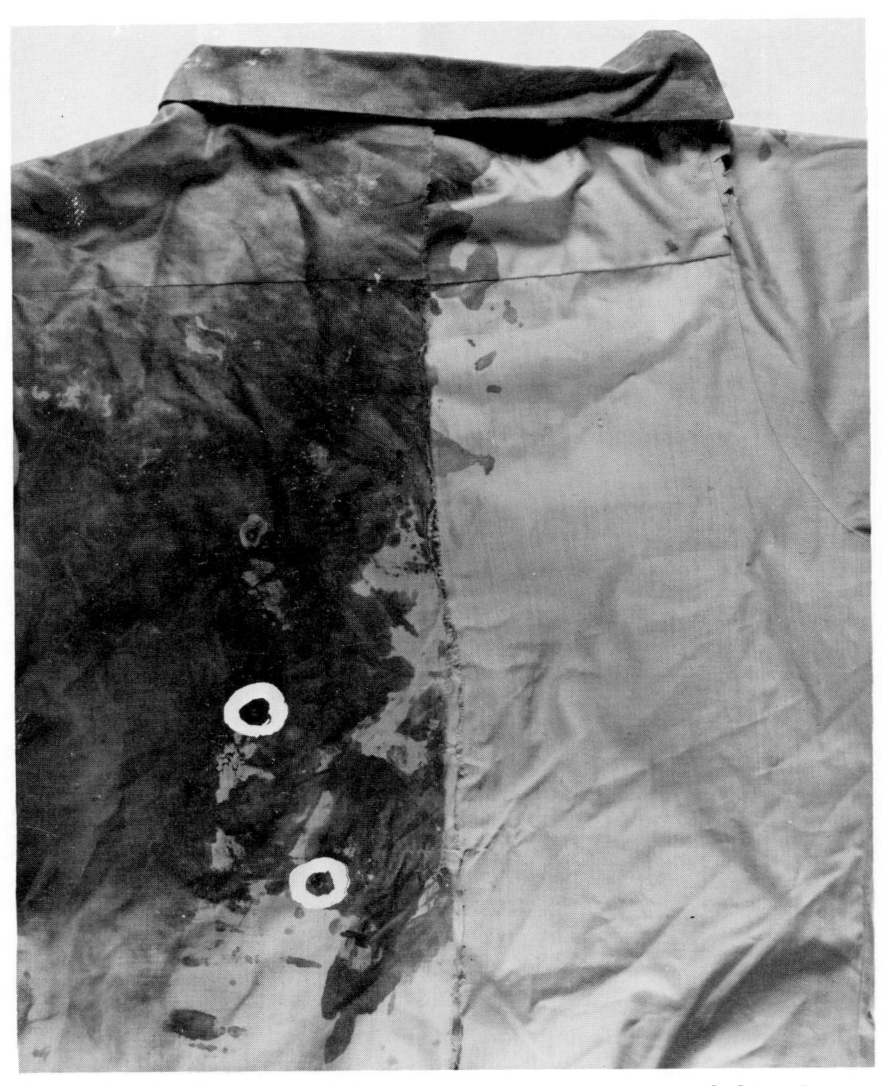

FIGURE 10. An illustration of the proper way to cut or tear clothing from a shooting victim (or stab-wound victims, etc.). This shirt was torn off along a seam away from the area of the bullet holes. An avoidance of any marring or destruction of the area of clothing through which the injury was sustained can be a favorable critical factor in a case investigation or subsequent court trial.

hit-and-run automobile accident. A torn piece of clothing lodged in the undercarriage of a suspected vehicle may be matched with a torn area in the clothing of the victim.

Removed articles of clothing should be handled as little as possible and without any deliberate shaking or dusting. They should be placed into *clean* plastic bags or other suitable *clean* containers. Separate bags or containers should be used for each article, and all the bags or containers must be properly labeled, as illustrated in Figure 11.

Gastric washings and specimens of blood, urine, or other substances removed from a patient require the same careful attention for criminal case investigation purposes as was previously recommended with respect to bullets and other objects. Their handling, labeling, and preservation may be crucial.

In suspected poisoning cases, vomitus and gastric washings should be preserved in their entirety. Nothing should be discarded. All too fre-

FIGURE 11. A plastic bag of this type is an ideal container for removed clothing. It should bear a tag giving the name of the victim, the date, and the name of the physician, and whatever other identifying data are deemed appropriate. The bag should be sealed.

quently, multiple stomach washings collected from a patient who has ingested a poison are all thrown together and a sample of this mixed washing is all that the toxicologist receives for analysis. And even when several washings are saved separately, if they are not labeled to establish sequence, it will be impossible to determine which was obtained first and, therefore, which has the greatest potential for recovery of the toxic material.

Blood specimens taken in suspected poisoning cases also require special attention if the physician is to aid rather than hinder the police investigation. Frequently the first specimen of blood obtained in an emergency situation is one for typing of the patient for possible blood transfusion. After several hours of observation, the subject is now thought to be the victim of an overdose of a toxic substance, and blood is procured at this time for toxicological examination. The several hours that elapsed between the time the first sample of blood was drawn for blood typing and the time that poisoning was suspected and a sample of blood drawn for toxicological analysis may have given the body sufficient time to metabolize the toxic substance. The first sample of blood would be much more apt to contain a measurable quantity of the poison than the second sample, but this is frequently overlooked by the physician and the opportunity for toxicological proof of the poisoning is lost.

There are occasions when the police may wish to have blood samples taken from an injured person for the purpose of chemical tests for alcoholic intoxication. Many physicians are reluctant to comply, out of concern that they may not legally do so. In almost all cases, however, there is a perfectly legal justification for the extraction of blood for medical purposes—for example, blood typing for possible transfusions—and there is no sound reason that some of the blood sample should not be turned over to the police for the auxiliary purpose of chemical testing for alcoholic intoxication, and for blood grouping tests in effecting comparisons with blood on weapons or on a suspect's clothing or on other objects. At least one state (New York) has even declared, by statute, that a physician who extracts blood solely for such a police purpose is immune from civil liability.[1] The immunity extends to registered professional nurses and laboratory technicians.

In certain sorts of criminal cases, especially sex crimes, the police investigators will be interested in vaginal smears as well as oral and rectal smears from the victim for crime laboratory examination purposes. They may also want to have specimens of pubic as well as head hair for possible comparison with loose hair found on a suspect. Fingernail clippings will also be desired for examination of blood, body tissue, or other material

[1] N.Y. VEHICLE & TRAFFIC LAW, §1194 (Supp. 1969).

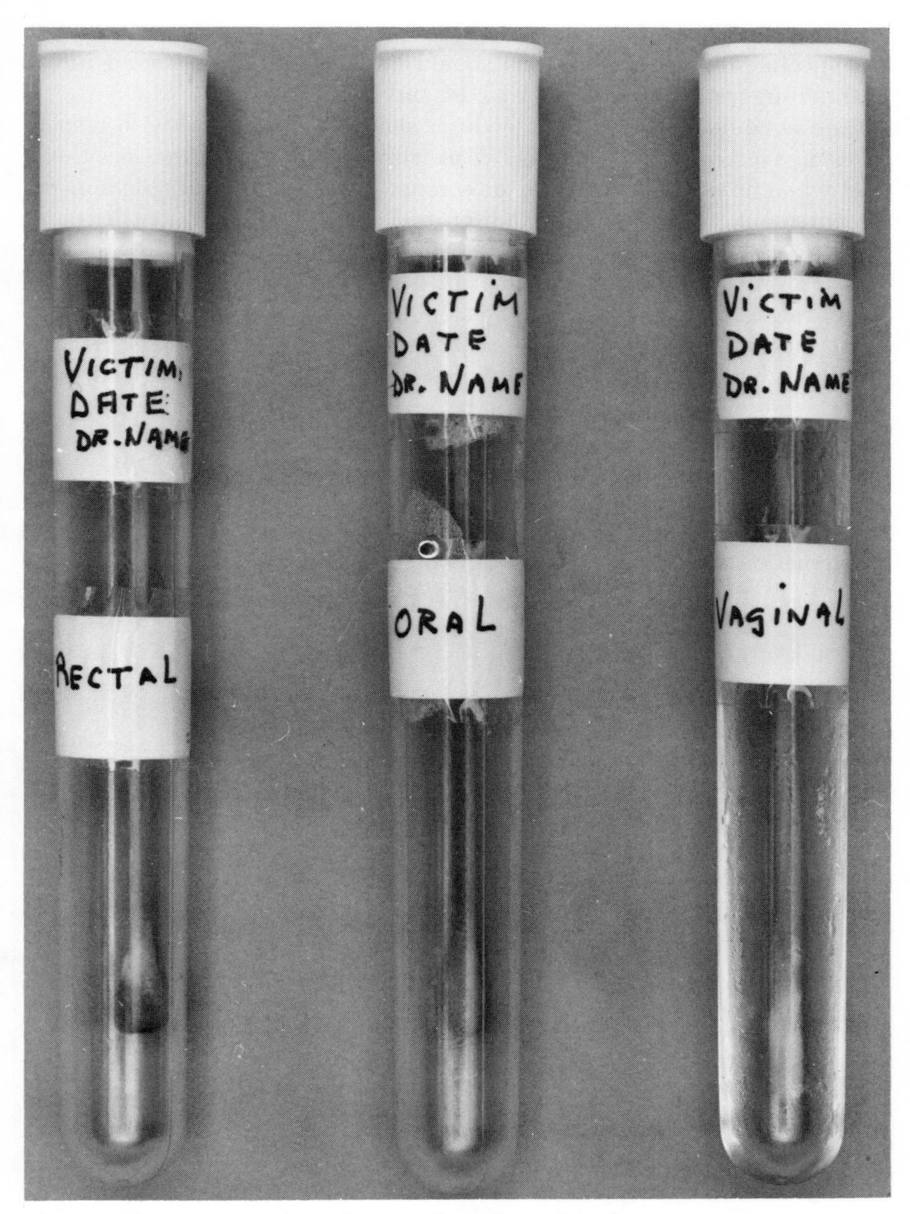

FIGURE 12. Rectal, oral, and vaginal swabs, taken from a sex crime victim patient, should be placed in containers such as these and labeled as indicated.

that they may have picked up in the process of resisting the attacker. As to all of this the physician should afford his full cooperation. And when the specimens are obtained they should be labeled and preserved in the manner suggested in Figures 12, 13, 14, and 15.

The same documentation procedures should be employed with respect to crime victims who are already dead when the physician first sees them, and when no medical examiner or coroner facilities are available and the procurement and the preservation of evidence rest solely upon the practitioner.

For an illustration of the manner in which foreign particles of possible significance to police investigators should be removed from the surface of a victim's body and preserved, see Figues 16*A* and 16*B*.

Where medical examiner or coroner facilities are available, the body should be left undisturbed until the arrival of members of the staff of either office.

Whenever a physician has any reason to suspect criminality as the cause of death, he should notify law enforcement authorities as quickly as possible. And most certainly this should be done before embalming, burial, or cremation of the body.

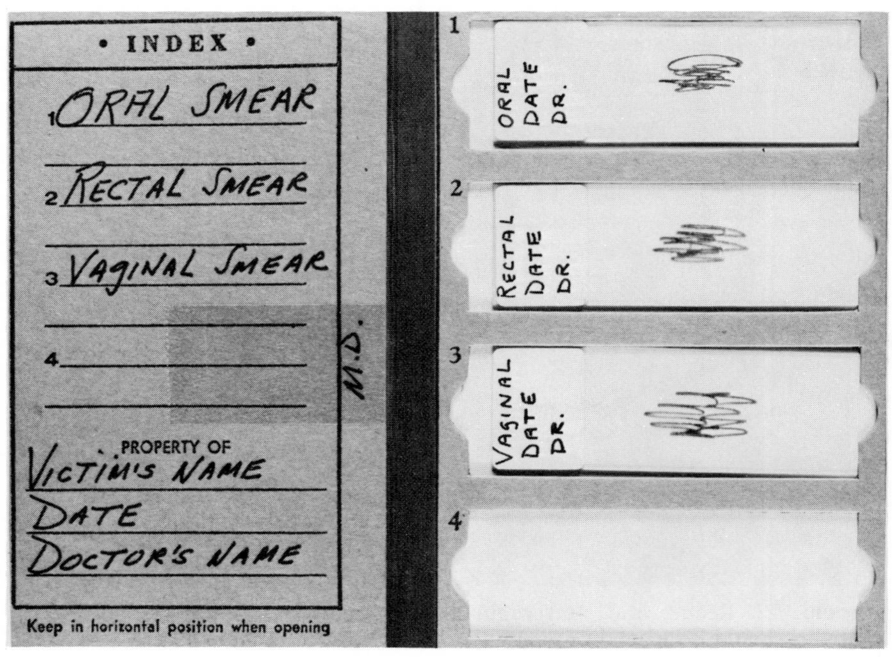

FIGURE 13. Illustration of suitable containers for the smears taken from a sex-crime victim.

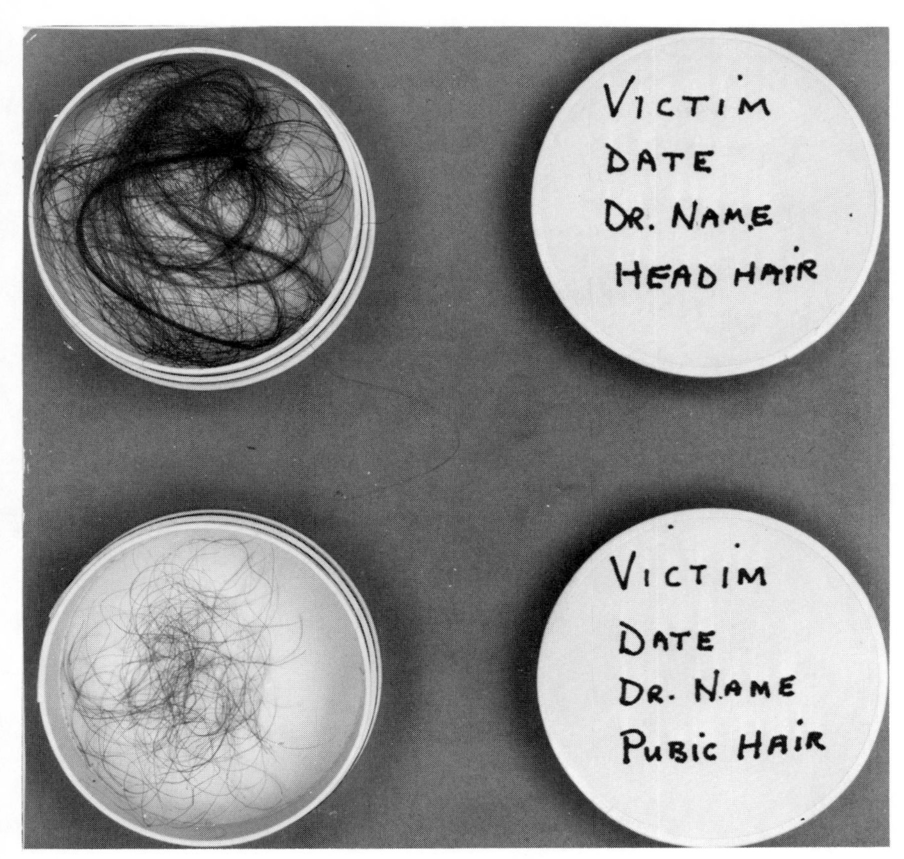

Figure 14. Hair specimens removed from the victim of a sex offense or other crime of violence should be placed in pillboxes, such as the ones shown here, and labeled as indicated.

X-rays taken on an emergency basis (and an emergency is involved in most of the types of cases that are the subject of this discussion) are usually not labeled properly; indeed, they may not even be identified or dated in any way. Many are the instances when x-rays taken under emergency conditions have been lost, mislaid, misfiled, or otherwise made unavailable for future use simply because they were not properly labeled. The crucial evidence needed in a subsequent court trial may have been lost forever. A physician can render a valuable public service, therefore, by suggesting to the x-ray technician that a proper documentation be made in order to preserve the value of the x-ray as evidence.

Whenever a physician indulges in therapeutic efforts on a shotgun or stabbing victim that leave markings which may be confused later on with

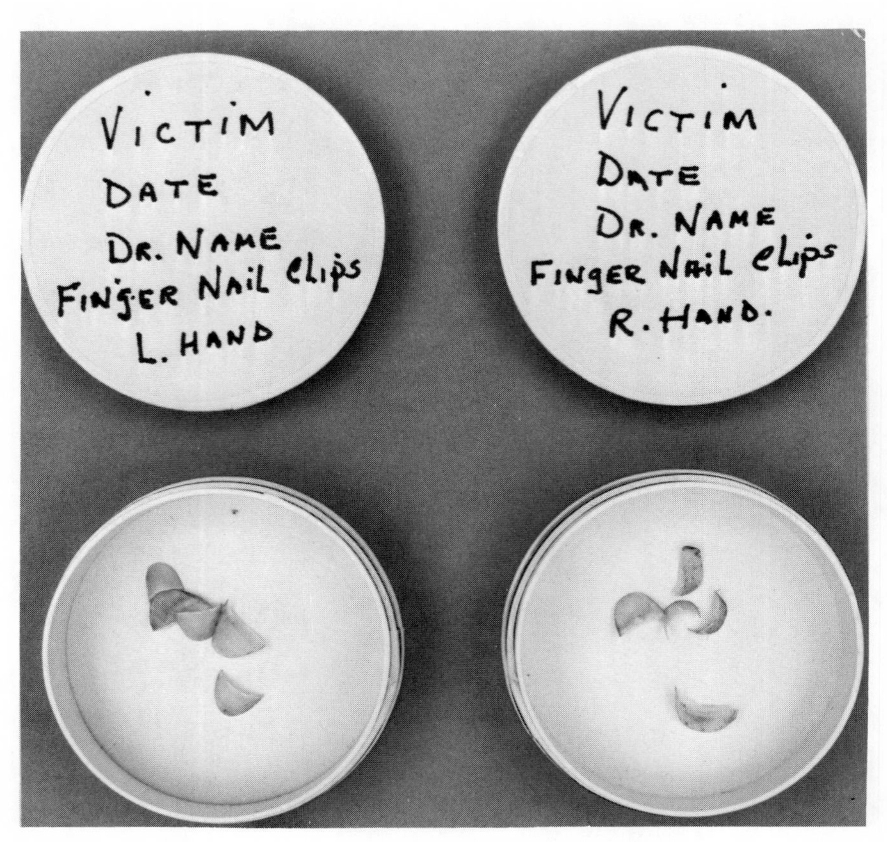

FIGURE 15. Pillbox containers with proper labeling for fingernail clips taken from victim of sex offense or other crime of violence involving close contact between victim and offender.

FIGURE 16. *A.* A simple yet very satisfactory way to remove foreign particles of possible significance to police investigators. Here Scotch tape is used to remove a paint particle from a crime victim. Such objects may be of considerable investigative value.

B. A pillbox is a suitable container for the preservation of foreign particles. If a pillbox is not readily available, a Petri dish can be used. In either event, the top should contain the necessary identification data as here illustrated.

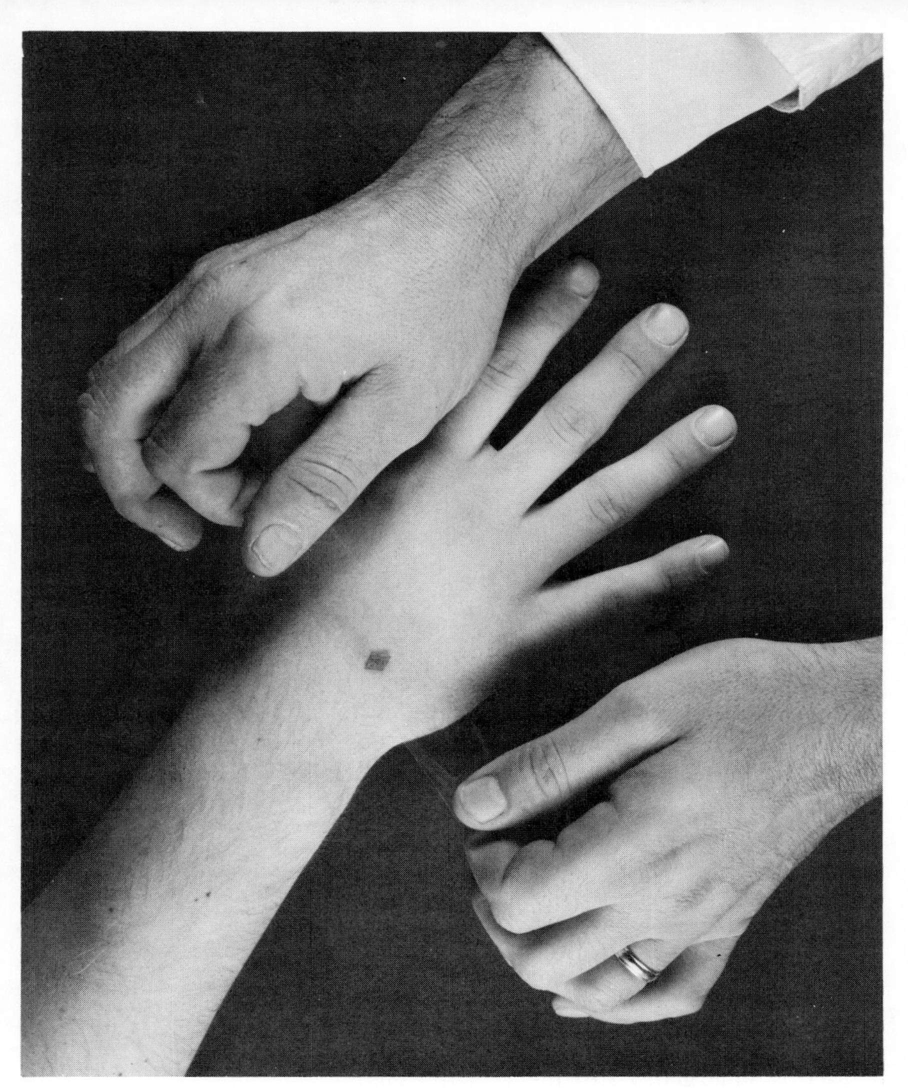

A

B

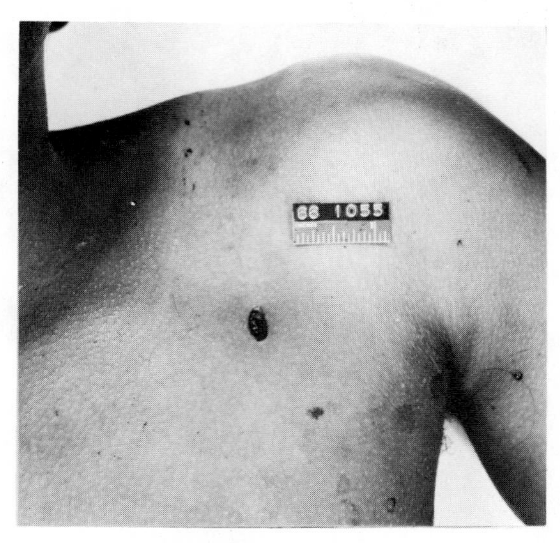

FIGURE 17. A surgical "stab wound" made in the course of emergency treatment to a gunshot victim can be very confusing to police investigators and to the courts. In the absence of proper documentation a serious question may be raised as to whether the victim was stabbed as well as shot. The consequences of this confusion could be very serious.

the effects of the criminally inflicted injuries, he should be particularly careful to document that fact. For instance, if a surgical "stab wound" is made in the thoracic area for the purpose of draining the pleural cavities, that wound may be externally indistinguishable from one made with criminal intent. Figure 17 is a good example. The "stab wound" shown in that photograph was made by the accident room physician who was rendering emergency treatment to the victim's gunshot wounds. In the absence of documentation, there was some question as to whether or not the victim had been both shot and stabbed by his criminal assailant. Figure 18 is a similar example of the possible consequences of lack of documentation. The victim in this case was shot by one person and stabbed by another. The gunshot wound is shown in *A;* the stab wounds in *B.* (Note the similarity to the therapeutic "stab wound" in Figure 17.)

Large trocars used for the purpose of therapy might leave skin defects that could be mistaken for gunshot wounds, so far as the external appearances are concerned. Figure 19*A* is an example of the former; Figure 19*B* is an example of the gunshot wound in the same patient. If surgical wounds are made, adequate documentation of their location and nature must be made by the physician in his own records or on the hospital chart so as to

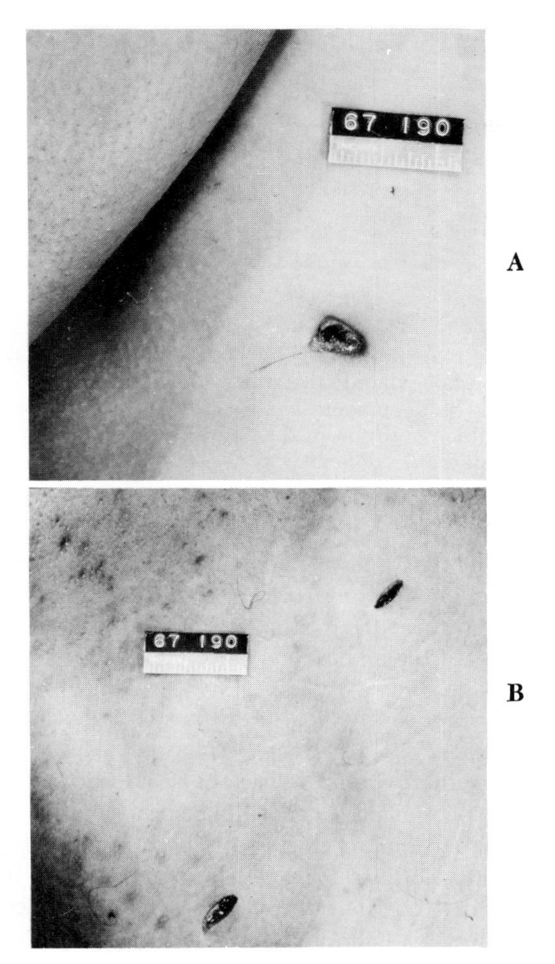

FIGURE 18. *A* and *B* show three wounds on a victim who was shot by one assailant and stabbed by another. The gunshot wound is shown in *A*. *B* shows two stab wounds, but only one was criminally inflicted; the other was made by the treating physician. In the absence of proper documentation regarding the physician's therapeutic incision there would be no way of accounting for both wounds.

prevent confusion if the patient should expire and an autopsy be undertaken by a physician unfamiliar with the particular case.

A careless manipulation of a patient's body, or the body of a person killed by bullet wounding, may result in the loss of crucial evidence. Figure 20 is a good illustration. It shows a partially exited bullet in a woman's breast. Any unnecessarily rough handling of the body might

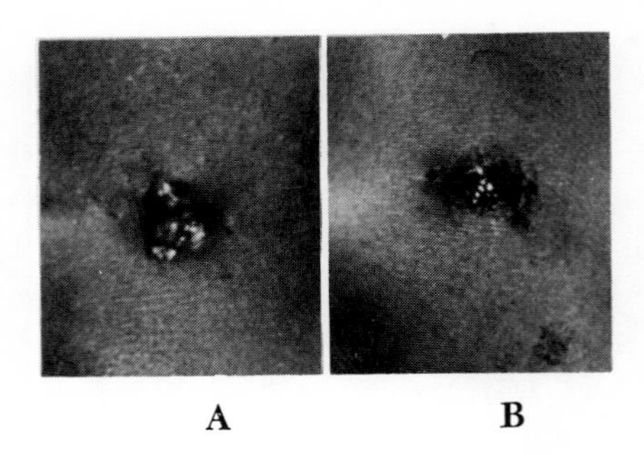

FIGURE 19. Of the two wounds shown here, only one, *B*, was made by a criminally inflicted gunshot wound; the other, *A*, was made by a surgeon using a large trocar. Lack of documentation regarding the therapeutic wound could result in considerable confusion in the course of the case investigation. It could also produce considerable difficulty at a criminal trial.

easily have caused the bullet to drop out of the skin and be lost. The reader may recall that one of the bullets fired by President Kennedy's assassin was found on a hospital stretcher without anyone having observed its being deposited there. Had his assassin been brought to trial, considerable difficulty might have been encountered in authenticating the exhibit for courtroom usage.

It is very important for medical-legal purposes that the physician guard against rough handling of a patient who has been the victim of a shooting, stabbing, or other such wound infliction. In addition, it would be well to have a covering sheet or plastic cloth placed under and about the victim's body at all times, particularly during any body location change. Moreover, the sheet or plastic cloth itself should be preserved for the police investigators, in order that they may recover whatever evidence may have been deposited upon it. This will afford protection against the loss of valuable evidence.

There is an adage in homicide investigation that states: "If the visible wounds do not seem to account for death, look in other areas where a wound may be hidden." This holds true in clinical medicine also. The practitioner should remember that wounds may be present in hard-to-examine areas such as the scalp, axilla, and perineal regions and that wounds in these regions may be responsible for the patient's problem. If the physician fails to recognize this, treatment may be directed only toward the less severe wounds found in areas most apt to be examined by the physician.

The problem of the unapparent wound is one frequently encountered in the examination of victims of homicide or accident. Figure 21 illustrates this well. *A* shows the overall appearance of the anterior aspect of a man

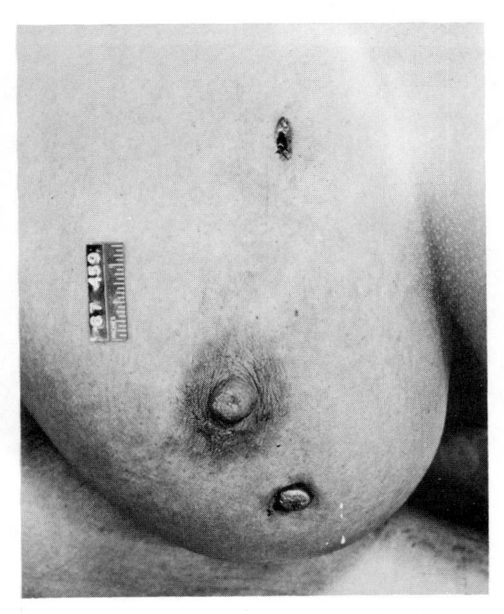

FIGURE 20. An illustration of the need, from a medical-legal standpoint, for an avoidance of rough handling of a patient who is a victim of a shooting, stabbing, or other such wound infliction. Very little movement of the body of this woman would be required to shake loose the partially exited bullet lodged in her breast. Crucial evidence of criminal guilt is often lost in this manner.

found dead in a house fire. *B* shows the entrance bullet wound in the badly charred skin and subcutaneous tissue overlying the right anterior chest wall. The small hairline passing through the entrance wound itself is a scapel incision. *C* shows the skin and subcutaneous tissue partially exposed by bending the tissue. The wound was not apparent when the initial examination of the body was made. Indeed, the entrance wound in this charred area is superficially indistinguishable from many other points in the thoracic skin. Such concealed homicides must be kept in mind when dealing with apparent victims of fire.

When death occurs to a crime victim or to a victim of an accident with possible criminal implications, particular care should be taken to leave endotracheal tubes, drains, and other paraphernalia attached to or within the several orifices of the body. It may be of utmost importance, for example, to know where the distal end of the endotracheal tube is in relation to the carinas of the mainstem bronchi. Of equal importance is the placement of nasogastric tubes and nasal catheters. Tubing and other apparatus left in place will be of great significance in the interpretation of the death when the autopsy is commenced.

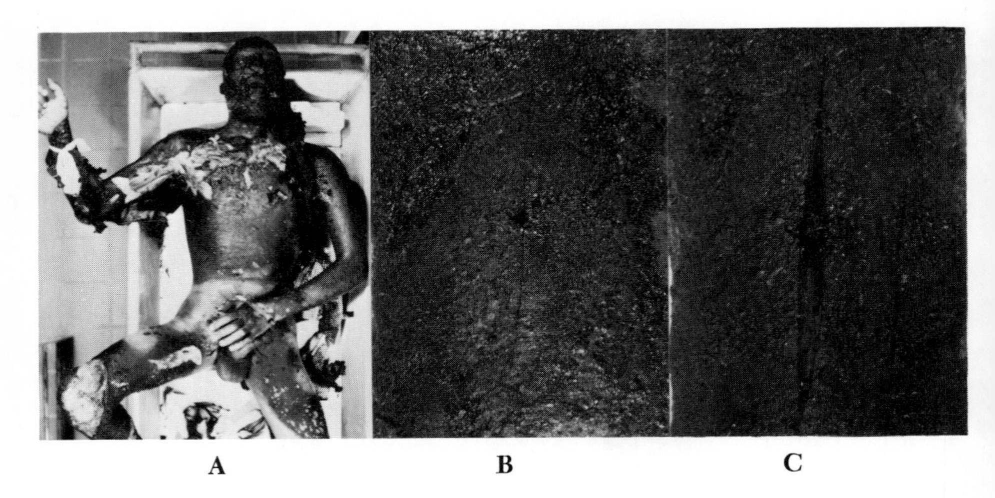

A B C

FIGURE 21. A case illustration of the necessity for expert pathological examinations of burned bodies. To unsuspecting eyes the source of death may be written off as asphyxiation or burning. As a matter of fact, however, the deceased in this case was killed by a bullet wound. The wound is shown in *B*. The small hairline passing through the wound itself is a scalpel incision. *C* shows the skin and subcutaneous tissue partially exposed by a bending of the tissue.

Once death has occurred there should be no probing of gunshot or stab wounds. Probing will not clearly establish the wound track, and it may easily create false and misleading passages.

It is also highly inadvisable for an attending physician to perform a "mini-autopsy" for the purpose of ascertaining the cause of death. First of all, in the particular state where he is practicing he may lack legal authorization to do so, either with or without the consent of relatives of the deceased.[2] In any event, the autopsy function should be left for the medical-legal expert in the office of the medical examiner or coroner.

Among the many difficulties encountered by the forensic pathologist in his efforts to arrive at a satisfactory diagnosis as to the precise cause of a crime victim's death is the interpretation of the written records made by physicians and hospital staff following hospitalization or the death of the patient.

Probably the single most neglected item in the hospital chart is the dating and timing of notes made by the physician. As if this were not confusing enough, frequently the notes are found on several pages in the record and these are not arranged in any orderly, chronological fashion.

[2] See Chapter 13.

The time and energy required to insert the date and the time of the note entry constitute a very slight burden, whereas the time and energy required to interpret undated and untimed notes may be considerable. Moreover, in many instances a determination of date and time may be impossible, particularly in view of the rapid change-over in hospital physician populations.

A second problem that is frequently encountered with hospital records is that there are no notes dealing with the therapy rendered the patient. If the hospital is one that requires notes to be made by the nursing staff, it may be possible to rectify this omission by examination of the nurses' notes. When such nursing notes are not provided, however, it is an impossible task to reconstruct properly the therapeutic endeavors of the physician unless he himself provides written notes regarding them.

Whenever possible, consistent with the welfare of the patient, a physician should cooperate with the police in their need to talk to the patient. All too often a physician either will flatly refuse police permission to do so, or else will be overly cautious with regard to the time when he will authorize the patient-police contact. Most enforcement officers recognize that the patient must not be exposed to early or too intense interrogation. They would be the first not to want to endanger the patient's recovery by virtue of prolonged questioning. Indeed, it is not in the best interest of law enforcement officers to push the patient farther than his physical stamina will allow. In the long run, the interests of justice would only be jeopardized by doing so. The overprotectiveness sometimes exhibited by physicians and the apparent guarding of their patients to prevent police questioning is genuinely reprehensible.

Physicians should realize that ultimately the police will have access to the patient anyway, and they should endeavor to cooperate with law enforcement officials as soon as it appears that questioning will not adversely affect the condition of the patient. The earlier the police can talk to a crime victim, the sooner they can embark upon a search for the offender and for the required evidence of guilt.

BIBLIOGRAPHY

BOOKS

Franchini, A.: FORENSIC MEDICINE IN THE FIELD OF CRIMINAL LAW. Cedam, Padua, Italy, 1966. (In Italian.)

Gonzales, T. A., *et al.*: LEGAL MEDICINE, PATHOLOGY AND TOXICOLOGY. Appleton-Century-Crofts, New York, 1954.

Gross, H. G. A.: CRIMINAL INVESTIGATION, 5th ed. (Jackson, R. L., ed.). Sweet & Maxwell, London, 1962.

Richardson, J. R.: MODERN SCIENTIFIC EVIDENCE, CIVIL AND CRIMINAL. W. H. Anderson Co., Cincinnati, 1961.

Simpson, C. K.: FORENSIC MEDICINE, 5th ed. E. Arnold, London, 1964.

Snyder, L.: HOMICIDE INVESTIGATION, 2d ed. Charles C Thomas, Springfield, Ill., 1967.

Svensson, A., and Wendel, O.: TECHNIQUES OF CRIME SCENE INVESTIGATION, revised American ed. American Elsevier Publishing Co., Inc., New York, 1965.

ARTICLE

Gordon, M. L.: *The Use of Scientific Evidence and Its Legal Limitations,* 9 JOURNAL OF FORENSIC SCIENCES 301 (1964).

COMMENT

Comment, *Evolving Methods of Scientific Proof,* 13 NEW YORK LAW FORUM 679 (1967).

chapter 23

ESTIMATION OF TIME OF DEATH AND THE INTERVAL BETWEEN OCCURRENCE OF INJURY AND DEATH

All too often a physician without special training in forensic pathology is requested, and agrees, to look at a dead body and tell the police how long it has been dead, or how long the individual lived after sustaining his injury.

Any physician who ventures to answer such questions after merely viewing the body or making a cursory examination of it risks the real possibility of a subsequent disclosure of gross error. Moreover, an inaccurate estimate can have a seriously misleading effect upon the police investigation. For instance, if a physician gives an opinion that the body has been dead six hours, or two days, or for some other period of time, or that the cause of death (shooting, stabbing, etc.) occurred at a specified time prior to death, the police investigators may erroneously eliminate from suspect consideration a guilty person who was nowhere near the deceased at the incorrectly estimated time of death or injury.

Even the most qualified forensic pathologist will avoid guesswork of the type we have mentioned. He also knows that in many instances a reliable estimate is impermissible even when a complete autopsy and various laboratory tests have been made of stomach contents, body fluids, and tissues.

A reliable estimate of postmortem interval, or of the elapsed time between injury and death, can seldom be made upon medical evidence alone. Ordinarily required is the existence of a number of factors, both medical and circumstantial. This has been referred to as the association method. For instance, in attempting to estimate the postmortem interval, or the elapsed time between physical incapacitation and death, where time in terms of days is concerned, the medical examiner, coroner, or other investigator must take into account such nonmedical and unspectacular events as the date when the last milk bottle or newspaper was taken to the deceased person's place of residence. This information can then be correlated with the time of death indications revealed by a medical determination of the state of digestion of stomach contents, the stage of body deterioration, and the like.

A body condition that can be seriously misinterpreted by a physician untrained in forensic pathology is the presence or absence of rigor mortis. The onset and disappearance of rigor mortis are dependent upon a number of factors—for example, environmental and internal body temperatures (heat will accentuate both onset and disappearance); the presence or absence of physical activity at the time of death (activity increases the onset); muscular condition of the deceased (in a muscular person the onset is delayed).

Another body condition that can be misleading is the deceased person's body temperature. Many factors can influence the rate of cooling, such as room temperature, the amount and kind of body clothes or covering, fat and muscle. To consider body temperature as a gauge of postmortem interval, without giving due attention to extraneous influences, is a hazardous undertaking.

Postmortem decomposition can also be affected considerably by the conditions of the environment. Bacterial development is influenced by the surrounding temperature, as well as by the presence of bacterial sepsis prior to death.

With this brief discussion we hope to have alerted the reader to the pitfalls that exist with regard to the estimation of time of death and the interval between occurrence of injury and death. For the physician or the lawyer who wishes to explore the medical intricacies we submit the following extensive bibliography:

BIBLIOGRAPHY *

BOOKS (SPECIFIC)

Gonzales, T. A., *et al.:* LEGAL MEDICINE, PATHOLOGY AND TOXICOLOGY. Appleton-Century-Crofts, New York, 1954.

Regan, L. J., and Moritz, A. R.: HANDBOOK OF LEGAL MEDICINE 106. The C. V. Mosby Company, St. Louis, 1956.

Simpson, K.: FORENSIC MEDICINE 16–17, 5th ed. E. Arnold, London, 1964.

BOOKS (RELEVANT)

Cannon, W. B.: THE MECHANICAL FACTORS OF DIGESTION. E. Arnold, London, 1911.

Cannon, W. B.: BODILY CHANGES IN PAIN, HUNGER, FEAR AND RAGE: AN AC-

* For their cooperation in the compilation of this bibliography, the authors are indebted to Mr. G. Arthur Martin, Q.C., of Toronto, Canada, and to Miss Joan P. Davis, Research Librarian of Northwestern University Medical School.

COUNT OF RECENT RESEARCHES INTO THE FUNCTION OF EMOTIONAL EXCITEMENT, 2d ed. Harper & Row, New York, 1963.

Glaister, J., and Rentoul, E.: *Examination of the Stomach,* in MEDICAL JURISPRUDENCE AND TOXICOLOGY 34, 11th ed. Williams and Wilkins, Baltimore, 1962.

James, A. H.: THE PHYSIOLOGY OF GASTRIC DIGESTION. E. Arnold, London, 1957.

Moritz, A. R.: *The Medicolegal Autopsy* in PATHOLOGY OF TRAUMA 391–407, 2d ed. Lea and Febiger, Philadelphia, 1954.

Simpson, C. K.: A DOCTOR'S GUIDE TO COURT: A HANDBOOK ON MEDICAL EVIDENCE, 2d ed. Butterworth, London, 1967.

Thompson, C. M., *et al.* (eds.): THE STOMACH, INCLUDING RELATED AREAS IN THE ESOPHAGUS AND DUODENUM. Grune & Stratton, New York, 1967.

Wolf, S. G., and Wolff, H. G.: HUMAN GASTRIC FUNCTION: AN EXPERIMENTAL STUDY OF MAN AND HIS STOMACH, 2d ed. Oxford University Press, London and New York, 1947.

Wolf, S. G.: THE STOMACH. Oxford University Press, New York, 1965.

PROCEEDINGS

Abridged Proceedings . . . Excerpta Medica International Congress Series, No. 80: INTERNATIONAL MEETING IN FORENSIC IMMUNOLOGY, MEDICINE, PATHOLOGY AND TOXICOLOGY. Excerpta Medica Foundation, Amsterdam, 1964.

Proceedings of the Symposium Held at the Faculty of Medicine, University of Alberta, Edmonton, Canada, 1965: GASTRIC SECRETION: MECHANISMS AND CONTROL. Symposium Publications, Division of Pergamon Press, Oxford and New York, 1967.

ARTICLES (SPECIFIC)

Bardzik, S.: *The Efficiency of Methods of Estimating the Time of Death by Pharmacological Means,* 13 J. FORENSIC MED. 141 (1966).

Cazzaniga, A.: *Chronologic Problems of Legal Medicine,* 60 ARCH. DI ANTROPOL. CRIM. 187–404 (1940). (In Italian.)

Fatteh, A.: *Estimation of Time of Death by Chemical Changes,* 163 MEDICOLEG. BULL. 1–6 (1966).

Ford, R.: *Critical Times in Murder Investigation (Time of Assault, Incapacitation, and Death),* 43 J. CRIMINAL LAW, CRIMINOLOGY AND POLICE SCIENCE 672 (1953).

Frache, G.: *Forensic Studies of Death: Modern Aspects,* 73 MINERVA MEDICOLEG. (Atti Assoc. ital. med. leg. e assicurazioni) 25–51 (1953). (In Italian.)

Helpern, M.: *Postmortem Examination in Cases of Suspected Homicide,* 24 ANN. INT. MED. 666–700 (1946).

Jetter, W. W., and McLean, R.: *Biochemical Changes in Body Fluids After Death,* 13 AM. J. CLIN. PATH. 178 (1943).

Kulsdom, M. E.: *Moment of Death: Statistical Study of 344 Cases,* 84 NEDERL. T. GENEESK. 3681 (1940). (In Dutch.)

Lundquist, F.: *Physical and Chemical Methods for the Estimation of Time of Death,* Spec. No. 9 ACTA MED. LEG. SOCIAL 205 (1956).

Morgan, A. D.: *Misleading Evidence (Related to Peristalsis) in Establishing Time of Death,* 2 BRIT. M. J. 255 (1945).

Moritz, A. R.: *Classical Mistakes in Forensic Pathology,* 26 AM. J. CLIN. PATH. 1383 (1956).

Mortiz, A. R.: *Scientific Evidence in Establishing the Time of Death,* 6 ANN. WEST. MED. & SURG. 302 (1952).

Omero, F.: *Contribution to the Study of Gastric Contents in Relation to Chronology of Death,* 15 RASS. GIULIA MED. 335 (1959). (In Italian.)

Pfeiffer, C. J., *et al.: Physiological Correlates Dependent Upon Mode of Death,* 10 TOXIC. APPL. PHARMACOL. 253 (1967).

Recine, H.: *Forensic Hemothanatology: Relations Between pH, Blood Platelet Count and the Time of Death,* 78 MINERVA MEDICOLEG. 148 (1958). (In Italian.)

Schleyer, von F.: *On Physical, Chemical, Hematological and Histological Methods of Determining Time of Death,* 99 ZBL. ALLG. PATH. 509 (1959). (In German.)

Simpson, K.: *The Moment of Death—A New Medico-Legal Problem,* 41 S. AFR. MED. J. 1188 (1967).

Zsako, I.: *Determining Exact Time of Death,* 39 BUDAPESTI ORVOSI UJSAG 121 (1941). (In Hungarian.)

[*The following four articles are based upon the well-known Steven Truscott homicide case in Canada, in which a determination of time of death was a critical issue based on stomach contents. Thereafter we list articles bearing on analysis of stomach contents to determine time of death.*]

Case of Steven Truscott. (Evidence Given at the Supreme Court of Canada, October, 1966, in the Case of Steven Truscott), 10 TRAUMA 25 (1969).

Camps, F. E.: *Time of Death,* 10 TRAUMA 9 (1969).

Houts, M.: *Time of Death: Still the Dark Age of Proof,* 10 TRAUMA 1 (1969).

Simpson, K.: *The Case Against Steven Truscott in Canada,* 36 MEDICOLEG. J. 58, Suppl. 4 (1968).

ARTICLES (RELEVANT)

Babkin, B.: *The Digestive Work of the Stomach,* 8 PHYSIOL. REV. 365 (1928).

BONORINO, P. C.: *Gastric Secretion: Changes and Factors Influencing Them,* 6 REV. ESPAN. ENFERM. APAR DIG. 201 (1947). (In Spanish.)

BORGSTROM, B., *et al.: Intestinal Digestion and Absorption in the Human,* 36 J. CLIN. INVEST. 1521 (1957).

Cannon, W. B.: *Influence of Emotional States on the Functions of the Alimentary Canal,* 137 AM. J. MED. SCI. 480 (1909).

Doret, J. P.: *Normal and Pathologic Motility Analyzed by Gastrography,* 77 GASTROENTEROLOGIA 231 (1951). (In French.)

Gershon, M. D.: *Inhibition of Gastrointestinal Movement by Sympathetic Nerve Stimulation: The Site of Action,* 189 J. PHYSIOL. 317 (1967).

Gibb, W. T.: *Theory Concerning the Manner in Which the Stomach Empties Itself*, 16 ANN. INT. MED. 94 (1942).

Gorham, F. D.: *Variations of Acid Concentration in Different Portions of Gastric Chyme and Its Relation to Clinical Methods of Gastric Analysis*, 27 ARCH. INT. MED. 434 (1921).

GRIFFITH, G. H., *et al*: *Measurement of Rate of Gastric Emptying Using Chromium-51*, 1 LANCET 1244 (1966).

Hardy, J. D., *et al.*: *Pain Threshold in Man (Scientific Proof and the Relations of Law and Medicine)*, 99 AM. J. PSYCHIAT. 744 (1943).

Henning, N., and Kinzlmeier, H.: *Continuous Registration of Various Gastric Functions in Man Under Influence of Substances Stimulating Secretion and Motility*, 118 ZTSCHR. GES. EXP. MED. 177 (1952). (In German.)

Hildes, J. A., and Dunlop, D. L.: *Method for Estimating Rates of Gastric Secretion and Emptying*, 29 CANAD. J. M. SC. 83 (1951).

Hopkins, A.: *The Pattern of Gastric Emptying: A New View of Old Results*, 182 J. PHYSIOL. 144 (1966).

Hunt, J. N.: *Gastric Emptying and Secretion in Man*, 39 PHYSIOL. REV. 491 (1959).

Hunt, J. N., and MacDonald, I.: *Influence of Volume on Gastric Emptying*, 126 J. PHYSIOL. 459 (1959).

Hunt, J. N.: *The Investigation of Gastric Digestive Function in Man*, 5 LECT. SCI. BASIS MED. 348 (1955).

Hunt, J. N., and Spurrell, W. R.: *Pattern of Emptying of the Human Stomach*, 113 J. PHYSIOL. 157 (1951).

Hunt, J. N.: *The Secretory Pattern of the Stomach of Man*, 113 J. PHYSIOL. 169 (1951).

Jactot, B.: *Physiology of Gastric Digestion*, 73 GAZ. MED. FRANCE 605 (1966). (In French.)

Jungmann, H., and Venning, P.: *Some Data on the Normal Variation of the Stomach Observed Radiologically*, 25 BRIT. J. RADIOL. 25 (1952).

Kovziridze, Z. Z.: *Secretory Activity of the Stomach in Various Combinations of Time Intervals Between Physical Loadings and Ingestion of Food of Different Qualitative Composition*, 24 VOP. PITAN 50 (1965). (In Russian.)

Maggi, A. L. C., and Borre, H. A.: *Gastric Juice: Determination of Total Chloride Content in Its Normal and Pathologic Variations*, 6 AN. D. INST. INVEST. FIS. APL. A LA PAT. HUMANA, 203 (1944). (In Spanish.)

Maile, W. C. D., and Scott, K. J. L.: *Digestibility of Common Foodstuffs as Determined by Radiography*, 1 LANCET 21 (1935).

Masuda, H., *et al.*: *Temperature of the Gastrointestinal Tract: Relation of Intragastric Temperature to Secretion*, 58 TOHOKU J. EXP. MED. 57 (1953). (In English.)

Michetti, G., and Beltrami, G.: *Behavior of Gastric Juice in Various Phases of Female Genital Life (Menstruation, pregnancy and menopause)*, 54 ACCAD. MED. GENOVA 561 (1939). (In Italian.)

Nimeh, W.: *Emptying of Normal Stomach in Altitudes*, 14 REV. GASTROENTEROL. 763 (1947).

Piper, D. W.: *Gastric Secretion,* 12 AUST. ANN. MED. 171 (1963).
Quigley, J. P., *et al.*: *Evidence That Body Irritation or Emotions Retard Gastric Evacuation, not by Producing Pylorospasm but by Depressing Motility,* 22 J. CLIN. INVEST. 839 (1943).
Quigley, J. P.: *Modern Explanation of Gastric Emptying Mechanism,* 10 AM. J. DIGEST. DIS. 418 (1943).
Rhodes, J., *et al.*: *Mechanics of Gastroduodenal Emptying: A Study of Gastric and Duodenal Emptying with Miniature Balloons and Intestinal Glass Electrodes,* 7 GUT 515 (1966).
Saito, H., and Matsuoka, F.: *Influence of Exposure to Heat or Cold Upon Gastric Secretion and Evacuation,* 37 J. SCI. LABOUR 268 (1961). (In Japanese.)
Scaffidi, V.: *Some Aspects of the Physiology and Physiopathology of Gastric Secretion,* 51 MINERVA MED. 4305 (1960). (In Italian.)
Sleeth, C. K., and Van Liere, E. J.: *Effect of Environmental Temperature on Emptying Time of the Stomach,* 118 AM. J. PHYSIOL. 272 (1937).
Thomas, J. E.: *Mechanics and Regulation of Gastric Emptying,* 37 PHYSIOL. REV. 453 (1957).
Tidwell, H. C., and Cameron, E. S.: *Relation Between Chemical Structure of Fats and Their Ability to Produce Gastric Inhibition,* 70 BULL. JOHNS HOPKINS HOSP. 362 (1942).
Triolo, A.: *Connection Between Gastric Secretion and Gastric Motility,* 1 MINERVA MED. 517 (1949). (In Italian.)
Van Liere, E. J., *et al.*: *Effect of Anoxia on Peristalsis of Small and Large Intestine,* 140 AM. J. PHYSIOL. 119 (1943).
Van Liere, E. J.: *Effect of Senescence on Gastric Emptying,* 38 WEST VIRGINIA M. J. 114 (1942).
Van Liere, E. J., and Northrup, D. W.: *Emptying Time of Normal Human Stomach in the Young Adult,* 1 GASTROENTEROLOGY 279 (1943).
Van Liere, E. J., and Northrup, D. W.: *Emptying Time of Old People,* 134 AM. J. PHYSIOL. 719 (1941).
Van Liere, E. J., and Sleeth, C. K.: *Emptying Time of Normal Human Stomach as Influenced by Acid and Alkali, with Review of the Literature,* 7 AM. J. DIGEST. DIS. 118 (1940).
Van Liere, E. J., and Sleeth, C. K.: *Relation of Size of Meal to Emptying Time of Human Stomach,* 119 AM. J. PHYSIOL. 480 (1937).
Wolf, S. G., and Wolff, H. G.: *Life Situations, Emotions and Gastric Function: Summary,* 3 AM. PRACT. 1 (1948).
Wolff, H. G.: *Emotions and Function,* 98 SCIENCE 481 (1943).

chapter 24

CRIMINAL LAWS OF SPECIAL IMPORTANCE TO THE PHYSICIAN

There are several serious criminal offenses with which physicians should be at least generally familiar. Perhaps the most pertinent of all is the crime of abortion, but there are several others that also dictate physician interest.

ABORTION

Until 1967 almost all of the states outlawed abortions except those necessary to save the life of the pregnant woman.[1] Only one state, Louisiana, made no exceptions whatever in its abortion statute, although in that state a separate statute stated that the performance of an abortion was not a cause for the revocation of a physician's license when "done for the relief of a woman whose life appears in peril." In a few other states, and in the District of Columbia, abortions were allowed not only to save the woman's life but also to preserve her health.

A liberalization trend developed in 1967–1968 when California, Colorado, Maryland, and North Carolina revised their abortion laws.[2] They provided, in general, that abortions were permissible when the pregnancy was the result of rape, incest, or other felonious intercourse, or whenever a substantial risk existed that a continuance of the pregnancy would

[1] Citations to the abortion statutes referred to in this chapter can be found in Ziff, H. L.: *Recent Abortion Law Reforms (Or Much Ado About Nothing)*, 60 Journal of Criminal Law, Criminology & Police Science 3 (1969). As originally employed in abortion statutes, the word "life" meant *physical* existence, but in a 1938 English case, *Rex* v. *Bourne,* [1938] 3 All Eng. 615, it was held that "life" covered a situation in which the continued pregnancy of a fourteen-year-old rape victim would probably make a "mental wreck" of her.

[2] Calif. Health & Safety Code. §§25950-25960 (Supp. 1970); Colo. Rev. Stat., §40-2-50 (Supp. 1970); Md. Code Ann., art. 43, §149E (Supp. 1969); N.C. Gen. Stat., §14-45.1 (Supp. 1969). These four states relied heavily upon the 1962 proposal contained in the Model Penal Code, §230.3, of the American Law Institute.

gravely impair the physical or mental health of the woman or that the child would be born with a serious physical or mental defect. Various conditions are attached to the statutes of these four states, however, in an effort to discourage abuses of the newly created exemptions.

In 1970 the legislatures of New York and Hawaii practically eliminated the offense of abortion if it is performed by a licensed physician.

The present New York law provides that any licensed physician may perform a consensual abortion within twenty-four weeks from the commencement of the pregnancy. No other controls or qualifications are prescribed.[3]

Although the Hawaii statute sets a pregnancy limitation, it does so in terms of a "nonviable" fetus rather than a specific period of time, such as the twenty-four-week period in the New York statute. Also in contrast to the New York statute, the Hawaiian enactment requires that the operation be performed in a licensed hospital and that the pregnant woman be domiciled in the state and physically present there for at least ninety days immediately preceding the abortion.[4]

The precedent set by New York and Hawaii is likely to be followed soon by legislatures in other jurisdictions.[5] Moreover, court decisions can be expected which will effect a liberalization of the abortion laws that remain unchanged by legislative amendment; in fact, there may even be a complete judicial nullification of them on constitutional grounds, particularly two newly articulated ones: The Supreme Court of California has already declared an abortion law unconstitutional because of (1) the "vagueness" of the phrase "necessary to preserve the life" and (2) the statute's violation of the fundamental right of a woman to choose whether or not to bear a child. The California court's decision resulted in the reversal of a physician's conviction for a conspiracy to commit an abortion. He had referred the pregnant woman to an abortionist after she had pleaded for help that would provide her with an alternative to the risk, which she insisted she otherwise intended to incur, of entrusting herself to an unreliable abortionist in Mexico.[6]

[3] (1970) LAWS OF N.Y., ch. 127, amending §125.05 of New York's Penal Code.

[4] (1970) HAWAII REV. STAT., ch. 768.

[5] After surveying the statutory and case law governing abortions and considering the relevant medical and social issues, Ziff recommends unregulated medical control during the first 16 weeks of pregnancy. Ziff, H. L.: *Recent Abortion Law Reforms (Or Much Ado About Nothing)*, 60 JOURNAL OF CRIMINAL LAW, CRIMINOLOGY & POLICE SCIENCE 3 (1969).

[6] In its decision, *People* v. *Belous*, 458 P.2d 194 (S. Ct. Cal. 1969), the court relied heavily on a case decided in 1965 by the U.S. Supreme Court, *Griswold* v. *Connecticut*, 381 U.S. 479 (1965), which held unconstitutional, as a violation of the constitutional "right of privacy," a state statute that made it unlawful to use contraceptives or to advise or assist anyone in the use of them. The defendant in *Griswold* was a

CRIMINAL HOMICIDE

The unlawful or unjustifiable killing of one human by another is criminal homicide. It may be either murder or manslaughter, depending upon the circumstances of the particular case.

Insofar as the physician is concerned, three case illustrations will suffice to explain the law regarding criminal homicide. They are (1) a "mercy killing" (that is, euthanasia); (2) a death resulting from the commission of the felony of unlawful abortion; and (3) a death resulting from gross negligence in administering medical care and treatment.

"Mercy Killing"

Although the law condones certain types of deliberate killings—for example, in self-defense or in the prevention of a dangerous felony—it does not tolerate an affirmative hastening of death for the purpose of relieving a dying person of great pain and suffering. Withholding medication that would extend a dying person's life for a limited period of time is legally permissible, but an affirmative act calculated to expedite death is prohibited.[7] An example of the latter would be the injection of air into the bloodstream of a person in the terminal stages of cancer.[8] Any such "mercy killing" constitutes the crime of murder, punishable by death or long imprisonment. Rarely are there any such prosecutions, however, due in large measure to the fact that such conduct, if it occurs with any frequency at all, is performed in the absence of witnesses.[9]

---

physician on the medical faculty of a university. The *Belous* case arose prior to California's enactment of a liberalized abortion statute. See Noonan, J. T.: *The Constitutionality of the Regulation of Abortion,* 21 Hastings Law Journal 51 (1969).

In *Babbitz* v. *McCann,* 310 F. Supp. 293 (E.D. Wis. 1970), a three-judge court held in accord with the California Supreme Court on the issue of invasion of privacy, but it also held that the word "necessary" and the expression of "to save the life of the mother" in the Wisconsin abortion statute were sufficiently clear to satisfy constitutional requirements.

Another federal case, *U.S.* v. *Vuitch,* 305 F. Supp. 1032 (D.D.C. 1969), decided by a single judge rather than a three-judge court, held that the phrase "necessary for the preservation of the mother's life or health" was constitutionally faulty because of vagueness. See also *Hall* v. *Lefkowitz,* 305 F. Supp. 1030 (S.D.N.Y. 1969).

[7] See Note, *Criminal Law—Humanitarian Motive As a Defense to Homicide,* 48 Michigan Law Review 1199 (1950).

[8] This was the charge in the celebrated case of *State* v. *Sander,* tried in New Hampshire in 1950. The defendant physician, although expressly disavowing euthanasia as a defense, was acquitted by a sympathetic jury. New York Times, March 10, 1950, p. 23. Motive, although not legally a defense to a charge of crime, often plays a significant practical role in criminal cases tried to a jury.

[9] See Richardson, J. R.: Doctors, Lawyers, and the Courts 145–48. The W. H. Anderson Company, Cincinnati, 1965.

Abortion Deaths

A general criminal law concept labels as murder any killing that results from the commission of a dangerous felony. An unlawful abortion is considered a dangerous felony, and a death resulting therefrom is punishable as murder.[10] This is the so-called felony-murder doctrine.

Death Due to Gross Negligence

A death caused by another person's gross negligence is punishable as manslaughter or as negligent homicide.[11]

Although ordinary negligence may subject a person to civil liability, a greater degree of negligence—negligence of a gross nature—is required before criminal punishment can be imposed.

For an illustration of the kind of negligence that would be required for a successful manslaughter prosecution, consider the hypothetical case of a surgeon who performs a delicate operation while in a state of intoxication at a time when the unimpaired skill of another surgeon was available.

FAILURE TO REPORT CRIMINALLY INFLICTED INJURIES AND HABITUAL USE OF NARCOTIC DRUGS

Many states and municipalities have statutes and ordinances that require physicians or hospital administrators to report to the local police any case where a patient appears for treatment of gunshot injuries or serious injuries that appear to have been inflicted by knives or other sharp instruments. The New York statute,[12] for example, requires the reporting by physicians of "a bullet wound, gunshot wound, powder burn or any other injury arising from or caused by the discharge of a gun or firearm, and every case of a wound which is likely to or may result in death and is actually or apparently inflicted by a knife, icepick or other sharp or pointed instrument." The report must be made "at once" to the local police department by the attending physician. Failure to make the required report is a misdemeanor.

[10] See, *e.g.*, *Clark* v. *State*, 57 So.2d 375 (Ala. App. 1951). It is the reasoning of *Keller* v. *Superior Court*, 80 Cal. Rptr. 865 (Cal. App. 1969), that an abortion performed after the fetus has become viable may constitute the crime of murder without reliance upon an abortion statute and the felony-murder doctrine. In *Keller* the defendant kicked his wife in the abdomen, thereby destroying a five-pound fetus between thirty-one and thirty-six weeks old. The lower California court sustained a murder conviction. The California Supreme Court reversed, however. See 470 P.2d 617 (1970).

[11] See *e.g.*, N.Y. PENAL CODE, §125.10 (Supp. 1969).

[12] N.Y. PENAL CODE, §265.25 (Supp. 1969).

Statutes also require attending or consulting physicians to report the name of any person known to be "a habitual user of any narcotic drug." [13] Legal reporting requirements override the usual confidentiality provided by the physician-patient testimonial privilege.[14]

BIBLIOGRAPHY

BOOKS

Blum, R. H., and Associates: UTOPIATES: THE USE AND USERS OF LSD-25. Atherton Press, New York, 1964.

Burdick, W.: LAW OF CRIME. Matthew Bender & Co., Inc., New York, 1946.

Dickens, B. M.: ABORTION AND THE LAW. McGibbon & Kee, London, 1966.

Downing, A. B.: EUTHANASIA AND THE RIGHT TO DEATH. Peter Owen, Ltd., London, 1969.

Guttmacher, A. F., ed.: THE CASE FOR LEGALIZED ABORTION NOW. Diablo Press, Berkeley, California, 1967.

Inbau, F. E., and Aspen, M. E.: CRIMINAL LAW FOR THE POLICE. Chilton Book Co., Philadelphia, 1969.

Kaplan, J.: MARIJUANA—THE NEW PROHIBITION. World Publishing Co., New York and Cleveland, 1970.

Lindesmith, A. R.: THE ADDICT AND THE LAW. Indiana University Press, Bloomington, 1965.

Nyswander, M.: THE DRUG ADDICT AS A PATIENT. Grune and Stratton, New York and London, 1956.

Perkins, R.: CRIMINAL LAW, 2d ed. Foundation Press, Inc., Mineola, New York, 1969.

Rosen, H., ed: ABORTION IN AMERICA: MEDICAL, PSYCHIATRIC, LEGAL, ANTHROPOLOGICAL, AND RELIGIOUS CONSIDERATIONS. Beacon Press, Boston, 1967.

Williams, G.: THE SANCTITY OF LIFE AND THE CRIMINAL LAW. Alfred Knopf, New York, 1957.

Williams, J. B., ed.: NARCOTICS AND HALLUCINOGENICS—A HANDBOOK 45–97. Glencoe Press, Beverly Hills, California, 1967.

ARTICLES

Finestone, H.: *Narcotics and Criminality,* 22 LAW & CONTEMPORARY PROBLEMS 69 (1956).

[13] N.Y. PUBLIC HEALTH LAW, §3344 (Supp. 1969). See also *Grossman* v. *Hilleboe,* 228 N.Y.S.2d 835 (App. Div. N.Y. 1962). The U.S. Supreme Court, however, has held unconstitutional a state law making drug addiction a crime. *Robinson* v. *California,* 370 U.S. 660 (1962). The scope of a doctor's right to treat drug addicts is discussed in Lindesmith, A. R.: THE ADDICT AND THE LAW, 4, 6–11, 13–15, 17, 145–48. Indiana University Press, Bloomington, 1965. See also Lindesmith, A. R.: ADDICTION AND OPIATES, Aldine Publishing Company, Chicago, 1968; Nyswander, M.: THE DRUG ADDICT AS A PATIENT, Grune and Stratton, New York and London, 1956.

[14] See Chapter 15.

Morris, A. A.: *Voluntary Euthanasia,* 45 WASHINGTON LAW REVIEW 239 (1979).
Moyers, T. G.: *Abortion Laws: A Study in Social Change,* 7 SAN DIEGO LAW REVIEW 237 (1970).
Sanders, J.: *Euthanasia: None Dare Call It Murder,* 60 JOURNAL OF CRIMINAL LAW, CRIMINOLOGY & POLICE SCIENCE 351 (1969).
Williams, G.: *Euthanasia and Abortion,* 38 UNIVERSITY OF COLORADO LAW REVIEW 178 (1966).
Winick, C.: *Narcotics Addiction and Its Treatment,* 22 LAW & CONTEMPORARY PROBLEMS 69 (1956).

COMMENT

Comment, *Abortion Reform: History, Status, and Prognosis,* 21 CASE WESTERN RESERVE LAW REVIEW 521 (1970).

part three

THE PHYSICIAN IN COURT

chapter 25

THE PHYSICIAN AS A COURTROOM WITNESS

Although physicians are usually exempted from jury service, they are more likely to encounter a courtroom experience than many classes of citizens who are eligible for jury duty.

A doctor who happens to witness an automobile accident or other occurrence that subsequently develops into a lawsuit, either civil or criminal, may be subpoenaed to testify in court. His status as a physician is no legal excuse for ignoring the subpoena. Moreover, as an ordinary witness he is not entitled to any compensation other than the modest, standard witness fee payable to any nonprofessional person who happens to be a so-called occurrence witness.

If subpoenaed to testify in court on behalf of a patient or former patient as to injuries allegedly caused by the other party to the lawsuit, the physician is legally obligated to appear at the designated time and place. (However, the attorney calling the physician as a witness may have informally arranged with him, as a matter of courtesy, to appear in court at a time other than that specified in the subpoena.) In this instance also the physician is ordinarily entitled, under the law, to no more compensation than any other witness—although it is customary, in civil cases, for the patient to compensate him at a reasonable level for the loss of professional earnings occasioned by his courtroom appearance. If asked in the courtroom by opposing counsel whether the patient is paying him "to testify in this case," the physician will rightly respond, "He's not paying me to testify but I expect to be reimbursed for the loss of my time."

In the event a physician is subpoenaed on behalf of the party opponent of his patient or former patient, he should promptly report that fact to the patient or to the patient's attorney. The attorney may be able to have the subpoena set aside (quashed) on the basis of the physician-patient privilege,[1] thereby sparing the physician from appearing in court. Unless the

[1] See Chapter 15.

subpoena is quashed, however, the physician cannot avoid the order to appear. A failure or outright refusal to comply would subject him to the inconvenience, not to mention embarrassment, of being taken into custody and brought to court by the police.

Doctors generally view with disdain the requirement that they personally appear in court to give their testimony. They frequently ask why a written statement would not suffice, especially if it were made under an oath administered by a notary public or other authorized out-of-court official. The lawyer's answer—and the law's—is that our adversary legal system places great emphasis on the opportunity for cross-examination afforded opposing counsel, so that he can engage in a face-to-face inquiry into the competency, accuracy, and possible bias of any witness—all in the presence of the judge and the jury so that they will be adequately equipped to evaluate the testimony given by the witness during the preceding friendly direct examination. Trial lawyers believe, and experience has taught, that cross-examination is a powerful engine for the discovery of truth. Only under special circumstances will a substitute for actual appearance in court be acceptable. One such exception is where there is good reason to believe that the prospective witness will be unavailable at the time of trial—for example, deceased, on vacation, or in military service. In this event a deposition can be taken for reading to the judge and the jury when the case comes to trial.[2] But even at a deposition an opportunity must be afforded opposing counsel to ask questions by way of cross-examination.

A physician with special expertise in a particular field of medicine may be consulted by an attorney with a view toward the physician's appearance in court to express an expert opinion upon some issue in the case. He may be asked to examine an injured person and to give an opinion—first in the form of a written report and, later, in courtroom testimony—as to the nature and extent of the injury or to offer a prognosis as to its ultimate consequences. He may be consulted for the purpose of expressing an opinion in court in response to a so-called hypothetical question that describes a person's condition on the basis of the antecedent testimony of other physicians or lay witnesses. Or, as we have seen in earlier chapters,[3] a physician may be requested to serve as an expert witness in a medical malpractice case. In any of these instances, of course, the physician has a free choice as to whether to become involved. Moreover, he may condition his willingness upon an understanding as to the fee he is to receive for his participation. That fee, however, should never be made contingent upon the outcome of the lawsuit.

[2] See Chapter 1.
[3] See Chapters 5 and 6.

Prior to a physician's appearance in court as a witness, the lawyer who has sought his testimony should arrange for a discussion of the testimony to be presented. This discussion should also focus on the anticipated content of cross-examination. Without such preparation the physician's testimony may be ineffective, and he will probably encounter a degree of unpleasantness in the courtroom that could have been avoided, particularly as regards the tactics employed by opposing counsel in his cross-examination.

This suggested pre-trial conference is a perfectly ethical procedure, invariably engaged in by competent trial counsel. No physician should ever hesitate to give a "Yes" answer if he is asked on cross-examination, "Have you talked to the other lawyer about this case before coming here today?" It would be strange indeed if the answer, in truth, were "No."

The initial phase of a physician's testimony—the *direct examination,* which takes up immediately after a court attaché has administered the testimonial oath—will consist of questions put by the lawyer who summoned the physician as a witness, and the physician's answers, regarding such preliminary matters as his name, his place of residence, and his office location. Thereafter the medical witness will be asked questions bearing upon his qualifications—the medical school from which he receiver his M.D. degree, his residence training, his graduate studies or special courses or research, his medical society and hospital affiliations, specialty board certifications, his professional writings, and the like. At this juncture opposing counsel may, if he chooses, request court permission to cross-examine the physician on the subject of his qualifications. In some jurisdictions such a cross-examination must be conducted at this point or else any objection to the witness's qualifications will be considered to have been waived.

After eliciting qualifying testimony, the lawyer who called the witness will proceed to ask questions concerning the nature and extent of the plaintiff's injuries or illness, the nature of the therapy undertaken, and other pertinent medical information depending on the character of the issues raised by the particular lawsuit. Opposing counsel is then accorded an opportunity to ask questions by way of cross-examination.

Unlike the practice in most European countries, where the witness stands up and delivers a lengthy narrative concerning what he knows about the case, in Anglo-American law the witnesses, including the expert witnesses, relate their evidence through the question-and-answer method. Although some lawyers argue that by focusing the witness's attention on specific details, our method actually is simpler and faster than the European method, most lawyers would agree that it is in fact slower and more cumbersome. The reason it is used is that the rules of evidence in our jurisprudence are vastly more detailed, complicated, and strict than those of most other countries. Relying on a jury untrained in the law, we make every possible effort to keep from its members the sort of information that they might rely on but which experience teaches is either unfair to one side or the other or for some reason dangerously misleading. We therefore require the witness to give his answers in response to relatively pointed questions so that the opposing attorney, forewarned by the question that the jury may be about to hear legally inadmissible material, can object in time to prevent receipt of the damaging answer.

In Anglo-American law not only must the parties proceed by question and answer, but they must adhere to certain forms of questions. And the restrictions are far more severe on the side calling the witness to the stand. The examination of one's own witness—the direct examination—must be made without the use of leading questions, that is, questions that suggest their own answer. A typical leading question is, "Did the defendant doctor look in on his patient each and every day of her hospitalization?" The witness may answer "Yes" but it is the attorney's version of the story that the jury hears. Leading questions, although technically prohibited, are generally used to save time on unimportant and background matters. "Is your name Clyde Bushmat?" However, as soon as important matters are reached, most trial lawyers automatically switch from leading questions to avoid a barrage of objections which are properly sustained by the judge.

A second major restriction encountered in direct examination is that the side calling the witness is, as lawyers say, "bound by his testimony." This means not that the lawyer must assume the truth of every fact testified to by his own witness but rather that he cannot argue with the witness or seek by further questioning to modify his testimony unless he can convince the judge that the witness is hostile or has taken him by surprise.

In cross-examination these restrictive rules do not apply. The cross-examiner can ask as many leading questions as he wishes, and if the answers prove unsatisfactory to him, he can go at the matter again and again in as many different ways as he can devise to press the witness into delivering the desired answers.

Following the cross-examination, there may be re-direct examination. It is worth noting that on re-direct examination the lawyer who called the witness can afford him full opportunity to expand upon or explain answers given by him during cross-examination. After the re-direct there may be re-cross. In most jurisdictions each examination is restricted to the scope of the examination that preceded it. In other words, the cross-examiner can properly inquire only into matters brought out in the witness's direct examination, the re-direct is limited to the scope of the cross-examination, and so on.

In the course of direct examination, and perhaps also during the cross-examination, exhibits, such as x-ray plates or hospital records, may be shown to the witness as a foundation for questions relating to them.

Following are some basic suggestions that may serve the purpose of rendering a physician's courtroom experience less unpleasant than originally anticipated. They will also enhance the effectiveness of his testimony.

Be Prepared

A medical witness should not attempt to testify as an expert unless he is satisfied that he is qualified in any specialty that is involved in the litigated matter. Beyond that, the medical witness should be certain before going to court that he is thoroughly conversant with all of the facts bearing upon the opinions that he expects to express during his testimony and with any other medical data relevant to the case. The lawyer whose task it is to cross-examine an expert will have studied the medical aspects of the case with great care; he will have read the literature and he will have been briefed by his own medical experts. He will be prepared to engage in a knowledgeable and penetrating cross-examination that is calculated to reveal any weaknesses in a medical witness's testimony.

Confer with the Lawyer Calling You as a Witness

Within a few days of going to court, the prospective medical witness should meet with the lawyer who has called him to testify. The lawyer should be asked to explain any matters that may be unknown or unclear to the physician, such as the location and layout of the courthouse and of the specific courtroom to which the case has been assigned; the procedures that will be employed when the witness appears in court; the nature and purpose of the questions that he will be asked on direct examination; the probable approach that will be taken by opposing counsel in conducting his cross-examination of the witness; the personality and courtroom manner of the judge assigned to the case; and the like. The lawyer should be advised of any available visual aids that might enhance the witness's testimony.

Do Not Be Nervous or Frightened

The honest and prepared physician who comes to court to tell the truth has nothing to fear from either direct or cross-examination. Consequently, he should not permit baseless apprehensions to detract from the force of his testimony. There is nothing mystical about courtroom testimony, and most trial lawyers conduct themselves as gentlemen. Furthermore, the competent, prepared, and truthful expert witness cannot be embarrassed or unsettled by a lawyer's questions.

Be Courteous

A medical witness will be courteous—as all other witnesses should be—to the judge, the jury, and the lawyers. There is no need, however, to appear obsequious.

Do Not Be Patronizing or Smug

Jurors—who come from all stations of life, high as well as low—are not likely to respond favorably to a condescending or smug attitude on the part of any witness. An attitude of modesty is far more impressive. The attorney who summoned the physician as an expert witness will ask him questions fully eliciting his qualifications; thereafter, the witness's informative answers to questions, given with straightforward candor, will adequately convey to the jurors the worth of both testifier and testimony.

Avoid Esoteric Terminology

The expert witness's function is to explain, not to confuse. The witness must keep it firmly in mind that his testimony is addressed to a jury composed of nonexperts, at least so far as the field of medicine is concerned. Consistent with accurate narration, therefore, the witness should avoid the use of technical medical terms that the jurors will not understand. If necessary, the witness can adopt the technique of employing technical terminology first, followed by an explanation of it in layman's terms.

Tell the Truth, No More and No Less

The medical witness cannot be compelled to compromise with accuracy. He is free to tell the truth, which he will do without exaggeration or unwarranted reservations. For example, often a question is not susceptible to a categorical answer. The medical witness cannot be required to answer flatly "Yes" or "No" if the question calls for a conditioned or qualified response. Frequently the only valid answer will commence with "If . . . ." And occasionally the witness, in all frankness, must and should indicate that his opinion is not conclusive. Jurors do not react adversely to a physician who states, "I can't be absolutely positive that my opinion is the only correct one. It *is* my belief, however, based on my training and years of experience, that the opinion I have expressed in this case is correct." Above all, the medical witness should avoid the adoption of a partisan stance.

Maintain Composure

A medical witness should remain calm even though his opinions or his memory of factual details are vigorously challenged by a lawyer during cross-examination. A few trial lawyers, unable to refute the testimony of a medical witness in any more direct way, will resort to a mode of inquiry calculated to irritate the physician and cause him to lose his temper. A witness gains nothing by overreacting to sarcastic or insulting questions. He has fallen into a trap deliberately set if he becomes angry or attempts to argue with the offensive lawyer. Opposing counsel will object to the cross-examiner's questions if they are truly improper. Furthermore, jurors can be expected to discount irrelevant and demeaning cross-questions.

Do Not Answer a Question to Which Objection Has Been Made Until the Judge Has Announced His Ruling

A witness should not answer a question to which an objection has been interposed until the judge has had an opportunity to make his ruling, which may sustain the objection and render a response from the witness unnecessary.

Do Not Volunteer Information from the Witness Stand

Every person called upon to give testimony should listen carefully and be scrupulous to answer only the precise question put to him by the examining lawyer. A witness, in other words, should not volunteer information uncalled for by the examining attorney's question. Unresponsive answers, if objected to by opposing counsel, will be stricken from the court record and the jurors will be instructed by the judge to disregard them.

Once a physician has presented his evidence in court to the best of his ability, he should not be disturbed when later on he learns that a jury verdict has been rendered contrary to the thrust of his testimony. The physician should not assume that the jury concluded that he was mistaken or that he lied, for there are extraneous factors that sometimes enter into jury verdicts.

Take the case, for instance, of a prosecution of a husband for the killing of his wife's paramour. In all but three states (Texas, New Mexico, and Utah) such killings are punishable as criminal homicides—murder or manslaughter, depending upon the particular surrounding circumstances. But what happens when such cases come to trial? Ordinarily the accused will claim that he killed in self-defense. And he may get by with that defense even though a forensic pathologist testifies that the killing resulted from an injury inflicted in such a manner as to belie the defendant's version of the ocurrence.

In reaching its "not guilty" verdict the jury may not have doubted at all the accuracy or integrity of the pathologist's testimony. What counteracted it, however, may have been the jury's attitude that the paramour deserved to be killed; that they—the male jurors, anyway—probably would have done the same thing under similar circumstances; and that, furthermore, no useful social purpose would be served by sending the defendant to the penitentiary, and particularly so in situations where his children would be left destitute or where his courtroom demeanor clearly indicated to the jurors that his release would entail no risk of future violent conduct. A "not guilty" verdict in cases of this type is usually referred to by the news media as an acquittal upon "unwritten law." For that outcome, of course, the forensic pathologist who testified in the case bears neither responsibility nor blame.

A "mercy killing" situation affords another example of a jury verdict based on factors extraneous to scientific evidence. Clearly established facts may be set aside by jurors because of compassion for the defendant who acted without selfish motives and solely for the purpose of sparing a loved-one or a patient from severe pain and suffering when death was inevitable anyway. The jury verdict might be in the form of a complete exoneration or, where the facts are so overwhelming as to be too difficult to set aside, "not guilty by reason of insanity."

Additional illustrations could be offered but the foregoing should be sufficient to establish that a jury verdict at variance with a medical witness's testimony should not be viewed as a reflection upon his competency or integrity.

BIBLIOGRAPHY

BOOKS

Goldstein, I., and Shabat, L. W.: MEDICAL TRIAL TECHNIQUE. Callaghan and Company, Chicago, 1942.

Houts, M.: MEDICAL PROOF. Matthew Bender, New York, 1966.

Inbau, F. E., and Aspen, M. E.: CRIMINAL LAW FOR THE LAYMAN. Chilton Book Co., Philadelphia, 1970.

Joiner, C. W.: TRIALS AND APPEALS. Prentice-Hall, Inc., Englewood Cliffs, N.J., 1957.

Kaplan, J., and Waltz, J. R.: THE TRIAL OF JACK RUBY 120–21, 189–92, 253, 270–71, 286–87. The Macmillan Company, New York, 1965.

Keeton, R. E.: TRIAL TACTICS AND METHODS. Little, Brown and Company, Boston, 1954.

ARTICLE

Inbau, F. E.: *Scientific Reasoning and Jury Verdicts,* 16 POSTGRADUATE MEDICINE, No. 4 (1954).

APPENDICES

appendix I

NUREMBERG CODE OF ETHICS IN MEDICAL RESEARCH

2 Trials of War Criminals Before the Nuremberg Military Tribunals Under Control Council Law No. 10 181–82 (1949)

[Note: Early in 1946 the Allied Military Tribunal was preparing to try twenty-three Nazi physicians and scientists charged with performing cruel experiments on political prisoners. At the request of the Secretary of State and the Secretary of War, the American Medical Association appointed Dr. Andrew C. Ivy of Chicago to serve as an adviser to the lawyers assigned to prosecute the defendants. Dr. Ivy was to consult with the prosecutors on the ethics of medical research. He drafted ten principles of ethics governing the use of human subjects in medical research. This code, with some modifications, was adopted as the cornerstone of the Allied cases against the Nazi physicians. Presented during the trials by General Telford Taylor, it has become a significant guidepost in the Western world. The full, final text of the code follows.]

1. The voluntary consent of the human subject is absolutely essential. This means that the person involved should have legal capacity to give consent; should so be situated as to be able to exercise free power of choice without the intervention of any element of force, fraud, deceit, duress, overreaching, or other ulterior form of constraint or coercion; and should have sufficient knowledge and comprehension of the elements of the subject matter involved as to enable him to make an understanding and enlightened decision. This latter element requires that before the acceptance of an affirmative decision by the experimental subject there should be made known to him the nature, duration, and purpose of the experiment; the method and means by which it is to be conducted; all inconveniences and hazards reasonably to be expected; and the effects upon his health or person which may possibly come from his participation in the experiment.

The duty and responsiblity for ascertaining the quality of the consent rests upon each individual who initiates, directs, or engages in the experiment. It is a personal duty and responsibility which may not be delegated to another with impunity.

2. The experiment should be such as to yield fruitful results for the good of society, unprocurable by other methods or means of study, and not random and unnecessary in nature.

3. The experiment should be so designed and based on the results of animal experimentation and a knowledge of the natural history of the disease or other problem under study that the anticipated results will justify the performance of the experiment.

4. The experiment should be so conducted as to avoid all unnecessary physical and mental suffering and injury.

5. No experiment should be conducted where there is an *a priori* reason to believe that death or disabling injury will occur; except, perhaps, in those experiments where the experimental physicians also serve as subjects.

6. The degree of risk to be taken should never exceed that determined by the humanitarian importance of the problem to be solved by the experiment.

7. Proper preparations should be made and adequate facilities provided to protect the experimental subject against even remote possibilities of injury, disability, or death.

8. The experiment should be conducted only by scientifically qualified persons. The highest degree of skill and care should be required through all stages of the experiment of those who conduct or engage in the experiment.

9. During the course of the experiment the human subject should be at liberty to bring the experiment to an end if he has reached the physical or mental state where continuation of the experiment seems to him to be impossible.

10. During the course of the experiment the scientist in charge must be prepared to terminate the experiment at any stage, if he has probable cause to believe, in the exercise of the good faith, superior skill, and careful judgment required of him, that a continuation of the experiment is likely to result in injury, disability, or death to the experimental subject.

appendix II

DECLARATION OF HELSINKI

RECOMMENDATIONS GUIDING DOCTORS IN CLINICAL RESEARCH
67 ANNALS OF INTERNAL MEDICINE, Supp. 7, 74–75 (1967)

[Note: The Declaration of Helsinki was issued by the World Medical Association in 1964. In 1967 it was endorsed by the American Medical Association and seven other influential medical societies in the United States.[1] The full text of the declaration follows.]

It is the mission of the doctor to safeguard the health of the people. His knowledge and conscience are dedicated to the fulfillment of this mission.

The Declaration of Geneva of the World Medical Association binds the doctor with the words, "The health of my patient will be my first consideration"; and the International Code of Medical Ethics which declares that "Any act or advice which could weaken physical or mental resistance of a human being may be used only in his interest."

Because it is essential that the results of laboratory experiments be applied to human beings to further scientific knowledge and to help suffering humanity, the World Medical Association has prepared the following recommendations as a guide to each doctor in clinical research. It must be stressed that the standards as drafted are only a guide to physicians all over the world. *Doctors are not relieved from criminal, civil and ethical responsibilities under the laws of their own countries.*

In the field of clinical research a fundamental distinction must be recognized between clincal research in which the aim is essentially therapeutic for a patient, and clinical research the essential object of which is purely

[1] American Federation for Clinical Research; American Society for Clinical Investigation; Central Society for Clinical Research; American College of Physicians; American College of Surgeons; Society for Pediatric Research; American Academy of Pediatrics.

scientific and without therapeutic value to the person subjected to the research.

I. ***Basic Principles***

1. Clinical research must conform to the moral and scientific principles that justify medical research, and should be based on laboratory and animal experiments or other scientifically established facts.
2. Clinical research should be conducted only by scientifically qualified persons and under the supervision of a qualified medical man.
3. Clinical research cannot legitimately be carried out unless the importance of the objective is in proportion to the inherent risk to the subject.
4. Every clinical research project should be preceded by careful assessment of inherent risks in comparison to foreseeable benefits to the subject or to others.
5. Special caution should be exercised by the doctor in performing clinical research in which the personality of the subject is liable to be altered by drugs or experimental procedure.

II. ***Clinical Research Combined With Professional Care***

1. In the treatment of the sick person the doctor must be free to use a new therapeutic measure if in his judgment it offers hope of saving life, re-establishing health, or alleviating suffering.

   If at all possible, consistent with patient psychology, the doctor should obtain the patient's freely given consent after the patient has been given a full explanation. In case of legal incapacity consent should also be procured from the legal guardian; in case of physical incapacity the permission of the legal guardian replaces that of the patient.

2. The doctor can combine clinical research with professional care, the objective being the acquistion of new medical knowledge, only to the extent that clinical research is justified by its therapeutic value for the patient.

III. ***Non-Therapeutic Clinical Research***

1. In the purely scientific application of clinical research carried out on a human being it is the duty of the doctor to remain the protector of the life and health of that person on whom clinical research is being carried out.
2. The nature, the purpose, and the risk of clinical research must be explained to the subject by the doctor.

3a. Clincal research on a human being cannot be undertaken without his free consent after he has been fully informed; if he is legally incompetent the consent of the legal guardian should be procured.

3b. The subject of clinical research should be in such a mental, physical, and legal state as to be able to exercise fully his power of choice.

3c. Consent should as a rule be obtained in writing. However, the responsibility for clinical research always remains with the research worker; it never falls on the subject, even after consent is obtained.

4a. The investigator must respect the right of each individual to safeguard his personal integrity, especially if the subject is in a dependent relationship to the investigator.

4b. At any time during the course of clinical research the subject or his guardian should be free to withdraw permission for research to be continued. The investigator or the investigating team should discontinue the research if in his or their judgment, it may, if continued, be harmful to the individual.

appendix III

AMERICAN MEDICAL ASSOCIATION, ETHICAL GUIDELINES FOR CLINICAL INVESTIGATION

A.M.A., DECLARATION OF HELSINKI AND AMA ETHICAL GUIDELINES FOR CLINICAL INVESTIGATION (1966) (pamphlet)

[Note: In 1957 the Law Department of the American Medical Association provided the following advice to its members: [1]

In order to avoid legal liability for use of experimental procedures in treatment of a patient, the following requirements must not vary too radically from the accepted methods of procedure; and usual and accepted procedures must have been tried previously without success. Medical ethics prohibit human experimentation except (1) with the voluntary informed consent of the person on whom the experiment is to be performed; (2) after the danger of the experiment has been investigated previously by animal experimentation; and (3) under proper medical protection and management.

On November 30, 1966, the House of Delegates of the American Medical Association adopted a full set of ethical guidelines to govern clinical investigation. These guidelines, the text of which follows, were intended to enlarge upon the fundamental concepts of the Declaration of Helsinki [2] and the A.M.A.'s earlier Principles of Medical Ethics.[3]]

At the 1966 Annual Convention of its House of Delegates, the American Medical Association endorsed the ethical principles set forth in the 1964 *Declaration of Helsinki* of the World Medical Association concerning human experimentation. These principles conform to and express fundamental concepts already embodied in the *Principles of Medical Ethics* of the American Medical Association.

[1] A.M.A., PRINCIPLES OF MEDICAL ETHICS (1957) (pamphlet).
[2] Appendix II, *supra*.
[3] A.M.A., PRINCIPLES OF MEDICAL ETHICS (1957) (pamphlet).

The following guidelines, enlarging on these fundamental concepts, are intended to aid physicians in fulfilling their ethical responsibilities when they engage in the clinical investigation of new drugs and procedures.

1. A physician may participate in clinical investigation only to the extent that his activities are a part of a systematic program competently designed, under accepted standards of scientific research, to produce data which is scientifically valid and significant.
2. In conducting clinical investigation, the investigator should demonstrate the same concern and caution for the welfare, safety and comfort of the person involved as is required of a physician who is furnishing medical care to a patient independent of any clinical investigation.
3. In clinical investigation *primarily for treatment*—
   A. The physician must recognize that the physician-patient relationship exists and that he is expected to exercise his professional judgment and skill in the best interest of the patient.
   B. Voluntary consent must be obtained from the patient, or from his legally authorized representative if the patient lacks the capacity to consent, following: (a) disclosure that the physician intends to use an investigational drug or experimental procedure, (b) a reasonable explanation of the nature of the drug or procedure to be used, risks to be expected, and possible therapeutic benefits, (c) an offer to answer any inquiries concerning the drug or procedure, and (d) a disclosure of alternative drugs or procedures that may be available.
      i. In exceptional circumstances and to the extent that disclosure of information concerning the nature of the drug or experimental procedure or risks would be expected to materially affect the health of the patient and would be detrimental to his best interests, such information may be withheld from the patient. In such circumstances such information shall be disclosed to a responsible relative or friend of the patient where possible.
      ii. Ordinarily, consent should be in writing, except where the physician deems it necessary to rely upon consent in other than written form because of the physical or emotional state of the patient.
      iii. Where emergency treatment is necessary and the patient is incapable of giving consent and no one is available who has authority to act on his behalf, consent is assumed.
4. In clinical investigation *primarily for the accumulation of scientific knowledge*—
   A. Adequate safeguards must be provided for the welfare, safety and comfort of the subject.
   B. Consent, in writing, should be obtained from the subject, or from his legally authorized representative if the subject lacks the capacity to consent, following: (a) a disclosure of the fact that an investigational drug or procedure is to be used, (b) a reasonable explanation of the

nature of the procedure to be used and risks to be expected, and (c) an offer to answer any inquiries concerning the drug or procedure.

C. Minors or mentally incompetent persons may be used as subjects only if:
   i. The nature of the investigation is such that mentally competent adults would not be suitable subjects.
   ii. Consent, in writing, is given by a legally authorized representative of the subject under circumstances in which an informed and prudent adult would reasonably be expected to volunteer himself or his child as a subject.

D. No person may be used as a subject against his will.

INDEX

A

B

C

G

H

I

J

L

M

S

T